Parallel and High Performance Computing

Parallel and High Performance Computing

ROBERT (BOB) ROBEY
AND YULIANA (YULIE) ZAMORA

MANNING

SHELTER ISLAND

Manning Publications Co.
20 Baldwin Road
PO Box 761
Shelter Island, NY 11964

Development editor:	Marina Michaels
Technical development editor:	Christopher Haupt
Review editor:	Aleksandar Dragosavljević
Production editor:	Deirdre S. Hiam
Copy editor:	Frances Buran
Proofreader:	Jason Everett
Technical proofreader:	Tuan A. Tran
Typesetter:	Dennis Dalinnik
Cover designer:	Marija Tudor

ISBN: 9781617296468
Printed in the United States of America

To my wife, Peggy, who has supported not only my journey in high performance comput-
ing, but also that of our son Jon and daughter Rachel. Scientific programming is far
from her medical expertise, but she has accompanied me and made it our journey.
To my son, Jon, and daughter, Rachel, who have rekindled the flame and for your
promising future.

—Bob Robey

To my husband Rick, who supported me the entire way, thank you for taking the
early shifts and letting me work into the night. You never let me give up on myself.
To my parents and in-laws, thank you for all your help and support.
And to my son, Derek, for being one of my biggest inspirations; you are the reason
I leap instead of jump.

—Yulie Zamora

brief contents

contents

12 GPU languages: Getting down to basics   417

13 GPU profiling and tools   460

From the authors

Bob Robey, Los Alamos, New Mexico

> *It's a dangerous business, Frodo, going out your door. You step onto the road, and*
> *if you don't keep your feet, there's no knowing where you might be swept off to.*

> — Bilbo Baggins

I could not have foreseen where this journey into parallel computing would take us. "Us" because the journey has been shared by numerous colleagues over the years. My journey into parallel computing began in the early 1990s, while I was at the University of New Mexico. I had written some compressible fluid dynamics codes to model shock tube experiments and was running these on every system I could get my hands on. As a result, I along with Brian Smith, John Sobolewski, and Frank Gilfeather, was asked to submit a proposal for a high performance computing center. We won the grant and established the Maui High Performance Computing Center in 1993. My part in the project was to offer courses and lead 20 graduate students in developing parallel computing at the University of New Mexico in Albuquerque.

The 1990s were a formative time for parallel computing. I remember a talk by Al Geist, one of the original developers of Parallel Virtual Machine (PVM) and a member of the MPI standards committee. He talked about the soon-to-be released MPI standard (June, 1994). He said it would never go anywhere because it was too complex. Al was right about the complexity, but despite that, it took off, and within months it was used by nearly every parallel application. One of the reasons for the success of MPI is that there were implementations ready to go. Argonne had been developing Chameleon, a portability tool that would translate between the message-passing languages at that time, including P4, PVM, MPL, and many others. The project was quickly changed to MPICH, which became the first high-quality MPI implementation. For over a decade, MPI became synonymous with parallel computing. Nearly every parallel application was built on top of MPI libraries.

Now let's fast forward to 2010 and the emergence of GPUs. I came across a Dr. Dobb's article on using a Kahan sum to compensate for the only single-precision arithmetic available on the GPU. I thought that maybe the approach could help resolve a long-standing issue in parallel computing, where the global sum of an array changes depending on the number of processors. To test this out, I thought of a fluid dynamics code that my son Jon wrote in high school. He tested the mass and energy conservation in the problem over time and would stop running and exit the program if it changed more than a specified amount. While he was home over Spring break from his freshman year at University of Washington, we tried out the method and were pleasantly surprised by how much the mass conservation improved. For production codes, the impact of this simple technique would prove to be important. We cover the enhanced precision sum algorithm for parallel global sums in section 5.7 in this book.

In 2011, I organized a summer project with three students, Neal Davis, David Nicholaeff, and Dennis Trujillo, to see if we could get more complex codes like adaptive mesh refinement (AMR) and unstructured arbitrary Lagrangian-Eulerian (ALE) applications to run on a GPU. The result was CLAMR, an AMR mini-app that ran entirely on a GPU. Much of the application was easy to port. The most difficult part was determining the neighbor for each cell. The original CPU code used a k-d tree algorithm, but tree-based algorithms are difficult to port to GPUs. Two weeks into the summer project, the Las Conchas Fire erupted in the hills above Los Alamos and the town was evacuated. We left for Santa Fe, and the students scattered. During the evacuation, I met with David Nicholaeff in downtown Santa Fe to discuss the GPU port. He suggested that we try using a hash algorithm to replace the tree-based code for the neighbor finding. At the time, I was watching the fire burning above the town and wondering if it had reached my house. In spite of that, I agreed to try it, and the hashing algorithm resulted in getting the entire code running on the GPU. The hashing technique was generalized by David, my daughter Rachel while she was in high school, and myself. These hash algorithms form the basis for many of the algorithms presented in chapter 5.

In following years, the compact hashing techniques were developed by Rebecka Tumblin, Peter Ahrens, and Sara Hartse. The more difficult problem of compact hashing for remapping operations on the CPU and GPU was tackled by Gerald Collom and Colin Redman when they were just out of high school. With these breakthroughs in parallel algorithms for the GPU, the barriers to getting many scientific applications running on the GPU were toppling.

In 2016, I started the Los Alamos National Laboratory (LANL) Parallel Computing Summer Research Internship (PCSRI) program along with my co-founders, Hai Ah Nam and Gabe Rockefeller. The goal of the parallel computing program was to address the growing complexity of high-performance computing systems. The program is a 10-week summer internship with lectures on various parallel computing topics, followed by a research project mentored by staff from Los Alamos National Laboratory. We have had anywhere from 12 to 18 students participating in the summer program, and many have used it as a springboard for their careers. Through this program, we continue to tackle some of the newest challenges facing parallel and high performance computing.

Yulie Zamora, University of Chicago, Illinois

> *If there's a book that you want to read, but it hasn't been written yet, then you must write it.*

> —Toni Morrison

My introduction to parallel computing began with, "Before you start, go into the room at the end of the 4th floor and install those Knights Corner processors in our cluster." This request from a professor at Cornell University encouraged me to try something new. What I thought would be a simple endeavor turned into a tumultuous journey into high performance computing. I started with learning the basics of how a small cluster worked through physically lifting 40-lb servers to working with the BIOS and running my first application, and then optimizing these applications across the nodes I installed.

After a short family break, daunting as it was, I applied for a research internship. Being accepted into the first Parallel Computing Summer Research Internship program in New Mexico gave me the opportunity to explore the intricacies of parallel computing on today's hardware and that is where I met Bob. I became enthralled with the gains in performance that were possible with just some knowledge of how to properly write parallel code. I personally explored how to write more effective OpenMP code. My excitement and progress in optimization of applications opened the door to other opportunities, such as attending conferences and presenting my work at the Intel User's Group meeting and at the Intel booth at Supercomputing. I was also invited to attend and present at the 2017 Salishan Conference. That was a great opportunity to exchange ideas with some of the leading visionaries of high performance computing.

Another great experience was applying for and participating in a GPU hackathon. At the hackathon, we ported a code over to OpenACC and, within a week, the code achieved a speedup by a factor of 60. Think of this—a calculation that previously took a month could now be done overnight. Fully diving into the potential of long-term research, I applied to graduate schools and chose University of Chicago, acknowledging its close relationship with Argonne National Laboratory. At the University of Chicago, I was advised by Ian Foster and Henry Hoffmann.

From my experiences, I realized how valuable personal interactions are to learning how to write parallel code. I also was frustrated by the lack of a textbook or reference that discusses the current hardware. To fill this gap, we have written this book to make it much easier for those new to parallel and high performance computing. Taking on the challenge of creating and teaching an introduction to computer science for incoming University of Chicago students helped me gain an understanding of those new to the field. On the other hand, explaining the parallel programming techniques as a teaching assistant in the Advanced Distributed Systems course allowed me to work with students with a higher level of understanding. Both these experiences helped me to attain the ability to explain complex topics at different levels.

I believe that everyone should have the opportunity to learn this important material on writing performant code and that it should be easily accessible to everyone. I was lucky enough to have mentors and advisors that steered me to the right website links or hand me their old manuscripts to read and learn. Though some of the techniques can be difficult, the greater problem is the lack of a coherent documentation or access to leading scientists in the field as mentors. I understand not everyone has the same resources and, therefore, I hope that creating this book fills a void that currently exists.

How we came to write this book

Beginning in 2016, a team of LANL scientists led by Bob Robey developed lecture materials for the Los Alamos National Laboratory (LANL) Parallel Computing Summer Research Internships (PCSRI). Much of this material addressed the latest hardware that is quickly coming to market. Parallel computing is changing at a rapid rate and there is little documentation to accompany it. A book covering the materials was clearly needed. It was at this point that Manning Publications contacted Bob about writing a book on parallel computing. We had a rough draft of the materials, so how hard could this be? Thus began a two-year effort to put it all into a high quality format.

The topics and chapter outline were well-defined at an early stage, based on the lectures for our summer program. Many of the ideas and techniques are drawn from the greater high performance computing community as we strive towards an exascale level of computing—a thousand-fold improvement in computational performance over the previous Petascale milestone. This community includes the Department of Energy (DOE) Centers of Excellence, the Exascale Computing Project, and a series of Performance, Portability, and Productivity workshops. The breadth and depth of the materials in our computing lectures reflect the deep challenges of the complex heterogeneous computing architectures.

We call the material in this book "an introduction with depth." It starts at the basics of parallel and high-performance computing, but without gaining knowledge of the computing architecture, it is not possible to achieve optimal performance. We try to give an insight into a deeper level of understanding as we go along because it is not enough to just travel along the trail without any idea of where you are or where you are going. We provide the tools to develop a map and to show how far the distance is to the goal that we are striving towards.

At the outset of this book, Joe Schoonover was tapped to write the GPU materials and Yulie Zamora the OpenMP chapter. Joe provided the design and layout of the GPU sections, but had to quickly drop out. Yulie has written papers and given many presentations on how OpenMP fit into this brave new world of exascale computing, so this material was especially well-suited for the OpenMP chapter of the book. Yulie's deep understanding of the challenges of exascale computing and her ability to break it down for newcomers to the field has been a critical contribution to the creation of this book.

acknowledgments

We'd like to thank all who helped shape this book. First on our list is Joe Schoonover of Fluid Dynamics, who has gone above and beyond in teaching parallel computing, particularly with GPUs. Joe was one of the co-leads of our parallel computing program and instrumental in formulating what the book should cover. Our other co-leads, Hai Ah Nam, Gabe Rockefeller, Kris Garrett, Eunmo Koo, Luke Van Roekel, Robert Bird, Jonas Lippuner, and Matt Turner, have contributed to the success of the parallel computing school and its content. The founding of the parallel computing summer program would not have occurred without the support and vision of the Institute Director, Stephan Eidenbenz. Also thanks to Scott Runnels and Daniel Israel, who have led the LANL Computational Physics summer school and pioneered the school's concept, giving us a model to follow.

We are fortunate to be surrounded by experts in parallel computing and book publishing. Thanks to Kate Bowman, whose expertise on writing helped guide the revisions of the early chapters. Kate is incredibly talented in all aspects of publishing and has been a book indexer for many years. We have also had informal reviews from Bob's son, Jon; daughter, Rachel; and son-in-law, Bob Bird, each of whom have some of their technical work mentioned in the book. Yulie's husband, Rick, helped provide expertise with some topics, and Dov Shlachter reviewed some early drafts and provided some helpful feedback.

We'd also like to acknowledge expertise from collaborators who found their way into specific chapters. This includes Rao Garimella and Shane Fogerty of Los Alamos and Matt Martineau of Lawrence Livermore National Laboratory whose work is incorporated in chapter 4. A special thanks goes to the innovative work of the many students mentioned earlier whose work fills much of chapter 5. Ron Green of Intel has for some years led the effort to document how to use the vectorization provided by the Intel compiler, forming the basis for chapter 6. The tsunami simulation in chapter 13 originated from the McCurdy High School team composed of Sarah Armstrong, Joseph Koby, Juan-Antonio Vigil, and Vanessa Trujillo, participating in the New Mexico Supercomputing Challenge in 2007. Also, thanks to Cristian Gomez for helping with the tsunami illustration. Work on process placement and affinity with Doug Jacobsen of Intel and Hai Ah Nam and Sam Gutiérrez of Los Alamos National Laboratory laid the foundation for chapter 14. Also, work with the Datalib team of Galen Shipman and Brad Settlemyer of Los Alamos National Laboratory, Rob Ross, Rob Latham, Phil Carns, Shane Snyder of Argonne National Laboratory, and Wei-Keng Liao of Northwestern University is reflected in chapter 16 and the section on the Darshan tool for profiling file operations in chapter 17.

We also appreciate the efforts of the Manning Publications professionals in creating a more polished and professional product. Our copy editor, Frances Buran, did a remarkable job improving the writing and making it more readable. She handled the highly technical and precise language and did it at an amazing pace. Also thanks to Deirdre Hiam, our production editor, for transforming the graphics, formulas, and text into a polished product for our readers. We would also like to thank Jason Everett, our proofreader. Paul Wells, the book's Production Manager, kept all of this effort on a tight schedule.

Manning Publications incorporates numerous reviews into the writing process, including writing style, copyediting, proofreading, and technical content. First is the Manning Acquisitions Editor, Mike Stephens, who saw the need for a book on this topic. Our Development Editor, Marina Michaels, helped keep us on track for this huge effort. Marina was especially helpful in making the material more accessible to a general audience. Christopher Haupt as the Technical Development Editor gave us valuable feedback on the technical content. We especially thank Tuan Tran, our Technical Proofer, who reviewed the source code for all the examples. Tuan did a great job tackling the difficulties of handling the challenge of high-performance computing software and hardware configurations. Our review editor, Aleksandar Dragosavljević, recruited a great set of reviewers that spanned a broad cross-section of readers. These reviewers, Alain Couniot, Albert Choy, Alessandro Campeis, Angelo Costa, Arav Kapish Agarwal, Dana Robinson, Domingo Salazar, Hugo Durana, Jean-François Morin, Patrick Regan, Phillip G Bradford, Richard Tobias, Rob Kielty, Srdjan Santic, Tuan A. Tran, and Vincent Douwe gave us valuable feedback which substantially improved the final product.

about this book

One of the most important tasks for an explorer is to draw a map for those who follow. This is especially true for those of us pushing the boundaries of science and technology. Our goal in this book is to provide a roadmap for those just starting to learn about parallel and high performance computing and for those who want to broaden their knowledge of the field. High performance computing is a rapidly changing field, where languages and technologies are constantly in flux. For this reason, we'll focus on the fundamentals that stay steady over time. For the computer languages for CPUs and GPUs, we stress the common patterns across the many languages, so that you can quickly select the most appropriate language for your current task.

Who should read this book

This book is targeted at both upper division undergraduate parallel computing classes and as state-of-the-art literature for computing professionals. If you are interested in performance, whether it be run time, scale, or power, this book will give you the tools to improve your application and outperform your competition. With processors reaching the limits of scale, heat, and power, we cannot count on the next generation computer to speed up our applications. Increasingly, highly skilled and knowledgeable programmers are critical for getting maximum performance from today's applications.

In this book, we hope to get across key ideas true for today's high performance computing hardware. These are the basic truths of programming for performance. These themes underlie the entire book.

> *In high performance computing, it is not how fast you write the code, it is how fast the code you write runs.*

This one thought sums up what it means to write applications for high performance computing. For most other applications, the focus is on how fast you can write an application. Today, computer languages are typically designed to promote quicker programming rather than better performing code. Although this programming approach has long infused high performing computing applications, it has not been widely documented or described. In chapter 4, we discuss this different focus in a programming methodology that has recently been coined as data-oriented design.

It is all about memory: how much you use and how often you load it.

Even when you know that available memory and memory operations are almost always the limiting factor in performance, we still tend to spend a lot of time thinking about floating-point operations. With most current computing hardware capable of 50 floating-point operations for every memory load, floating-point operations are a secondary concern. In almost every chapter, we use our implementation of the STREAM benchmark, a memory performance test, to verify that we are getting reasonable performance from the hardware and programming language.

If you load one value, you get eight or sixteen.

It's like buying eggs. You can't get just one. Memory loads are done by cache lines of 512 bits. For a double-precision value of 8 bytes, eight values will be loaded whether you want them or not. Plan your program to use more than one value, and preferably eight contiguous values, for best performance. And while you are at it, use the rest of the eggs.

If there are any flaws in your code, parallelization will expose them.

Code quality requires more attention in high performance computing than a comparable serial application. This applies to before beginning parallelization, during parallelization, and after parallelization. With parallelization, you are more likely to trigger a flaw in your program and will also find debugging more challenging, especially at large scale. We introduce the techniques for improving software quality in chapter 2, then throughout the chapters we mention important tools, and finally, in chapter 17, we list other tools that can prove valuable.

These key themes transcend hardware types applying equally to all CPUs and GPUs. These exist because of the current physical constraints imposed on the hardware.

How this book is organized: A roadmap

This book does not expect that you have any knowledge of parallel programming. It does expect that readers are proficient programmers, preferably in a compiled, high performance computing language such as C, C++, or Fortran. It is also expected that readers have some knowledge of computing terminology, operating system basics, and networking. Readers should also be able to find their way around their computer, including installing software and light system administration tasks.

The knowledge of computing hardware is perhaps the most important requirement for readers. We recommend opening up your computer, looking at each component, and getting an understanding of its physical characteristics. If you cannot open up your computer, see the photos of a typical desktop system at the end of appendix C. For example, look at the bottom of the CPU in figure C.2 and at the forest of pins going into the chip. Can you fit any more pins there? Now you can see why there is a physical limit to how much data can be transferred to the CPU from other parts of the system. Flip back to these photos and the glossary in appendix A when you need to have a better understanding of the computing hardware or computing terminology.

We have divided this book into four parts that comprise the world of high performance computing. These are

- Part 1: Introduction to parallel computing (chapters 1–5)
- Part 2: Central processing unit (CPU) technologies (chapters 6–8)
- Part 3: Graphics processing unit (GPU) technologies (chapters 9–13)
- Part 4: High performance computing (HPC) ecosystems (chapters 14–17)

The order of topics is oriented towards someone tackling a high performance computing project. For example, for an application project, the software engineering topics in chapter 2 are necessary before starting a project. Once the software engineering is in place, the next decisions are the data structures and algorithms. Then come the implementations for the CPU and GPU. Finally, the application is adapted for the parallel file system and other unique characteristics of a high performance computing system.

On the other hand, some of our readers are more interested in gaining fundamental skills in parallel programming and might want to go directly into the MPI or OpenMP chapters. But don't stop there. Today, there is so much more to parallel computing. From GPUs that can speed up your application another order of magnitude to tools that can improve your code quality or point out sections of code to optimize—the potential gains are only limited by your time and expertise.

If you are using this book for a class on parallel computing, the scope of the material is sufficient for at least two semesters. You might think of the book as a buffet of materials that can be individualized to the audience. By selecting the topics to cover, you can customize it for your own course objectives. Here is a possible sequence of material:

- Chapter 1 provides an introduction to parallel computing
- Chapter 3 approaches measuring hardware and application performance
- Sections 4.1–4.2 describe the data-oriented design concept of programming, multi-dimensional arrays, and cache basics
- Chapter 7 covers OpenMP (Open Multi-Processing) to get on-node parallelism
- Chapter 8 covers MPI (Message Passing Interface) to get distributed parallelism across multiple nodes
- Sections 14.1–14.5 introduce affinity and process placement concepts
- Chapters 9 and 10 describe GPU hardware and programming models
- Sections 11.1–11.2 focus on OpenACC to get applications running on the GPU

You can add topics such as algorithms, vectorization, parallel file handling, or more GPU languages to this list. Or you can remove a topic so that you can spend more time on the remaining topics. There still are additional chapters to tempt students to continue to explore the world of parallel computing on their own.

About the code

You cannot learn parallel computing without actually writing code and running it. For this purpose, we provide a large set of examples that accompanies the book. The examples are freely available at https://github.com/EssentialsOfParallelComputing. You can download these examples either as a complete set or individually by chapter.

With the scope of the examples, hardware, and software, there will inevitably be flaws and errors in the accompanying examples. If you find something that is in error or just not complete, we encourage contributions to the examples. We have already merged in some change requests from readers, which were greatly appreciated. Additionally, the source code repository will be the best place to look for corrections and source code discussions.

Software/hardware requirements

Perhaps the biggest challenge in parallel and high performance computing is the wide range of hardware and software that is involved. In the past, these specialized systems were only available at specific sites. Recently, the hardware and software has become more democratized and widely available even at the desktop or laptop level. This is a substantial shift that can make software for high performance computing much easier to develop. However, the setup of the hardware and software environment is the most difficult part of the task. If you have access to a parallel computing cluster where these are already set up, we encourage you to take advantage of it. Eventually, you may want to set up your own system. The examples are easiest to use on a Linux or Unix system, but should also work on Windows and the MacOS in many cases with some additional effort. We have provided alternatives with Docker container templates and VirtualBox setup scripts when you find that the example doesn't run on your system.

The GPU exercises require GPUs from the different vendors, including NVIDIA, AMD Radeon, and Intel. Anyone who has struggled to get GPU graphics drivers installed on their system will not be surprised that these present the greatest difficulty in setting up your local system for the examples. Some of the GPU languages also can work on the CPU, allowing the development of code on a local system for hardware that you do not have. You may also find that debugging on the CPU is easier. But to see the actual performance, you will have to have the actual GPU hardware.

Other examples requiring special installation include the batch system and the parallel file examples. A batch system requires more than a single laptop or workstation to set it up to look like a real installation. Similarly, the parallel file examples work best with a specialized filesystem like Lustre, though the basic examples will work on a laptop or workstation.

liveBook discussion forum

Purchase of *Parallel and High Performance Computing* includes free access to a private web forum run by Manning Publications where you can make comments about the book, ask technical questions, and receive help from the authors and from other users. To access the forum, go to https://livebook.manning.com/#!/book/parallel-and-high-performance-computing/discussion. You can also learn more about Manning's forums and the rules of conduct at https://livebook.manning.com/#!/discussion. Manning's commitment to our readers is to provide a venue where a meaningful dialogue between individual readers and between readers and the authors can take place. It is not a commitment to any specific amount of participation on the part of the authors, whose contribution to the forum remains voluntary (and unpaid). We suggest you try asking the authors some challenging questions lest their interest stray! The forum and the archives of previous discussions will be accessible from the publisher's website as long as the book is in print.

Other online resources

Manning Publications also provides an online discussion forum called livebook for each book. Our site is at https://livebook.manning.com/book/parallel-and-high-performance-computing. This is a good place to add comments or expand on the materials in the chapters.

About the cover illustration

The figure on the cover of *Parallel and High Performance Computing* is captioned "M'de de brosses à Vienne," or "Seller of brushes in Vienna." The illustration is taken from a collection of dress costumes from various countries by Jacques Grasset de Saint-Sauveur (1757-1810), titled *Costumes de Différents Pays*, published in France in 1797. Each illustration is finely drawn and colored by hand. The rich variety of Grasset de Saint-Sauveur's collection reminds us vividly of how culturally apart the world's towns and regions were just 200 years ago. Isolated from each other, people spoke different dialects and languages. In the streets or in the countryside, it was easy to identify where they lived and what their trade or station in life was just by their dress.

The way we dress has changed since then and the diversity by region, so rich at the time, has faded away. It is now hard to tell apart the inhabitants of different continents, let alone different towns, regions, or countries. Perhaps we have traded cultural diversity for a more varied personal life—certainly for a more varied and fast-paced technological life.

At a time when it is hard to tell one computer book from another, Manning celebrates the inventiveness and initiative of the computer business with book covers based on the rich diversity of regional life of two centuries ago, brought back to life by Grasset de Saint-Sauveur's pictures.

about the authors

Robert (Bob) Robey is a technical staff scientist in the Computational Physics Division at Los Alamos National Laboratory and an adjunct researcher at the University of New Mexico. He is a founder of the Parallel Computing Summer Research Internships started in 2016. He is a member of the NSF/IEEE-TCPP Curriculum Initiative on Parallel and Distributed Computing. Bob is a board member of the New Mexico Supercomputing Challenge, a high school and middle school educational program in its 30th year. He has mentored hundreds of students over the years and has twice been recognized as a Los Alamos Distinguished Student Mentor. Bob co-taught a parallel computing class at University of New Mexico and has given guest lectures at other universities.

Bob began his scientific career by operating explosive-driven and compressible gas-driven shock tubes at the University of New Mexico. This includes the largest explosively-driven shock tube in the world at 20 feet in diameter and over 800 feet long. He conducted hundreds of experiments with explosions and shock waves. To support his experimental work, Bob has written several compressible fluid dynamics codes since the early 1990s and has authored many articles in international journals and publications. Full 3D simulations were a rarity at the time, stressing compute resources to the limit. The search for more compute resources led to his involvement in high performance computing research.

Bob worked 12 years at the University of New Mexico conducting experiments, writing, and running compressible fluid dynamics simulations, and started a high performance computing center. He was a lead proposal writer and brought tens of millions of dollars of research grants to the university. Since 1998, he has held a position at the Los Alamos National Laboratory. While there, he contributed to large multi-physics codes running on a variety of the latest hardware.

Bob is a world-class kayaker with first descents down previously unrun rivers in Mexico and New Mexico. He is also a mountaineer with ascents of peaks on three continents up to over 18,000 feet in elevation. He is a leader in the co-ed Los Alamos Venture crew and helps out with multi-day trips down western rivers.

Bob is a graduate of Texas A&M University with a Masters in Business Administration and a Bachelors degree in Mechanical Engineering. He has taken graduate coursework at University of New Mexico in the Mathematics Department.

Yuliana (Yulie) Zamora is completing her PhD in Computer Science at the University of Chicago. Yulie is a 2017 fellow at the CERES Center of Unstoppable Computing at the University of Chicago and a National Physical Science Consortium (NPSC) graduate fellow.

Yulie has worked at the Los Alamos National Laboratory and interned at Argonne National Laboratory. At Los Alamos National Laboratory, she optimized the Higrad Firetec code used for simulating wildland fires and other atmospheric physics for some of the top high performance computing systems. At Argonne National Laboratory, she worked at the intersection of high performance computing and machine learning. She has worked on projects ranging from performance prediction on NVIDIA GPUs to machine learning surrogate models for scientific applications.

Yulie developed and taught an Introduction to Computer Science course for incoming University of Chicago students. She incorporated many of the basic concepts of parallel computing fundamentals into the material. The course was so successful, she was asked to teach it again and again. Wanting to gain more teaching experience, she volunteered for a teaching assistant position for an Advanced Distributed Systems course at the University of Chicago.

Yulie's Bachelors degree is in Civil Engineering from Cornell University. She finished her Masters of Computer Science from University of Chicago and will soon complete her PhD in Computer Science, also from the University of Chicago.

Part 1

Introduction to parallel computing

T he first part of this book covers topics of general importance to parallel computing. These topics include

- Understanding the resources in a parallel computer
- Estimating the performance and speedup of applications
- Looking at software engineering needs particular to parallel computing
- Considering choices for data structures
- Selecting algorithms that perform and parallelize well

While these topics should be considered first by a parallel programmer, these will not have the same importance to all readers of this book. For the parallel application developer, all of the chapters in this part address upfront concerns for a successful project. A project needs to select the right hardware, the right type of parallelism, and the right kind of expectations. You should determine the appropriate data structures and algorithms before starting your parallelization efforts; it's much harder to change these later.

Even if you are a parallel application developer, you may not need the full depth of material discussed. Those desiring only modest parallelism or serving a particular role on a team of developers might find a cursory understanding of the content sufficient. If you just want to explore parallel computing, we suggest reading chapter 1 and chapter 5, then skimming the others to get the terminology that is used in discussing parallel computing.

We include chapter 2 for those who may not have a software engineering background or for those who just need a refresher. If you are new to all of the details of CPU hardware, then you may need to read chapter 3 in small increments. An understanding of the current computing hardware and your application is important in extracting performance, but it doesn't have to come all at once. Be sure to return to chapter 3 when you are ready to purchase your next computing system so you can cut through all the marketing claims to what is really important for your application.

The discussion of data design and performance modeling in chapter 4 can be challenging because it requires an understanding of hardware details, their performance, and compilers to fully appreciate. Although it's an important topic due to the impact the cache and compiler optimizations have on performance, it's not necessary for writing a simple parallel program.

We encourage you to follow along with the accompanying examples for the book. You should spend some time exploring the many examples that are available in these software repositories at https://github.com/EssentialsOfParallelComputing.

The examples are organized by chapter and include detailed information for setup on various hardware and operating systems. For helping to deal with portability issues, there are sample container builds for Ubuntu distributions in Docker. There are also instructions for setting up a virtual machine through VirtualBox. If you have a need for setting your own system up, you may want to read the section on Docker and virtual machines in chapter 13. But containers and virtual machines come with restricted environments that are not easy to work around.

Our work is ongoing for the container builds and other system environment setups to work properly for the many possible system configurations. Getting the system software installed correctly, especially the GPU driver and associated software, is the most challenging part of the journey. The wide variety of operating systems, hardware including graphics processing units (GPUs), and the often overlooked quality of installation software makes this a difficult task. One alternative is to use a cluster where the software is already installed. Still, it is helpful at some point to get some software installed on your laptop or desktop for a more convenient development resource. Now it is time to turn the page and enter the world of parallel computing. It is a world of nearly unlimited performance and potential.

Why parallel computing?

1

This chapter covers

- What parallel computing is and why it's growing in importance
- Where parallelism exists in modern hardware
- Why the amount of application parallelism is important
- Software approaches to exploit parallelism

In today's world, you'll find many challenges requiring extensive and efficient use of computing resources. Most of the applications requiring performance traditionally are in the scientific domain. But artificial intelligence (AI) and machine learning applications are projected to become the predominant users of large-scale computing. Some examples of these applications include

- Modeling megafires to assist fire crews and to help the public
- Modeling tsunamis and storm surges from hurricanes (see chapter 13 for a simple tsunami model)
- Voice recognition for computer interfaces
- Modeling virus spread and vaccine development

- Modeling climatic conditions over decades and centuries
- Image recognition for driverless car technology
- Equipping emergency crews with running simulations of hazards such as flooding
- Reducing power consumption for mobile devices

With the techniques covered in this book, you will be able to handle larger problems and datasets, while also running simulations ten, a hundred, or even a thousand times faster. Typical applications leave much of the compute capability of today's computers untapped. Parallel computing is the key to unlocking the potential of your computer resources. So what is parallel computing and how can you use it to supercharge your applications?

Parallel computing is the execution of many operations at a single instance in time. Fully exploiting parallel computing does not happen automatically. It requires some effort from the programmer. First, you must identify and expose the potential for parallelism in an application. Potential parallelism, or *concurrency*, means that you certify that it is safe to conduct operations in any order as the system resources become available. And, with parallel computing, there is an additional requirement: these operations must occur at the same time. For this to happen, you must also properly leverage the resources to execute these operations simultaneously.

Parallel computing introduces new concerns that are not present in a serial world. We need to change our thought processes to adapt to the additional complexities of parallel execution, but with practice, this becomes second nature. This book begins your discovery in how to access the power of parallel computing.

Life presents numerous examples of parallel processing, and these instances often become the basis for computing strategies. Figure 1.1 shows a supermarket checkout line, where the goal is to have customers quickly pay for the items they want to purchase. This can be done by employing multiple cashiers to process, or check out, the customers one at a time. In this case, the skilled cashiers can more quickly execute the checkout process so customers leave faster. Another strategy is to employ many self-checkout stations and allow customers to execute the process on their own. This strategy requires fewer human resources from the supermarket and can open more lanes to process customers. Customers may not be able to check themselves out as efficiently as a trained cashier, but perhaps more customers can check out quickly due to increased parallelism resulting in shorter lines.

We solve computational problems by developing *algorithms*: a set of steps to achieve a desired result. In the supermarket analogy, the process of checking out is the algorithm. In this case, it includes unloading items from a basket, scanning the items to obtain a price, and paying for the items. This algorithm is sequential (or serial); it must follow this order. If there are hundreds of customers that need to execute this task, the algorithm for checking out many customers contains a parallelism that can be taken advantage of. Theoretically, there is no dependency between any two customers going through the checkout process. By using multiple checkout lines or self-checkout stations, supermarkets expose parallelism, thereby increasing the rate at which

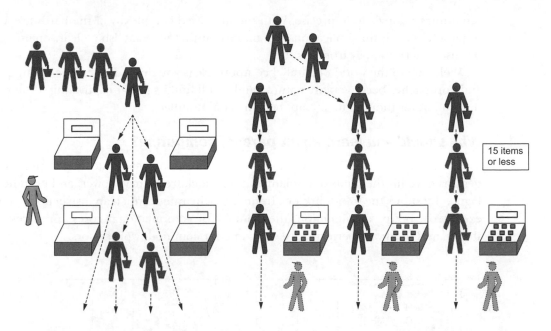

Figure 1.1 Everyday parallelism in supermarket checkout queues. The checkout cashiers (with caps) process their queue of customers (with baskets). On the left, one cashier processes four self-checkout lanes simultaneously. On the right, one cashier is required for each checkout lane. Each option impacts the supermarket's costs and checkout rates.

customers buy goods and leave the store. Each choice in how we implement this parallelism results in different costs and benefits.

> **DEFINITION** *Parallel computing* is the practice of identifying and exposing parallelism in algorithms, expressing this in our software, and understanding the costs, benefits, and limitations of the chosen implementation.

In the end, parallel computing is about *performance*. This includes more than just speed, but also the size of the problem and energy efficiency. Our goal in this book is to give you an understanding of the breadth of the current parallel computing field and familiarize you with enough of the most commonly used languages, techniques, and tools so that you can tackle a parallel computing project with confidence. Important decisions about how to incorporate parallelism are often made at the outset of a project. A reasoned design is an important step toward success. Avoiding the design step can lead to problems much later. It is equally important to keep expectations realistic and to know both the available resources and the nature of the project.

Another goal of this chapter is to introduce the terminology used in parallel computing. One way to do that is to point you to the glossary in appendix C for a quick reference on terminology as you read this book. Because this field and the technology has grown incrementally, the use of many of the terms by those in the parallel community is oftentimes sloppy and imprecise. With the increased complexity of the hardware and of parallelism within applications, it's important that we establish a clear, unambiguous use of terminology from the start.

Welcome to the world of parallel computing! As you delve deeper, the techniques and approaches become more natural, and you'll find its power captivating. Problems that you never thought to attempt become commonplace.

1.1 Why should you learn about parallel computing?

The future is parallel. The increase in serial performance has plateaued as processor designs have hit the limits of miniaturization, clock frequency, power, and even heat. Figure 1.2 shows the trends in clock frequency (the rate at which an instruction can be executed), power consumption, the number of computational cores (or cores for short), and hardware performance over time for commodity processors.

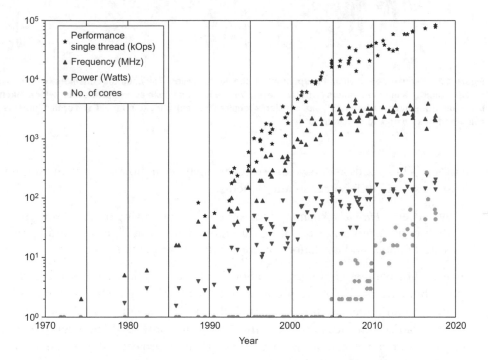

Figure 1.2   Single thread performance, CPU clock frequency (MHz), CPU power consumption (watts), and the number of CPU cores from 1970 to 2018. The parallel computing era begins about 2005, when the core count in CPU chips begins to rise, while the clock frequency and power consumption plateaus, yet performance steadily increases (Horowitz et al. and Rupp, https://github.com/karlrupp/microprocessor-trend-data).

In 2005, the number of cores abruptly increased from a single core to multiple cores. At the same time, clock frequency and power consumption flattened out. Theoretical performance steadily increased because performance is proportional to the product of clock frequency and the number of cores. This shift towards increasing the core count rather than the clock speed indicates that achieving the most ideal performance of a central processing unit (CPU) is only available through parallel computing.

Modern consumer-grade computing hardware comes equipped with multiple central processing units (CPUs) and/or graphics processing units (GPUs) that process multiple instruction sets simultaneously. These smaller systems often rival the computing power of supercomputers of two decades ago. Making full use of compute resources (on laptops, workstations, smart phones, and so forth) requires you, the programmer, to have a working knowledge of the tools available for writing parallel applications. You must also understand the hardware features that boost parallelism.

Because there are many different parallel hardware features, this presents new complexities to the programmer. One of these features is hyperthreading, introduced by Intel. Having two instruction queues interleaving work to the hardware logic units allows a single physical core to appear as two cores to the operating system (OS). Vector processors are another hardware feature that began appearing in commodity processors in about 2000. These execute multiple instructions at once. The width in bits of the vector processor (also called a vector unit) specifies the number of instructions to execute simultaneously. Thus, a 256 bit-wide vector unit can execute four 64-bit (doubles) or eight 32-bit (single-precision) instructions at one time.

Example

Let's take a 16-core CPU with hyperthreading and a 256 bit-wide vector unit, commonly found in home desktops. A serial program using a single core and no vectorization only uses 0.8% of the theoretical processing capability of this processor! The calculation is

16 cores × 2 hyperthreads × (256 bit-wide vector unit)/(64-bit double) = 128-way parallelism

where 1 serial path/128 parallel paths = .008 or 0.8%. The following figure shows that this is a small fraction of the total CPU processing power.

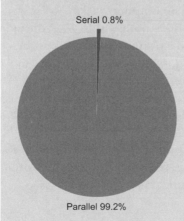

Serial 0.8%

Parallel 99.2%

A serial application only accesses 0.8% of the processing power of a 16-core CPU.

> **(continued)**
> Calculating theoretical and realistic expectations for serial and parallel performance as shown in this example is an important skill. We'll discuss this in more depth in chapter 3.

Some improvement in software development tools has helped to add parallelism to our toolkits, and currently, the research community is doing more, but it is still a long way from addressing the performance gap. This puts a lot of the burden on us, the software developers, to get the most from a new generation of processors.

Unfortunately, software developers have lagged in adapting to this fundamental change in computing power. Further, transitioning current applications to make use of modern parallel architectures can be daunting due to the explosion of new programming languages and application programming interfaces (APIs). But a good working knowledge of your application, an ability to see and expose parallelism, and a solid understanding of the tools available can result in substantial benefits. Exactly what kind of benefits would applications see? Let's take a closer look.

1.1.1   *What are the potential benefits of parallel computing?*

Parallel computing can reduce your time to solution, increase the energy efficiency in your application, and enable you to tackle larger problems on currently existing hardware. Today, parallel computing no longer is the sole domain of the largest computing systems. The technology is now present in everyone's desktop or laptop, and even on handheld devices. This makes it possible for every software developer to create parallel software on their local systems, thereby greatly expanding the opportunity for new applications.

Cutting edge research from both industry and academia reveals new areas for parallel computing as interest broadens from scientific computing into machine learning, big data, computer graphics, and consumer applications. The emergence of new technologies such as self-driving cars, computer vision, voice recognition, and AI requires large computational capabilities both within the consumer device and in the development sphere, where massive training datasets must be consumed and processed. And in scientific computing, which has long been the exclusive domain of parallel computing, there are also new, exciting possibilities. The proliferation of remote sensors and handheld devices that can feed data into larger, more realistic computations to better inform decision-making around natural and man-made disasters allows for more extensive data.

It must be remembered that parallel computing itself is not the goal. Rather, the goals are what results from parallel computing: reducing run time, performing larger calculations, or decreasing energy consumption.

FASTER RUN TIME WITH MORE COMPUTE CORES

Reduction of an application's run time, or the *speedup*, is often thought to be the primary goal of parallel computing. Indeed, this is usually its biggest impact. Parallel computing can speed up intensive calculations, multimedia processing, and big data operations, whether your applications take days or even weeks to process or the results are needed in real-time now.

In the past, the programmer would spend greater efforts on serial optimization to squeeze out a few percentage improvements. Now, there is the potential for orders of magnitude of improvement with multiple avenues to choose from. This creates a new problem in exploring the possible parallel paradigms—more opportunities than programming manpower. But, a thorough knowledge of your application and an awareness of parallelism opportunities can lead you down a clearer path towards reducing your application's run time.

LARGER PROBLEM SIZES WITH MORE COMPUTE NODES

By exposing parallelism in your application, you can scale up your problem's size to dimensions that were out of reach with a serial application. This is because the amount of compute resources dictates what *can* be done, and exposing parallelism permits you to operate on larger resources, presenting opportunities that were never considered before. The larger sizes are enabled by greater amounts of main memory, disk storage, bandwidth over networks and to disk, and CPUs. In analogy with the supermarket as mentioned earlier, exposing parallelism is equivalent to employing more cashiers or opening more self-checkout lanes to handle a larger and growing number of customers.

ENERGY EFFICIENCY BY DOING MORE WITH LESS

One of the new impact areas of parallel computing is energy efficiency. With the emergence of parallel resources in handheld devices, parallelism can speed up applications. This allows the device to return to sleep mode sooner and permits the use of slower, but more parallel processors that consume less power. Thus, moving heavyweight multimedia applications to run on GPUs can have a more dramatic effect on energy efficiency while also resulting in vastly improved performance. The net result of employing parallelism reduces power consumption and extends battery life, which is a strong competitive advantage in this market niche.

Another area where energy efficiency is important is with remote sensors, network devices, and operational field-deployed devices, such as remote weather stations. Often, without large power supplies, these devices must be able to function in small packages with few resources. Parallelism expands what can be done on these devices and offloads the work from the central computing system in a growing trend that is called *edge compute*. Moving the computation to the very edge of the network enables processing at the source of the data, condensing it into a smaller result set that can be more easily sent over the network.

Accurately calculating the energy costs of an application is challenging without direct measurements of power usage. However, you can estimate the cost by multiplying the manufacturer's thermal design power by the application's run time and the number of processors used. Thermal design power is the rate at which energy is expended under typical operational loads. The energy consumption for your application can be estimated using the formula

$$P = (N\,\text{Processors}) \times (R\,\text{Watts/Processors}) \times (T\,\text{hours})$$

where P is the energy consumption, N is the number of processors, R is the thermal design power, and T is the application run time.

Example

Intel's 16-core Xeon E5-4660 processor has a thermal design power of 120 W. Suppose that your application uses 20 of these processors for 24 hours to run to completion. The estimated energy usage for your application is

$$P = (20\ \text{Processors}) \times (120\ \text{W/Processors}) \times (24\ \text{hours}) = 57.60\ \text{kWhrs}$$

In general, GPUs have a higher thermal design power than modern CPUs, but can potentially reduce run time or require only a few GPUs to obtain the same result. The same formula can be used as before, where N is now seen as the number of GPUs.

Example

Suppose that you've ported your application to a multi-GPU platform. You can now run your application on four NVIDIA Tesla V100 GPUs in 24 hrs! NVIDIA's Tesla V100 GPU has a maximum thermal design power of 300 W. The estimated energy usage for your application is

$$P = (4\ \text{GPUs}) \times (300\ \text{W/GPUs}) \times (24\ \text{hrs}) = 28.80\ \text{kWhrs}$$

In this example, the GPU accelerated application runs at half the energy cost as the CPU-only version. Note that, in this case, even though the time to solution remains the same, the energy expense is cut in half!

Achieving a reduction in energy cost through accelerator devices like GPUs requires that the application has sufficient parallelism that can be exposed. This permits the efficient use of the resources on the device.

PARALLEL COMPUTING CAN REDUCE COSTS

Actual monetary cost is becoming a more visible concern for software developer teams, software users, and researchers alike. As the size of applications and systems grows, we need to perform a cost-benefit analysis on the resources available. For example, with the next large High Performance Computing (HPC) systems, the power costs are projected to be three times the cost of the hardware acquisition.

Usage costs have also promoted cloud computing as an alternative, which is being increasingly adopted across academia, start-ups, and industries. In general, cloud providers bill by the type and quantity of resources used and the amount of time spent using these. Although GPUs are generally more expensive than CPUs per unit time, some applications can leverage GPU accelerators such that there are sufficient reductions in run time relative to the CPU expense to yield lower costs.

1.1.2 Parallel computing cautions

Parallel computing is not a panacea. Many applications are neither large enough or require enough run time to need parallel computing. Some may not even have enough inherent parallelism to exploit. Also, transitioning applications to leverage multi-core and many-core (GPU) hardware requires a dedicated effort that can temporarily shift attention away from direct research or product goals. The investment of time and effort must first be deemed worthwhile. It is always more important that the application runs and generates the desired result before making it fast and scaling it up to larger problems.

We strongly recommend that you start your parallel computing project with a plan. It's important to know what options are available for accelerating the application, then select the most appropriate for your project. After that, it is crucial to have a reasonable estimate of the effort involved and the potential payoffs (in terms of dollar cost, energy consumption, time to solution, and other metrics that can be important). In this chapter, we begin to give you the knowledge and skills to make decisions on parallel computing projects up front.

1.2 The fundamental laws of parallel computing

In serial computing, all operations speed up as the clock frequency increases. In contrast, with parallel computing, we need to give some thought and modify our applications to fully exploit parallel hardware. Why is the amount of parallelism important? To understand this, let's take a look at the parallel computing laws.

1.2.1 The limit to parallel computing: Amdahl's Law

We need a way to calculate the potential speedup of a calculation based on the amount of the code that is parallel. This can be done using Amdahl's Law, proposed by Gene Amdahl in 1967. This law describes the speedup of a fixed-size problem as the processors increase. The following equation shows this, where P is the parallel fraction of the code, S is the serial fraction, which means that $P + S = 1$, and N is the number of processors:

$$SpeedUp(N) = \frac{1}{S + \frac{P}{N}}$$

Amdahl's Law highlights that no matter how fast we make the parallel part of the code, we will always be limited by the serial portion. Figure 1.3 visualizes this limitation. This scaling of a fixed-size problem is referred to as strong scaling.

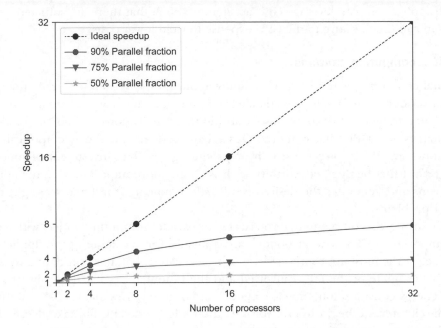

Figure 1.3   Speedup for a fixed-size problem according to Amdahl's Law is shown as a function of the number of processors. Lines show ideal speedup when 100% of an algorithm is parallelized, and for 90%, 75%, and 50%. Amdahl's Law states that speedup is limited by the fractions of code that remain serial.

> **DEFINITION**   *Strong scaling* represents the time to solution with respect to the number of processors for a fixed total size.

1.2.2   *Breaking through the parallel limit: Gustafson-Barsis's Law*

Gustafson and Barsis pointed out in 1988 that parallel code runs should increase the size of the problem as more processors are added. This can give us an alternate way to calculate the potential speedup of our application. If the size of the problem grows proportionally to the number of processors, the speedup is now expressed as

$$SpeedUp(N) = N - S * (N - 1)$$

where N is the number of processors, and S is the serial fraction as before. The result is that a larger problem can be solved in the same time by using more processors. This provides additional opportunities to exploit parallelism. Indeed, growing the size of the problem with the number of processors makes sense because the application

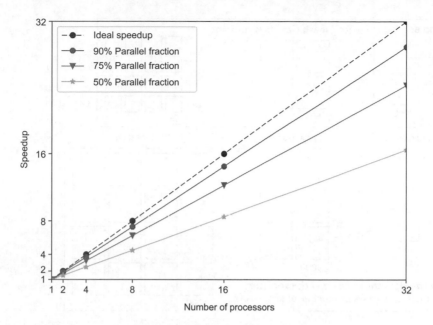

Figure 1.4   Speedup for when the size of a problem grows with the number of available processors according to Gustafson-Barsis's Law is shown as a function of the number of processors. Lines show ideal speedup when 100% of an algorithm is parallelized, and for 90%, 75%, and 50%.

user wants to benefit from more than just the power of the additional processor and wants to use the additional memory. The run-time scaling for this scenario, shown in figure 1.4, is called weak scaling.

> **DEFINITION**   *Weak scaling* represents the time to solution with respect to the number of processors for a fixed-sized problem per processor.

Figure 1.5 shows the difference between strong and weak scaling in a visual representation. The weak scaling argument that the mesh size should stay constant on each processor makes good use of the resources of the additional processor. The strong scaling perspective is primarily concerned with speedup of the calculation. In practice, *both* strong scaling and weak scaling are important because these address different user scenarios.

The term *scalability* is often used to refer to whether more parallelism can be added in either the hardware or the software and whether there is an overall limit to how much improvement can occur. While the traditional focus is on the run-time scaling, we will make the argument that memory scaling is often more important.

Figure 1.6 shows an application with limited memory scalability. A *replicated array* (R) is a dataset that is duplicated across all the processors. A *distributed array* (D) is partitioned and split across the processors. For example, in a game simulation, 100

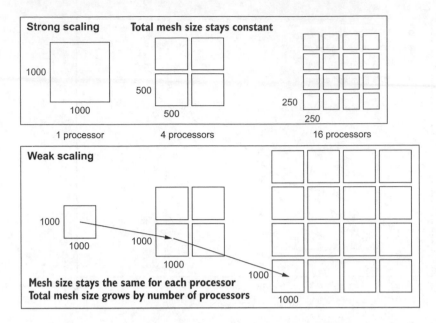

Figure 1.5 Strong scaling keeps the same overall size of a problem and splits it across additional processors. In weak scaling, the size of the mesh stays the same for each processor and the total size increases.

characters can be distributed across 4 processors with 25 characters on each processor. But the map of the game board might be copied to every processor. In figure 1.6, the replicated array is duplicated across the mesh. Because this figure is for weak scaling, the problem size grows as the number of processors increases. For 4 processors, the array is 4 times as large on each processor. As the number of processors and the

Memory sizes for weak scaling with replicated and distributed arrays

	1 proc	2 proc		4 proc	
	Proc 0	Proc 0	Proc 1	Proc 0	Proc 1
Array R	100 MB	200 MB	200 MB	400 MB	400 MB
Array D	100 MB	100 MB	100 MB	100 MB	100 MB
				Proc 2	Proc 3
				400 MB	400 MB
				100 MB	100 MB

Array R – Array is replicated (copied) to every processor
Array D – Array is distributed across processors

Figure 1.6 Distributed arrays stay the same size as the problem and number of processors doubles (weak scaling). But replicated (copied) arrays need all the data on each processor, and memory grows rapidly with the number of processors. Even if the run time weakly scales (stays constant), the memory requirements limit scalability.

size of the problem grows, soon there is not enough memory on a processor for the job to run. Limited run-time scaling means the job runs slowly; limited memory scaling means the job can't run at all. It is also the case that if the application's memory can be distributed, the run time usually scales as well. The reverse, however, is not necessarily true.

One view of a computationally intensive job is that every byte of memory gets touched in every cycle of processing, and run time is a function of memory size. Reducing memory size will necessarily reduce run time. The initial focus in parallelism should thus be to reduce the memory size as the number of processors grows.

1.3 How does parallel computing work?

Parallel computing requires combining an understanding of hardware, software, and parallelism to develop an application. It is more than just message passing or threading. Current hardware and software give many different options to bring parallelization to your application. Some of these options can be combined to yield even greater efficiency and speedup.

It is important to have an understanding of the parallelization in your application and the way different hardware components allow you to expose it. Further, developers need to recognize that between your source code and the hardware, your application must traverse additional layers, including a compiler and an OS (figure 1.7).

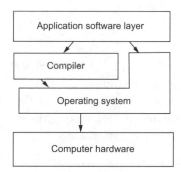

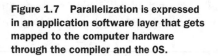

Figure 1.7 Parallelization is expressed in an application software layer that gets mapped to the computer hardware through the compiler and the OS.

As a developer, you are responsible for the application software layer, which includes your source code. In the source code, you make choices about the programming language and parallel software interfaces you use to leverage the underlying hardware. Additionally, you decide how to break up your work into parallel units. A compiler is designed to translate your source code into a form the hardware can execute. With these instructions at hand, an OS manages executing these on the computer hardware.

We will show you with an example how to introduce parallelization to an algorithm through a prototype application. This process takes place in the application software layer but requires an understanding of computer hardware. For now, we'll refrain from discussing the choice in compiler and OS. We will incrementally add each layer of parallelization so that you can see how this works. With each parallel strategy, we will explain how the available hardware influences the choices that are made. The purpose in doing this is to demonstrate how hardware features influence the parallel strategies. We categorize the parallel approaches a developer can take into

- Process-based parallelization
- Thread-based parallelization
- Vectorization
- Stream processing

Following the example, we will introduce a model to help you think about modern hardware. This model breaks down modern compute hardware into individual components and the variety of compute devices. A simplified view of memory is included in this chapter. A more detailed look at the memory hierarchy is presented in chapters 3 and 4. Finally, we will discuss in more detail the application and software layers.

As mentioned, we categorize the parallel approaches a developer can take into process-based parallelization, thread-based parallelization, vectorization, and stream processing. Parallelization based on individual processes with their own memory spaces can be distributed memory on different nodes of a computer or within a node. Stream processing is generally associated with GPUs. The model for modern hardware and application software will help you better understand how to plan to port your application to current parallel hardware.

1.3.1   *Walking through a sample application*

For this introduction to parallelization, we will look at a data parallel approach. This is one of the most common parallel computing application strategies. We'll perform the computation on a spatial mesh composed of a regular two-dimensional (2D) grid of rectangular elements or cells. The steps (summarized here and described in detail later) to create the spatial mesh and prepare for the calculation are

1 Discretize (break up) the problem into smaller cells or elements
2 Define a computational kernel (operation) to conduct on each element of the mesh
3 Add the following layers of parallelization on CPUs and GPUs to perform the calculation:
   - *Vectorization*—Work on more than one unit of data at a time
   - *Threads*—Deploy more than one compute pathway to engage more processing cores
   - *Processes*—Separate program instances to spread out the calculation into separate memory spaces
   - *Off-loading the calculation to GPUs*—Send the data to the graphics processor to calculate

We start with a 2D problem domain of a region of space. For purposes of illustration, we will use a 2D image of the Krakatau volcano (figure 1.8) as our example. The goal of our calculation could be to model the volcanic plume, the resulting tsunami, or the early detection of a volcanic eruption using machine learning. For all of these options, calculation speed is critical if we want real-time results to inform our decisions.

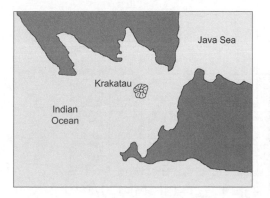

Figure 1.8 An example 2D spatial domain for a numerical simulation. Numerical simulations typically involve stencil operations (see figure 1.11) or large matrix-vector systems. These types of operations are often used in fluids modeling to yield predictions of tsunami arrival times, weather forecasts, smoke plume spreading, and other processes necessary for informed decisions.

STEP 1: DISCRETIZE THE PROBLEM INTO SMALLER CELLS OR ELEMENTS

For any detailed calculation, we must first break up the domain of the problem into smaller pieces (figure 1.9), a process that is called *discretization*. In image processing, this is often just the pixels in a bitmap image. For a computational domain, these are called cells or elements. The collection of cells or elements form a *computational mesh* that covers the spatial region for the simulation. Data values for each cell might be integers, floats, or doubles.

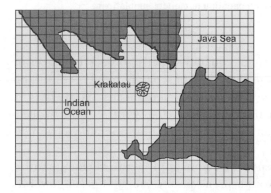

Figure 1.9 The domain is discretized into cells. For each cell in the computational domain, properties such as wave height, fluid velocity, or smoke density are solved for according to physical laws. Ultimately, a stencil operation or a matrix-vector system represents this discrete scheme.

STEP 2: DEFINE A COMPUTATIONAL KERNEL, OR OPERATION, TO CONDUCT ON EACH ELEMENT OF THE MESH

The calculations on this discretized data are often some form of a stencil operation, so-called because it involves a pattern of adjacent cells to calculate the new value for each cell. This can be an average (a blur operation, which blurs the image or makes it fuzzier), a gradient (edge-detection, which sharpens the edges in the image), or another more complex operation associated with solving physical systems described by partial differential equations (PDEs). Figure 1.10 shows a stencil operation as a five-point stencil that performs a blur operation by using a weighted average of the stencil values.

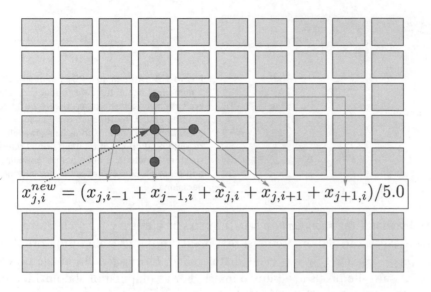

$$x_{j,i}^{new} = (x_{j,i-1} + x_{j-1,i} + x_{j,i} + x_{j,i+1} + x_{j+1,i})/5.0$$

Figure 1.10 **A five-point stencil operator as a cross pattern on the computational mesh. The data marked by the stencil are read in the operation and stored in the center cell. This pattern is repeated for every cell. The blur operator, one of the simpler stencil operators, is a weighted sum of the five points marked with the large dots and updates a value at the central point of the stencil. This type of operation is done for smoothing operations or wave propagation numerical simulations.**

But what are these partial differential equations? Let's go back to our example and imagine this time it is a color image composed of separate red, green, and blue arrays to make an RGB color model. The term "partial" here means that there is more than one variable and that we are separating out the change of red with space and time from that of green and blue. Then we carry out the blur operator separately on each of these colors.

There is one more requirement: we need to apply a rate of change with time and space. In other words, the red would spread at one rate and green and blue at others. This could be to produce a special effect on an image, or it can describe how real colors bleed and merge in a photographic image during development. In the scientific world, instead of red, green, and blue, we might have mass and *x* and *y* velocity. With the addition of a little more physics, we might have the motion of a wave or an ash plume.

STEP 3: VECTORIZATION TO WORK ON MORE THAN ONE UNIT OF DATA AT A TIME

We start introducing parallelization by looking at vectorization. What is vectorization? Some processors have the ability to operate on more than one piece of data at a time; a capability referred to as *vector operations*. The shaded blocks in figure 1.11 illustrate how multiple data values are operated on simultaneously in a vector unit in a processor with one instruction in one clock cycle.

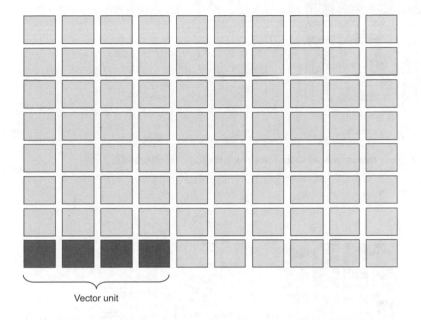

Vector unit

Figure 1.11   A special vector operation is conducted on four doubles. This operation can be executed in a single clock cycle with little additional energy costs to the serial operation.

STEP 4: THREADS TO DEPLOY MORE THAN ONE COMPUTE PATHWAY TO ENGAGE MORE PROCESSING CORES

Because most CPUs today have at least four processing cores, we use threading to operate the cores simultaneously across four rows at a time. Figure 1.12 shows this process.

STEP 5: PROCESSES TO SPREAD OUT THE CALCULATION TO SEPARATE MEMORY SPACES

We can further split the work between processors on two desktops, often called *nodes* in parallel processing. When the work is split across nodes, the memory spaces for each node are distinct and separate. This is indicated by putting a gap between the rows as in figure 1.13.

Even for this fairly modest hardware scenario, there is a potential speedup of 32x. This is shown by the following:

$$\text{2 desktops (nodes)} \times \text{4 cores} \times \text{(256 bit-wide vector unit)}/\text{(64-bit double)} =$$
$$\text{32x potential speedup}$$

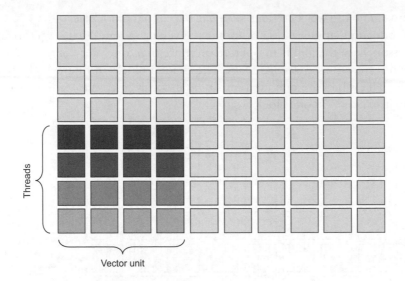

Figure 1.12   Four threads process four rows of vector units simultaneously.

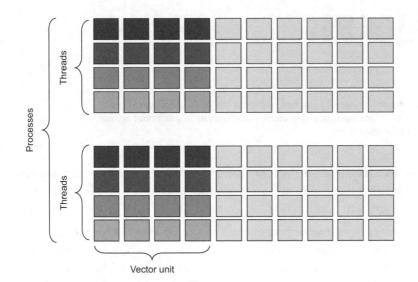

Figure 1.13   This algorithm can be parallelized further by distributing the 4×4 blocks among distinct processes. Each process uses four threads, each handling a four-node-wide vector unit in a single clock cycle. Additional white space in the figure illustrates the process boundaries.

If we look at a high-end cluster with 16 nodes, 36 cores per node, and a 512-bit vector processor, the potential theoretical speedup is 4,608 times faster than a serial process:

16 nodes × 36 cores × (512 bit-wide vector unit)/(64-bit double) =
4,608x potential speedup

STEP 6: OFF-LOADING THE CALCULATION TO GPUS

The GPU is another hardware resource for supercharging parallelization. With GPUs, we can harness lots of *streaming multiprocessors* for work. For example, figure 1.14 shows how the work can be split up separately into 8x8 tiles. Using the hardware specifications for the NVIDIA Volta GPU, these tiles can be operated on by 32 double-precision cores spread out over 84 streaming multiprocessors, giving us a total of 2,688 double-precision cores that work simultaneously. If we have one GPU per node in a 16-node cluster, each with a 2,688 double-precision streaming multiprocessor, this is a 43,008-way parallelization from 16 GPUs.

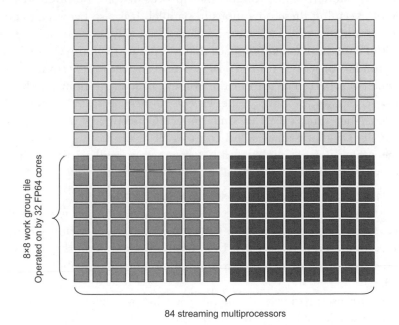

Figure 1.14 On a GPU, the vector length is much larger than on a CPU. Here, 8×8 tiles are distributed across GPU work groups.

These are impressive numbers, but at this point, we must temper expectations by acknowledging that actual speedup falls far short of this full potential. Our challenge now becomes organizing such extreme and disparate layers of parallelization to obtain as much speedup as possible.

For this high-level application walk-through, we left out a lot of important details, which we will cover in later chapters. But even this nominal level of detail highlights some of the strategies for exposing parallelization of an algorithm. To be able to develop similar strategies for other problems, an understanding of modern hardware and software is necessary. We now dive deeper into the current hardware and software models. These conceptual models are simplified representations of the diverse real-world hardware to avoid complexity and maintain generality over quickly evolving systems.

1.3.2   *A hardware model for today's heterogeneous parallel systems*

To build a basic understanding of how parallel computing works, we'll explain the components in today's hardware. To begin, Dynamic Random Access Memory, called DRAM, stores information or data. A computational core, or core for short, performs arithmetic operations (add, subtract, multiply, divide), evaluates logical statements, and loads and stores data from DRAM. When an operation is performed on data, the instructions and data are loaded from memory onto the core, operated on, and stored back into memory. Modern CPUs, often called processors, are outfitted with many cores capable of executing these operations in parallel. It is also becoming common to find systems outfitted with accelerator hardware, like GPUs. GPUs are equipped with thousands of cores and a memory space that is separate from the CPU's DRAM.

A combination of a processor (or two), DRAM, and an accelerator compose a compute node, which can be referred to in the context of a single home desktop or a "rack" in a supercomputer. Compute nodes can be connected to each other with one or more networks, sometimes called an interconnect. Conceptually, a node runs a single instance of the OS that manages and controls all of the hardware resources. As hardware is becoming more complex and heterogeneous, we'll start with simplified models of the system's components so that each is more obvious.

DISTRIBUTED MEMORY ARCHITECTURE: A CROSS-NODE PARALLEL METHOD

One of the first and most scalable approaches to parallel computing is the distributed memory cluster (figure 1.15). Each CPU has its own local memory composed of DRAM and is connected to other CPUs by a communication network. Good scalability of distributed memory clusters arises from its seemingly limitless ability to incorporate more nodes.

This architecture also provides some memory locality by dividing the total addressable memory into smaller subspaces for each node, which makes accessing memory

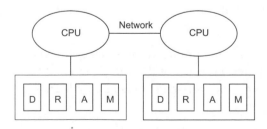

Figure 1.15   **The distributed memory architecture links nodes composed of separate memory spaces. These nodes can be workstations or racks.**

off-node clearly different than on-node. This forces the programmer to explicitly access different memory regions. The disadvantage of this is that the programmer must manage the partitioning of the memory spaces at the outset of the application.

SHARED MEMORY ARCHITECTURE: AN ON-NODE PARALLEL METHOD

An alternative approach connects the two CPUs directly to the same shared memory (figure 1.16). The strength of this approach is that the processors share the same address space, which simplifies programming. But this introduces potential memory conflicts, resulting in correctness and performance issues. Synchronizing memory access and values between CPUs or the processing cores on a multi-core CPU is complicated and expensive.

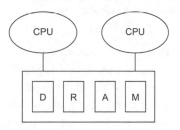

Figure 1.16   The shared memory architecture provides parallelization within a node.

The addition of more CPUs and processing cores does not increase the amount of memory available to the application. This and the synchronization costs limit the scalability of the shared memory architecture.

VECTOR UNITS: MULTIPLE OPERATIONS WITH ONE INSTRUCTION

Why not just increase the clock frequency for the processor to get greater throughput as done in the past? The biggest limitation in increasing CPU clock frequencies is that it requires more power and produces more heat. Whether it is an HPC supercomputing center with limits on installed power lines or your cell phone with limited battery capacity, devices today all have power limitations. This problem is called *the power wall*.

Rather than increasing the clock frequency, why not do more than one operation per cycle? This is the idea behind the resurgence of vectorization on many processors. It takes only a little more energy to do multiple operations in a vector unit, compared to a single operation (more formally called a *scalar operation*). With vectorization, we can process more data in a single clock cycle than with a serial process. There is little change to the power requirements for multiple operations (versus just one), and a reduction in execution time can lead to a decrease in energy consumption for an application. Much like a four-lane freeway that allows four cars to move simultaneously in comparison to a single lane road, the vector operation gives greater processing throughput. Indeed, the four pathways through the vector unit, shown in different shadings in figure 1.17, are commonly called *lanes* of a vector operation.

Most CPUs and GPUs have some capability for vectorization or equivalent operations. The amount of data processed in one clock cycle, the *vector length*, depends on the size of the vector units on the processor. Currently, the most commonly available vector length is 256-bits. If the discretized data are 64-bit doubles, then we can do four floating-point operations simultaneously as a vector operation. As figure 1.17 illustrates, vector hardware units load one block of data at a time, perform a single operation on the data simultaneously, and then store the result.

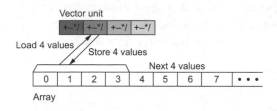

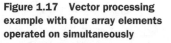

Figure 1.17   Vector processing example with four array elements operated on simultaneously

ACCELERATOR DEVICE: A SPECIAL-PURPOSE ADD-ON PROCESSOR

An *accelerator device* is a discrete piece of hardware designed for executing specific tasks at a fast rate. The most common accelerator device is the GPU. When used for computation, this device is sometimes referred to as a general-purpose graphics processing unit (GPGPU). The GPU contains many small processing cores, called streaming multiprocessors (SMs). Although simpler than a CPU core, SMs provide a massive amount of processing power. Usually, you'll find a small integrated GPU on the CPU.

Most modern computers also have a separate, discrete GPU connected to the CPU by the Peripheral Component Interface (PCI) bus (figure 1.18). This bus introduces a communication cost for data and instructions, but the discrete card is often more powerful than an integrated unit. In high-end systems, for example, NVIDIA uses NVLink and AMD Radeon uses their Infinity Fabric to reduce data communication costs, but this cost still is substantial. We will discuss the interesting GPU architecture more in chapters 9–12.

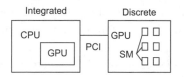

Figure 1.18   GPUs come in two varieties: integrated and discrete. Discrete or dedicated GPUs typically have a large number of streaming multiprocessors and their own DRAM. Accessing data on a discrete GPU requires communication over a PCI bus.

GENERAL HETEROGENEOUS PARALLEL ARCHITECTURE MODEL

Now let's combine all of these different hardware architectures into one model (figure 1.19). Two nodes, each with two CPUs, share the same DRAM memory. Each CPU is a dual-core processor with an integrated GPU. A discrete GPU on the PCI bus also attaches to one of the CPUs. Though the CPUs share main memory, these are commonly in different Non-Uniform Memory Access (NUMA) regions. This means that accessing the second CPU's memory is more expensive than getting at it's own memory.

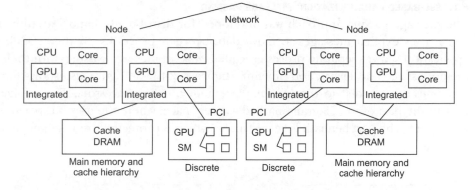

Figure 1.19 A general heterogeneous parallel architecture model consisting of two nodes connected by a network. Each node has a multi-core CPU with an integrated and discrete GPU and some memory (DRAM). Modern compute hardware normally has some arrangement of these components.

Throughout this hardware discussion, we have presented a simplified model of the memory hierarchy, showing just DRAM or main memory. We've shown a cache in the combined model (figure 1.19), but no detail on its composition or how it functions. We reserve our discussion of the complexities of memory management, including multiple levels of cache, for chapter 3. In this section, we simply presented a model for today's hardware to help you identify the available components so that you can select the parallel strategy best suited for your application and hardware choices.

1.3.3 *The application/software model for today's heterogeneous parallel systems*

The software model for parallel computing is necessarily motivated by the underlying hardware but is nonetheless distinct from it. The OS provides the interface between the two. Parallel operations do not spring to life on their own; rather, source code must indicate how to parallelize work by spawning processes or threads; offloading data, work, and instructions to a compute device; or operating on blocks of data at a time. The programmer must first expose the parallelization, determine the best technique to operate in parallel, and then explicitly direct its operation in a safe, correct, and efficient manner. The following methods are the most common techniques for parallelization, then we'll go through each of these in detail:

- *Process-based parallelization*—Message passing
- *Thread-based parallelization*—Shared data via memory
- *Vectorization*—Multiple operations with one instruction
- *Stream processing*—Through specialized processors

PROCESS-BASED PARALLELIZATION: MESSAGE PASSING

The message passing approach was developed for distributed memory architectures, which uses explicit messages to move data between processes. In this model, your application spawns separate processes, called *ranks* in message passing, with their own memory space and instruction pipeline (figure 1.20). The figure also shows that the processes are handed to the OS for placement on the processors. The application lives in the part of the diagram marked as user space, where the user has permissions to operate. The part beneath is kernel space, which is protected from dangerous operations by the user.

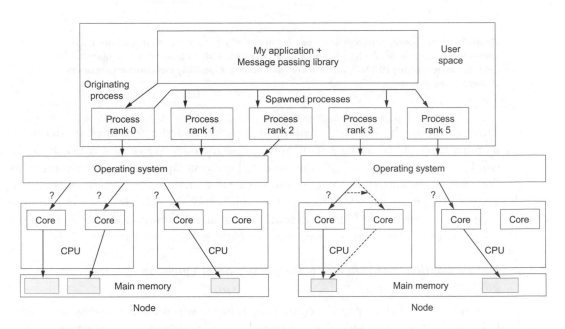

Figure 1.20   The message passing library spawns processes. The OS places the processes on the cores of two nodes. The question marks indicate that the OS controls the placement of the processes and can move these during run time as indicated by the dashed arrows. The OS also allocates memory for each process from the node's main memory.

Keep in mind that processors—CPUs—have multiple processing cores that are not equivalent to the processes. Processes are an OS concept, and processors are a hardware component. For however many processes the application spawns, these are scheduled by the OS to the processing cores. You can actually run eight processes on your quad-core laptop and these will just swap in and out of the processing cores. For this reason, mechanisms have been developed to tell the OS how to place processes and whether to "bind" the process to a processing core. Controlling binding is discussed in more detail in chapter 14.

To move data between processes, you'll need to program explicit messages into the application. These messages can be sent over a network or via shared memory. The many message-passing libraries coalesced into the Message Passing Interface (MPI) standard in 1992. Since then, MPI has taken over this niche and is present in almost all parallel applications that scale beyond a single node. And, yes, you'll also find many different implementations of MPI libraries as well.

Distributed computing versus parallel computing

Some parallel applications use a lower-level approach to parallelization, called distributed computing. We define *distributed computing* as a set of loosely-coupled processes that cooperate via OS-level calls. While distributed computing is a subset of parallel computing, the distinction is important. Examples of distributed computing applications include peer-to-peer networks, the World Wide Web, and internet mail. The Search for Extraterrestrial Intelligence (SETI@home) is just one example of many scientific distributed computing applications.

The location of each process is usually on a separate node and is created through the OS using something like a remote procedure call (RPC) or a network protocol. The processes then exchange information through the passing of messages between the processes by *inter-process communication* (IPC), of which there are several varieties. Simple parallel applications often use a distributed computing approach, but often through a higher-level language such as Python and specialized parallel modules or libraries.

THREAD-BASED PARALLELIZATION: SHARED DATA VIA MEMORY

The thread-based approach to parallelization spawns separate instruction pointers within the same process (figure 1.21). As a result, you can easily share portions of the process memory between threads. But this comes with correctness and performance pitfalls. The programmer is left to determine which sections of the instruction set and

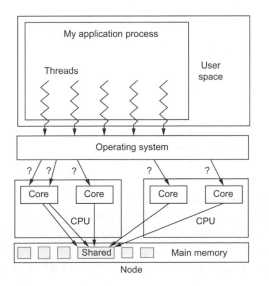

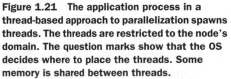

Figure 1.21 The application process in a thread-based approach to parallelization spawns threads. The threads are restricted to the node's domain. The question marks show that the OS decides where to place the threads. Some memory is shared between threads.

data are independent and can support threading. These considerations are discussed in more detail in chapter 7, where we will look at OpenMP, one of the leading threading systems. OpenMP provides the capability to spawn threads and divide up the work among the threads.

There are many varieties of threading approaches, ranging from heavy to lightweight and managed by either the user space or the OS. While threading systems are limited to scaling within a single node, these are an attractive option for modest speedup. The memory limitations of the single node, however, have larger implications for the application.

VECTORIZATION: MULTIPLE OPERATIONS WITH ONE INSTRUCTION

Vectorizing an application can be far more cost-effective than expanding compute resources at an HPC center, and this method might be absolutely necessary on portable devices like cell phones. When vectorizing, work is done in blocks of 2-16 data items at a time. The more formal term for this operation classification is single instruction, multiple data (SIMD). The term SIMD is used a lot when talking about vectorization. SIMD is just one category of parallel architectures that will be discussed later in section 1.4.

Invoking vectorization from a user's application is most often done through source code pragmas or through compiler analysis. Pragmas and directives are hints given to the compiler to guide how to parallelize or vectorize a section of code. Both pragmas and compiler analysis are highly dependent on the compiler capabilities (figure 1.22). Here we are dependent on the compiler, where the previous parallel mechanisms were dependent on the OS. Also, without explicit compiler flags, the generated code is for the least powerful processor and vector length, significantly reducing the effectiveness of the vectorization. There are mechanisms where the compiler can be bypassed, but these require much more programming effort and are not portable.

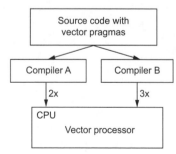

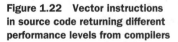

Figure 1.22   Vector instructions in source code returning different performance levels from compilers

STREAM PROCESSING THROUGH SPECIALIZED PROCESSORS

Stream processing is a dataflow concept, where a stream of data is processed by a simpler special-purpose processor. Long used in embedded computing, the technique was adapted for rendering large sets of geometric objects for computer displays in a specialized processor, the GPU. These GPUs were filled with a broad set of arithmetic operations and multiple SMs to process geometric data in parallel. Scientific programmers soon found ways to adapt stream processing to large sets of simulation data such as cells, expanding the role of the GPU to a GPGPU.

In figure 1.23, the data and kernel are shown offloaded over the PCI bus to the GPU for computation. GPUs are still limited in functionality in comparison to CPUs, but where the specialized functionality can be used, these provide extraordinary compute capability at a lower power requirement. Other specialized processors also fit this category, though we focus on the GPU for our discussions.

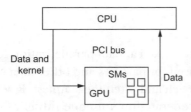

Figure 1.23 In the stream processing approach, data and compute kernel are offloaded to the GPU and its streaming multiprocessors. Processed data, or output, transfers back to the CPU for file IO or other work.

1.4 Categorizing parallel approaches

If you read more about parallel computing, you will encounter acronyms such as SIMD (single instruction, multiple data) and MIMD (multiple instruction, multiple data). These terms refer to categories of computer architectures proposed by Michael Flynn in 1966 in what has become known as *Flynn's Taxonomy*. These classes help to view potential parallelization in architectures in different ways. The categorization is based on breaking up instructions and data into either serial or multiple operations (figure 1.24). Be aware that though the taxonomy is useful, some architectures and algorithms do not fit neatly within a category. The usefulness comes from recognizing patterns in categories such as SIMD that have potential difficulties with conditionals. This is because each data item might want to be in a different block of code, but the threads have to execute the same instruction.

		Instruction	
		Single	Multiple
Data	Single	SISD Single instruction single data	MISD Multiple instruction single data
	Multiple	SIMD Single instruction multiple data	MIMD Multiple instruction multiple data

Figure 1.24 Flynn's Taxonomy categorizes different parallel architectures. A serial architecture is single data, single instruction (SISD). Two categories only have partial parallelization in that either the instructions or data are parallel, but the other is serial.

In the case where there is more than one instruction sequence, the category is called multiple instruction, single data (MISD). This is not a common architecture; the best example is a redundant computation on the same data. This is used in highly fault-tolerant approaches such as spacecraft controllers. Because spacecraft are in high radiation environments, these often run two copies of each calculation and compare the output of the two.

Vectorization is a prime example of SIMD in which the same instruction is performed across multiple data. A variant of SIMD is single instruction, multi-thread (SIMT), which is commonly used to describe GPU work groups.

The final category has parallelization in both instructions and data and is referred to as MIMD. This category describes multi-core parallel architectures that comprise the majority of large parallel systems.

1.5   *Parallel strategies*

So far in our initial example in section 1.3.1, we looked at data parallelization for cells or pixels. But data parallelization can also be used for particles and other data objects. Data parallelization is the most common approach and often the simplest. Essentially, each process executes the same program but operates on a unique subset of data as illustrated in the upper right of figure 1.25. The data parallel approach has the advantage that it scales well as the problem size and number of processors grow.

Another approach is *task parallelism*. This includes the main controller with worker threads, pipeline, or bucket-brigade strategies also shown in figure 1.25. The pipeline approach is used in superscalar processors where address and integer calculations are done with a separate logic unit rather than the floating-point processer, allowing these calculations to be done in parallel. The bucket-brigade uses each processor to operate on and transform the data in a sequence of operations. In the main-worker approach, one processor schedules and distributes the tasks for all the workers, and each worker checks for the next work item as it returns the previous completed task. It is also possible to combine different parallel strategies to expose a greater degree of parallelism.

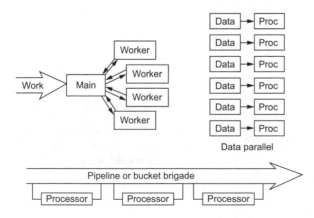

Data parallel

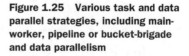

Figure 1.25   Various task and data parallel strategies, including main-worker, pipeline or bucket-brigade and data parallelism

1.6   *Parallel speedup versus comparative speedups: Two different measures*

We will present a lot of comparative performance numbers and speedups throughout this book. Often the term *speedup* is used to compare two different run times with little explanation or context to fully understand what it means. Speedup is a general term that is used in many contexts such as quantifying the effects of optimization, for example. To clarify the difference between the two major categories of parallel performance numbers, we'll define two different terms.

- *Parallel speedup*—We should really call this *serial-to-parallel speedup*. The speedup is relative to a baseline serial run on a standard platform, usually a single CPU. The parallel speedup can be due to running on a GPU or with OpenMP or MPI on all the cores on the node of a computer system.
- *Comparative speedup*—We should really call this *comparative speedup between architectures*. This is usually a performance comparison between two parallel implementations or other comparison between reasonably constrained sets of hardware. For example, it may be between a parallel MPI implementation on all the cores of the node of a computer versus the GPU(s) on a node.

These two categories of performance comparisons represent two different goals. The first is to understand how much speedup can be obtained through adding a particular type of parallelism. It is not a fair comparison between architectures, however. It is about parallel speedup. For example, comparing a GPU run time to a serial CPU run is not a fair comparison between a multi-core CPU and the GPU. Comparative speedups between architectures are more appropriate when trying to compare a multi-core CPU to the performance of one or more GPUs on a node.

In recent years, some have normalized the two architectures so that relative performance is compared for similar power or energy requirements rather than an arbitrary node. Still, there are so many different architectures and possible combinations that any performance numbers to justify a conclusion can be obtained. You can pick a fast GPU and a slow CPU or a quad-core CPU versus a 16-core processor. We are therefore suggesting you add the following terms *in parenthesis* to performance comparisons to help give these more context:

- Add (Best 2016) to each term. For example, parallel speedup (Best 2016) and comparative speedup (Best 2016) would indicate that the comparison is between the best hardware released in a particular year (2016 in this example), where you might compare a high-end GPU to a high-end CPU.
- Add (Common 2016) or (2016) if the two architectures were released in 2016 but are not the highest-end hardware. This might be relevant to developers and users who have more mainstream parts than that found in the top-end systems.

- Add (Mac 2016) if the GPU and the CPU were released in a 2016 Mac laptop or desktop, or something similar for other brands with fixed components over a period of time (2016 in this example). Performance comparisons of this type are valuable to users of a commonly available system.
- Add (GPU 2016:CPU 2013) to show that there is a possible mismatch in the hardware release year (2016 versus 2013 in this example) of the components being compared.
- No qualifications added to comparison numbers. Who knows what the numbers mean?

Because of the explosion in CPU and GPU models, performance numbers will necessarily be more of a comparison between apples and oranges rather than a well-defined metric. But for more formal settings, we should at least indicate the nature of the comparison so that others have a better idea of the meaning of the numbers and to be more fair to the hardware vendors.

1.7   *What will you learn in this book?*

This book is written with the application code developer in mind and no previous knowledge of parallel computing is assumed. You should simply have a desire to improve the performance and scalability of your application. The application areas include scientific computing, machine learning, and analysis of big data on systems ranging from a desktop to the largest supercomputers.

To fully benefit from this book, readers should be proficient programmers, preferably with a compiled, HPC language such as C, C++, or Fortran. We also assume a rudimentary knowledge of hardware architectures. In addition, readers should be comfortable with computer technology terms such as bits, bytes, ops, cache, RAM, etc. It is also helpful to have a basic understanding of the functions of an OS and how it manages and interfaces with the hardware components. After reading this book, some of the skills you will gain include

- Determining when message passing (MPI) is more appropriate than threading (OpenMP) and vice-versa
- Estimating how much speedup is possible with vectorization
- Discerning which sections of your application have the most potential for speedup
- Deciding when it might be beneficial to leverage a GPU to accelerate your application
- Establishing what is the peak potential performance for your application
- Estimating the energy cost for your application

Even after this first chapter, you should feel comfortable with the different approaches to parallel programming. We suggest that you work through the exercises in each chapter to help you integrate the many concepts that we present. If you are beginning to feel a little overwhelmed by the complexity of the current parallel architectures, you are not alone. It's challenging to grasp all the possibilities. We'll break it down, piece-by-piece, in the following chapters to make it easier for you.

1.7.1 Additional reading

A good basic introduction to parallel computing can be found on the Lawrence Livermore National Laboratory website:

Blaise Barney, "Introduction to Parallel Computing." https://computing.llnl.gov/tutorials/parallel_comp/.

1.7.2 Exercises

1 What are some other examples of parallel operations in your daily life? How would you classify your example? What does the parallel design appear to optimize for? Can you compute a parallel speedup for this example?

2 For your desktop, laptop, or cell phone, what is the theoretical parallel processing power of your system in comparison to its serial processing power? What kinds of parallel hardware are present in it?

3 Which parallel strategies do you see in the store checkout example in figure 1.1? Are there some present parallel strategies that are not shown? How about in your examples from exercise 1?

4 You have an image-processing application that needs to process 1,000 images daily, which are 4 mebibytes (MiB, 2^{20} or 1,048,576 bytes) each in size. It takes 10 min in serial to process each image. Your cluster is composed of multi-core nodes with 16 cores and a total of 16 gibibytes (GiB, 2^{30} bytes, or 1024 mebibytes) of main memory storage per node. (Note that we use the proper binary terms, MiB and GiB, rather than MB and GB, which are the metric terms for 10^6 and 10^9 bytes, respectively.)

   a What parallel processing design best handles this workload?

   b Now customer demand increases by 10x. Does your design handle this? What changes would you have to make?

5 An Intel Xeon E5-4660 processor has a thermal design power of 130 W; this is the average power consumption rate when all 16 cores are used. NVIDIA's Tesla V100 GPU and AMD's MI25 Radeon GPU have a thermal design power of 300 W. Suppose you port your software to use one of these GPUs. How much faster should your application run on the GPU to be considered more energy efficient than your 16-core CPU application?

Summary

- Because this is an era where most of the compute capabilities of hardware are only accessible through parallelism, programmers should be well versed in the techniques used to exploit parallelism.

- Applications must have parallel work. The most important job of a parallel programmer is to expose more parallelism.
- Improvements to hardware are nearly all-enhancing parallel components. Relying on increasing serial performance will not result in future speedup. The key to increasing application performance will all be in the parallel realm.
- A variety of parallel software languages are emerging to help access the hardware capabilities. Programmers should know which are suitable for different situations.

Planning for parallelization

This chapter covers

- Planning steps for a parallel project
- Version control and team development workflows
- Understanding performance capabilities and limitations
- Developing a plan to parallelize a routine

Developing a parallel application or making an existing application run in parallel can feel challenging at first. Often, developers new to parallelism are unsure of where to begin and what pitfalls they might encounter. This chapter focuses on a workflow model for developing parallel applications as illustrated in figure 2.1. This model provides the context for where to get started and how to maintain

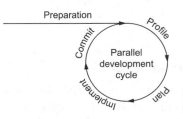

Figure 2.1 Our suggested parallel development workflow begins with preparing the application and then repeating four steps to incrementally parallelize an application. This workflow is particularly suited to an agile project management technique.

progress in developing your parallel application. Generally, it is best to implement parallelism in small increments so that if problems are encountered, the last few commits can be reversed. This kind of pattern is suited to agile project management techniques.

Let's imagine that you have been assigned a new project to speed up and parallelize an application from the spatial mesh presented in figure 1.9 (the Krakatau volcano example). This could be an image detection algorithm, a scientific simulation of the ash plume, or a model of the resulting tsunami waves, or all three of these. What steps can you take to have a successful parallelism project?

It is tempting to just jump into the project. But without thought and preparation, you greatly reduce your chance of success. As a start, you will need a project plan for this parallelism effort, so we begin here with a high-level overview of the steps in this workflow. Then we'll dive deeper into each step as this chapter progresses, with a focus on the characteristics typical for a parallel project.

Rapid development: The parallel workflow

You first need to prepare your team and your application for rapid development. Because you have an existing serial application that works on the spatial mesh from figure 1.9, there will likely be lots of small changes with frequent tests to ensure that the results do not change. Code preparation includes setting up version control, developing a test suite, and ensuring code quality and portability. Team preparation will be centered around processes for the development procedures. As always, project management will address task management and scope control.

To set the stage for the development cycle, you will need to determine the capabilities of the computing resources available, the demands of your application, and your performance requirements. System benchmarking helps to determine compute resource limitations, while profiling aids your understanding of the application's demands and its most expensive computational kernels. *Computational kernels* refer to sections of the application that are both computationally intensive and conceptually self-contained.

From the kernel profiles, you will plan the tasks for parallelizing routines and implementing the changes. The implementation stage is only complete once the routine is parallelized and the code maintains portability and correctness. With these requirements satisfied, the changes will be committed to a version control system. After committing the incremental changes, the process begins again with an application and kernel profile.

2.1   *Approaching a new project: The preparation*

Figure 2.2 presents the recommended components in the preparation step. These are the items proven to be important specifically for parallelization projects.

At this stage, you will need to set up version control, develop a test suite for your application, and clean up existing code. Version control allows you to track the changes

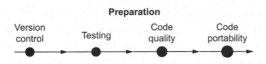

Figure 2.2 **The recommended preparation components address issues that are important for parallel code development.**

you make to your application over time. It permits you to quickly undo mistakes and track down bugs in your code at a later date. A test suite allows you to verify the correctness of your application with each change that is made to your code. When coupled with version control, this can be a powerful setup for rapidly developing your application.

With version control and code testing in place, you can now tackle the task of cleaning up your code. Good code is easy to modify and extend, and does not exhibit unpredictable behavior. Good, clean code can be ensured with modularity and checks for memory issues. *Modularity* means that you implement kernels as independent subroutines or functions with well-defined input and output. Memory issues can include memory leaks, out-of-bounds memory access, and use of uninitialized memory. Starting your parallelism work with predictable and quality code promotes rapid progress and predictable development cycles. It is hard to match your serial code if the original results are due to a programming error.

Finally, you will want to make sure your code is *portable*. This means that multiple compilers can compile your code. Having and maintaining compiler portability allows your application to target additional platforms, beyond the one you may currently have in mind. Further, experience shows that developing code to work with multiple compilers helps to find bugs before these are committed to your code's version history. With the high performance computing landscape changing rapidly, portability allows you to adapt to changes much quicker down the line.

It is not unusual that the preparation time rivals that spent on the actual parallelism, especially for complex code. Including this preparation in your project scope and time estimates avoids frustrations with your project's progress. In this chapter, we assume that you are starting from a serial or prototype application. However, you can still benefit from this workflow strategy even if you've already started parallelizing your code. Next, we discuss the four components of project preparation.

2.1.1 *Version control: Creating a safety vault for your parallel code*

It is inevitable with the many changes that occur during parallelism that you will suddenly find the code is broken or returning different results. Being able to recover from this situation by backing up to a working version is critically important.

> **NOTE** Check to see what kind of version control is in place for your application before beginning any parallelism work.

For your image detection project in our scenario, you find that there is already a version control system in place. But the ash plume model never had any version control.

As you dig deeper, you find that there are actually four versions of the ash plume code in various developer's directories. When there is a version control system in operation, you may want to review the processes your team uses for day-to-day operations. Perhaps the team thinks it is a good idea to switch to a "pull request" model, where changes are posted for review by other team members before being committed. Or you and your team may feel that the direct commit of the "push" model is more compatible with the rapid, small commits of parallelism tasks. In the push model, commits are made directly to the repository without review. In our example of the ash plume application without version control, the priority is to get something in place to tame the uncontrolled divergence of code among developers.

There are many options for version control. If you have no other preferences, we would suggest Git, the most common distributed version control system. A *distributed version control system* is one that allows multiple repository databases, rather than a single centralized system used in *centralized version control.* Distributed version control is advantageous for open source projects and where developers work on laptops, in remote locations, or other situations where they are not connected to a network or close to the central repository. In today's development environment, this is a huge advantage. But it comes with the cost of additional complexity. Centralized version control is still popular and more appropriate for the corporate environment because there is only one place where all the information about the source code exists. Centralized control also provides better security and protection for proprietary software.

There are many good books, blogs, and other resources on how to use Git; we list a few at the end of the chapter. We also list some other common version control systems in chapter 17. These include free distributed version control systems such as Mercurial and Git, commercial systems such as PerForce and ClearCase, and for centralized version control, CVS and SVN. Regardless of which system you use, you and your team should commit frequently. The following scenario is especially common with parallelism tasks:

- I'll commit after I add the next small change. . . .
- Just one more. . . . Then all of a sudden the code is not working.
- It's too late to commit now!

This happens to me far too often. So I try to avoid the problem by committing regularly.

> **TIP** If you do not want lots of small commits in the main repository, you can collapse the commits with some version control systems such as Git, or you can maintain a temporary version control system just for yourself.

The commit message is where the commit author can communicate what task is being addressed and why certain changes were made, whether for self or for current or future team members. Every team has their own preference for how detailed these messages should be; we recommend using as much detail as possible in your commit messages. This is your opportunity to save yourself from later confusion by being diligent today.

In general, commit messages include a summary and a body. The summary provides a short statement indicating clearly what new changes the commit covers. Additionally, if you use an issue tracking system, the summary line will reference an issue number from that system. Finally, the body contains most of the "why" and "how" behind the commit.

Examples of commit messages

- Bad commit message:

```
Fixed a bug
```

- Good commit message:

```
Fixed the race condition in the OpenMP version of the blur operator
```

- Great commit message:

```
[Issue #21] Fixed the race condition in the OpenMP version of the
blur operator.
* The race condition was causing non-reproducible results amongst
GCC, Intel, and PGI compilers. To fix this, an OMP BARRIER was
introduced to force threads to synchronize just before calculating
the weighted stencil sum.
* Confirmed that the code builds and runs with GCC, Intel, and PGI
compilers and produces consistent results.
```

The first message doesn't really help anyone understand what bug was fixed. The second message helps pinpoint the resolution to problems that involve race conditions in the blur operator. The last message references an issue number (#21) in an outside issue tracking system and provides the commit summary on the first line. The commit body, the two bullet points beneath the summary, provides more details about what specifically was needed and why, and indicates to other developers that you took the time to test your version before committing it.

With a plan for version control and at least a rough agreement on your team's development processes, we are ready to move on to the next step.

2.1.2 Test suites: The first step to creating a robust, reliable application

A *test suite* is a set of problems that exercise parts of an application to guarantee that related parts of the code still work. Test suites are a necessity for all but the simplest of codes. With each change, you should test to see that the results that you get are the same. This sounds simple, but some code can reach slightly different results with different compilers and numbers of processors.

Example: Krakatau scenario test for validated results

Your project has an ocean wave simulation application that generates validated results. *Validated results* are simulation results that are compared to experimental or real-world data. Simulation code that has been validated is valuable. You don't want to lose that while you parallelize the code.

In our scenario, you and your team used two different compilers for development and production. The first is the C compiler in the GNU Compiler Collection (GCC), the ubiquitous, freely-available compiler dispersed with all Linux distributions and many other operating systems. The C compiler is colloquially referred to as the GCC compiler. Your application also uses the commercially available Intel C compiler.

The following figure shows the hypothetical results for the validated test problem that predicts wave height and total mass. The output varies slightly depending on which compiler and the number of processors used in the simulation.

Which differences between calculations with various compilers and numbers of processors are acceptable?

In this example, there are variations in the two metrics reported from the program. Without additional information, it is difficult to determine which is correct and which variations in the solution are acceptable. In general, differences in your program output can be due to

- Changes in the compiler or the compiler version
- Changes in hardware
- Compiler optimizations or small differences between compilers or compiler versions
- Changes in the order of operations, especially due to code parallelism

In the following sections, we'll discuss why such differences can arise, how to determine which variations are reasonable, and how to design tests that catch real bugs before these are committed to your repository.

UNDERSTANDING CHANGES IN RESULTS DUE TO PARALLELISM

The parallelism process inherently changes the order of operations, which slightly modifies the numerical results. But errors in parallelism also generate small differences. This is crucial to understand in parallel code development because we need to compare to a single processor run to determine if our parallelism coding is correct.

We'll discuss a way to reduce the numerical errors so that the parallelism errors are more obvious in section 5.7, when we discuss techniques for global sums.

For our test suite, we will need a tool that compares numerical fields with a small tolerance for differences. In the past, test suite developers would have to create a tool for this purpose, but a few numerical diff utilities have appeared on the market in recent years. Two such tools are

- Numdiff from https://www.nongnu.org/numdiff/
- ndiff from https://www.math.utah.edu/~beebe/software/ndiff/

Alternatively, if your code outputs its state in HDF5 or NetCDF files, these formats come with utilities that allow you to compare values stored in the files with varying tolerances.

- HDF5® is version 5 of the software originally known as Hierarchical Data Format, now called HDF. It is freely available from The HDF Group (https://www.hdfgroup.org/) and is a common format used to output large data files.
- NetCDF or the Network Common Data Form is an alternate format used by the climate and geosciences community. Current versions of NetCDF are built on top of HDF5. You can find these libraries and data formats at the Unidata Program Center's website (https://www.unidata.ucar.edu/software/netcdf/).

Both of these file formats use binary data for speed and efficiency. *Binary data* is the machine representation of the data. This format just looks like gibberish to you and me, but HDF5 has some useful utilities that allow us to look at what's inside. The h5ls utility lists the objects in the file, such as the names of all the data arrays. The h5dump utility dumps the data in each object or array. And most importantly for our purposes here, the h5diff utility compares two HDF files and reports the difference above a numeric tolerance. HDF5 and NetCDF along with other parallel input/output (I/O) topics will be discussed in more detail in chapter 16.

USING CMAKE AND CTEST TO AUTOMATICALLY TEST YOUR CODE

Many testing systems have become available in recent years. This includes CTest, Google test, pFUnit test, and others. You can find more information on tools in chapter 17. For now, let's look at a system created using CTest and ndiff.

CTest is a component of the CMake system. CMake is a configuration system that adapts generated makefiles to different systems and compilers. Incorporating the CTest testing system into CMake couples the two tightly together into a unified system. This provides a lot of convenience to the developer. The process of implementing tests using CTest is relatively easy. The individual tests are written as any sequence of commands. To incorporate these into the CMake system requires adding the following to the CMakeLists.txt:

- `enable_testing()`
- `add_test(<testname> <executable name> <arguments to executable>)`

Then you can invoke the tests with make test, ctest, or you can select individual tests with ctest -R mpi, where mpi is a regular expression that runs any matching test names. Let's just walk through an example of creating a test using the CTest system.

Example: CTest prerequisites

You will need MPI, CMake, and ndiff installed to run this example. For MPI (Message Passing Interface), we'll use OpenMPI 4.0.0 and CMake 3.13.3 (includes CTest) on the Mac with older versions on Ubuntu. We'll use the GCC compiler, version 8, installed on a Mac rather than the default compiler. Then OpenMPI, CMake, and GCC (GNU Compiler Collection) are installed with a package manager. We'll use Homebrew on the Mac and Apt, and Synaptic on Ubuntu Linux. Be sure to get the development headers from libopenmpi-dev if these are split out from the run time. ndiff is installed manually by downloading the tool from https://www.math.utah.edu/~beebe/software/ndiff/ and running ./configure, make, and make install.

Make two source files as shown in listing 2.1 to create applications for this simple testing system. We'll use a timer to produce small differences in output from both a serial and a parallel program. Note that you'll find the source code for this chapter at https://github.com/EssentialsofParallelComputing/Chapter2.

Listing 2.1   Simple timing programs for demonstrating the testing system

```
C Program, TimeIt.c
 1 #include <unistd.h>
 2 #include <stdio.h>
 3 #include <time.h>
 4 int main(int argc, char *argv[]){
 5    struct timespec tstart, tstop, tresult;
 6    clock_gettime(CLOCK_MONOTONIC, &tstart);          Starts timer, calls sleep,
 7    sleep(10);                                        then stops the timer
 8    clock_gettime(CLOCK_MONOTONIC, &tstop);
 9    tresult.tv_sec =
          tstop.tv_sec - tstart.tv_sec;               Timer has two values for resolution
10    tresult.tv_usec =                                and to prevent overflows.
          tstop.tv_nsec - tstart.tv_nsec;
11    printf("Elapsed time is %f secs\n",
          (double)tresult.tv_sec +                     Prints calculated time
12        (double)tresult.tv_nsec*1.0e-9);
13 }


MPI Program, MPITimeIt.c
 1 #include <unistd.h>
 2 #include <stdio.h>
 3 #include <mpi.h>
 4 int main(int argc, char *argv[]){
 5    int mype;
 6    MPI_Init(&argc, &argv);                           Initializes MPI and
 7    MPI_Comm_rank(MPI_COMM_WORLD, &mype);             gets processor rank
 8    double t1, t2;
```

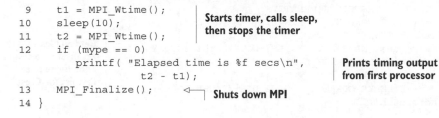

```
 9    t1 = MPI_Wtime();
10    sleep(10);
11    t2 = MPI_Wtime();
12    if (mype == 0)
          printf( "Elapsed time is %f secs\n",
                      t2 - t1);
13    MPI_Finalize();
14 }
```

Starts timer, calls sleep, then stops the timer

Prints timing output from first processor

Shuts down MPI

Now you need a test script that runs the applications and produces a few different output files. After these run, there should be numerical comparisons of the output. Here is an example of the process you can put in a file called mympiapp.ctest. You should do a chmod +x to make it executable.

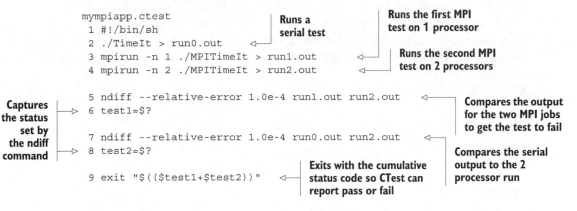

```
mympiapp.ctest
 1 #!/bin/sh
 2 ./TimeIt > run0.out
 3 mpirun -n 1 ./MPITimeIt > run1.out
 4 mpirun -n 2 ./MPITimeIt > run2.out

 5 ndiff --relative-error 1.0e-4 run1.out run2.out
 6 test1=$?

 7 ndiff --relative-error 1.0e-4 run0.out run2.out
 8 test2=$?

 9 exit "$(($test1+$test2))"
```

Runs a serial test

Runs the first MPI test on 1 processor

Runs the second MPI test on 2 processors

Compares the output for the two MPI jobs to get the test to fail

Captures the status set by the ndiff command

Compares the serial output to the 2 processor run

Exits with the cumulative status code so CTest can report pass or fail

This test first compares the output for a parallel job with 1 and 2 processors with a tolerance of 0.1% on line 5. Then it compares the serial run to the 2 processor parallel job on line 7. To get the tests to fail, try reducing the tolerance to 1.0e–5. CTest uses the exit code on line 9 to report pass or fail. The simplest way to add a bunch of CTest files to the test suite is to use a loop that finds all the files ending in .ctest and adds these to the CTest list. Here is an example of a CMakeLists.txt file with the additional instructions to create the two applications:

```
CMakeLists.txt
 1 cmake_minimum_required (VERSION 3.0)
 2 project (TimeIt)
 3
 4 enable_testing()
 5
 6 find_package(MPI)
 7
 8 add_executable(TimeIt TimeIt.c)
 9
10 add_executable(MPITimeIt MPITimeIt.c)
11 target_include_directories(MPITimeIt PUBLIC.
       ${MPI_INCLUDE_PATH})
12 target_link_libraries(MPITimeIt ${MPI_LIBRARIES})
13
```

Enables CTest functionality in CMake

CMake built-in routine to find most MPI packages

Adds TimeIt and MPITimeIt build targets with their source code files

Needs an include path to the mpi.h file and to the MPI library

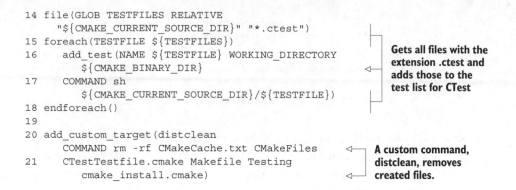

```
14 file(GLOB TESTFILES RELATIVE
      "${CMAKE_CURRENT_SOURCE_DIR}" "*.ctest")
15 foreach(TESTFILE ${TESTFILES})
16    add_test(NAME ${TESTFILE} WORKING_DIRECTORY
          ${CMAKE_BINARY_DIR}
17    COMMAND sh
          ${CMAKE_CURRENT_SOURCE_DIR}/${TESTFILE})
18 endforeach()
19
20 add_custom_target(distclean
      COMMAND rm -rf CMakeCache.txt CMakeFiles
21    CTestTestfile.cmake Makefile Testing
          cmake_install.cmake)
```

Gets all files with the extension .ctest and adds those to the test list for CTest

A custom command, distclean, removes created files.

The find_package(MPI) command on line 6 defines MPI_FOUND, MPI_INCLUDE_
PATH, and MPI_LIBRARIES. These variables include the language in newer CMake
versions of MPI_<lang>_INCLUDE_PATH, and MPI_<lang>_LIBRARIES so that there
are different paths for C, C++, and Fortran. Now all that remains is to run the test with

```
mkdir build && cd build
cmake ..
make
make test
```

or

```
ctest
```

You can also get the output for failed tests with

```
ctest --output-on-failure
```

You should get some results like the following:

```
Running tests...
Test project /Users/brobey/Programs/RunDiff
    Start 1: mpitest.ctest
1/1 Test #1: mpitest.ctest ..................    Passed    30.24 sec

100% tests passed, 0 tests failed out of 1

Total Test time (real) =  30.24 sec
```

This test is based on the sleep function and timers, so it may or may not pass. Test
results are in Testing/Temporary/*.

   In this test, we compared the output between individual runs of the application. It
is also good practice to store a gold standard file from one of the runs along with the
test script to compare against as well. This comparison detects changes that will cause
a new version of the application to get different results than earlier versions. When

this happens, it is a red flag; check if the new version is still correct. If so, you should update the gold standard.

Your test suite should exercise as many parts of the code as is practical. The metric *code coverage* quantifies how well the test suite does its task, which is expressed as a percentage of the lines of source code. There is an old saying from test developers that the part of the code that doesn't have a test is broken because even if it isn't now, it will be eventually. With all of the changes made when parallelizing code, breakage is inevitable. While high code coverage is important, for our parallelism efforts, it is more critical that there are tests for the parts of the code you are parallelizing. Many compilers have the capability to generate code coverage statistics. For GCC, gcov is the profiling tool, and for Intel, it is Codecov. We'll take a look at how this works for GCC.

Code coverage with GCC

1 Add the flags `-fprofile-arcs` and `-ftest-coverage` when compiling and linking
2 Run the instrumented executable on a series of tests
3 Run `gcov <source.c>` to get the coverage for each file

> **NOTE** For builds with CMake, add an extra .c extension to the source filename; for example, gcov CMakeFiles/stream_triad.dir/stream_triad.c.c handles the extension added by CMake.

4 You will get output something like this:

```
88.89% of 9 source lines executed in file <source>.c
Creating <source>.c.gcov
```

The gcov output file contains a listing with each line prepended with the number of times it was executed.

UNDERSTANDING THE DIFFERENT KINDS OF CODE TESTS

There are also different kinds of testing systems. In this section, we'll cover the following types:

- *Regression tests*—Run at regular intervals to keep the code from backsliding. This is typically done nightly or weekly using the cron job scheduler that launches jobs at specified times.
- *Unit tests*—Tests the operation of subroutines or other small parts of code during development.
- *Continuous integration tests*—Gaining in popularity, these tests are automatically triggered to run by a commit to the code.
- *Commit tests*—A small set of tests that can be run from the command line in a fairly short time and are used before commits.

All of these testing types are important for a project and, rather than just relying on one, these should be used together as figure 2.3 illustrates. Testing is particularly

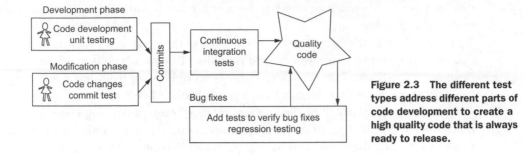

Figure 2.3 **The different test types address different parts of code development to create a high quality code that is always ready to release.**

important for parallel applications because detecting bugs earlier in the development cycle means that you are not debugging 1,000 processors 6 hours into a run.

Unit tests are best created as you develop the code. True aficionados of unit tests use test-driven development (TDD), where the tests are created first and then the code is written to pass these. Incorporating these type of tests into parallel code development includes testing their operation in the parallel language and implementation. Identifying problems at this level is far easier to resolve.

Commit tests are the first tests that you should add to a project to be heavily used in the code modification phase. These tests should exercise all of the routines in the code. By having these tests readily available, team members can run these before making a commit to the repository. We recommend that developers invoke these tests from the command line like a Bash or Python script, or a makefile, prior to a commit.

Example: A development workflow with commit tests using CMake and CTest

To make a commit test within CMakeLists.txt, create the three files shown in the following listing. Use the Timeit.c from the previous test, but change the sleep interval from 10 to 30.

Creating a commit test with CTest

```
blur_short.ctest
1 #!/bin/sh
2 make


blur_long.ctest
1 #!/bin/sh
2 ./TimeIt


CMakeLists.txt
1 cmake_minimum_required (VERSION 3.0)
2 project (TimeIt)
3                                        Enables CTest
4 enable_testing()       ◁─┘            functionality in CMake
5
6 add_executable(TimeIt TimeIt.c)
```

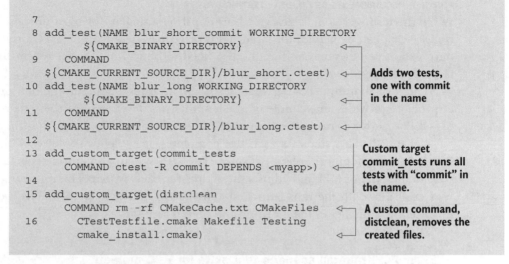

```
 7
 8 add_test(NAME blur_short_commit WORKING_DIRECTORY
       ${CMAKE_BINARY_DIRECTORY}
 9   COMMAND
   ${CMAKE_CURRENT_SOURCE_DIR}/blur_short.ctest)
10 add_test(NAME blur_long WORKING_DIRECTORY
       ${CMAKE_BINARY_DIRECTORY}
11   COMMAND
   ${CMAKE_CURRENT_SOURCE_DIR}/blur_long.ctest)
12
13 add_custom_target(commit_tests
     COMMAND ctest -R commit DEPENDS <myapp>)
14
15 add_custom_target(distclean
     COMMAND rm -rf CMakeCache.txt CMakeFiles
16     CTestTestfile.cmake Makefile Testing
       cmake_install.cmake)
```

Adds two tests, one with commit in the name

Custom target commit_tests runs all tests with "commit" in the name.

A custom command, distclean, removes the created files.

The commit tests can be run with `ctest -R commit` or with the custom target added to the CMakeLists.txt with `make commit_tests`. A `make test` or `ctest` command runs all the tests including the long test, which takes a while. The commit test command picks out the tests with *commit* in the name to get a set of tests that covers critical functionality but runs a little faster. Now the workflow is

1. Edit the source code: `vi mysource.c`
2. Build code: `make`
3. Run the commit tests: `make commit_tests`
4. Commit the code changes: `git commit`

And repeat. Continuous integration tests are invoked by a commit to the main code repository. This is an additional guard against committing bad code. The tests can be the same as the commit tests or can be more extensive. Top continuous integration tools for these types of tests are

- Jenkins (https://www.jenkins.io)
- Travis CI for GitHub and Bitbucket (https://travis-ci.com)
- GitLab CI (https://about.gitlab.com/stages-devops-lifecycle/continuous-integration/)
- CircleCI (https://circleci.com)

Regression tests are usually set up to run overnight through a cron job. This means that the test suites can be more extensive than the test suites for other testing types. These tests can be longer but should complete by the morning report. Additional tests, such as memory checks and code coverage are often run as regression tests due to the longer run times and the periodicity of the reports. The results of regression tests are often tracked over time and a "wall of passes" is considered as an indication of the project's well-being.

FURTHER REQUIREMENTS OF AN IDEAL TESTING SYSTEM

While the testing system as described previously is sufficient for most purposes, there is more that can be helpful for larger HPC projects. These types of HPC projects can have extensive test suites and might also need to be run in a batch system to access larger resources.

The Collaborative Testing System (CTS) at https://sourceforge.net/projects/ ctsproject/ provides an example of a system that was developed for these demands. It uses a Perl script to run a fixed set of test servers, typically 10, launching the tests in parallel to a batch system. As each test completes, it launches the next. This avoids flooding the system with jobs all at once. The CTS system also autodetects the batch system and type of MPI and adjusts the scripts for each system. The reporting system uses cron jobs with the tests launched early in the overnight period. The cross-platform report launches in the morning and then is sent out.

Example: Krakatau scenario test suite for HPC projects

After reviewing your applications, you find there is a large user base for the image detection application. So your team decides to set extensive regression tests before every commit to avoid impacting the users. Longer running memory correctness tests run overnight, and the performance tracked weekly. The ocean wave simulation is new, however, and has fewer users, but you want to ensure the validated problem continues to give the same answer. It is too long to run for a commit test, so you run a shortened version and the full version weekly.

For both applications, a continuous integration test is set up to build the code and run a few smaller tests. The ash plume model just started being developed, so you decide to use unit tests to check each new section of code as it is added.

2.1.3   Finding and fixing memory issues

Good code quality is paramount. Parallelizing often causes any code flaw to appear; this might be uninitialized memory or memory overwrites.

- *Uninitialized memory is memory that is accessed before its values are set.* When you allocate memory to your program, it gets whatever values are in those memory locations. This leads to unpredictable behavior if it is used before being set.
- *Memory overwrites occur when data is written to a memory location that isn't owned by a variable.* An example of this is writing past the bounds of an array or string.

To catch these sorts of problems, we suggest using memory correctness tools to thoroughly check your code. One of the best of these is the freely-available Valgrind program. Valgrind is an instrumentation framework that operates at the machine-code level by executing instructions through a synthetic CPU. There are many tools that have been developed under the Valgrind umbrella. The first step is to install Valgrind on your system using a package manager. If you are running the latest version of macOS, you may find that it takes a few months for Valgrind to be ported to the new kernel. Your best bet for this is to run Valgrind on a different computer, an older macOS or spin up a virtual machine or Docker image.

To run Valgrind, execute your program as usual, inserting the `valgrind` command at the front. For MPI jobs, the `valgrind` command gets placed after `mpirun` and before your executable name. Valgrind works best with the GCC compiler because that development team adopted it, working to eliminate false positives that can clutter the diagnostic output. It is suggested that when using Intel compilers, compile without vectorization to avoid warnings about the vector instructions. You can also try the other memory correctness tools that are listed in section 17.5.

USING VALGRIND MEMCHECK TO FIND MEMORY ISSUES

The Memcheck tool is the default tool in the Valgrind tool suite. It intercepts every instruction and checks it for various types of memory errors, generating diagnostics at the start, during, and at the end of the run. This slows down the run by an order of magnitude. If you have not used it before, be prepared for a lot of output. One memory error leads to many others. The best strategy is to start with the first error, fix it, and run again. To see how Valgrind works, try the example code in listing 2.2. To execute Valgrind, insert the `valgrind` command before the executable name either as

```
valgrind <./my_app>
```

or

```
mpirun -n 2 valgrind <./myapp>
```

Listing 2.2   Example code for Valgrind memory errors

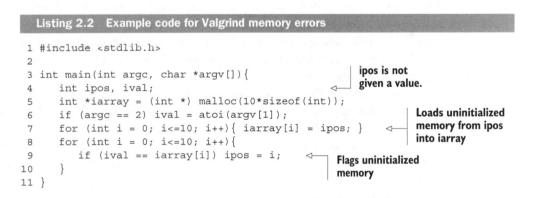

```
 1 #include <stdlib.h>
 2
 3 int main(int argc, char *argv[]){        ipos is not
 4    int ipos, ival;                        given a value.
 5    int *iarray = (int *) malloc(10*sizeof(int));
 6    if (argc == 2) ival = atoi(argv[1]);   Loads uninitialized
 7    for (int i = 0; i<=10; i++){ iarray[i] = ipos; }   memory from ipos
 8    for (int i = 0; i<=10; i++){            into iarray
 9       if (ival == iarray[i]) ipos = i;    Flags uninitialized
10    }                                       memory
11 }
```

Compile this code with `gcc -g -o test test.c` and then run it with `valgrind --leak-check=full ./test 2`. The output from Valgrind is interspersed within the program's output and can be identified by the prefix with double equal signs (==). The following shows some of the more important parts of the output from this example:

```
==14324== Invalid write of size 4
==14324==    at 0x400590: main (test.c:7)
==14324==
==14324== Conditional jump or move depends on uninitialized value(s)
```

```
==14324==      at 0x4005BE: main (test.c:9)
==14324==
==14324== Invalid read of size 4
==14324==      at 0x4005B9: main (test.c:9)
==14324==
==14324== 40 bytes in 1 blocks are definitely lost in loss record 1 of 1
==14324==      at 0x4C29C23: malloc (vg_replace_malloc.c:299)
==14324==      by 0x40054F: main (test.c:5)
```

This output displays reports on several memory errors. The trickiest one to understand is the uninitialized memory report. Valgrind reports the error on line 9 when a decision was made with the uninitialized value. The error is actually on line 7 where iarray is set to ipos, which was not given a value. It can take some careful analysis in a more complex program to determine the source of the error.

2.1.4 *Improving code portability*

A last code preparation requirement improves code portability to a wider range of compilers and operating systems. Portability begins with the base HPC language, generally C, C++, or Fortran. Each of these languages maintains standards for compiler implementations, and new standard releases occur periodically. But this does not mean that compilers implement these readily. Often the lag time from release to full implementation by compiler vendors can be long. For example, the Polyhedron Solutions website (http://mng.bz/yYne) reports that no Linux Fortran compiler fully implements the 2008 standard, and less than half fully implement the 2003 standard. Of course, what matters is if the compilers have implemented the features that you want. C and C++ compilers are usually more up-to-date in their implementations of new standards, but the lag time can still cause problems for aggressive development teams. Also, even if the features are implemented, it does not mean these work in a wide variety of settings.

Compiling with a variety of compilers helps to detect coding errors or identify where code is pushing the "edge" on language interpretations. Portability provides flexibility when using tools that work best in a particular environment. For example, Valgrind works best with GCC, but Intel® Inspector, a thread correctness tool, works best when you compile the application with Intel compilers. Portability also helps when using parallel languages. For example, CUDA Fortran is only available with the PGI compiler. The current set of implementations of GPU directive-based languages OpenACC and OpenMP (with the target directive) are only available on a small set of compilers. Fortunately, MPI and the OpenMP for CPUs are widely available for many compilers and systems. At this point, we need to it make clear that there are three distinct OpenMP capabilities: 1) vectorization through SIMD directives, 2) CPU threading from the original OpenMP model, and 3) offloading to an accelerator, generally a GPU, through the new target directives.

> **Example: Krakatau scenario and code portability**
>
> Your image detection application only compiles with the GCC compiler. Your parallelism project adds OpenMP threading. Your team decides to get it to compile with the Intel compiler so that you can use the Intel Inspector to find thread race conditions. The ash plume simulation is written in Fortran and targeted to run on GPUs. Based on your research of current GPU languages, you decide to include PGI as one of your development compilers so you can use CUDA Fortran.

2.2 Profiling: Probing the gap between system capabilities and application performance

Profiling (figure 2.4) determines the hardware performance capabilities and compares that with your application performance. The difference between the capabilities and current performance yields the potential for performance improvement.

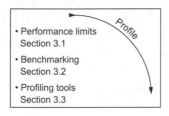

Figure 2.4   The purpose of the profiling step is to identify the most important parts of the application code that need to be addressed.

The first part of the profiling process is to determine what is the limiting aspect of your application's performance. We'll detail possible performance limitations for applications in section 3.1. Briefly, most applications today are limited by memory bandwidth or a limitation that closely tracks memory bandwidth. A few applications might be limited by available floating-point operations (flops). We'll present ways to calculate theoretical performance limits in section 3.2. We'll also describe benchmark programs that can measure the achievable performance for that hardware limitation.

Once the potential performance is understood, then you can profile your application. We'll present the process of using some profiling tools in section 3.3. The gap between the current performance of your application and the hardware capabilities for the limiting aspect of your application then become the target for improvement for the next steps in parallelism.

2.3 Planning: A foundation for success

Armed with the information gathered on your application and the targeted platforms, it is time to put some details into a plan. Figure 2.5 shows parts of this step. With the effort that's required in parallelism, it is sensible to research prior work before starting the implementation step.

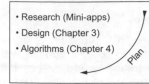

Figure 2.5 **The planning steps lay the foundation for a successful project.**

It is likely that similar problems were encountered in the past. You'll find many research articles on parallelism projects and techniques published in recent years. But one of the richest sources of information includes the benchmarks and mini-apps that have been released. With mini-apps, you have not only the research but also the actual code to study.

2.3.1 Exploring with benchmarks and mini-apps

The high performance computing community has developed many benchmarks, kernels, and sample applications for use in benchmarking systems, performance experiments, and algorithm development. We'll list some of these in section 17.4. You can use benchmarks to help select the most appropriate hardware for your application, and mini-apps provide help on the best algorithms and coding techniques.

Benchmarks are intended to highlight a specific characteristic of hardware performance. Now that you have a sense of what is the performance limit of your application, you should look at the benchmarks most applicable to your situation. If you compute on large arrays that are accessed in a linear fashion, then the stream benchmark is appropriate. If you have an iterative matrix solver as your kernel, then the High Performance Conjugate Gradient (HPCG) benchmark might be better. *Mini-apps* are more focused on a typical operation or pattern found in a class of scientific applications.

It is worthwhile to see if any of these benchmarks or mini-apps are similar to the parallel application you are developing. If so, studying how these do similar operations can save a lot of effort. Often, a lot of work has been done with the code to explore how to get the best performance, to port to other parallel languages and platforms, or to quantify performance characteristics.

Currently benchmarks and mini-apps are predominantly from the field of scientific computing. We'll use some of these in our examples, and you are encouraged to use these for your experimentation and as example code. Many of the key operations and parallel implementations are demonstrated in these examples.

Example: Ghost cell updates

Many mesh-based applications distribute their mesh across processors in a distributed memory implementation (see figure 1.13). Because of this, these applications need to update the boundaries of their mesh with values from an adjacent processor.

This operation is called a *ghost cell update*. Richard Barrett at Sandia National Laboratories developed the MiniGhost mini-app to experiment with different ways to perform this type of operation. The MiniGhost mini-app is part of the Mantevo suite of mini-apps available at https://mantevo.org/default.php.

2.3.2 Design of the core data structures and code modularity

The design of data structures has a long ranging impact on your application. This is one of the decisions that needs to be made up front, realizing that changing the design later becomes difficult. In chapter 4, we go through some of the considerations that are important, along with a case study that demonstrates the analysis of the performance of different data structures.

To begin, focus on the data and data movement. This is the dominant consideration with today's hardware platforms. It also leads into an effective parallel implementation where the careful movement of data becomes even more important. If we consider the filesystem and network as well, data movement dominates everything.

2.3.3 Algorithms: Redesign for parallel

At this point, you should evaluate the algorithms in your application. Can these be modified for parallel coding? Are there algorithms that have better scalability? For example, your application may have a section of code that only takes 5% of the run time but has an N^2 algorithmic scaling, while the rest of the code scales with N, where N is the number of cells or some other data component. As the problem size grows, the 5% soon becomes 20% and then even higher. Soon it is dominating the run time. To identify these kinds of issues, you might want to profile a larger problem and then look at the *growth* in the run time rather than the absolute percentage.

Example: Data structure for the ash plume model

Your ash plume model is in the early stages of development. There are several proposed data structures and breakdowns of the functional steps. Your team decides to spend a week analyzing the alternatives before they become fixed in the code, knowing that it will be difficult to change in the future. One of the decisions is which multi-material data structure to use and, because many materials will only be in small regions of the mesh, whether there is a good way to take advantage of this. You decide to explore a sparse data storage data structure to save memory (some are discussed in section 4.3.2) and for a faster code.

Example: Algorithm selection for the wave simulation code

The parallelism work on the wave simulation code is projected to add OpenMP and vectorization. You have heard of different implementation styles for each of these

(continued)

parallelism approaches. You assign two team members to review recent papers for insights on the approaches that work best. One of your team members expresses concerns about the parallelism of one of the more difficult routines, which has a complicated algorithm. The current technique does not look straightforward to parallelize. You agree and ask the team member to look into alternative algorithms that might be different than what is currently being done.

2.4   *Implementation: Where it all happens*

This is the step I think of as hand-to-hand combat. Down in the trenches, line-by-line, loop-by-loop, and routine-by-routine the code is transformed to parallel code. This is where all your knowledge of parallel implementations on CPUs and GPUs comes to effect. As figure 2.6 shows, this material will be covered in much of the rest of the book. The chapters on parallel programming languages, chapters 6–8 for CPUs and chapters 9–13 for GPUs, begin your journey to developing this expertise.

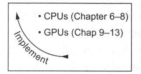

Figure 2.6   The implementation step utilizes parallel languages and skills developed in the rest of the book.

During the implementation step, it is important to keep track of your overall goals. You may or may not have decided on your parallel language at this point. Even if you have, you should be willing to reassess your choice as you get deeper into the implementation. Some of the initial considerations for your choice of direction for the project include

- Are your speedup requirements fairly modest? You should explore vectorization and shared memory (OpenMP) parallelism in chapters 6 and 7.
- Do you need more memory to scale up? If so, you will want to explore distributed memory parallelism in chapter 8.
- Do you need large speedups? Then GPU programming is worth looking into in chapters 9–13.

The key in this implementation step is to break down the work into manageable chunks and divide out the work among your team members. There is both the exhilaration of getting an order of magnitude speedup in a routine and realizing that the overall impact is small, and there is still a lot of work to do. Perseverance and teamwork are important in reaching the goal.

> ### Example: Reassessment of parallel language
>
> Your project to add OpenMP and vectorization to the wave simulation code is going well. You have gotten an order of magnitude speedup for typical calculations. But as the application speeds up, your users want to run larger problems and they don't have enough memory. Your team begins to think about adding MPI parallelism to access additional nodes where more memory is available.

2.5 Commit: Wrapping it up with quality

The commit step finalizes this part of the work with careful checks to verify that code quality and portability are maintained. Figure 2.7 shows the components of this step. How extensive these checks are is highly dependent on the nature of the application. For production applications with many users, the tests need to be far more thorough.

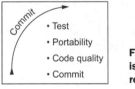

Figure 2.7 The goal of the commit step is to create a solid rung on the ladder to reaching your end goal.

NOTE At this point, it is easier to catch relatively small-scale problems than it is to debug complications six days into a run on a thousand processors.

The team must buy-in to the commit process and work together to follow it. It is suggested that there be a team meeting to develop the procedures for all to follow. The processes used during the initial efforts to improve code quality and portability can be exploited in creating your procedures. Lastly, the commit process should be re-evaluated periodically and adapted for the current project needs.

> ### Example: Re-evaluating your team's code development process
>
> Your wave simulation application team has gotten the first increment of work for adding OpenMP to the application. But now the application is occasionally crashing with no explanation. One of your team members realizes that it might be due to thread race conditions. Your team implements an additional step to check for these conditions as part of the commit process.

2.6 Further explorations

In this chapter, we have only brushed the surface of how to approach a new project and what the available tools can do. For more information, explore the resources and try some of the exercises in the following sections.

2.6.1 *Additional reading*

Additional expertise with today's distributed version control tools benefits your project. At least one member of your team should research the many resources on the web that discuss how to use your chosen version control system. If you use Git, the following books from Manning are good resources:

- Mike McQuaid, *Git in Practice* (Manning, 2014).
- Rick Umali, *Learn Git in a Month of Lunches* (Manning, 2015).

Testing is vitally important in the parallel development workflow. Unit testing is perhaps the most valuable but also the most difficult to implement well. Manning has a book that gives a much more thorough discussion of unit testing:

Vladimir Khorikov, *Unit Testing Principles, Practices, and Patterns* (Manning, 2020).

Floating-point arithmetic and precision is an underappreciated topic, despite its importance to every computational scientist. The following is a good read and overview on floating-point arithmetic:

David Goldberg, "What every computer scientist should know about floating-point arithmetic," *ACM Computing Surveys (CSUR)* 23, no. 1 (1991): 5-48.

2.6.2 *Exercises*

1 You have a wave height simulation application that you developed during graduate school. It is a serial application and because it was only planned to be the basis for your dissertation, you didn't incorporate any software engineering techniques. Now you plan to use it as the starting point for an available tool that many researchers can use. You have three other developers on your team. What would you include in your project plan for this?

2 Create a test using CTest

3 Fix the memory errors in listing 2.2

4 Run Valgrind on a small application of your choice

This chapter has covered a lot of ground with many of the details necessary for a parallel project plan. The estimation of performance capabilities and uses of tools to extract information on hardware characteristics and application performance give solid, concrete data points to populate the plan. The proper use of these tools and skills can help build a solid foundation for a successful parallel project.

Summary

- Code preparation is a significant part of parallelism work. Every developer is surprised at the amount of effort spent preparing the code for the project. But this time is well spent in that it is the foundation for a successful parallelism project.
- You should improve your code quality for parallel code. Code quality must be an order of magnitude better than typical serial code. Part of this need for quality

resides in the difficulty of debugging at scale and part is due to flaws that are exposed in the parallelism process or simply due to the sheer number of iterations that each line of code is executed. Perhaps this is because the probability of encountering a flaw is quite small, but when a thousand processors are running the code, it becomes a thousand times more likely to occur.

- The profiling step is important to determine where to focus optimization and parallelism work. Chapter 3 provides more details on how to profile your application.

- There is an overall project plan and another separate plan for each iteration of development. Both of these plans should include some research to include mini-apps, data structure designs, and new parallel algorithms to lay the foundation for the next steps.

- With the commit step, we need to develop processes to maintain good code quality. This should be an ongoing effort and not pushed to later when the code is put into production or when the existing user base starts encountering problems with large, long-running simulations.

Performance limits and profiling 3

This chapter covers

- Understanding the limiting aspect of application performance
- Evaluating performance for the limiting hardware components
- Measuring the current performance of your application

Programmer resources are scarce. You need to target these resources so that they have the most impact. How do you do this if you don't know the performance characteristics of your application and the hardware you plan to run on? That is what this chapter means to address. By measuring the performance of your hardware and your application, you can determine where it's most effective to spend your development time.

> **NOTE** We encourage you to follow along with the exercises for this chapter. The exercises can be found at https://github.com/EssentialsofParallel Computing/Chapter3.

3.1   *Know your application's potential performance limits*

Computational scientists still consider floating-point operations (flops) as the primary performance limit. While this might have been true years ago, the reality is that flops seldom limit performance in modern architectures. But limits can be for bandwidth or for latency. *Bandwidth* is the best rate at which data can be moved through a given path in the system. For bandwidth to be the limit, the code should use a streaming approach, where the memory usually needs to be contiguous and all the values used. When a streaming approach is not possible, latency is the more appropriate limit. *Latency* is the time required for the first byte or word of data to be transferred. The following shows some of the possible hardware performance limits:

- Flops (floating-point operations)
- Ops (operations) that include all types of computer instructions
- Memory bandwidth
- Memory latency
- Instruction queue (instruction cache)
- Networks
- Disk

We can break down all of these limitations into two major categories: speeds and feeds. *Speeds* are how fast operations can be done. It includes all types of computer operations. But to be able to do the operations, you must get the data there. This is where feeds come in. *Feeds* include the memory bandwidth through the cache hierarchy, as well as network and disk bandwidth. For applications that cannot get streaming behavior, the latency of memory, network and disk feed are more important. Latency times can be orders of magnitude slower than those for bandwidth. One of the biggest factors in whether applications are controlled by latency limits or streaming bandwidths is the quality of the programming. Organizing your data so that it can be consumed in a streaming pattern can yield dramatic speedups.

The relative performance of different hardware components is shown in figure 3.1. Let's use the 1 word loaded per cycle and 1 flop per cycle marked by the large dot as our starting point. Most scalar arithmetic operations like addition, subtraction, and multiplication, can be done in 1 cycle. The division operation can take longer at 3–5 cycles. In some arithmetic mixes, 2 flops/cycle are possible with the fused multiply-add instruction. The number of arithmetic operations that can be done increases further with vector units and multi-core processors. Hardware advances, mostly through parallelism, greatly increase the flops/cycle.

Looking at the sloped memory limits, we see that the performance increase through a deeper hierarchy of caches means that memory accesses can only match the speedup of operations if the data is contained in the L1 cache, typically about 32 KiB. But if we only have that much data, we wouldn't be so worried about the time it takes. We really want to operate on large amounts of data that can only be contained in main memory (DRAM) or even on the disk or network. The net result is that the floating-point

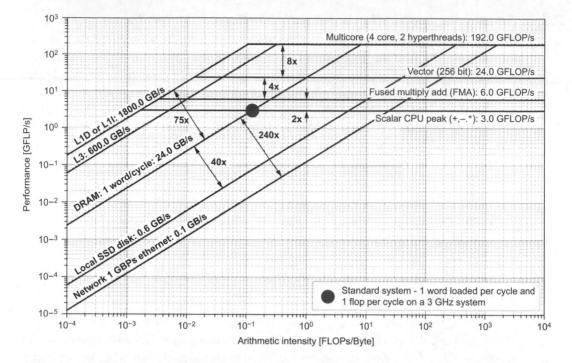

Figure 3.1   Feeds and speeds shown on a roofline plot. The conventional scalar CPU is close to the 1 word loaded per cycle and 1 flop per cycle indicated by the shaded circle. The multipliers for the increase in flops are due to the fused multiply-add instruction, vectorization, multiple cores, and hyperthreads. The relative speeds of memory movement are also shown. We'll discuss the roofline plot more in section 3.2.4.

capabilities of processors have increased far faster than memory bandwidth. This has led to many *machine balances* of the order of 50 flops capability for every 8-byte word loaded. To understand this impact on applications, we measure its arithmetic intensity.

- *Arithmetic intensity*—In an application, measures the number of flops executed per memory operations, where memory operations can be either in bytes or words (a word is 8 bytes for a double and 4 bytes for a single-precision value).
- *Machine balance*—Indicates for computing hardware the total number of flops that can be executed divided by the memory bandwidth.

Most applications have an arithmetic intensity close to 1 flop per word loaded, but there are also applications that have a higher arithmetic intensity. The classic example of a high arithmetic intensity application uses a dense matrix solver to solve a system of equations. The use of these solvers used to be much more common in applications than is true today. The Linpack benchmark uses the kernel from this operation to represent this class of applications. The arithmetic intensity for this benchmark is reported by Peise to be 62.5 flops/word (see reference in appendix A, Peise, 2017, pg. 201). This is sufficient for most systems to max out the floating-point capability. The heavy use of the Linpack benchmark for the top 500 ranking of the largest computing systems has become a leading reason for current machine designs that target a high flop-to-memory load ratio.

For many applications, even achieving the memory bandwidth limit can be difficult. Some understanding of the memory hierarchy and architecture is necessary to understand memory bandwidth. Multiple caches between memory and the CPU help hide the slower main memory (figure 3.5 in section 3.2.3) in the memory hierarchy. Data is transported up the memory hierarchy in chunks called *cache lines*. If memory is not accessed in a contiguous, predictable fashion, the full memory bandwidth is not achieved. Merely accessing data in columns for a 2D data structure that is stored in row order will stride across memory by the row length. This can result in as little as one value being used out of each cache line. A rough estimate of the memory bandwidth from this data access pattern is 1/8th of the stream bandwidth (1 out of every 8 cache values used). This can be generalized for other cases where more cache usage occurs by defining a non-contiguous bandwidth (B_{nc}) in terms of the percentage of cache used (U_{cache}) and the empirical bandwidth (B_E):

$$B_{nc} = U_{cache} \times B_E = \text{Average Percentage of Cache Used} \times \text{Empirical Bandwidth}$$

There are other possible performance limits. The instruction cache may not be able to load instructions fast enough to keep a processor core busy. Integer operations are also a more frequent limiter than commonly assumed, especially with higher dimensional arrays where the index calculations become more complex.

For applications that require significant network or disk operations (such as big data, distributed computing, or message passing), network and disk hardware limits can be the most serious concern. To get an idea of the magnitude of these device performance limitations, consider the rule of thumb that for the time taken for the first byte transferred over a high performance computer network, you can do over 1,000 flops on a single processor core. Standard mechanical disk systems are orders of magnitude slower for the first byte, which has led to the highly asynchronous, buffered operation of today's filesystems and to the introduction of solid-state storage devices.

> **Example**
>
> Your image detection application has to process a lot of data. Right now it comes in over the network and is stored to disk for processing. Your team reviews the performance limits and decides to try and eliminate the storage to disk as an unnecessary intermediate operation. One of your team members suggests that you can do additional floating-point operations almost for free so the team should consider a more sophisticated algorithm. But you think that the limiting aspect of the wave simulation code is memory bandwidth. You add a task to the project plan to measure the performance and confirm your hunch.

3.2   *Determine your hardware capabilities: Benchmarking*

Once you have prepared your application and your test suites, you can begin characterizing the hardware that you are targeting for production runs. To do this, you need to develop a conceptual model for the hardware that allows you to understand its performance. Performance can be characterized by a number of metrics:

- The rate at which floating-point operations can be executed (FLOPs/s)
- The rate at which data can be moved between various levels of memory (GB/s)
- The rate at which energy is used by your application (Watts)

The conceptual models allow you to estimate the theoretical peak performance of various components of the compute hardware. The metrics you work with in these models, and those you aim to optimize, depend on what you and your team value in your application. To complement this conceptual model, you can also make empirical measurements on your target hardware. The empirical measurements are made with micro-benchmark applications. One example of a micro-benchmark is the STREAM Benchmark that is used for bandwidth-limited cases.

3.2.1   *Tools for gathering system characteristics*

In determining hardware performance, we use a mixture of theoretical and empirical measurements. Although complementary, the theoretical value provides an upper bound to performance, and the empirical measurement confirms what can be achieved in a simplified kernel in close to actual operating conditions.

It is surprisingly difficult to get hardware performance specifications. The explosion of processor models and the focus of marketing and media reviews for the broader public often obscure the technical details. Good resources for such include

- For Intel processors, https://ark.intel.com
- For AMD processors, https://www.amd.com/en/products/specifications/processors

One of the best tools for understanding the hardware you run is the lstopo program. It is bundled with the hwloc package that comes with nearly every MPI distribution. This command outputs a graphical view of the hardware on your system. Figure 3.2 shows the output for a Mac laptop. The output can be graphical or text-based. To get the picture in figure 3.2 currently requires a custom installation of hwloc and the cairo packages to enable the X11 interface. The text version works with the standard package manager installs. Linux and Unix versions of hwloc usually work as long as you can display an X11 window. A new command, `netloc`, is being added to the hwloc package to display the network connections.

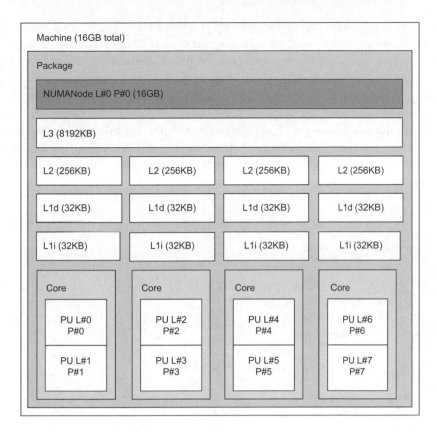

Figure 3.2 **Hardware topology for a Mac laptop using the** `lstopo` **command**

To install cairo v1.16.0

1 Download cairo from https://www.cairographics.org/releases/
2 Configure it with the following commands:

```
./configure --with-x --prefix=/usr/local
make
make install
```

To install hwloc v2.1.0a1-git

1 Clone the hwloc package from Git: https://github.com/open-mpi/hwloc.git
2 Configure it with the following commands:

```
./configure --prefix=/usr/local
make
make install
```

Some other commands for probing hardware details are lscpu on Linux systems, wmic on Windows, and sysctl or system_profiler on Mac. The Linux lscpu command outputs a consolidated report of the information from the /proc/cpuinfo file. You can see the full information for every logical core by viewing /proc/cpuinfo directly. The information from the lscpu command and the /proc/cpuinfo file helps to determine the number of processors, the processor model, the cache sizes, and the clock frequency for the system. The flags contain important information on the vector instruction set for the chip. In figure 3.3, we see that the AVX2 and various forms of the SSE vector instruction set are available. We'll discuss vector instruction sets more in chapter 6.

```
Architecture:          x86_64
CPU op-mode(s):        32-bit, 64-bit
Byte Order:            Little Endian
CPU(s):                4
On-line CPU(s) list: 0-3
Thread(s) per core:  1
Core(s) per socket:  4
Socket(s):             1
NUMA node(s):          1
Vendor ID:             GenuineIntel
CPU family:            6
Model:                 94
Model name:            Intel(R) Core(TM) i5-6500 CPU @ 3.20GHz
Stepping:              3
CPU MHz:               871.241
CPU max MHz:           3600.0000
CPU min MHz:           800.0000
BogoMIPS:              6384.00
Virtualization:        VT-x
L1d cache:             32K
L1i cache:             32K
L2 cache:              256K
L3 cache:              6144K
NUMA node0 CPU(s):   0-3
Flags:          .      fpu vme de pse tsc msr pae mce cx8 apic sep mtrr pge mca
cmov pat pse36 clflush dts acpi mmx fxsr sse sse2 ss ht tm pbe syscall nx pdpe1gb
rdtscp lm constant_tsc art arch_perfmon pebs bts rep_good nopl xtopology
nonstop_tsc cpuid aperfmperf tsc_known_freq pni pclmulqdq dtes64 monitor ds_cpl
vmx smx est tm2 ssse3 sdbg fma cx16 xtpr pdcm pcid sse4_1 sse4_2 x2apic movbe
popcnt tsc_deadline_timer aes xsave avx f16c rdrand lahf_lm abm 3dnowprefetch
cpuid_fault epb invpcid_single pti ssbd ibrs ibpb stibp tpr_shadow vnmi flexpriority
ept vpid fsgsbase tsc_adjust bmi1 hle avx2 smep bmi2 erms invpcid rtm mpx
rdseed adx smap clflushopt intel_pt xsaveopt xsavec xgetbv1 xsaves dtherm ida
arat pln pts hwp hwp_notify hwp_act_window hwp_epp flush_l1d
```

Figure 3.3   Output from lscpu for a Linux desktop that shows a 4-core i5-6500 CPU @ 3.2 GHz with AVX2 instructions

Obtaining information on the devices on the PCI bus can be helpful, particularly for identifying the number and type of the graphics processor. The lspci command reports all the devices (figure 3.4). From the output in the figure, we can see that there is one GPU and that it is an NVIDIA GeForce GTX 960.

```
00:00.0 Host bridge: Intel Corporation Skylake Host Bridge/DRAM Registers (rev 07)
00:01.0 PCI bridge: Intel Corporation Skylake PCIe Controller (x16) (rev 07)
00:14.0 USB controller: Intel Corporation Sunrise Point-H USB 3.0 xHCI Controller (rev 31)
00:14.2 Signal processing controller: Intel Corporation Sunrise Point-H Thermal subsystem (rev 31)
00:16.0 Communication controller: Intel Corporation Sunrise Point-H CSME HECI #1 (rev 31)
00:17.0 SATA controller: Intel Corporation Sunrise Point-H SATA controller [AHCI mode] (rev 31)
00:1b.0 PCI bridge: Intel Corporation Sunrise Point-H PCI Root Port #19 (rev f1)
00:1c.0 PCI bridge: Intel Corporation Sunrise Point-H PCI Express Root Port #3 (rev f1)
00:1d.0 PCI bridge: Intel Corporation Sunrise Point-H PCI Express Root Port #9 (rev f1)
00:1f.0 ISA bridge: Intel Corporation Sunrise Point-H LPC Controller (rev 31)
00:1f.2 Memory controller: Intel Corporation Sunrise Point-H PMC (rev 31)
00:1f.3 Audio device: Intel Corporation Sunrise Point-H HD Audio (rev 31)
00:1f.4 SMBus: Intel Corporation Sunrise Point-H SMBus (rev 31)
00:1f.6 Ethernet controller: Intel Corporation Ethernet Connection (2) I219-V (rev 31)
01:00.0 VGA compatible controller: NVIDIA Corporation GM206 [GeForce GTX 960] (rev a1)
01:00.1 Audio device: NVIDIA Corporation Device 0fba (rev a1)
```

Figure 3.4 Output from the `lspci` command from a Linux desktop that shows an NVIDIA GeForce GTX 960 GPU.

3.2.2 Calculating theoretical maximum flops

Let's run through the numbers for a mid-2017 MacBook Pro laptop with an Intel Core i7-7920HQ processor. This is a 4-core processor running at a nominal frequency of 3.1 GHz with hyperthreading. With its turbo boost feature, it can run at 3.7 GHz when using four processors and up to 4.1 GHz when using a single processor. The theoretical maximum flops (F_T) can be calculated with

$$F_T = C_v \times f_c \times I_c = \text{Virtual Cores} \times \text{Clock Rate} \times \text{Flops/Cycle}$$

The number of cores includes the effects of hyperthreads that make the physical cores (C_h) appear to be a greater number of virtual or logical cores (C_v). Here we have two hyperthreads that make the virtual number of processors appear to be eight. The clock rate is the turbo boost rate when all the processors are engaged. For the processor, it is 3.7 GHz. Finally, the flops per cycle, or more generally instructions per cycle (I_c), includes the number of simultaneous operations that can be executed by the vector unit.

To determine the number of operations that can be performed, we take the vector width (VW) and divide by the word size in bits (W_{bits}). We also include the fused multiply-add (FMA) instruction as another factor of two operations per cycle. We refer to this as fused operations (F_{ops}) in the equation. For this specific processor, we get

$$I_c = VW/W_{bits} \times F_{ops} = (256\text{-bit Vector Unit}/64 \text{ bits}) \times (2\ FMA) = 8 \text{ Flops/Cycle}$$

$$C_v = C_h \times HT = (4 \text{ Hardware Cores} \times 2 \text{ Hyperthreads})$$

$$F_T = (8 \text{ Virtual Cores}) \times (3.7 \text{ GHz}) \times (8 \text{ Flops/Cycle}) = 236.8 \text{ GFlops/s}$$

3.2.3   *The memory hierarchy and theoretical memory bandwidth*

For most large computational problems, we can assume that there are large arrays that need to be loaded from main memory through the cache hierarchy (figure 3.5). The memory hierarchy has grown deeper over the years with the addition of more levels of cache to compensate for the increase in processing speed relative to the main memory access times.

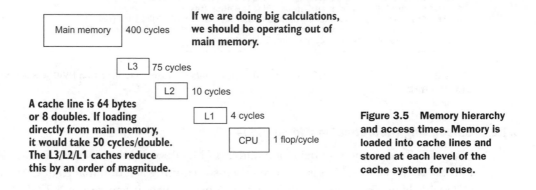

If we are doing big calculations, we should be operating out of main memory.

A cache line is 64 bytes or 8 doubles. If loading directly from main memory, it would take 50 cycles/double. The L3/L2/L1 caches reduce this by an order of magnitude.

Figure 3.5   Memory hierarchy and access times. Memory is loaded into cache lines and stored at each level of the cache system for reuse.

We can calculate the theoretical memory bandwidth of the main memory using the memory chips specifications. The general formula is

$$B_T = MTR \times M_c \times T_w \times N_s = \text{Data Transfer Rate} \times$$
$$\text{Memory Channels} \times \text{Bytes Per Access} \times \text{Sockets}$$

Processors are installed in a socket on the motherboard. The *motherboard* is the main system board of the computer, and the *socket* is the location where the processor is inserted. Most motherboards are single-socket, where only one processor can be installed. Dual-socket motherboards are more common in high-performance computing systems. Two processors can be installed in a dual-socket motherboard, giving us more processing cores and more memory bandwidth.

The data or memory transfer rate (*MTR*) is usually given in millions of transfers per sec (MT/s). The double data rate (DDR) memory performs transfers at the top and bottom of the cycle for two transactions per cycle. This means that the memory bus clock rate is half of the transfer rate in MHz. The memory transfer width (T_w) is 64 bits and because there are 8 bits/byte, 8 bytes are transferred. There are two memory channels (M_c) on most desktop and laptop architectures. If you install memory in both memory channels, you will get better bandwidth, but this means you cannot simply buy another DRAM module and insert it. You will have to replace all the modules with larger modules.

For the 2017 MacBook Pro with LPDDR3-2133 memory and for two channels, the theoretical memory bandwidth (B_T) can be calculated from the memory transfer rate

(*MTR*) of 2133 MT/s, the number of channels (M_c), and the number of sockets on the motherboard:

$$B_T = 2133 \text{ MT/s} \times 2 \text{ channels} \times 8 \text{ bytes} \times 1 \text{ socket} = 34{,}128 \text{ MiB/s or } 34.1 \text{ GiB/s}$$

The achievable memory bandwidth is lower than the theoretical bandwidth due to the effects of the rest of the memory hierarchy. You'll find complex theoretical models for estimating the effects of the memory hierarchy, but that is beyond what we want to consider in our simplified processor model. For this, we will turn to empirical measurements of bandwidth at the CPU.

3.2.4 *Empirical measurement of bandwidth and flops*

The *empirical bandwidth* is the measurement of the fastest rate that memory can be loaded from main memory into the processor. If a single byte of memory is requested, it takes 1 cycle to retrieve it from a CPU register. If it is not in the CPU register, it comes from the L1 cache. If it is not in the L1 cache, the L1 cache loads it from L2 and so on to main memory. If it goes all the way to main memory, for a single byte of memory, it can take around 400 clock cycles. This time required for the first byte of data from each level of memory is called the *memory latency*. Once the value is in a higher cache level, it can be retrieved faster until it gets *evicted* from that level of the cache. If all memory has to be loaded a byte at a time, this would be painfully slow. So when a byte of memory is loaded, a whole chunk of data (called a *cache line*) is loaded at the same time. If nearby values are subsequently accessed, these are then already in the higher cache levels.

The cache lines, cache sizes, and number of cache levels are sized to try to provide as much of the theoretical bandwidth of the main memory as possible. If we load contiguous data as fast as possible to make the best use of the caches, we get the CPU's maximum possible data transfer rate. This maximum data transfer rate is called the *memory bandwidth*. To determine the memory bandwidth, we can measure the time for reading and writing a large array. From the following empirical measurements, the measured bandwidth is about 22 GiB/s. This measured bandwidth is what we'll use in the simple performance models in the next chapter.

Two different methods are used for measuring the bandwidth: the STREAM Benchmark and the roofline model measured by the Empirical Roofline Toolkit. The STREAM Benchmark was created by John McCalpin around 1995 to support his argument that memory bandwidth is far more important than the peak floating-point capability. In comparison, the roofline model (see the figure in the sidebar entitled "Measuring bandwidth using the empirical Roofline Toolkit" and the discussion later in this section) integrates both the memory bandwidth limit and the peak flop rate into a single plot with regions that show each performance limit. The Empirical Roofline Toolkit was created by Lawrence Berkeley National Laboratory to measure and plot the roofline model.

The *STREAM Benchmark* measures the time to read and write a large array. For this, there are four variants, depending on the operations performed on the data by the CPU as it is being read: the copy, scale, add, and triad measurements. The copy does no floating-point work, the scale and add do one arithmetic operation, and the triad does two. These each give a slightly different measure of the maximum rate that data can be expected to be loaded from main memory when each data value is only used once. In this regime, the flop rate is limited by how fast memory can be loaded.

		Bytes	Arithmetic Operations
Copy:	a(i) = b(i)	16	0
Scale:	a(i) = q*b(i)	16	1
Sum:	a(i) = b(i) + c(i)	24	1
Triad:	a(i) = b(i) + q*c(i)	24	2

The following exercise shows how to use the STREAM Benchmark to measure bandwidth on a given CPU.

Exercise: Measuring bandwidth using the STREAM Benchmark

Jeff Hammond, a scientist at Intel, put the McCalpin STREAM Benchmark code into a Git repository for more convenience. We use his version in this example. To access the code

1 Clone the image at https://github.com/jeffhammond/STREAM.git

2 Edit the makefile and change the compile line to

```
-O3 -march=native -fstrict-aliasing -ftree-vectorize -fopenmp
      -DSTREAM_ARRAY_SIZE=80000000 -DNTIMES=20
make ./stream_c.exe
```

Here are the results for the 2017 Mac Laptop:

Function	Best Rate MB/s	Avg time	Min time	Max time
Copy:	22086.5	0.060570	0.057954	0.062090
Scale:	16156.6	0.081041	0.079225	0.082322
Add:	16646.0	0.116622	0.115343	0.117515
Triad:	16605.8	0.117036	0.115622	0.118004

We can select the best bandwidth from one of the four measurements as our empirical value of maximum bandwidth.

If a calculation can reuse the data in cache, much higher flop rates are possible. If we assume that all data being operated on is in a CPU register or maybe the L1 cache, then the maximum flop rate is determined by the CPU's clock frequency and how many flops it can do per cycle. This is the theoretical maximum flop rate calculated in the preceding example.

Now we can put these two together to create a plot of the roofline model. The roofline model has a vertical axis of flops per second and a horizontal axis of arithmetic intensity. For high arithmetic intensity, where there are a lot of flops compared to the data loaded, the theoretical maximum flop rate is the limit. This produces a horizontal line on the plot at the maximum flop rate. As the arithmetic intensity decreases, the time for the memory loads starts to dominate, and we no longer can reach the maximum theoretical flops. This then creates the sloped roof in the roofline model, where the achievable flop rate slopes down as the arithmetic intensity drops. The horizontal line on the right of the plot and the sloped line on the left produce the characteristic shape reminiscent of a roofline and what has become known as the roofline model or plot. You can determine the roofline plot for a CPU or even a GPU as shown in the following exercise.

Exercise: Measuring bandwidth using the empirical Roofline Toolkit

To prepare for this exercise, install either OpenMPI or MPICH to get a working MPI. Install gnuplot v4.2 and Python v3.0. On Macs, download the GCC compiler to replace the default compiler. These installs can be done using a package manager (brew on Mac and apt or synaptic on Ubuntu Linux).

1 Clone the Roofline Toolkit from Git:

```
git clone https://bitbucket.org/berkeleylab/cs-roofline-toolkit.git
```

2 Then type

```
cd cs-roofline-toolkit/Empirical_Roofline_Tool-1.1.0
cp Config/config.madonna.lbl.gov.01 Config/MacLaptop2017
```

3 Edit Config/MacLaptop2017. (The following figure shows the file for a 2017 Mac laptop.)
4 Run tests `./ert Config/MacLaptop2017`.
5 View the Results.MacLaptop2017/Run.001/roofline.ps file.

(continued)

```
# Mac Laptop, MPI and OpenMP (4-core Intel Core I7 3.1 GHz)

ERT_RESULTS Results.MacLaptop.01
ERT_DRIVER driver1
ERT_KERNEL kernel1                  mpicc --show can help with these paths.

ERT_MPI        True
ERT_MPI_CFLAGS    -I/usr/local/Cellar/open-mpi/4.0.0/include
ERT_MPI_LDFLAGS   -L/usr/local/opt/libevent/lib -L/usr/local/Cellar/open-mpi/4.0.0/lib -lmpi

ERT_OPENMP        True
ERT_OPENMP_CFLAGS -fopenmp
ERT_OPENMP_LDFLAGS -fopenmp

ERT_FLOPS  1,2,4,8,16          -march=native to compile for this CPU's vector unit
ERT_ALIGN  64

ERT_CC     gcc-8
ERT_CFLAGS  -O3 -march=native -fstrict-aliasing -ftree-vectorize
ERT_LD     gcc-8
ERT_LDFLAGS
ERT_LDLIBS

ERT_RUN    export OMP_NUM_THREADS=ERT_OPENMP_THREADS; mpirun -np ERT_MPI_PROCS ERT_CODE

ERT_PROCS_THREADS       1-8
ERT_MPI_PROCS           1,2,4      Sets number of MPI ranks and threads. The
ERT_OPENMP_THREADS      1,2,4,8    lspci command may help. Core I7 has
                                   hyperthreads, I5 does not.
ERT_NUM_EXPERIMENTS 3
ERT_MEMORY_MAX 1073741824
ERT_WORKING_SET_MIN 1
ERT_TRIALS_MIN 1

ERT_GNUPLOT gnuplot
```

Config/MacLaptop2017

The following figure shows the roofline for the 2017 Mac laptop. The empirical measurement of the maximum flops is a little higher than we calculated analytically. This is probably due to a higher clock frequency for a short period of time. Trying different configuration parameters like turning off vectorization or running one process can help to determine whether you have the right hardware specifications. The sloped lines are the bandwidth limits at different arithmetic intensities. Because these are determined empirically, the labels for each slope might not be correct and extra lines may be present.

From these two empirical measurements, we get a similar maximum bandwidth through the cache hierarchy of around 22 MB/s or about 65% of the theoretical bandwidth at the DRAM chips (22 GiB/s / 34.1 GiB/s).

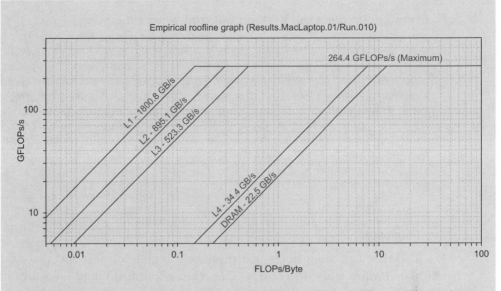

Roofline for 2017 Mac Laptop shows the maximum FLOPs as a horizontal line, and the maximum bandwidth from various cache and memory levels as sloped lines.

3.2.5 *Calculating the machine balance between flops and bandwidth*

Now we can determine the machine balance. The *machine balance* is the flops divided by the memory bandwidth. We can calculate both a theoretical machine balance (MB_T) and an empirical machine balance (MB_F) like so:

$$MB_T = F_T / B_T = 236.8 \text{ GFlops/s} / 34.1 \text{ GiB/s} \times (8 \text{ bytes/word}) = 56 \text{ Flops/word}$$

$$MB_E = F_E / B_E = 264.4 \text{ GFlops/s} / 22 \text{ GiB/s} \times (8 \text{ bytes/word}) = 96 \text{ Flops/word}$$

In the roofline figure in the previous section, the machine balance is the intersection of the DRAM bandwidth line with the horizontal flop limit line. We see that intersection is just above 10 Flops/Byte. Multiplying by 8 would give a machine balance above 80 Flops/word. We get a few different estimates of the machine balance from these different methods, but the conclusion for most applications is that we are in the bandwidth-bound regime.

3.3 *Characterizing your application: Profiling*

Now that you have some sense of what performance you can get with the hardware, you need to determine what are the performance characteristics of your application. Additionally, you should develop an understanding of how different subroutines and functions depend on each other.

Example: Profiling the Krakatu tsunami wave simulation

You decide to profile your wave simulation application to see where the time is spent and decide how to parallelize and speed up the code. Some high-fidelity simulations can take days to run, so your team wants to understand how parallelization with OpenMP and vectorization might improve the performance. You decide to study a similar mini-app, CloverLeaf, that solves the compressible fluid dynamics equations. These equations are just slightly more complicated than the ones in your wave simulation application. CloverLeaf has versions in several parallel languages. For this profiling study, your team wants to compare the serial version to the parallel version with OpenMP and vectorization. Understanding CloverLeaf performance gives you a good frame of reference for the second step of profiling your serial wave simulation code.

3.3.1   *Profiling tools*

We'll focus on profiling tools that produce a high-level view and that also provide additional information or context. There are a lot of profiling tools, but many produce more information than can be absorbed. As time permits, you may want to explore the other profiling tools listed in section 17.3. We'll also present a mix of freely available tools and commercial tools so that you have options depending on your available resources.

It is important to remember your goal here is to isolate where it is best to spend your time parallelizing your application. The goal is *not* to understand every last detail of your current performance. It is easy to make the mistake of either not using these tools at all or getting lost in the tools and the data those produce.

USING CALL GRAPHS FOR HOT-SPOT AND DEPENDENCY ANALYSIS

We'll start with tools that highlight hot spots and graphically display how each subroutine relates to others within code. *Hot spots* are kernels that occupy the largest amount of time during execution. Additionally, a *call graph* is a diagram that shows which routines call other routines. We can merge these two sets of information for an even more powerful combination as we will see in the next exercise.

A number of tools can generate call graphs, including valgrind's cachegrind tool. Cachegrind's call graphs highlight both hot spots and display subroutine dependencies. This type of graph is useful for planning development activities to avoid merge conflicts. A common strategy is to segregate tasks among the team so that work done by each team member takes place in a single call stack. The following exercise shows how to produce a call graph with the Valgrind tool suite and Callgrind. Another tool in the Valgrind suite, either KCacheGrind or QCacheGrind, then displays the results. The only difference is that one uses X11 graphics and the other uses Qt graphics.

Exercise: Call graph using cachegrind

For this exercise, the first step is to generate a call graph file using the Callgrind tool and then visualize it with KCacheGrind.

1 Install Valgrind and KcacheGrind or QCacheGrind using a package manager
2 Download the CloverLeaf miniapp from https://github.com/UK-MAC/CloverLeaf

```
git clone --recursive https://github.com/UK-MAC/CloverLeaf.git
```

3 Build the serial version of CloverLeaf

```
cd CloverLeaf/CloverLeaf_Serial
make COMPILER=GNU IEEE=1 C_OPTIONS="-g -fno-tree-vectorize" \
           OPTIONS="-g -fno-tree-vectorize"
```

4 Run Valgrind with the Callgrind tool

```
cp InputDecks/clover_bm256_short.in clover.in
edit clover.in and change cycles from 87 to 10
valgrind --tool=callgrind -v ./clover_leaf
```

5 Start QCacheGrind with the command `qcachegrind`
6 Load a specific callgrind.out.*XXX* file into the QCacheGrind GUI
7 Right click Call Graph and change the image settings

The following figure shows the CloverLeaf call graph. Each box in the call graph shows the name of the kernel and the percentage of time consumed by the kernel at each level of the call stack. A *call stack* is the chain of routines that call the present location in the code. As each routine calls a subroutine, it pushes its address onto the stack. At the end of the routine, the program simply pops the address off the stack as it returns to the prior calling routine. Each of the other "leaves" of the tree have their own call stacks. The call stack describes the hierarchy of data sources for the values in the "leaf" routine with the variables being passed down through the call chain. Timings can be either *exclusive*, where each routine excludes the timing of the routines it calls, or *inclusive*, where it includes the timing of all the routines below. The timings shown in the figure in the sidebar entitled "Measuring bandwidth using the empirical Roofline Toolkit" are inclusive with each level containing the levels below and summing up to 100% at the main routine.

In the figure, the call hierarchy is shown for the most expensive routines, along with the number of times called and the percentage of run time. We can see from this that the majority of the run time is in the `advection` routines that move materials and energy from one cell to another. We need to focus our efforts there. The call graph is also helpful in tracing the path through the source code to follow.

(continued)

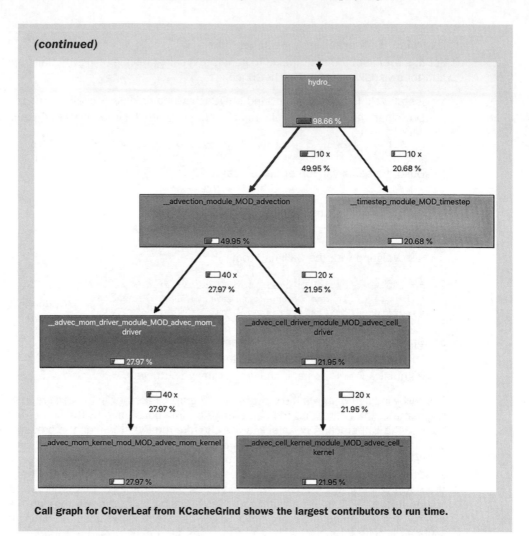

Call graph for CloverLeaf from KCacheGrind shows the largest contributors to run time.

Another useful profiling tool is Intel® Advisor. This is a commercial tool with helpful features for getting the most performance from your application. Intel Advisor is part of the Parallel Studio package that also bundles the Intel compilers, Intel Inspector, and VTune. There are options for a student, educator, open source developer and trial licenses at https://software.intel.com/en-us/qualify-for-free-software/student. These Intel tools have also been released for free in the OneAPI package at https://software.intel.com/en-us/oneapi. Recently, Intel Advisor has added a profiling feature incorporating the roofline model. Let's take a look at it in operation.

Exercise: Intel® Advisor

This exercise shows how to generate the roofline for the CloverLeaf mini-app, a regular grid compressible fluid dynamics (CFD) hydrocode.

1 Build the OpenMP version of CloverLeaf:

```
git clone --recursive https://github.com/UK-MAC/CloverLeaf.git
cd CloverLeaf/CloverLeaf_OpenMP
make COMPILER=INTEL IEEE=1 C_OPTIONS="-g -xHost" OPTIONS="-g -xHost"
```

or

```
make COMPILER=GNU IEEE=1 C_OPTIONS="-g -march=native" \
    OPTIONS="g -march=native"
```

2 Run the application in the Intel Advisor tool:

```
cp InputDecks/clover_bm256_short.in clover.in
advixe-gui
```

3 Set the executable to clover_leaf in the CloverLeaf_OpenMP directory. The working directory can be set to the application directory or CloverLeaf_OpenMP.

  a For the GUI operation, select the Start Survey Analysis pull-down menu and choose Start Roofline Analysis
  b On the command line, type the following:

```
advixe-cl --collect roofline --project-dir ./advixe_proj -- ./clover_leaf
```

4 Start the GUI and click the folder icon to load the run data.
5 To view the results, click Survey and Roofline, then click on the far left side of the top panel of performance results (where it says roofline in vertical text).

The following figure shows the summary statistics for the Intel Advisor profiler. It reports an arithmetic intensity of approximately .11 FLOPS/byte or .88 FLOPS/word. The floating-point computational rate is 36 GFLOPS/s.

Program metrics

Elapsed Time	217.54s
Vector Instruction Set	AVX512, AVX2, AVX, SSE2
Total GFLOP Count	7814.08
Total Arithmetic Intensity	0.10980

Number of CPU Threads	88
Total GFLOPS	35.92

Loop metrics

Metrics	Total	
Total CPU time	19123.80s	100.0%
Time in **71** vectorized loops	17750.90s	92.8%
Time in scalar code	1372.92s	7.2%
Total GFLOP Count	7814.08	100.0%
Total GFLOPS	35.92	

Summary output from Intel Advisor reporting an arithmetic intensity of 0.11 FLOPS/byte.

(continued)

The next figure shows the roofline plot from Intel Advisor for the CloverLeaf mini-app. The performance of various kernels is shown as points relative to the roofline performance of the Skylake processor. The size and color of the points indicate the percentage of overall time for each of the kernels. Even at a glance, it is clear that the algorithm is bandwidth limited and far to the left of the compute-bound region. Because this mini-app uses double precision, multiply the arithmetic intensity of .01 by 8 to get an arithmetic intensity well below 1 flop/word. The machine balance is the intersection of the double-precision FMA peak and the DRAM bandwidth.

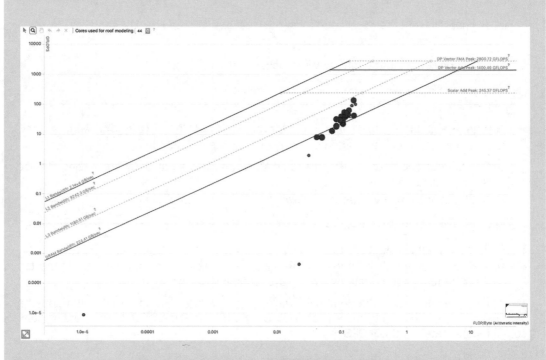

Roofline from Intel® Advisor for Cloverleaf (clover_bm256_short.in) on a Skylake Gold_6152 processor

In this plot, the machine balance is above 10 flops/byte or, multiplying by 8, greater than 80 flops/word, where the word size is a double. The sections of code that are most important for performance are identified by the names associated with each dot. The routines that have the most potential for improvement can be determined by how far these are below the bandwidth limit. We also can see that it would be helpful to improve the arithmetic intensity in the kernels.

We can also use the freely available likwid tool suite to get an arithmetic intensity. *Likwid* is an acronym for "Like I Knew What I'm Doing" and is authored by Treibig, Hager, and Wellein at the University of Erlangen-Nuremberg. It is a command-line tool that only runs on Linux and utilizes the machine-specific registers (MSR). The MSR module must be enabled with modprobe msr. The tool uses hardware counters to measure and report various information from the system, including run time, clock frequency, energy and power usage, and memory read and write statistics.

Exercise: likwid perfctr

1 Install likwid from package manager or with the following commands:

```
git clone https://github.com/RRZE-HPC/likwid.git
cd likwid
edit config.mk
make
make install
```

2 Enable MSR with `sudo modprobe msr`

3 Run `likwid-perfctr -C 0-87 -g MEM_DP ./clover_leaf`
   (In the output, there's also min and max columns. These have been removed to save space.)

```
+-------------------------------------------+--------------+------------+
|                   Metric                  |     Sum      |    Avg     |
+-------------------------------------------+--------------+------------+
|           Runtime (RDTSC) [s] STAT        |  47646.0600  |  541.4325  |
|           Runtime unhalted [s] STAT       |  56963.3936  |  647.3113  |
|              Clock [MHz] STAT             | 223750.6676  | 2542.6212  |
|                  CPI STAT                 |    170.1285  |    1.9333  |
|               Energy [J] STAT             | 151590.4909  | 1722.6192  |
|                Power [W] STAT             |    279.9804  |    3.1816  |
|            Energy DRAM [J] STAT           |  37986.9191  |  431.6695  |
|             Power DRAM [W] STAT           |     70.1601  |    0.7973  |
|              DP MFLOP/s STAT              |  22163.8134  |  251.8615  |
|            AVX DP MFLOP/s STAT            |   4777.5260  |   54.2901  |
|            Packed MUOPS/s STAT            |   1194.3827  |   13.5725  |
|            Scalar MUOPS/s STAT            |  17386.2877  |  197.5715  |
|  Memory read bandwidth [MBytes/s] STAT    |  96817.7018  | 1100.2012  |
|  Memory read data volume [GBytes] STAT    |  52420.2526  |  595.6847  |
|  Memory write bandwidth [MBytes/s] STAT   |  26502.2674  |  301.1621  |
|  Memory write data volume [GBytes] STAT   |  14349.1896  |  163.0590  |
|    Memory bandwidth [MBytes/s] STAT       | 123319.9692  | 1401.3633  |
|     Memory data volume [GBytes] STAT      |  66769.4422  |  758.7437  |
|         Operational intensity STAT        |      0.3609  |    0.0041  |
+-------------------------------------------+--------------+------------+
```

```
Computation Rate = (22163.8134+4*4777.5260) = 41274 MFLOPs/sec = 41.3
         GFLOPs/sec
Arithmetic Intensity = 41274/123319.9692 = .33 FLOPs/byte
Operational Intensity = .3608 FLOPs/byte

For a serial run:
Computation Rate = 2.97 GFLOPS/sec
Operational intensity = 0.2574 FLOPS/byte
Energy = 212747.7787 Joules
Energy DRAM = 49518.7395 Joules
```

We can also use the output from likwid to calculate the energy reduction for Clover-Leaf due to running in parallel.

> **Exercise: Calculate the energy savings for parallel run relative to serial**
>
> Energy reduction is (212747.7787 - 151590.4909) / 212747.7787 = 28.7 %.
>
> DRAM energy reduction is (49518.7395 - 37986.9191) / 49518.7395 = 23.2 %.

INSTRUMENT SPECIFIC SECTIONS OF CODE WITH LIKWID-PERFCTR MARKERS

Markers can be used in likwid to get performance for one or multiple sections of code. This capability will be used in the next chapter in section 4.2.

1 Compile the code with `-DLIKWID_PERFMON -I<PATH_TO_LIKWID>/include`
2 Link with `-L<PATH_TO_LIKWID>/lib` and `-llikwid`
3 Insert the lines from listing 3.1 into your code

> **Listing 3.1   Inserting markers into code to instrument specific sections of code**

```
LIKWID_MARKER_INIT;
LIKWID_MARKER_THREADINIT;
LIKWID_MARKER_REGISTER("Compute")

LIKWID_MARKER_START("Compute");
// ...  Your code to measure
LIKWID_MARKER_STOP("Compute");
LIKWID_MARKER_CLOSE;
```

A single threaded region

Requires daemon with suid (root) permissions

GENERATING YOUR OWN ROOFLINE PLOTS

Charlene Yang, NERSC, has created and released a Python script for generating a roofline plot. This is extremely convenient for generating a high-quality, custom graphic with data from your explorations. For these examples, you may want to install the anaconda3 package. It contains the matplotlib library and Jupyter notebook support. Use the following code to customize a roofline plot using Python and matplotlib:

```
git clone https://github.com/cyanguwa/nersc-roofline.git
cd nersc-roofline/Plotting
modify data.txt
python plot_roofline.py data.txt
```

We'll use modified versions of this plotting script in a couple of exercises. In this first one, we embedded parts of the roofline plotting script into a Jupyter notebook. Jupyter notebooks (https://jupyter.org/install.html) allow you to intersperse Markdown documentation with Python code for an interactive experience. We use this to dynamically calculate the theoretical hardware performance and then create a roofline plot of your arithmetic intensity and performance.

Exercise: Plotting script embedded in a Jupyter notebook

Install Python3 using a package manager. Then use the Python installer, pip, to install NumPy, SciPy, matplotlib, and Jupyter:

```
brew install python3
pip install numpy scipy matplotlib jupyter
```

Run the Jupyter notebook:

1   Download the Jupyter notebook at https://github.com/EssentialsofParallelComputing/Chapter3
2   Open the Jupyter notebook HardwarePlatformCharacterization.ipynb
3   In HardwarePlatformCharacterization.ipynb, change the settings for the hardware in the first section for your platform of interest as shown in the following figure:

Hardware Platform Characterization

```
In [1]: CPUDescription="Mid-2017 MacBook Pro laptop with an Intel Core i7-7920HQ processor"
        MemoryDescription="LPDDR3-2133"
        print (CPUDescription)
        print (MemoryDescription)

        Mid-2017 MacBook Pro laptop with an Intel Core i7-7920HQ processor
        LPDDR3-2133
```

Processor Characteristics

Processor Frequency [GHz]
Processor Cores
Hyperthreads
Vector Width [bits]
Word Size in Bits [64 for double, 32 for single precision]
FMA [2 for Fused Multiple Add, 1 otherwise]

```
In [2]: ProcessorFrequency=3.7
        ProcessorCores=4
        Hyperthreads=2
        VectorWidth=256
        WordSizeBits=64
        FMA=2
```

Main Memory Characteristics

Data Transfer Rate [MT/s]
Bytes Transferred per Access [Bytes]
Number Channels

```
In [3]: DataTransferRate=2133
        MemoryChannels=2
        BytesTransferredPerAccess=8
```

Once you change the hardware settings, you are ready to run the calculations for the theoretical hardware characteristics. Run all cells in the notebook and look for calculations in the next part of the notebook as shown in the next figure.

```
In [4]: TheoreticalMaximumFlops=ProcessorCores*Hyperthreads*ProcessorFrequency*VectorWidth/WordSizeBits*FMA
        print ("Theoretical Maximum Flops =",TheoreticalMaximumFlops, "GFLOPS/s")

        Theoretical Maximum Flops = 236.8 GFLOPS/s
```

```
In [5]: TheoreticalMemoryBandwidth=DataTransferRate*MemoryChannels*BytesTransferredPerAccess/1000
        print ("Theoretical Maximum Bandwidth (at main memory) =", TheoreticalMemoryBandwidth, "GiB/s")

        Theoretical Maximum Bandwidth (at main memory) = 34.128 GiB/s
```

```
In [6]: WordSizeBytes=WordSizeBits/8
        TheoreticalMachineBalance=TheoreticalMaximumFlops/TheoreticalMemoryBandwidth
        print ("Theoretical Machine Balance = ",TheoreticalMachineBalance, "Flops/byte")
        print ("Theoretical Machine Balance = ",TheoreticalMachineBalance*WordSizeBytes, "Flops/word")

        Theoretical Machine Balance =  6.938584153774028 Flops/byte
        Theoretical Machine Balance =  55.50867323019222 Flops/word
```

(continued)

The next notebook section contains the measured performance data you want to plot on the roofline plot. Enter this data from performance measurements. We use the data collected using the likwid performance counters for a serial run of CloverLeaf and one with OpenMP and vectorization.

```
In [7]:  smemroofs = [21000.0, 9961.16, 1171.55, 224.08]
         scomproofs = [2801.24, 1400.26]
         smem_roof_name = ["L1 Bandwidth", "L2 Bandwidth", "L3 Bandwidth", "DRAM Bandwidth"]
         scomp_roof_name = ["DP Vector FMA Peak", "DP Vector Add Peak"]
         AI = [.3608, .2106]
         FLOPS = [41.3, 2.735]
         labels = ["CloverLeaf w/OpenMP and Vectorization", "CloverLeaf Serial"]

         print ('memroofs', smemroofs)
         print ('mem_roof_names', smem_roof_name)
         print ('comproofs', scomproofs)
         print ('comp_roof_names', scomp_roof_name)
         print ('AI', AI)
         print ('FLOPS', FLOPS)
         print ('labels', labels)

         memroofs [21000.0, 9961.16, 1171.55, 224.08]
         mem_roof_names ['L1 Bandwidth', 'L2 Bandwidth', 'L3 Bandwidth', 'DRAM Bandwidth']
         comproofs [2801.24, 1400.26]
         comp_roof_names ['DP Vector FMA Peak', 'DP Vector Add Peak']
         AI [0.3608, 0.2106]
         FLOPS [41.3, 2.735]
         labels ['CloverLeaf w/OpenMP and Vectorization', 'CloverLeaf Serial']
```

Now the notebook starts the code to plot the roofline using matplotlib. Shown here is the first half of the plotting script. You can change the plot extent, scales, labels, and other settings.

```
In [8]:  %matplotlib inline

         import numpy as np
         import matplotlib.pyplot as plt

         font = { 'size'   : 20}
         plt.rc('font', **font)

         markersize = 16
         colors = ['b','g','r','y','m','c']
         styles = ['o','s','v','^','D','>',"<","*","h","H","+","1","2","3","4","8","p","d","|","_","-.",",","."]

         fig = plt.figure(1,figsize=(20.67,12.6))
         plt.clf()
         ax = fig.gca()
         ax.set_xscale('log')
         ax.set_yscale('log')
         ax.set_xlabel('Arithmetic Intensity [FLOPs/Byte]')
         ax.set_ylabel('Performance [GFLOP/sec]')
         ax.grid()
         ax.grid(which='minor', linestyle=':', linewidth='0.5', color='black')

         nx = 10000
         xmin = -3
         xmax = 2
         ymin = 0.1
         ymax = 10000

         ax.set_xlim(10**xmin, 10**xmax)
         ax.set_ylim(ymin, ymax)

         ixx = int(nx*0.02)
         xlim = ax.get_xlim()
         ylim = ax.get_ylim()
```

The plotting script then finds the "elbows" where the lines intersect to plot only the relative segments. It also works out the location and orientation of the text to be placed on the plot.

```
x = np.logspace(xmin,xmax,nx)
for roof in scomproofs:
    for ix in range(1,nx):
        if smemroofs[0] * x[ix] >= roof and smemroofs[0] * x[ix-1] < roof:
            scomp_x_elbow.append(x[ix-1])
            scomp_ix_elbow.append(ix-1)
            break


for roof in smemroofs:
    for ix in range(1,nx):
        if (scomproofs[0] <= roof * x[ix] and scomproofs[0] > roof * x[ix-1]):
            smem_x_elbow.append(x[ix-1])
            smem_ix_elbow.append(ix-1)
            break

for i in range(0,len(scomproofs)):
    y = np.ones(len(x)) * scomproofs[i]
    ax.plot(x[scomp_ix_elbow[i]:],y[scomp_ix_elbow[i]:],c='k',ls='-',lw='2')

for i in range(0,len(smemroofs)):
    y = x * smemroofs[i]
    ax.plot(x[:smem_ix_elbow[i]+1],y[:smem_ix_elbow[i]+1],c='k',ls='-',lw='2')


marker_handles = list()
for i in range(0,len(AI)):
    ax.plot(float(AI[i]),float(FLOPS[i]),c=colors[i],marker=styles[i],linestyle='None',ms=markersize,label=labels[i])
    marker_handles.append(ax.plot([],[],c=colors[i],marker=styles[i],linestyle='None',ms=markersize,label=labels[i])[0])

for roof in scomproofs:
    ax.text(x[-ixx],roof,
            scomp_roof_name[scomproofs.index(roof)] + ': ' + '{0:.1f}'.format(float(roof)) + ' GFLOP/s',
            horizontalalignment='right',
            verticalalignment='bottom')

for roof in smemroofs:
    ang = np.arctan(np.log10(xlim[1]/xlim[0]) / np.log10(ylim[1]/ylim[0])
                    * fig.get_size_inches()[1]/fig.get_size_inches()[0] )
    ax.text(x[ixx],x[ixx]*roof*(1+0.25*np.sin(ang)**2),
            smem_roof_name[smemroofs.index(roof)] + ': ' + '{0:.1f}'.format(float(roof)) + ' GiB/s',
            horizontalalignment='left',
            verticalalignment='bottom',
            rotation=180/np.pi*ang)


legl = plt.legend(handles = marker_handles,loc=4, ncol=2)
ax.add_artist(legl)

plt.savefig('roofline.png')
plt.savefig('roofline.eps')
plt.savefig('roofline.pdf')
plt.savefig('roofline.svg')

plt.show()
```

Plotting this arithmetic intensity and computation rate gives the result in figure 3.6. Both the serial and the parallel runs are plotted on the roofline. The parallel run is about 15 times faster and with slightly higher operational (arithmetic) intensity.

There are a couple more tools that can measure arithmetic intensity. The Intel® Software Development Emulator (SDE) package (https://software.intel.com/en-us/articles/intel-software-development-emulator) generates lots of information that can be used to calculate arithmetic intensity. The Intel® Vtune™ performance tool (part of the Parallel Studio package) can also be used to gather performance information.

When we compare the results from Intel Advisor and likwid, there is a difference in the arithmetic intensity. There are many different ways to count operations, counting the whole cache line when loaded or just the data used. Similarly, the counters can count the entire vector width and not just the part that is used. Some tools count just

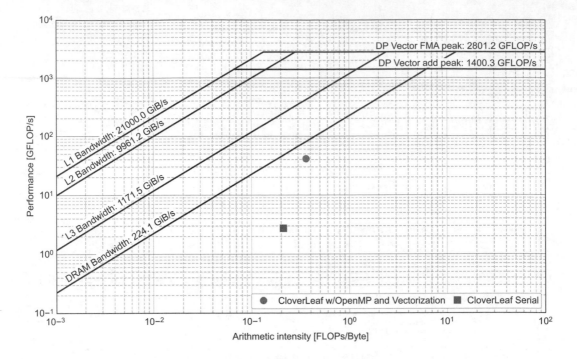

Figure 3.6   Overall performance of Clover Leaf on a Skylake Gold processor

floating-point operations, whereas others count different types of operations (such as integer) as well.

3.3.2   *Empirical measurement of processor clock frequency and energy consumption*

Recent processors have a lot of hardware performance counters and control capabilities. These include processor frequency, temperature, power, and many others. New software applications and libraries are emerging to make accessing this information easier. These applications ease the programming difficulty, but these may also help work around the need for elevated permissions so that the data is more accessible to normal users. This is a welcome development because programmers cannot optimize what they cannot see.

With the aggressive management of processor frequency, processors seldom are at their nominal frequency setting. The clock frequency is reduced when processors are at idle and increased to a turbo-boost mode when busy. Two easy interactive commands to see the behavior of the processor frequency are

```
watch -n 1 "lscpu | grep MHz"
watch -n 1 "grep MHz /proc/cpuinfo"
```

The likwid tool suite also has a command-line tool, likwid-powermeter, to look at processor frequencies and power statistics. The likwid-perfctr tool also reports some of these statistics in a summary report. Another handy little app is the Intel® Power Gadget, with versions for the Mac and Windows and a more limited one for Linux. It graphs frequency, power, temperature, and utilization.

The CLAMR mini-app (http://www.github.com/LANL/CLAMR.git) is developing a small library, PowerStats, that will track energy and frequency from within an application and report it at the end of the run. Currently, PowerStats works on the Mac, using the Intel Power Gadget library interface. A similar capability is being developed for Linux systems. The application code needs to add just a few calls as shown in the following listing.

Listing 3.2 PowerStats code to track energy and frequency

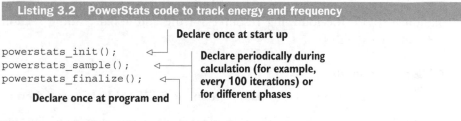

When run, the following table is printed:

```
Processor       Energy(mWh) =    94.47181
IA              Energy(mWh) =    70.07562
DRAM            Energy(mWh) =     3.09289
Processor       Power (W)   =    71.07833
IA              Power (W)   =    54.73608
DRAM            Power (W)   =     2.32194
Average Frequency           =  3721.19422
Average Temperature (C)     =    94.78369
Time Expended (secs)        =    12.13246
```

3.3.3 Tracking memory during run time

Memory usage is also another aspect of performance that isn't easily visible to the programmer. You can use the same sort of interactive command for processor frequency as in the previous listing, but for memory statistics instead. First, get your process ID from the top or the ps command. Then use one of the following commands to track memory usage:

```
watch -n 1 "grep VmRSS /proc/<pid>/status"
watch -n 1 "ps <pid>"
top -s 1 -p <pid>
```

To integrate this into your program, perhaps to see what happens with memory in different phases, the MemSTATS library in CLAMR provides four different memory-tracking calls:

```
long long memstats_memused()
long long memstats_mempeak()
long long memstats_memfree()
long long memstats_memtotal()
```

Insert these calls into your program to return the current memory statistics at the point of the call. MemSTATS is a single C source and header file, so it should be easy to integrate into your program. To get the source, go to http://github.com/LANL/ CLAMR/ and look in the MemSTATS directory. It is also available at https://github .com/EssentialsofParallelComputing/Chapter3 in the code samples.

3.4   *Further explorations*

This chapter only brushes the surface of what all these tools can do. For more information, explore the following resources in the additional reading section and try some of the exercises.

3.4.1   *Additional reading*

You can find more information and data on the STREAM Benchmark here:

John McCalpin. 1995. "STREAM: Sustainable Memory Bandwidth in High Performance Computers." https://www.cs.virginia.edu/stream/.

The roofline model originated at Lawrence Berkeley National Laboratory. Their website has many resources exploring its use:

"Roofline Performance Model." https://crd.lbl.gov/departments/computer-science/ PAR/research/roofline/.

3.4.2   *Exercises*

1 Calculate the theoretical performance of a system of your choice. Include the peak flops, memory bandwidth, and machine balance in your calculation.
2 Download the Roofline Toolkit from https://bitbucket.org/berkeleylab/ cs-roofline-toolkit.git and measure the actual performance of your selected system.
3 With the Roofline Toolkit, start with one processor and incrementally add optimization and parallelization, recording how much improvement you get at each step.
4 Download the STREAM Benchmark from https://www.cs.virginia.edu/stream/ and measure the memory bandwidth of your selected system.
5 Pick one of the publicly available benchmarks or mini-apps listed in section 17.1 and generate a call graph using KCacheGrind.
6 Pick one of the publicly available Benchmarks or mini-apps listed in section 17.1 and measure its arithmetic intensity with either Intel Advisor or the likwid tools.

7 Using the performance tools presented in this chapter, determine the average processor frequency and energy consumption for a small application.

8 Using some of the tools from section 3.3.3, determine how much memory an application uses.

This chapter has covered a lot of ground with many necessary details for a parallel project plan. Estimating performance capabilities and using tools to extract information on hardware characteristics and application performance give solid, concrete data points to populate the plan. The proper use of these tools and skills can help build a foundation for a successful parallel project.

Summary

- There are several possible performance limitations for an application. These range from the peak number of floating-point operations (flops) to memory bandwidth and hard disk reads and writes.

- Applications on current computing systems are generally more limited by memory bandwidth than flops. Although identified two decades ago, it has become even more true than projected at that time. But computational scientists have been slow to adapt their thinking to this new reality.

- You can use profiling tools to measure your application performance and to determine where to focus optimization and parallelization work. This chapter shows examples using Intel® Advisor, Valgrind, Callgrind, and likwid, but there are many other tools including Intel® VTune, Open|Speedshop (O|SS), HPC Toolkit, or Allinea/ARM MAP. (A more complete list is given in section 17.3.) However, the most valuable tools are those that provide actionable information rather than quantity.

- You can use hardware performance utilities and apps to determine energy consumption, processor frequency, memory usage, and much more. By making these performance attributes more visible, it becomes easier to optimize for these considerations.

Data design and performance models

This chapter covers

- Why real applications struggle to achieve performance
- Addressing kernels and loops that significantly underperform
- Choosing data structures for your application
- Assessing different programming approaches before writing code
- Understanding how the cache hierarchy delivers data to the processor

This chapter has two topics that are intimately coupled: (1) the introduction of performance models increasingly dominated by data movement and, thus, necessarily (2) the underlying design and structure of data. Although it may seem secondary to performance, the data structure and its design are critical. This must be determined in advance because it dictates the entire form of the algorithms, code, and later, the parallel implementation.

The choice of data structures and, thereby, the data layout often determines the performance that you can achieve and in ways that are not always obvious when the design decisions are made. Thinking about the data layout and its performance impacts is at the core of a new and growing programming approach called *data-oriented design*. This approach considers the patterns of how data will be used in the program and proactively designs around it. Data-oriented design gives us a data-centric view of the world, which is also consistent with our focus on memory bandwidth rather than floating-point operations (flops). In summary, for performance, our approach is to think about

- Data rather than code
- Memory bandwidth rather than flops
- Cache line instead of individual data elements
- Operations prioritized on data already in cache

Simple performance models based on the data structures and the algorithms that naturally follow can roughly predict performance. A *performance model* is a simplified representation of how a computer system executes the operations in a kernel of code. We use simplified models because reasoning about the full complexity of the computer operation is difficult and obscures the key aspects we need to think about for performance. These simplified models should capture the computer's operational aspects that are most important for performance. Also, every computer system varies in the details of its operation. Because we want our application to run on a wide range of systems, we need a model that abstracts a general view of the operations that all systems have in common.

A model helps us to understand the current functioning of our kernel performance. It helps build expectations for the performance and how it might improve with changes to the code. Changes to the code can be a lot of work, and we'll want to know what the result should be before embarking on the effort. It also helps us to focus on the critical factors and resources for our application's performance.

A performance model is not limited to flops, and indeed, we will focus on the data and memory aspects. In addition to flops and memory operations, integer operations, instructions and instruction types can be important and should be counted. But the limits associated with these additional considerations usually track memory performance and can be treated as a small reduction in the performance from that limit.

The first part of the chapter looks at simple data structures and how these impact performance. Next, we'll introduce performance models to use for quickly making design decisions. These performance models are then put to use in a case study to look at more complicated data structures for compressed, sparse multi-material arrays to assess which data structure is likely to perform well. The impact of these decisions on data structures often shows up much later in the project when changes are far more difficult. The last portion of this chapter focuses on advanced programming models; it introduces the more complex models that are appropriate for deeper dives into performance issues or understanding how computer hardware and its design influences performance. Let's dig into what this means when looking at your code and performance issues.

NOTE We encourage you to follow along with the examples for this chapter at https://github.com/EssentialsofParallelComputing/Chapter4.

4.1 *Performance data structures: Data-oriented design*

Our goal is to design data structures that lead to good performance. We'll start with a way to allocate multidimensional arrays and then move on to more complex data structures. To achieve this goal requires

- Understanding how data is laid out in the computer
- How data is loaded into cache lines and then the CPU
- How data layout impacts performance
- The increasing importance of data movement to performance in today's computers

In most modern programming languages, data is grouped in structures of one kind or another. For example, the use of data structures in C or classes in object-oriented programming (also called OOP) bring related items together for the convenience of organizing the source code. The members of the class are gathered together with the methods that operate on it. While the philosophy of object-oriented programming offers a lot of value from a programmer's perspective, it completely ignores how the CPU operates. Object-oriented programming results in frequent method calls with few lines of code in between (figure 4.1).

For method invocation, the class must first be brought into the cache. Next the data is brought into cache and then adjacent elements of the class. This is convenient when you are operating on one object. But for applications with intensive computations, there are large numbers of each item. For these situations, we don't want to invoke a method on one item at a time with each invocation requiring the transversal of a deep call stack. These lead to instruction cache misses, poor data cache usage, branching, and lots of function call overhead.

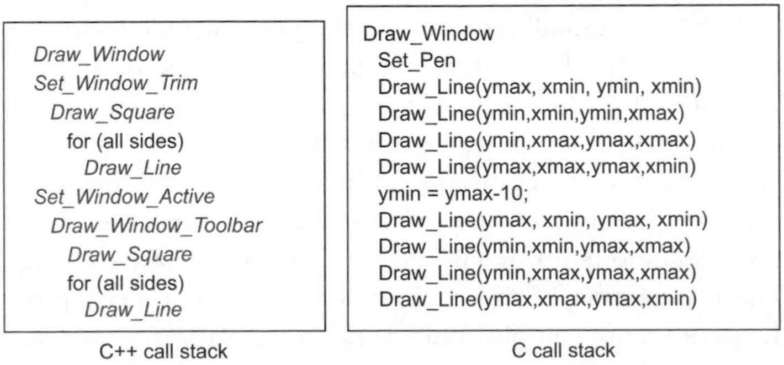

```
Draw_Window
  Set_Window_Trim
    Draw_Square
      for (all sides)
        Draw_Line
  Set_Window_Active
    Draw_Window_Toolbar
      Draw_Square
        for (all sides)
          Draw_Line
```

C++ call stack

```
Draw_Window
  Set_Pen
  Draw_Line(ymax, xmin, ymin, xmin)
  Draw_Line(ymin,xmin,ymin,xmax)
  Draw_Line(ymin,xmax,ymax,xmax)
  Draw_Line(ymax,xmax,ymax,xmin)
  ymin = ymax-10;
  Draw_Line(ymax, xmin, ymax, xmin)
  Draw_Line(ymin,xmin,ymax,xmax)
  Draw_Line(ymin,xmax,ymax,xmax)
  Draw_Line(ymax,xmax,ymax,xmin)
```

C call stack

Figure 4.1   Object-oriented languages have deep call stacks with lots of method calls (shown on the left), while procedural languages have long sequences of operations at one level of the call stack.

C++ methods make it much easier to write concise code, but nearly every line is a method invocation as figure 4.1 illustrates. In numerical simulation code, the `Draw_Line` call would more than likely be a complex mathematical expression. But even here, if the `Draw_Line` function is inlined into the source code, there will be no jumps into functions for the C code. *Inlining* is where the compiler copies the source from a subroutine into the location where it is used rather than making a call to it. The compiler can only inline for simple, short routines, however. But object-oriented code has method calls that won't inline because of complexity and deep call stacks. This causes instruction cache misses and other performance issues. If we are only drawing one window, the loss in performance is offset by the simpler programming. If we are going to draw a million windows, we can't afford the performance hit.

So let's flip this around and design our data structures for performance rather than programming convenience. Object-oriented programming and other modern programming styles are powerful but introduce many performance traps. At CppCon in 2014, Mike Acton's presentation, "Data-oriented design and C++," summarized work from the gaming industry that identified why modern programming styles impede performance. Advocates of the data-oriented design programming style address this issue by creating a programming style that focuses squarely on performance. This approach is coined *data-oriented design*, which focuses on the best data layout for the CPU and the cache. This style has much in common with the techniques long used by high-performance computing (HPC) developers. In HPC, data-oriented design is the norm; it follows naturally from the way people wrote programs in Fortran. So, what does data-oriented design look like? It

- Operates on arrays, not individual data items, avoiding the call overhead and the instruction and data cache misses
- Prefers arrays rather than structures for better cache usage in more situations
- Inlines subroutines rather than transversing a deep call hierarchy
- Controls memory allocation, avoiding undirected reallocation behind the scenes
- Uses contiguous array-based linked lists to avoid the standard linked list implementations used in C and C++, which jump all over memory with poor data locality and cache usage

As we move into parallelization in the next chapters, we'll note that our experience shows that large data structures or classes also cause problems with shared memory parallelization and vectorization. In shared memory programming, we need to be able to mark variables as private to a thread or as global across all threads. But currently, all the items in the data structure have the same attribute. The problem is particularly acute during incremental introduction of OpenMP parallelization. When implementing vectorization, we want long arrays of homogeneous data, while classes usually group heterogeneous data. This complicates things.

4.1.1 *Multidimensional arrays*

In this section, we'll cover the ubiquitous multidimensional array data structure in scientific computing. Our goal will be to understand

- How to lay out multidimensional arrays in memory
- How to access the arrays to avoid performance problems
- How to call numerical libraries that are in Fortran from a C program

Handling multidimensional arrays is the most common problem with regard to performance. The first two subfigures in figure 4.2 show the conventional C and Fortran data layouts.

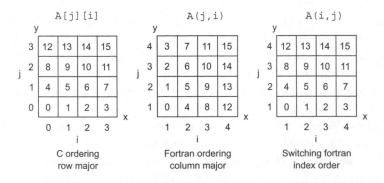

Figure 4.2 Conventional C ordering is row major while Fortran ordering is column major. Switching either the Fortran or C index order makes these compatible. Note that convention has Fortran array indices starting at 1 while C starts at 0. Also, C convention numbers the elements from 0 to 15 in contiguous order.

The C data order is referred to as *row major*, where data across the row varies faster than data in the column. This means that row data is contiguous in memory. In contrast, the Fortran data layout is *column major*, where the column data varies fastest. Practically, as programmers, we must remember which index should be in the inner loop to leverage the contiguous memory in each situation (figure 4.3).

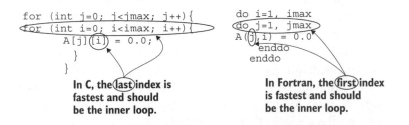

Figure 4.3 For C, the important thing to remember is that the last index varies fastest and should be the inner loop of a nested loop. For Fortran, the first index varies fastest and should be the inner loop of a nested loop.

Beyond the differences in data ordering between languages, there is a further issue that must be considered. Is the memory for the whole 2D array contiguous? Fortran doesn't guarantee that the memory is contiguous unless you use the CONTIGUOUS attribute on the array as this example shows:

```
real, allocatable, contiguous :: x(:,:)
```

In practice, using the contiguous attribute is not as critical as it might seem. All popular Fortran compilers allocate contiguous memory for arrays with or without this attribute. The possible exceptions are padding for cache performance or passing an array through a subroutine interface with a slice operator. A *slice operator* is a construct in Fortran that allows you to refer to a subset of an array as in the example of a copy of a row of a 2D array to a 1D array with the syntax y(:) = x(1,:). Slice operators can also be used in a subroutine call; for example,

```
call write_data_row(x(1,:))
```

Some research compilers handle this by simply modifying the *stride* between data elements in the dope vector for the array. In Fortran, the *dope vector* is the metadata for the array containing the start location, length of the array, and the stride between elements for each dimension. Dope in this context is from "give me the dope (info)" on someone or something (in this case, the array). Figure 4.4 illustrates the concepts of a dope vector, the slice operator, and stride. The idea is that by modifying the stride in the dope vector from 1 to 4, the data is then traversed as a row rather than a column. But in practice, production Fortran compilers usually make a copy of the data and pass it into the subroutine to avoid breaking code that is expecting contiguous data. This also means that you should avoid using the slice operator in calling Fortran subroutines because of the hidden copy and its resulting performance cost.

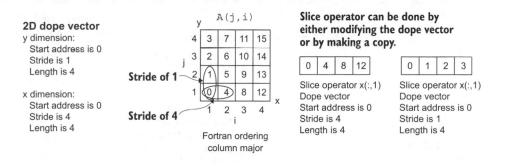

Figure 4.4   Different views of a Fortran array created by modifying the dope vector, a set of metadata describing the start, stride, and length in each dimension. The slice operator returns a section of a Fortran array with all of the elements in the dimension with the colon (:). More complicated sections can be created, such as the lower four elements with A(1:2,1:2), where the upper and lower bounds are specified with the colon.

C has its own issues with contiguous memory for a 2D array. This is due to the conventional way of dynamically allocating a 2D array in C as shown in the following listing.

Listing 4.1 Conventional way of allocating a 2D array in C

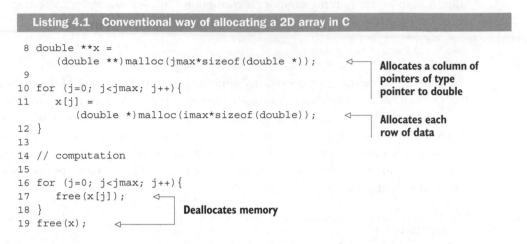

```
 8 double **x =
       (double **)malloc(jmax*sizeof(double *));          ◁──  Allocates a column of
 9                                                              pointers of type
10 for (j=0; j<jmax; j++){                                      pointer to double
11     x[j] =
           (double *)malloc(imax*sizeof(double));        ◁──  Allocates each
12 }                                                           row of data
13
14 // computation
15
16 for (j=0; j<jmax; j++){
17     free(x[j]);    ◁─┐
18 }                    ├─  Deallocates memory
19 free(x);          ◁─┘
```

This listing uses 1+jmax allocations, and each allocation can come from a different place in the heap. With larger-sized 2D arrays, the layout of the data in memory has only a small impact on cache efficiency. The bigger problem is that the use of noncontiguous arrays is severely limited; it's impossible to pass these to Fortran, write those in a block to a file, and then pass these to a GPU or to another processor. Instead, each of these operations needs to be done row by row. Fortunately, there is an easy way to allocate a contiguous block of memory for C arrays. Why isn't it standard practice? It's because everyone learns the conventional method as in listing 4.1 and doesn't think about it. The following listing shows how to allocate a contiguous block of memory for a 2D array.

Listing 4.2 Allocating a contiguous 2D array in C

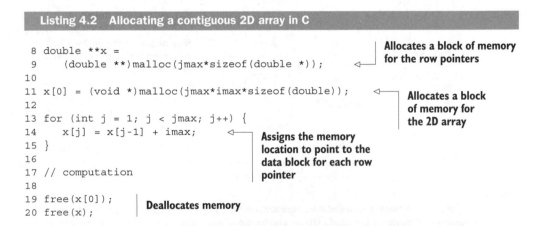

```
 8 double **x =
 9     (double **)malloc(jmax*sizeof(double *));      ◁─┘  Allocates a block of memory
10                                                          for the row pointers
11 x[0] = (void *)malloc(jmax*imax*sizeof(double));  ◁─┐  Allocates a block
12                                                       │  of memory for
13 for (int j = 1; j < jmax; j++) {                      │  the 2D array
14     x[j] = x[j-1] + imax;    ◁──  Assigns the memory
15 }                                 location to point to the
16                                   data block for each row
17 // computation                    pointer
18
19 free(x[0]);    │  Deallocates memory
20 free(x);       │
```

This method not only gives you a contiguous memory block, but it also only takes two memory allocations! We can optimize this even further by bundling the row pointers into the memory block at the start of the contiguous memory allocation on line 11 of listing 4.2, thereby combining the two memory allocations into one (figure 4.5).

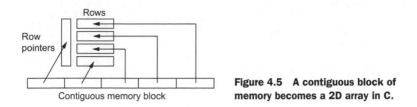

Figure 4.5 A contiguous block of memory becomes a 2D array in C.

The following listing shows the implementation of a single contiguous memory allocation for a 2D array in malloc2D.c.

Listing 4.3 Single contiguous memory allocation for a 2D array

malloc2D.c

```
 1 #include <stdlib.h>
 2 #include "malloc2D.h"
 3
 4 double **malloc2D(int jmax, int imax)
 5 {
 6     double **x = (double **)malloc(jmax*sizeof(double *) +
 7                   jmax*imax*sizeof(double));         ◁────┐  Allocates a block of
 8                                                            memory for the row
 9     x[0] = (double *)x + jmax;         ◁──────┐           pointers and the 2D array
10
11     for (int j = 1; j < jmax; j++) {
12         x[j] = x[j-1] + imax;         ◁────┐
13     }
14
15     return(x);
16 }
```

Allocates a block of memory for the row pointers and the 2D array

Assigns the start of the memory block for the 2D array after the row pointers

Assigns the memory location to point to the data block for each row pointer

malloc2D.h

```
1 #ifndef MALLOC2D_H
2 #define MALLOC2D_H
3 double **malloc2D(int jmax, int imax);
4 #endif
```

Now we have only one memory block, including the row pointer array. This should improve memory allocation and cache efficiency. The array can also be indexed as a 1D or a 2D array as shown in listing 4.4. The 1D array reduces the integer address calculation and is easier to vectorize or thread (when we come to that in chapters 6 and 7). The listing also shows a manual 2D index calculation into a 1D array.

Listing 4.4   1D and 2D access of contiguous 2D array

calc2d.c

```
 1 #include "malloc2D.h"
 2
 3 int main(int argc, char *argv[])
 4 {
 5     int i, j;
 6     int imax=100, jmax=100;
 7
 8     double **x = (double **)malloc2D(jmax,imax);
 9
10     double *x1d=x[0];
11     for (i = 0; i< imax*jmax; i++){       1D access of the
12         x1d[i] = 0.0;                     contiguous 2D array
13     }
14
15     for (j = 0; j< jmax; j++){
16         for (i = 0; i< imax; i++){        2D access of the
17             x[j][i] = 0.0;                contiguous 2D array
18         }
19     }
20
21     for (j = 0; j< jmax; j++){
22         for (i = 0; i< imax; i++){        Manual 2D index
23             x1d[i + imax * j] = 0.0;      calculation for a 1D array
24         }
25     }
26 }
```

Fortran programmers take for granted the first-class treatment of multidimensional arrays in the language. Although C and C++ have been around for decades, these still do not have a native multidimensional array built into the language. There are proposals to the C++ standard to add native multidimensional array support for the 2023 revision (see the Hollman, et al. reference in appendix A). Until then, the multidimensional array memory allocation covered in listing 4.4 is essential.

4.1.2   *Array of Structures (AoS) versus Structures of Arrays (SoA)*

In this section, we'll cover the implications of structures and classes on data layout. Our goals are to understand

- The different ways structures can be laid out in memory
- How to access arrays to avoid performance problems

There are two different ways to organize related data into data collections. These are the *Array of Structures* (AoS), where the data is collected into a single unit at the lowest level and then an array is made of the structure, or the *Structure of Arrays* (SoA), where each data array is at the lowest level and then a structure is made of the arrays. A third way, which is a hybrid of these two data structures, is the *Array of Structures of Arrays* (AoSoA). We will discuss this hybrid data structure in section 4.1.3.

One common example of an AoS is the color values used to draw graphic objects. The following listing shows the red, green, blue (RGB) color system structure in C.

Listing 4.5   Array of Structures (AoS) in C

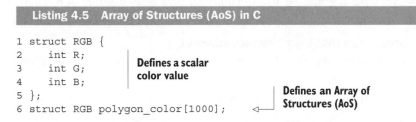

```
1 struct RGB {
2     int R;                  Defines a scalar
3     int G;                  color value
4     int B;
5 };                                   Defines an Array of
6 struct RGB polygon_color[1000];      Structures (AoS)
```

Listing 4.5 shows an AoS where the data is laid out in memory (figure 4.6). In the figure, note the blank space at bytes 12, 28, and 44 where the compiler inserts padding to get the memory alignment on a 64-bit boundary (128 bits or 16 bytes). A 64-byte cache line holds four values of the structure. Then in line 6, we create the `polygon_color` array composed of 1,000 of the RGB data structure type. This data layout is reasonable because, generally, the RGB values are used together to draw each polygon.

```
R  G  B     R  G  B     R  G  B
0  4  8  12 16 20 24 28 32 36 40 44 bytes
```

Figure 4.6   Layout in memory of an RGB color model in an Array of Structures (AoS).

The SoA is an alternative data layout. The following listing shows the C code for this.

Listing 4.6   Structure of Arrays (SoA) in C

```
 1 struct RGB {
 2     int *R;                 Defines an integer
 3     int *G;                 array of a color value
 4     int *B;
 5 };                                  Defines a Structure
 6 struct RGB polygon_color;            of Arrays (SoA)
 7
 8 polygon_color.R = (int *)malloc(1000*sizeof(int));
 9 polygon_color.G = (int *)malloc(1000*sizeof(int));
10 polygon_color.B = (int *)malloc(1000*sizeof(int));
11
12 free(polygon_color.R);
13 free(polygon_color.G);
14 free(polygon_color.B);
```

The memory layout has all 1,000 R values in contiguous memory. The G and B color values could follow the R values in memory, but these can also be elsewhere in the heap, depending on where the memory allocator finds space. The *heap* is a separate region of memory that is used to allocate dynamic memory with the `malloc` routine or the new operator. We can also use the contiguous memory allocator (listing 4.3) to force the memory to be located together.

Our concern here is performance. Each of these data structures is equally reasonable to use from the programmer's perspective, but the important questions are how does the data structure appear to the CPU and how does it affect performance. Let's look at the performance of these data structures in a couple of different scenarios.

ARRAY OF STRUCTURES (AoS) PERFORMANCE ASSESSMENT

In our color example, assume that when the data is read, all three components for a point are accessed but not a single R, G, or B value, so the AoS representation works well. And for graphics operations, this data layout is commonly used.

> **NOTE** If the compiler adds padding, it increases the number of memory loads by 25% for the AoS representation, but not all compilers insert this padding. Still it is worth considering for those compilers that do.

If only one of the RGB values is accessed in a loop, the cache usage would be poor because the loop skips over unneeded values. When this access pattern is vectorized by the compiler, it would need to use a less efficient gather/scatter operation.

STRUCTURE OF ARRAYS (SoA) PERFORMANCE ASSESSMENT

For the SoA layout, the RGB values have separate cache lines (figure 4.7). Thus, for small data sizes where all three RGB values are needed, there's good cache usage. But as the arrays grow larger and more arrays are presented, the cache system struggles, causing performance to suffer. In these cases, the interactions of the data and the cache become too complicated to fully predict the performance.

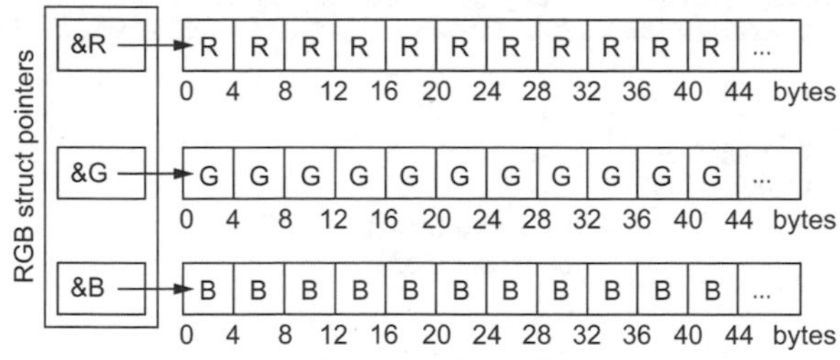

Figure 4.7   In the Structure of Arrays (SoA) data layout, the pointers are adjacent in memory, pointing to separate contiguous arrays for each color.

Another data layout and access pattern that is often encountered is the use of variables as 3D spatial coordinates in a computational application. The following listing shows the typical C structure definition for this.

Listing 4.7   Spatial coordinates in a C Array of Structures (AoS)

```
1 struct point {
2    double x, y, z;        Defines the spatial
3 };                        coordinate of point
```

```
4 struct point cell[1000];         ←——┐  Defines an array
5 double radius[1000];                 │  of point locations
6 double density[1000];
7 double density_gradient[1000];
```

One use of this data structure is to calculate the distance from the origin (radius) as follows:

```
10 for (int i=0; i < 1000; i++){
11    radius[i] = sqrt(cell[i].x*cell[i].x + cell[i].y*cell[i].y +
      cell[i].z*cell[i].z);
12 }
```

The values of x, y, and z are brought in together in one cache line and written out to the radius variable in a second cache line. The cache usage for this case is reasonable. But in a second plausible case, a computational loop might use the x location to calculate a gradient in density in the x-direction like this:

```
20 for (int i=1; i < 1000; i++){
21   density_gradient[i] = (density[i] - density[i-1])/
                           (cell[i].x - cell[i-1].x);
22 }
```

Now the cache access for x skips over the y and z data so that only one-third (or even one-quarter if padded) of the data in the cache is used. Thus, the optimal data layout depends entirely on usage and the particular data access patterns.

In mixed use cases, which are likely to appear in real applications, sometimes the structure variables are used together and sometimes not. Generally, the AoS layout performs better overall on CPUs, while the SoA layout performs better on GPUs. In reported results, there is enough variability that it is worth testing for a particular usage pattern. In the density gradient case, the following listing shows the SoA code.

> ### Listing 4.8 Spatial coordinate Structure of Arrays (SoA)

```
 1 struct point{                        Defines arrays of
 2     double *x, *y, *z;      ←——┐     spatial locations
 3 };                             │
 4 struct point cell;          ←——┘  Defines structure of
 5 cell.x = (double *)malloc(1000*sizeof(double));   cell spatial locations
 6 cell.y = (double *)malloc(1000*sizeof(double));
 7 cell.z = (double *)malloc(1000*sizeof(double));
 8 double *radius = (double *)malloc(1000*sizeof(double));
 9 double *density = (double *)malloc(1000*sizeof(double));
10 double *density_gradient = (double *)malloc(1000*sizeof(double));
11 // ... initialize data
12
13 for (int i=0; i < 1000; i++){         ←——┐  This loop uses contiguous
14    radius[i] = sqrt(cell.x[i]*cell.x[i] +   │  values of arrays.
                       cell.y[i]*cell.y[i] +
                       cell.z[i]*cell.z[i]);
```

```
15 }
16
17 for (int i=1; i < 1000; i++){          This loop uses contiguous
18    density_gradient[i] = (density[i] - density[i-1])/    values of arrays.
                            (cell.x[i] - cell.x[i-1]);
19 }
20
21 free(cell.x);
22 free(cell.y);
23 free(cell.z);
24 free(radius);
25 free(density);
26 free(density_gradient);
```

With this data layout, each variable is brought in on a separate cache line, and cache usage will be good for both kernels. But as the number of required data members get sufficiently larger, the cache has difficulty efficiently handling the multitude of memory streams. In a C++ object-oriented implementation, you should be wary of other pitfalls. The next listing presents a cell class with the cell spatial coordinate and the radius as its data components and a method to calculate the radius from x, y, and z.

Listing 4.9   Spatial coordinate class example with C++

```
1 class Cell{
2       double x;
3       double y;
4       double z;
5       double radius;
6    public:
7       void calc_radius() {                    Invokes radius
             radius = sqrt(x*x + y*y + z*z);     function for each cell
          }
8       void big_calc();
9 }
10
11 Cell my_cells[1000];         Defines an array of objects
                                as an array of structs
12
13 for (int i = 0; i < 1000; i++){
14    my_cells[i].calc_radius();
15 }
16
17 void Cell::big_calc(){
18    radius = sqrt(x*x + y*y + z*z);
19    // ... lots more code, preventing in-lining
20 }
```

Running this code results in a couple of instruction cache misses and overhead from subroutine calls for each cell. Instruction cache misses occur when the sequence of instructions jumps and the next instruction is not in the instruction cache. There are two level 1 caches: one for the program data and the second for the processor's instructions. Subroutine calls require the additional overhead to push the arguments onto the stack before the call and an instruction jump. Once in the routine, the arguments need to be popped off the stack and then, at the end of the routine, there is another instruction jump. In this case, the code is simple enough that the compiler can inline the routine to avoid these costs. But in more complex cases, such as with a big_calc routine, it cannot. Additionally, the cache line pulls in x, y, z, and the radius. The cache helps speed up the load of the position coordinates that actually need to be read. But the radius, which needs to be written, is also in the cache line. If different processors are writing the values for the radius, this could invalidate the cache lines and require other processors to reload the data into their caches.

There are many features of C++ that make programming easier. These should generally be used at a higher level in the code, using the simpler procedural style of C and Fortran where performance counts. In the previous listing, the radius calculation can be done as an array instead of as a single scalar element. The class pointer can be dereferenced once at the start of the routine to avoid repeated dereferencing and possible instruction cache misses. *Dereferencing* is an operation where the memory address is obtained from the pointer reference so that the cache line is dedicated to the memory data instead of the pointer. Simple hash tables can also use a structure to group the key and value together as the following listing shows.

Listing 4.10   Hash Array of Structures (AoS)

```
1 struct hash_type {
2     int key;
3     int value;
4 };
5 struct hash_type hash[1000];
```

The problem with this code is that it reads multiple keys until it finds one that matches and then reads the value for that key. But the key and value are brought into a single cache line, and the value ignored until the match occurs. It is better to have the key as one array and the value as another to facilitate a faster search through the keys as shown in the next listing.

Listing 4.11   Hash Structure of Arrays (SoA)

```
1 struct hash_type {
2     int *key;
3     int *value;
4 } hash;
5 hash.key   = (int *)malloc(1000*sizeof(int));
6 hash.value = (int *)malloc(1000*sizeof(int));
```

As a final example, take a physics state structure that contains density, 3D momentum, and total energy. The following listing shows this structure.

Listing 4.12   Physics state Array of Structures (AoS)

```
1 struct phys_state {
2    double density;
3    double momentum[3];
4    double TotEnergy;
5 };
```

When processing only density, the next four values in cache go unused. Again, it is better to have this as an SoA.

4.1.3   *Array of Structures of Arrays (AoSoA)*

There are cases where hybrid groupings of structures and arrays are effective. The Array of Structures of Arrays (AoSoA) can be used to "tile" the data into vector lengths. Let's introduce the notation A[len/4]S[3]A[4] to represent this layout. A[4] is an array of four data elements and is the inner, contiguous block of data. S[3] represents the next level of the data structure of three fields. The combination of S[3]A[4] gives the data layout that figure 4.8 shows.

R	R	R	R	G	G	G	G	B	B	B	B	...
0	4	8	12	16	20	24	28	32	36	40	44 bytes	

Figure 4.8   An Array of Structures of Arrays (AoSoA) is used with the last array length, matching the vector length of the hardware for a vector length of four.

We need to repeat the block of 12 data values A[len/4] times to get all the data. If we replace the 4 with a variable, we get

A[len/V]S[3]A[V], where V=4

In C or Fortran, respectively, the array could be dimensioned as

var[len/V][3][V], var(1:V,1:3,1:len/V)

In C++, this would be implemented naturally as the following listing shows.

Listing 4.13   RGB Array of Structures of Arrays (AoSoA)

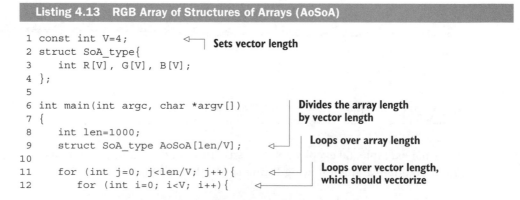

```
1 const int V=4;              ← Sets vector length
2 struct SoA_type{
3    int R[V], G[V], B[V];
4 };
5
6 int main(int argc, char *argv[])    Divides the array length
7 {                                    by vector length
8    int len=1000;
9    struct SoA_type AoSoA[len/V];  ←  Loops over array length
10
11   for (int j=0; j<len/V; j++){  ←  Loops over vector length,
12      for (int i=0; i<V; i++){   ←  which should vectorize
```

```
13              AoSoA[j].R[i] = 0;
14              AoSoA[j].G[i] = 0;
15              AoSoA[j].B[i] = 0;
16          }
17      }
18  }
```

By varying V to match the hardware vector length or the GPU work group size, we create a portable data abstraction. In addition, by defining V=1 or V=len, we recover the AoS and SoA data structures, respectively. This data layout then becomes a way to adapt for the hardware and the program's data use patterns.

There are many details to address about the implementation of this data structure to minimize indexing costs and decide whether to pad the array for performance. The AoSoA data layout has some of the properties of both the AoS and SoA data structures so the performance is generally close to the better of the two as shown in a study by Robert Bird from Los Alamos National Laboratory (figure 4.9).

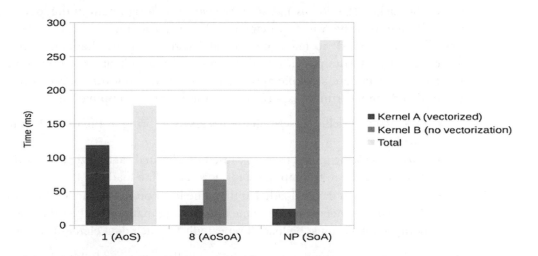

Figure 4.9   Performance of the Array of Structures of Arrays (AoSoA) generally matches the best of the AoS and SoA performances. The 1, 8 and NP array length in the x-axis legend is the value for the last array in AoSoA. These values mean that the first set reduces to an AOS, the last set reduces to an SoA, and the middle set has a second array length of 8 to match the vector length of the processor.

4.2   *Three Cs of cache misses: Compulsory, capacity, conflict*

Cache efficiency dominates the performance of intensive computations. As long as the data is cached, the computation proceeds quickly. When the data is not cached, a *cache miss* occurs. The processor then has to pause and wait for the data to be loaded. The cost of a cache miss is on the order of 100 to 400 cycles; 100s of flops can be done in the same time! For performance, we must minimize cache misses. But minimizing cache misses requires an understanding of how data moves from main memory to the CPU. This is done with a simple performance model that separates cache misses into three C's: *compulsory*, *capacity*, and *conflict*. First we must understand how the cache works.

When data is loaded, it is loaded in blocks, called *cache lines*, that are typically 64 bytes long. These are then inserted into a cache location based on its address in memory. In a *direct-mapped cache*, there is only one location to load data into the cache. This is important when two arrays get mapped to the same location. With a direct-mapped cache, only one array can be cached at a time. To avoid this, most processors have an *N-way set associative cache* that provides *N* locations into which data are loaded. With regular, predictable memory accesses of large arrays, it is possible to *prefetch data*. That is, you can issue an instruction to preload data before it is needed so that it's already in the cache. This can be done either in hardware or in software by the compiler.

Eviction is the removal of a cache line from one or more cache levels. This can be caused by the load of a cache line at the same location (*cache conflict*) or the limited size of the cache (*capacity miss*). A *store operation* by an assignment in the loop causes a write allocate in cache, where a new cache line is created and modified. This cache line is evicted (stored) to main memory, although it may not happen immediately. There are various write policies used that affect the details of write operations. The three C's of caches are a simple approach to understanding the source of the cache misses that dominate run-time performance for intensive computations.

- *Compulsory*—Cache misses that are necessary to bring in the data when it is first encountered.
- *Capacity*—Cache misses that are caused by a limited cache size, which evicts data from the cache to free up space for new cache line loads.
- *Conflict*—When data is loaded at the same location in the cache. If two or more data items are needed at the same time but are mapped to the same cache line, both data items must be loaded repeatedly for each data element access.

When cache misses occur due to capacity or conflict evictions followed by reloads of the cache lines, this is sometimes referred to as *cache thrashing*, which can lead to poor performance. From these definitions, we can easily calculate a few characteristics of a kernel and at least get an idea of the expected performance. For this, we will use the blur operator kernel from figure 1.10.

Listing 4.14 shows the stencil.c kernel. We also use the 2D contiguous memory allocation routine in malloc2D.c from section 4.1.1. The timer code is not shown here but is in the online source code. Included are timers and calls to the likwid ("Like I Knew What I'm Doing") profiler. Between iterations, there is a write to a large array to flush the cache so that there is no relevant data in it that can distort the results.

Listing 4.14   Stencil kernel for the Krakatau blur operator

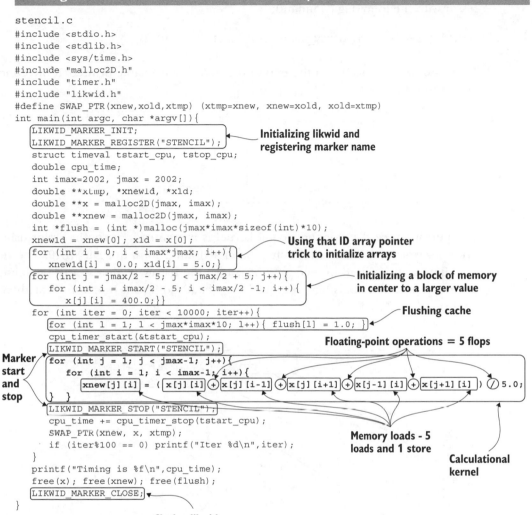

```
stencil.c
#include <stdio.h>
#include <stdlib.h>
#include <sys/time.h>
#include "malloc2D.h"
#include "timer.h"
#include "likwid.h"
#define SWAP_PTR(xnew,xold,xtmp) (xtmp=xnew, xnew=xold, xold=xtmp)
int main(int argc, char *argv[]){
    LIKWID_MARKER_INIT;
    LIKWID_MARKER_REGISTER("STENCIL");          Initializing likwid and
    struct timeval tstart_cpu, tstop_cpu;        registering marker name
    double cpu_time;
    int imax=2002, jmax = 2002;
    double **xtmp, *xnew1d, *x1d;
    double **x = malloc2D(jmax, imax);
    double **xnew = malloc2D(jmax, imax);
    int *flush = (int *)malloc(jmax*imax*sizeof(int)*10);
    xnew1d = xnew[0]; x1d = x[0];            Using that ID array pointer
    for (int i = 0; i < imax*jmax; i++){     trick to initialize arrays
        xnew1d[i] = 0.0; x1d[i] = 5.0;}
    for (int j = jmax/2 - 5; j < jmax/2 + 5; j++){     Initializing a block of memory
        for (int i = imax/2 - 5; i < imax/2 -1; i++){   in center to a larger value
            x[j][i] = 400.0;}}
    for (int iter = 0; iter < 10000; iter++){
        for (int l = 1; l < jmax*imax*10; l++){ flush[l] = 1.0; }    Flushing cache
        cpu_timer_start(&tstart_cpu);
        LIKWID_MARKER_START("STENCIL");
        for (int j = 1; j < jmax-1; j++){        Floating-point operations = 5 flops
            for (int i = 1; i < imax-1; i++){
                xnew[j][i] = ( x[j][i] + x[j][i-1] + x[j][i+1] + x[j-1][i] + x[j+1][i] ) / 5.0;
        } }
        LIKWID_MARKER_STOP("STENCIL");
        cpu_time += cpu_timer_stop(tstart_cpu);
        SWAP_PTR(xnew, x, xtmp);
        if (iter%100 == 0) printf("Iter %d\n",iter);
    }
    printf("Timing is %f\n",cpu_time);
    free(x); free(xnew); free(flush);
    LIKWID_MARKER_CLOSE;
}
```

Marker start and stop

Memory loads - 5 loads and 1 store

Calculational kernel

Closing likwid

If we have a perfectly effective cache, once the data is loaded into memory, it is kept there. Of course, this is far from reality in most cases. But with this model, we can calculate the following:

- Total memory used = 2000 × 2000 × (5 references + 1 store) × 8 bytes = 192 MB
- Compulsory memory loaded and stored = 2002 × 2002 × 8 bytes × 2 arrays = 64.1 MB
- Arithmetic intensity = 5 flops × 2000 × 2000 / 64.1 Mbytes = .312 flops/byte or 2.5 flops/word

The program is then compiled with the likwid library and run on a Skylake 6152 processor with the following command:

```
likwid-perfctr -C 0 -g MEM_DP -m ./stencil
```

The result that we need is at the end of the performance table printed at the conclusion of the run:

```
+----------------------------------------+------------+
|   ...                                  |            |
|              DP MFLOP/s                |  3923.4952 |
|             AVX DP MFLOP/s             |  3923.4891 |
|   ...                                  |            |
|        Operational intensity           |     0.247  |
+----------------------------------------+------------+
```

The performance data for the stencil kernel is presented as a roofline plot using a Python script (available in the online materials) and shown in figure 4.10. The roofline plot, as introduced in section 3.2.4, shows the hardware limits of the maximum floating-point operations and the maximum bandwidth as a function of arithmetic intensity.

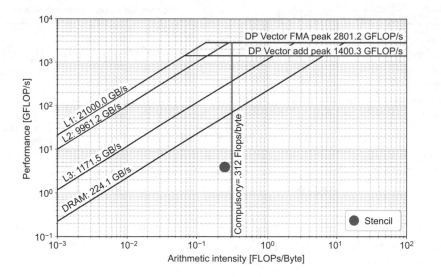

Figure 4.10 The roofline plot of the stencil kernel for the Krakatau example in chapter 1 shows the compulsory upper bound to the right of the measured performance.

This roofline plot shows the compulsory data limit to the right side of the measured arithmetic intensity of 0.247 (shown with a large dot in figure 4.10). The kernel cannot do better than the compulsory limit if it has a cold cache. A *cold cache* is one that does not have any relevant data in it from whatever operations were being done before entering the kernel. The distance between the large dot and the compulsory limit gives us an idea of how effective the cache is in this kernel. The kernel in this case is simple, and the capacity and conflict cache loads are only about 15% greater than the compulsory cache loads. Thus, there is not much room for improvement for the kernel performance. The distance between the large dot and the DRAM roofline is because this is a serial kernel with vectorization, while the rooflines are parallel with OpenMP. Thus, there is a potential to improve performance by adding parallelism.

Because this is a log-log plot, differences are greater than they might appear. Looking closely, the possible improvement from parallelism is nearly an order of magnitude. Improving cache usage can be accomplished by using other values in the cache line or reusing data multiple times while it is in the cache. These are two different cases, referred to as either spatial locality or temporal locality:

- *Spatial locality* refers to data with nearby locations in memory that are often referenced close together.
- *Temporal locality* refers to recently referenced data that is likely to be referenced again in the near future.

For the stencil kernel (listing 4.14), when the value of x[1][1] is brought into cache, x[1][2] is also brought into cache. This is spatial locality. In the next iteration of the loop to calculate x[1][2], x[1][1] is needed. It should still be in the cache and gets reused as a case of temporal locality.

A fourth C is often added to the three C's mentioned earlier that will become important in later chapters. This is called coherency.

DEFINITION *Coherency* applies to those cache updates needed to synchronize the cache between multiprocessors when data that is written to one processor's cache is also held in another processor's cache.

The cache updates required to maintain coherency can sometimes lead to heavy traffic on the memory bus and are sometimes referred to as *cache update storms*. These cache update storms can lead to slowdowns in performance rather than speedups when additional processors are added to a parallel job.

4.3 Simple performance models: A case study

This section looks at an example of using simple performance models to make informed decisions on what data structure to use for multi-material calculations in a physics application. It uses a real case study to show the effects of:

- Simple performance models for a real programming design question
- Compressed sparse data structures to stretch your computational resources

Some segments of computational science have long used compressed sparse matrix representations. Most notable is the Compressed Sparse Row (CSR) format used for sparse matrices since the mid 1960s with great results. For the compressed sparse data structure evaluated in this case study, the memory savings are greater than 95%, and the run time approaches 90% faster than the simple 2D array design. The simple performance models used predicted the performance within a 20–30% error of actual measured performance (see Fogerty, Mattineau, et al., in the section on additional reading later in this chapter). But there is a cost to using this compressed scheme—programmer effort. We want to use the compressed sparse data structure where its benefits outweigh the costs. Making this decision is where the simple performance model really shows its usefulness.

> ### Example: Modeling the Krakatau ash plume
> Your team is considering the modeling of the ash plume in the example from chapter 1. They realize that the ash materials in the plume may eventually number in the 10s or even up to 100, yet these materials do not need to be in every cell. Could a compressed sparse representation be useful for this situation?

Simple performance models are useful to the application developer when addressing more complex programming problems than just a doubly-nested loop over a 2D array. The goal of these models is to get a rough assessment of performance through simple counts of operations in a characteristic kernel to make decisions on programming alternatives. Simple performance models are slightly more complicated than the three C's model. The basic process is to count and note the following:

- Memory loads and stores (memops)
- Floating-point operations (flops)
- Contiguous versus non-contiguous memory loads
- Presence of branches
- Small loops

We'll count memory loads and stores (collectively referred to as *memops*) and flops, but we'll also note whether the memory loads are contiguous and if there are branches that might affect the performance. We'll also use empirical data such as stream bandwidth and generalized operation counts to transform the counts into performance estimates. If the memory loads are not contiguous, only 1 out of 8 values in the cache line are used, so we divide the stream bandwidth by up to 8 for those cases.

For the serial part of this study, we'll use the hardware performance of a MacBook Pro with 6 MB L3 cache. The processor frequency (v) is 2.7 GHz. The measured stream bandwidth is 13,375 MB/s using the technique introduced in section 3.2.4 with the stream benchmark code.

In algorithms with branching, if we take the branch almost all the time, the branch cost is low. When the branch taken is infrequent, we add a branch prediction cost (B_c) and possibly a missed prefetch cost (P_c). A simple model of the branch predictor uses the most frequent case in the last few iterations as the likely path. This lowers the cost if there is some clustering in branch paths due to data locality. The branch penalty (B_p) becomes $N_b B_f (B_c + P_c)/v$. For typical architectures, the branch prediction cost (B_c) is about 16 cycles and the missing prefetch cost (P_c) is empirically determined to be about 112 cycles. N_b is the number of times the branch is encountered and B_f is the *branch miss frequency*. Loop overhead for small loops of unknown length are also assigned a cost (L_c) to account for branching and control. The loop cost is estimated at about 20 cycles per exit. The loop penalty (L_p) becomes L_c/v.

We will use simple performance models in a design study looking at possible multi-material data structures for physics simulations. The purpose of this design study is to determine which data structures would give the best performance before writing any code. In the past, the choice was made on subjective judgement rather than an objective basis. The particular case that is being examined is the sparse case, where there are many materials in the computational mesh but only one or few materials in any computational cell. We'll reference the small sample mesh with four materials in figure 4.11 in the discussion of possible data layouts. Three of the cells have only a single material, whereas cell 7 has four materials.

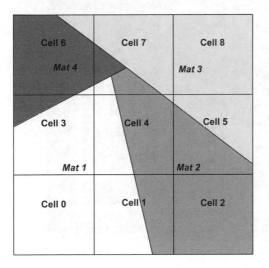

Figure 4.11 A 3×3 computational mesh shows that cell 7 contains four materials.

The data structure is only half the story. We also need to evaluate the data layout in a couple of representative kernels by

1 Computing pavg[C], the average density of materials in cells of a mesh
2 Evaluating p[C][m], the pressure in each material contained in each cell using the ideal gas law: p(p,t) = nrt/v

Both of these computations have an arithmetic intensity of 1 flop per word or lower. We also expect that these kernels will be bandwidth limited. We'll use two large data sets to test the performance of the kernels. Both are 50 material (N_m), 1 million cell problems (N_c) with four state arrays (N_v). The state arrays are density (p), temperature (t), pressure (p), and volume fraction (V_f). The two data sets are

- *Geometric Shapes Problem*—A mesh initialized from nested rectangles of materials (figure 4.12). The mesh is a regular rectangular grid. With the materials in separate rectangles rather than scattered, most cells only have one or two materials. The result is that there are 95% pure cells (P_f) and 5% mixed cells (M_f). This mesh has some data locality so the branch prediction miss (B_p) is roughly estimated to be 0.7.

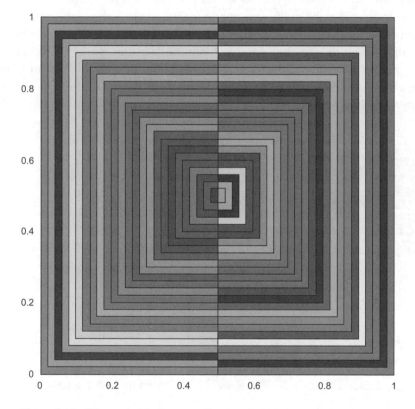

Figure 4.12   Fifty nested half rectangles used to initialize mesh for the geometric shapes test case

- *Randomly Initialized Problem*—A randomly initialized mesh with 80% pure cells and 20% mixed cells. Because there is little data locality, the branch prediction miss (B_p) is estimated to be 1.0.

In the performance analysis in sections 4.3.1 and 4.3.2, there are two major design considerations: data layout and loop order. We refer to the data layout as either cell- or material-centric, depending on the larger organizing factor in the data. The data layout factor has the large stride in the data order. We refer to the loop access pattern as either cell- or material-dominant to indicate which is the outer loop. The best situation occurs when the data layout is consistent with the loop access pattern. There is no perfect solution; one of the kernels prefers one layout and the second kernel prefers the other.

4.3.1 Full matrix data representations

The simplest data structure is a *full matrix* storage representation. This assumes that every material is in every cell. These full matrix representations are similar to the 2D arrays discussed in the previous section.

FULL MATRIX CELL-CENTRIC STORAGE

For the small problem in figure 4.11 (the 3x3 computational mesh), figure 4.13 shows the cell-centric data layout. The data order follows the C language convention with the materials stored contiguously for each cell. In other words, the programming representation is `variable[C][m]` with `m` varying fastest. In the figure, the shaded elements are mixed materials in a cell. Pure cells just have a 1.0 entry. The elements with dashes indicate that none of that material is in the cell and is therefore given a zero in this representation. In this simple example, about half of the entries have zeros, but in the bigger problem, the number of entries that are zero will be greater than 95%. The number of non-zero entries is referred to as the *filled fraction* (F_f), and for our design scenario is typically less than 5%. Thus, if a compressed sparse storage scheme is used, the memory savings will be greater than 95%, even accounting for the additional storage overhead of the more complex data structures.

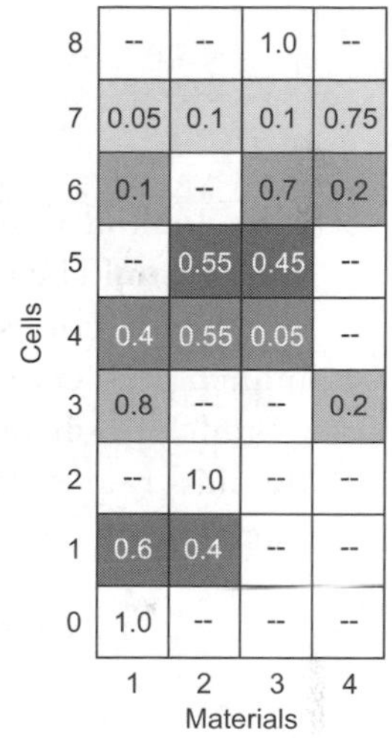

Figure 4.13 The cell-centric, full matrix data structure with materials stored contiguously for each cell

The full matrix data approach has the advantage that it is simpler and, thus, easier to parallelize and optimize. The memory savings is substantial enough that it is probably worth using the compressed sparse data structure. But what are the performance implications of the method? We can guess that having more memory for data potentially increases the memory bandwidth and makes the full matrix representation slower. But what if we test for the volume fraction and, if it is zero, we skip the mixed material access? Figure 4.14 shows how we tested this approach, where the pseudo-code for the cell-dominant loop is shown along with the counts for each operation to the left of the line of code. The cell-dominant loop structure has the cell index in the outer loop, which matches with the cell index as the first index in the cell-centric data structure.

```
1: for all cells, C, up to Nc do
2:    ave ← 0.0
3:    for all material IDs, m, up to Nm do        # NcNm loads (Vf)
4:        if Vf [C][m] > 0.0 then                 # BpNcNm branch penalty
                                                  # 2Ff NcNm loads (ρ, f)
5:            ave ← ave + ρ [C][m] * f [C][m]     # 2Ff NcNm flops (+, *)
6:        end if
7:    end for
8:        ρave [C] ← ave/V[C]                      # Nc stores (ρave), Nc loads (V)
                                                  # Nc flops (I)
9: end for
```

Figure 4.14   Modified cell-dominant algorithm to compute average density of cells using the full matrix storage

The counts are summarized from the line notes (beginning with #) in figure 4.14 as:

$$memops = N_c(N_m + 2F_fN_m + 2) = 54.1 \ Mmemops$$

$$flops = N_c(2F_fN_m + 1) = 3.1 \ Mflops$$

$$N_c = 1e6; \ N_m = 50; \ F_f = .021$$

If we look at flops, we would conclude that we have been efficient and the performance would be great. But this algorithm is clearly going to be dominated by memory bandwidth. For estimating memory bandwidth performance, we need to factor in the branch prediction miss. Because the branch is taken so infrequently, the probability of a branch prediction miss is high. The geometric shapes problem has some locality, so the miss rate is estimated to be 0.7. Putting this all together, we get the following for our performance model (PM):

$$PM = N_c(N_m + F_fN_m + 2) * 8/Stream + B_pF_fN_cN_m = 67.2 \ ms$$

$$B_f = 0.7; \ B_c = 16; \ P_c = 16; \ \upsilon = 2.7$$

The cost of the branch prediction miss makes the run time high; higher than if we just skipped the conditional and added in zeros. Longer loops would amortize the penalty cost, but clearly a conditional that is rarely taken is not the best scenario for performance. We could also insert a prefetch operation before the conditional to force loading the data in case the branch is taken. But this would increase the memops so the actual performance improvement would be small. It would also increase the traffic on the memory bus, causing congestion that would trigger other problems, especially when adding thread parallelism.

FULL MATRIX MATERIAL-CENTRIC STORAGE

Now let's take a look at the material-centric data structure (figure 4.15). The C notation for this is variable[m][C] with the rightmost index of C (or cells) varying fastest. In the figure, the dashes indicate elements that are filled with zeros. Many of the characteristics of this data structure are similar to the cell-centric full matrix data representation, but with the indices of the storage flipped.

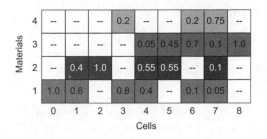

Figure 4.15 The material-centric full matrix data structure stores cells contiguously for each material. The array indexing in C would be `density[m][C]` with the cell index contiguous. The cells with dashes are filled with zeros.

The algorithm for computing the average density of each of the cells can be done with contiguous memory loads and a little thought. The natural way to implement this algorithm is to have the outer loop over the cells, initialize it to zero there, and divide by the volume at the end. But this strides over the data in a non-contiguous fashion. We want to loop over cells in the inner loop, requiring separate loops before and after the main loop. Figure 4.16 shows the algorithm along with annotations for memops and flops.

```
1: for all cells, C, up to N_c do
2:   ρ_ave[C] ← 0.0                              # N_c stores (ρ_ave)
3: end for
4: for all material IDs, m, up to N_m do
5:   for all cells, C, up to N_c do
6:     ρ_ave[C] ← ρ_ave[C] + ρ[m][C]*V_f[m][C]   # N_cN_m stores (ρ_ave)
                                                  # 3N_cN_m loads (ρ_ave,ρ,V_f)
                                                  # 2N_cN_m flops (+,*)
8:   end for
7: end for
8: end for
9: for all cells, C, up to N_c do
10:  ρ_ave[C] ← ρ_ave[C]/V[C]                     # 3N_c loads/stores (ρ_ave,V)
                                                  # N_c flops (/)
11: end for
```

Figure 4.16 Material-dominant algorithm to compute average density of cells using full matrix storage

Collecting all the annotations for operations, we get

$$memops = 4N_c(N_m + 1) = 204 \; Mmemops$$

$$flops = 2N_cN_m + N_c = 101 \; Mflops$$

This kernel is bandwidth limited, so the performance model is

$$PM = 4N_c(N_m + 1) * 8/\text{Stream} = 122 \; ms$$

The performance of this kernel is half of what the cell-centric data structure achieved. But this computational kernel favors the cell-centric data layout, and the situation is reversed for the pressure calculation.

4.3.2 *Compressed sparse storage representations*

Now we'll discuss the advantages and limitations of a couple of compressed storage representations. The compressed sparse storage data layouts clearly save memory, but the design for both cell- and material-centric layouts takes some thought.

CELL-CENTRIC COMPRESSED SPARSE STORAGE

The standard approach is a linked list of materials for each cell. But linked lists are generally short and jump all over memory. The solution is to put the linked list into a contiguous array with the link pointing to the start of the material entries. The next cell will have its materials follow right afterwards. Thus, during normal traversal of the cells and materials, these will be accessed in contiguous order. Figure 4.17 shows the cell-centric data storage scheme. The values for pure cells are kept in cell state arrays. In the figure, 1.0 is the volume fraction of the pure cells, but it can also be the pure cell values for density, temperature, and pressure. The second array is the number of materials in the mixed cell. A −1 indicates that it is a pure cell. Then the material linked list index, *imaterial*, is in the third array. If it is less than 1, the absolute value of the entry is the index into the mixed data storage arrays. If it is 1 or greater, then it is the index into the compressed pure cell arrays.

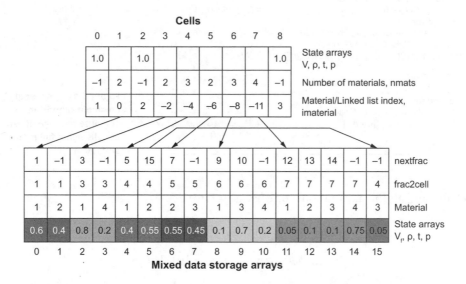

Figure 4.17   The mixed material arrays for the cell-centric data structure use a linked list implemented in a contiguous array. The different shading at the bottom indicates the materials that belong to a particular cell and match the shading used in figure 4.13.

Mixed data storage arrays are basically a linked list implemented in a standard array so that the data is contiguous for good cache performance. The mixed data starts with an array called `nextfrac`, which points to the next material for that cell. This enables the addition of new materials in the cell by adding these to the end of the array. Figure 4.17 shows this with the mixed material list for cell 4, where the arrow shows the third material to be added at the end. The `frac2cell` array is a backward mapping to the cell that contains the material. The third array, `material`, contains the material number for the entry. These are the arrays that provide the navigation around the compressed sparse data structure. The fourth array is the set of state arrays for each material in each cell with the volume fraction (V_f), density (ρ), temperature (t) and pressure (p).

The mixed material arrays keep extra memory at the end of the array to quickly add new material entries on the fly. Removing the data link and setting it to zero deletes the materials. To give better cache performance, the arrays are periodically reordered back into contiguous memory.

Figure 4.18 shows the algorithm for the calculation of the average density for each cell for the compressed sparse data layout. We first retrieve the material index, `imaterial`, to see if this is a cell with mixed materials by testing if it is zero or less. If it is a pure cell, we do nothing because we already have the density in the cell array. If it is a mixed material cell, we enter a loop to sum up the density multiplied by the volume fraction for each of the materials. We test for the end condition of the index becoming negative and use the `nextfrac` array to get the next entry. Once we reach the end of the list, we calculate the cell's density (ρ). To the right side of the lines of code are the annotations for the operational costs.

```
1: for all cells, C, up to N_c do
2:    ave ← 0.0
3:    ix ← imaterial [C]                # N_c loads (imaterial )
4:    if ix <= 0 then
5:        for ix ← -ix,Untill ix < 0 do      # L_p small loop overhead
6:            ave ← ave + ρ[ix]*V_f [ix]      # 2M_L loads (ρ, V_f)
                                               # M_L flops (+,*)
7:            ix ← nextfrac[ix]               # M_L loads (nextfrac)
8:        end for
9:        ρ[C] ← ave/V[C]                     # M_fN_c stores (ρ_ave)
                                               # M_fN_c loads (V)
                                               # M_fN_c flops (l)
10:   end if
11: end for
```

Figure 4.18   Cell-dominant algorithm to compute average cell density using compact storage

To the right of the lines of code are the annotations for the operational costs. For this analysis, we will have 4-byte integer loads, so we convert *memops* to *membytes*. Collecting the counts, we obtain

$$membytes = (4 + 2M_f * 8)\,N_c + (2 * 8 + 4) = 6.74\ Mbytes$$

$$flops = 2M_L + M_fN_c = .24\ Mflops$$

$$M_f = .04895;\ M_L = 97970$$

Again, this algorithm is memory bandwidth limited. The estimated run time from the performance model is a 98% reduction from the full cell-centric matrix.

$$PM = membytes/\text{Stream} + L_p M_f N_c = .87 \; ms$$

$$L_p = 20/2.7e6; \; M_f = .04895$$

MATERIAL-CENTRIC COMPRESSED SPARSE STORAGE

The material-centric compressed sparse data structure subdivides everything into separate materials. Returning to the small test problem in figure 4.9, we see that there are six cells with material 1: 0, 1, 3, 4, 6, and 7 (shown in figure 4.19 in subset 1). There are two mappings in the subset: one from mesh to subset, mesh2subset, and one from the subset back to the mesh, subset2mesh. The list in the subset to mesh has the indices of the six cells. The mesh array contains −1 for each cell that does not have the material and numbers the ones that do sequentially to map to the subset. The nmats array at the top of figure 4.19 has the number of materials contained in each cell. The volume fraction (V_f), and density (ρ) arrays on the right side of the figure have values for each cell in that material. The C nomenclature for this would be Vf[imat][icell]

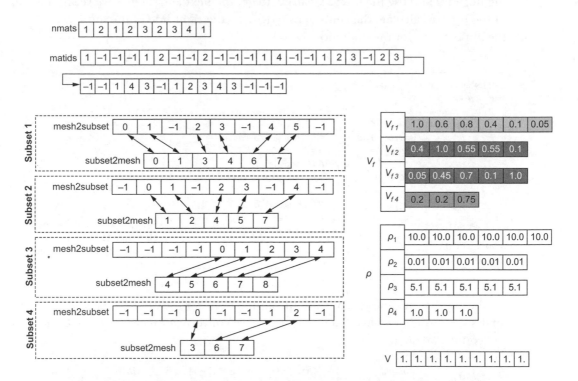

Figure 4.19   The material-centric compressed sparse data layout is organized around materials. For each material, there is a variable-length array with a list of the cells that contain the material. The shading corresponds to the shading in figure 4.15. The illustration maps between the full mesh and subsets and the volume fraction and density variables for each subset.

```
 1: for all cells, C, up to N_c do
 2:    ρ_ave[C] ← 0.0                          # N_c stores
 3: end for
 4: for all material IDs, m up to N_m do
 5:    ncmat ← ncellsmat[m]                    # N_m loads (ncellsmat)
 6:    Subset ← Subset2mesh[m]                 # N_m loads (subset2mesh)
 7:    for all cells, c, up to ncmat do
 8:       C ← subset[c]                        # F_f N_c N_m loads (subset)
 9:       ρ_ave[C] ← ρ_ave[C] + ρ[m][c] * V_f[m][c]   # 3F_f N_c N_m loads (ρ_ave, ρ, V_f)
                                               # F_f N_c N_m stores (ρ_ave)
                                               # 2F_f N_c N_m flops (+, *)
10:    end for
11: end for
12: for all cells, C, up to N_c do
13:    ρ_ave[C] ← ρ_ave[C]/V[C]               # 2N_c loads (ρ_ave, V)
                                               # N_c stores (ρ_ave)
                                               # N_c flops (/)
14: end for
```

Figure 4.20 Material-dominant algorithm computes the average density of cells using the material-centric compact storage scheme.

and p[imat][icell]. Because there are relatively few materials with long lists of cells, we can use regular 2D array allocations rather than forcing these to be contiguous. To operate on this data structure, we mostly work with each material subset in sequence.

The material-dominant algorithm in figure 4.20 for the compressed sparse algorithm looks like the algorithm in figure 4.13 with the addition of the retrieval of the pointers in lines 5, 6, and 8. But the loads and flops in the inner loop are only done for the material subset of the mesh rather than the full mesh. This provides considerable savings in flops and memops. Collecting all the counts, we get

$$membytes = 5 * 8 * F_f N_m N_c + 4 * 8 * N_c + (8 + 4) * N_m = 74 \ Mbytes$$

$$flops = (2F_f N_m + 1) N_c = 3.1 \ Mflops$$

The performance model shows more than a 95% reduction in estimated run time from the material-centric full matrix data structure:

$$PM = membytes/Stream = 5.5 \ ms$$

Table 4.1 summarizes the results for these four data structures. The difference between the estimated and measured run time is remarkably small. This shows that even rough counts of memory loads can be a good predictor of performance.

Table 4.1 The sparse data structures are faster and use less memory than the full 2D matrices.

	Memory load (MBs)	Flops	Estimated run time	Measured run time
Cell-centric full	424	3.1	67.2	108
Material-centric full	1632	101	122	164
Cell-centric compressed sparse	6.74	.24	.87	1.4
Material-centric compressed sparse	74	3.1	5.5	9.6

The advantage of the compressed sparse representations is dramatic, with savings in both memory and performance. Because the kernel we analyzed was more suited for the cell-centric data structures, the cell-centric compressed sparse data structure is clearly the best performer both in memory and run time. If we look at the other kernel that shows the material-centric data layout, the results are slightly in favor of the material-centric data structures. But the big takeaway is that either of the compressed sparse representations is a vast improvement over the full matrix representations.

While this case study focused on multi-material data representations, there are many diverse applications with sparse data that can benefit from the addition of a compressed sparse data structure. A quick performance analysis similar to the one done in this section can determine whether the benefits are worth the additional effort in these applications.

4.4   *Advanced performance models*

There are more advanced performance models that better capture aspects of the computer hardware. We will briefly cover these advanced models to understand what these offer and the possible lessons to be learned. The details of the performance analysis are not as important as the takeaways.

In this chapter, we focused primarily on bandwidth-limited kernels because these represent the performance limitations of most applications. We counted the bytes loaded and stored by the kernel and estimated the time required for this data movement based on the stream benchmark or roofline model (chapter 3). By now, you should realize that the unit of operation for computer hardware is not really bytes or words but cache lines, and we can improve the performance models by counting the cache lines that need to be loaded and stored. At the same time, we can estimate how much of the cache line is used.

The stream benchmark is actually composed of four individual kernels: the copy, scale, add, and triad kernels. So why the variation in the bandwidth (16156.6–22086.5 MB/s) among these kernels as seen in the STREAM Benchmark exercise in 3.2.4? It was implied then that the cause was the difference in arithmetic intensity among the kernels shown in the table in section 3.2.4. This is only partly true. The small difference in arithmetic operations is really a pretty minor influence as long as we are in the bandwidth-limited regime. The correlation with the arithmetic operations is also not high. Why does the scale operation have the lowest bandwidth? The real culprits are the details in the cache hierarchy of the system. The cache system is not like a pipe with water flowing steadily through it as might be implied by the stream benchmark. It is more like a bucket brigade ferrying data up the cache levels with varying numbers of buckets and sizes as figure 4.21 shows. This is exactly what the Execution Cache Memory (ECM) model developed by Treibig and Hager tries to capture. Although it requires knowledge of the hardware architecture, it can predict the performance extremely well for streaming kernels. Movement between levels can be limited by the number of operations (µops), called micro-ops, that can be performed in a single

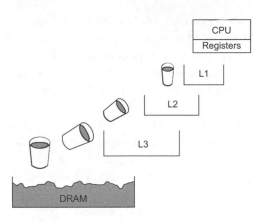

Figure 4.21 The movement of data between cache levels is a series of discrete operations, more like a bucket brigade than a flow through a pipe. The details of the hardware and how many loads can be issued at each level and in each direction largely impact the efficiency of loading data through the cache hierarchy.

cycle. The ECM model works in terms of cache lines and cycles, modeling the movement between the different cache levels.

Let's just take a quick look at the ECM model for the stream triad (A[i] = B[i] + s*C[i]) to see how this model works (figure 4.22). This calculation must be done for the specific kernel and hardware. We'll use a Haswell EP system for the hardware for this analysis. We start at the computational core with the equation $T_{core} = \max(T_{nOL}, T_{OL})$, where T is time in cycles. T_{OL} is generally the arithmetic operations that overlap the data transfer time, and T_{nOL} is the non-overlapping data transfer time.

For the stream triad, we have a cache line of multiply-add operations. If this is done with a scalar operation, it takes 8 cycles to complete. But we can do this with the new Advanced Vector Extensions (AVX) instructions. The Haswell chip has two fused

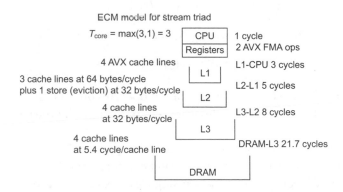

Figure 4.22 The Execution Cache Memory (ECM) model for the Haswell processor provides a detailed timing for the data transfer of the stream triad computation between cache levels. If the data is in main memory, the time it takes to get the data to the CPU is the sum of the transfer times between each cache level or 21.7 + 8 + 5 + 3 = 37.7 cycles. The floating-point operations only take 3 cycles, so the memory loads are the limiting aspect for the stream triad.

multiply-add (FMA) AVX 256-bit vector units. Each of these units processes four double-precision values. There are eight values in a cache line, so two FMA AVX vector units can process this in one cycle. T_{nOL} is the data transfer time. We need to load cache lines for B and C, and we need to load and store a cache line for A. This takes 3 cycles for the Haswell chip because of a limitation of the address generation units (AGUs).

Moving the four cache lines from L2 to L1 at 64 bytes/cycle takes 4 cycles. But the use of A[i] is a store operation. A store generally requires a special load called a *write-allocate*, where the memory space is allocated in the virtual data manager, and the cache line created at the necessary cache levels. Then the data is modified and *evicted* (stored) from the cache. This can only operate at 32 bytes/cycle at this level of cache, resulting in an additional cycle or a total of 5 cycles. From L3–L2, the data transfer is 32 bytes/cycle, so it takes 8 cycles. And finally, using the measured bandwidth of 27.1 GB/s, the number of cycles to move the cache lines from main memory is about 21.7 cycles. ECM uses this special notation to summarize these numbers:

$$\{T_{OL} \parallel T_{nOL} \mid T_{L1L2} \mid T_{L2L3} \mid T_{L3Mem}\} = \{1 \parallel 3 \mid 5 \mid 8 \mid 21.7\} \text{ cycles}$$

The T_{core} is shown by the $T_{OL} \parallel T_{nOL}$ in the notation. These are essentially the times (in cycles) to move between each level, with a special case for the T_{core}, where some of the operations on the computational core can overlap some of the data transfer operations from L1 to the registers. Then the model predicts the number of cycles it would take to load from each level of the cache by summing the data transfer time, including the non-overlapping data transfers from L1 to registers. The max of the T_{OL} and the data transfer time is then used as the predicted time:

$$T_{ECM} = \max(T_{nOL} + T_{data}, T_{OL})$$

This special ECM notation shows the resulting prediction for each cache level:

$$\{3|8|16|37.7\} \text{ cycles}$$

This notation says that the kernel takes 3 cycles when it operates out of the L1 cache, 8 out of L2 cache, 16 out of L3, and 37.7 cycles when the data has to be retrieved from main memory.

What can be learned from this example is that bumping up against a discrete hardware limit on a particular chip with a particular kernel can force another cycle or two at one of the transfers between cache levels, causing slower performance. A slightly different version of the processor might not have the same problem. For example, later versions of Intel chips add another AGU, which changes the L1-register cycles from 3 to 2.

This example also demonstrates that the vector units have value for both arithmetic operations and data movement. The vector load, also known as a quad-load operation, is not new. Much of the focus in the discussion on vector processors is on the arithmetic operations. But for bandwidth-limited kernels, it is likely that the vector memory operations are more important. An analysis by Stengel, et al. using the ECM model shows that the AVX vector instructions can give a two times performance improvement over loops that the compiler naively schedules. This is perhaps because the compiler does not have enough information available. More recent vector units also implement a *gather/scatter* memory load operation where the data loaded into the vector unit does not have to be in contiguous memory locations (gather) and the store from the vector to memory does not have to be contiguous memory locations (scatter).

> **NOTE** This new gather/scatter memory load feature is welcomed as many real numerical simulation codes need it to perform well. But there are still performance issues with the current gather/scatter implementation and more improvement is needed.

We can also analyze the performance of the cache hierarchy with the *streaming store.* The streaming store bypasses the cache system and writes directly to main memory. There is an option in most compilers to use streaming stores, and some invoke it as an optimization on their own. Its effect is to reduce the number of cache lines being moved between levels of the cache hierarchy, reducing congestion and the slower eviction operation between levels of the cache. Now that you have seen the effect of the cache-line movement, you should be able to appreciate its value.

The ECM model is used to evaluate and optimize stencil kernels by several researchers. Stencil kernels are streaming operations and can be analyzed with these techniques. It gets a little messy to keep track of all the cache lines and hardware characteristics without making mistakes, so performance counting tools can help. We'll refer you to a couple of references listed in appendix A for further information on these.

The advanced models are great for understanding the performance of relatively simple streaming kernels. *Streaming kernels* are those that load data in a nearly optimal way to effectively use the cache hierarchy. But kernels in scientific and HPC applications are often complex with conditionals, imperfectly nested loops, reductions, and loop-carried dependencies. In addition, compilers can transform the high-level language to assembler operations in unexpected ways, which complicate the analysis. There are usually a lot of kernels and loops to deal with as well. It is not feasible to analyze these complex kernels without specialized tools, so we try to develop general ideas from the simple kernels that we can apply to the more complex ones.

4.5   *Network messages*

We can extend our data transfer models for use in analyzing the computer network. A simple network performance model between nodes of a cluster or an HPC system is

$$\text{Time (ms)} = \text{latency (μsecs)} + \text{bytes\_moved (MBytes)} / (\text{bandwidth (GB/s)})$$
$$\text{(with unit conversions)}$$

Note that this is a network bandwidth rather than the memory bandwidth we have been using. There is an HPC benchmark site for latency and bandwidth at

http://icl.cs.utk.edu/hpcc/hpcc_results_lat_band.cgi

We can use the network micro-benchmarks from the HPC benchmark site to get typical latency and bandwidth numbers. We'll use 5 µsecs for the latency and 1 GB/s for the bandwidth. This gives us the plot shown in figure 4.23. For larger messages, we can estimate about 1 s for every MB transferred. But the vast majority of messages are small. We look at two different communication examples, first a larger message and then a smaller one, to understand the importance of latency and bandwidth in each.

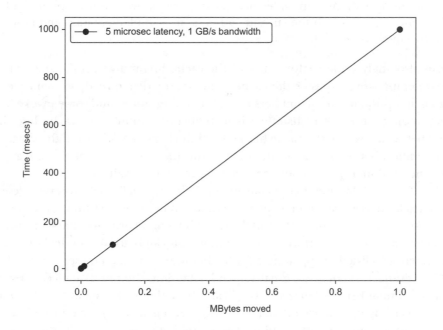

Figure 4.23   Typical network transfer time as a function of the size of the message gives us a rule of thumb: 1 MB takes 1 s (second), 1 KB takes 1 ms (millisecond), or 1 byte takes 1 microsec.

Example: Ghost cell communication

Let's take a 1000×1000 mesh. We need to communicate the outside cells of our processor as shown in the following figure to the adjacent processor so that it can complete its calculation. The extra cells placed on the outside of the mesh for the processor are called *ghost cells*.

1000 elements in outside cells * 8 bytes = 8 KB

Communication time = 5 µsecs + 8 ms

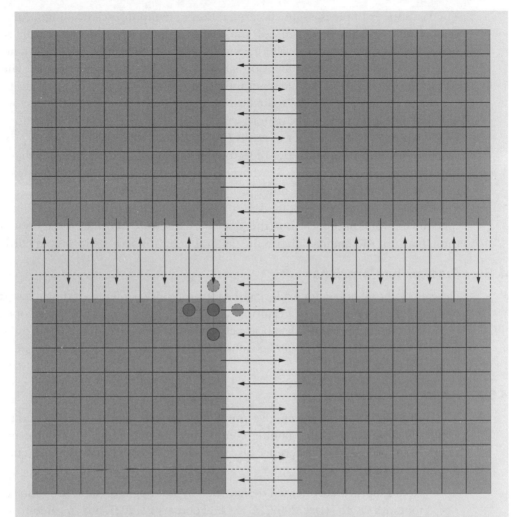

Outer cell data is exchanged with adjacent processors so that the stencil calculation is operating on current values. The dashed cells are called ghost cells because these hold duplicated data from another processor. The arrows only show the data exchange for every other cell for clarity.

Example: Sum number of cells across processors

We need to transfer the number of cells to the adjacent processor to sum and then return the sum. There are two communications of a 4-byte integer.

Communication time = (5 µsecs + 4 µsecs) * 2 = 18 µsecs

In this case, the latency is significant in the overall time taken for the transmission of the message.

The last sum example is a reduction operation in computer science lingo. An array of cell counts across the processors is reduced into a single value. More generally, a *reduction operation* is any operation where a multidimensional array from 1 to N dimensions is reduced to at least one dimension smaller and often to a scalar value. These are common operations in parallel computing and involve cooperation among the processors to complete. Also, the reduction sum in the last example can be performed in pair-wise fashion in a tree-like pattern with the number of communication hops being $log_2 N$, where N is the number of ranks (processors). When the number of processors reaches into the thousands, the time for the operation grows larger. Perhaps more importantly, all of the processors have to synchronize at the operation, leading to many of those waiting for the other processors to get to the reduction call.

There are more complex models for network messages that might be useful for specific network hardware. But the details of network hardware vary enough that these may not shed much light on the general behavior across all possible hardware.

4.6   *Further explorations*

Here are some resources for exploring the topics in this chapter, including data-oriented design, data structures, and performance models. Most application developers find the additional materials on data-oriented design to be interesting. Many applications can exploit sparsity, and we can learn how from the case study on compressed sparse data structures.

4.6.1   *Additional reading*

The following two references give good descriptions of the data-oriented design approach developed in the gaming community for building performance into program design. The second reference also gives the location of the video of Acton's presentation at CppCon.

- Noel Llopis, "Data-oriented design (or why you might be shooting yourself in the foot with OOP)" (Dec, 2009). Accessed February 21, 2021. http://gamesfromwithin.com/data-oriented-design.
- Mike Acton and Insomniac Games, "Data-oriented design and C++." Presentation at CppCon (September, 2014):
  - Powerpoint at https://github.com/CppCon/CppCon2014
  - Video at https://www.youtube.com/watch?v=rX0ItVEVjHc

The following reference is good for going into more detail on the case study of compressed sparse data structures using simple performance models. You'll also find measured performance results on multi-core and GPUs:

Shane Fogerty, Matt Martineau, et al., "A comparative study of multi-material data structures for computational physics applications." In *Computers & Mathematics with Applications* Vol. 78, no. 2 (July, 2019): 565–581. The source code is available at https://github.com/LANL/MultiMatTest.

The following paper introduces the shorthand notation used for the Execution Cache Model:

Holger Stengel, Jan Treibig, et al., "Quantifying performance bottlenecks of stencil computations using the execution-cache-memory model." In *Proceedings of the 29th ACM on International Conference on Supercomputing* (ACM, 2015): 207–216.

4.6.2   Exercises

1   Write a 2D contiguous memory allocator for a lower-left triangular matrix.
2   Write a 2D allocator for C that lays out memory the same way as Fortran.
3   Design a macro for an Array of Structures of Arrays (AoSoA) for the RGB color model in section 4.1.
4   Modify the code for the cell-centric full matrix data structure to *not* use a conditional and estimate its performance.
5   How would an AVX-512 vector unit change the ECM model for the stream triad?

Summary

- Data structures are at the foundation of application design and often dictate performance and the resulting implementation of parallel code. It is worth a little additional effort to develop a good design for the data layout.
- You can use the concepts of data-oriented design to develop higher performing applications.
- There are ways to write contiguous memory allocators for multidimensional arrays or special situations to minimize memory usage and improve performance.
- You can use compressed storage structures to reduce your application's memory usage while also improving performance.
- Simple performance models based on counting loads and stores can predict the performance of many basic kernels.
- More complex performance models shed light on the performance of the cache hierarchy with respect to low-level details in the hardware architecture.

Parallel algorithms
and patterns

5

This chapter covers

- What parallel algorithms and patterns are and their importance
- How to compare the performance of different algorithms
- What distinguishes parallel algorithms from other algorithms

Algorithms are at the core of computational science. Along with data structures, covered in the previous chapter, algorithms form the basis of all computational applications. For this reason, it is important to give careful thought to the key algorithms in your code. To begin, let's define what we mean by parallel algorithms and parallel patterns.

- *A parallel algorithm is a well-defined, step-by-step computational procedure that emphasizes concurrency to solve a problem.* Examples of algorithms include sorting, searching, optimization, and matrix operations.
- *A parallel pattern is a concurrent, separable fragment of code that occurs in diverse scenarios with some frequency.* By themselves, these code fragments generally do not solve complete problems of interest. Some examples include reductions, prefix scans, and ghost cell updates.

We will show the reduction in section 5.7, the prefix scan in section 5.6, and ghost cell updates in section 8.4.2. In one context, a parallel procedure can be considered an algorithm, and in another, it can be a pattern. The real difference is whether it is accomplishing the main goal or just part of a larger context. Recognizing patterns that are "parallel friendly" is important to prepare for later parallelization efforts.

5.1   *Algorithm analysis for parallel computing applications*

The development of parallel algorithms is a young field. Even the terminology and techniques to analyze parallel algorithms are still stuck in the serial world. One of the more traditional ways to evaluate algorithms is by looking at their algorithmic complexity. Our definition of algorithmic complexity follows.

> **DEFINITION**   *Algorithmic complexity* is a measure of the number of operations that it would take to complete an algorithm. Algorithmic complexity is a property of the algorithm and is a measure of the amount of work or operations in the procedure.

Complexity is usually expressed in *asymptotic notation.* Asymptotic notation is a type of expression that specifies the limiting bounds of performance. Basically, the notation identifies whether the run time grows linearly or whether it progresses at a more accelerated rate with the problem's size. The notation uses various forms of the letter O, such as $O(N)$, $O(N \log N)$ or $O(N^2)$. N is the size of a long array such as the number of cells, particles, or elements. The combination of $O()$ and N refers to how the cost of the algorithm scales as the size N of the array grows. The O can be thought of as "order" as in "scales on the order of." Generally, a simple loop over N items will be $O(N)$, a double-nested loop will be $O(N^2)$, and a tree-based algorithm will be $O(N \log N)$. By convention, the leading constants are dropped. The most commonly used asymptotic notations are

- *Big O*—This is the worst case limit of an algorithm's performance. Examples are a doubly nested `for` loop for a large array of size N, which would be $O(N^2)$ complexity.
- *Big Ω (Big Omega)*—The best case performance of an algorithm.
- *Big Θ (Big Theta)*—The average case performance of an algorithm.

Traditional analysis of algorithms uses algorithmic complexity, computational complexity, and time complexity interchangeably. We will define the terms a bit differently to help us evaluate algorithms on today's parallel computing hardware. Time doesn't scale with the amount of work and neither does the computational effort or cost. We thus make the following adjustments to the definitions for computational complexity and time complexity:

- *Computational complexity (also called step complexity) is the number of steps that are needed to complete an algorithm.* This complexity measurement is an attribute of the implementation and the type of hardware that is used for the calculation. It includes the amount of parallelism that is possible. If you're using a vector or multi-core computer, a step (cycle) can be four or more floating-point operations. Can you use these additional operations to reduce the number of steps?

- *Time complexity takes into account the actual cost of an operation on a typical modern computing system.* The largest adjustment for time is to consider the cost of memory loads and the caching of data.

We'll use complexity analysis for some of our algorithm comparisons, such as the prefix sum algorithms in section 5.5. But for applied computer scientists, the asymptotic complexity of an algorithm is somewhat one-dimensional and of limited use. It only tells us the cost of an algorithm in the limit as it grows larger. In an applied setting, we need a more complete model of an algorithm. We'll see why in the next section.

5.2   *Performance models versus algorithmic complexity*

We first introduced performance models in chapter 4 to analyze the relative performance of different data structures. In a performance model, we build a much more complete description of the performance of an algorithm than in algorithmic complexity analysis. The biggest difference is that *we don't hide the constant multiplier in front of the algorithm.* But there is also a difference in the terms such as log N for scaling. The actual count of operations is from a binary tree and should be $\log_2 N$.

In traditional algorithmic complexity analysis, the difference between the two logarithmic terms is a constant that gets absorbed into the constant multiplier. In common world problems, these constants could matter and don't cancel out; therefore, we need to use a performance model to differentiate between different approaches of a similar algorithm. To further understand the benefits of using performance models, let's start with an example from everyday life.

Example

You are one of the organizers of a conference with 100 participants. You want to hand out registration packets to each participant. Here are some algorithms that you can use:

1   Have all 100 participants form a line as you search through 100 folders to find the packet to hand to each participant in turn. The worst case is that you will have to look through all 100 folders. On average, you will look through 50. If there is no packet, you have to look through all 100.
2   Presort the packets alphabetically prior to registration. Now you can use a bisection search to find each folder.

Returning to the first algorithm in the example, let's assume for simplicity's sake that the folders remain after the packets are handed out to a participant, such that the number of folders stays constant at the original number. There are N participants and N folders, creating a doubly nested loop. The computation is of order N^2 operations, or $O(N^2)$ in Big O asymptotic notation for the worst case. If the folders decreased each time, the computation would be $(N + N - 1 + N - 2 \ldots)$ or an $O(N^2)$ algorithm. The second algorithm can exploit the sorted order of the folders with a bisection search so the algorithm can be done for the worst case in $O(N \log N)$ operations.

Asymptotic complexity tells us how the algorithm performs as we reach large sizes, such as one million participants. But we won't ever have one million participants. We will have a finite size of 100 participants. For finite sizes, a more complete picture of the algorithmic performance is needed.

To illustrate this, we apply a performance model to one of the most basic computer algorithms to see how it might give us more insight. We'll use a time-based model where we include the real hardware costs rather than an operation-based count. In this example, we look at a bisection search, also known as a binary search. It is one of the most common computer algorithms and numerical optimization techniques. Conventional asymptotic analysis says that the binary search is much faster than a linear search. We'll show that accounting for how real computers function, the increase in speed is not as much as might be expected. This analysis also helps to explain the table lookup results in section 5.5.1.

> ### Example: Bisection search versus linear search
>
> The bisection search algorithm can be used to find the correct entry in a sorted array of 256 integer elements. This algorithm takes the midpoint, bisecting the remaining possible range in a recursive manner. In a performance model, a bisection search would have $\log_2 256$ steps or 8, while a linear search would have a worst case of 256 steps and an average of 128. If we count cache line loads for a 4-byte integer array, the linear search would only be 16 cache line loads for the worst case and 8 on average. The binary search would require 4 cache line loads for the worst case and about 4 for the average case. It is imperative to highlight that this linear search would only be two times slower than a binary search, instead of the 16 times slower that we might expect.
>
> In this analysis, we assume any operation on data in the cache is essentially free (actually a couple of cycles), while a cache line load is on the order of about 100 cycles. We just count the cache line loads and ignore the comparison operations. For our time-based performance model, we would say the cost of the linear search is $(n / 16) / 2 = 8$ and the bisection search is $\log_2(n / 16) = 4$.
>
> *How the cache behaves changes the result by a large amount for these short array lengths.* The bisection search is still faster, but not by as much as the simpler analysis would have us expect.

Though asymptotic complexity is used to understand performance as an algorithm scales, it does not provide an equation for absolute performance. For a given problem, linear search, which scales linearly, might outperform a bisection search, which scales logarithmically. This is especially true when you parallelize the algorithm as it is much simpler to scale a linearly scaled algorithm than a logarithmically scaled algorithm. In addition, the computer is designed to linearly walk through an array and prefetch data, which can speedup performance a little more. Finally, the specific problem can have the item occurring at the beginning of the array, where a bisection search performs much worse than a linear search.

As an example of other parallel considerations, let's look at the implementation of the search on 32 threads of a multi-core CPU or a GPU. The set of threads must wait for the slowest to complete during each operation. The bisection search always takes 4 cache loads. The linear search varies in the number of cache lines required for each thread. The worst case controls how long the operation takes, making the cost closer to 16 cache lines than the average of 8 cache lines.

So you ask, how does this work in practice? Let's look at the two variations of the table lookup code described in the example. You can test the following algorithms on your system with the perfect hash code included in the accompanying source code for this chapter at https://github.com/EssentialsofParallelComputing/Chapter5. First, the following listing shows the linear search algorithm version of the table lookup code.

Listing 5.1   Linear search algorithm in a table lookup

PerfectHash/table.c

```
268 double *interpolate_bruteforce(int isize, int xstride,
        int d_axis_size, int t_axis_size, double *d_axis, double *t_axis,
269    double *dens_array, double *temp_array, double *data)
270 {
271    int i;
272
273    double *value_array=(double *)malloc(isize*sizeof(double));
274
275    for (i = 0; i<isize; i++){
276      int tt, dd;
277
276      int tt, dd;
277
278      for (tt=0; tt<t_axis_size-2 &&
             temp_array[i] > t_axis[tt+1]; tt++);
279      for (dd=0; dd<d_axis_size-2 &&
             dens_array[i] > d_axis[dd+1]; dd++);
280
281      double xf = (dens_array[i]-d_axis[dd])/
                    (d_axis[dd+1]-d_axis[dd]);
282      double yf = (temp_array[i]-t_axis[tt])/
                    (t_axis[tt+1]-t_axis[tt]);
283      value_array[i] =
                 xf *     yf *data(dd+1,tt+1)
284      + (1.0-xf)*     yf *data(dd,   tt+1)
285      +     xf *(1.0-yf)*data(dd+1,tt)
286      + (1.0-xf)*(1.0-yf)*data(dd,   tt);
287
288    }
```

Specifies a linear search from 0 to axis_size

Interpolation

```
289
290   return(value_array);
291 }
```

The linear search of the two axes is done in lines 278 and 279. The coding is simple and straightforward, resulting in a cache-friendly implementation. Now let's look at the bisection search in the following listing.

Listing 5.2   Bisection search algorithm in a table lookup

PerfectHash/table.c

```
293 double *interpolate_bisection(int isize, int xstride,
        int d_axis_size, int t_axis_size, double *d_axis, double *t_axis,
294    double *dens_array, double *temp_array, double *data)
295 {
296   int i;
297
298   double *value_array=(double *)malloc(isize*sizeof(double));
299
300   for (i = 0; i<isize; i++){
301     int tt = bisection(t_axis, t_axis_size-2,              ┐ Bisection
                        temp_array[i]);                        │ calls
302     int dd = bisection(d_axis, d_axis_size-2,              │
                        dens_array[i]);                        ┘
303
304     double xfrac = (dens_array[i]-d_axis[dd])/            ┐
                        (d_axis[dd+1]-d_axis[dd]);             │
305     double yfrac = (temp_array[i]-t_axis[tt])/             │
                        (t_axis[tt+1]-t_axis[tt]);             │
306     value_array[i] =                                       ├ Interpolation
                  xfrac *      yfrac *data(dd+1,tt+1)          │
307     + (1.0-xfrac)*      yfrac *data(dd,  tt+1)             │
308     +      xfrac *(1.0-yfrac)*data(dd+1,tt)                │
309     + (1.0-xfrac)*(1.0-yfrac)*data(dd,  tt);               ┘
310   }
311
312   return(value_array);
313 }
314
315 int bisection(double *axis, int axis_size, double value)
316 {
317   int ibot = 0;                                            ┐
318   int itop = axis_size+1;                                  │
319                                                            │
320   while (itop - ibot > 1){          ┐ Bisection            │
321     int imid = (itop + ibot) /2;    │ algorithm            │
322     if ( value >= axis[imid] )      │                      │
323       ibot = imid;                  │                      │
324     else                            │                      │
325       itop = imid;                  │                      │
326   }                                 ┘                      │
327   return(ibot);
328 }
```

The bisection code is slightly longer than the linear search (listing 5.1), but it should have less operational complexity. We'll look at other table search algorithms in section 5.5.1 and show their relative performance in figure 5.8.

   Spoiler: the bisection search is not much faster than the linear search as you might expect, even accounting for the cost of the interpolation. Although this is the case, this analysis shows the linear search is not as slow as you might expect either.

5.3   *Parallel algorithms: What are they?*

Now let's take another example from everyday life to introduce some ideas for parallel algorithms. This first example demonstrates how an algorithmic approach that is comparison-free and less synchronous can be easier to implement and can perform better for highly parallel hardware. We discuss additional examples in the following sections that highlight spatial locality, reproducibility, and other important attributes for parallelism and then summarize all of the ideas in section 5.8 at the end of the chapter.

Example: Comparison sort versus hash sort

You want to sort the 100 participants in the auditorium from the previous example. First, you try a comparison sort.

1   Sort a room by having each person compare their last name to their neighbor in their row and move left if their last name is earlier in alphabetical sequence and right if later.
2   Continue for up to *N* steps, where *N* is the number of people in the room.

For GPUs, a workgroup cannot communicate with another workgroup. Let's assume each row in the auditorium is a workgroup. When you reach the end of the row, it is like you have reached the limit of the GPU workgroup, and you have to exit the kernel to do a comparison with the next row. Having to exit the kernel means that it takes multiple kernel invocations, adding to coding complexity and to run time. There will be more on how a GPU functions in chapters 9 and 10.

Now, let's look at a different sorting algorithm: the hash sort. The best way to understand a hash sort is through the following example. We'll go into more detail on the elements of a hash function in section 5.4.

1   Place a sign for each letter at the front of the room.
2   Each person goes to the table with the first letter of their last name.
3   For letters with large numbers of participants, repeat for the second letter in the last name. For small numbers of participants, do any simple sort, including the one described previously.

The first sort is a comparison sort using a bubble sort algorithm, which generally performs poorly. The *bubble sort* steps through a list, compares adjacent elements, and swaps these if they are in an incorrect order. The algorithm goes repeatedly through the list until the list is sorted. The best comparison sort has an algorithmic complexity limit of $O(N \log N)$. The *hash sort* breaks this barrier because it doesn't use comparisons. On average, the hash sort is an $\Theta(1)$ operation for each participant and $\Theta(N)$ for all participants. The faster performance is significant; more importantly, the operations for each participant are completely independent. Having the operations completely independent makes the algorithm easy to parallelize, even on less synchronous GPU architectures.

Combining this all together, we can use the hash sort to put the participants and folders in alphabetical order and add parallelism by having multiple lines divide up by the alphabet at the registration table. The two hash sorts will be $\Theta(N)$ and in parallel will be $\Theta(N/P)$ where P is the number of processors. For 16 processors and 100 participants, the parallel speedup from the serial, brute-force method is $100^2/(100/16) =$ 1,600x. We recognize that the hash design is similar to what we see in well-organized conferences or school registration lines.

5.4 *What is a hash function?*

In this section, we will discuss the importance of a hash function. Hashing techniques originated in the 1950s and 60s, but have been slow to be adapted to many application areas. Specifically, we will go through what constitutes a perfect hash, spatial hashing, perfect spatial hashing, along with all the promising use cases.

A *hash function* maps from a key to a value, much like a dictionary uses a word as the lookup key to its definition. In figure 5.1, the word *Romero* is the key that is hashed to look up the value, which in this case is the moniker or username. Unlike a physical dictionary, a computer needs at least 26 possible storage locations times the maximum length of the dictionary key. So for a computer, it is absolutely necessary to encode the key into a shorter form called a hash. The term *hash* or *hashing* refers to "chopping up" the key into a shorter form to use as an index to store the value. The location for storing the collection of values for a specific key is called a *bucket* or *bin*. There are many different ways to generate a hash from a key; the best approaches are generally problem-specific.

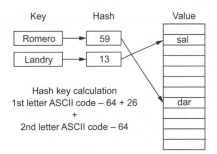

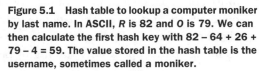

Figure 5.1 Hash table to lookup a computer moniker by last name. In ASCII, *R* is 82 and *O* is 79. We can then calculate the first hash key with 82 − 64 + 26 + 79 − 4 = 59. The value stored in the hash table is the username, sometimes called a moniker.

A *perfect hash* is one where there is one entry in each bucket at most. Perfect hashes are simple to handle, but can take more memory. A *minimal perfect hash* is just one entry in each bucket and with no empty buckets. It takes longer to calculate minimal perfect hashes, but for example, for fixed sets of programming keywords, the extra time is worth it. For most of the hashes we'll discuss here, the hashes will be created on the fly, queried, and thrown away, so a faster creation time is more important than memory size. Where a perfect hash is not feasible or takes too much memory, a compact hash can be employed. A *compact hash* compresses the hash so that it requires less storage memory. As always, there are tradeoffs in programming complexity, run time, and required memory among the different hashing methods.

The *load factor* is the fraction of the hash that is filled. It is computed by n/k, where n is the number of entries in the hash table and k is the number of buckets. Compact hashes still work at load factors of .8 to .9, but the efficiency drops off after that due to collisions. *Collisions* occur when more than one key wants to store its value in the same bucket. It is important to have a good hash function that distributes keys more uniformly, avoiding the clustering of entries, thereby allowing higher load factors. With a compact hash, both the key and the value are stored so that on retrieval, the key can be checked to see if it is the right entry.

In the previous examples, we used the first letter of the last name as a simple hash key. While effective, there are certainly flaws with using the first letter. One is that the number of last names starting with each letter in the alphabet is not evenly distributed, leading to unequal numbers of entries in each bucket. We could instead use the integer representation of the string, which produces a hash for the first four letters of the name. But the character set gives only 52 possible values for the 256 storage locations for each byte, leading to only a fraction of possible integer keys. A special hash function that expects only characters would need far fewer storage locations.

5.5   *Spatial hashing: A highly-parallel algorithm*

Our discussion in chapter 1 used a uniform-sized, regular grid from the Krakatau example in figure 1.9. For this discussion on parallel algorithms and spatial hashing, we need to use more complex computational meshes. In scientific simulations, more complex meshes define with more detail the areas that we are interested in. In big data, specifically image analysis and categorization, these more complex meshes are not widely adopted. Yet the technique would have great value there; when a cell in the image has mixed characteristics, just split the cell.

The biggest impediment to using more complex meshes is that coding becomes more complicated and we must incorporate new computational techniques. For complex meshes, it is a greater challenge to find methods that work and scale well on parallel architectures. In this section, we'll show you how you can handle some of the common spatial operations with highly parallel algorithms.

Example: Krakatau wave simulation

Your team is working on their wave application and decides they need more resolution for the simulation in some areas at the wave front and at the shoreline as shown in figure 1.9. They don't, however, need fine resolution in other parts of the grid. The team decides to take a look at adaptive mesh refinement (AMR), where they can put finer mesh resolution in areas that need it.

Cell-based adaptive mesh refinement (AMR) belongs to a class of unstructured mesh techniques that no longer have the simplicity of a structured grid to locate data. In cell-based AMR (figure 5.2), the cell data arrays are one-dimensional, and the data can be in any order. The mesh locations are carried along in additional arrays that have the size and location information for each cell. Thus, there is some structure to the grid, but the data is completely unstructured. Taking this further into unstructured territory, a fully-unstructured mesh could have cells of triangles, polyhedra, or other complex shapes. This allows the cells to "fit" the boundaries between land and ocean, but at the cost of more complex numerical operations. Because many of the same parallel algorithms for unstructured data apply to both, we'll work mostly with the cell-based AMR example.

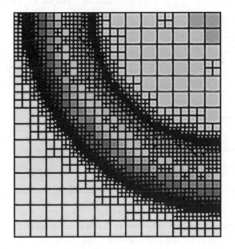

Figure 5.2   A cell-based AMR mesh for a wave simulation from the CLAMR mini-app. The black squares are the cells and the variously-shaded squares represent the height of a wave radiating outward from the upper right corner.

AMR techniques can be broken down into patch, block, and cell-based approaches. The patch and block methods use various size patches or fixed-size blocks that can at least partially exploit the regular structure of these groups of cells. Cell-based AMR has truly unstructured data that can be in any order. A shallow-water, cell-based AMR mini-app, CLAMR (https://github.com/lanl/CLAMR.git), was developed by Davis, Nicholaeff, and Trujillo while they were summer students in 2011 at Los Alamos National Laboratory. They wanted to see if cell-based AMR applications could run on GPUs. In the process, they found breakthrough parallel algorithms that also made CPU implementations run faster. The most important of these was a spatial hash.

Spatial hashing is a technique where the key is based on spatial information. The hashing algorithm retains the same average algorithmic complexity of $\Theta(1)$ operations for each lookup. All spatial queries can be performed with a spatial hash; many are much faster than alternative methods. The basic principle is to map objects onto a grid of buckets arranged in a regular pattern.

A spatial hash is shown in the center of figure 5.3. The sizing of the buckets is selected based on the characteristic size of the objects to map. For a cell-based AMR mesh, the minimum cell size is used. For particles or objects, as shown on the right in the figure, the cell size is based on the interaction distance. This choice means that only the cells immediately adjacent need to be queried for interaction or collision calculations. Collision calculations are one of the great application areas for spatial hashes, not only in scientific computing for smooth particle hydrodynamics, molecular dynamics, and astrophysics, but also in gaming engines and computer graphics. There are many situations where we can exploit spatial locality to reduce computational costs.

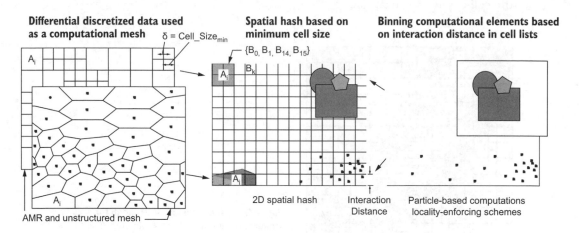

Figure 5.3 Computational meshes, particles, and objects mapped onto a spatial hash. The polyhedra of the unstructured mesh and the rectangular cells of the cell-based adaptive refinement mesh can be mapped to a spatial hash for spatial operations. Particles and geometric objects can also benefit from being mapped to a spatial hash to provide information about their spatial locality so that only nearby items need to be considered.

Both the AMR and the unstructured mesh on the left in the figure are referred to as *differential discretized data* because the cells are smaller where the gradients are steeper to better resolve the physical phenomena. But these have a limit to how much smaller the cells can get. The limit keeps the bucket sizes from getting too small. Both meshes store their cell indices in all the underlying buckets of the spatial hash. For the particles and geometric objects, the particle indices and object identifiers are stored in the buckets. This provides a form of locality that keeps the computational cost from increasing as the problem size increases. For example, if the problem domain is increased on the left and top, the interaction calculation in the lower right of the spatial hash stays the same. The algorithmic complexity thus stays $\Theta(N)$ for the particle calculations instead of growing to $\Theta(N^2)$. The following listing shows the pseudo code for the interaction loop, which is over nearby locations for the inner loop instead of having to search through all the particles.

> **Listing 5.3   Particle interaction pseudo-code**

```
1 forall particles, ip, in NParticles{
2     forall particles, jp, in Adjacent_Buckets{
3         if (distance between particles < interaction_distance){
4             perform collision or interaction calculation
5         }
6     }
7 }
```

5.5.1   *Using perfect hashing for spatial mesh operations*

We'll first look at perfect hashing to focus on the use of hashing rather than the mechanics internal to hashing. These methods all rely on being able to guarantee that there will be only one entry in each bucket, avoiding the issues of handling collisions where a bucket might have more than one data entry. For perfect hashing, we'll investigate the four most important spatial operations:

- *Neighbor finding*—Locating the one or two neighbors on each side of a cell
- *Remapping*—Mapping another AMR mesh onto a current AMR mesh
- *Table lookup*—Locating the intervals in the 2D table to perform the interpolation
- *Sorting*—A 1D or 2D sort of the cell data

All of the source code for the examples for the four operations in 1D and 2D is available at https://github.com/lanl/PerfectHash.git under an open source license. The source is also linked into the examples for this chapter. The perfect hash code uses CMake and tests for the availability of OpenCL. If you do not have OpenCL capability, the code detects that and will not compile the OpenCL implementations. The rest of the cases on the CPU will still run.

NEIGHBOR FINDING USING A SPATIAL PERFECT HASH

Neighbor finding is one of the most important spatial operations. In scientific computing, the material moved out of one cell has to move into the adjacent cell. We need to know which cell to move to in order to compute the amount of material and move it. In image analysis, the characteristics of the adjacent cell can give important information on the composition of the current cell.

The rules for the AMR mesh in CLAMR are that there can be only a single-level jump in refinement across a face of a cell. Also, the neighbor list of each cell on each side is just one of the neighbor cells, and the choice is to be the lower cell or the cell to the left of each pair as figure 5.4 shows. The second of the pair is found by using the neighbor list of the first cell; for example, `ntop[nleft[ic]]`. The problem then becomes setting up the neighbor arrays for every cell.

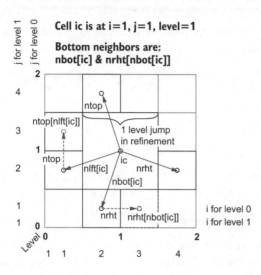

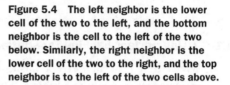

Figure 5.4   **The left neighbor is the lower cell of the two to the left, and the bottom neighbor is the cell to the left of the two below. Similarly, the right neighbor is the lower cell of the two to the right, and the top neighbor is to the left of the two cells above.**

What are the possible algorithms for finding neighbors? The naive way is to search all the other cells for the cell that is adjacent. This can be done by looking at the i, j, and *level* variables in each cell. The naive algorithm is $O(N^2)$. It performs well with small numbers of cells, but the run-time complexity grows large quickly. Some common alternative algorithms are tree-based, such as the k-D tree and quadtree algorithms (octree in three dimensions). These are comparison-based algorithms that scale as $O(N \log N)$, which are defined later. The code for the 2D neighbor calculation, including the k-D tree, brute force, CPU, and GPU hash implementations is available at https://github.com/lanl/PerfectHash.git, along with the other spatial perfect hash applications discussed later in this chapter.

The k-D tree splits the mesh into two equal halves in the x-dimension and then two equal halves in the y-dimension, repeating until it finds the object. The algorithm to build the k-D tree is $O(N \log N)$, and each search is also $O(N \log N)$.

The quadtree has four children for each parent, one for each quadrant. This exactly maps to the subdivision of the cell-based AMR mesh. A full quadtree starts from the top, or root, with one cell and subdivides to the finest level of the AMR mesh. A "truncated" quadtree starts from the coarsest level of the mesh and has a quadtree for each coarse cell to map down to the finest level. The quadtree algorithm is a comparison-based algorithm: $O(N \log N)$.

The limitation of just one level jump across a face is called a *graded mesh*. In cell-based AMR, graded meshes are common, but other quadtree applications such as *n*-body applications in astrophysics result in much larger jumps in the quadtree data structure.

The one-level jump in refinement allows us to improve the algorithm design for finding neighbors. We can start our search at the leaf that represents our cell and, at most, we only have to go up two levels of the tree to find our neighbor. For searching for a near neighbor of similar size, the search should start at the leaves and use a quadtree. For searches for large irregular objects, the k-D tree should be used and the search should start from the root of the tree. Proper use of tree-based search algorithms can provide a viable implementation on CPUs, but the comparisons and tree construction present difficulties on GPUs, where comparisons beyond the work group cannot be done easily.

This sets the stage for the design of a spatial hash to perform the neighbor finding operation. We can guarantee that there are no collisions in our spatial hash by making the buckets in the hash the size of the finest cells in the AMR mesh. The algorithm then becomes

- Allocate a spatial hash the size of the finest level of the cell-based AMR mesh
- For each cell in the AMR mesh, write the cell number to the hash buckets underlying the cell
- Compute the index for a finer cell one cell outside the current cell on each side
- Read the value placed in the hash bucket at that location

For the mesh shown in figure 5.5, the write phase is followed by a read phase to look up the index of the right neighbor cell.

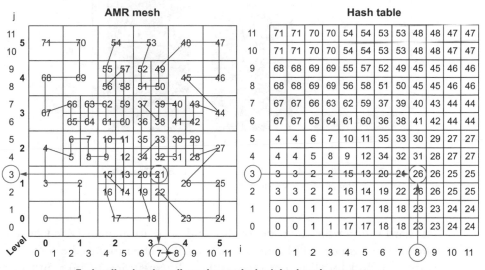

Each cell writes its cell number to the hash buckets it covers.
Right neighbor of cell 21 is at col 8, row 3. Look up in hash and it is cell 26.

Figure 5.5   Finding the right neighbor of cell 21 using a spatial perfect hash

This algorithm is well suited to GPUs and is shown in listing 5.5. The first implementation took less than a day to port from the CPU to the GPU. The original k-D tree would take weeks or months to implement on the GPU. The algorithmic complexity also breaks the $O(\log N)$ threshold and is, on average, $\Theta(N)$ for N cells.

This first implementation of the perfect hash neighbor calculation was an order of magnitude faster on the CPU than the k-D tree method, and an additional order of magnitude faster on the GPU than a single core of a CPU for a total of 3,157x speedup (figure 5.6). The algorithm performance study was done on an NVIDIA V100 GPU and a Skylake Gold 5118 CPU with a nominal clock frequency of 2.30 GHz. All the results in this chapter used this architecture as well. The CPU core and GPU architecture are the best available around 2018, giving a *Best(2018)* parallel speedup comparison (see section 1.6 for speedup notation). But it isn't an architecture comparison between the CPU and the GPU. If the 24 virtual cores on this CPU were utilized, the CPU would also see a considerable parallel speedup.

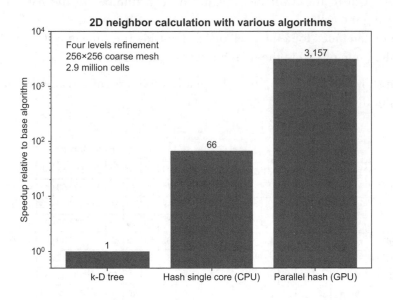

Figure 5.6   The algorithm and parallel speedup total 3,157x. The new algorithm enables the parallel speedup on the GPU.

How hard is it to write the code for this kind of performance? Let's take a look at the code for the hash table in listing 5.4 for the CPU. The input to the routine are the 1D arrays, `i`, `j`, and `level`, where `level` is the refinement level, and `i` and `j` are the row and column of the cell in the mesh at that cell's refinement level. The whole listing is about a dozen lines.

Listing 5.4 Writing out a spatial hash table for the CPU

```
neigh2d.c from PerfectHash
452 int *levtable = (int *)malloc(levmx+1);          Constructs a table
453 for (int lev=0; lev<levmx+1; lev++)              of powers of two
        levtable[lev] = (int)pow(2,lev);             (1, 2, 4, ...)
454
455 int jmaxsize = mesh_size*levtable[levmx];        Sets the number of rows and
456 int imaxsize = mesh_size*levtable[levmx];        columns at the finest level
457 int **hash = (int **)genmatrix(jmaxsize,
                imaxsize, sizeof(int));               Allocates the hash table
458
459 for(int ic=0; ic<ncells; ic++){    ◄──────────┐  Maps cells to
460     int lev = level[ic];                        │  hash table
461     for (int jj=j[ic]*levtable[levmx-lev];
            jj<(j[ic]+1)*levtable[levmx-lev]; jj++) {
462         for (int ii=i[ic]*levtable[levmx-lev];
                ii<(i[ic]+1)*levtable[levmx-lev]; ii++) {
463             hash[jj][ii] = ic;
464         }
465     }
466 }
```

The loops at lines 459, 461, and 462 reference the 1D arrays i, j, and level; level is the refinement level where 0 is the coarse level and 1 to levmax are the levels of refinement. The arrays i and j are the row and column of the cell in the mesh at that cell's refinement level.

Listing 5.5 shows the code for writing out the spatial hash in OpenCL for the GPU, which is similar to listing 5.4. Although we haven't covered OpenCL yet, the simplicity of the GPU code is clear, even without understanding all the details. Let's do a brief comparison to get a sense of how code has to change for the GPU. We define a macro to handle the 2D indexing and to make the code look more like the CPU version. Then the biggest difference is that there is no cell loop. This is typical of GPU code, where the outer loops are removed and are instead handled by the kernel launch. The cell index is provided for each thread by a call to the get_global_id intrinsic. There will be more on this example and writing OpenCL code, in general, in chapter 12.

Listing 5.5 Writing out a spatial hash table on the GPU in OpenCL

```
neigh2d_kern.cl from PerfectHash
77 #define hashval(j,i) hash[(j)*imaxsize+(i)]
78
79 __kernel void hash_setup_kern(
80      const uint isize,
81      const uint mesh_size,
82      const uint levmx,
83      __global const int  *levtable,      Passes in the table
84      __global const int  *i,             of powers of 2 along
85      __global const int  *j,             with i, j, and level
86      __global const int  *level,
```

```
87        __global int   *hash
88      ) {
89
90    const uint ic = get_global_id(0);
91    if (ic >= isize) return;
92
93    int imaxsize = mesh_size*levtable[levmx];
94    int lev = level[ic];
95    int ii = i[ic];
96    int jj = j[ic];
97    int levdiff = levmx - lev;
98
99    int iimin =  ii    *levtable[levdiff];
100   int iimax = (ii+1)*levtable[levdiff];
101   int jjmin =  jj    *levtable[levdiff];
102   int jjmax = (jj+1)*levtable[levdiff];
103
104   for (   int jjj = jjmin; jjj < jjmax; jjj++) {
105      for (int iii = iimin; iii < iimax; iii++) {
106         hashval(jjj, iii) = ic;
107      }
108   }
109 }
```

The loop across the cells is implied by the GPU kernel; each thread is a cell. (line 90)

The return is important to avoid reading past end of the arrays. (line 91)

Computes the bounds of the underlying hash buckets to set (lines 99–102)

Sets the hash table value to the thread ID (the cell number) (line 106)

The code for retrieving the neighbor indexes is also simple as shown in listing 5.6, with just a loop across the cells and a read of the hash table at where the neighbor location would be on the finest level of the mesh. You can find the locations of the neighbors by incrementing the row or column by one cell in the direction needed. For the left or bottom neighbor, the increment is 1, while for the right or top neighbor, the increment is the full width of the mesh in the x-direction or `imaxsize`.

Listing 5.6 Finding neighbors from a spatial hash table on the CPU

```
neigh2d.c from PerfectHash
472 for (int ic=0; ic<ncells; ic++){
473   int ii = i[ic];
474   int jj = j[ic];
475   int lev = level[ic];
476   int levmult = levtable[levmx-lev];
477   int nlftval =
          hash[     jj    *levmult                 ]
               [MAX( ii    *levmult-1,0          )];
478   int nrhtval =
          hash[     jj    *levmult                 ]
               [MIN((ii+1)*levmult,  imaxsize-1)];
480   int nbotval =
          hash[MAX( jj    *levmult-1,0)            ]
               [     ii    *levmult               ];
481   int ntopval =
          hash[MIN((jj+1)*levmult,  jmaxsize-1)]
               [     ii    *levmult               ];
```

Calculates the neighbor cell location for the query, using a max/min to keep it in bounds (lines 477–481)

```
482    neigh2d[ic].left  = nlftval;
483    neigh2d[ic].right = nrhtval;         Assigns the neighbor
484    neigh2d[ic].bot   = nbotval;         value for output
485    neigh2d[ic].top   = ntopval;         arrays
486}
```

For the GPU, we again remove the loop for the cells and replace it with a get_
global_id call as shown in the following listing.

Listing 5.7   Finding neighbors from a spatial hash table on the GPU in OpenCL

```
neigh2d_kern.cl from PerfectHash
113 #define hashval(j,i) hash[(j)*imaxsize+(i)]
114
115 __kernel void calc_neighbor2d_kern(
116       const int isize,
117       const uint mesh_size,
118       const int levmx,
119       __global const int *levtable,
120       __global const int *i,
121       __global const int *j,
122       __global const int *level,
123       __global const int *hash,
124       __global struct neighbor2d *neigh2d
125       ) {
126                                           Gets the cell ID
127    const uint ic  = get_global_id(0);     for the thread
128    if (ic >= isize) return;
129
130    int imaxsize = mesh_size*levtable[levmx];
131    int jmaxsize = mesh_size*levtable[levmx];
132
133    int ii = i[ic];          The rest of code is similar
134    int jj = j[ic];          to the CPU version.
135    int lev = level[ic];
136    int levmult = levtable[levmx-lev];
137
138    int nlftval = hashval(    jj    *levmult                    ,
                             max( ii    *levmult-1,0            ));
139    int nrhtval = hashval(    jj    *levmult                    ,
                             min((ii+1)*levmult,  imaxsize-1));
140    int nbotval = hashval(max( jj    *levmult-1,0            )    ,
                                ii    *levmult                );
141    int ntopval = hashval(min((jj+1)*levmult,  jmaxsize-1),
                                ii    *levmult                );
142    neigh2d[ic].left   = nlftval;
143    neigh2d[ic].right  = nrhtval;
144    neigh2d[ic].bottom = nbotval;
145    neigh2d[ic].top    = ntopval;
146 }
```

Compare the simplicity of this code to the k-D tree code for the CPU, which is a thousand lines long!

REMAP CALCULATIONS USING A SPATIAL PERFECT HASH

Another important numerical mesh operation is a remap from one mesh to another. Fast remaps can permit different physics to be performed on meshes optimized for their individual needs.

In this case, we will look at remapping the values from one cell-based AMR mesh to another cell-based AMR mesh. Mesh remaps can also involve unstructured meshes or particle-based simulations, but the techniques are more complicated. The setup phase is identical to the neighbor case, where the cell index for every cell is written to the spatial hash. In this case, the spatial hash is created for the source mesh. Then the read phase, shown in listing 5.8, queries the spatial hash for the cell numbers underlying each cell of the target mesh and sums up the values from the source mesh into the target mesh after adjusting for the size difference of the cells. For this demonstration, we have simplified the source code from the example at https://github.com/Essentials ofParallelComputing/Chapter5.git.

Listing 5.8   The read phase of the remapping of a value on the CPU

```
remap2.c from PerfectHash
211 for(int jc = 0; jc < ncells_target; jc++) {
212     int ii = mesh_target.i[jc];                    Gets the location
213     int jj = mesh_target.j[jc];                    of the target
214     int lev = mesh_target.level[jc];               mesh cell
215     int lev_mod = two_to_the(levmx - lev);
216     double value_sum = 0.0;
217     for(int jjj = jj*lev_mod;
                jjj < (jj+1)*lev_mod; jjj++) {          Queries the spatial
                                                        hash for source
218       for(int iii = ii*lev_mod;                     mesh cells
                iii < (ii+1)*lev_mod; iii++) {
219         int ic = hash_table[jjj*i_max+iii];
220         value_sum += value_source[ic] /             Sums the values
              (double)four_to_the(                      from the source
                levmx-mesh_source.level[ic]             mesh, adjusting for
              );                                        relative cell sizes
221       }
222     }
223     value_remap[jc] += value_sum;
224 }
```

Figure 5.7 shows the performance improvement from the remap using the spatial perfect hash. There is a speedup due to the algorithm and then an additional parallel speedup running on the GPU for a total speedup of over 1,000 times faster. The parallel speedup on the GPU is made possible by the ease of the algorithm implementation on the GPU. Good parallel speedup should also be possible on the multi-core processor as well.

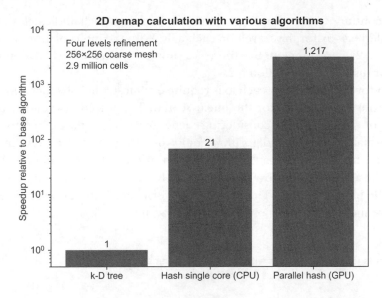

Figure 5.7 The speedup of the remap algorithm due to the change of the algorithm from a k-D tree to a hash on a single core of the CPU and then ported to the GPU for a parallel speedup.

TABLE LOOKUPS USING A SPATIAL PERFECT HASH

The operation of looking up values from tabular data presents a different kind of locality that can be exploited by a spatial hash. You can use hashing for searching for the intervals on both axes for the interpolation. For this example, we used a 51x23 lookup table of equation-of-state values. The two axes are density and temperature, with an equal spacing used between values on each axis. We will use n for the length of the axis and N for the number of table lookups that are to be performed. We used three algorithms in this study:

- The first is a linear search (brute force) starting at the first column and row. The brute force should be an $O(n)$ algorithm for each data query or for all N, $O(N * n)$, where n is the number of columns or rows, respectively, for each axis.
- The second is a bisection search that looks at the midpoint value of the possible range and recursively narrows the location for the interval. The bisection search should be an $O(\log n)$ algorithm for each data query.
- Finally, we used a hash to do an $O(1)$ lookup of the interval for each axis. We measured the performance of the hash on both a single core of a CPU and a GPU. The test code searches for the interval on both axes and a simple interpolation of the data values from the table to get the result.

Figure 5.8 shows the performance results for the different algorithms. The results have some surprises. The bisection search is no faster than the brute force (linear search) despite being an $O(N \log n)$ algorithm instead of an $O(N * n)$ algorithm. This seems to be contrary to the simple performance model, which indicates that the speedup should be 4–5x for the search on each axis. With the interpolation, we'd still expect around a 2x improvement. But there is a simple explanation, which you might guess from our discussions in section 5.2.

The search for the interval on each axis requires, at most, only two cache loads on one axis and four on the other for the linear search! The bisection would need the same number of cache loads. By considering cache loads, we would expect no difference in performance. The hash algorithm could directly go to the correct interval, but it would still need a cache load. The reduction in cache loads would be about a factor of 3x. The additional improvement is probably due to the reduction in the conditionals for the hash algorithm. The observed performance is in line with the expectations once we include the effect of the cache hierarchy.

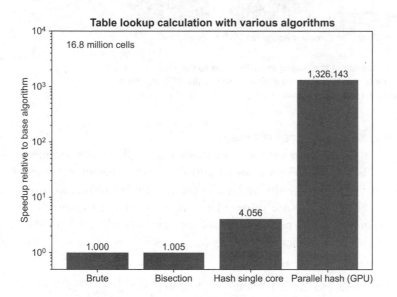

Figure 5.8   The algorithms used for table lookup show a large speedup for the hash algorithm on the GPU.

Porting the algorithm to the GPU is a bit more involved and shows what performance enhancements are possible in the process. To understand what was done, let's first look at the hash implementation on the CPU in listing 5.9. The code loops over all of the 16 million values, finding the intervals on each axis, and then interpolates the data in the table to get the resulting value. By using the hashing technique, we can find the interval locations by using a simple arithmetic expression with no conditionals.

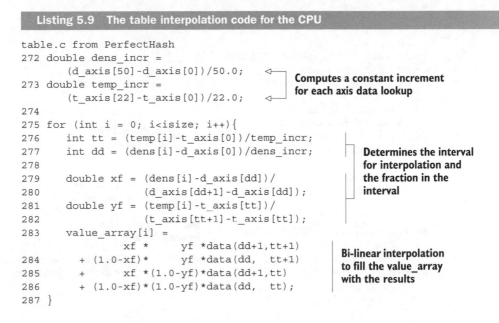

We could simply port this to the GPU as was done in the earlier cases by removing the for loop and replacing it with a call to get_global_id. But the GPU has a small local memory cache that is shared by each work group, which can hold about 4,000 double-precision values. We have 1,173 values in the table and 51+23 axis values. These can fit in the local memory cache that can be accessed quickly and shared among all the threads in the workgroup. The code in listing 5.10 shows how this is done. The first part of the code cooperatively loads the data values into local memory using all of the threads. A synchronization is then required to guarantee that all the data is loaded before moving on to the interpolation kernel. The remaining code looks much the same as the code for the CPU in listing 5.9.

Listing 5.10   The table interpolation code in OpenCL for the GPU

```
table_kern.cl from PerfectHash
45 #define dataval(x,y) data[(x)+((y)*xstride)]
46
47 __kernel void interpolate_kernel(
48    const uint isize,
49    const uint xaxis_size,
50    const uint yaxis_size,
51    const uint dsize,
52    __global const double *xaxis_buffer,
53    __global const double *yaxis_buffer,
54    __global const double *data_buffer,
55    __local        double *xaxis,
56    __local        double *yaxis,
57    __local        double *data,
58    __global const double *x_array,
59    __global const double *y_array,
```

```
60      __global        double *value
61      )
62 ·{
63      const uint tid = get_local_id(0);
64      const uint wgs = get_local_size(0);
65      const uint gid = get_global_id(0);
66
67      if (tid < xaxis_size)
            xaxis[tid]=xaxis_buffer[tid];        ◁─┐  Loads the axis
68      if (tid < yaxis_size)                       │  data values
            yaxis[tid]=yaxis_buffer[tid];        ◁─┘
69
70      for (uint wid = tid; wid<d_size; wid+=wgs){   │ Loads the
71         data[wid] = data_buffer[wid];              │ data table
72      }
73
74      barrier(CLK_LOCAL_MEM_FENCE);   ◁─┤ Needs to synchronize
75                                         before table queries
76      double x_incr = (xaxis[50]-xaxis[0])/50.0;    │ Computes a constant increment
77      double y_incr = (yaxis[22]-yaxis[0])/22.0;    │ for each axis data lookup
78
79      int xstride = 51;
80
81      if (gid < isize) {
82         double xdata = x_array[gid];    │ Loads the next
83         double ydata = y_array[gid];    │ data value
84
85         int is = (int)((xdata-xaxis[0])/x_incr);
86         int js = (int)((ydata-yaxis[0])/y_incr);   │ Determines the interval
87         double xf = (xdata-xaxis[is])/             │ for interpolation and the
                        (xaxis[is+1]-xaxis[is]);       │ fraction in the interval
88         double yf = (ydata-yaxis[js])/
                        (yaxis[js+1]-yaxis[js]);
89
90         value[gid] =
                   xf *      yf *dataval(is+1,js+1)
91          + (1.0-xf)*      yf *dataval(is,  js+1)   │ Bi-linear
92          +      xf *(1.0-yf)*dataval(is+1,js)      │ interpolation
93          + (1.0-xf)*(1.0-yf)*dataval(is,  js);
94      }
95 }
```

The performance result for the GPU hash code shows the impact of this optimization with a larger speedup than from the single core CPU performance for the other kernels.

SORTING MESH DATA USING A SPATIAL PERFECT HASH

The sort operation is one of the most studied algorithms and forms the basis for many other operations. In this section, we look at the special case of sorting spatial data. You can use a spatial sort to find the nearest neighbors, eliminate duplicates, simplify range finding, graphics output, and a host of other operations.

For simplicity, we'll work with 1D data with a minimum cell size of 2.0. All cells must be a power of two larger than the minimum cell size. The test case allows up to four levels of coarsening, in addition to the minimum cell size for the following possibilities: 2.0, 4.0, 8.0, 16.0, and 32.0. Cell sizes are randomly generated, and the cells randomly ordered. The sort is performed with a quicksort and then with a hash sort on the CPU and the GPU. The calculation for the spatial hash sort exploits the information about the 1D data. We know the minimum and maximum value for X and the minimum cell size. With this information, we can calculate a bucket index that guarantees a perfect hash with

$$b_k = \left\lceil \frac{X_i - X_{min}}{\Delta_{min}} \right\rceil$$

where b_k is the bucket to place the entry, X_i is the x coordinate for the cell, X_{min} is the minimum value of X, and Δ_{min} is the minimum distance between any two adjacent values of X.

We can demonstrate the hash sort operation (figure 5.9). The minimum difference between values is 2.0, so the bucket size of 2 guarantees that there are no collisions. The minimum value is 0, so the bucket location can be calculated with $B_i = X_i / \Delta_{min} = X_i / 2.0$. We could store either the value or the index in the hash table. For example, 8, the first key, could be stored in bucket 4, or the original index location of 0 could also be stored. If the value is stored, we retrieve the 8 with hash[4]. If the index is stored, then we retrieve the value with keys[hash[4]]. Storing the index loca-

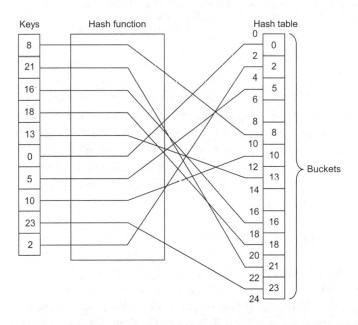

Figure 5.9 Sorting using a spatial perfect hash. This method stores the value in the hash with a bucket, but it could also store the index location of the value in the original array. Note that the bucket size of 2 with a range of 0 to 24 is indicated by the small numbers on the left of the hash table.

tion is a little slower in this case, but it is more general. It can also be used to reorder all the arrays in a mesh. In the test case for the performance study, we use the method of storing the index.

The spatial hash sort algorithm is $\Theta(N)$, while the quicksort is $\Theta(N \log N)$. But the spatial hash sort is more specialized to the problem at hand and can temporarily take more memory. The remaining questions are how difficult is this algorithm to write and how does it perform? The following listing shows the code for the write phase of the spatial hash implementation.

Listing 5.11   The spatial hash sort on the CPU

```
sort.c from PerfectHash
283 uint hash_size =
        (uint)((max_val - min_val)/min_diff);         Creates a hash table with
284 hash = (int*)malloc(hash_size*sizeof(int));        buckets of size min_diff
285 memset(hash, -1, hash_size*sizeof(int));   ◁
286                                                     Sets all the elements
287 for(uint i = 0; i < length; i++) {                 of hash array to –1
288     hash[(int)((arr[i]-min_val)/min_diff)] = i;  ◁
289 }                                                   Places the index of
290                                                     current array element
291 int count=0;                                        into hash according to
292 for(uint i = 0; i < hash_size; i++) {   Sweeps     where the arr value goes
293     if(hash[i] >= 0) {                  through hash
294         sorted[count] = arr[hash[i]];   and puts set
295         count++;                        values in a
296     }                                   sorted array
297 }
298
299 free(hash);
```

Note that the code in the listing is barely more than a dozen lines. Compare this to a quicksort code that is five times as long and far more complicated.

Figure 5.10 shows the performance of the spatial sort on both a single core of the CPU and the GPU. As we shall see, the parallel implementation on the CPU and GPU takes some effort for good performance. The read phase of the algorithm needs a well implemented prefix sum so that the retrieval of the sorted values can be done in parallel. The prefix sum is an important pattern for many algorithms; we'll discuss it further in section 5.6.

The GPU implementation for this example uses a well implemented prefix sum, and the performance of the spatial hash sort is excellent as a result. In earlier tests with an array size of two million, this GPU sort was 3x faster than the fastest general GPU sort, and the serial CPU version was 4x faster than the standard quicksort. With current CPU architectures and a larger array size of 16 million, our spatial hash sort is shown to be nearly 6x faster (figure 5.10). It is remarkable that our sort written in two or three months is much faster than the current fastest reference sorts on the CPU and GPU, especially since the reference sorts are the results of decades of research and the effort of many researchers!

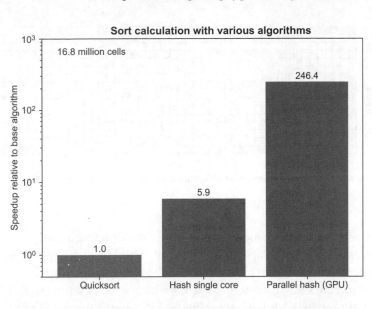

Figure 5.10 **Our spatial hash sort shows a speedup on a single core of the CPU and a further parallel speedup on the GPU. Our sort is 6x faster than the current fastest sort.**

5.5.2 *Using compact hashing for spatial mesh operations*

We are not done yet with exploring hashing methods. The algorithms in the perfect hashing section can be greatly improved. In the previous section, we explored using compact hashes for the neighbor finding and the remap operations. The key observations are that we don't need to write to every spatial hash bin, and we can improve the algorithms by handling collisions. This thereby allows the spatial hashes to be compressed and use less memory. This gives us more options on algorithm choice with different memory requirements and run times.

NEIGHBOR FINDING WITH WRITE OPTIMIZATIONS AND COMPACT HASHING

The previous simple perfect hash algorithm for finding neighbors performs well for small numbers of mesh refinement levels in an AMR mesh. But when there are six or more levels of refinement, a coarse cell writes to 64 hash buckets, and a fine cell only has to write to one, leading to a load imbalance and a problem with thread divergence for parallel implementations.

Thread divergence is when the amount of work for each thread varies and the threads end up waiting for the slowest. We can improve the perfect hash algorithm further with the optimizations shown in figure 5.11. The first optimization is realizing that the neighbor queries only sample the outer hash buckets of a cell, so there is no need to write to the interior. Further analysis shows that only the corners or midpoints of the cell's representation in the hash will be queried, reducing the needed writes even further. In the figure, the example shown to the far right of the sequence further

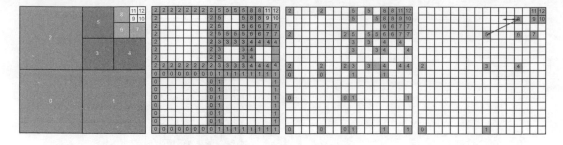

Figure 5.11   Optimizing the neighbor-finding calculation using the perfect spatial hash by reducing the number of writes and reads

optimizes the writes to only one per cell and does multiple reads where the entry exists for a finer, same size, or coarser neighbor cell. This last technique requires initializing the hash table to a sentinel value such as −1 to indicate no entry.

But now that less data is written to the hash, we have a lot of empty space, or sparsity, and can compress the hash table to as low as 1.25x times the number of entries, greatly reducing the memory requirements of the algorithm. The inverse of the size multiplier is known as the *hash load factor* and is defined as the number of filled hash table entries divided by the hash table size. For a 1.25 size multiplier, the hash load factor is 0.8. We typically use a much smaller load factor, typically around 0.333 or a size multiplier of 3. This is because in parallel processing, we want to avoid one processor being slower than the others. *Hash sparsity* represents the empty space in the hash. Sparsity indicates the opportunity for compression.

Figure 5.12 shows the process of creating a compact hash. Because of the compression to a compact hash, two entries try to store their value in bucket 1. The second

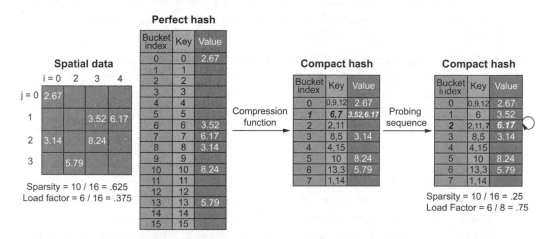

Figure 5.12   This sequence from left to right shows the storing of spatial data in a perfect spatial hash, compressing it into a smaller hash and then, where there is a collision, looking for the next available empty slot to store it.

entry sees that there is already a value there, so it looks for the next open slot in a technique called *open addressing*. In open addressing, we look for the next open slot in the hash table and store the value in that slot. There are other hashing methods than open addressing, but these often require the ability to allocate memory during an operation. Allocating memory is more difficult on the GPU, so we stick with open addressing where collisions are resolved by finding alternate storage locations within the already allocated hash table.

In open addressing, there are a few choices that we can use as the trial for the next open slot. These are

- *Linear probing*—Where the next entry is just the next bucket in sequence until an open bucket is found
- *Quadratic probing*—Where the increment is squared so that the attempted buckets are +1, +4, +9, and so forth from the original location
- *Double hashing*—Where a second hashing function is used to jump to a deterministic, but pseudo-random distance from the first trial location

The reason for the more complex choices for the next trial is to avoid clustering of values in part of the hash table, leading to longer store and query sequences. We use the quadratic probing method because the first couple of tries are in the cache, which leads to better performance. Once a slot is found, both the key and the value are stored. When reading the hash table, the stored key is compared to the read key, and if they aren't the same, then the read tries the next slot in the table.

We could make a performance estimate of the improvement of these optimizations by counting the number of writes and reads. But we need to adjust these write and read numbers to account for the number of cache lines and not just the raw number of values. Also, the code with the optimizations has more conditionals. Thus, the run-time improvement is modest and only better for higher levels of mesh refinement. The parallel code on the GPU shows more benefit because the thread divergence is reduced.

Figure 5.13 shows the measured performance results for the different hash table optimizations for a sample AMR mesh that has a relatively modest sparsity factor of 30. The code is available at https://github.com/lanl/CompactHash.git. The last performance numbers shown in figure 5.13 for both the CPU and GPU are for compact hash runs. The cost of the compact hash is offset by not having as much memory to initialize to the sentinel value of −1. The effect is that the compact hash has a competitive performance compared to the perfect hashing methods. With more sparsity in the hash table than the 30x compression factor in this test case, the compact hash can even be faster than the perfect hash methods. Cell-based AMR methods in general should have at least a 10x compression and can often exceed 100x.

These hashing methods have been implemented in the CLAMR mini-app. The code switches between a perfect hash algorithm for low levels of sparsity and the compact hash when there is a lot of empty space in the hash.

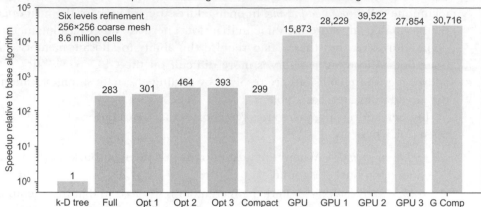

Figure 5.13 **The optimized versions shown for the CPU and GPU correspond to the methods shown in figure 5.11. Compact is the CPU compact, and G Comp is the GPU compact for the last method in each set. The compact method is faster than the original perfect hash, requiring considerably less memory. At higher levels of refinement, the methods that reduce the number of writes show some performance benefit as well.**

FACE NEIGHBOR FINDING FOR UNSTRUCTURED MESHES

So far, we haven't discussed algorithms for unstructured meshes because it's hard to guarantee that a perfect hash can easily be created for these. The most practical methods require a way to handle collisions and, thus, compact hashing techniques. Let's explore one case where the use of a hash is fairly straightforward. Finding the neighbor face for a polygonal mesh can be an expensive search procedure. Many unstructured codes store the neighbor map because it is so expensive. The technique we show next is so fast that the neighbor map can be calculated on the fly.

Example: Finding the face neighbor for an unstructured mesh

The following figure presents a small part of an unstructured mesh with polygonal cells. One of the computational challenges for this type of mesh is to find the connectivity map for each face of the polygons. A brute force search of every other element seems reasonable for small numbers of polygons, but for larger numbers of cells, this can soon take minutes or hours. A k-D tree search reduces the time, but is there an even faster way? Let's try a hash-based method instead. We overlay the figure on top of the hash table to the right of the figure. The algorithm is as follows:

- We place a dot for the center of each face in the hash bucket where it falls.
- Every cell writes its cell number into the bin at the center of each face. If the face is to the left and up from the center, it writes its index to the first of two places in the bin; otherwise, it writes to the second place.
- Every cell checks for each face to see if there is a number in the other bucket. If there is, it is the neighbor cell. If not, it is an external face with no neighbor.

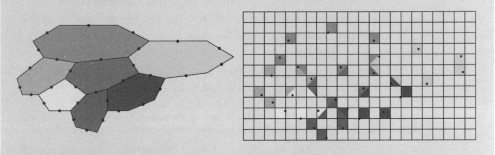

We have found our neighbors in a single write and single read!

Finding the neighbor for each face of each cell using a spatial hash. Each face writes to one of two bins in the spatial hash. If the face is towards the left and up from center, it writes to the first bin. If towards the right and down, it writes to the second. In the read pass, it looks to see if the other bin has been filled and if it is, that cell number is its neighbor. (Graphic and algorithm courtesy of Rachel Robey.)

The proper size of the hash table is difficult to specify. The best solution is to pick a reasonable size based on the number of faces or the minimum face length and then handle collisions if these occur.

REMAPS WITH WRITE OPTIMIZATIONS AND COMPACT HASHING

Another operation, the remap, is a little more difficult to optimize and set up for a compact hash because the perfect hash approach reads all the underlying cells. First, we have to come up with a way that doesn't require every hash bucket to be filled.

We write the cell indices for each cell to the lower left corner of the underlying hash. Then, during the read, if a value is not found or the level of the cell in the input mesh is not correct, we look for where a cell in the input mesh would write if it were at the next coarser level. Figure 5.14 shows this approach, where cell 1 in the output mesh queries the hash location (0,2) and finds a –1, so it then looks for where the next coarser cell would be at (0,0) and finds the cell index of 1. The density of cell 1

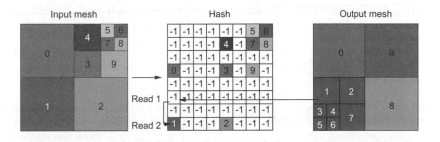

Figure 5.14 A single write, multiple read implementation of a spatial hash remap. The first query is where a cell of the same size from the input mesh would write, and then if no value is found, the next query looks for where a cell at the next coarser level would write.

in the output mesh is then set to the density of cell 1 in the input mesh. For cell 9 in the output mesh, it looks in the hash at (4,4) and finds an input cell index of 3. It then looks up the level of cell 3 in the input mesh, and because the input mesh cell level is finer, it must also query hash locations (6,4) to get the cell index of 9 and location (4,6), which returns cell index 4 and location (6,6) to get cell index of 7. The first two cell indices are at the same level, so these do not need to go any further. The cell index of 7 is at a finer level, so we must recursively descend into that location to find cell indices of 8, 5, and 6. Listing 5.12 shows the code.

Listing 5.12 The setup phase for the single-write spatial hash remap on the CPU

```
singlewrite_remap.cc and meshgen.cc from CompactHashRemap/AMR_remap
47 #define two_to_the(ishift)      (1u <<(ishift) )        ◁  Defines 2n power
48                                                             function as the shift
49 typedef struct {                    ◁  Structure to hold     operator for speed
50     uint ncells;                       characteristics of a mesh
51     uint ibasesize;      ◁
52     uint levmax;         ◁  Number of cells
53     uint *dist;             in the mesh
54     uint *i;
55     uint *j;             Number of coarse cells
56     uint *level;         across the x-dimension
57     double *values;
58 } cell_list;            Number of refinement levels
59                          in addition to the base mesh
60 cell_list icells, ocells;        ◁
61                                      Sets up input
                                        and output
<... lots of code to create mesh ...>   ◁  meshes


120 size_t hash_size = icells.ibasesize*two_to_the(icells.levmax)*
121                    icells.ibasesize*two_to_the(icells.levmax);
122 int *hash = (int *) malloc(hash_size *           Allocates the hash table
                         sizeof(int));               for a perfect hash
123 uint i_max = icells.ibasesize*two_to_the(icells.levmax);
```

Distribution of cells across levels of refinement → (line 53)

Before the write, a perfect hash table is allocated and initialized to the sentinel value of −1 (figure 5.10). Then the cell indices from the input mesh are written to the hash (listing 5.13). The code is available at https://github.com/lanl/CompactHashRemap .git in the file AMR_remap/singlewrite_remap.cc, along with variants for using a compact hash table and OpenMP. The OpenCL version for the GPU is in AMR_remap/ h_remap_kern.cl.

Listing 5.13 The write phase for the single-write spatial hash remap on the CPU

```
AMR_remap/singlewrite_remap.cc from CompactHashRemap     The actual read part of the
127 for (uint i = 0; i < icells.ncells; i++) {           hash write is just four lines.
128     uint lev_mod =
            two_to_the(icells.levmax -           The multiplier to convert
                 icells.level[i]);               between mesh levels
```

```
129      hash[((icells.j[i] * lev_mod) * i_max)      | Computes the index
             + (icells.i[i] * lev_mod)] = i;         | for the ID hash table
130 }
```

The code for the read phase (listing 5.14) has an interesting structure. The first part is basically split into two cases: the cell at the same location in the input mesh is the same level or coarser or it is a set of finer cells. In the first case, we loop up the levels until we find the right level and set the value in the output mesh to the value in the input mesh. If it is finer, we recurse down the levels, summing up the values as we go.

Listing 5.14   The read phase for the single-write spatial hash remap on the CPU

```
AMR_remap/singlewrite_remap.cc from CompactHashRemap
132 for (uint i = 0; i < ocells.ncells; i++) {
133      uint io = ocells.i[i];
134      uint jo = ocells.j[i];
135      uint lev = ocells.level[i];
136
137      uint lev_mod = two_to_the(ocells.levmax - lev);
138      uint ii = io*lev_mod;
139      uint ji = jo*lev_mod;
140
141      uint key = ji*i_max + ii;
142      int probe = hash[key];
144
145      if (lev > ocells.levmax){lev = ocells.levmax;}
146
147      while(probe < 0 && lev > 0) {      <--| If a sentinel value is found,
148          lev--;                            | continues to coarser levels
149          uint lev_diff = ocells.levmax - lev;
150          ii >>= lev_diff;
151          ii <<= lev_diff;
152          ji >>= lev_diff;
153          ji <<= lev_diff;                            | Because this is at the
154          key = ji*i_max + ii;                        | same level or coarser,
155          probe = hash[key];                          | sets the value of the
156      }                                               | found cell ID in the
157      if (lev >= icells.level[probe]) {               | input mesh
158          ocells.values[i] = icells.values[probe]; <--|
159      } else {
160          ocells.values[i] =                    | For finer cells, recursively
                 avg_sub_cells(icells, ji, ii,      | descends and sums the
                            lev, hash);             | contributors
161      }
162 }
163 double avg_sub_cells (cell_list icells, uint ji, uint ii,
             uint level, int *hash) {
164      uint key, i_max, jump;
165      double sum = 0.0;
166      i_max = icells.ibasesize*two_to_the(icells.levmax);
167      jump = two_to_the(icells.levmax - level - 1);
168
169      for (int j = 0; j < 2; j++) {
170          for (int i = 0; i < 2; i++) {
```

```
171              key = ((ji + (j*jump)) * i_max) + (ii + (i*jump));
172              int ic = hash[key];
173              if (icells.level[ic] == (level + 1)) {          Accumulates to
174                  sum += icells.values[ic];              ◁        the new value
175              } else {
176                  sum += avg_sub_cells(icells, ji + (j*jump),
                         ii + (i*jump), level+1, hash);       ◁
177              }                                                Recursively
178          }                                                   descends
179      }                                                       again
180
181      return sum/4.0;
182 }
```

Ok, this seems fine for the CPU, but how is it going to work on the GPU? Supposedly, recursion is not supported on the GPU. There doesn't seem to be any easy way to write this without recursion. But we tested it on the GPU and found that it works. It runs fine on all of the GPUs that we tried for the limited number of levels of refinement that will be used in any practical mesh. Evidently, a limited amount of recursion works on a GPU! We then implemented compact hash versions of this approach and these show good performance.

HIERARCHICAL HASH TECHNIQUE FOR THE REMAP OPERATION

Another innovative approach to using hashing for a remap operation involves a hierarchical set of hashes and a "breadcrumb" technique. A breadcrumb trail of sentinel values has the benefit that we do not need to initialize the hash tables to a sentinel value at the start (figure 5.15).

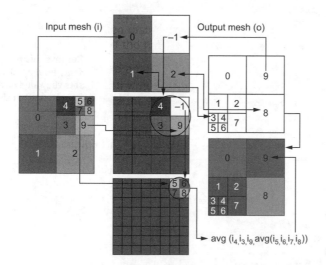

Figure 5.15 A hierarchical hash table with a separate hash for each level. When a write is done in one of the finer levels, a sentinel value is placed in each level above to form a "breadcrumb" trail to inform queries that there is data at finer levels.

The first step is to allocate a hash table for each level of the mesh. Then the cell indices are written to the appropriate level hash and recurse upward through the coarser hashes, leaving a sentinel value so that queries know there are values in the finer-level hash tables. Looking at figure 5.15 for cell 9 in the input mesh, we see that

- The cell index is written to the mid-level hash table, then a sentinel value is written to the hash bins in the coarser hash table.
- The read operation for cell 9 first goes to the coarsest level of the hash table, where it finds a sentinel value of -1. It now knows that it must go to the finer levels.
- It finds three cells at the mid-level hash table and another sentinel value to tell the read operation to recursively descend to the finest level, where it finds four more values to add to the summation.
- The other queries are all found in the coarsest hash table, and the values assigned to the output mesh.

Each of the hash tables can be either a perfect hash or a compact hash. The method has a recursive structure, similar to the previous technique. It also runs fine on GPUs.

5.6 Prefix sum (scan) pattern and its importance in parallel computing

The prefix sum was a critical element of making the hash sort work in parallel in section 5.5.1. The prefix sum operation, also known as a scan, is a common operation in computations with irregular sizes. Many computations with irregular sizes need to know where to start writing to be able to operate in parallel. A simple example is where each processor has a different number of particles. To be able to write to the output array or access data on other processors or threads, each processor needs to know the relationship of the local indices to the global indices. In the prefix sum, the output array, y, is a running sum of all of the numbers previous to it in the original array:

$$y_j = \sum_{i=0}^{j-1} x_i$$

The prefix sum can either be an inclusive scan, where the current value is included, or an exclusive scan, where it isn't included. The previous equation is for an exclusive scan. Figure 5.16 shows both an exclusive and an inclusive scan. The exclusive scan is the starting index for the global array, while the inclusive scan is the ending index for each process or thread.

The following listing shows the standard serial code for the scan operation.

x	3	4	6	3	8	7	5	4	
y	0	3	7	13	16	24	31	36	Exclusive scan
y	3	7	13	16	24	31	36	40	Inclusive scan

Figure 5.16   The array x gives the number of particles in each cell. The exclusive and inclusive scan of an array gives the starting and ending address in the global data set.

Listing 5.15   The serial inclusive scan operation

```
1 y[0] = x[0];
2 for (int i=1; i<n; i++){
3    y[i] = y[i-1] + x[i];
4 }
```

Once the scan operation is complete, each process is free to perform its operation in parallel because the process knows where to put its result. The scan operation itself, though, appears to be intrinsically serial. Each iteration is dependent on the previous. But there are effective ways to parallelize it. We'll look at a step-efficient, a work-efficient, and a large array algorithm in this section.

5.6.1   *Step-efficient parallel scan operation*

A step-efficient algorithm uses the fewest number of steps. But this might not be the fewest number of operations because a different number of operations is possible with each step. This was discussed earlier when defining computational complexity in section 5.1.

The prefix sum operation can be made parallel with a tree-based reduction pattern as figure 5.17 shows. Rather than waiting for the previous element to sum up its values, each element sums its value and the preceding value. Then it does the same operation, but with the value two elements over, four elements over, and so on. The end result is an inclusive scan; during the operation all of the processes have been busy.

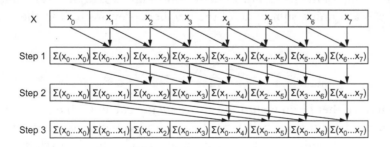

Figure 5.17   The step-efficient inclusive scan uses $O(\log_2 n)$ steps to compute a prefix sum in parallel.

Now we have a parallel prefix that operates in just $\log_2 n$ steps, but the amount of work increases from the serial algorithm. Can we design a parallel algorithm that has the same amount of work?

5.6.2 Work-efficient parallel scan operation

A work-efficient algorithm uses the least number of operations. This might not be the fewest number of steps because a different number of operations is possible with each step. The choice of a work-efficient or a step-efficient algorithm is dependent on the number of parallel processes that can exist.

The work-efficient parallel scan operation uses two sweeps through the arrays. The first sweep is called an upsweep, though it is more of a right sweep. It is shown in figure 5.18 from top to bottom, rather than the traditional bottom to top for easier comparison to the step-efficient algorithm.

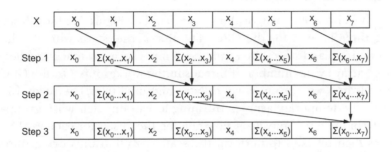

Figure 5.18 The upsweep phase of the work-efficient scan shown from top to bottom, which has far fewer operations than the step-efficient scan. Essentially, every other value is left unmodified.

The second phase, known as the downsweep phase, is more of a left sweep. It starts by setting the last value to zero and then does another tree-based sweep (figure 5.19) to get the final result. The amount of work is reduced significantly, but with the requirement of more steps.

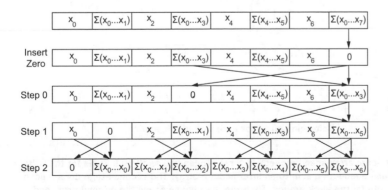

Figure 5.19 The downsweep phase of the work-efficient exclusive scan operation has far fewer operations than the step-efficient scan.

When shown this way, the work-efficient scan has an interesting pattern, with a right sweep starting with half the threads and decreasing until only one is operating. Then it begins a sweep back to the left with one thread at the start and finishing with all threads busy. The additional steps allow the earlier calculations to be reused so that the total operations are only $O(N)$.

These two parallel prefix sum algorithms give us a couple of different options on how to incorporate parallelism in this essential operation. But both of these are limited to the number of threads available in a workgroup on the GPU or the number of processors on a CPU.

5.6.3   *Parallel scan operations for large arrays*

For larger arrays, we also need an algorithm that is parallel. Figure 5.20 shows such an algorithm using three kernels for the GPU. The first kernel starts with a reduction sum on each workgroup and stores the result in a temporary array that is smaller than the original large array by the number of threads in the workgroup. On the GPU, the number of threads in a workgroup is typically as high as 1,024. The second kernel then loops across the temporary array performing a scan on each work group-sized block. This results in the temporary array now holding the offsets for each work group. A third kernel is then invoked to perform the scan operation on work group-sized chunks of the original array, and an offset calculated for each thread at this level.

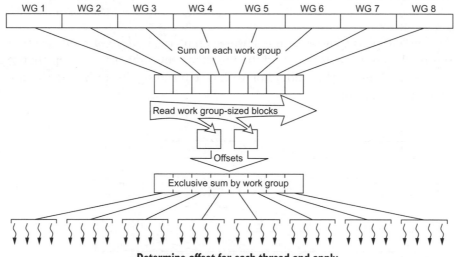

Determine offset for each thread and apply

Figure 5.20   The large array scan proceeds in three stages and as three kernels for the GPU. The first stage does a reduction sum to an intermediate array. The second stage does a scan to create the offsets for the work groups. Then the third phase scans the original array and applies the work group offsets to get the scan results for each element of the array.

Because the parallel prefix sum is so important in operations like sorts, it is heavily optimized for GPU architectures. We don't go into that level of detail in this book. Instead, we suggest that application developers use libraries or freely available implementations for their work. For the parallel prefix scan available for CUDA, you'll find implementations such as the CUDA Data Parallel Primitives Library (CUDPP), available at https://github.com/cudpp/cudpp. For OpenCL, we suggest either the implementation from its parallel primitives library, CLPP, or the scan implementation from our hash-sorting code available in the sort_kern.cl file at https://github.com/LANL/PerfectHash.git. We'll present a version of the prefix scan for OpenMP in chapter 7.

5.7 Parallel global sum: Addressing the problem of associativity

Not all parallel algorithms are about speeding up calculations. The global sum is a prime example of such a case. Parallel computing has been plagued since the earliest days with the non-reproducibility of sums across processors. In this section, we show one example of an algorithm that improves the reproducibility of a parallel calculation so that it gets nearer to the results of the original serial calculation.

Changing the order of additions changes the answer in finite-precision arithmetic. This is problematic because a parallel calculation changes the order of the additions. The problem is due to finite-precision arithmetic not being associative. And the problem gets worse as the problem size gets larger because the addition of the last value becomes a smaller and smaller part of the overall sum. Eventually the addition of the last value might not change the sum at all. There is even a worse case for additions of finite-precision values when adding two values that are almost identical, but of different signs. This subtraction of one value from another when these are nearly the same causes a *catastrophic cancellation*. The result is only a few significant digits with noise filling the rest.

Example: Catastrophic cancellation

The subtraction of two nearly similar values will have a result with only a small number of significant figures. Put the following code in a file called catastrophic.py and run the program with `python catastrophic.py`.

Catastrophic cancellation in a short Python code

```
x = 12.15692174374373 - 12.15692174374372
print x          ◁──── Returns
                       1.06581410364e-14
```

The result in the example has only a couple of significant digits left! And where do the rest of the digits in the printed value come from? The problem in parallel computing is that instead of the sum being a linear addition of the values in the array, on two processors the sum is a linear sum of half of the array and then the two partial sums added at the end. The change in the order causes the global sum to be different. The difference can be small, but now the question is whether the parallelization of the code has been done properly. Exacerbating the problem is that all of the new parallelization techniques and hardware, such as vectorization and threads, also cause this problem. The pattern for this global sum operation is called a reduction.

DEFINITION   A *reduction* is an operation where an array of one or more dimensions is reduced to at least one dimension less and often to a scalar value.

This operation is one of the most common in parallel computing and is often a concern for performance, and in this case, correctness. An example of this is calculating the total mass or energy in a problem. This takes a global array of the mass in each cell and results in a single scalar value.

As with all computer calculations, the results of the global sum reduction are not exact. In serial calculations, this does not pose a serious problem because we always get the same inexact result. In parallel, we most likely get a more accurate result with more correct significant digits, but it is different than the serial result. This is known as the *global sum issue*. Anytime the results between the serial and parallel versions were slightly different, the cause was attributed to this problem. But often, when time was taken to dig more deeply into the code, the problem turned out to be a subtle parallel programming error such as failing to update the ghost cells between processors. *Ghost cells* are cells that hold the adjacent processor values needed by the local processor, and if they are not updated, the slightly older values cause a small error compared to the serial run.

For years, I thought, like other parallel programmers, that the only solution was to sort the data into a fixed order and sum it up in a serial operation. But because this was too expensive, we just lived with the problem. In about 2010, several parallel programmers, including myself, realized that we were looking at the problem wrong. It is not solely an order problem, but also a precision problem. In real number arithmetic, addition is associative! So adding precision is also a way to solve the problem and at a far lower cost than sorting the data.

To gain a better understanding of the problem and how to solve it, let's take a look at a problem from compressible fluid dynamics called the Leblanc problem, also known as "the shock tube from hell." In the Leblanc problem, a high pressure region is separated from a low pressure region by a diaphragm that is removed at time zero. It is a challenging problem because of the strong shock that results. But the feature we are most interested in is the large dynamic range in both the density and energy variables. We'll use the energy variable with a high value at $1.0e{-}1$ and a low value of $1.0e{-}10$. The *dynamic range* is the range of the working set of real numbers, or in this case, the ratio of the maximum and the minimum values. The dynamic range is nine orders of magnitude, which means that when adding the small value to the large value for double-precision, floating-point numbers with about 16 significant digits, in reality, we only have about 7 significant digits in the result.

Let's look at a problem size of 134,217,728 on a single processor with half the values at the high energy state and the other half at the low energy state. These two regions are separated by a diaphragm at the beginning of the problem. The problem size is large for a single processor, but for a parallel computation, it is relatively small. If the high energy values are summed first, the next single low value that is added will have few significant digits to contribute. Reversing the order of the sum so that the low energy values are summed first makes the small values of near equal size in their sum, and by the time the high energy value is added, there will be more significant digits, thus a more accurate sum. This gives us a possible sorting-based solution. Just sort the values in order from the lowest magnitude to the highest and you will get a more accurate sum. There are several solutions for addressing the global sum that are much more tractable than the sorting technique. The list of possible techniques presented here includes

- Long-double data type
- Pairwise summation
- Kahan summation
- Knuth summation
- Quad-precision summation

You can try the various methods in the exercises that accompany the chapter at https://github.com/EssentialsOfParallelComputing/Chapter5.git. The original study looked at parallel OpenMP implementations and truncation techniques that we won't go into here.

The easiest solution is to use the long-double data type on a x86 architecture. On this architecture, a long-double is implemented as an 80-bit floating-point number in hardware giving an extra 16-bits of precision. Unfortunately, this is not a portable technique. The long double on some architectures and compilers is only 64-bits, and on others it's 128-bits and implemented in software. Some compilers also force rounding between operations to maintain consistency with other architectures. Check your compiler documentation carefully on how it implements a long-double when using this technique. The code shown in the next listing is simply a regular sum with the data type of the accumulator set to long double.

> ### Listing 5.16   Long-double data type sum on x86 architectures

GlobalSums/do_ldsum.c
```
1 double do_ldsum(double *var, long ncells)
2 {
3     long double ldsum = 0.0;
4     for (long i = 0; i < ncells; i++){
5         ldsum += (long double)var[i];        ◁── var is an array of doubles, while the accumulator is a long double.
6     }
7     double dsum = ldsum;        ◁────────── The return type of the function
8     return(dsum);        ◁── Returns    can also be long double and the
9 }                              a double   value of ldsum returned.
```

At line 8 in the listing, a double is returned to stay consistent with the concept of a higher precision accumulator returning the same data type as the array. We see how this performs later, but first let's cover the other methods for addressing the global sum.

The pairwise summation is a surprisingly simple solution to the global sum problem, especially within a single processor. The code is relatively straightforward as the following listing shows but requires an additional array half the size of the original.

Listing 5.17 Pairwise summation on processor

```
GlobalSums/do_pair_sum.c
 4 double do_pair_sum(double *var, long ncells)
 5 {
 6     double *pwsum =
         (double *)malloc(ncells/2*sizeof(double));       ⟵  Needs temporary space
                                                              to do the pairwise
 7                                                            recursive sums
 8     long nmax = ncells/2;
 9     for (long i = 0; i<nmax; i++){                       Adds the initial
10         pwsum[i] = var[i*2]+var[i*2+1];                 pairwise sum into
11     }                                                    new array
12
13     for (long j = 1; j<log2(ncells); j++){
14         nmax /= 2;                                      Recursively sums the
15         for (long i = 0; i<nmax; i++){                  remaining log₂ steps,
16             pwsum[i] = pwsum[i*2]+pwsum[i*2+1];         reducing array size by
17         }                                               two for each step
18     }
19     double dsum = pwsum[0];      ⟵
20     free(pwsum);          ⟵  Frees      Assigns the result
21     return(dsum);            temporary  to a scalar value
22 }                            space      for return
```

The simplicity of the pairwise summation becomes a little more complicated when working across processors. If the algorithm remains true to its basic structure, a communication may be needed at each step of the recursive sum.

Next is the Kahan summation. The Kahan summation is the most practical method of the possible global sum methods. It uses an additional double variable to carry the remainder of the operation, in effect doubling the effective precision. The technique was developed by William Kahan in 1965 (Kahan later became one of the key contributors to the early IEEE floating-point standards). The Kahan summation is most appropriate for a running summation when the accumulator is the larger of two values. The following listing shows this technique.

Listing 5.18 Kahan summation

```
GlobalSums/do_kahan_sum.c
 1 double do_kahan_sum(double *var, long ncells)
 2 {
 3     struct esum_type{
 4         double sum;                    Declares a double-
 5         double correction;             double data type
 6     };
```

```
 7
 8    double corrected_next_term, new_sum;
 9    struct esum_type local;
10
11    local.sum = 0.0;
12    local.correction = 0.0;
13    for (long i = 0; i < ncells; i++) {
14       corrected_next_term = var[i] + local.correction;
15       new_sum            = local.sum + local.correction;
16       local.correction = corrected_next_term -
                             (new_sum - local.sum);
17       local.sum          = new_sum;
18    }
19
20    double dsum = local.sum + local.correction;
21    return(dsum);
22 }
```

(line 16) **Computes the remainder to carry to the next iteration**

(lines 20–21) **Returns the double-precision result**

The Kahan summation takes about four floating-point operations instead of one. But the data can be kept in registers or the L1 cache, making the operation less expensive than we might initially expect. Vectorized implementations can make the operation cost the same as the standard summation. This is an example where we use the excess floating-point capability of the processor to get a better answer.

We'll look at a vector implementation of the Kahan sum in section 6.3.4. Some new numerical methods are attempting a similar approach, using the excess floating-point capability of current processors. These view the current machine balance of 50 flops per data load as an opportunity and implement higher-order methods that require more floating-point operations to exploit the unused floating-point resource because it is essentially free.

The Knuth summation method handles additions where either term can be larger. The technique was developed by Donald Knuth in 1969. It collects the error for both terms at a cost of seven floating-point operations as the following listing shows.

> **Listing 5.19   Knuth summation**

GlobalSums/do_knuth_sum.c

```
 1 double do_knuth_sum(double *var, long ncells)
 2 {
 3    struct esum_type{
 4       double sum;
 5       double correction;
 6    };
 7
 8    double u, v, upt, up, vpp;
 9    struct esum_type local;
10
11    local.sum = 0.0;
12    local.correction = 0.0;
13    for (long i = 0; i < ncells; i++) {
14       u = local.sum;
15       v = var[i] + local.correction;
```

(lines 3–6) **Defines a double-double data type**

```
16      upt = u + v;
17      up = upt - v;            Carries the values
18      vpp = upt - up;          for each term
19      local.sum = upt;                              Combined into
20      local.correction = (u - up) + (v - vpp);      one correction
21   }
22
23   double dsum = local.sum + local.correction;      Returns the double-
24   return(dsum);                                     precision result
25 }
```

The last technique, the quad-precision sum, has the advantage of simplicity in coding, but because the quad-precision types are almost always done in software, it is expensive. Portability is also something to beware of as not all compilers have implemented the quad-precision type. The following listing presents this code.

Listing 5.20   Quad precision global sum

```
GlobalSums/do_qdsum.c
1 double do_qdsum(double *var, long ncells)
2 {
3     __float128 qdsum = 0.0;              Quad precision
4     for (long i = 0; i < ncells; i++){  data type
5        qdsum += (__float128)var[i];      Casts the input
6     }                                    value from array
7     double dsum =qdsum;                  to quad precision
8     return(dsum);
9 }
```

Now on to the assessment of how these different approaches work. Because half the values are 1.0e–1 and the other half are 1.0e–10, we can get an accurate answer to compare against by multiplying instead of adding:

```
accurate_answer = ncells/2 * 1.0e-1 + ncells/2 * 1.0e-10
```

Table 5.1 shows the results of comparing the global sum values actually obtained versus the accurate answer and measuring the run time. We essentially get nine digits of accuracy with a regular summation of doubles. The long double on a system with an 80-bit floating-point representation improves it somewhat, but doesn't completely eliminate the error. The pairwise, Kahan and Knuth summations all reduce the error to zero with a modest increase in run time. A vectorized implementation of the Kahan and Knuth summation (shown in section 6.3.4) eliminates the increase in run time. Even so, when considering cross-processor communications and the cost of MPI calls, the increase in run time is insignificant.

Now that we understand the behavior of the global sum techniques on a processor, we can consider the problem when the arrays are distributed across multiple processors. We need some understanding of MPI to tackle this problem, so we will show how to do this in section 8.3.3, after learning the basics of MPI.

Table 5.1 Precision and run-time results for various global sum techniques

Method	Error	Run time
Double	–1.99e–09	0.116
Long double	–1.31e–13	0.118
Pairwise summation	0.0	0.402
Kahan summation	0.0	0.406
Knuth summation	0.0	0.704
Quad double	5.55e–17	3.010

5.8 Future of parallel algorithm research

We have seen some of the characteristics of parallel algorithms including those suitable for extremely parallel architectures. Let's summarize these so that we can look for them in other situations:

- *Locality*—Often-used term in describing good algorithms but without any definition. It can have multiple meanings. Here are a couple:
  - *Locality for cache*—Keeps the values that will be used together close together so that cache utilization is improved.
  - *Locality for operations*—Avoids operating on all the data when not all is needed. The spatial hash for particle interactions is a classic example that keeps an algorithm's complexity $O(N)$ instead of $O(N^2)$.
- *Asynchronous*—Avoids coordination between threads that can cause synchronization.
- *Fewer conditionals*—Besides the additional performance hit from conditional logic, thread divergence can be a problem on some architectures.
- *Reproducibility*—Often a highly parallel technique violates the lack of associativity of finite-precision arithmetic. Enhanced-precision techniques can help counter this issue.
- *Higher arithmetic intensity*—Current architectures have added floating-point capability faster than memory bandwidth. Algorithms that increase arithmetic intensity can make good use of parallelism such as the vector operations.

5.9 Further explorations

The development of parallel algorithms is still a young field of research, and there are many new algorithms to be discovered. But there are also many known techniques that have not been widely disseminated or used. Particularly challenging is that the algorithms are often in wildly different fields of computer or computational science.

5.9.1   *Additional reading*

For more on algorithms, we recommend a popular textbook:

> Thomas Cormen, et al., *Introduction to Algorithms*, 3rd ed (MIT Press, 2009).

For more information on patterns and algorithms, here are two good books for further reading:

- Michael McCool, Arch D. Robison, and James Reinders, *Structured Parallel Programming: Patterns for Efficient Computation* (Morgan Kaufmann, 2012).
- Timothy G. Mattson, Beverly A. Sanders, and Berna L. Massingill, *Patterns for Parallel Programming* (Addison-Wesley, 2004).

The concepts of spatial hashing have been developed by some of my students ranging from high school level through graduate students. The section on perfect hashing in the following resource draws from work by Rachel Robey and David Nicholaeff. David also implemented spatial hashing in the CLAMR mini-app.

> Rachel N. Robey, David Nicholaeff, and Robert W. Robey, "Hash-based algorithms for discretized data," *SIAM Journal on Scientific Computing* 35, no. 4 (2013): C346–C368.

The ideas for parallel compact hashing for neighbor finding came from Rebecka Tumblin, Peter Ahrens, and Sara Hartse. These were built from the methods to reduce the writes and reads developed by David Nicholaeff.

> Rebecka Tumblin, Peter Ahrens, et al., "Parallel compact hash algorithms for computational meshes," *SIAM Journal on Scientific Computing* 37, no. 1 (2015): C31–C53.

Developing optimized methods for the remap operation was much more challenging. Gerald Collom and Colin Redman tackled the problem and came up with some really innovative techniques and implementations on the GPU and in OpenMP. This chapter only touches on some of these. There are far more ideas in their paper:

> Gerald Collom, Colin Redman, and Robert W. Robey, "Fast Mesh-to-Mesh Remaps Using Hash Algorithms," *SIAM Journal on Scientific Computing* 40, no. 4 (2018): C450–C476.

I first developed the concept of enhanced-precision global sums in about 2010. Jonathan Robey implemented the technique in his Sapient hydrocode and Rob Aulwes, Los Alamos National Laboratory, helped develop the theoretical foundations. The following two references give more details on the method:

- Robert W. Robey, Jonathan M. Robey, and Rob Aulwes, "In search of numerical consistency in parallel programming," *Parallel Computing* 37, no. 4–5 (2011): 217–229.

- Robert W. Robey, "Computational Reproducibility in Production Physics Applications," Numerical Reproducibility at Exascale Workshop (NRE2015), International Conference for High Performance Computing, Networking, Storage and Analysis, 2015. Available at https://github.com/lanl/ExascaleDocs/blob/master/ComputationalReproducibilityNRE2015.pdf

5.9.2   Exercises

1   A cloud collision model in an ash plume is invoked for particles within a 1 mm distance. Write pseudocode for a spatial hash implementation. What complexity order is this operation?

2   How are spatial hashes used by the postal service?

3   Big data uses a map-reduce algorithm for efficient processing of large data sets. How is it different than the hashing concepts presented here?

4   A wave simulation code uses an AMR mesh to better refine the shoreline. The simulation requirements are to record the wave heights versus time for specified locations where buoys and shore facilities are located. Because the cells are constantly being refined, how could you implement this?

Summary

- Algorithms and patterns are one of the foundations of computational applications. Selecting algorithms that have low computational complexity and lend themselves to parallelization is important when first developing an application.
- A comparison-based algorithm has a lower complexity limit of $O(N \log N)$. Non-comparison algorithms can break this lower algorithmic limit.
- Hashing is a non-comparison technique that has been used in spatial hashing to achieve $\Theta(N)$ complexity for spatial operations.
- For any spatial operation, there is a spatial hashing algorithm that scales as $O(N)$. In this chapter, we provide examples of techniques that can be used in many scenarios.
- Certain patterns have been shown to be adaptable to parallelism and the asynchronous nature of GPUs. The prefix scan and hashing techniques are two such patterns. The prefix scan is important for parallelizing irregular-sized arrays. Hashing is a non-comparison, asynchronous algorithm that is highly scalable.
- Reproducibility is an important attribute in developing robust production applications. This is especially important for reproducible global sums and for dealing with finite-precision arithmetic operations that are not associative.
- Enhanced precision is a new technique that restores associativity, allowing reordering of operations, and thus, more parallelism.

Part 2

CPU: The parallel workhorse

Today, every developer should understand the growing parallelism available within modern CPU processors. Unlocking the untapped performance of CPUs is a critical skill for parallel and high performance computing applications. To show how to take advantage of CPU parallelism, we cover

- Using vector hardware
- Using threads for parallel work across multi-core processors
- Coordinating work on multiple CPUs and multi-core processors with message passing

The CPU's parallel capabilities need to be at the core of your parallel strategy. Because it's the central workhorse, the CPU controls all the memory allocations, memory movement, and communication. The application developer's knowledge and skill are the most important factors for fully using the CPU's parallelism. CPU optimization is not automatically done by some magic compiler. Commonly, many of the parallel resources on the CPU go untapped by applications. We can break down the available CPU parallelism into three components in increasing order of effort. These are

- *Vectorization*—Exploits the specialized hardware that can do more than one operation at a time
- *Multi-core and threading*—Spreads out work across the many processing cores in today's CPUs
- *Distributed memory*—Harnesses multiple nodes into a single, cooperative computing application

Thus, we begin with vectorization. Vectorization is a highly underused capability with notable gains when implemented. Though compilers can do some vectorization, compilers don't do enough. The limitations are especially noticeable for complicated code. Compilers are just not there yet. Although compilers are improving, there is not sufficient funding or manpower for this to happen quickly. Consequently, the application programmer has to help in a variety of ways. Unfortunately, there is little documentation on vectorization. In chapter 6, we present an introduction to the arcane knowledge of getting more from vectorization for your application.

With the explosion in processing cores on each CPU, the need and knowledge for exploiting on-node parallelism is growing rapidly. Two common CPU resources for this include threading and shared memory. There are dozens of different threading systems and shared memory approaches. In chapter 7, we present a guide to using OpenMP, the most commonly used threading package for high performance computing.

The dominant language for parallelism across nodes, and even within nodes, is the open source standard, the Message Passing Interface (MPI). The MPI standard grew out of a consolidation of many message-passing libraries from the early days of parallel programming. MPI is a well-designed language that has withstood the test of time and changes to hardware architectures. It has also adapted with new features and improvements that have been incorporated into its implementations. Still, most application programmers just use the most basic features of the language. In chapter 8, we give an introduction to the basics of MPI, as well as some advanced features that can be useful in many scientific and big data applications.

The key to getting high performance on the CPU is to pay attention to memory bandwidth, supplying the data to parallel engines. Good parallel performance begins with good serial performance (and an understanding of the topics presented in the first five chapters of this book). CPUs provide the most general parallelism for the widest variety of applications. From modest parallelism through extreme scale, the CPU often delivers the goods. The CPU is also where you must begin your journey into the parallel world. Even in solutions that use accelerators, the CPU remains an essential component in the system.

Up until now, the solution to increasing performance was to add more compute power in the form of physically adding more nodes to your cluster or high performance computer. The parallel and high performance computing community has gone as far as it can with that approach and is beginning to hit power and energy consumption limits. Additionally, the number of nodes and processors cannot continue to grow without running into the limitations of scaling applications. In response to this, we must turn to other avenues to improve performance. Within the processing node, there are a lot of underutilized parallel hardware capabilities. As we first mentioned in section 1.1, parallelism within the node will continue to grow.

Even with continuing limitations of compute power and other looming thresholds, key insights and knowledge of lesser-known tools can unlock substantial performance. Through this book and your studies, we can help tackle these challenges. In the end, your skills and knowledge are important commodities for unlocking the promises of parallel performance.

The examples that accompany the three chapters in part 2 of this book are at https://github.com/EssentialsofParallelComputing, with a separate repository for each chapter. Docker container builds for each chapter should install and work well on any operating system. The container builds for the first two chapters in this part (chapters 6 and 7) use a graphical interface to allow the use of performance and correctness tools.

Vectorization: FLOPs for free

6

This chapter covers

- The importance of vectorization
- The kind of parallelization provided by a vector unit
- Different ways you can access vector parallelization
- Performance benefits you can expect

Processors have special vector units that can load and operate on more than one data element at a time. If we're limited by floating-point operations, it is absolutely necessary to use vectorization to reach peak hardware capabilities. *Vectorization* is the process of grouping operations together so more than one can be done at a time. But, adding more flops to hardware capability when an application is memory bound has limited benefit. Take note, most applications are memory bound. Compilers can be powerful, but as you will see, real performance gain with vectorization might not be as easy as the compiler documentation suggests. Still, the performance gain from vectorization can be achieved with a little effort and should not be ignored.

In this chapter, we will show how programmers, with a little bit of effort and knowledge, can achieve a performance boost through vectorization. Some of these

175

techniques simply require the use of the right compiler flags and programming styles, while others require much more work. Real-world examples demonstrate the various ways vectorization is achieved.

> **NOTE**   We encourage you to follow along with the examples for this chapter at https://github.com/EssentialsofParallelComputing/Chapter6.

6.1   *Vectorization and single instruction, multiple data (SIMD) overview*

We introduced the single instruction, multiple data (SIMD) architecture in section 1.4 as one component of Flynn's Taxonomy. This taxonomy is used as a parallelization classification of instruction and data streams on an architecture. In the SIMD case, as the name indicates, there is a single instruction that is executed across multiple data streams. One vector add instruction replaces eight individual scalar add instructions in the instruction queue, which reduces the pressure on the instruction queue and cache. The biggest benefit is that it takes about the same power to perform eight additions in a vector unit as one scalar addition. Figure 6.1 shows a vector unit that has a 512-bit vector width, offering a vector length of eight double-precision values.

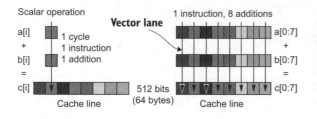

Figure 6.1   **A scalar operation does a single double-precision addition in one cycle. It takes eight cycles to process a 64-byte cache line. In comparison, a vector operation on a 512-bit vector unit can process all eight double-precision values in one cycle.**

Let's briefly summarize vectorization terminology:

- *Vector (SIMD) lane*—A pathway through a vector operation on vector registers for a single data element much like a lane on a multi-lane freeway.
- *Vector width*—The width of the vector unit, usually expressed in bits.
- *Vector length*—The number of data elements that can be processed by the vector in one operation.
- *Vector (SIMD) instruction sets*—The set of instructions that extend the regular scalar processor instructions to utilize the vector processor.

Vectorization is produced through both a software and a hardware component. The requirements are

- *Generate instructions*—The vector instructions must be generated by the compiler or manually specified through intrinsics or assembler coding.
- *Match instructions to the vector unit of the processor*—If there is a mismatch between the instructions and the hardware, newer hardware can usually process the

instructions, but older hardware will just fail to run. (AVX instructions do not run on ten-year-old chips. Sorry!)

There is no fancy process that converts regular scalar instructions on the fly. If you use an older version of your compiler, as many programmers do, it will not have the capability to generate the instructions for the latest hardware. Unfortunately, it takes time for compiler writers to include new hardware capabilities and instruction sets. It can also take a while for the compiler writers to optimize these capabilities.

> *Take away: When you use the latest processors, make sure to use the latest versions of the compiler.*

You should also specify the appropriate vector instruction set to generate. By default, most compilers take the safe route and generate SSE2 (Streaming SIMD Extensions) instructions so that the code works on any hardware. SSE2 instructions only execute two double-precision operations at a time instead of the four or eight operations that can be done on more recent processors. For performance applications, there are better choices:

- You can compile for the architecture you are running on.
- You can compile for any architecture manufactured within the last 5 or 10 years. Specifying AVX (Advanced Vector Extensions) instructions would give a 256-bit width vector and would run on any hardware since 2011.
- You can ask the compiler to generate more than one vector instruction set. It then falls back to the best one for the hardware being used.

> *Take away: Specify the most advanced vector instruction set in your compiler flags that you can reasonably use.*

6.2 *Hardware trends for vectorization*

To implement the choices discussed previously, it is helpful to know the historical dates of hardware and instruction set release for selecting which vector instruction set to use. Table 6.1 highlights the key releases, and figure 6.2 shows the trends in the vector unit size.

Table 6.1 The vector hardware releases over the last decade have dramatically improved vector functionality.

Release	Functionality
MMX (trademark with no official meaning)	Targeted towards the graphics market, but GPUs soon took over this function. Vector units shifted their focus to computation rather than graphics. AMD released its version under the name 3DNow! with single-precision support.
SSE (Streaming SIMD Extensions)	First Intel vector unit to offer floating-point operations with single-precision support
SSE2	Double-precision support added

Table 6.1   The vector hardware releases over the last decade have dramatically improved vector functionality. *(continued)*

Release	Functionality
AVX (Advanced Vector Extensions)	Twice the vector length. AMD added a fused multiply-add FMA vector instruction in its competing hardware, effectively doubling the performance for some loops.
AVX2	Intel added a fused multiply-add (FMA) to its vector processor.
AVX512	First offered on the Knights Landing processor; it came to the main-line multi-core processor hardware lineup in 2017. From the years 2018 and on, Intel and AMD (Advanced Micro Devices, Inc.) have created multiple variants of AVX512 as incremental improvements to vector hardware architectures.

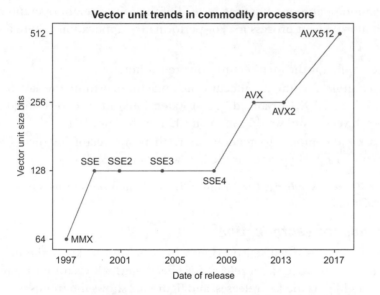

Figure 6.2   The appearance of vector unit hardware for commodity processors began around 1997 and has slowly grown over the last twenty years, both in vector width (size) and in types of operations supported.

6.3   *Vectorization methods*

There are several ways to achieve vectorization in your program. In ascending order of programmer effort, these include

- Optimized libraries
- Auto-vectorization
- Hints to the compiler
- Vector intrinsics
- Assembler instructions

6.3.1 Optimized libraries provide performance for little effort

For the least effort to achieve vectorization, programmers should research what libraries are available that they can use for their application. Many low-level libraries provide highly-optimized routines for programmers seeking performance. Some of the most commonly used libraries include

- BLAS (Basic Linear Algebra System)—A base component of high-performance linear algebra software
- LAPACK—A linear algebra package
- SCALAPACK—A scalable linear algebra package
- FFT (Fast Fourier transform)—Various implementation packages available
- Sparse Solvers—Various implementations of sparse solvers available

The Intel® Math Kernel Library (MKL) implements optimized versions of the BLAS, LAPACK, SCALAPACK, FFTs, sparse solvers, and mathematical functions for Intel processors. Though available as a part of some Intel commercial packages, the library is also offered freely. Many other library developers release packages for a variety of purposes. Additionally, hardware vendors supply optimized libraries for their hardware under different licensing arrangements.

6.3.2 Auto-vectorization: The easy way to vectorization speedup (most of the time[1])

Auto-vectorization is the recommended choice for most programmers because implementation requires the least amount of programming effort. That being said, compilers cannot always recognize where vectorization can be applied safely. In this section, we first look at what kind of code a compiler might automatically vectorize. Then, we show how to verify that you get the actual vectorization you expect. You will also learn about programming styles that make it possible for the compiler to vectorize code and perform other optimizations. This includes the use of the `restrict` keyword for C and `__restrict` or `__restrict__` attributes for C++.

With ongoing improvements of architectures and compilers, auto-vectorization can provide significant performance improvement. The proper compiler flags and programming style can improve this further.

> **DEFINITION** *Auto-vectorization* is the vectorization of the source code by the compiler for standard C, C++, or Fortran languages.

---

[1] It is important to note that although auto-vectorization often yields significant performance gains, it can sometimes slow down the code. This is due to the overhead of setting up the vector instructions being greater than the performance gain. The compiler generally makes a decision to vectorize using a cost function. The compiler vectorizes if the cost function shows that the code would be faster, but it is guessing at the array lengths and assumes all the data is from the first level of the cache.

Example: Auto-vectorization

Let's see how auto-vectorization works on the simple loop from the STREAM Triad from the STREAM Benchmark introduced in section 3.2.4. We separate out the triad code from the STREAM Benchmark into a standalone test problem with this listing.

Auto vectorization of stream_triad.c

```
autovec/stream_triad.c
 1 #include <stdio.h>
 2 #include <sys/time.h>
 3 #include "timer.h"
 4
 5 #define NTIMES 16
 6 #define STREAM_ARRAY_SIZE 80000000
 7 static double a[STREAM_ARRAY_SIZE],
                 b[STREAM_ARRAY_SIZE],
                 c[STREAM_ARRAY_SIZE];
 8
 9 int main(int argc, char *argv[]){
10    struct timeval tstart;
11    double scalar = 3.0, time_sum = 0.0;
12    for (int i=0; i<STREAM_ARRAY_SIZE; i++) {
13        a[i] = 1.0;
14        b[i] = 2.0;
15    }
16
17    for (int k=0; k<NTIMES; k++){
18        cpu_timer_start(&tstart);
19        for (int i=0; i<STREAM_ARRAY_SIZE; i++){
20            c[i] = a[i] + scalar*b[i];
21        }
22        time_sum += cpu_timer_stop(tstart);
23        c[1] = c[2];
24    }
25    printf("Average runtime is %lf msecs\n", time_sum/NTIMES);
26 }
```

Lines 7: **Large enough to force into main memory**

Lines 12–15: **Initializes data and arrays**

Lines 19–21: **Stream triad loop has three operands with a multiply and an add.**

Line 23: ← **Keeps the compiler from optimizing out the loop**

```
Makefile for the GCC compiler
CFLAGS=-g -O3 -fstrict-aliasing \
       -ftree-vectorize -march=native -mtune=native \
       -fopt-info-vec-optimized

stream_triad: stream_triad.o timer.o
```

We will discuss compiler flags in more detail in section 6.4, and the timer.c and timer.h files in section 17.2. Compiling the stream_triad.c file with version 8 of the GCC compiler gives the following compiler feedback:

```
stream_triad.c:19:7: note: loop vectorized
stream_triad.c:12:4: note: loop vectorized
```

GCC vectorizes both the initialization loop and the stream triad loop! We can run the stream triad with

```
./stream_triad
```

We can verify that the compiler uses vector instructions with the likwid tool (section 3.3.1).

```
likwid-perfctr -C 0 -f -g MEM_DP ./stream_triad
```

Look in the report output from this command for these lines:

```
| FP_ARITH_INST_RETIRED_128B_PACKED_DOUBLE |  PMC0 |         0 |
|    FP_ARITH_INST_RETIRED_SCALAR_DOUBLE   |  PMC1 |        98 |
| FP_ARITH_INST_RETIRED_256B_PACKED_DOUBLE |  PMC2 | 640000000 |
| FP_ARITH_INST_RETIRED_512B_PACKED_DOUBLE |  PMC3 |         0 |
```

In the output, you can see most of the operation counts are in the `256B_PACKED_DOUBLE` category on the third line. Why all the 256 bit operations? Some versions of the GCC compiler, including the 8.2 version used in this test, generate 256 bits instead of the 512-bit vector instructions for the Skylake processor. Without a tool like likwid, we would need to carefully check the vectorization reports or inspect the generated assembler instructions to find out the compiler was not generating the proper instructions. For the GCC compiler, we can change the generated instructions by adding the compiler flag `-mprefer-vector-width=512` and then try again. Now we'll get AVX512 instructions with eight double-precision values computed at once:

```
| FP_ARITH_INST_RETIRED_256B_PACKED_DOUBLE |  PMC2 |         0 |
| FP_ARITH_INST_RETIRED_512B_PACKED_DOUBLE |  PMC3 | 320000000 |
```

Example: Auto-vectorization in a function

In this example, we try a slightly more complicated version of the code from the previous example with the stream triad loop in a separate function. The following listing shows how.

Stream triad loop in a separate function

```
autovec_function/stream_triad.c
 1 #include <stdio.h>
 2 #include <sys/time.h>
 3 #include "timer.h"
 4
 5 #define NTIMES 16
 6 #define STREAM_ARRAY_SIZE 80000000
 7 static double a[STREAM_ARRAY_SIZE], b[STREAM_ARRAY_SIZE],
               c[STREAM_ARRAY_SIZE];
 8
```

(continued)

```
 9 void stream_triad(double* a, double* b,          Stream triad loop in
       double* c, double scalar){                    a separate function
10    for (int i=0; i<STREAM_ARRAY_SIZE; i++){
11        a[i] = b[i] + scalar*c[i];
12    }
13 }
14
15 int main(int argc, char *argv[]){
16    struct timeval tstart;
17    double scalar = 3.0, time_sum = 0.0;
18    for (int i=0; i<STREAM_ARRAY_SIZE; i++) {
19        a[i] = 1.0;
20        b[i] = 2.0;
21    }
22
23    for (int k=0; k<NTIMES; k++){
24        cpu_timer_start(&tstart);
25        stream_triad(a, b, c, scalar);              Stream triad
26        time_sum += cpu_timer_stop(tstart);         function call
27        // to keep the compiler from optimizing out the loop
28        c[1] = c[2];
29    }
30    printf("Average runtime is %lf msecs\n", time_sum/NTIMES);
31 }
```

Let's look at the output from the GCC compiler for the code in the previous stream triad loop listing:

```
stream_triad.c:10:4: note: loop vectorized
stream_triad.c:10:4: note: loop versioned for vectorization because of
  possible aliasing
stream_triad.c:10:4: note: loop vectorized
stream_triad.c:18:4: note: loop vectorized
```

The compiler cannot tell if the arguments to the function point to the same or to overlapping data. This causes the compiler to create more than one version and produces code that tests the arguments to determine which to use. We can fix this by adding to the function definition the restrict attribute as part of the arguments. The C99 standard added this keyword. Unfortunately, C++ has not standardized the restrict keyword, but the __restrict attribute works for GCC, Clang, and Visual C++. Another common form of the attribute in C++ compilers is __restrict__:

```
9 void stream_triad(double* restrict a, double* restrict b,
                    double* restrict c, double scalar){
```

We used GCC to compile the code with the restrict keyword added and got

```
stream_triad.c:10:4: note: loop vectorized
stream_triad.c:10:4: note: loop vectorized
stream_triad.c:18:4: note: loop vectorized
```

Now this compiler generates fewer versions of the function. We need to also point out that the `-fstrict-aliasing` flag tells the compiler to aggressively generate code with the assumption that there is no aliasing.

> **DEFINITION** *Aliasing* is where pointers point to overlapping regions of memory. In this situation, the compiler cannot tell if it is the same memory, and it would be unsafe to generate vectorized code or other optimizations.

In recent years, the strict aliasing option has become the default with GCC and other compilers (optimization levels `-O2` and `-O3` set `-fstrict-aliasing`). This broke a lot of code where aliased variables actually existed. As a result, compilers have dialed back how aggressively they generate more efficient code. All of this is to tell you that you may get different results with various compilers and even different compiler versions.

By using the `restrict` attribute, you make a promise to the compiler that there is no aliasing. We recommend using both the `restrict` attribute and the `-fstrict-aliasing` compiler flag. The attribute is portable with the source across all architectures and compilers. You'll need to apply the compiler flags for each compiler, but these affect all of your source.

From these examples, it would seem that the best course of action for programmers to get vectorization is to just let the compiler auto-vectorize. While compilers are improving, for more complex code compilers often fail to recognize that they can safely vectorize the loop. Thus, the programmer needs to help the compiler with hints. We discuss this technique next.

6.3.3 *Teaching the compiler through hints: Pragmas and directives*

Ok, the compiler is not quite able to figure it out and generate vectorized code; is there something we can do? In this section, we will present how to give more precise directions to the compiler. In return, this gives you more control over the vectorization process of your code. Here, you will learn how to use pragmas and directives to convey information to the compiler for portable implementation of vectorization.

> **DEFINITION** *Pragma* is an instruction to a C or C++ compiler to help it interpret the source code. The form of the instruction is a preprocessor statement starting with #pragma. (In Fortran, where it is called a directive, the form is a comment line starting with !$).

Example: Using manual hints to the compiler for vectorization

We need an example where the compiler does not vectorize the code without help. For this we use the example code in the following listings. Together these calculate the wave speed in a cell to determine the timestep to use in the calculation. The timestep

(continued)

can be no greater than the minimum time it takes for a wave to cross any cell in the mesh.

Timestep calculation using a minimum reduction loop in timestep/main.c

```
timestep/main.c
 1 #include <stdio.h>
 2 #include "timestep.h"
 3 #define NCELLS 10000000
 4 static double H[NCELLS], U[NCELLS], V[NCELLS], dx[NCELLS],
          dy[NCELLS];
 5 static int celltype[NCELLS];
 6
 7 int main(int argc, char *argv[]){
 8    double mymindt;
 9    double g = 9.80, sigma = 0.95;
10    for (int ic=0; ic<NCELLS ; ic++) {
11       H[ic] = 10.0;
12       U[ic] = 0.0;
13       V[ic] = 0.0;
14       dx[ic] = 0.5;
15       dy[ic] = 0.5;
16       celltype[ic] = REAL_CELL;
17    }
18    H[NCELLS/2] = 20.0;
19
20    mymindt = timestep(NCELLS, g, sigma,
             celltype, H, U, V, dx, dy);
21
22    printf("Minimum dt is %lf\n",mymindt);
23 }
```

⎫ **Initializes arrays and data** (lines 10–18)

⎱ **Calls the timestep calculation** (line 20)

Timestep calculation using a minimum reduction loop in timestep/timestep.c

```
timestep/timestep.c
 1 #include <math.h>
 2 #include "timestep.h"
 3 #define REAL_CELL 1
 4
 5 double timestep(int ncells, double g, double sigma, int* celltype,
 6          double* H, double* U, double* V, double* dx, double* dy){
 7    double wavespeed, xspeed, yspeed, dt;
 8    double mymindt = 1.0e20;
 9    for (int ic=0; ic<ncells ; ic++) {
10       if (celltype[ic] == REAL_CELL) {
11          wavespeed = sqrt(g*H[ic]);
12          xspeed = (fabs(U[ic])+wavespeed)/dx[ic];
13          yspeed = (fabs(V[ic])+wavespeed)/dy[ic];
14          dt=sigma/(xspeed+yspeed);
```

← **The velocity of wave** (line 11)

← **Time for wave to cross cell times safety factor (sigma)** (lines 12–14)

```
15              if (dt < mymindt) mymindt = dt;     ⟵┐  Gets the minimum
16          }                                           time for all cells
17      }                                               and uses for
18      return(mymindt);                                timestep
19  }


Makefile for GCC
CFLAGS=-g -O3 -fstrict-aliasing -ftree-vectorize -fopenmp-simd \
  -march=native -mtune=native -mprefer-vector-width=512 \
  -fopt-info-vec-optimized -fopt-info-vec-missed

stream_triad: main.o timestep.o timer.o
```

For this example, we added the `-fopt-info-vec-missed` compiler flag to get a report on the missed loop vectorizations. Compiling this code gives us

```
main.c:10:4: note: loop vectorized

timestep.c:9:4: missed: couldn't vectorize loop
timestep.c:9:4: missed: not vectorized: control flow in loop.
```

This vectorization report tells us that the timestep loop was not vectorized due to the conditional in the loop. Let's see if we can get the loop to optimize by adding a pragma. Add the following line just before the `for` loop in timestep.c (at line 9):

```
#pragma omp simd reduction(min:mymindt)
```

Now compiling the code shows conflicting messages about whether the timestep loop was vectorized:

```
main.c:10:4: note: loop vectorized
timestep_opt.c:9:9: note: loop vectorized
timestep_opt.c:11:7: note: not vectorized: control flow in loop.
```

We need to check the executable with a performance tool such as likwid to see if it actually vectorizes:

```
likwid-perfctr -g MEM_DP -C 0 ./timestep_opt
```

The output from the likwid tool shows that no vector instructions are being executed:

```
|           DP MFLOP/s        |  451.4928 |
|           AVX DP MFLOP/s    |         0 |
|           Packed MUOPS/s    |         0 |
```

With the GCC 9.0 version of the compiler, we have been able to get this to vectorize by adding the `-fno-trapping-math` flag. If there is a division in a conditional block, this flag tells the compiler not to worry about throwing an error exception, so it will then vectorize. If there is a `sqrt` in the conditional block, the `-fno-math-errno` flag will allow the compiler to vectorize. For better portability, the pragma should also tell the compiler that some variables are not preserved across loop iterations and, hence, are not a flow or anti-flow dependency. These dependencies will be discussed after the listing in the following example.

```
#pragma omp simd private(wavespeed, xspeed, yspeed, dt) reduction(min:mymindt)
```

An even better way to indicate that the scope of the variables is limited to each iteration of the loop is to declare the variables in the scope of the loop:

```
double wavespeed = sqrt(g*H[ic]);
double xspeed = (fabs(U[ic])+wavespeed)/dx[ic];
double yspeed = (fabs(V[ic])+wavespeed)/dy[ic];
double dt=sigma/(xspeed+yspeed);
```

Now we can remove the `private` clause and the declaration of the variables prior to the loop. We can also add the `restrict` attribute to the function interface to inform the compiler the pointers do not overlap:

```
double timestep(int ncells, double g, double sigma, int* restrict celltype,
                double* restrict H, double* restrict U, double* restrict V,
                double* restrict dx, double* restrict dy);
```

Even with all of these changes, we were not able to get the GCC compiler to vectorize the code. With further investigation using version 9 of the GCC compiler, we finally were successful by adding the `-fno-trapping-math` flag. If there is a division in a conditional block, this flag tells the compiler not to worry about throwing an error exception so it will then vectorize. If there is a `sqrt` in the conditional block, the `-fno-math-errno` flag allows the compiler to vectorize. The Intel compiler, however, vectorizes all of the versions.

One of the more common operations is a sum of an array. Back in section 4.5, we introduced this type of operation as a reduction. We'll add a little complexity to the operation by including a conditional that limits the sum to the real cells in a mesh. Here *real cells* are considered elements not on the boundary or ghost cells from other processors. We discuss ghost cells in chapter 8.

Listing 6.1   Mass sum calculation using a sum reduction loop

```
mass_sum/mass_sum.c
1 #include "mass_sum.h"
2 #define REAL_CELL 1                                        Sets the reduction
3                                                            variable to zero
4 double mass_sum(int ncells, int* restrict celltype, double* restrict H,
5                 double* restrict dx, double* restrict dy){
6    double summer = 0.0;
7 #pragma omp simd reduction(+:summer)      ◁──┐ Thread loop treats summer
8    for (int ic=0; ic<ncells ; ic++) {          as a reduction variable.
```

```
 9        if (celltype[ic] == REAL_CELL) {
10            summer += H[ic]*dx[ic]*dy[ic];
11        }
12    }
13    return(summer);
14 }
```

> The conditional can be implemented with a mask.

The OpenMP SIMD pragma should automatically set the reduction variable to zero, but when the pragma is ignored, the initialization on line 6 is necessary. The OpenMP SIMD pragma on line 7 tells the compiler that we use the summer variable in a reduction sum. In the loop, the conditional on line 9 can be implemented in the vector operations with a mask. Each vector lane has its own copy of summer and these will then be combined at the end of the for loop.

The Intel compiler successfully recognizes the sum reduction and automatically vectorizes the loop without the OpenMP SIMD pragma. GCC also vectorizes with versions 9 and later of the compiler.

Example: Using the compiler vectorization report as a guide for adding pragmas

Because the Intel compiler generates better vectorization reports, we will use it for this example. The source code for this example is taken from listing 4.14. The main loop is shown in this listing with line numbers.

Main loop of stencil example from listing 4.14

```
56    for (int j = 1; j < jmax-1; j++){
57        for (int i = 1; i < imax-1; i++){
58            xnew[j][i] = (x[j][i] + x[j  ][i-1] + x[j  ][i+1]
                                + x[j-1][i  ] + x[j+1][i  ])/5.0;
59        }
60    }
```

For this example, we used the Intel v19 compiler with these compiler flags:

```
CFLAGS=-g -O3 -std=c99 -qopenmp-simd -ansi-alias -xHost \
  -qopt-zmm-usage=high -qopt-report=5 -qopt-report-phase=vec,loop
```

The vectorization report shows that the compiler did not vectorize the inner loop at line 57 and the outer loop at line 56:

```
LOOP BEGIN at stencil.c(56,7)
    remark #15344: loop was not vectorized: vector dependence prevents
                vectorization
    remark #15346: vector dependence: assumed OUTPUT dependence between
                xnew[j][i] (58:13)and xnew[j][i] (58:13)
    remark #15346: vector dependence: assumed OUTPUT dependence between
                xnew[j][i] (58:13)and xnew[j][i] (58:13)
```

```
(continued)
    LOOP BEGIN at stencil.c(57,10)
        remark #15344: loop was not vectorized: vector dependence prevents
                       vectorization
        remark #15346: vector dependence: assumed FLOW dependence between
                       xnew[j][i] (58:13)and x[j][i] (58:13)
        remark #15346: vector dependence: assumed ANTI dependence between
                       x[j][i] (58:13)and xnew[j][i] (58:13)
        remark #25438: unrolled without remainder by 4
    LOOP END
LOOP END
```

In the previous example, the flow and anti-flow dependencies arise due to the possibility of aliasing between x and xnew. The compiler is being more conservative in this case than it needs to be. The output dependency is only called out in the attempt to vectorize the outer loop. The compiler cannot be certain that the subsequent iterations of the inner loop won't write to the same location as a prior iteration. Before we continue, let's define a few terms:

- *Flow dependency*—A variable within the loop is read after being written, known as a read-after-write (RAW).
- *Anti-flow dependency*—A variable within the loop is written after being read, known as a write-after-read (WAR).
- *Output dependency*—A variable is written to more than once in the loop.

For the GCC v8.2 compiler, the vectorization report is

```
stencil.c:57:10: note: loop vectorized
stencil.c:57:10: note: loop versioned for vectorization because of
                 possible aliasing
stencil.c:51:7: note: loop vectorized
stencil.c:37:7: note: loop vectorized
stencil.c:37:7: note: loop versioned for vectorization because of
                 possible aliasing
```

The GCC compiler chooses to create two versions and tests which to use at run time. The report is nice enough to give us a clear idea of the cause of the problem. There are two ways that we can fix these problems. We can help guide the compiler by adding a pragma before the loop at line 57 like this:

```
#pragma omp simd
        for (int i = 1; i < imax-1; i++){
```

Another approach to solving this problem is to add a restrict attribute to the definition of x and xnew:

```
double** restrict x = malloc2D(jmax, imax);
double** restrict xnew = malloc2D(jmax, imax);
```

The vectorization report for Intel now shows that the inner loop is vectorized with a vectorized peel loop, main vectorized loop, and a vectorized remainder loop. This calls for a few more definitions.

- *Peel loop*—A loop to execute for misaligned data so that the main loop would then have aligned data. Often the peel loop is conditionally executed at run time if the data is discovered to be misaligned.
- *Remainder loop*—A loop that executes after the main loop to handle a partial set of data that is too small for a full vector length.

The peel loop is added to deal with the unaligned data at the start of the loop, and the remainder loop takes care of any extra data at the end of the loop. The reports for all three loops look similar. Looking at the main loop report, we see that the estimated speedup is over six times faster:

```
LOOP BEGIN at stencil.c(55,21)
   remark #15388: vec support: reference xnew[j][i] has aligned access
   [ stencil.c(56,13) ]
   remark #15389: vec support: reference x[j][i] has unaligned access
   [ stencil.c(56,28) ]
   remark #15389: vec support: reference x[j][i-1] has unaligned access
   [ stencil.c(56,38) ]
   remark #15389: vec support: reference x[j][i+1] has unaligned access
   [ stencil.c(56,50) ]
   remark #15389: vec support: reference x[j-1][i] has unaligned access
   [ stencil.c(56,62) ]
   remark #15389: vec support: reference x[j+1][i] has unaligned access
   [ stencil.c(56,74) ]
   remark #15381: vec support: unaligned access used inside loop body
   remark #15305: vec support: vector length 8
   remark #15399: vec support: unroll factor set to 2
   remark #15309: vec support: normalized vectorization overhead 0.236
   remark #15301: OpenMP SIMD LOOP WAS VECTORIZED
   remark #15449: unmasked aligned unit stride stores: 1
   remark #15450: unmasked unaligned unit stride loads: 5
   remark #15475: --- begin vector cost summary ---
   remark #15476: scalar cost: 43
   remark #15477: vector cost: 6.620
   remark #15478: estimated potential speedup: 6.370
   remark #15486: divides: 1
   remark #15488: --- end vector cost summary ---
   remark #25015: Estimate of max trip count of loop=125
LOOP END
```

Take note that the estimated speedup is carefully labeled as *potential speedup*. It is unlikely that you will get the full estimated speedup unless

- Your data is in a high level of the cache.
- The actual array length is long.
- You are not bandwidth-limited with data loads from main memory.

In the preceeding implementation, the actual measured speedup on a Skylake Gold processor with the Intel compiler is 1.39 times faster than the unvectorized version. This vectorization report is for the speedup of the processor, but we still have a memory bandwidth-limited kernel from main memory to contend with.

For the GCC compiler, the SIMD pragma is successful at eliminating the versioning of the two loops. In fact, adding the restrict clause had no effect, and both loops are still versioned. Additionally, because there is a vectorized version in all these cases, performance doesn't change. To understand speedup, we can compare the performance to a version where the vectorization is turned off to find that the speedup for vectorization with GCC is about 1.22 times faster.

6.3.4   *Crappy loops, we got them: Use vector intrinsics*

For troublesome loops that just don't vectorize even with hints, vector intrinsics are another option. In this section, we'll see how to use intrinsics for more control over vectorization. The downside of vector intrinsics is that these are less portable. Here, we will look at some examples that use vector intrinsics for successful vectorization to show the use of intrinsics to vectorize the Kahan sum introduced in section 5.7. In that section, we said the cost of the Kahan sum in a normal sum operation was about four floating-point operations instead of one. But if we can vectorize the Kahan sum operation, the cost becomes much less.

The implementations in these examples use a 256-bit vector intrinsic to speed up the operation by nearly a factor of four over the serial version. We show three different ways to implement a Kahan sum kernel in the listings for the following examples. You will find the full implementation at https://github.com/lanl/GlobalSums.git, which is extracted from the global sums example. It is included in the GlobalSumsVectorized directory in the code for this chapter.

Example: Implementation of the Kahan sum using vector intrinsics

The first intrinsics example, by Andy Dubois and Brett Neuman of Los Alamos National Laboratory, uses the Intel x86 vector intrinsics. This is the most commonly used set of intrinsics and can run on both Intel and AMD processors that support AVX vector instructions.

> **Intel x86 vector intrinsics version of the enhanced precision Kahan sum**

```
GlobalSumsVectorized/kahan_intel_vector.c
1 #include <x86intrin.h>
2
3 static double
      sum[4] __attribute__ ((aligned (64)));
4
5 double do_kahan_sum_intel_v(double* restrict var, long ncells)
6 {
7     double const zero = 0.0;
```

Include file with Intel and AMD x86 vector intrinsics definitions

Defines a regularly aligned array of four double-precision values

```
 8    __m256d local_sum = _mm256_broadcast_sd(
                         (double const*) &zero);
 9    __m256d local_corr = _mm256_broadcast_sd(
                         (double const*) &zero);

10
11    #pragma simd
12    #pragma vector aligned
13    for (long i = 0; i < ncells; i+=4) {
14        __m256d var_v = _mm256_load_pd(&var[i]);
15        __m256d corrected_next_term =
                 var_v + local_corr;
16        __m256d new_sum =
                 local_sum + local_corr;
17        local_corr = corrected_next_term -
                 (new_sum - local_sum);
18        local_sum = new_sum;
19    }
20    __m256d sum_v;
21    sum_v  = local_corr;
22    sum_v += local_sum;
23    _mm256_store_pd(sum, sum_v);
24
25    struct esum_type{
26       double sum;
27       double correction;
28    } local;
29    local.sum = 0.0;
30    local.correction = 0.0;
31
32    for (long i = 0; i < 4; i++) {
33       double corrected_next_term_s =
                 sum[i] + local.correction;
34       double new_sum_s =
                 local.sum + local.correction;
35       local.correction =
                 corrected_next_term_s -
                 (new_sum_s - local.sum);
36       local.sum       = new_sum_s;
37    }
38    double final_sum =
          local.sum + local.correction;
39    return(final_sum);
40 }
```

Fills a four-wide, double-precision vector variable with zeros

Pragmas to instruct the compiler to operate on the aligned vector variables

Loads four values from a standard array into a vector variable

Does the standard Kahan operation on all four-wide vector variables

Stores the four vector lanes into a regularly aligned array of four values

Sums the four sums from the four vector lanes using scalar variables

Example: Implementation of the Kahan sum using GCC vector intrinsics

The second implementation of the Kahan sum uses the GCC vector extensions. These vector instructions can support other architectures than the AVX vector units on x86 architectures. But the GCC vector extensions' portability is limited to where you can use the GCC compiler. If a longer vector length is specified than the hardware supports, the compiler generates instructions using combinations of shorter vector lengths.

(continued)

GCC vector extensions version of the enhanced precision Kahan sum

```
GlobalSumsVectorized/kahan_gcc_vector.c
 1 static double
      sum[4] __attribute__ ((aligned (64)));
 2
 3 double do_kahan_sum_gcc_v(double* restrict var, long ncells)
 4 {
 5    typedef double vec4d __attribute__
         ((vector_size(4 * sizeof(double))));
 6
 7    vec4d local_sum = {0.0};
 8    vec4d local_corr = {0.0};
 9
10    for (long i = 0; i < ncells; i+=4) {
11       vec4d var_v = *(vec4d *)&var[i];
12       vec4d corrected_next_term =
            var_v + local_corr;
13       vec4d new_sum =
            local_sum + local_corr;
14       local_corr = corrected_next_term -
            (new_sum - local_sum);
15       local_sum = new_sum;
16    }
17    vec4d sum_v;
18    sum_v  = local_correction;
19    sum_v += local_sum;
20    *(vec4d *)sum = sum_v;
21
22    struct esum_type{
23       double sum;
24       double correction;
25    } local;
26    local.sum = 0.0;
27    local.correction = 0.0;
28
29    for (long i = 0; i < 4; i++) {
30       double corrected_next_term_s =
            sum[i] + local.correction;
31       double new_sum_s =
            local.sum + local.correction;
32       local.correction =
            corrected_next_term_s
            (new_sum_s - local.sum);
33       local.sum = new_sum_s;
34    }
35    double final_sum =
            local.sum + local.correction;
36    return(final_sum);
37 }
```

Annotations:

- **Defines a regularly aligned array of four double-precision values** (lines 1)
- **Declares the vec4d vector data type** (line 5)
- **Fills a four-wide, double-precision vector variable with zeros** (lines 7–8)
- **Loads four values from a standard array into a vector variable** (line 11)
- **The standard Kahan operation is done on all four-wide vector variables.** (lines 12–15)
- **Stores the four vector lanes into a regularly aligned array of four values** (line 20)
- **Sums the four sums from the four vector lanes using scalar variables** (lines 29–35)

Example: Implementation of the Kahan sum using C++ vector intrinsics

For C++ code, Agner Fog of the Technical University of Denmark wrote a C++ vector class library under an open source license. This class library is portable across hardware architectures and automatically adapts to older hardware with shorter vector lengths. The Fog vector class library is well-designed and has an extensive manual. More details on this library are given in the additional reading section at the end of the chapter.

In this example, we'll write the vector version of the Kahan sum in C++ and then call it from our C main program. We'll also handle a remainder block of values that doesn't fit a full vector width by using the partial_load function. We won't always have arrays that are evenly divided into 4-wide groupings. We can sometimes pad the arrays with extra zeros to make an array the right size, but the better approach is to handle the remaining values in a separate block of code at the end of the loop. Note that the Vec4d data type is defined in the vector class header file.

Agner Fog's C++ vector class library for enhanced precision for Kahan sum

```
GlobalSumsVectorized/kahan_fog_vector.cpp
 1 #include "vectorclass.h"          ◁────  Includes the vector
 2                                           class header file
 3 static double
     sum[4] __attribute__ ((aligned (64)));   Defines a regularly aligned array
 4                                             of four double-precision values
 5 extern "C" {
 6 double do_kahan_sum_agner_v(double* var,    Specifies that we
                              long ncells);    want a C-style
 7 }                                           subroutine
 8
 9 double do_kahan_sum_agner_v(double* var, long ncells)
10 {
11     Vec4d local_sum(0.0);        Fills a four-wide, double-precision
12     Vec4d local_corr(0.0);       vector variable with zeros
13     Vec4d var_v;
14
15     int ncells_main=(ncells/4)*4;         Defines a vector
16     int ncells_remainder=ncells%4;        double-precision
17     for (long i = 0; i < ncells_main; i+=4) {   variable of 256 bits
18         var_v.load(var+i);        ◁────    (or four doubles)
19         Vec4d corrected_next_term =
             var_v + local_corr;
20         Vec4d new_sum =           Loads four values
             local_sum + local_corr;  from a standard
21         local_corr = corrected_next_term -  array into a
             (new_sum - local_sum);   vector variable
22         local_sum = new_sum;
23     }
24     if (ncells_remainder > 0) {
25         var_v.load_partial(ncells_remainder,var+ncells_main);
26         Vec4d corrected_next_term = var_v + local_corr;
27         Vec4d new_sum = local_sum + local_corr;
```

(continued)

```
28        local_corr = corrected_next_term - (new_sum - local_sum);
29        local_sum = new_sum;
30    }
31
32    Vec4d sum_v;
33    sum_v  = local_corr;
34    sum_v += local_sum;
35    sum_v.store(sum);
36
37    struct esum_type{
38       double sum;
39       double correction;
40    } local;
41    local.sum = 0.0;
42    local.correction = 0.0;
43    for (long i = 0; i < 4; i++) {
44       double corrected_next_term_s =
             sum[i] + local.correction;
45       double new_sum_s =
             local.sum + local.correction;
46       local.correction =
             corrected_next_term_s -
             (new_sum_s - local.sum);
47       local.sum = new_sum_s;
48    }
49    double final_sum =
          local.sum + local.correction;
50    return(final_sum);
51 }
```

The standard Kahan operation is done on all four-wide vector variables.

Stores the four vector lanes into a regularly aligned array of four values

Sums the four sums from the four vector lanes using scalar variables

The `load` and `store` commands are more natural in this vector class library than some of the other vector-intrinsic syntax.

We then tested the Kahan sum implemented with the three vector intrinsics against the original serial sum and original Kahan sum. We used version 8.2 of the GCC compiler and ran the tests on a Skylake Gold processor. The GCC compiler fails to vectorize the serial sum and the original Kahan sum code. Adding an OpenMP pragma gets the serial sum to vectorize, but the loop-carried dependency in the Kahan sum prevents the compiler from vectorizing the code.

It is important to note in the following performance results that the vectorized versions for serial and Kahan sums with all three vector intrinsics (bolded) have nearly identical run times. We can do more floating-point operations in the same time and simultaneously reduce the numerical error. This is a great example that with some effort, floating-point operations can come for free.

```
SETTINGS INFO -- ncells 1073741824 log 30
Initializing mesh with Leblanc problem, high values first
  relative diff  runtime   Description
```

```
    8.423e-09       1.273343    Serial sum
            0       3.519778    Kahan sum with double double accumulator
4 wide vectors serial sum
   -3.356e-09       0.683407    Intel vector intrinsics Serial sum
   -3.356e-09       0.682952    GCC vector intrinsics Serial sum
   -3.356e-09       0.682756    Fog C++ vector class Serial sum
4 wide vectors Kahan sum
            0       1.030471    Intel Vector intrinsics Kahan sum
            0       1.031490    GCC vector extensions Kahan sum
            0       1.032354    Fog C++ vector class Kahan sum
8 wide vector serial sum
   -1.986e-09       0.663277    Serial sum (OpenMP SIMD pragma)
   -1.986e-09       0.664413    8 wide Intel vector intrinsic Serial sum
   -1.986e-09       0.664067    8 wide GCC vector intrinsic Serial sum
   -1.986e-09       0.663911    8 wide Fog C++ vector class Serial sum
8 wide vector Kahan sum
   -1.388e-16       0.689495    8 wide Intel Vector intrinsics Kahan sum
   -1.388e-16       0.689100    8 wide GCC vector extensions Kahan sum
   -1.388e-16       0.689472    8 wide Fog C++ vector class Kahan sum
```

6.3.5 *Not for the faint of heart: Using assembler code for vectorization*

In this section, we will cover when it is appropriate to write vector assembly in your application. We'll also discuss what vector assembler code looks like, how to disassemble your compiled code, and how to tell which vector instruction set the compiler generated.

Programming vector units directly with vector assembly instructions has the greatest opportunity to achieve maximum performance. But it takes a deep understanding of the performance behavior of the large number of vector instructions across many different processors. Programmers without this expertise will probably get better performance from using vector intrinsics as shown in the previous section than from directly writing vector assembler instructions. In addition, the portability of vector assembly code is limited; it will only work on a small set of processor architectures. For these reasons, it is rare that writing vector assembly instructions makes sense.

Example: Looking at vector assembly instructions

To see what vector assembly instructions look like, we can display these from the object file using the `objdump` command. The listing shows the output from the following command:

```
objdump -d -M=intel --no-show-raw-insn <object code file.o>
```

Assembler code for GCC vector extensions version of Kahan sum

```
0000000000000000 <do_kahan_sum_gcc_v>:
0:   test    %rsi,%rsi
3:   jle     90 <do_kahan_sum_gcc_v+0x90>
9:   vxorpd  %xmm2,%xmm2,%xmm2
d:   xor     %eax,%eax
f:   vmovapd %ymm2,%ymm0
```

(continued)

```
13:    nopl    0x0(%rax,%rax,1)
18:    vmovapd %ymm0,%ymm1
1c:    vaddpd  %ymm2,%ymm0,%ymm0
20:    vaddpd  (%rdi,%rax,8),%ymm2,%ymm3
25:    add     $0x4,%rax
29:    vsubpd  %ymm1,%ymm0,%ymm1
2d:    vsubpd  %ymm1,%ymm3,%ymm2
31:    cmp     %rax,%rsi
34:    jg      18 <do_kahan_sum_gcc_v+0x18>
36:    vaddpd  %ymm2,%ymm0,%ymm0
3a:    vmovapd %ymm0,0x0(%rip)                  # 42 <do_kahan_sum_gcc_v+0x42>
42:    vxorpd  %xmm2,%xmm2,%xmm2
46:    vaddsd  0x0(%rip),%xmm2,%xmm0            # 4e <do_kahan_sum_gcc_v+0x4e>
4e:    vaddsd  %xmm2,%xmm0,%xmm2
52:    vaddsd  0x0(%rip),%xmm0,%xmm0            # 5a <do_kahan_sum_gcc_v+0x5a>
5a:    vsubsd  %xmm2,%xmm0,%xmm0
5e:    vaddsd  %xmm2,%xmm0,%xmm3
62:    vaddsd  0x0(%rip),%xmm0,%xmm1            # 6a <do_kahan_sum_gcc_v+0x6a>
6a:    vsubsd  %xmm2,%xmm3,%xmm2
6e:    vsubsd  %xmm2,%xmm1,%xmm1
72:    vaddsd  %xmm1,%xmm3,%xmm2
76:    vaddsd  0x0(%rip),%xmm1,%xmm0            # 7e <do_kahan_sum_gcc_v+0x7e>
7e:    vsubsd  %xmm3,%xmm2,%xmm3
82:    vsubsd  %xmm3,%xmm0,%xmm0
86:    vaddsd  %xmm2,%xmm0,%xmm0
8a:    vzeroupper
8d:    retq
8e:    xchg    %ax,%ax
90:    vxorpd  %xmm0,%xmm0,%xmm0
94:    jmp     3a <do_kahan_sum_gcc_v+0x3a>
```

If you see ymm registers, vector instructions were generated. zmm registers indicate that there are AVX512 vector instructions. The xmm registers are generated for both scalar and SSE vector instructions. We can tell the listing was from the kahan_gcc_vector.c.o file because there are no zmm instructions in the output. If we look at the kahan_gcc _vector8.c.o file that generates 512-bit instructions, you'll see zmm instructions.

Because it seldom makes sense to do more than simply look at the assembler instructions that the compiler generates, we won't go through a programming example of writing a routine in assembler from scratch.

6.4   *Programming style for better vectorization*

We suggest that you adopt a programming style that is more compatible with the needs of vectorization and other forms of loop parallelization. Based on the lessons learned from the examples throughout the chapter, certain programming styles can help the compiler generate vectorized code. Adopting the following programming styles leads to better performance out of the box and less work needed for optimization efforts.

General suggestions:

- Use the `restrict` attribute on pointers in function arguments and declarations (C and C++).
- Use pragmas or directives where needed to inform the compiler.
- Be careful with optimizing for the compiler with `#pragma unroll` and other techniques; you might limit the possible options for the compiler transformations.[2]
- Put exceptions and error checks with print statements in a separate loop.

Concerning data structures:

- Try to use a data structure with a long length for the innermost loop.
- Use the smallest data type needed (`short` rather than `int`).
- Use contiguous memory accesses. Some newer instruction sets implement gather/scatter memory loads, but these are less efficient.
- Use Structure of Arrays (SOA) rather than Array of Structures (AOS).
- Use memory-aligned data structures where possible.

Related to loop structures:

- Use simple loops without special exit conditions.
- Make loop bounds a local variable by copying global values and then using them.
- Use the loop index for array addresses when possible.
- Expose the loop bound size so it is known to the compiler. If the loop is only three iterations long, the compiler might unroll the loop rather than generate a four-wide vector instruction.
- Avoid array syntax in performance-critical loops (Fortran).

In the loop body:

- Define local variables within a loop so that it is clear that these are not carried to subsequent iterations (C and C++).
- Variables and arrays within a loop should be write-only or read-only (only on the left side of the equal sign or on the right side, except for reductions).
- Don't reuse local variables for a different purpose in the loop—create a new variable. The memory space you waste is far less important than the confusion this creates for the compiler.
- Avoid function calls and inline instead (manually or with the compiler).
- Limit conditionals within the loop and, where necessary, use simple forms that can be masked.

---

[2] A `#pragma unroll` tells the compiler to insert the specified number of statements to replace iterations of the loop and to reduce the loop iterations in the loop control statement or remove it altogether.

Concerning compiler settings and flags:

- Use the latest version of a compiler and prefer compilers that do better vectorization.
- Use a strict aliasing compiler flag.
- Generate code for the most powerful vector instruction set you can get away with.

6.5 Compiler flags relevant for vectorization for various compilers

Tables 6.2 and 6.3 show the compiler flags that are recommended for vectorization for the latest version of various compilers. Compiler flags for vectorization frequently change, so check the documentation for the compiler version that you are using.

The strict aliasing flag listed in column two of table 6.2 should help with auto-vectorization for C and C++, but verify that it doesn't break any code. Column three in table 6.2 has the various options to specify which vectorization instruction set to use for some of the compilers. The ones shown in the table should be a good starting point. Vectorization reports can be generated with the compiler flags in column two of table 6.2. The compiler reports are still improving for most of the compilers and are likely to change. For GCC, the optimized and missed flags are recommended. Getting the loop optimization reports at the same time as the vectorization can be helpful so that you can see if loops have been unrolled or interchanged. If not using the rest of OpenMP, but using OpenMP SIMD directives, the flags in the last column of table 6.3 should be used.

Table 6.2   Vectorization flags for various compilers

Compiler	Strict aliasing	Vectorization	Floating-point flags

GCC, G++, GFortran v9	`-fstrict-aliasing`	`-ftree-vectorize`
		`-march=native`
		`-mtune=native`
		
		ver 8.0+:
		`-mprefer-vector`
		`-width=512`
			`-fno-trapping-math`
			`-fno-math-errno`

Clang v9	`-fstrict-aliasing`	`-fvectorize`
		`-march=native`
		`-mtune=native`
			`-fno-math-errno`

Intel icc v19	`-ansi-alias`	`-restrict`
		`-xHost`
		`-vecabi=cmdtarget`
		
		ver 18.0+:
		`-qopt-zmm-usage=high`	

MSVC	Not implemented	On by default	

IBM XLC v16	`-qalias=ansi`
	`-qalias=restrict`
		`-qsimd=auto`
		`-qhot`
		`-qarch=pwr9`
		`-qtune=pwr9`	

Table 6.2   Vectorization flags for various compilers

Compiler	Strict aliasing	Vectorization	Floating-point flags

Cray	`-h restrict=[a,f]`	`-h vector3`
		`-h preferred_vector_width=#`
		`where # can be [64,128,256,512]`	

Table 6.3   OpenMP SIMD and vectorization report flags for various compilers

Compiler	Vectorization report	OpenMP SIMD

GCC, G++,
GFortran v9
	`-fopt-info-vec-optimized[=file]`
	`-fopt-info-vec-missed[=file]`
	`-fopt-info-vec-all[=file]`
	Same for loop optimizations
	replace `vec` with `loop`
		`-fopenmp-simd`

Clang v9	`-Rpass-analysis=loop-vectorize`	`-fopenmp-simd`

Intel icc v19	`-qopt-report=[1-5]`
	`-qopt-report-phase=vec,loop`
	`-qopt-report-filter=`
	`   "filename,ln1-ln2"`
		`-qopenmp-simd`

MSVC	`-Qvec-report:[1,2]`	`-openmp:experimental`
IBM XLC v16	`-qreport`	`-qopenmp`
Cray	`-h msgs -h negmsgs` `-h list=a`	`-h omp` (default)

You can set the vector instructions to any single set such as AVX2 or multiple sets. We'll show you how to do both. For a single instruction set, the flags shown in the previous tables request that the compiler should use the vector instruction set for the processor that is used for compiling (`march=native`, `-xHost`, and `-qarch=pwer9`). Without this flag, the compiler uses the SSE2 set. If you are interested in running across a wide range of processors, you may want to specify an older instruction set or just use the default. There is some loss in performance from older sets.

Support for more than one vector instruction set can be added with the Intel compiler. This is common practice for the Intel Knights Landing processor, where the instruction set for the host processor might be different. For this, you must specify both instruction sets:

```
-axmic-avx512 -xcore-avx2
```

The `-ax` adds the additional set. Note that the `host` keyword cannot be used when requesting two instruction sets.

We briefly mentioned the use of a floating-point flag to encourage vectorization in the sum reduction kernel when discussing listing 6.1. When vectorizing loops with a conditional, the compiler inserts a mask that uses only part of the vector results. But the masked operations can generate a floating-point error by dividing by zero or taking the square root of a negative number. GCC and Clang compilers require that the extra floating-point flags shown in the last column of table 6.2 be set to vectorize loops with conditionals and any potentially problematic floating-point operations.

There are some situations where you might want to turn off vectorization. Turning off vectorization allows you to see the improvement and speedup you achieved with vectorization. It allows you to check that you get the same answer with and without vectorization. Sometimes auto-vectorization gives you the wrong answer and, thus, you would want to turn it off. You may also want to only vectorize the computationally intensive files and skip the rest.

Table 6.4   Compiler flags to turn off vectorization

Compiler	Flag
GCC	`-fno-tree-vectorize` (default is on at –O3)
Clang	`-fno-vectorize` (default is on)
Intel	`-no-vec` (default is on with –O2 or higher)
MSVC	There is no compiler flag to turn off vectorization (by default is on)
XLC	`-qsimd=noauto` (default is on at –O3 level)
Cray	`-h vector0 -hpf0 or -hfp1` (default vectorization level is `-h vector2`)

The vectorization and performance results in this chapter were with GCC v8 and v9 and with the Intel compiler v19. As noted in table 6.1, the 512-bit vector support was added to GCC starting in version 8 and in Intel in version 18. So the capability for the new 512-bit vector hardware is recent.

A CMAKE MODULE FOR SETTING COMPILER FLAGS

Setting all of the flags for compiler vectorization is messy and difficult to get right. So we have created a CMake module that you can use, which is similar to the FindOpenMP .cmake and FindMPI.cmake modules. Then the main CMakeLists.txt file just needs

```
find_package(Vector)
if (CMAKE_VECTOR_VERBOSE)
   set(VECTOR_C_FLAGS "${VECTOR_C_FLAGS} ${VECTOR_C_VERBOSE}")
endif()
set(CMAKE_C_FLAGS "${CMAKE_C_FLAGS} ${VECTOR_C_FLAGS}")
```

The CMake module is shown in FindVector.cmake in the main directory for this chapter's examples at https://github.com/EssentialsofParallelComputing/Chapter6.git. Also see the GlobalSumsVectorized code example for using the FindVector.cmake module. We'll migrate the module to other examples to help clean up our CMake-Lists.txt file as well. The following listing is an excerpt from the module for the C compiler. The flags for C++ and Fortran are also set with similar code in the Find-Vector.cmake module.

Listing 6.2   Excerpt from FindVector.cmake for C compiler

Sets all flags and turns on vectorization

Sets all flags but disables vectorization

Turns on verbose messages when compiling for vectorization feedback

Set to compile for architecture that it's on

Stricter aliasing option to help auto-vectorization

Set so that Kahan sum does not get optimized out (unsafe optimizations)

Turns on vectorization

Turns off vectorization for debugging and performance measurement

```
FindVector.cmake
 8 # Main output flags
 9 #     VECTOR_<LANG>_FLAGS
10 #     VECTOR_NOVEC_<LANG>_FLAGS
11 #     VECTOR_<LANG>_VERBOSE
12 # Component flags
13 #     VECTOR_ALIASING_<LANG>_FLAGS
14 #     VECTOR_ARCH_<LANG>_FLAGS
15 #     VECTOR_FPMODEL_<LANG>_FLAGS
16 #     VECTOR_NOVEC_<LANG>_OPT
17 #     VECTOR_VEC_<LANG>_OPTS
...
25 if(CMAKE_C_COMPILER_LOADED)
26   if ("${CMAKE_C_COMPILER_ID}" STREQUAL "Clang") # using Clang
27     set(VECTOR_ALIASING_C_FLAGS "${VECTOR_ALIASING_C_FLAGS}
         -fstrict-aliasing")
28     if ("${CMAKE_SYSTEM_PROCESSOR}" STREQUAL "x86_64")
29       set(VECTOR_ARCH_C_FLAGS "${VECTOR_ARCH_C_FLAGS}
           -march=native -mtune=native")
30     elseif ("${CMAKE_SYSTEM_PROCESSOR}" STREQUAL "ppc64le")
31       set(VECTOR_ARCH_C_FLAGS "${VECTOR_ARCH_C_FLAGS}
           -mcpu=powerpc64le")
32     elseif ("${CMAKE_SYSTEM_PROCESSOR}" STREQUAL "aarch64")
33       set(VECTOR_ARCH_C_FLAGS "${VECTOR_ARCH_C_FLAGS}
           -march=native -mtune=native")
34     endif ("${CMAKE_SYSTEM_PROCESSOR}" STREQUAL "x86_64")
35
36     set(VECTOR_OPENMP_SIMD_C_FLAGS "${VECTOR_OPENMP_SIMD_C_FLAGS}
         -fopenmp-simd")
37     set(VECTOR_C_OPTS "${VECTOR_C_OPTS} -fvectorize")
38     set(VECTOR_C_FPOPTS "${VECTOR_C_FPOPTS} -fno-math-errno")
39     set(VECTOR_NOVEC_C_OPT "${VECTOR_NOVEC_C_OPT} -fno-vectorize")
40     set(VECTOR_C_VERBOSE "${VECTOR_C_VERBOSE} -Rpass=loop-vectorize
         -Rpass-missed=loop-vectorize -Rpass-analysis=loop-vectorize")
41
42   elseif ("${CMAKE_C_COMPILER_ID}" STREQUAL "GNU") # using GCC
43     set(VECTOR_ALIASING_C_FLAGS "${VECTOR_ALIASING_C_FLAGS}
         -fstrict-aliasing")
44     if ("${CMAKE_SYSTEM_PROCESSOR}" STREQUAL "x86_64")
45       set(VECTOR_ARCH_C_FLAGS "${VECTOR_ARCH_C_FLAGS}
           -march=native -mtune=native")
46     elseif ("${CMAKE_SYSTEM_PROCESSOR}" STREQUAL "ppc64le")
47       set(VECTOR_ARCH_C_FLAGS "${VECTOR_ARCH_C_FLAGS}
           -mcpu=powerpc64le")
```

```
48    elseif ("${CMAKE_SYSTEM_PROCESSOR}" STREQUAL "aarch64")
49      set(VECTOR_ARCH_C_FLAGS "${VECTOR_ARCH_C_FLAGS}
          -march=native -mtune=native")
50    endif ("${CMAKE_SYSTEM_PROCESSOR}" STREQUAL "x86_64")
51
52    set(VECTOR_OPENMP_SIMD_C_FLAGS "${VECTOR_OPENMP_SIMD_C_FLAGS}
          -fopenmp-simd")
53    set(VECTOR_C_OPTS "${VECTOR_C_OPTS} -ftree-vectorize")
54    set(VECTOR_C_FPOPTS "${VECTOR_C_FPOPTS} -fno-trapping-math
          -fno-math-errno")
55    if ("${CMAKE_SYSTEM_PROCESSOR}" STREQUAL "x86_64")
56      if ("${CMAKE_C_COMPILER_VERSION}" VERSION_GREATER "7.9.0")
57        set(VECTOR_C_OPTS "${VECTOR_C_OPTS} -mprefer-vector-width=512")
58      endif ("${CMAKE_C_COMPILER_VERSION}" VERSION_GREATER "7.9.0")
59    endif ("${CMAKE_SYSTEM_PROCESSOR}" STREQUAL "x86_64")
60
61    set(VECTOR_NOVEC_C_OPT "${VECTOR_NOVEC_C_OPT} -fno-tree-vectorize")
62    set(VECTOR_C_VERBOSE "${VECTOR_C_VERBOSE} -fopt-info-vec-optimized
          -fopt-info-vec-missed -fopt-info-loop-optimized
          -fopt-info-loop-missed")
63
64  elseif ("${CMAKE_C_COMPILER_ID}" STREQUAL "Intel") # using Intel C
65    set(VECTOR_ALIASING_C_FLAGS "${VECTOR_ALIASING_C_FLAGS}
          -ansi-alias")
66    set(VECTOR_FPMODEL_C_FLAGS "${VECTOR_FPMODEL_C_FLAGS}
          -fp-model:precise")
67
68    set(VECTOR_OPENMP_SIMD_C_FLAGS "${VECTOR_OPENMP_SIMD_C_FLAGS}
          -qopenmp-simd")
69    set(VECTOR_C_OPTS "${VECTOR_C_OPTS} -xHOST")
70    if ("${CMAKE_C_COMPILER_VERSION}" VERSION_GREATER "17.0.4")
71      set(VECTOR_C_OPTS "${VECTOR_C_OPTS} -qopt-zmm-usage=high")
72    endif ("${CMAKE_C_COMPILER_VERSION}" VERSION_GREATER "17.0.4")
73    set(VECTOR_NOVEC_C_OPT "${VECTOR_NOVEC_C_OPT} -no-vec")
74    set(VECTOR_C_VERBOSE "${VECTOR_C_VERBOSE} -qopt-report=5
          -qopt-report-phase=openmp,loop,vec")
75
76  elseif (CMAKE_C_COMPILER_ID MATCHES "PGI")
77    set(VECTOR_ALIASING_C_FLAGS "${VECTOR_ALIASING_C_FLAGS}
          -alias=ansi")
78    set(VECTOR_OPENMP_SIMD_C_FLAGS "${VECTOR_OPENMP_SIMD_C_FLAGS}
          -Mvect=simd")
79
80    set(VECTOR_NOVEC_C_OPT "${VECTOR_NOVEC_C_OPT} -Mnovect ")
81    set(VECTOR_C_VERBOSE "${VECTOR_C_VERBOSE} -Minfo=loop,inline,vect")
82
83  elseif (CMAKE_C_COMPILER_ID MATCHES "MSVC")
84    set(VECTOR_C_OPTS "${VECTOR_C_OPTS}" " ")
85
86    set(VECTOR_NOVEC_C_OPT "${VECTOR_NOVEC_C_OPT}" " ")
87    set(VECTOR_C_VERBOSE "${VECTOR_C_VERBOSE} -Qvec-report:2")
88
89  elseif (CMAKE_C_COMPILER_ID MATCHES "XL")
90    set(VECTOR_ALIASING_C_FLAGSS "${VECTOR_ALIASING_C_FLAGS}
          -qalias=restrict")
```

```
 91      set(VECTOR_FPMODEL_C_FLAGSS "${VECTOR_FPMODEL_C_FLAGS} -qstrict")
 92      set(VECTOR_ARCH_C_FLAGSS "${VECTOR_ARCH_C_FLAGS} -qhot -qarch=auto
           -qtune=auto")
 93
 94      set(CMAKE_VEC_C_FLAGS "${CMAKE_VEC_FLAGS} -qsimd=auto")
 95      set(VECTOR_NOVEC_C_OPT "${VECTOR_NOVEC_C_OPT} -qsimd=noauto")
 96      # "long vector" optimizations
 97      #set(VECTOR_NOVEC_C_OPT "${VECTOR_NOVEC_C_OPT} -qhot=novector")
 98      set(VECTOR_C_VERBOSE "${VECTOR_C_VERBOSE} -qreport")
 99
100  elseif (CMAKE_C_COMPILER_ID MATCHES "Cray")
101      set(VECTOR_ALIASING_C_FLAGS "${VECTOR_ALIASING_C_FLAGS}
           -h restrict=a")
102      set(VECTOR_C_OPTS "${VECTOR_C_OPTS} -h vector=3")
103
104      set(VECTOR_NOVEC_C_OPT "${VECTOR_NOVEC_C_OPT} -h vector=0")
105      set(VECTOR_C_VERBOSE "${VECTOR_C_VERBOSE} -h msgs -h negmsgs
           -h list=a")
106
107  endif()
108
109  set(VECTOR_BASE_C_FLAGS "${VECTOR_ALIASING_C_FLAGS}
         ${VECTOR_ARCH_C_FLAGS} ${VECTOR_FPMODEL_C_FLAGS}")
110  set(VECTOR_NOVEC_C_FLAGS "${VECTOR_BASE_C_FLAGS}
         ${VECTOR_NOVEC_C_OPT}")
111  set(VECTOR_C_FLAGS "${VECTOR_BASE_C_FLAGS} ${VECTOR_C_OPTS}
         ${VECTOR_C_FPOPTS} ${VECTOR_OPENMP_SIMD_C_FLAGS}")
112 endif()
```

6.6   *OpenMP SIMD directives for better portability*

With the release of the OpenMP 4.0 standard, we have the option of using a more portable set of SIMD directives. These directives are implemented as commands rather than hints. We have already seen the use of these directives in section 6.3.3. The directives can be used to only request vectorization, or these can be combined with the for/do directive to request both threading and vectorization. The general syntax for C and C++ pragmas is

```
#pragma omp simd      / Vectorizes the following loop or block of code
#pragma omp for simd  / Threads and vectorizes the following loop
```

The general syntax for Fortran directives is

```
!$omp simd      / Vectorizes the following loop or block of code
!$omp do simd   / Threads and vectorizes the following loop
```

The basic SIMD directive can be supplemented with additional clauses to communicate more information. The most common additional clause is some variant of the private clause. This clause breaks false dependencies by creating a separate, private variable for each vector lane. An example of the syntax is

```
#pragma omp simd private(x)
   for (int i=0; i<n; i++){
      x=array(i);
      y=sqrt(x)*x;
   }
```

For a simple `private` clause, the recommended approach for C and C++ programmers is to just define the variable in the loop to make clear your intent:

```
double x=array(i);
```

The `firstprivate` clause initializes the private variable for each thread with the value coming into the loop, while the `lastprivate` clause sets the variable after the loop to the logically last value it would have in a sequential form of the loop.

The `reduction` clause creates a private variable for each lane and then performs the specified operation between the values for each lane at the end of the loop. The reduction variables are initialized for each vector lane as would make sense for the specified operation.

The `aligned` clause tells the compiler that the data is aligned on a 64-byte boundary so that peel loops do not need to be generated. Aligned data can be loaded into vector registers more efficiently. But first, the memory needs to be allocated with memory alignment. There are many different functions that you can use to get aligned memory, but there are still issues with portability. Here are some of the possibilities:

```
void *memalign(size_t alignment, size_t size);
int posix_memalign(void **memptr, size_t alignment, size_t size);
void *aligned_alloc(size_t alignment, size_t size);
void *aligned_malloc(size_t alignment, size_t size);
```

You can also use attributes to a memory definition to specify memory alignment:

```
double x[100] __attribute__((aligned(64)));
```

Another important modifier is the `collapse` clause. It tells the compiler to combine nested loops into a single loop for the vectorized implementation. The argument to the clause indicates how many loops to collapse:

```
#pragma omp collapse(2)
   for (int j=0; j<n; j++){
      for (int i=0; i<n; i++){
         x[j][i] = 0.0;
      }
   }
```

The loops are required to be *perfectly* nested. Perfectly nested loops only have statements in the innermost loop, with no extraneous statements before or after each loop block. The following clauses are for more specialized cases:

- The `linear` clause says that the variable changes for every iteration by some linear function.
- The `safelen` clause tells the compiler that the dependencies are separated by the specified length, which allows the compiler to vectorize for vector lengths shorter than or equal to the safe length clause argument.
- The `simdlen` clause generates vectorization of the specified length instead of the default length.

OpenMP SIMD FUNCTIONS

We can also vectorize an entire function or subroutine so that it can be called from within a vectorized region of the code. The syntax is a little different for C/C++ and Fortran. For C/C++, we'll use an example where the radial distance of an array of points is calculated using the Pythagorean theorem:

```
#pragma omp declare simd
double pythagorean(double a, double b){
    return(sqrt(a*a + b*b));
}
```

For Fortran, the subroutine or function name must be specified as an argument to the SIMD clause:

```
subroutine pythagorean(a, b, c)
!$omp declare simd(pythagorean)
real*8 a, b, c
    c = sqrt(a**2+b**2)
end subroutine pythagorean
```

The OpenMP SIMD function directive can also take some of the same clauses and some new ones as follows:

- The `inbranch` or `notinbranch` clause informs the compiler whether the function is called from within a conditional or not.
- The `uniform` clause says that the argument specified in the clause stays constant for all calls and does not need to be set up as a vector in the vectorized call.
- The `linear(ref, val, uval)` clause specifies to the compiler that the variable in the clause argument is linear in some form. For example, Fortran passes arguments by reference and when it passes subsequent array locations. In the previous Fortran example, the clause would look like this:

  ```
  !$omp declare simd(pythagorean) linear(ref(a, b, c))
  ```

  The clause can also be used to specify that the value is linear and whether the step is a larger constant as might occur in a strided access.
- The `aligned` and `simdlen` clauses are similar to the uses in the loop-oriented OpenMP SIMD clauses.

6.7   *Further explorations*

You won't find a lot of available materials on vectorization. The best approach for further explorations is to try vectorizing a smaller code block and experiment with the compilers that you commonly use. That being said, Intel has a lot of brief vectorization guides that are the best and most current resources. Look on the Intel website for the latest materials.

6.7.1   *Additional reading*

John Levesque, Cray Corporation, has authored a recent book with a good chapter on vectorization:

> John Levesque and Aaron Vose, *Programming for Hybrid Multi/Manycore MPP Systems*, (CRC Press, 2017).

Agner Fog has some of the best references on vectorization in his optimization guides, for example:

- Agner Fog, "Optimizing software in C++: An optimization guide for Windows, Linux and Mac platforms," 2004–2018 (last updated Aug, 2018).
- Agner Fog, "VCL C++ vector class library," v. 1.30 (2012–2017) available as a PDF at https://www.agner.org/optimize/vectorclass.pdf.

6.7.2   *Exercises*

1   Experiment with auto-vectorizing loops from the multimaterial code in section 4.3 (https://github.com/LANL/MultiMatTest.git). Add the vectorization and loop report flags and see what your compiler tells you.
2   Add OpenMP SIMD pragmas to help the compiler vectorize loops to the loop you selected in the first exercise.
3   For one of the vector-intrinsic examples, change the vector length from four double-precision values to an eight-wide vector width. Check the source code for this chapter for examples of working code for eight-wide implementations.
4   If you are on an older CPU, does your program from exercise 3 successfully run? What is the performance impact?

Summary

Both auto- and manual vectorization can provide significant performance improvements for your code. To underscore this

- We show several different methods for vectorizing code with different levels of control, effort, and performance.
- We summarize the proper compiler flags and their usage.
- We provide a list of programming styles to achieve vectorization.

OpenMP that performs

This chapter covers

- Planning and designing a correct and performant OpenMP program
- Writing loop-level OpenMP for modest parallelism
- Detecting correctness problems and improving robustness
- Fixing performance issues with OpenMP
- Writing scalable OpenMP for high performance

As many-core architectures grow in size and popularity, the details of thread-level parallelism become a critical factor in software performance. In this chapter, we first introduce the basics of Open Multi-Processing (OpenMP), a shared memory programming standard, and why it's important to have a fundamental understanding of how OpenMP functions. We will look at sample problems ranging in difficulty from a simple common "Hello World" example to a complex split-direction stencil implementation with OpenMP parallelization. We will thoroughly analyze the interaction between OpenMP directives and the underlying OS kernel, as well as the memory hierarchy and hardware features. Finally, we will investigate a promising high-level approach to OpenMP programming for future extreme-scale applications.

We show that high-level OpenMP is efficient for algorithms containing many short loops of computational work.

When compared to more standard-threading approaches, the high-level OpenMP paradigm leads to a reduction in thread overhead costs, synchronization waits, cache thrashing, and memory usage. Given these advantages, it is essential that the modern parallel computing programmer (you) knows both shared and distributed memory programming paradigms. We discuss the distributed memory programming paradigm in chapter 8 on the Message Passing Interface (MPI).

> **NOTE** You'll find the accompanying source code for this chapter at https://github.com/EssentialsofParallelComputing/Chapter7.

7.1 *OpenMP introduction*

OpenMP is one of the most widely supported open standards for threads and shared-memory parallel programming. In this section, we will explain the standard, ease of use, expected gains, difficulties, and the memory models.

The version of OpenMP that you see today took some time to develop and is still evolving. The origin of OpenMP began when several hardware vendors introduced their implementations in the early 1990s. A failed attempt was made in 1994 to standardize these implementations in the ANSI X3H5 draft standard. It was not until the introduction of wide-scale, multi-core systems in the late '90s that a re-emergence of the OpenMP approach was spurred, leading to the first OpenMP standard in 1997.

Today, OpenMP provides a standard and portable API for writing shared-memory parallel programs using threads; it's known to be easy to use, allowing for fast implementation, and requires only a small increase in code, normally seen in the context of pragmas or directives. A pragma (C/C++) or directive (Fortran) indicates to the compiler where to initiate OpenMP threads. These terms, pragma and directive, are often used interchangeably. *Pragmas* are preprocessor statements in C and C++. *Directives* are written as comments in Fortran in order for the program to retain the standard language syntax when OpenMP is not used. Although using OpenMP requires a compiler that supports it, most compilers come standard with that support.

OpenMP makes parallelization achievable for a beginner, thus allowing for an easy and fun introduction to scaling an application beyond one core. With the easy use of OpenMP pragmas and directives, a block of code can be quickly executed in parallel. In figure 7.1, you can see a conceptual view of the effort required and the performance obtained for OpenMP and MPI (discussed in chapter 8). Using OpenMP will often be the first exciting step into scaling an application.

7.1.1 *OpenMP concepts*

Although it is easy to achieve modest parallelism with OpenMP, thorough optimization can be a challenge. The source of the difficulty is the relaxed memory model that permits thread race conditions to exist. By *relaxed*, we mean that the value of the variables in main memory are not updated immediately. It would be too expensive to do

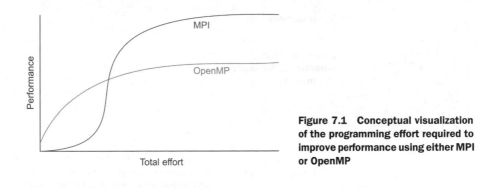

Figure 7.1 Conceptual visualization of the programming effort required to improve performance using either MPI or OpenMP

so for every change in variables. Because of the delay in the updates, minor timing differences between memory operations by each thread on shared variables have the potential to cause different results from run-to-run. Let's look at some definitions:

- *Relaxed memory model*—The value of the variables in main memory or caches of all the processors are not updated immediately.
- *Race condition*—A situation where multiple outcomes are possible, and the result is dependent on the timing of the contributors.

OpenMP was initially used to parallelize highly regular loops using threads on shared memory multiprocessors. Within a threaded parallel construct, each variable can be either shared or private. The terms *shared* and *private* have a particular meaning for OpenMP. Here are their definitions:

- *Private variable*—In the context of OpenMP, a private variable is local and only visible to its thread.
- *Shared variable*—In the context of OpenMP, a shared variable is visible and modifiable by any thread.

Truly understanding these terms requires a fundamental view of how memory is managed for a threaded application. As figure 7.2 shows, each thread has a private memory in its stack and shares memory in the heap.

OpenMP directives specify work sharing but say nothing about the memory or data location. As a programmer, you must understand the implicit rules for the memory scope of variables. The OS kernel can use several techniques to manage memory for OpenMP and threading. The most common technique is the first touch concept, where memory is allocated nearest to the thread where it is first touched. We define work sharing and first touch as

- *Work sharing*—To split the work across a number of threads or processes.
- *First touch*—The first touch of an array causes the memory to be allocated. The memory is allocated near the thread location where the touch occurs. Prior to the first touch, the memory only exists as an entry in a virtual memory table. The physical memory that corresponds to the virtual memory is created when it is first accessed.

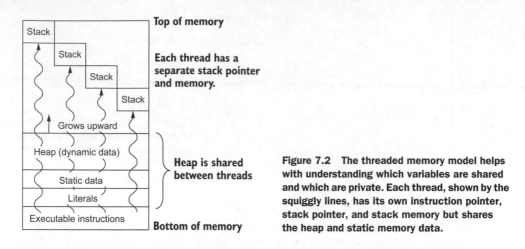

Figure 7.2 **The threaded memory model helps with understanding which variables are shared and which are private. Each thread, shown by the squiggly lines, has its own instruction pointer, stack pointer, and stack memory but shares the heap and static memory data.**

The reason that first touch is important is that on many high-end, high-performance computing nodes, there are multiple memory regions. When there are multiple memory regions, there is often Non-Uniform Memory Access (NUMA) from a CPU and its processes to different portions of memory, adding an important consideration for optimizing code performance.

> **DEFINITION**   On some computing nodes, blocks of memory are closer to some processors than others. This situation is called *Non-Uniform Memory Access* (NUMA). This is often the case when a node has two CPU sockets with each socket having its own memory. A processor's access to memory in the other NUMA domain typically takes twice the time (penalty) as it does to access its own memory.

Moreover, because OpenMP has a relaxed memory model, an OpenMP barrier or flush operation is required for the memory view of a thread to be communicated to other threads. A *flush operation* guarantees that a value moves between two threads, preventing race conditions. An OpenMP barrier flushes all the locally modified values and synchronizes the threads. How this updating of the values is done is a complicated operation in the hardware and operating system.

On a shared-memory, multi-core system, the modified values in cache must be flushed to the main memory and updated. Newer CPUs use specialized hardware to determine what actually changed, so the cache in dozens of cores only updates if necessary. But it is still an expensive operation and forces threads to stall while waiting for updates. In many ways, it is a similar kind of operation to what you need to do when you want to remove a thumb drive from your computer; you have to tell the operating system to flush all the thumb drive caches and then wait. Codes that use frequent barriers and flushes combined with smaller parallel regions often have excessive synchronization leading to poor performance.

OpenMP addresses a single node, not multiple nodes with distributed memory architectures. Thus, its memory scalability is limited to the memory on the node. For parallel applications that have larger memory requirements, OpenMP needs to be used in conjunction with a distributed-memory parallel technique. We discuss the most common of these, the MPI standard, in chapter 8.

Table 7.1 shows some common OpenMP concepts, terminology, and directives. We will demonstrate the use of these in the rest of the chapter.

Table 7.1   Roadmap of OpenMP topics in this chapter

OpenMP topic	OpenMP pragma	Description
Parallel regions (see listing 7.2)	`#pragma omp parallel`	Spawns threads within the region following this directive.
Loop work sharing (see listing 7.7)	*#pragma omp for* For Fortran: `#pragma do for`	Splits work equally between threads. Scheduling clauses include `static`, `dynamic`, `guided`, and `auto`.
Combined parallel region and work sharing (see listing 7.7)	`#pragma omp parallel for`	Directives can also be combined for specific calls within routines.
Reduction (see section 7.3.5)	`#pragma omp parallel for reduction (+: sum)`, `(min: xmin)`, or `(max: xmax)`	
Synchronization (see listing 7.15)	`#pragma omp barrier`	With multiple threads running, this call creates a stopping point so that all the threads can regroup before moving to the next section.
Serial sections (see listing 7.4 and 7.5)	`#pragma omp masked` executes on thread zero with no barrier at the end[a] `#pragma omp single)` one thread with an implicit barrier at the end of the block	This directive prevents multiple threads from executing the code. Use this directive when you have a function within a parallel region that you only want to run on one thread.
Locks	`#pragma omp critical or atomic`	For advanced implementations and used only in special cases

[a] `#pragma omp masked` was `#pragma omp master`. With the release of OpenMP standard v 5.1 in Nov. 2020, the term "master" was changed to "masked" to address concerns that it is offensive to many in the technical community. We are strong advocates of inclusion and, thus, use the new syntax throughout this chapter. Readers are warned that compilers may take some time to implement the change. Note that the examples that accompany the chapter will use the older syntax until most compilers are updated.

7.1.2   A simple OpenMP program

Now we'll show you how to apply each of the OpenMP concepts and directives. In this section, you will learn how to create a region of code with multiple threads using the OpenMP parallel pragma on a traditional "Hello World" problem distributed among threads. You will see how easy it is to use OpenMP and, potentially, to achieve performance gains. There are several ways to control how many threads you have in the parallel region. These are

- *Default*—The default is usually the maximum number of threads for the node, but it can be different, depending on the compiler and if MPI ranks exist.
- *Environment variable*—Set the size with the OMP_NUM_THREADS environment variable; for example

```
export OMP_NUM_THREADS=16
```

- *Function call*—Call the OpenMP function omp_set_threads, for example

```
omp_set_threads(16)
```

- *Pragma*—For example, #pragma omp parallel num_threads(16)

The simple example in listings 7.1 through 7.6 shows how to get your thread ID and the number of threads. Listing 7.1 shows our first attempt at writing a Hello World program.

> **Listing 7.1 A simple hello OpenMP program that prints** Hello OpenMP

```
HelloOpenMP/HelloOpenMP.c
 1 #include <stdio.h>
 2 #include <omp.h>          ◁──┘  Includes OpenMP header file for the
                                   OpenMP function calls (mandatory)
 3
 4 int main(int argc, char *argv[]){
 5    int nthreads, thread_id;              Function calls to get
 6    nthreads = omp_get_num_threads();     the number of threads
 7    thread_id = omp_get_thread_num();     and the thread ID
 8    printf("Goodbye slow serial world and Hello OpenMP");
 9    printf("I have %d thread(s) and my thread id is %d\n",nthreads,thread_id);
10 }
```

To compile with GCC

```
gcc -fopenmp -o HelloOpenMP HelloOpenMP.c
```

where -fopen is the compiler flag to turn on OpenMP.

Next, we'll set the number of threads for the program to use by setting an environment variable. We could also use the function call omp_set_num_threads() or just let OpenMP pick the number of threads based on the hardware that we are running on. To set the number of threads, use this command to set the environment variable:

```
export OMP_NUM_THREADS=4
```

Now, run your executable with ./HelloOpenMP, we get

```
Goodbye slow serial world and Hello OpenMP!
  I have 1 thread(s) and my thread id is 0
```

Not quite what we wanted; there is only one thread. We have to add a parallel region to get multiple threads. Listing 7.2 shows how to add the parallel region.

> **NOTE** In listings throughout the chapter, you'll see the annotations >> Spawn threads >> and Implied Barrier Implied Barrier. These are visual cues to show where threads are spawned and where barriers are inserted by the compiler. In later listings, we'll use the same annotations for Explicit Barrier Explicit Barrier where we have inserted a barrier directive.

Listing 7.2   Adding a parallel region to Hello OpenMP

```
HelloOpenMP/HelloOpenMP_fix1.c
 1 #include <stdio.h>
 2 #include <omp.h>
 3
 4 int main(int argc, char *argv[]){
 5    int nthreads, thread_id;
 6    #pragma omp parallel >> Spawn threads >>      ⟵  Adds the
 7    {                                                parallel region
 8        nthreads = omp_get_num_threads();
 9        thread_id = omp_get_thread_num();
10        printf("Goodbye slow serial world and Hello OpenMP!\n");
11        printf("  I have %d thread(s) and my thread id is
       %d\n",nthreads,thread_id);
12    } Implied Barrier        Implied Barrier
13 }
```

With these changes, we get the following output:

```
Goodbye slow serial world and Hello OpenMP!
  I have 4 thread(s) and my thread id is 3
Goodbye slow serial world and Hello OpenMP!
  I have 4 thread(s) and my thread id is 3
Goodbye slow serial world and Hello OpenMP!
Goodbye slow serial world and Hello OpenMP!
  I have 4 thread(s) and my thread id is 3
  I have 4 thread(s) and my thread id is 3
```

As you can see, all of the threads report that they are thread number 3. This is because nthreads and thread_id are shared variables. The value that is assigned at run time to these variables is the one written by the last thread to execute the instruction. This is a typical race condition as figure 7.3 illustrates. It is a common issue in threaded programs of any type.

Also note that the order of the printout is random, depending on the order of the writes from each processor and how they get flushed to the standard output device. To get the right thread numbers, we define the thread_id variable in the loop so that the scope of the variable becomes private to the thread as the following listing shows.

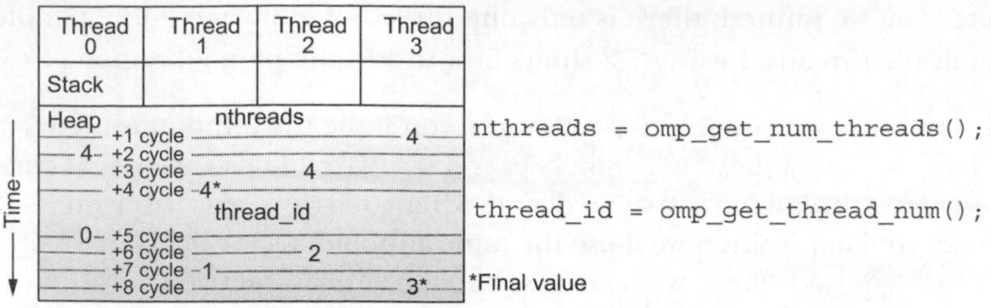

Figure 7.3 Variables in the previous example are defined before the parallel region, thus these are shared variables in the heap. Each thread writes to these, and the final value is determined by which one writes last. The shading represents progression through time with writes at different clock cycles by various threads in a non-deterministic fashion. This situation and similar situations are called *race conditions* because the results can vary from run to run.

Listing 7.3 Defining variables where these are used in Hello OpenMP

```
HelloOpenMP/HelloOpenMP_fix2.c
 1 #include <stdio.h>
 2 #include <omp.h>
 3
 4 int main(int argc, char *argv[]){
 5    #pragma omp parallel >> Spawn threads >>
 6    {
 7       int nthreads = omp_get_num_threads();
 8       int thread_id = omp_get_thread_num();
 9       printf("Goodbye slow serial world and Hello OpenMP!\n");
10       printf("   I have %d thread(s) and my thread id is
    %d\n",nthreads,thread_id);
11    } Implied Barrier        Implied Barrier
12 }
```

> Definition of nthreads and thread_id moved into the parallel region.

And we get

```
Goodbye slow serial world and Hello OpenMP!
Goodbye slow serial world and Hello OpenMP!
   I have 4 thread(s) and my thread id is 2
Goodbye slow serial world and Hello OpenMP!
   I have 4 thread(s) and my thread id is 3
Goodbye slow serial world and Hello OpenMP!
   I have 4 thread(s) and my thread id is 0
   I have 4 thread(s) and my thread id is 1
```

> Now we get a different thread ID for each thread.

Say we really didn't want every thread printing out. Let's minimize the output and put the print statement in a single OpenMP clause as the following listing shows, so only one thread writes output.

Listing 7.4 Adding a single pragma to print output for Hello OpenMP

HelloOpenMP/HelloOpenMP_fix3.c

```
 1 #include <stdio.h>
 2 #include <omp.h>
 3
 4 int main(int argc, char *argv[]){
 5    #pragma omp parallel >> Spawn threads >>
 6    {
 7        int nthreads = omp_get_num_threads();
 8        int thread_id = omp_get_thread_num();
 9        #pragma omp single
10        {
11            printf("Number of threads is %d\n",nthreads);
12            printf("My thread id %d\n",thread_id);
13        } Implied Barrier        Implied Barrier
14    } Implied Barrier        Implied Barrier
15 }
```

Variables defined in a parallel region are private.

Places output statements into an OpenMP single pragma block

And the output is now:

```
Goodbye slow serial world and Hello OpenMP!
  I have 4 thread(s) and my thread id is 2
```

The thread ID is a different value on each run. Here, we really wanted the thread that prints out to be the first thread, so we change the OpenMP clause in the next listing to use masked instead of single.

Listing 7.5 Changing a single pragma to a masked pragma in Hello OpenMP

HelloOpenMP/HelloOpenMP_fix4.c

```
 1 #include <stdio.h>
 2 #include <omp.h>
 3
 4 int main(int argc, char *argv[]){
 5    #pragma omp parallel >> Spawn threads >>
 6    {
 7        int nthreads = omp_get_num_threads();
 8        int thread_id = omp_get_thread_num();
 9        #pragma omp masked
10        {
11            printf("Goodbye slow serial world and Hello OpenMP!\n");
12            printf("  I have %d thread(s) and my thread id is
    %d\n",nthreads,thread_id);
13        }
14    } Implied Barrier        Implied Barrier
15 }
```

Adds directive to run only on main thread

Running this code now returns what we were first trying to do:

```
Goodbye slow serial world and Hello OpenMP!
  I have 4 thread(s) and my thread id is 0
```

We can make this operation even more concise and use fewer pragmas as we show in listing 7.6. The first print statement does not need to be in the parallel region. Also, we can limit the second printout to thread zero by simply using a conditional on the thread number. The implied barrier is from the `omp parallel` pragma.

Listing 7.6   Reducing the number of pragmas in Hello OpenMP

```
HelloOpenMP/HelloOpenMP_fix5.c
 1 #include <stdio.h>
 2 #include <omp.h>
 3
 4 int main(int argc, char *argv[]){
 5     printf("Goodbye slow serial world and Hello OpenMP!\n");
 6     #pragma omp parallel >> Spawn threads >>
 7     if (omp_get_thread_num() == 0) {
 8         printf("  I have %d thread(s) and my thread id is %d\n",
                omp_get_num_threads(), omp_get_thread_num());
 9     }
10     Implied Barrier       Implied Barrier
11 }
```

Moves print statement out of parallel region (points to lines 5–6)

Replaces OpenMP masked pragma with conditional for thread zero (points to line 7)

Pragma applies to next statement or a scoping block delimited by curly braces.

We have learned a few important things from this example:

- Variables that are defined outside a parallel region are by default *shared* in the parallel region.
- We should always strive to have the smallest program scope for a variable that is still correct. By defining the variable in the loop, the compiler can better understand our intent and handle it correctly.
- Using the `masked` clause is more restrictive than the `single` clause because it requires thread 0 to execute the code block. The `masked` clause also does not have an implicit barrier at the end.
- We need to watch out for possible race conditions between the operations of different threads.

OpenMP is continuously updating and releasing new versions. Before using an OpenMP implementation, you should know the version and the features that are supported. OpenMP started with the ability to harness threads across a single node. New capabilities, such as vectorization, and offloading tasks to accelerators, such as GPUs, have been added to the OpenMP standard. The following table shows some of the major features added in the last decade.

Version 3.0 (2008)	Introduction of task parallelism, and improvements to loop parallelism. These improvements to loop parallelism include loop collapse and nested parallelism.
Version 3.1 (2011)	Adds reduction `min` and `max` operators to C and C++ (other operators already in C and C++; `min` and `max` already in Fortran) and thread binding control

Version 4.0 (2013)	Adds OpenMP SIMD (vectorization) directive, target directive for offloading to GPUs and other accelerator devices, and thread affinity control
Version 4.5 (2015)	Substantial improvements to accelerator device support for GPUs
Version 5.0 (2018)	Further improvements to accelerator device support

One thing to note is that to deal with the substantial changes in hardware that are occurring, the pace of changes to OpenMP has increased since 2011. While the changes in version 3.0 and 3.1 dealt mostly with the standard CPU threading model, since then the changes in versions 4.0, 4.5, and 5.0 have mostly dealt with other forms of hardware parallelism, such as accelerators and vectorization.

7.2 Typical OpenMP use cases: Loop-level, high-level, and MPI plus OpenMP

OpenMP has three specific use-case scenarios to meet the needs of three different types of users. The first decision you need to make is which scenario is appropriate for your situation. The strategy and techniques vary for each of these cases: loop-level OpenMP, high-level OpenMP, and OpenMP to enhance MPI implementations. In the following sections, we will elaborate on each of these, when to use them and why, and how to use them. Figure 7.4 shows the recommended material to be carefully read for each of the use cases.

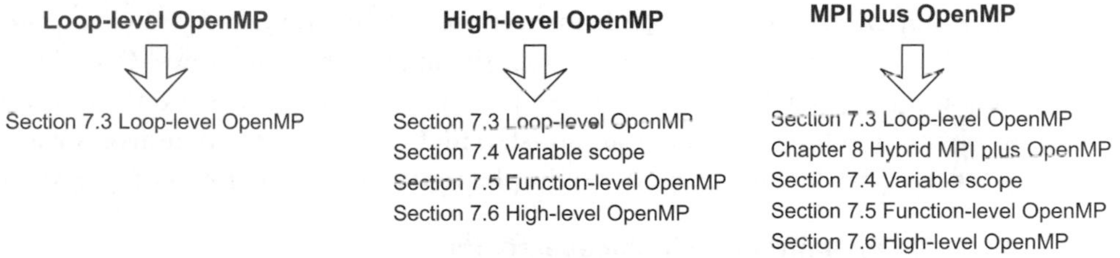

Loop-level OpenMP　　**High-level OpenMP**　　**MPI plus OpenMP**

Section 7.3 Loop-level OpenMP

Section 7.3 Loop-level OpenMP
Section 7.4 Variable scope
Section 7.5 Function-level OpenMP
Section 7.6 High-level OpenMP

Section 7.3 Loop-level OpenMP
Chapter 8 Hybrid MPI plus OpenMP
Section 7.4 Variable scope
Section 7.5 Function-level OpenMP
Section 7.6 High-level OpenMP

Figure 7.4　The recommended reading for each of the scenarios depends on the use case for your application.

7.2.1 Loop-level OpenMP for quick parallelization

A standard use case for loop-level OpenMP is when your application only needs a modest speedup and has plenty of memory resources. By this we mean that its requirements can be satisfied by the memory on a single hardware node. In this use case, it might be sufficient to use loop-level OpenMP. The following list summarizes the application characteristics of loop-level OpenMP:

- Modest parallelism
- Has plenty of memory resources (low memory requirements)
- Expensive part of calculation is in just a few `for` or `do` loops

We use loop-level OpenMP in these cases because it takes little effort and can be done quickly. With separate `parallel for` pragmas, the issue of thread race conditions is reduced. By placing OpenMP `parallel for` pragmas or `parallel do` directives before key loops, the parallelism of the loop can be easily achieved. Even when the end goal is a more efficient implementation, this loop-level approach is often the first step when introducing thread parallelism to an application.

> **NOTE** If your use case requires only modest speedup, go to section 7.3 for examples of this approach.

7.2.2   *High-level OpenMP for better parallel performance*

Next we discuss a different scenario, high-level OpenMP, where higher performance is desired. Our high-level OpenMP design has a radical difference from the strategies for standard loop-level OpenMP. Standard OpenMP starts from the bottom-up and applies the parallelism constructs at the loop level. Our high-level OpenMP approach takes a whole system view to the design with a top-down approach that addresses the memory system, the system kernel, and the hardware. The OpenMP language does not change, but the method of its use does. The end result is that we eliminate many of the thread startup costs and the costs of synchronization that hobble the scalability of loop-level OpenMP.

If you need to extract every last bit of performance out of your application, then high-level OpenMP is for you. Begin by learning loop-level OpenMP in section 7.3 as a starting point for your application. Then you will need to gain a deeper understanding of OpenMP variable scope from sections 7.4 and 7.5. Finally, dive into section 7.6 for a look at how the diametrically opposite approach of high-level OpenMP from the loop-level approach results in better performance. In that section, we'll look at the implementation model and a step-by-step method to reach the desired structure. This is followed by detailed examples of implementations for high-level OpenMP.

7.2.3   *MPI plus OpenMP for extreme scalability*

We can also use OpenMP to supplement distributed memory parallelism (as discussed in chapter 8). The basic idea of using OpenMP on a small subset of processes adds another level of parallel implementation that helps for extreme scaling. This could be within the node, or better yet, the set of processors that uniformly share quick access to shared memory, commonly referred to as a Non-Uniform Memory Access (NUMA) region.

We first discussed NUMA regions in OpenMP concepts in section 7.1.1 as an additional consideration for performance optimization. By using threading only within one memory region where all memory accesses have the same cost, some of the complexity and performance traps of OpenMP are avoided. In a more modest hybrid implementation, OpenMP can be used to harness the two-to-four hyperthreads for each processor. We'll discuss this scenario, the hybrid MPI + OpenMP, in chapter 8 after describing the basics of MPI.

For the OpenMP skills needed for this hybrid approach with small thread counts, it is sufficient to learn the loop-level OpenMP techniques in section 7.3. Then move incrementally to a more efficient and scalable OpenMP implementation, which allows more and more threads to replace MPI ranks. This requires at least some of the steps on the path to high-level OpenMP as presented in section 7.6. Now that you know what sections are important for your application's use case, let's jump into the details of how to make each strategy work.

7.3 *Examples of standard loop-level OpenMP*

In this section, we will look at examples of loop-level parallelization. The loop-level use case was introduced in section 7.2.1; here we will show you the implementation details. Let's begin.

Parallel regions are initiated by inserting pragmas around blocks of code that can be divided among independent threads (e.g., do loops, for loops). OpenMP relies on the OS kernel for its memory handling. This reliance for memory handling can often be an important factor that limits OpenMP from reaching its peak potential. We'll look at why this happens. Each variable within a parallel construct can be either shared or private. Moreover, OpenMP has a relaxed memory model. Each thread has a temporary view of memory so that it doesn't have the cost of storing memory with every operation. When the temporary view finally must be reconciled with main memory, an OpenMP barrier or flush operation is required to synchronize memory. Each of these synchronizations comes with a cost, due to the time that it takes to perform the flush, but also because it requires fast threads to wait for slower ones to complete. An understanding of how OpenMP functions can reduce these performance bottlenecks.

Performance is not the only concern for an OpenMP programmer. You should also watch for correctness issues caused by thread race conditions. Threads might progress at different speeds on the processors and, in combination with the relaxed memory synchronization, serious errors can suddenly occur in even well-tested code. Careful programming and the use of specialized tools as discussed in section 7.9.2 is essential for robust OpenMP applications.

In this section, we'll take a look at a few loop-level OpenMP examples to get an idea of how it is used in practice. The source code that accompanies the chapter has more variants of each example. We strongly encourage you to experiment with each of these on the architecture and compiler that you commonly work with. We ran each of the examples on a Skylake Gold 6152 dual socket system, as well as a 2017 Mac laptop. Threads are allocated by cores, and thread binding is enabled using the following OpenMP environment variables to reduce the performance variation of runs:

```
export OMP_PLACES=cores
export OMP_CPU_BIND=true
```

We'll explore thread placement and binding more in chapter 14. For now, to help you get experience with loop-level OpenMP, we'll present three different examples: vector addition, stream triad, and a stencil code. We'll show the parallel speedup of the three examples after the last example in section 7.3.4.

7.3.1   *Loop level OpenMP: Vector addition example*

In the vector addition example (listing 7.7), you can see the interaction between the three components: OpenMP work-sharing directives, implied variable scope, and memory placement by the operating system. These three components are necessary for OpenMP program correctness and performance.

> **Listing 7.7   Vector add with a simple loop-level OpenMP pragma**

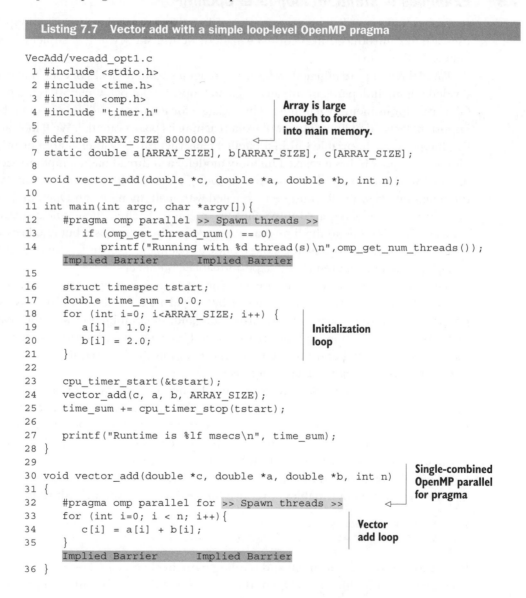

```
VecAdd/vecadd_opt1.c
 1 #include <stdio.h>
 2 #include <time.h>
 3 #include <omp.h>
 4 #include "timer.h"                        Array is large
 5                                           enough to force
 6 #define ARRAY_SIZE 80000000    ◁───       into main memory.
 7 static double a[ARRAY_SIZE], b[ARRAY_SIZE], c[ARRAY_SIZE];
 8
 9 void vector_add(double *c, double *a, double *b, int n);
10
11 int main(int argc, char *argv[]){
12     #pragma omp parallel  >> Spawn threads >>
13         if (omp_get_thread_num() == 0)
14             printf("Running with %d thread(s)\n",omp_get_num_threads());
    Implied Barrier        Implied Barrier
15
16     struct timespec tstart;
17     double time_sum = 0.0;
18     for (int i=0; i<ARRAY_SIZE; i++) {
19        a[i] = 1.0;                        Initialization
20        b[i] = 2.0;                        loop
21     }
22
23     cpu_timer_start(&tstart);
24     vector_add(c, a, b, ARRAY_SIZE);
25     time_sum += cpu_timer_stop(tstart);
26
27     printf("Runtime is %lf msecs\n", time_sum);
28 }
29                                                        Single-combined
30 void vector_add(double *c, double *a, double *b, int n) OpenMP parallel
31 {                                                       for pragma
32     #pragma omp parallel for  >> Spawn threads >>  ◁───
33     for (int i=0; i < n; i++){
34        c[i] = a[i] + b[i];                Vector
35     }                                     add loop
    Implied Barrier        Implied Barrier
36 }
```

This particular implementation style produces modest parallel performance on a single node. Take note, this implementation could be better. All the array memory is first touched by the main thread during the initialization prior to the main loop as shown on the left in figure 7.5. This can cause the memory to be located in a different memory region, where the memory access time is greater for some of the threads.

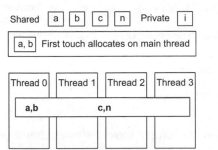

Simple OpenMP loop ignores
memory allocation.
Memory ends up on main thread.

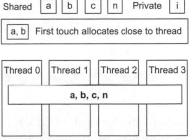

Distributing initialization loop mimics
thread access for proper first touch.
Memory ends up close to threads.

Figure 7.5 Adding a single OpenMP pragma on the main vector add computation loop (on the left) results in the a and b arrays being touched first by the main thread; the data is allocated near thread zero. The c array is first touched during the computation loop and, therefore, the memory for the c array is close to each thread. On the right, adding an OpenMP pragma on the initialization loop results in the memory for the a and b arrays being placed near the thread where the work is done.

Now, to improve the OpenMP performance, we insert pragmas in the initialization loops as listing 7.8 shows. The loops are distributed in the same static threading partition, so the threads that touch the memory in the initialization loop will have the memory located near to them by the operating system (shown on the right side of figure 7.5).

> **Listing 7.8 Vector add with first touch**

```
VecAdd/vecadd_opt2.c
11 int main(int argc, char *argv[]){
12    #pragma omp parallel  >> Spawn threads >>
13       if (omp_get_thread_num() == 0)
14          printf("Running with %d thread(s)\n",omp_get_num_threads());
      Implied Barrier       Implied Barrier
15
16    struct timespec tstart;
17    double time_sum = 0.0;
18    #pragma omp parallel for  >> Spawn threads >>        ◁─┐
19    for (int i=0; i<ARRAY_SIZE; i++) {
20       a[i] = 1.0;
21       b[i] = 2.0;
22    }
      Implied Barrier        Implied Barrier
```

Initialization in a "parallel for" pragma so first touch gets memory in the proper location

Initializes the a and b arrays

```
23
24    cpu_timer_start(&tstart);
25    vector_add(c, a, b, ARRAY_SIZE);
26    time_sum += cpu_timer_stop(tstart);
27
28    printf("Runtime is %lf msecs\n", time_sum);
29 }
30
31 void vector_add(double *c, double *a, double *b, int n)
32 {
33    #pragma omp parallel for  >> Spawn threads >>
34    for (int i=0; i < n; i++){
35       c[i] = a[i] + b[i];
36    }
      Implied Barrier      Implied Barrier
37 }
```

OpenMP for pragma to distribute work for vector add loop across threads

Vector add loop

The threads in the second NUMA region no longer have a slower memory access time. This improves the memory bandwidth for the threads in the second NUMA region and also improves the load balance across the threads. First touch is an OS policy that was mentioned earlier in section 7.1.1. Good first touch implementations may often gain a 10 to 20% performance improvement. For evidence that this is the case, see table 7.2 in section 7.3.4 for the performance improvement on these examples.

If NUMA is enabled in the BIOS, the Skylake Gold 6152 CPU has a factor of about two decrease in performance when accessing remote memory. As with most tunable parameters, the configuration of individual systems can vary. To see your configuration, you can use the numactl and numastat commands for Linux. You may have to install the numactl-libs or numactl-devel packages for these commands.

Figure 7.6 shows the output for the Skylake Gold test platform. The node distances listed at the end of the output roughly capture the cost of accessing memory on a remote node. You can think of this as the relative number of hops to get to memory. Here the memory access cost is a little over a factor of two (21 versus 10). Note that sometimes two NUMA region systems are listed with a cost of 20 versus 10 as a default configuration instead of their real costs.

The NUMA configuration information can tell you what is important to optimize. If you only have one NUMA region, or the difference in memory access costs is small, you may not need to worry as much about first touch optimizations. If the system is configured for interleaved memory accesses to the NUMA regions, optimizing for the faster local memory accesses will not help. In the absence of specific information or when trying to optimize in general for larger HPC systems, you should use first touch optimizations to get local, faster memory accesses.

7.3.2   *Stream triad example*

The following listing shows another similar example for the stream triad benchmark. This example runs multiple iterations of the kernel to get an average performance.

```
•  numactl --hardware
   available: 2 nodes (0-1)
   node 0 cpus: 0 1 2 3 4 5 6 7 8 9 10 11 12 13 14 15 16 17 18 19 20 21 44 45 46 47 48 49 50 51
   52 53 54 55 56 57 58 59 60 61 62 63 64 65
   node 0 size: 195243 MB
   node 0 free: 189993 MB
   node 1 cpus: 22 23 24 25 26 27 28 29 30 31 32 33 34 35 36 37 38 39 40 41 42 43 66 67 68 69 70
   71 72 73 74 75 76 77 78 79 80 81 82 83 84 85 86 87
   node 1 size: 196608 MB
   node 1 free: 190343 MB
   node distances:
   node   0   1
     0:  10  21
     1:  21  10

•  numastat
                         node0            node1
   numa_hit          311179492        298484169
   numa_miss                 0                0
   numa_foreign              0                0
   interleave_hit       106713           106520
   local_node        310521578        296233768
   other_node           657914          2250401
```

Figure 7.6 Output from the `numactl` and `numastat` commands. The distance between memory regions is highlighted. Note that the NUMA utilities use the term "node" differently than we have defined it. In their terminology, each NUMA region is a node. We reserve the node terminology for a separate distributed memory system such as another desktop or tray in a rack-mounted system.

Listing 7.9 Loop-level OpenMP threading of the stream triad

StreamTriad/stream_triad_opt2.c

```c
 1 #include <stdio.h>
 2 #include <time.h>
 3 #include <omp.h>
 4 #include "timer.h"
 5
 6 #define NTIMES 16
 7 #define STREAM_ARRAY_SIZE 80000000        Large enough to force
 8 static double a[STREAM_ARRAY_SIZE], b[STREAM_ARRAY_SIZE],   into main memory
   c[STREAM_ARRAY_SIZE];
 9
10 int main(int argc, char *argv[]){
11    #pragma omp parallel >> Spawn threads >>
12       if (omp_get_thread_num() == 0)
13          printf("Running with %d thread(s)\n",omp_get_num_threads());
   Implied Barrier      Implied Barrier
14
15    struct timeval tstart;
16    double scalar = 3.0, time_sum = 0.0;
17    #pragma omp parallel for >> Spawn threads >>      Initializes data
18    for (int i=0; i<STREAM_ARRAY_SIZE; i++) {         and arrays
19       a[i] = 1.0;
20       b[i] = 2.0;
21    }
   Implied Barrier      Implied Barrier
```

```
22
23    for (int k=0; k<NTIMES; k++){
24       cpu_timer_start(&tstart);
25       #pragma omp parallel for >> Spawn threads >>
26       for (int i=0; i<STREAM_ARRAY_SIZE; i++){
27          c[i] = a[i] + scalar*b[i];
28       }
      Implied Barrier      Implied Barrier
29       time_sum += cpu_timer_stop(tstart);
30       c[1]=c[2];      <──┐
31    }                    │  Keeps the compiler from
32                         │  optimizing the loop
33    printf("Average runtime is %lf msecs\n", time_sum/NTIMES);
34 }
```

Stream
triad loop

Again, we just need one pragma to implement the OpenMP threaded computation at line 25. A second pragma inserted at line 17 further improves performance because of the better memory placement obtained by a proper first touch technique.

7.3.3   *Loop level OpenMP: Stencil example*

The third example of loop-level OpenMP is the stencil operation first introduced in chapter 1 (figure 1.10). This stencil operator adds the surrounding neighbors and takes an average for the new value of the cell. Listing 7.10 has more complex memory read access patterns and, as we optimize the routine, it shows us the effect of threads accessing memory written by other threads. In this first loop-level OpenMP implementation, each parallel for block is synchronized by default, which prevents potential race conditions. In later, more optimized versions of the stencil, we'll add explicit synchronization directives.

Listing 7.10   Loop-level OpenMP threading in the stencil example with first touch

```
Stencil/stencil_opt2.c
 1 #include <stdio.h>
 2 #include <stdlib.h>
 3 #include <time.h>
 4 #include <omp.h>
 5
 6 #include "malloc2D.h"
 7 #include "timer.h"
 8
 9 #define SWAP_PTR(xnew,xold,xtmp) (xtmp=xnew, xnew=xold, xold=xtmp)
10
11 int main(int argc, char *argv[])
12 {
13    #pragma omp parallel >> Spawn threads >>
14    #pragma omp masked
15       printf("Running with %d thread(s)\n",omp_get_num_threads());
      Implied Barrier       Implied Barrier
16
17    struct timeval tstart_init, tstart_flush, tstart_stencil, tstart_total;
```

```
18    double init_time, flush_time, stencil_time, total_time;
19    int imax=2002, jmax = 2002;
20    double** xtmp;
21    double** x = malloc2D(jmax, imax);
22    double** xnew = malloc2D(jmax, imax);
23    int *flush = (int *)malloc(jmax*imax*sizeof(int)*4);
24
25    cpu_timer_start(&tstart_total);
26    cpu_timer_start(&tstart_init);
27    #pragma omp parallel for >> Spawn threads >>          ◁─────────┐
28    for (int j = 0; j < jmax; j++){                                 │
29       for (int i = 0; i < imax; i++){                    Initializes with
30          xnew[j][i] = 0.0;                               OpenMP pragma
31          x[j][i] = 5.0;                                  for first-touch
32       }                                                  memory allocation
33    } Implied Barrier      Implied Barrier                          │
34                                                                    │
35    #pragma omp parallel for >> Spawn threads >>          ◁─────────┘
36    for (int j = jmax/2 - 5; j < jmax/2 + 5; j++){
37       for (int i = imax/2 - 5; i < imax/2 -1; i++){
38          x[j][i] = 400.0;
39       }
40    } Implied Barrier      Implied Barrier
41    init_time += cpu_timer_stop(tstart_init);
42
43    for (int iter = 0; iter < 10000; iter++){
44       cpu_timer_start(&tstart_flush);
45       #pragma omp parallel for >> Spawn threads >>       ◁──────┐
46       for (int l = 1; l < jmax*imax*4; l++){                    │
47          flush[l] = 1.0;                                 Inserts parallel
48       } Implied Barrier      Implied Barrier              for pragma to
49       flush_time += cpu_timer_stop(tstart_flush);        thread loop
50       cpu_timer_start(&tstart_stencil);                         │
51       #pragma omp parallel for >> Spawn threads >>       ◁──────┘
52       for (int j = 1; j < jmax-1; j++){
53          for (int i = 1; i < imax-1; i++){
54             xnew[j][i]=(x[j][i] + x[j][i-1] + x[j][i+1] +
55                                   x[j-1][i] + x[j+1][i])/5.0;
56          }
57       } Implied Barrier      Implied Barrier
58       stencil_time += cpu_timer_stop(tstart_stencil);
59
60       SWAP_PTR(xnew, x, xtmp);
61       if (iter%1000 == 0) printf("Iter %d\n",iter);
62    }
63    total_time += cpu_timer_stop(tstart_total);
64
65    printf("Timing: init %f flush %f stencil %f total %f\n",
66           init_time,flush_time,stencil_time,total_time);
67
68    free(x);
69    free(xnew);
70    free(flush);
71 }
```

For this example, we inserted a flush loop at line 46 to empty the cache of the x and xnew arrays. This is to mimic the performance where a code does not have the variables in cache from a prior operation. The case without data in cache is termed a *cold cache*, and when the data is in cache it is called a *warm cache*. Both cold and warm caches are valid cases to analyze for different use-case scenarios. Simply, both cases are possible in a real application, and it may be difficult to even know which will happen without a deep analysis.

7.3.4   *Performance of loop-level examples*

Let's review the performance of the earlier examples in this section. As seen in listings 7.8, 7.9, and 7.10, introducing loop-level OpenMP requires few changes to the source code. As table 7.2 demonstrates, the performance improvement is on the order of 10x faster. This is a pretty good performance return for the effort required. But for a system with 88 threads, the achieved parallel efficiency is modest, at about 19% as calculated below, giving us some room for improvement. To calculate the speedup, we first take the serial run time divided by the parallel run time like this:

Stencil speedup = (serial run-time)/(parallel run-time) = 17.0 times faster

If we get perfect speedup on 88 threads, it would be 88. We take the actual speedup and divide by the ideal speedup of 88 to calculate the parallel efficiency:

Stencil parallel efficiency = (stencil speedup)/(ideal speedup) = 17 / 88 = 19%

Parallel efficiency is much better at smaller thread counts; at four threads, parallel efficiency is at 85%. The effect of getting memory allocated close to the thread is small, but significant. In the timings in table 7.2, the first optimization, simple loop-level OpenMP, has just OpenMP `parallel for` pragmas on the computation loops. The second optimization with first touch adds the OpenMP `parallel for` pragmas for the initialization loops. Table 7.2 summarizes the performance improvements for simple OpenMP with the addition of a first touch optimization. The timings used `OMP_PLACES=cores` and `OMP_CPU_BIND=true`.

Table 7.2   Shown are the run times in msecs. The speedup on a Skylake Gold 6152 dual socket node with the GCC version 8.2 compiler is a factor of ten on 88 threads. Adding an OpenMP pragma on the initialization to get proper first-touch memory allocation returns an additional speedup.

	Serial	Simple loop-level OpenMP	Adding first touch
Vector Add	0.253	0.0301	0.0175
Stream Triad	0.164	0.0203	0.0131
Stencil	62.56	3.686	3.311

Profiling the stencil application threaded with OpenMP, we observe that 10-15% of the run time is consumed by OpenMP overhead, consisting of thread waits and thread startup costs. We can reduce the OpenMP overhead by adopting a high-level OpenMP design as we'll discuss in section 7.6.

7.3.5 *Reduction example of a global sum using OpenMP threading*

Another common type of loop is a reduction. Reductions are a common pattern in parallel programming that were introduced in section 5.7. *Reductions* are any operation that starts with an array and calculates a scalar result. In OpenMP, this can also be handled easily in the loop-level pragma with the addition of a `reduction` clause as the following listing shows.

Listing 7.11 Global sum with OpenMP threading

GlobalSums/serial_sum_novec.c

```
 1 double do_sum_novec(double* restrict var, long ncells)
 2 {
 3     double sum = 0.0;
 4     #pragma omp parallel for reduction(+:sum)
 5     for (long i = 0; i < ncells; i++){
 6         sum += var[i];
 7     }
 8
 9     return(sum);
10 }
```

Global sum reduction code → lines 3–7

OpenMP parallel for loop with reduction clause → line 4

The reduction operation computes a local sum on each thread and then sums all the threads together. The reduction variable, `sum`, is initialized to the appropriate value for the operation. In the code in listing 7.11, the reduction variable is initialized to zero. The initialization of the `sum` variable to zero on line 3 is still needed for proper operation when we don't use OpenMP.

7.3.6 *Potential loop-level OpenMP issues*

Loop-level OpenMP can be applied to most, but not all loops. The loop must have a canonical form so that the OpenMP compiler can apply the work-sharing operation. The canonical form is the traditional, straightforward loop implementation that is first learned by programmers. The requirements are that

- The loop index variable must be an integer.
- The loop index cannot be modified in the loop.
- The loop must have standard exit conditions.
- The loop iterations must be countable.
- The loop must not have any loop-carried dependencies.

You can test the last requirement by reversing the order of the loop or by changing the order of the loop operations. If the answer changes, the loop has loop-carried dependencies. There are similar restrictions on loop-carried dependencies for vectorization on the CPU and threading implementations on the GPU. The similarities of this loop-carried dependency requirement have been described as *fine-grained* parallelization versus the *coarse-grained* structure used in a distributed-memory, message-passing approach. Here are some definitions:

- *Fine-grained parallelization*—A type of parallelism where computational loops or other small blocks of code are operated on by multiple processors or threads and may need frequent synchronization.
- *Coarse-grained parallelization*—A type of parallelism where the processor operates on large blocks of code with infrequent synchronization.

Many programming languages have proposed a modified loop-type that tells the compiler that loop-level parallelism is allowed to be applied in some form. For now, supplying a pragma or directive before the loop supplies this information.

7.4   *Variable scope importance for correctness in OpenMP*

To convert an application or routine to high-level OpenMP, you need to understand variable scope. The OpenMP specifications are vague on many scoping details. Figure 7.7 shows the scoping rules for compilers. Generally, a variable on the stack is considered private, and those that are placed in the heap are shared (figure 7.2). For high-level OpenMP, the most important case is how to manage scope in a called routine in a parallel region.

Scoping rules

Specification		Shared	Private	Reduction
	Parallel construct	Variables declared outside parallel construct or in a shared clause	Automatic variables within parallel construct or in a `private` or `firstprivate` clause	Reduction clause
Parallel region	Fortran routine	`save` attribute, initialized variables, common block, module variables	All local variables or declared `threadprivate`. Also dynamically allocated	
	C routine	File scope variables, `extern`, or `static`		
	Arguments	Inherited from calling environment		
	Always	All loop indices will be private		

Figure 7.7   Summary of thread scoping rules for OpenMP applications

When determining the scope of variables, you should put more focus on variables on the left-hand side of an expression. The scope for variables that are being written to is more important to get correct. Note that private variables are undefined at entry and after the exit of a parallel region as listing 7.12 shows. The `firstprivate` and `lastprivate` clauses can modify this behavior in special cases. If a variable is private, we should see it set before it is used in the parallel block and not used after the parallel region. If a variable is intended to be private, it is best to declare the variable within the loop because a locally declared variable has exactly the same behavior as a private OpenMP variable. Long story short, declaring the variable within the loop eliminates any confusion on what the behavior should be. It does not exist before the loop or afterward, so incorrect uses are not possible.

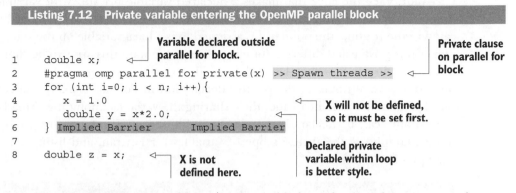

Listing 7.12 Private variable entering the OpenMP parallel block

On the directive in line 4 in listing 7.11, we added a reduction clause to note the special treatment needed for the `sum` variable. On line 2 of listing 7.12, we showed the `private` directive. There are other clauses that can be used on the parallel directive and other program blocks, for example:

- `shared(var,var)`
- `private(var,var)`
- `firstprivate(var,var)`
- `lastprivate(var, var)`
- `reduction([+,min,max]:<var,var>)`
- `*threadprivate` (a special directive used in a thread-parallel function)

We highly recommend using tools such as Intel® Inspector and Allinea/ARM MAP to develop more efficient code and to implement high-level OpenMP. We discuss some of these tools in section 7.9. Becoming familiar with a variety of essential tools is necessary before beginning the implementation of high-level OpenMP. After running your application through these tools, a better understanding of the application allows for a smoother transition to the implementation of high-level OpenMP.

7.5 *Function-level OpenMP: Making a whole function thread parallel*

We will introduce the concept of high-level OpenMP in section 7.6. But before we attempt high-level OpenMP, it is necessary to see how the loop-level implementations can be expanded to cover larger sections of code. The purpose for expanding the loop-level implementation is to lower the overhead and increase parallel efficiency. When expanding the parallel region, it eventually covers an entire subroutine. Once we convert the whole function into an OpenMP parallel region, OpenMP provides far less control over the thread scope of the variables. The clauses for a parallel region no longer help as there is no place to add scoping clauses. So how do we control variable scope?

While the defaults for variable scope in functions usually work well, there are cases where they don't. The only OpenMP pragma control for functions is the threadprivate directive that makes a declared variable private. Most variables in a function are on the stack and are already private. If there is an array dynamically allocated in the routine, the pointer it is assigned to is a local variable on the stack, which means it is private and different for every thread. We want this array to be shared, but there is no directive for that. Using the specific compiler scoping rules from figure 7.7, we add a save attribute to the pointer declaration in Fortran, making the compiler put the variable in the heap and, thus, sharing the variable among the threads. In C, the variable can be declared static or made file scope. The following listing shows some examples of the thread scope of variables for Fortran, and listing 7.14 shows examples for C and C++.

Listing 7.13   Function-level variable scope in Fortran

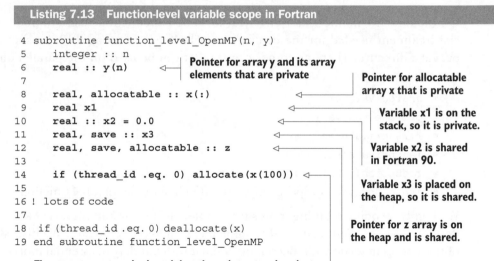

```
 4 subroutine function_level_OpenMP(n, y)
 5    integer :: n
 6    real :: y(n)              ◄─┐  Pointer for array y and its array
 7                                 │  elements that are private
 8    real, allocatable :: x(:)  ◄      Pointer for allocatable
 9    real x1                    ◄      array x that is private
10    real :: x2 = 0.0           ◄      Variable x1 is on the
11    real, save :: x3           ◄      stack, so it is private.
12    real, save, allocatable :: z  ◄   Variable x2 is shared
13                                      in Fortran 90.
14    if (thread_id .eq. 0) allocate(x(100))  ◄
15                                      Variable x3 is placed on
16 ! lots of code                      the heap, so it is shared.
17
18  if (thread_id .eq. 0) deallocate(x)   Pointer for z array is on
19 end subroutine function_level_OpenMP   the heap and is shared.
```

The x array memory is shared, but the pointer to x is private.

The pointer for array y on line 6 is the scope of the variable at the location of the subroutine. In this case, it is in a parallel region, making it private. Both the pointer for x and the variable x1 are private. The scope of variable x2 on line 10 is more complicated. It is shared in Fortran 90 and private in Fortran 77. Initialized variables in Fortran 90 are on the heap and are only initialized (to zero in this case) on their first occurrence! The variables x3 and z on lines 11 and 12 are shared because these are in the heap. The memory allocated for x on line 14 is on the heap and shared, but the pointer is private, which results in memory only accessible on thread zero.

Listing 7.14   Function-level variable scope in C/C++

```
 5 void function_level_OpenMP(int n, double *y)   ◄─┐  The pointer to
 6 {                                                 │  array y is private.
```

```
 7      double *x;                                    The pointer to
 8      static double *x1;                            array x is private.
 9
10      int thread_id;                                The pointer to
11 #pragma omp parallel                               array x1 is shared.
12      thread_id = omp_get_thread_num();
13
14      if (thread_id == 0) x = (double *)malloc(100*sizeof(double));
15      if (thread_id == 0) x1 = (double *)malloc(100*sizeof(double));
16
17 // lots of code
18      if (thread_id ==0) free(x);                   Memory for the x1
19      if (thread_id ==0) free(x1);                  array is shared.
20 }
                                                      Memory for the x
                                                      array is shared.
```

The pointer to array y in the argument list on line 5 is on the stack. It has the scope of the variable at the calling location. In a parallel region, the pointer to y is private. The memory for the x array is on the heap and shared, but the pointer is private, so the memory is only accessible from thread zero. Memory for the x1 array is on the heap and shared, and the pointer is shared so the memory is accessible and shared across all the threads.

You need to be always on guard for unexpected effects of variable declarations and definitions that impact the thread scope. For example, initializing a local variable with a value in a Fortran 90 subroutine automatically gives the variable the save attribute and the variable is now shared.[1] We recommend explicitly adding the save attribute to the declaration to avoid any issues or confusion.

7.6   *Improving parallel scalability with high-level OpenMP*

Why use high-level OpenMP? The central high-level OpenMP strategy is to improve on standard loop-level parallelism by minimizing fork/join overhead and memory latency. Reduction of thread wait times is often seen as another major motivating factor of high-level OpenMP implementations. By explicitly dividing the work among the threads, threads are no longer implicitly waiting on other threads and can therefore go on to the next part of the calculation. This allows explicit control of the synchronization point. In figure 7.8, unlike the typical fork-join model of standard OpenMP, high-level OpenMP keeps the threads dormant but alive, thus reducing overhead tremendously.

In this section, we'll review the explicit steps needed to implement high-level OpenMP. Then we'll show you how to go from a loop-level implementation to a high-level implementation.

---

[1] This is not the case under the Fortran 77 standard! But even with Fortran 77, some compilers such as the DEC Fortran compiler mandate that every variable in a routine have the save attribute, causing obscure bugs and portability problems. Knowing this, we could make sure we are compiling with the Fortran 90 standard and potentially fix the private scoping issue by initializing the array pointer, which causes it to be moved to the heap, making the variable shared.

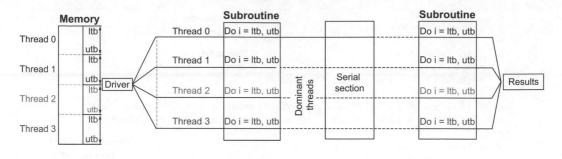

Figure 7.8   Visualization of high-level OpenMP threading. Threads are spawned once and left dormant when not needed. Thread bounds are specified manually and synchronization is minimized.

7.6.1   *How to implement high-level OpenMP*

Implementation of high-level OpenMP is often more time-consuming because it requires the use of advanced tools and extensive testing. Implementing high-level OpenMP can also be difficult as it is more prone to race conditions than the standard loop-level implementation. Additionally, it is often not apparent how to get from the starting point (loop-level implementation) to the ending point (high-level implementation).

The common use for the more tedious high-level open implementation would be when you want more efficiency and want to get rid of thread spawning and synchronization costs. For more information on high-level OpenMP, see section 7.11. You can implement efficient high-level OpenMP by having a good understanding of the memory bounds of all loops in your application, enabling the use of profiling tools, and methodically working through the following steps. We suggest and show an implementation strategy that is incremental, methodical, and can provide a successful, smooth transition to a high-level OpenMP implementation. Steps to a high-level OpenMP implementation include

- *Base implementation*—Implement loop-level OpenMP
- *Step 1: Reduce thread start up*—Merge the parallel regions and join all the loop-level parallel constructs into larger parallel regions
- *Step 2: Synchronization*—Add `nowait` clauses to `for` loops, where synchronization is not needed, and calculate and manually partition the loops across the threads, which allows for removal of barriers and required synchronization.
- *Step 3: Optimize*—Make arrays and variables private to each thread when possible.
- *Step 4: Code correctness*—Check thoroughly for race conditions (after every step).

Figures 7.9 and 7.10 show the pseudocode corresponding to the previous four steps, starting with a typical loop-level implementation using `omp parallel do` pragmas and transitioning to more efficient high-level parallelism.

In our steps to a high-level OpenMP implementation, the thread start-up time is reduced in the first step of high-level OpenMP. The entire code is placed in a single

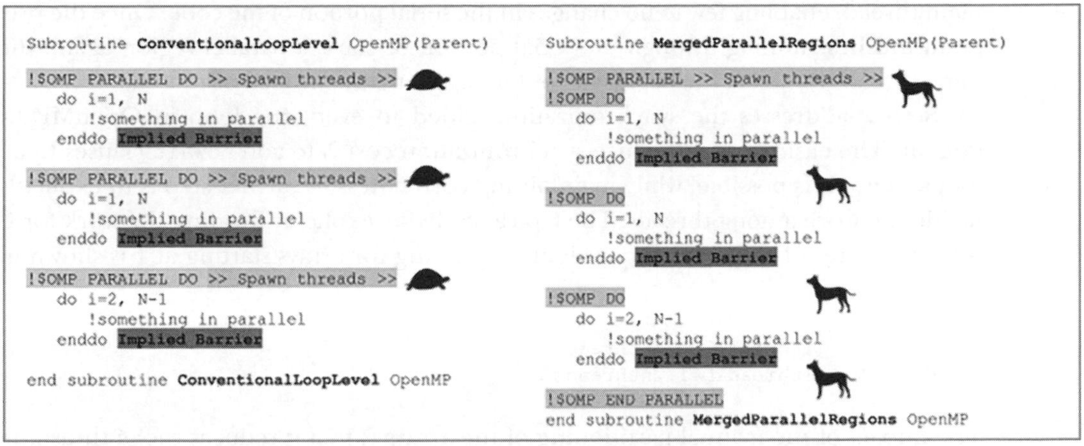

Figure 7.9 High-level OpenMP starts with a loop-level OpenMP implementation and merges parallel regions together to reduce the cost of thread spawning. We use the animal images to represent where the changes are made and the relative speed of the actual implementation. The conventional loop level OpenMP shown with the turtle is faster, but there is overhead with each `parallel do` that limits speedup. The dog represents the relative gain in speed from merging parallel regions.

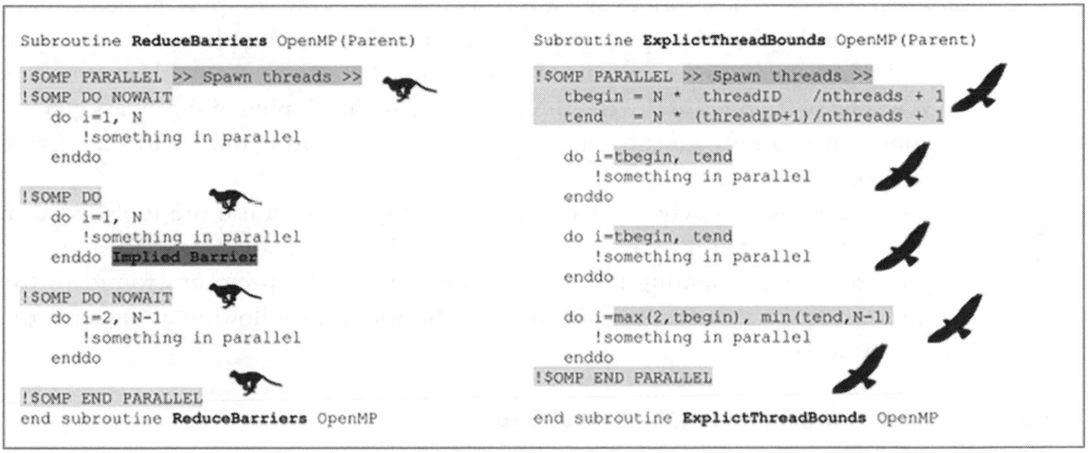

Figure 7.10 The next steps for high-level OpenMP add `nowait` clauses to `do` or `for` loops, which reduce synchronization costs. Then we calculate the loop bounds ourselves and explicitly use these in the loops to avoid even more synchronization. Here, the cheetah and the hawk identify the changes made in both implementations. The hawk (on the right) is faster than the cheetah (on the left) as the overhead of the OpenMP is reduced.

parallel region in order to minimize the overhead of forking and joining. In high-level OpenMP, threads are generated by the `parallel` directive once, at the beginning of the execution of the program. Unused threads do not die but remain dormant when running through a serial portion. To guarantee this, the serial portion is executed by the main thread, enabling few to no changes in the serial portion of the code. Once the program finishes running through the serial portion or starts a parallel region again, the same threads forked at the beginning of the program are invoked or reused.

Step 2 addresses the synchronization added to every `for` loop in OpenMP by default. The easiest way to reduce synchronization cost is to add `nowait` clauses to all loops where it is possible, while maintaining correctness. A further step is to explicitly divide the work among threads. The typical code for explicitly dividing the work for C is shown here. (The Fortran equivalent accounting for arrays starting at 1 is shown in figure 7.10.)

```
tbegin = N *  threadID   /nthreads
tend   = N * (threadID+1)/nthreads
```

The impact of the manual partitioning of the arrays is that it reduces cache thrashing and race conditions by not allowing threads to share the same space in memory.

Step 3, optimization, means that we explicitly state whether certain variables are shared or private. By giving the threads a specific space in memory, the compiler (and programmer) can forgo guessing about the state of the variables. This can be done by applying the variable scoping rules from figure 7.7. Furthermore, compilers cannot properly parallelize loops that include complex loop-carried dependencies and loops that are not in canonical form. High-level OpenMP helps the compiler by being more explicit about the thread scoping of variables, thus allowing complex loops to be parallelized. This leads into the last part of this step for the high-level OpenMP approach. Arrays will be partitioned across the threads. Explicit partitioning of the arrays guarantees that a thread only touches memory assigned to it and allows us to start fixing memory locality issues.

And in the last step, code correctness, it is important to use the tools listed in section 7.9 to detect and fix race conditions. In the next section, we will show you the process of implementing the steps we described. The programs found in the GitHub source for this chapter will prove to be useful in following along with the stepwise process.

7.6.2   *Example of implementing high-level OpenMP*

You can complete a full implementation of high-level OpenMP in a series of steps. You should first look at where the bottleneck(s) of the code are in your application, in addition to finding the most compute-intensive loop in the code. You can then find the innermost level loop of the code and add the standard loop-based OpenMP directives. The scoping of the variables in the most intensive loops and inner loops needs to be understood, referring to figure 7.7 for guidance.

In step 1, you should focus on reducing the thread start-up costs. This is done in listing 7.15 by merging parallel regions to include the entire iteration loop in a single parallel region. We start slowly moving the OpenMP directives outward, expanding the parallel region. The original OpenMP pragmas on lines 49 and 57 can be merged into one parallel region between lines 44 to 70. The extent of the parallel region is defined by the curly braces on lines 45 and 70 thus only starting the parallel region once instead of 10,000 times.

Listing 7.15 Merging parallel regions into a single parallel region

```
HighLevelOpenMP_stencil/stencil_opt4.c                    Single OpenMP
44 #pragma omp parallel >> Spawn threads >>    <————      parallel region
45 {
46    int thread_id = omp_get_thread_num();
47    for (int iter = 0; iter < 10000; iter++){
48       if (thread_id ==0) cpu_timer_start(&tstart_flush);
49       #pragma omp for nowait              <————   OpenMP for pragma
50       for (int l = 1; l < jmax*imax*4; l++){       with no synchronization
51          flush[l] = 1.0;                            barrier at end of loop
52       }
53       if (thread_id == 0){
54          flush_time += cpu_timer_stop(tstart_flush);
55          cpu_timer_start(&tstart_stencil);
56       }
57       #pragma omp for >> Spawn threads >>    <————  Second OpenMP
58       for (int j = 1; j < jmax-1; j++){              for pragma
59          for (int i = 1; i < imax-1; i++){
60             xnew[j][i]=(x[j][i] + x[j][i-1] + x[j][i+1] + x[j-1][i] +
   x[j+1][i])/5.0;
61          }
62       } Implied Barrier        Implied Barrier
63       if (thread_id == 0){
64          stencil_time += cpu_timer_stop(tstart_stencil);
65
66          SWAP_PTR(xnew, x, xtmp);
67          if (iter%1000 == 0) printf("Iter %d\n",iter);
68       }
69    }
70 } // end omp parallel
   Implied Barrier        Implied Barrier
```

Portions of the code that are required to be run in serial are placed in control of the main thread, allowing for the parallel region to be expanded across large portions of the code that encompass both serial and parallel regions. With each step, use the tools discussed in section 7.9 to make sure that the application still runs correctly.

In the second part of the implementation, you begin the transition to high-level OpenMP by carrying the main OpenMP parallel loop to the beginning of the program. After that, you can move on to calculating upper and lower loop bounds. Listing 7.16 (and the online examples in stencil_opt5.c and stencil_opt6.c) shows how you calculate the upper and lower bounds specific to the parallel region. Remember, arrays start at different points depending on language: Fortran starts at 1 and C starts at 0. Loops with the same upper and lower bound can use the same thread without having to recalculate the bounds.

NOTE You must be careful to insert barriers in required locations to prevent race conditions. Much care also needs to be taken when placing these pragmas as too many could become detrimental to the overall performance of the application.

Listing 7.16   Precalculating loop lower and upper bounds

```
HighLevelOpenMP_stencil/stencil_opt6.c
29 #pragma omp parallel >> Spawn threads >>
30 {
31     int thread_id = omp_get_thread_num();
32     int nthreads = omp_get_num_threads();
33
34     int jltb = 1 + (jmax-2) * ( thread_id     ) / nthreads;
35     int jutb = 1 + (jmax-2) * ( thread_id + 1 ) / nthreads;
36
37     int ifltb = (jmax*imax*4) * ( thread_id     ) / nthreads;
38     int ifutb = (jmax*imax*4) * ( thread_id + 1 ) / nthreads;
39
40     int jltb0 = jltb;
41     if (thread_id == 0) jltb0--;
42     int jutb0 = jutb;
43     if (thread_id == nthreads-1) jutb0++;
44
45     int kmin = MAX(jmax/2-5,jltb);
46     int kmax = MIN(jmax/2+5,jutb);
47
48     if (thread_id == 0) cpu_timer_start(&tstart_init);
49     for (int j = jltb0; j < jutb0; j++){
50         for (int i = 0; i < imax; i++){
51             xnew[j][i] = 0.0;
52             x[j][i] = 5.0;
53         }
54     }
55
56     for (int j = kmin; j < kmax; j++){
57         for (int i = imax/2 - 5; i < imax/2 -1; i++){
58             x[j][i] = 400.0;
59         }
60     }
61     #pragma omp barrier
62     if (thread_id == 0) init_time += cpu_timer_stop(tstart_init);
63
64     for (int iter = 0; iter < 10000; iter++){
65         if (thread_id == 0) cpu_timer_start(&tstart_flush);
66         for (int l = ifltb; l < ifutb; l++){
67             flush[l] = 1.0;
68         }
69         if (thread_id == 0){
70             flush_time += cpu_timer_stop(tstart_flush);
71             cpu_timer_start(&tstart_stencil);
72         }
73         for (int j = jltb; j < jutb; j++){
```

Computes loop bounds

Uses thread ID instead of OpenMP masked pragma to eliminate synchronization

Uses manually calculated loop bounds

Barrier to synchronize with other threads

Explicit Barrier   Explicit Barrier

```
74            for (int i = 1; i < imax-1; i++){
75                xnew[j][i]=( x[j][i] + x[j][i-1] + x[j][i+1] + x[j-1][i] +
    x[j+1][i] )/5.0;
76            }
77        }
78        #pragma omp barrier
          Explicit Barrier        Explicit Barrier
79        if (thread_id == 0){
80            stencil_time += cpu_timer_stop(tstart_stencil);
81
82            SWAP_PTR(xnew, x, xtmp);
83            if (iter%1000 == 0) printf("Iter %d\n",iter);
84        }
85        #pragma omp barrier
          Explicit Barrier        Explicit Barrier
86    }
87 } // end omp parallel
   Implied Barrier        Implied Barrier
```

Barrier to synchronize with other threads (annotation pointing to lines 78 and 85)

Uses thread ID instead of OpenMP masked pragma to eliminate synchronization (annotation pointing to lines 79–84)

To obtain a correct answer, it is crucial to start from the innermost loop and have an understanding of which variables need to stay private or become shared among the threads. As you start enlarging the parallel region, serial portions of the code will be placed into a masked region. This region has one thread that does all the work, while the other threads remain alive but dormant. Zero or only a few changes are required when placing serial portions of the code into a main thread. Once the program finishes running through the serial region or gets into a parallel region, the past dormant threads start working again to parallelize the current loop.

For the final step, comparing results for steps along the way to a high-level OpenMP implementation, in listings 7.14 and 7.15 and the provided online stencil examples, you can see that the number of pragmas is greatly reduced while also yielding better performance (figure 7.11).

```
Stencil_opt2    Timing: init 0.003746 flush 3.495596 stencil 3.306887 total 6.808650
Stencil_opt3    Timing: init 0.003081 flush 3.158420 stencil 3.568470 total 6.735474
Stencil_opt4    Timing: init 0.002930 flush 2.853069 stencil 3.491407 total 6.355609
Stencil_opt5    Timing: init 0.002973 flush 3.077176 stencil 3.140370 total 6.227241
Stencil_opt6    Timing: init 0.002831 flush 2.947900 stencil 3.186743 total 6.255831
```

Figure 7.11 Optimizing the OpenMP pragmas both reduces the number of pragmas required and improves the performance of the stencil kernel.

7.7 *Hybrid threading and vectorization with OpenMP*

In this section, we will combine topics from chapter 6 with what you have learned in this chapter. This combination yields to better parallelization and utilizes the vector processor. The OpenMP threaded loop can be combined with the vectorized loop by adding the simd clause to the parallel for as in #pragma omp parallel for simd. The following listing shows this for the stream triad.

Listing 7.17   Loop-level OpenMP threading and vectorization of the stream triad

StreamTriad/stream_triad_opt3.c

```
 1 #include <stdio.h>
 2 #include <time.h>
 3 #include <omp.h>
 4 #include "timer.h"
 5   .
 6 #define NTIMES 16
 7 #define STREAM_ARRAY_SIZE 80000000        ◁──   Large enough to
 8 static double a[STREAM_ARRAY_SIZE], b[STREAM_ARRAY_SIZE],   force into main
    c[STREAM_ARRAY_SIZE];                                     memory
 9
10 int main(int argc, char *argv[]){
11    #pragma omp parallel >> Spawn threads >>
12       if (omp_get_thread_num() == 0)
13          printf("Running with %d thread(s)\n",omp_get_num_threads());
      Implied Barrier        Implied Barrier
14
15    struct timeval tstart;
16    double scalar = 3.0, time_sum = 0.0;
17    #pragma omp parallel for simd >> Spawn threads >>     Initializes
18    for (int i=0; i<STREAM_ARRAY_SIZE; i++) {             data and
19       a[i] = 1.0;                                        arrays
20       b[i] = 2.0;
21    }
      Implied Barrier        Implied Barrier
22    for (int k=0; k<NTIMES; k++){
23       cpu_timer_start(&tstart);
24       #pragma omp parallel for simd >> Spawn threads >>
25       for (int i=0; i<STREAM_ARRAY_SIZE; i++){          Stream
26          c[i] = a[i] + scalar*b[i];                     triad loop
27       }
         Implied Barrier        Implied Barrier
28       time_sum += cpu_timer_stop(tstart);
29       c[1]=c[2];           ◁──   Keeps the compiler from
30    }                              optimizing out the loop
31
32    printf("Average runtime is %lf msecs\n", time_sum/NTIMES);
33}.
```

The hybrid implementation of the stencil example with both threading and vectorization puts the for pragma on the outer loop and the simd pragma on the inner loop as the following listing shows. Both the threaded and the vectorized loops work best with loops over large arrays as would usually be the case for the stencil example.

Listing 7.18   Stencil example with both threading and vectorization

HybridOpenMP_stencil/stencil_hybrid.c

```
26 #pragma omp parallel >> Spawn threads >>
27 {
```

```
28      int thread_id = omp_get_thread_num();
29      if (thread_id == 0) cpu_timer_start(&tstart_init);
30      #pragma omp for
31      for (int j = 0; j < jmax; j++){
32          #ifdef OMP_SIMD
33          #pragma omp simd
34          #endif
35          for (int i = 0; i < imax; i++){
36              xnew[j][i] = 0.0;
37              x[j][i] = 5.0;
38          }
39      } Implied Barrier      Implied Barrier
40
41      #pragma omp for
42      for (int j = jmax/2 - 5; j < jmax/2 + 5; j++){
43          for (int i = imax/2 - 5; i < imax/2 -1; i++){
44              x[j][i] = 400.0;
45          }
46      } Implied Barrier      Implied Barrier
47      if (thread_id == 0) init_time += cpu_timer_stop(tstart_init);
48
49      for (int iter = 0; iter < 10000; iter++){
50          if (thread_id ==0) cpu_timer_start(&tstart_flush);
51          #ifdef OMP_SIMD
52          #pragma omp for simd nowait
53          #else
54          #pragma omp for nowait
55          #endif
56          for (int l = 1; l < jmax*imax*10; l++){
57              flush[l] = 1.0;
58          }
59          if (thread_id == 0){
60              flush_time += cpu_timer_stop(tstart_flush);
61              cpu_timer_start(&tstart_stencil);
62          }
63          #pragma omp for
64          for (int j = 1; j < jmax-1; j++){
65              #ifdef OMP_SIMD
66              #pragma omp simd
67              #endif
68              for (int i = 1; i < imax-1; i++){
69                  xnew[j][i]=(x[j][i] + x[j][i-1] + x[j][i+1] +
70                                          x[j-1][i] + x[j+1][i])/5.0;
                  }
71          } Implied Barrier      Implied Barrier
72          if (thread_id == 0){
73              stencil_time += cpu_timer_stop(tstart_stencil);
74
75              SWAP_PTR(xnew, x, xtmp);
76              if (iter%1000 == 0) printf("Iter %d\n",iter);
77          }
78          #pragma omp barrier
79      }
80  } // end omp parallel
    Implied Barrier      Implied Barrier
```

Adds OpenMP SIMD pragma for inner loops

Adds additional OpenMP SIMD pragma to for pragma on single loop

For the GCC compiler, the results with and without vectorization show a significant speedup with vectorization:

```
4 threads, GCC 8.2 compiler, Skylake Gold 6152
Threads only:      Timing init 0.006630 flush 17.110755 stencil 17.374676
     total 34.499799
Threads & vectors: Timing init 0.004374 flush 17.498293 stencil 13.943251
     total 31.454906
```

7.8   *Advanced examples using OpenMP*

The examples shown so far have been simple loops over a set of data with relatively few complications. In this section, we show you how to handle three advanced examples that require more effort:

- *Split-direction, two-step stencil*—Advanced handling for thread scoping of variables
- *Kahan summation*—A more complex reduction loop
- *Prefix scan*—Explicitly handling partitioning work among threads

The examples in this section reveal the various ways to handle more difficult situations and give you a deeper understanding of OpenMP.

7.8.1   *Stencil example with a separate pass for the x and y directions*

Here we will look at the potential difficulties that arise when implementing OpenMP for a split-direction, two-step stencil operator where a separate pass is made for each spatial direction. *Stencils* are building-blocks for numerical scientific applications and used to calculate dynamic solutions to partial differential equations.

In a two-step stencil, where values are calculated on the faces, data arrays have different data-sharing requirements. Figure 7.12 represents such a stencil with 2D-face data arrays. Furthermore, it is common that one of the dimensions of these 2D arrays needs to be shared among all the threads or processes. The *x*-face data is simpler to deal with because it is aligned with the thread data decomposition, but we don't need the full *x*-face array on every thread. The *y*-face data has a different problem because the data is across threads, necessitating sharing of the *y*-face 2D array. High-level OpenMP allows for a quick privatization of the dimension needed. Figure 7.12 shows how certain dimensions of a matrix can be kept either private, shared, or both.

The first touch principle of most kernels (defined in section 7.1.1) says that memory will most likely be local to the thread (except at the edges between threads on page boundaries). We can improve the memory locality by making the array sections completely private to the thread where possible, such as the *x*-face data. Due to the increasing number of processors, increasing the data locality is essential in minimizing the increasing speed gap between processors and memory. The following listing shows a serial implementation to begin with.

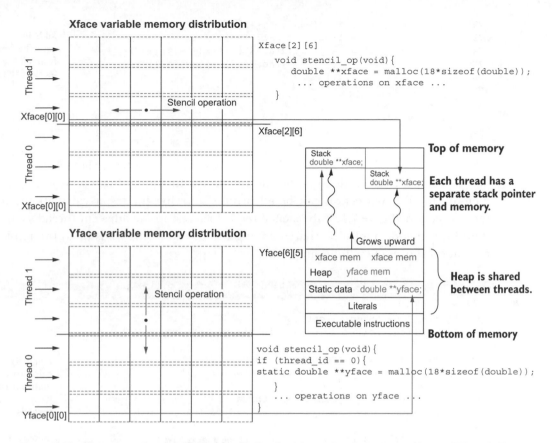

Figure 7.12 The *x* face of a stencil aligned with the threads needs private storage for each thread. The pointer should be on the stack, and each thread should have a different pointer. The *y* face needs to share the data, so we define one pointer in the static data region where both threads can access it.

Listing 7.19 Split-direction stencil operator

SplitStencil/SplitStencil.c

```
58 void SplitStencil(double **a, int imax, int jmax)
59 {
60     double** xface = malloc2D(jmax, imax);
61     double** yface = malloc2D(jmax, imax);
62     for (int j = 1; j < jmax-1; j++){
63         for (int i = 0; i < imax-1; i++){
64             xface[j][i] = (a[j][i+1]+a[j][i])/2.0;
65         }
66     }
67     for (int j = 0; j < jmax-1; j++){
68         for (int i = 1; i < imax-1; i++){
69             yface[j][i] = (a[j+1][i]+a[j][i])/2.0;
70         }
71     }
```

Calculates values on x and y faces of cells

x-face calculation requires only adjacent cells in the x direction.

y-face calculation requires adjacent cells in the y direction.

```
72    for (int j = 1; j < jmax-1; j++){
73       for (int i = 1; i < imax-1; i++){
74          a[j][i] = (a[j][i]+xface[j][i]+xface[j][i-1]+
75                            yface[j][i]+yface[j-1][i])/5.0;
76       }
77    }
78    free(xface);
79    free(yface);
80 }
```

Adds in contributions from all the faces of the cell

When using OpenMP with the stencil operator, you must determine whether the memory for each thread needs to be private or shared. In listing 7.18 (previously), the memory for the *x*-direction can be all private, allowing for faster calculations. In the *y*-direction (figure 7.12), the stencil requires access to the adjacent thread's data; therefore, this data must be shared among the threads. This leads us to the implementation shown in the following listing.

Listing 7.20   Split-direction stencil operator with OpenMP

```
SplitStencil/SplitStencil_opt1.c
86 void SplitStencil(double **a, int imax, int jmax)
87 {
88    int thread_id = omp_get_thread_num();
89    int nthreads = omp_get_num_threads();
90
91    int jltb = 1 + (jmax-2) * ( thread_id     ) / nthreads;
92    int jutb = 1 + (jmax-2) * ( thread_id + 1 ) / nthreads;
93
94    int jfltb = jltb;
95    int jfutb = jutb;
96    if (thread_id == 0) jfltb--;
97
98    double** xface = (double **)malloc2D(jutb-jltb, imax-1);
99    static double** yface;
100   if (thread_id == 0) yface = (double **)malloc2D(jmax+2, imax);
101 #pragma omp barrier
       Explicit Barrier        Explicit Barrier
102   for (int j = jltb; j < jutb; j++){
103      for (int i = 0; i < imax-1; i++){
104         xface[j-jltb][i] = (a[j][i+1]+a[j][i])/2.0;
105      }
106   }
107   for (int j = jfltb; j < jfutb; j++){
108      for (int i = 1; i < imax-1; i++){
109         yface[j][i] = (a[j+1][i]+a[j][i])/2.0;
110      }
111   }
112 #pragma omp barrier
       Explicit Barrier        Explicit Barrier
```

Manually calculates distribution of data across threads

Declares the y-face data pointer as static so it has shared scope.

The y faces have one less data value to distribute.

Allocates a private portion of the x-face data for each thread

Does the local x-face calculation on each thread

The y-face calculation has a j+1 and thus needs a shared array.

Inserts an OpenMP barrier so that all threads have the allocated memory

We need an OpenMP synchronization because the next loop uses an adjacent thread work.

Allocates one version of the y-face array to be shared across threads

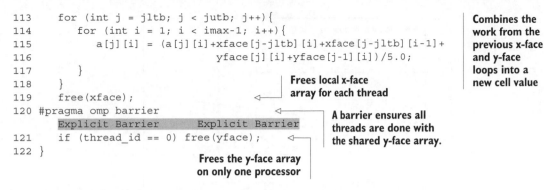

```
113    for (int j = jltb; j < jutb; j++){
114       for (int i = 1; i < imax-1; i++){
115          a[j][i] = (a[j][i]+xface[j-jltb][i]+xface[j-jltb][i-1]+
116                               yface[j][i]+yface[j-1][i])/5.0;
117       }
118    }
119    free(xface);
120 #pragma omp barrier
       Explicit Barrier      Explicit Barrier
121    if (thread_id == 0) free(yface);
122 }
```

Combines the work from the previous x-face and y-face loops into a new cell value

Frees local x-face array for each thread

A barrier ensures all threads are done with the shared y-face array.

Frees the y-face array on only one processor

To define the memory on the stack as shown in the *x*-direction, we need a pointer to a pointer to a double (`double **xface`) so that the pointer is on the stack and private to each thread. Then we allocate the memory using a custom 2D `malloc` call at line 98 in listing 7.20. We only need enough memory for each thread, so we compute the thread bounds in lines 91 and 92 and use these in the 2D `malloc` call. The memory is allocated from the heap and can be shared, but each thread only has its own pointer; therefore, each thread can't access the other threads' memory.

Rather than allocating memory from the heap, we could have used the automatic allocation, such as `double xface[3][6]`, where the memory is automatically allocated on the stack. The compiler automatically sees this declaration and pushes the memory space onto the stack. In cases where the arrays are large, the compiler might move the memory requirement to the heap. Each compiler has a different threshold on deciding whether to place memory on the heap or on the stack. If the compiler moves the memory to the heap, only one thread has the pointer to this location. In effect, it is private, even though it is in shared memory space.

For the *y*-faces, we define a static pointer to a pointer (`static double **yface`), where all threads can access the same pointer. In this case, only one thread needs to do this memory allocation, and all remaining threads can access this pointer and the memory itself. For this example, you can use figure 7.7 to see the different options of making the memory shared. In this case, you would go to the Parallel Region -> C Routine and pick one of the file scope variables, `extern` or `static`, to make the pointer shared among the threads. It is easy to get something wrong such as in the variable scope, the memory allocation, or the synchronization. For example, what happens if we just define a regular `double **yfaces` pointer. Now each thread has its own private pointer and only one of these gets memory allocated. The pointer for the second thread would not point to anything, generating an error when it is used.

Figure 7.13 shows the performance for running the threaded version of the code on the Skylake Gold processor. For a small number of threads, we get a super-linear speedup before falling off at above eight threads. Super-linear speedup happens on occasion because the cache performance improves as the data is partitioned across threads or processors.

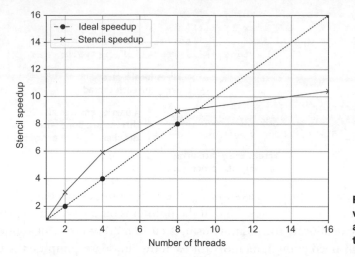

Figure 7.13 **The threaded version of the split stencil has a super-linear speedup for two to eight threads.**

DEFINITION   *Super-linear speedup* is performance that's better than the ideal scaling curve for strong scaling. This can happen because the smaller array sizes fit into a higher level of the cache, resulting in better cache performance.

7.8.2 *Kahan summation implementation with OpenMP threading*

For the enhanced-precision Kahan summation algorithm, introduced in section 5.7, we cannot use a pragma to get the compiler to generate a multi-threaded implementation because of the loop-carried dependencies. Therefore, we'll follow a similar algorithm as we used in the vectorized implementation in section 6.3.4. We first sum up the values on each thread in the first phase of the calculation. Then we sum the values across the threads to get the final sum as the following listing shows.

Listing 7.21   **An OpenMP implementation of the Kahan summation**

GlobalSums/kahan_sum.c

```
 1 #include <stdlib.h>
 2 #include <omp.h>
 3
 4 double do_kahan_sum(double* restrict var, long ncells)
 5 {
 6    struct esum_type{
 7       double sum;
 8       double correction;
 9    };
10
11    int nthreads = 1;          │  Gets the total number of
12    int thread_id   = 0;       │  threads and thread_id
13 #ifdef _OPENMP
14    nthreads = omp_get_num_threads();
15    thread_id = omp_get_thread_num();
16 #endif
17
```

```
18    struct esum_type local;
19    local.sum = 0.0;
20    local.correction = 0.0;
21
22    int tbegin = ncells * ( thread_id     ) / nthreads;
23    int tend   = ncells * ( thread_id + 1 ) / nthreads;
24
25    for (long i = tbegin; i < tend; i++) {
26       double corrected_next_term = var[i] + local.correction;
27       double new_sum             = local.sum + local.correction;
28       local.correction   = corrected_next_term - (new_sum - local.sum);
29       local.sum          = new_sum;
30    }
31
32    static struct esum_type *thread;
33    static double sum;
34
35 #ifdef _OPENMP
36 #pragma omp masked
37    thread = malloc(nthreads*sizeof(struct esum_type));
38 #pragma omp barrier
```

Computes the range for which this thread is responsible

Puts the variables in shared memory

Defines the compiler variable _OPENMP when using OpenMP

Allocates one thread in shared memory

Explicit Barrier   Explicit Barrier

```
39
40    thread[thread_id].sum = local.sum;
41    thread[thread_id].correction = local.correction;
42
43 #pragma omp barrier
```

Stores the summation of each thread in array

Waits until all threads get here and then sums across threads

Explicit Barrier   Explicit Barrier

```
44
45    static struct esum_type global;
46 #pragma omp masked
47    {
48       global.sum = 0.0;
49       global.correction = 0.0;
50       for ( int i = 0 ; i < nthreads ; i ++ ) {
51          double corrected_next_term = thread[i].sum +
52                   thread[i].correction + global.correction;
53          double new_sum   = global.sum + global.correction;
54          global.correction = corrected_next_term -
                                (new_sum - global.sum);
55          global.sum = new_sum;
56       }
57
58       sum = global.sum + global.correction;
59       free(thread);
60    } // end omp masked
61 #pragma omp barrier
```

Uses a single thread to compute the beginning offset for each thread

Explicit Barrier   Explicit Barrier

```
62 #else
63    sum = local.sum + local.correction;
64 #endif
65
66    return(sum);
67 }
```

7.8.3 *Threaded implementation of the prefix scan algorithm*

In this section, we look at the threaded implementation of the prefix scan operation. The prefix scan operation, introduced in section 5.6, is important for algorithms with irregular data. This is because a count to determine the starting location for ranks or threads allows the rest of the calculation to be done in parallel. As discussed in that section, the prefix scan can also be done in parallel, yielding another parallelization benefit. The implementation process has three phases:

- *All threads*—Calculates a prefix scan for each thread's portion of the data
- *Single thread*—Calculates the starting offset for each thread's data
- *All threads*—Applies the new thread offset across all the data for each thread

The implementation in listing 7.22 works for a serial application and when called from within an OpenMP parallel region. This has the benefit that you can use the code in the listing for both serial and threaded cases, reducing the code duplication for this operation.

> **Listing 7.22   An OpenMP implementation of the prefix scan**

```
PrefixScan/PrefixScan.c
 1 void PrefixScan (int *input, int *output, int length)
 2 {
 3     int nthreads = 1;
 4     int thread_id   = 0;                        Gets the total number
 5 #ifdef _OPENMP                                  of threads and
 6     nthreads = omp_get_num_threads();           thread_id
 7     thread_id = omp_get_thread_num();
 8 #endif
 9                                                 Computes the range
10     int tbegin = length * ( thread_id     ) / nthreads;   for which this thread
11     int tend   = length * ( thread_id + 1 ) / nthreads;   is responsible
12
13     if ( tbegin < tend ) {
14         output[tbegin] = 0;                     Does an
15         for ( int i = tbegin + 1 ; i < tend ; i++ ) {   exclusive scan
16             output[i] = output[i-1] + input[i-1];        for each thread
17         }
18     }
19     if (nthreads == 1) return;          For multiple threads only, do the
20                                          adjustment to prefix scan for the
21 #ifdef _OPENMP                           beginning value for each thread
22 #pragma omp barrier
       Explicit Barrier        Explicit Barrier
23
24     if (thread_id == 0) {                            Uses the main
25         for ( int i = 1 ; i < nthreads ; i ++ ) {    thread to compute
26             int ibegin = length * ( i - 1 ) / nthreads;   the beginning offset
27             int iend   = length * ( i     ) / nthreads;   for each thread
28
29             if ( ibegin < iend )
30                 output[iend] = output[ibegin] + input[iend-1];
```

Only performs this operation if there is a positive number of entries.

Waits until all threads get here

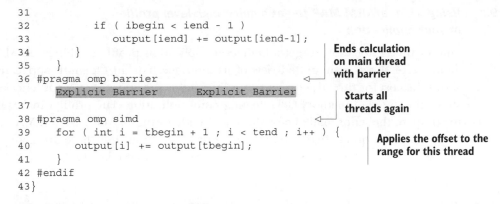

```
31
32          if ( ibegin < iend - 1 )
33              output[iend] += output[iend-1];
34      }
35  }
36 #pragma omp barrier
        Explicit Barrier        Explicit Barrier
37
38 #pragma omp simd
39    for ( int i = tbegin + 1 ; i < tend ; i++ ) {
40       output[i] += output[tbegin];
41    }
42 #endif
43 }
```

This algorithm should theoretically scale as

```
Parallel_timer = 2 * serial_time/nthreads
```

The performance on the Skylake Gold 6152 architecture peaks at about 44 threads, 9.4 times faster than the serial version.

7.9 *Threading tools essential for robust implementations*

Developing a robust OpenMP implementation is difficult without using specialized tools for detecting thread race conditions and performance bottlenecks. The use of tools becomes much more important as you try to get a higher performance OpenMP implementation. There are both commercial and openly available tools. The typical tool list when integrating advanced implementations of OpenMP in your application includes:

- *Valgrind*—A memory tool introduced in section 2.1.3. It also works with OpenMP and helps in finding uninitialized memory or out-of-bounds accesses in threads.
- *Call graph*—The cachegrind tool produces a call graph and a profile of your application. A call graph determines which functions call other functions to clearly show the call hierarchy and code path. An example of the cachegrind tool was presented in section 3.3.1.
- *Allinea/ARM Map*—A high-level profiler to get an overall cost of thread starts and barriers (for OpenMP apps).
- *Intel® Inspector*—To detect thread race conditions (for OpenMP apps).

We described the first two tools in earlier chapters; they can be referred to there. In this section, we will discuss the last two tools as these relate more to an OpenMP application. These tools are needed to profile the bottlenecks and understand where they lie within your application and, thus, are essential in knowing where to best start changing your code in an efficient manner.

7.9.1   Using Allinea/ARM MAP to get a quick high-level profile of your application

One of the better tools to get a high-level application profile is Allinea/ARM MAP. Figure 7.14 shows a simplified view of its interface. For an OpenMP application, it shows the cost for thread starts and waits, highlights the application's bottlenecks, and shows the usage of memory CPU floating point utilization. The profiler makes it easy to compare the gains made before and after code changes. Allinea/ARM MAP excels at producing a quick, high-level view of your application, but there are many other profilers that can be used. Some of these are reviewed in section 17.3.

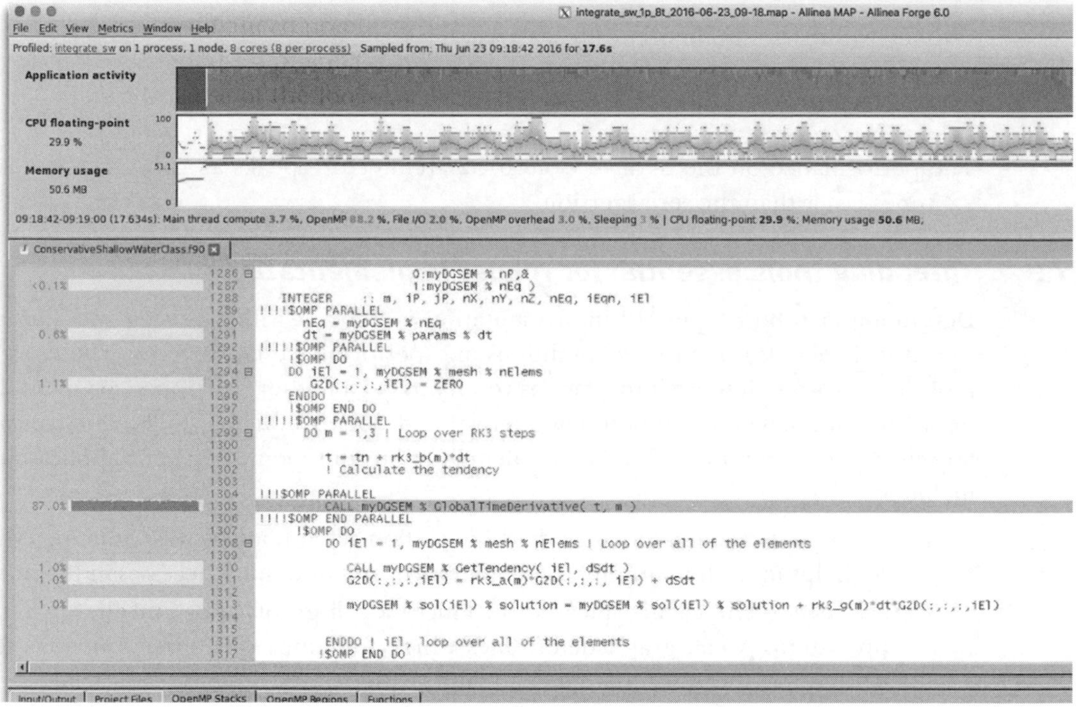

Figure 7.14   These are results from Allinea/ARM MAP showing the majority of the compute time on the highlighted line of code. We often use indicators like this to show us the location of bottlenecks.

7.9.2   Finding your thread race conditions with Intel® Inspector

It is essential to find and eliminate thread race conditions in an OpenMP implementation to produce a robust, production-quality application. For this purpose, tools are essential because it is impossible for even the best programmer to catch all the thread race conditions. As the application begins to scale, memory errors occur more frequently and can cause an application to break. Catching these memory errors early on saves time and energy on future runs.

There are not many tools that are effective at finding thread race conditions. We show the use of one of these tools, the Intel® Inspector, to detect and pinpoint the location of these race conditions. Having tools to understand thread race conditions in memory is also useful when scaling to larger thread counts. Figure 7.15 provides a sample screenshot of Intel® Inspector.

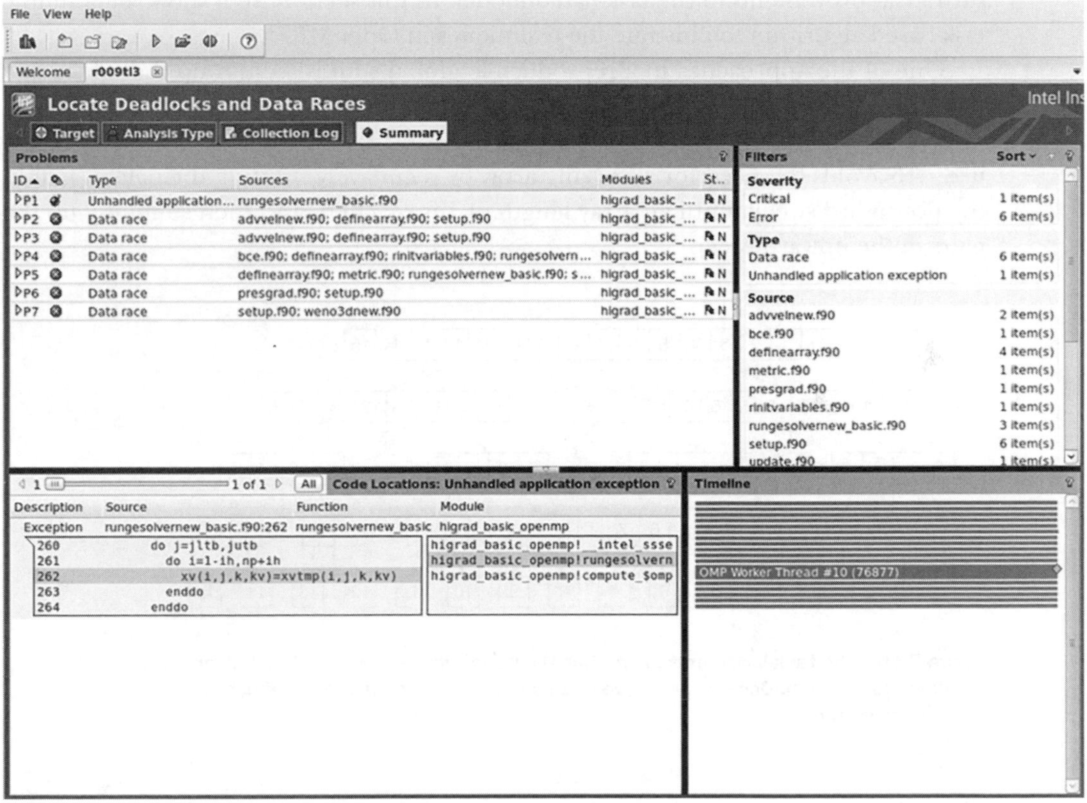

Figure 7.15 Intel® Inspector report showing detection of thread race conditions. Here the items listed as Data race under the Type heading on the panel to the upper left show all the places where there is currently a race condition.

Before changes in the initial application are made, it is critical to complete regression testing. Ensuring correctness is crucial to the successful implementation of OpenMP threading. A correct OpenMP code cannot be implemented unless an application or a whole subroutine is in its proper working state. This also requires that the section of code that is being threaded with OpenMP must also be exercised in a regression test. Without being able to do regression testing, it becomes difficult to make steady progress. In summary, these tools, along with regression testing, create a better understanding of the dependencies, efficiency, and correctness in most applications.

7.10 *Example of a task-based support algorithm*

The task-based parallel strategy was first introduced in chapter 1 and illustrated in figure 1.25. Using a task-based approach, you can divide work into separate tasks that can then be parceled out to individual processes. Many algorithms are more naturally expressed in terms of a task-based approach. OpenMP has supported this type of approach since its version 3.0. In the subsequent standard releases, there have been further improvements to the task-based model. In this section we'll show you a simple task-based algorithm to illustrate the techniques in OpenMP.

One of the approaches to a reproducible global sum is to sum up the values in a pairwise manner. The normal array approach requires the allocation of a working array and some complicated indexing logic. Using a task-based approach as in figure 7.16 avoids the need for a working array by recursively splitting the data in half in the downward sweep, until an array length of 1 is reached, and then summing up the pairs in the upward sweep.

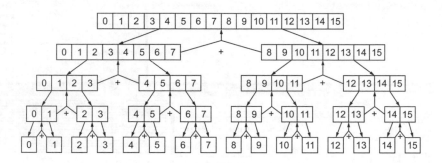

Figure 7.16   The task-based implementation recursively splits the array into half on the downward sweep. Once an array size of 1 occurs, the task sums pairs of data in the upward sweep.

Listing 7.23 shows the code for the task-based approach. The spawning of the task needs to be done in a parallel region but by only one thread, leading to the nested blocks of pragmas in lines 8 to 14.

Listing 7.23   A pair-wise summation using OpenMP tasks

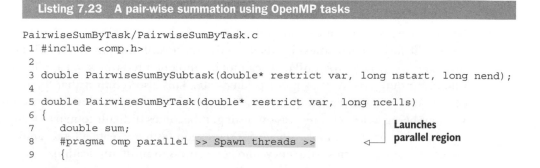

```
PairwiseSumByTask/PairwiseSumByTask.c
 1 #include <omp.h>
 2
 3 double PairwiseSumBySubtask(double* restrict var, long nstart, long nend);
 4
 5 double PairwiseSumByTask(double* restrict var, long ncells)
 6 {
 7    double sum;
 8    #pragma omp parallel >> Spawn threads >>          Launches
 9    {                                                 parallel region
```

```
10        #pragma omp masked
11        {
12            sum = PairwiseSumBySubtask(var, 0, ncells);
13        }
14    } Implied Barrier      Implied Barrier
15    return(sum);
16 }
17
18 double PairwiseSumBySubtask(double* restrict var, long nstart, long nend)
19 {
20    long nsize = nend - nstart;
21    long nmid = nsize/2;
22    double x,y;
23    if (nsize == 1){
24        return(var[nstart]);
25    }
26
27    #pragma omp task shared(x) mergeable final(nsize > 10)
28    x = PairwiseSumBySubtask(var, nstart, nstart + nmid);
29    #pragma omp task shared(y) mergeable final(nsize > 10)
30    y = PairwiseSumBySubtask(var, nend - nmid, nend);
31    #pragma omp taskwait
32
33    return(x+y);
34 }
```

Starts main task on one thread

Subdivides the array into two parts

Initializes sum at leaf with single value from array

Launches a pair of subtasks with half of the data for each

Waits for two tasks to complete

Sums the values from the two subtasks and returns to the calling thread

Getting good performance with a task-based algorithm takes a lot more tuning to prevent too many threads from being spawned and to keep granularity of the tasks reasonable. For some algorithms, task-based algorithms are a much more appropriate parallel strategy.

7.11 Further explorations

There are many materials on traditional thread-based OpenMP programming. With nearly every compiler supporting OpenMP, the best learning approach is to simply start adding OpenMP directives to your code. There are many training opportunities covering OpenMP, including the annual Supercomputing Conference held in November. For information, see https://sc21.supercomputing.org/. For those who are even more interested in OpenMP, there is an International Workshop on OpenMP held every year that covers the latest developments. For information, see http://www.iwomp.org/.

7.11.1 Additional reading

Barbara Chapman is one of the leading writers and authorities on OpenMP. Her book is the standard reference for OpenMP programming, especially for the threading implementation in OpenMP as of 2008:

Barbara Chapman, Gabriele Jost, and Ruud Van Der Pas, *Using OpenMP: portable shared memory parallel programming*, vol. 10 (MIT Press, 2008).

There are many researchers working on developing more efficient techniques of implementing OpenMP, which has come to be called *high-level OpenMP*. Here is a link to slides going into more detail on high-level OpenMP:

> Yuliana Zamora, "Effective OpenMP Implementations on Intel's Knights Landing," Los Alamos National Laboratory Technical Report LA-UR-16-26774, 2016. Available at: https://www.osti.gov/biblio/1565920-effective-openmp-implementations-intel-knights-landing.

A good textbook on OpenMP and MPI is one written by Peter Pacheco. It has some good examples of OpenMP code:

> Peter Pacheco, *An introduction to parallel programming* (Elsevier, 2011).

Blaise Barney at Lawrence Livermore National Laboratory has authored a well-written OpenMP reference that's also available online:

> Blaise Barney, *OpenMP Tutorial*, https://computing.llnl.gov/tutorials/openMP/

The OpenMP Architecture Review Board (ARB) maintains a website that is the authoritative location for all things OpenMP, from specifications to presentations and tutorials:

> OpenMP Architecture Review Board, *OpenMP*, https://www.openmp.org.

For a deeper discussion on the difficulties with threading:

> Edward A Lee, "The problem with threads." *Computer* 39, no. 5 (2006): 33-42.

7.11.2 Exercises

1 Convert the vector add example in listing 7.8 into a high-level OpenMP following the steps in section 7.2.2.
2 Write a routine to get the maximum value in an array. Add an OpenMP pragma to add thread parallelism to the routine.
3 Write a high-level OpenMP version of the reduction in the previous exercise.

We covered a substantial amount of material in this chapter. This solid foundation will help you in developing an effective OpenMP application.

Summary

- Loop-level implementations of OpenMP can be quick and easy to create.
- An efficient implementation of OpenMP can achieve promising application speed-up.
- Good first-touch implementations can often gain a 10–20% performance improvement.
- Understanding variable scope across threads is important in getting OpenMP code to work.

- High-level OpenMP can boost performance on current and upcoming many-core architectures.
- Threading and debugging tools are essential when implementing more complex versions of OpenMP.
- Some of the style guidelines that are suggested in this chapter include
  - Declaring variables where these are used so that they automatically become private, which is generally correct.
  - Modifying declarations to get the right threading scope for variables rather than using an extensive list in private and public clauses.
  - Avoiding the `critical` clause or other locking constructs where possible. Performance is generally impacted heavily by these constructs.
  - Reducing synchronization by adding `nowait` clauses to `for` loops and limiting the use of `#pragma omp barrier` to only where necessary.
  - Merging small parallel regions into fewer, larger parallel regions to reduce OpenMP overhead.

MPI: The parallel backbone

8

This chapter covers

- Sending messages from one process to another
- Performing common communication patterns with collective MPI calls
- Linking meshes on separate processes with communication exchanges
- Creating custom MPI data types and using MPI Cartesian topology functions
- Writing applications with hybrid MPI plus OpenMP

The importance of the Message Passing Interface (MPI) standard is that it allows a program to access additional compute nodes and, thus, run larger and larger problems by adding more nodes to the simulation. The name *message passing* refers to the ability to easily send messages from one process to another. MPI is ubiquitous in the field of high-performance computing. Across many scientific fields, the use of supercomputers entails an MPI implementation.

MPI was launched as an open standard in 1994 and, within months, became the dominant parallel computing library-based language. Since 1994, the use of MPI has led to scientific breakthroughs from physics to machine learning to self-driving cars! Several implementations of MPI are now in widespread use. MPICH from Argonne National Laboratories and OpenMPI are two of the most common. Hardware vendors often have customized versions of one of these two implementations for their platforms. The MPI standard, now up to version 3.1 as of 2015, continues to evolve and change.

In this chapter, we'll show you how to implement MPI in your application. We'll start with a simple MPI program and then progress to a more complicated example of how to link together separate computational meshes on separate processes through communicating boundary information. We'll touch on some advanced techniques that are important for well-written MPI programs, such as building custom MPI data types and the use of MPI Cartesian topology functions. Last, we'll introduce combining MPI with OpenMP (MPI plus OpenMPI) and vectorization to get multiple levels of parallelism.

NOTE We encourage you to follow along with the examples for this chapter at https://github.com/EssentialsofParallelComputing/Chapter8.

8.1 The basics for an MPI program

In this section, we will cover the basics that are needed for a minimal MPI program. Some of these basic requirements are specified by the MPI standard, while others are provided by convention by most MPI implementations. The basic structure and operation of MPI has stayed remarkably consistent since the first standard.

To begin, MPI is a completely library-based language. It does not require a special compiler or accommodations from the operating system. All MPI programs have a basic structure and process as figure 8.1 shows. MPI always begins with an `MPI_Init` call right at the start of the program and an `MPI_Finalize` at the program's exit. This is in contrast to OpenMP, as discussed in chapter 7, which needs no special startup and shutdown commands and just places parallel directives around key loops.

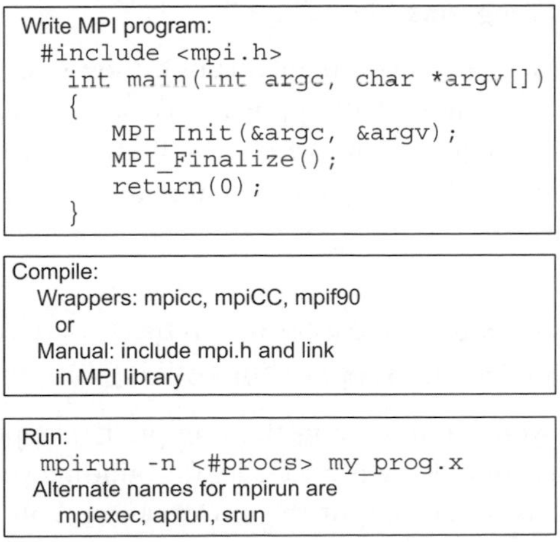

```
Write MPI program:
  #include <mpi.h>
    int main(int argc, char *argv[])
    {
        MPI_Init(&argc, &argv);
        MPI_Finalize();
        return(0);
    }
```

```
Compile:
  Wrappers: mpicc, mpiCC, mpif90
    or
  Manual: include mpi.h and link
    in MPI library
```

```
Run:
  mpirun -n <#procs> my_prog.x
  Alternate names for mpirun are
    mpiexec, aprun, srun
```

Figure 8.1 The MPI approach is library-based. Just compile, linking in the MPI library, and launch with a special parallel startup program.

Once you write an MPI parallel program, it is compiled with an include file and library. Then it is executed with a special startup program that establishes the parallel processes across nodes and within the node.

8.1.1   *Basic MPI function calls for every MPI program*

The basic MPI function calls include `MPI_Init` and `MPI_Finalize`. The call to `MPI_Init` should be right after program startup, and the arguments from the `main` routine must be passed to the initialization call. Typical calls look like the following and may or may not use the `return` variable:

```
iret = MPI_Init(&argc, &argv);
iret = MPI_Finalize();
```

Most programs will need the number of processes and the process rank within the group that can communicate, called a *communicator*. One of the main functions of MPI is to start up remote processes and lash these up so messages can be sent between the processes. The default communicator is `MPI_COMM_WORLD`, which is set up at the beginning of every parallel job by `MPI_Init`. Let's take a moment to look at a few definitions:

- *Process*—An independent unit of computation that has ownership of a portion of memory and control over resources in user space.
- *Rank*—A unique, portable identifier to distinguish the individual process within the set of processes. Normally this would be an integer within the set of integers from zero to one less than the number of processes.

The calls to get these important variables are

```
iret = MPI_Comm_rank(MPI_COMM_WORLD, &rank);
iret = MPI_Comm_size(MPI_COMM_WORLD, &nprocs);
```

8.1.2   *Compiler wrappers for simpler MPI programs*

Although MPI is a library, we can treat it like a compiler through the use of the MPI compiler wrappers. This makes the building of MPI applications easier because you don't need to know which libraries are required and where the libraries are located. These are especially convenient for small MPI applications. There are compiler wrappers for each programming language:

- `mpicc`—Wrapper for C code
- `mpicxx`—Wrapper for C++ (also can be `mpiCC` or `mpic++`)
- `mpifort`—Wrapper for Fortran (also can be `mpif77` or `mpif90`)

Using these wrappers is optional. If you are not using the compiler wrappers, they can still be valuable for identifying the compile flags necessary for building your application. The `mpicc` command has options that output this information. You can find these options for your MPI with `man mpicc`. For the two most popular MPI implementations, we list the command-line options for `mpicc`, `mpicxx`, and `mpifort` here.

- For OpenMPI, use these command options:
  - `--showme`
  - `--showme:compile`
  - `--showme:link`
- For MPICH, use these command options:
  - `-show`
  - `-compile_info`
  - `-link_info`

8.1.3 Using parallel startup commands

The startup of the parallel processes for MPI is a complex operation that is handled by a special command. At first, this command was often `mpirun`. But with the release of the MPI 2.0 standard in 1997, the startup command was recommended to be `mpiexec`, to try and provide more portability. Yet this attempt at standardization was not completely successful, and today there are several names used for the startup command:

- `mpirun -n <nprocs>`
- `mpiexec -n <nprocs>`
- `aprun`
- `srun`

Most MPI startup commands take the option `-n` for the number of processes, but others might take `-np`. With the complexity of recent computer node architectures, the startup commands have a myriad of options for affinity, placement, and environment (some of which we will discuss in chapter 14). These options vary with each MPI implementation and even with each release of their MPI libraries. The simplicity of the options available from the original startup commands has morphed into a confusing morass of options that have not yet stabilized. Fortunately, for the beginning MPI user, *most of these options can be ignored*, but they are important for advanced use and tuning.

8.1.4 Minimum working example of an MPI program

Now that we have learned all the basic components, we can combine them into the minimum working example that listing 8.1 shows: we start the parallel job and print out the rank and number of processes from each process. In the call to get the rank and size, we use the `MPI_COMM_WORLD` variable that is the group of all the MPI processes and is predefined in the MPI header file. Note that the displayed output can be in any order; the MPI program leaves it up to the operating system for when and how the output is displayed.

Listing 8.1   MPI minimum working example

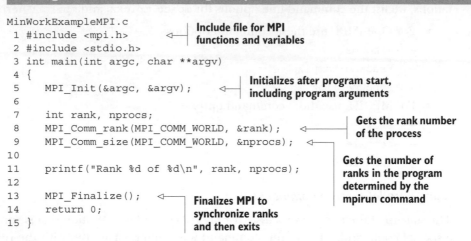

```
MinWorkExampleMPI.c
 1 #include <mpi.h>              ⟵—|  Include file for MPI
 2 #include <stdio.h>                 functions and variables
 3 int main(int argc, char **argv)
 4 {
 5    MPI_Init(&argc, &argv);    ⟵—|  Initializes after program start,
 6                                      including program arguments
 7    int rank, nprocs;
 8    MPI_Comm_rank(MPI_COMM_WORLD, &rank);     ⟵——  Gets the rank number
 9    MPI_Comm_size(MPI_COMM_WORLD, &nprocs);   ⟵—   of the process
10
11    printf("Rank %d of %d\n", rank, nprocs);      Gets the number of
12                                                   ranks in the program
13    MPI_Finalize();  ⟵—|  Finalizes MPI to        determined by the
14    return 0;              synchronize ranks       mpirun command
15 }                         and then exits
```

Listing 8.2 defines a simple makefile to build this example using the MPI compiler wrappers. In this case, we use the `mpicc` wrapper to supply the location of the mpi.h include file and the MPI library.

Listing 8.2   Simple makefile using MPI compiler wrappers

```
MinWorkExample/Makefile.simple

default:        MinWorkExampleMPI
all:    MinWorkExampleMPI

MinWorkExampleMPI: MinWorkExampleMPI.c Makefile
        mpicc MinWorkExampleMPI.c  -o MinWorkExampleMPI

clean:
        rm -f MinWorkExampleMPI MinWorkExampleMPI.o
```

For more elaborate builds on a variety of systems, you might prefer CMake. The following listing shows the CMakeLists.txt file for this program.

Listing 8.3   The CMakeLists.txt for building with CMake

```
MinWorkExample/CMakeLists.txt
cmake_minimum_required(VERSION 2.8)

project(MinWorkExampleMPI)

# Require MPI for this project:        Calls a special module to
find_package(MPI REQUIRED)   ⟵—        find MPI and sets variables

add_executable(MinWorkExampleMPI MinWorkExampleMPI.c)
```
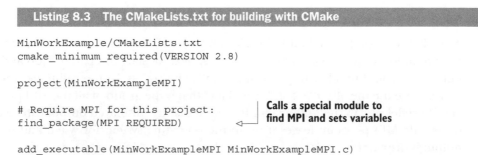

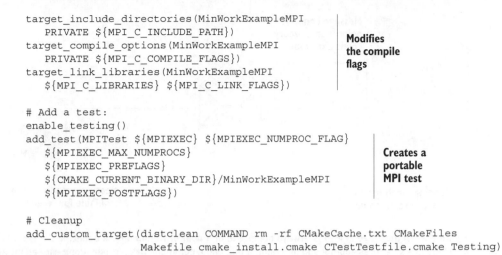

```
target_include_directories(MinWorkExampleMPI
   PRIVATE ${MPI_C_INCLUDE_PATH})
target_compile_options(MinWorkExampleMPI
   PRIVATE ${MPI_C_COMPILE_FLAGS})
target_link_libraries(MinWorkExampleMPI
   ${MPI_C_LIBRARIES} ${MPI_C_LINK_FLAGS})
```
Modifies the compile flags

```
# Add a test:
enable_testing()
add_test(MPITest ${MPIEXEC} ${MPIEXEC_NUMPROC_FLAG}
   ${MPIEXEC_MAX_NUMPROCS}
   ${MPIEXEC_PREFLAGS}
   ${CMAKE_CURRENT_BINARY_DIR}/MinWorkExampleMPI
   ${MPIEXEC_POSTFLAGS})
```
Creates a portable MPI test

```
# Cleanup
add_custom_target(distclean COMMAND rm -rf CMakeCache.txt CMakeFiles
               Makefile cmake_install.cmake CTestTestfile.cmake Testing)
```

Now using the CMake build system, let's configure, build, and then run the test with these commands:

```
cmake .
make
make test
```

The write operation from the `printf` command displays output in any order. Finally, to clean up after the run, use these commands:

```
make clean
make distclean
```

8.2 The send and receive commands for process-to-process communication

The core of the message-passing approach is to send a message from point-to-point or, perhaps more precisely, process-to-process. The whole point of parallel processing is to coordinate work. To do this, you need to send messages either for control or work distribution. We'll show you how these messages are composed and properly sent. There are many variants of the point-to-point routines; we'll cover those that are recommended to use in most situations.

Figure 8.2 shows the components of a message. There must be a mailbox at either end of the system. The size of the mailbox is important. The sending side knows the size of the message, but the receiving side does not. To make sure there is a place for the message to be stored, it is usually better to post the *receive* first. This avoids delaying the message by the receiving process having to allocate a temporary space to store the message until a receive is posted and it can copy it to the right location. For an analogy, if the receive (mailbox) is not posted (not there), the postman has to hangout until someone puts one up. Posting the receive first avoids the possibility

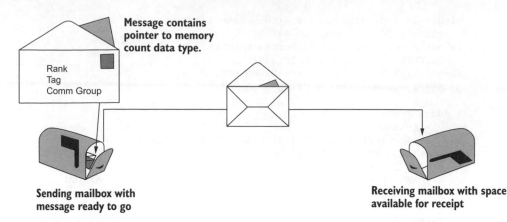

Figure 8.2   A message in MPI is always composed of a pointer to memory, a count, and a type. The envelope has an address composed of a rank, a tag, and a communication group along with an internal MPI context.

of insufficient memory space on the receiving end to allocate a temporary buffer to store the message.

The message itself is always composed of a triplet at both ends: a pointer to a memory buffer, a count, and a type. The type sent and type received can be different types and counts. The rationale for using types and counts is that it allows the conversion of types between the processes at the source and at the destination. This permits a message to be converted to a different form at the receiving end. In a heterogeneous environment, this might mean converting lower-endian to big-endian, a low-level difference in the byte order of data stored on different hardware vendors. Also, the receive size can be greater than the amount sent. This permits the receiver to query how much data is sent so it can properly handle the message. But the receiving size cannot be smaller than the sending size because it would cause a write past the end of the buffer.

The envelope also is composed of a triplet. It defines who the message is from, who it is sent to, and a message identifier to keep from getting multiple messages confused. The triplet consists of the rank, tag, and communication group. The rank is for the specified communication group. The tag helps the programmer and MPI distinguish which message goes to which receive. In MPI, the tag is a convenience. It can be set to MPI_ANY_TAG if an explicit tag number is not desired. MPI uses a context created internally within the library to separate the messages correctly. Both the communicator and the tag must match for a message to complete.

NOTE   One of the strengths of the message-passing approach is the memory model. Each process has clear ownership of its data plus the control and synchronization over when the data changes. You can be guaranteed that some other process cannot change your memory while your back is turned.

Now let's try an MPI program with a simple send/receive. We have to send data on one process and receive data on another. There are different ways that we could issue these calls on a couple of processes (figure 8.3). Some of the combinations of basic blocking send and receives are not safe and can hang, such as the two combinations on the left of figure 8.3. The third combination requires careful programming with conditionals. The method to the far right is one of several safe methods to schedule communications by using non-blocking sends and receives. These are also called *asynchronous* or *immediate* calls, which explains the *I* character preceding the send and receive keywords (the case shown on the far right of the figure).

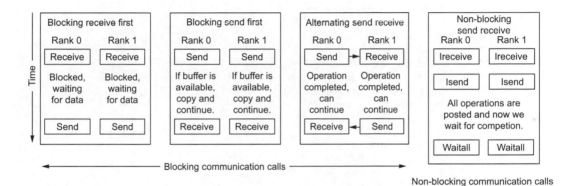

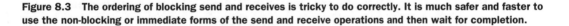

Figure 8.3 **The ordering of blocking send and receives is tricky to do correctly. It is much safer and faster to use the non-blocking or immediate forms of the send and receive operations and then wait for completion.**

The most basic MPI send and receive is `MPI_Send` and `MPI_Recv`. The basic send and receive functions have the following prototypes:

```
MPI_Send(void *data, int count, MPI_Datatype datatype, int dest, int tag,
         MPI_COMM comm)
MPI_Recv(void *data, int count, MPI_Datatype datatype, int source, int tag,
         MPI_COMM comm, MPI_Status *status)
```

Now let's go through each of the four cases in figure 8.3 to understand why some hang and some work fine. We'll begin with the `MPI_Send` and `MPI_Receive` that were shown in the previous function prototypes and in the left-most example in the figure. Both of these routines are *blocking*. Blocking means that these do not return until a specific condition is fulfilled. In the case of these two calls, the condition for return is that the buffer is safe to use again. On the send, the buffer must have been read and is no longer needed. On the receive, the buffer must be filled. If both processes in a communication are blocking, a situation known as a *hang* can occur. A hang occurs when one or more processes are waiting on an event that can never occur.

Example: A blocking send/receive program that hangs

This example highlights a common problem in parallel programming. You must always be on guard to avoid a situation that might hang (deadlock). In the following listing, we look at how this might occur so that we can avoid it.

A simple send/receive example in MPI (always hangs)

```
Send_Recv/SendRecv1.c
 1 #include <mpi.h>
 2 #include <stdio.h>
 3 #include <stdlib.h>
 4 int main(int argc, char **argv)
 5 {
 6    MPI_Init(&argc, &argv);
 7
 8    int count = 10;
 9    double xsend[count], xrecv[count];
10    for (int i=0; i<count; i++){
11       xsend[i] = (double)i;
12    }
13
14    int rank, nprocs;
15    MPI_Comm_rank(MPI_COMM_WORLD, &rank);
16    MPI_Comm_size(MPI_COMM_WORLD, &nprocs);
17    if (nprocs%2 == 1){
18       if (rank == 0){
19          printf("Must be called with an even number of processes\n");
20       }
21       exit(1);
22    }
23
24    int tag = rank/2;
25    int partner_rank = (rank/2)*2 + (rank+1)%2;
26    MPI_Comm comm = MPI_COMM_WORLD;
27
28    MPI_Recv(xrecv, count, MPI_DOUBLE,
                partner_rank, tag, comm,
                MPI_STATUS_IGNORE);
29    MPI_Send(xsend, count, MPI_DOUBLE,
                partner_rank, tag, comm);
30
31    if (rank == 0) printf("SendRecv successfully completed\n");
32
33    MPI_Finalize();
34    return 0;
35 }
```

Integer division pairs up the tags for the send and receive partners. (line 24)

Partner rank is the opposite member of the pair. (line 25)

Receives are posted first. (line 28)

Sends are done after the receives. (line 29)

The tag and rank of the communication partner are calculated through integer and modulo arithmetic that pairs up the tags for each send and receive and gets the rank of the other member of the pair. Then the receives are posted for every process with its partner. These are blocking receives that do not complete (return) until the buffer is filled. Because the send is not called until after the receives complete, the program hangs. Note that we wrote the send and receive calls without `if` statements (conditionals) based on rank. Conditionals are the source of many bugs in parallel code, so these are generally good to avoid.

Let's try reversing the order of the sends and receives. We list the changed lines in the following listing from the original listing in the previous example.

Listing 8.4   A simple send/receive example in MPI (sometimes fails)

```
Send_Recv/SendRecv2.c
28    MPI_Send(xsend, count, MPI_DOUBLE,        First calls send
              partner_rank, tag, comm);          operation
29    MPI_Recv(xrecv, count, MPI_DOUBLE,
              partner_rank, tag, comm,           Then calls receive operation
              MPI_STATUS_IGNORE);                after send completes
```

So does this one fail? Well, it depends. The send call returns after the use of the send data buffer is complete. Most MPI implementations will copy the data into preallocated buffers on the sender or receiver if the size is small enough. In this case, the send completes and the receive is called. If the message is large, the send waits for the receive call to allocate a buffer to put the message into before returning. But the receive never gets called, so the program hangs. We could alternate the posting of sends and receives by ranks so that hangs do not occur. We have to use a conditional for this variant as the following listing shows.

Listing 8.5   Send/receive with alternating sends and receives by rank

```
Send_Recv/SendRecv3.c                  Even ranks post
28    if (rank%2 == 0) {           ◄──  the send first.
29        MPI_Send(xsend, count, MPI_DOUBLE, partner_rank, tag, comm);
30        MPI_Recv(xrecv, count, MPI_DOUBLE, partner_rank, tag, comm,
                   MPI_STATUS_IGNORE);
31    } else {                                                        ◄─────┐
32        MPI_Recv(xrecv, count, MPI_DOUBLE, partner_rank, tag, comm,       │
                   MPI_STATUS_IGNORE);                                      │
33        MPI_Send(xsend, count, MPI_DOUBLE, partner_rank, tag, comm);      │
34    }                                                                     │
                                       Odd ranks do the receive first. ─────┘
```

But this is complicated to get right in more complex communication and requires careful use of conditionals. A better way to implement this is by using the `MPI_Sendrecv` call as the next listing shows. By using this call, you hand-off the responsibility for correctly executing the communication to the MPI library. This is a pretty good deal for the programmer.

Listing 8.6   Send/receive with the `MPI_Sendrecv` call

```
Send_Recv/SendRecv4.c
28     MPI_Sendrecv(xsend, count, MPI_DOUBLE,
                    partner_rank, tag,
29                 xrecv, count, MPI_DOUBLE,
                    partner_rank, tag, comm,
                    MPI_STATUS_IGNORE);
```

> **A combined send/receive call replaces the individual MPI_Send and MPI_Recv.**

The `MPI_Sendrecv` call is a good example of the advantages of using the collective communication calls that we'll present in section 8.3. It is good practice to use the collective communication calls when possible because these delegate responsibility for avoiding hangs and deadlocks, as well as the responsibility for good performance to the MPI library.

As an alternative to the blocking communication calls in previous examples, we look at using the `MPI_Isend` and `MPI_Irecv` in listing 8.7. These are called *immediate (I)* versions because these return immediately. This is often referred to as asynchronous or non-blocking calls. *Asynchronous* means that the call initiates the operation but does not wait for the completion of the work.

Listing 8.7   A simple send/receive example using `Isend` and `Irecv`

```
Send_Recv/SendRecv5.c
27     MPI_Request requests[2] =
           {MPI_REQUEST_NULL, MPI_REQUEST_NULL};
28
29     MPI_Irecv(xrecv, count, MPI_DOUBLE,
                 partner_rank, tag, comm,
                 &requests[0]);
30     MPI_Isend(xsend, count, MPI_DOUBLE,
                 partner_rank, tag, comm,
                 &requests[1]);
31     MPI_Waitall(2, requests, MPI_STATUSES_IGNORE);
```

> **Defines an array of requests and sets to null so these are defined when tested for completion**

> **The Irecv is posted first.**

> **The Isend is then called after the Irecv completes.**

> **Calls a Waitall to wait for the send and receive to complete**

Each process waits at the `MPI_Waitall` on line 31 of the listing for message completion. You should also see a measurable improvement in program performance by reducing the number of places that block from every send and receive call to just the single `MPI_Waitall`. But you must be careful not to modify the send buffer or access the receive buffer until the operation completes. There are other combinations that work. Let's look at the following listing, which uses one possibility.

Listing 8.8   A mixed immediate and blocking send/receive example

```
Send_Recv/SendRecv6.c
27     MPI_Request request;
28
29     MPI_Isend(xsend, count, MPI_DOUBLE,
                 partner_rank, tag, comm,
                 &request);
```

> **Posts the send with an MPI_Isend so that it returns**

```
30    MPI_Recv(xrecv, count, MPI_DOUBLE,
              partner_rank, tag, comm,
              MPI_STATUS_IGNORE);
31    MPI_Request_free(&request);
```

> **Calls the blocking receive. This process can continue as soon as it returns.**

> **Frees the request handle to avoid a memory leak**

We start the communication with an asynchronous send and then block with a blocking receive. Once the blocking receive completes, this process can continue even if the send has not completed. You still must free the request handle with an `MPI_Request_free` or as a side-effect of a call to `MPI_Wait` or an `MPI_Test` to avoid a memory leak. You can also call the `MPI_Request_free` immediately after the `MPI_Isend`.

Other variants of send/receive might be useful in special situations. The modes are indicated by a one- or two-letter prefix, similar to that seen in the immediate variant, as listed here:

- `B` (buffered)
- `S` (synchronous)
- `R` (ready)
- `IB` (immediate buffered)
- `IS` (immediate synchronous)
- `IR` (immediate ready)

The list of predefined MPI data types for C is extensive; the data types map to nearly all the types in the C language. MPI also has types corresponding to Fortran data types. We list just the most common ones for C:

- `MPI_CHAR` (a 1-byte C character type)
- `MPI_INT` (a 4-byte integer type)
- `MPI_FLOAT` (a 4-byte real type)
- `MPI_DOUBLE` (an 8-byte real type)
- `MPI_PACKED` (a generic byte-sized data type, usually used for mixed data types)
- `MPI_BYTE` (a generic byte-sized data type)

The `MPI_PACKED` and `MPI_BYTE` are special types and match any other type. `MPI_BYTE` indicates an untyped value and the count specifies the number of bytes. It bypasses any data conversion operations in heterogeneous data communications. `MPI_PACKED` is used with the `MPI_PACK` routine as the ghost exchange example in section 8.4.3 shows. You can also define your own data type to use in these calls. This is also demonstrated in the ghost exchange example. There are also many communication completion testing routines, which include

```
int MPI_Test(MPI_Request *request, int *flag, MPI_Status *status)
int MPI_Testany(int count, MPI_Request requests[], int *index, int *flag,
                MPI_Status *status)
int MPI_Testall(int count, MPI_Request requests[], int *flag,
                MPI_Status statuses[])
```

```
int MPI_Testsome(int incount, MPI_Request requests[], int *outcount,
                 int indices[], MPI_Status statuses[])
int MPI_Wait(MPI_Request *request, MPI_Status *status)
int MPI_Waitany(int count, MPI_Request requests[], int *index,
                MPI_Status *status)
int MPI_Waitall(int count, MPI_Request requests[], MPI_Status statuses[])
int MPI_Waitsome(int incount, MPI_Request requests[], int *outcount,
                 int indices[], MPI_Status statuses[])
int MPI_Probe(int source, int tag, MPI_Comm comm, MPI_Status *status)
```

There are additional variants of the MPI_Probe that are not listed here. MPI_Waitall is shown in several examples in this chapter. The other routines are useful in more specialized situations. The name of the routines gives a good idea of the capabilities that these provide.

8.3   Collective communication: A powerful component of MPI

In this section, we'll look at the rich set of collective communication calls in MPI. Collective communications operate on a group of processes contained in an MPI communicator. To operate on a partial set of processes, you can create your own MPI communicator for a subset of MPI_COMM_WORLD such as every other process. Then you can use your communicator in place of MPI_COMM_WORLD in collective communication calls. Most of the collective communication routines operate on data. Figure 8.4 gives a visual idea of what each collective operation does.

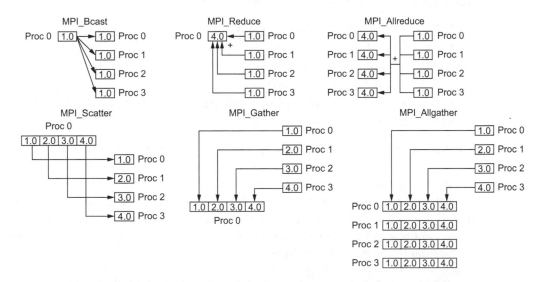

Figure 8.4   The data movement of the most common MPI collective routines provide important functions for parallel programs. Additional variants MPI_Scatterv, MPI_Gatherv, and MPI_Allgatherv allow a variable amount of data to be sent or received from the processes. Not shown are some additional routines such as the MPI_Alltoall and similar functions.

We'll present examples of how to use the most commonly used collective operations as these might be applied in an application. The first example (in section 8.3.1) shows how you might use the barrier. It is the only collective routine that does not operate on data. Then we'll show some examples with the broadcast (section 8.3.2), reduction (section 8.3.3), and finally, scatter/gather operations (sections 8.3.4 and 8.3.5). MPI also has a variety of all-to-all routines. But these are costly and rarely used, so we won't cover those here. These collective operations all operate on a group of processes represented by a communication group. All members of a communication group must call the collective or your program will hang.

8.3.1   *Using a barrier to synchronize timers*

The simplest collective communication call is `MPI_Barrier`. It is used to synchronize all of the processes in an MPI communicator. In most programs, it should not be necessary, but it is often used for debugging and for synchronizing timers. Let's look at how `MPI_Barrier` could be used to synchronize timers in the following listing. We also use the `MPI_Wtime` function to get the current time.

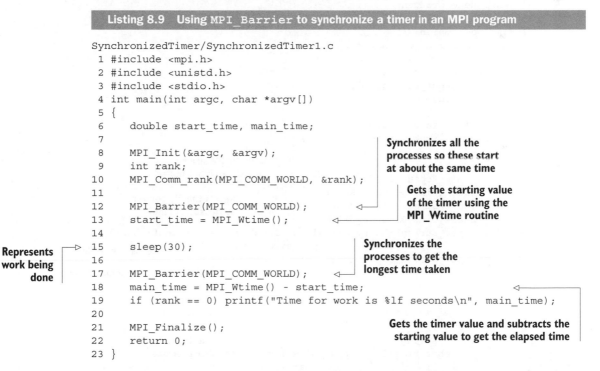

Listing 8.9   Using `MPI_Barrier` to synchronize a timer in an MPI program

```
SynchronizedTimer/SynchronizedTimer1.c
 1 #include <mpi.h>
 2 #include <unistd.h>
 3 #include <stdio.h>
 4 int main(int argc, char *argv[])
 5 {
 6    double start_time, main_time;
 7
 8    MPI_Init(&argc, &argv);
 9    int rank;
10    MPI_Comm_rank(MPI_COMM_WORLD, &rank);
11
12    MPI_Barrier(MPI_COMM_WORLD);
13    start_time = MPI_Wtime();
14
15    sleep(30);
16
17    MPI_Barrier(MPI_COMM_WORLD);
18    main_time = MPI_Wtime() - start_time;
19    if (rank == 0) printf("Time for work is %lf seconds\n", main_time);
20
21    MPI_Finalize();
22    return 0;
23 }
```

Synchronizes all the processes so these start at about the same time

Gets the starting value of the timer using the MPI_Wtime routine

Represents work being done

Synchronizes the processes to get the longest time taken

Gets the timer value and subtracts the starting value to get the elapsed time

The barrier is inserted before starting the timer and then just before stopping the timer. This forces the timers on all of the processes to start at about the same time. By inserting the barrier before stopping the timer, we get the maximum time across all of the processes. Sometimes using a synchronized timer gives a less confusing measure of time, but in others, an unsynchronized timer is better.

NOTE Synchronized timers and barriers should not be used in production runs; these can cause serious slowdowns in an application.

8.3.2 *Using the broadcast to handle small file input*

The broadcast sends data from one processor to all of the others. This operation is shown in figure 8.4 in the upper left. One of the uses of the broadcast, MPI_Bcast, is to send values read from an input file to all other processes. If every process tries to open a file at large process counts, it can take minutes to complete the file open. This is because file systems are inherently serial and one of the slower components of a computer system. For these reasons, for small file input, it is a good practice to only open and read a file from a single process. The following listing shows the way to do this.

Listing 8.10   Using MPI_Bcast to handle small file input

```
FileRead/FileRead.c
 1 #include <stdio.h>
 2 #include <string.h>
 3 #include <stdlib.h>
 4 #include <mpi.h>
 5 int main(int argc, char *argv[])
 6 {
 7    int rank, input_size;
 8    char *input_string, *line;
 9    FILE *fin;
10
11    MPI_Init(&argc, &argv);
12    MPI_Comm_rank(MPI_COMM_WORLD, &rank);
13
14    if (rank == 0){                                    Gets the file size to
15       fin = fopen("file.in", "r");                    allocate an input buffer
16       fseek(fin, 0, SEEK_END);
17       input_size = ftell(fin);                        Resets the file pointer
18       fseek(fin, 0, SEEK_SET);                        to the start of file
19       input_string = (char *)malloc((input_size+1)*sizeof(char));
20       fread(input_string, 1, input_size, fin);        Reads entire file
21       input_string[input_size] = '\0';
22    }                                                  Null terminating input buffer
23
24    MPI_Bcast(&input_size, 1, MPI_INT, 0,              Broadcasts size
              MPI_COMM_WORLD);                           of input buffer
25    if (rank != 0)
         input_string =                                 Allocates input buffer
             (char *)malloc((input_size+1)*             on other processes
                           sizeof(char));
26    MPI_Bcast(input_string, input_size,               Broadcasts
              MPI_CHAR, 0, MPI_COMM_WORLD);              input buffer
27
28    if (rank == 0) fclose(fin);
29
30    line = strtok(input_string,"\n");
```

```
31    while (line != NULL){
32       printf("%d:input string is %s\n",rank,line);
33       line = strtok(NULL,"\n");
34    }
35    free(input_string);
36
37    MPI_Finalize();
38    return 0;
39 }
```

It is better to broadcast larger chunks of data than it is to broadcast many small individual values. We therefore broadcast the entire file. To do this, we need to first broadcast the size so that every process can allocate an input buffer and then broadcast the data. The file read and broadcasts are done from rank 0, generally referred to as the main process.

MPI_Bcast takes a pointer for the first argument, so when sending a scalar variable, we send the reference by using the ampersand (&) operator to get the address of the variable. Then comes the count and the type to fully define the data to be sent. The next argument specifies the originating process. It is 0 in both of these calls because that is the rank where the data resides. All other processes in the MPI_COMM_WORLD communication then receive the data. This technique is for small input files. For larger file input or output, there are ways to conduct parallel file operations. The complex world of parallel input and output is discussed in chapter 16.

8.3.3 *Using a reduction to get a single value from across all processes*

The reduction pattern, discussed in section 5.7, is one of the most important parallel computing patterns. The reduction operation is shown in figure 8.4 in the upper middle. An example of the reduction in Fortran array syntax is xsum = sum(x(:)), where the Fortran sum intrinsic sums the x array and puts it in the scalar variable xsum. The MPI reduction calls take an array or multi-dimensional array and combine the values into a scalar result. There are many operations that can be done during the reduction. The most common are

- MPI_MAX (maximum value in an array)
- MPI_MIN (minimum value in an array)
- MPI_SUM (sum of an array)
- MPI_MINLOC (index of minimum value)
- MPI_MAXLOC (index of maximum value)

The following listing shows how we can use MPI_Reduce to get the minimum, maximum, and average of a variable from every process.

> **Listing 8.11 Using reductions to get min, max, and avg timer results**

SynchronizedTimer/SynchronizedTimer2.c
```
1 #include <mpi.h>
2 #include <unistd.h>
```

```
 3 #include <stdio.h>
 4 int main(int argc, char *argv[])
 5 {
 6    double start_time, main_time, min_time, max_time, avg_time;
 7
 8    MPI_Init(&argc, &argv);
 9    int rank, nprocs;
10    MPI_Comm_rank(MPI_COMM_WORLD, &rank);
11    MPI_Comm_size(MPI_COMM_WORLD, &nprocs);
12
13    MPI_Barrier(MPI_COMM_WORLD);
14    start_time = MPI_Wtime();
15
16    sleep(30);
17
18    main_time = MPI_Wtime() - start_time;
19    MPI_Reduce(&main_time, &max_time, 1,
              MPI_DOUBLE, MPI_MAX, 0, MPI_COMM_WORLD);
20    MPI_Reduce(&main_time, &min_time, 1,
              MPI_DOUBLE, MPI_MIN, 0,MPI_COMM_WORLD);
21    MPI_Reduce(&main_time, &avg_time, 1,
              MPI_DOUBLE, MPI_SUM, 0,MPI_COMM_WORLD);
22    if (rank == 0)
          printf("Time for work is Min: %lf  Max: %lf  Avg:  %lf seconds\n",
23                 min_time, max_time, avg_time/nprocs);
24
25    MPI_Finalize();
26    return 0;
27 }
```

- Line 13–14: **Synchronizes all the processes so these start at about the same time**
- Line 16: **Represents work being done**
- Line 18: **Gets the timer value and subtracts the starting value to get the elapsed time**
- Lines 19–21: **Uses reduction calls to compute the max, min, and average time**

The reduction result, the maximum in this case, is stored on rank 0 (argument 6 in the MPI_Reduce call), which in this case is the main process. If we wanted to just print it out on the main process, this would be appropriate. But if we wanted all of the processes to have the value, we would use the MPI_Allreduce routine.

You can also define your own operator. We'll use the example of the Kahan enhanced-precision summation we have been working with and first introduced in section 5.7. The challenge in a distributed memory parallel environment is to carry the Kahan summation across process ranks. We start by looking at the main program in the following listing before looking at two other parts of the program in listings 8.13 and 8.14.

Listing 8.12   An MPI version of the Kahan summation

```
GlobalSums/globalsums.c
57 int main(int argc, char *argv[])
58 {
59    MPI_Init(&argc, &argv);
60    int rank, nprocs;
61    MPI_Comm_rank(MPI_COMM_WORLD, &rank);
62    MPI_Comm_size(MPI_COMM_WORLD, &nprocs);
63
64    init_kahan_sum();
```

- Line 64: **Initializes the new MPI data type and creates a new operator**

```
65
66    if (rank == 0) printf("MPI Kahan tests\n");
67
68    for (int pow_of_two = 8; pow_of_two < 31; pow_of_two++){
69        long ncells = (long)pow((double)2,(double)pow_of_two);
70
71        int nsize;
72        double accurate_sum;
73        double *local_energy =
              init_energy(ncells, &nsize,       Gets a distributed
              &accurate_sum);                   array to work with
74
75        struct timespec cpu_timer;
76        cpu_timer_start(&cpu_timer);
77                                               Calculates the Kahan
78        double test_sum =                      summation of the energy
              global_kahan_sum(nsize, local_energy);  array across all processes
79
80        double cpu_time = cpu_timer_stop(cpu_timer);
81
82        if (rank == 0){
83            double sum_diff = test_sum-accurate_sum;
84            printf("ncells %ld log %d acc sum %-17.16lg sum %-17.16lg ",
85                    ncells,(int)log2((double)ncells),accurate_sum,test_sum);
86            printf("diff %10.4lg relative diff %10.4lg runtime %lf\n",
87                    sum_diff,sum_diff/accurate_sum, cpu_time);
88        }
89
90        free(local_energy);
91    }
92
93    MPI_Type_free(&EPSUM_TWO_DOUBLES);         Frees the custom data
94    MPI_Op_free(&KAHAN_SUM);                   type and operator
95    MPI_Finalize();
96    return 0;
97 }
```

The main program shows that the new MPI data type is created once at the start of the program and freed at the end, before MPI_Finalize. The call to perform the global Kahan summation is done multiple times within the loop, where the data size is increased by powers of two. Now let's look at the next listing to see what needs to be done to initialize the new data type and operator.

Listing 8.13 Initializing new MPI data type and operator for Kahan summation

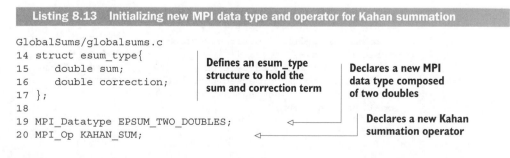

```
GlobalSums/globalsums.c
14 struct esum_type{
15     double sum;
16     double correction;
17 };
18
19 MPI_Datatype EPSUM_TWO_DOUBLES;
20 MPI_Op KAHAN_SUM;
```

```
21
22 void kahan_sum(struct esum_type * in,
                  struct esum_type * inout, int *len,
23     MPI_Datatype *EPSUM_TWO_DOUBLES)
24 {
25    double corrected_next_term, new_sum;
26    corrected_next_term = in->sum + (in->correction + inout->correction);
27    new_sum = inout->sum + corrected_next_term;
28    inout->correction = corrected_next_term - (new_sum - inout->sum);
29    inout->sum = new_sum;
30 }
31
32 void init_kahan_sum(void){
33    MPI_Type_contiguous(2, MPI_DOUBLE,
                            &EPSUM_TWO_DOUBLES);
34    MPI_Type_commit(&EPSUM_TWO_DOUBLES);
35
36    int commutative = 1;
37    MPI_Op_create((MPI_User_function *)kahan_sum,
                     commutative, &KAHAN_SUM);
38 }
```

Defines a function for the new operator using a predefined signature (lines 22–23)

Creates the type and commits it (lines 33–34)

Creates the new operator and commits it (lines 36–37)

We first create the new data type, EPSUM_TWO_DOUBLES, by combining two of the basic MPI_DOUBLE data type in line 33. We have to declare the type outside the routine at line 19 so that it is available to use by the summation routine. To create the new operator, we first write the function to use as the operator in lines 22-30. We then use esum_type to pass both double values in and back out. We also need to pass in the length and the data type that it will operate on as the new EPSUM_TWO_DOUBLES type.

In the process of creating a Kahan sum reduction operator, we showed you how to create a new MPI data type and a new MPI reduction operator. Now let's move on to actually calculating the global sum of the array across MPI ranks as the following listing shows.

Listing 8.14   Performing an MPI Kahan summation

```
GlobalSums/globalsums.c
40 double global_kahan_sum(int nsize, double *local_energy){
41    struct esum_type local, global;
42    local.sum = 0.0;
43    local.correction = 0.0;
44
45    for (long i = 0; i < nsize; i++) {
46       double corrected_next_term =
                 local_energy[i] + local.correction;
47       double new_sum =
                 local.sum + local.correction;
48       local.correction = corrected_next_term -
                              (new_sum - local.sum);
49       local.sum = new_sum;
50    }
51
```

Initializes both members of the esum_type to zero (lines 42–43)

Performs the on-process Kahan summation (lines 45–49)

```
52      MPI_Allreduce(&local, &global, 1, EPSUM_TWO_DOUBLES, KAHAN_SUM,   ◁┐
                    MPI_COMM_WORLD);
53
54      return global.sum;
55 }
```

Performs the reduction with the new KAHAN_SUM operator

Calculating the global Kahan summation is relatively easy now. We can do the local Kahan sum as shown in section 5.7. But we have to add `MPI_Allreduce` at line 52 to get the global result. Here, we defined the allreduce operation to end with the result on all processors as shown in figure 8.4 in the upper right.

8.3.4   *Using gather to put order in debug printouts*

A gather operation can be described as a collate operation, where data from all processors is brought together and stacked into a single array as shown in figure 8.4 in the lower center. You can use this collective communication call to bring order to the output to the console from your program. By now, you should have noticed that the output printed from multiple ranks of an MPI program comes out in random order, producing a jumbled, confusing mess. Let's look at a better way to handle this so that the only output is from the main process. By printing the output from only the main process, the order will be correct. The next listing shows a sample program that gets data from all of the processes and prints it out in a nice, orderly output.

> **Listing 8.15   Using a gather to print debug messages**

```
DebugPrintout/DebugPrintout.c
 1 #include <stdio.h>
 2 #include <time.h>
 3 #include <unistd.h>
 4 #include <mpi.h>
 5 #include "timer.h"
 6 int main(int argc, char *argv[])
 7 {
 8     int rank, nprocs;
 9     double total_time;
10     struct timespec tstart_time;
11
12     MPI_Init(&argc, &argv);
13     MPI_Comm_rank(MPI_COMM_WORLD, &rank);
14     MPI_Comm_size(MPI_COMM_WORLD, &nprocs);
15
16     cpu_timer_start(&tstart_time);
17     sleep(30);                                              ◁
18     total_time += cpu_timer_stop(tstart_time);
19
20     double times[nprocs];                                   ◁
21     MPI_Gather(&total_time, 1, MPI_DOUBLE,
              times, 1, MPI_DOUBLE, 0, MPI_COMM_WORLD);
22     if (rank == 0) {                                        ◁
23         for (int i=0; i<nprocs; i++){
```

Gets unique values on each process for our example

Needs an array to collect all the times

Uses a gather to bring all the values to process zero

Only prints on the main process

Loops over the processes for the print

```
24              printf("%d:Work took %lf secs\n",          Prints the time
                     i, times[i]);                         for each process
25          }
26      }
27
28      MPI_Finalize();
29      return 0;
30 }
```

MPI_Gather takes the standard triplet describing the data source. We need to use the ampersand to get the address of the scalar variable total_time. The destination is also a triplet with the destination array of times. An array is already an address, so no ampersand is needed. The gather is done to process 0 of the MPI world communication group. From there, it requires a loop to print the time for each process. We prepend every line with a number in the format #: so that it is clear which process the output refers to.

8.3.5   *Using scatter and gather to send data out to processes for work*

The scatter operation, shown in figure 8.4 in the lower left, is the opposite of the gather operation. For this operation, the data is sent from one process to all the others in the communication group. The most common use for a scattering operation is in the parallel strategy distributing data arrays out to other processes for work. This is provided by the MPI_Scatter and MPI_Scatterv routines. The following listing shows the implementation.

Listing 8.16   Using scatter to distribute data and gather to bring it back

ScatterGather/ScatterGather.c
```
 1 #include <stdio.h>
 2 #include <stdlib.h>
 3 #include <mpi.h>
 4 int main(int argc, char *argv[])
 5 {
 6     int rank, nprocs, ncells = 100000;
 7
 8     MPI_Init(&argc, &argv);
 9     MPI_Comm comm = MPI_COMM_WORLD;
10     MPI_Comm_rank(comm, &rank);
11     MPI_Comm_size(comm, &nprocs);
12
13     long ibegin = ncells *(rank   )/nprocs;     Computes the size
14     long iend   = ncells *(rank+1)/nprocs;      of the array on
15     int  nsize  = (int)(iend-ibegin);           every process
16
17     double *a_global, *a_test;
18     if (rank == 0) {
19         a_global = (double *)
20             malloc(ncells*sizeof(double));       Sets up data
21         for (int i=0; i<ncells; i++) {           on the main
22             a_global[i] = (double)i;             process
23         }
        }
```

```
24
25    int nsizes[nprocs], offsets[nprocs];
26    MPI_Allgather(&nsize, 1, MPI_INT, nsizes,
                  1, MPI_INT, comm);
27    offsets[0] = 0;
28    for (int i = 1; i<nprocs; i++){
29       offsets[i] = offsets[i-1] + nsizes[i-1];
30    }
31
32    double *a = (double *)
           malloc(nsize*sizeof(double));
33    MPI_Scatterv(a_global, nsizes, offsets,
34       MPI_DOUBLE, a, nsize, MPI_DOUBLE, 0, comm);
35
36    for (int i=0; i<nsize; i++){
37       a[i] += 1.0;
38    }
39
40    if (rank == 0) {
41       a_test = (double *)
             malloc(ncells*sizeof(double));
42    }
43
44    MPI_Gatherv(a, nsize, MPI_DOUBLE,
45                a_test, nsizes, offsets,
                  MPI_DOUBLE, 0, comm);
46
47    if (rank == 0){
48       int ierror = 0;
49       for (int i=0; i<ncells; i++){
50          if (a_test[i] != a_global[i] + 1.0) {
51             printf("Error: index %d a_test %lf a_global %lf\n",
52                    i,a_test[i],a_global[i]);
53             ierror++;
54          }
55       }
56       printf("Report: Correct results %d errors %d\n",
                ncells-ierror,ierror);
57    }
58
59    free(a);
60    if (rank == 0) {
61       free(a_global);
62       free(a_test);
63    }
64
65    MPI_Finalize();
66    return 0;
67 }
```

- **Gets the sizes and offsets into global arrays for communication** (lines 25–30)
- **Distributes the data onto the other processes** (lines 32–34)
- **Does the computation** (lines 36–38)
- **Returns array data to the main process, perhaps for output** (lines 41–45)

We first need to calculate the size of the data on each process. The desired distribution is to be as equal as possible. A simple way to calculate the size is shown in lines 13–15, using simple integer arithmetic. Now we need the global array, but we only need it on the main process. So we allocate and set it up on this process in lines 18-23. In order to distribute or gather the data, the sizes and offsets for all processes must be known. We see the typical calculation for this in lines 25-30. The actual scatter is done with an `MPI_Scatterv` on lines 32–34. The data source is described with the arguments `buffer`, `counts`, `offsets`, and the data type. The destination is handled with the standard triplet. Then the source rank that will send the data is specified as rank 0. Finally, the last argument is `comm`, the communication group that will receive the data.

`MPI_Gatherv` does the opposite operation, as shown in figure 8.4. We only need the global array on the main process, and so it is only allocated there on lines 40-42. The arguments to `MPI_Gatherv` start with the description of the source with the standard triplet. Then the destination is described with the same four arguments as were used in the scatter. The destination rank is the next argument, followed by the communication group.

It should be noted that the sizes and offsets used in the `MPI_Gatherv` call are all of integer type. This limits the size of the data that can be handled. There was an attempt to change the data type to the long data type so larger data sizes could be handled in version 3 of the MPI standard. It was not approved because it would break too many applications. Stay tuned for the addition of new calls that provide support for a long integer type in one of the next MPI standards.

8.4   *Data parallel examples*

The data parallel strategy, defined in section 1.5, is the most common approach in parallel applications. We'll look at a few examples of this approach in this section. First, we'll look at a simple case of the stream triad where no communication is necessary. Then we'll look at the more typical ghost cell exchange techniques used to link together the subdivided domains distributed to each process.

8.4.1   *Stream triad to measure bandwidth on the node*

The STREAM Triad is a bandwidth testing benchmark code introduced in section 3.2.4. This version uses MPI to get more processes working on the node and, possibly, on multiple nodes. The purpose of having more processes is to see what the maximum bandwidth is for the node when all processors are used. This gives a target bandwidth to aim for with more complicated applications. As listing 8.17 shows, the code is simple because no communication between ranks is required. The timing is only reported on the main process. You can run this first on one processor and then on all the processors on your node. Do you get the full parallel speedup that you would expect from the increase in processors? How much does the system memory bandwidth limit your speedup?

Listing 8.17   The MPI version of the STREAM Triad

```
StreamTriad/StreamTriad.c
  1 #include <stdio.h>
  2 #include <stdlib.h>
```

```
 3  #include <time.h>
 4  #include <mpi.h>
 5  #include "timer.h"
 6
 7  #define NTIMES 16
 8  #define STREAM_ARRAY_SIZE 80000000
 9
10  int main(int argc, char *argv[]){
11
12      MPI_Init(&argc, &argv);
13
14      int nprocs, rank;
15      MPI_Comm_size(MPI_COMM_WORLD, &nprocs);
16      MPI_Comm_rank(MPI_COMM_WORLD, &rank);
17      int ibegin = STREAM_ARRAY_SIZE *(rank   )/nprocs;
18      int iend   = STREAM_ARRAY_SIZE *(rank+1)/nprocs;
19      int nsize = iend-ibegin;
20      double *a = malloc(nsize * sizeof(double));
21      double *b = malloc(nsize * sizeof(double));
22      double *c = malloc(nsize * sizeof(double));
23
24      struct timespec tstart;
25      double scalar = 3.0, time_sum = 0.0;
26      for (int i=0; i<nsize; i++) {
27         a[i] = 1.0;
28         b[i] = 2.0;
29      }
30
31      for (int k=0; k<NTIMES; k++){
32         cpu_timer_start(&tstart);
33         for (int i=0; i<nsize; i++){
34            c[i] = a[i] + scalar*b[i];
35         }
36         time_sum += cpu_timer_stop(tstart);
37         c[1]=c[2];
38      }
39
40      free(a);
41      free(b);
42      free(c);
43
44      if (rank == 0)
            printf("Average runtime is %lf msecs\n", time_sum/NTIMES);
45      MPI_Finalize();
46      return(0);
47  }
```

Large enough to force into main memory ← (line 8)

Initializes data and arrays (lines 26–29)

The stream triad loop (lines 33–35)

Keeps the compiler from optimizing out the loop ← (line 37)

8.4.2 Ghost cell exchanges in a two-dimensional (2D) mesh

Ghost cells are the mechanism that we use to link the meshes on adjacent processors. These are used to cache values from adjacent processors so that fewer communications are needed. The ghost cell technique is the single most important method for enabling distributed memory parallelism in MPI.

Let's talk a little bit about the terminology of halos and ghost cells. Even before the age of parallel processing, a region of cells surrounding the mesh was often used to implement boundary conditions. These boundary conditions could be reflective, inflow, outflow, or periodic. For efficiency, programmers wanted to avoid `if` statements in the main computational loop. To do this, they added cells surrounding the mesh and set those to appropriate values before the main computational loop. These cells had the appearance of a halo, so the name stuck. *Halo cells* are any set of cells surrounding a computational mesh regardless of their purpose. A *domain-boundary halo* is then halo cells used for imposing a specific set of boundary conditions.

Once applications were parallelized, a similar outer region of cells was added to hold values from the neighboring meshes. These cells are not real cells but only exist as an aid to reduce communication costs. Because these are not real, these were soon given the name *ghost cells.* The real data for a ghost cell is on the adjacent processor and the local copy is just a ghost value. The ghost cells also look like halos and are also referred to as halo cells. *Ghost cell updates* or *exchanges* refer to the updating of the ghost cells and are only needed for parallel, multi-process runs when you need updates of real values from adjacent processes.

The boundary conditions need to be done for both serial and parallel runs. Confusion exists because these operations are often referred to as *halo updates*, although it's unclear exactly what is meant. In our terminology, *halo updates* refers to both the domain boundary updates and ghost cell updates. For optimizing MPI communication, we only need to look at the ghost cell updates or exchanges and put aside the boundary conditions calculations for the present.

Let's now look at how to set up ghost cells for the borders of the local mesh on each process and perform the communication between the subdomains. By using ghost cells, the needed communications are grouped into a fewer number of communications than if a single communication is done every time a cell's value is needed from another process. This is the most common technique to make the data parallel approach perform well. In the implementations of the ghost cell updates, we'll demonstrate the use of the `MPI_Pack` routine and load a communication buffer with a simple cell-by-cell array assignment. In later sections, we'll also see how to do the same communication with MPI data types, using the MPI topology calls for setup and communication.

Once we implement the ghost cell updates in a data parallel code, most of the needed communication is handled. This isolates the code that provides the parallelism into a small section of the application. This small section of the code is important to optimize for parallel efficiency. Let's look at some implementations of this functionality, starting with the setup in listing 8.18 and the work done by the stencil loops in listing 8.19. You may want to look at the full code in the GhostExchange/GhostExchange_Pack directory of the example code for the chapter at https://github.com/EssentialsOfParallelComputing/Chapter8.

Listing 8.18 Setup for ghost cell exchanges in a 2D mesh

-t do_timing synchronizes timing.

Input settings: -i <imax> -j <jmax> are the sizes of the grid.

-x <nprocx> -y <nprocy> are the number of processes in x- and y-directions.

-h <nhalo> -c is the number of halo cells and -c includes corner cells.

```
GhostExchange/GhostExchange_Pack/GhostExchange.cc
30      int imax = 2000, jmax = 2000;
31      int nprocx = 0, nprocy = 0;
32      int nhalo = 2, corners = 0;
33      int do_timing;
        ....
40      int xcoord = rank%nprocx;
41      int ycoord = rank/nprocx;
42
43      int nleft = (xcoord > 0         ) ?
                  rank - 1      : MPI_PROC_NULL;
44      int nrght = (xcoord < nprocx-1) ?
                  rank + 1      : MPI_PROC_NULL;
45      int nbot  = (ycoord > 0         ) ?
                  rank - nprocx : MPI_PROC_NULL;
46      int ntop  = (ycoord < nprocy-1) ?
                  rank + nprocx : MPI_PROC_NULL;
47
48      int ibegin = imax *(xcoord  )/nprocx;
49      int iend   = imax *(xcoord+1)/nprocx;
50      int isize  = iend - ibegin;
51      int jbegin = jmax *(ycoord  )/nprocy;
52      int jend   = jmax *(ycoord+1)/nprocy;
53      int jsize  = jend - jbegin;
```

xcoord and ycoord of processes. Row index varies fastest.

Neighbor rank for each process for neighbor communication

Size of computational domain for each process and the global begin and end index

We do memory allocation for the local size plus room for the halos on each process. To make the indexing a little simpler, we offset the memory indexing to start at -nhalo and end at isize+nhalo. The real cells then are always from 0 to isize-1, regardless of the width of the halo.

The following lines show a call to a special malloc2D with two additional arguments that offset the array addressing so that the real part of the array is from 0,0 to jsize,isize. This is done with some pointer arithmetic that moves the starting location of each pointer.

```
64      double** x    = malloc2D(jsize+2*nhalo, isize+2*nhalo, nhalo, nhalo);
65      double** xnew = malloc2D(jsize+2*nhalo, isize+2*nhalo, nhalo, nhalo);
```

We use the simple stencil calculation from the blur operator introduced in figure 1.10 to provide the work. Many applications have far more complex computations that take much more time. The following listing shows the stencil calculation loops.

Listing 8.19 Work is done in a stencil iteration loop

```
GhostExchange/GhostExchange_Pack/GhostExchange.cc
91      for (int iter = 0; iter < 1000; iter++){
```

Iteration loop

```
92        cpu_timer_start(&tstart_stencil);
93
94        for (int j = 0; j < jsize; j++){
95           for (int i = 0; i < isize; i++){
96              xnew[j][i] =
                    (x[j][i] + x[j][i-1] + x[j][i+1] +
                    x[j-1][i] + x[j+1][i])/5.0;
97           }
98        }
99
100       SWAP_PTR(xnew, x, xtmp);
101
102       stencil_time += cpu_timer_stop(tstart_stencil);
103
104       boundarycondition_update(x, nhalo, jsize,
             isize, nleft, nrght, nbot, ntop);
105       ghostcell_update(x, nhalo, corners,
             jsize, isize, nleft, nrght, nbot, ntop);
106    }
```

Stencil calculation (lines 94–98)

Pointer swap for old and new x arrays (line 100) ←

Ghost cell update call refreshes ghost cells. (line 105)

Iteration loop (line 106) ←

Now we can look at the critical ghost cell update code. Figure 8.5 shows the required operation. The width of the ghost cell region can be one, two, or more cells in depth. The corner cells may also be needed for some applications. Four processes (or ranks) each need data from this rank; to the left, right, top, and bottom. Each of these processes requires a separate communication and a separate data buffer. The width of the halo region varies in different applications, as well as whether the corner cells are needed.

Figure 8.5 shows an example of a ghost cell exchange for a 4-by-4 mesh on nine processes with a one-cell-wide halo and the corners included. The outer boundary halos are updated first and then a horizontal data exchange, a synchronization, and the vertical data exchange. If corners are not needed, the horizontal and vertical exchanges can be done at the same time. If the corners are desired, a synchronization is necessary between the horizontal and vertical exchanges.

A key observation of the ghost cell data updates is that in C, the row data is contiguous, whereas the column data is separated by a stride that is the size of the row. Sending individual values for the columns is expensive and so we need to group these together somehow.

You can perform the ghost cell update with MPI in several ways. In this first version in listing 8.20, we'll look at an implementation using the MPI_Pack call to pack the column data. The row data is sent with just a standard MPI_Isend call. The width of the ghost cell region is specified by the nhalo variable, and corners can be requested with the proper input.

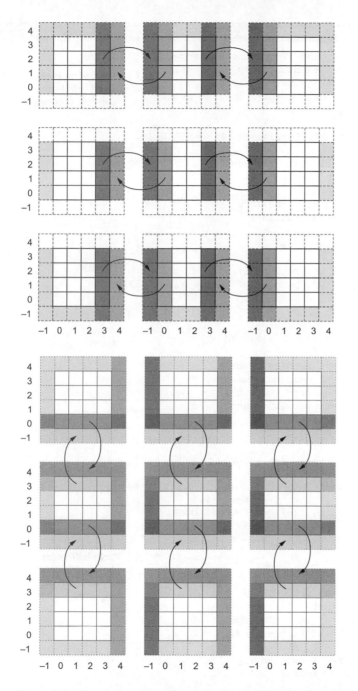

Figure 8.5 The corner cell version of the ghost cell update first exchanges data to the left and right (on the top half of the figure), followed by a top and bottom exchange (on the bottom half of the figure). With care, the left and right exchange can be smaller with just the real cells plus the outer boundary cells, although there is no harm in making it the full vertical size of the mesh. The updating of the boundary cells surrounding the mesh is done separately.

Listing 8.20   Ghost cell update routine for 2D mesh with `MPI_Pack`

GhostExchange/GhostExchange_Pack/GhostExchange.cc

```
167 void ghostcell_update(double **x, int nhalo,
        int corners, int jsize, int isize,
168     int nleft, int nrght, int nbot, int ntop,
        int do_timing)
169 {
170     if (do_timing) MPI_Barrier(MPI_COMM_WORLD);
171
172     struct timespec tstart_ghostcell;
173     cpu_timer_start(&tstart_ghostcell);
174
175     MPI_Request request[4*nhalo];
176     MPI_Status status[4*nhalo];
177
178     int jlow=0, jhgh=jsize;
179     if (corners) {
180         if (nbot == MPI_PROC_NULL) jlow = -nhalo;
181         if (ntop == MPI_PROC_NULL) jhgh = jsize+nhalo;
182     }
183     int jnum = jhgh-jlow;
184     int bufcount = jnum*nhalo;
185     int bufsize = bufcount*sizeof(double);
186
187     double xbuf_left_send[bufcount];
188     double xbuf_rght_send[bufcount];
189     double xbuf_rght_recv[bufcount];
190     double xbuf_left_recv[bufcount];
191
192     int position_left;
193     int position_right;
194     if (nleft != MPI_PROC_NULL){
195         position_left = 0;
196         for (int j = jlow; j < jhgh; j++){
197             MPI_Pack(&x[j][0], nhalo, MPI_DOUBLE,
198                 xbuf_left_send, bufsize,
                    &position_left,  MPI_COMM_WORLD);
199         }
200     }
201
202     if (nrght != MPI_PROC_NULL){
203         position_right = 0;
204         for (int j = jlow; j < jhgh; j++){
205             MPI_Pack(&x[j][isize-nhalo], nhalo,
                    MPI_DOUBLE, xbuf_rght_send,
206             bufsize, &position_right,
                    MPI_COMM_WORLD);
207         }
208     }
209
```

The update of the ghost cells from adjacent processes

Packs buffers for ghost cell update for left and right neighbors

```
210    MPI_Irecv(&xbuf_rght_recv, bufsize,
               MPI_PACKED, nrght, 1001,
211              MPI_COMM_WORLD, &request[0]);
212    MPI_Isend(&xbuf_left_send, bufsize,
               MPI_PACKED, nleft, 1001,
213              MPI_COMM_WORLD, &request[1]);
214
215    MPI_Irecv(&xbuf_left_recv, bufsize,
               MPI_PACKED, nleft, 1002,
216              MPI_COMM_WORLD, &request[2]);
217    MPI_Isend(&xbuf_rght_send, bufsize,
               MPI_PACKED, nrght, 1002,
218              MPI_COMM_WORLD, &request[3]);
219    MPI_Waitall(4, request, status);
220
221    if (nrght != MPI_PROC_NULL){
222       position_right = 0;
223       for (int j = jlow; j < jhgh; j++){
224         MPI_Unpack(xbuf_rght_recv, bufsize,
                 &position_right, &x[j][isize],
225            nhalo, MPI_DOUBLE, MPI_COMM_WORLD);
226       }
227    }
228
229    if (nleft != MPI_PROC_NULL){
230       position_left = 0;
231       for (int j = jlow; j < jhgh; j++){
232         MPI_Unpack(xbuf_left_recv, bufsize,
                 &position_left,  &x[j][-nhalo],
233            nhalo, MPI_DOUBLE, MPI_COMM_WORLD);
234       }
235    }
236
237    if (corners) {
238       bufcount = nhalo*(isize+2*nhalo);
239       MPI_Irecv(&x[jsize][-nhalo],
               bufcount, MPI_DOUBLE, ntop, 1001,
240              MPI_COMM_WORLD, &request[0]);
241       MPI_Isend(&x[0     ][-nhalo],
               bufcount, MPI_DOUBLE, nbot, 1001,
242               MPI_COMM_WORLD, &request[1]);
243
244       MPI_Irecv(&x[      -nhalo][-nhalo],
               bufcount, MPI_DOUBLE, nbot, 1002,
245              MPI_COMM_WORLD, &request[2]);
246       MPI_Isend(&x[jsize-nhalo][-nhalo],
               bufcount, MPI_DOUBLE,ntop, 1002,
247              MPI_COMM_WORLD, &request[3]);
248       MPI_Waitall(4, request, status);
249    } else {
```

Communication for left and right neighbors

Unpacks buffers for left and right neighbors

Ghost cell updates in one contiguous block for bottom and top neighbors

Waits for all communication to complete

```
250        for (int j = 0; j<nhalo; j++){
251            MPI_Irecv(&x[jsize+j][0],
                   isize, MPI_DOUBLE, ntop, 1001+j*2,
252               MPI_COMM_WORLD, &request[0+j*4]);
253            MPI_Isend(&x[0+j    ][0],
                   isize, MPI_DOUBLE, nbot, 1001+j*2,
254               MPI_COMM_WORLD, &request[1+j*4]);
255
256            MPI_Irecv(&x[      -nhalo+j][0],
                   isize, MPI_DOUBLE, nbot, 1002+j*2,
257               MPI_COMM_WORLD, &request[2+j*4]);
258            MPI_Isend(&x[jsize-nhalo+j][0],
                   isize, MPI_DOUBLE, ntop, 1002+j*2,
259               MPI_COMM_WORLD, &request[3+j*4]);
260        }
261        MPI_Waitall(4*nhalo, request, status);
262    }
263
264    if (do_timing) MPI_Barrier(MPI_COMM_WORLD);
265
266    ghostcell_time += cpu_timer_stop(tstart_ghostcell);
267 }
```

> Ghost cell updates one row at a time for bottom and top neighbors

> Waits for all communication to complete

The MPI_Pack call is particularly useful when there are multiple data types that need to be communicated in the ghost update. The values are packed into a type-agnostic buffer and then unpacked on the other side. The neighbor communication in the vertical direction is done with contiguous row data. When there are corners included, a single buffer works well. Without corners, individual halo rows are sent. There are usually only one or two halo cells, so this is a reasonable approach.

Another way to load the buffers for the communication is with an array assignment. Array assignments are a good approach when there is a single, simple data type like the double-precision float type used in this example. The following listing shows the code for replacing the MPI_Pack loops with array assignments.

Listing 8.21   Ghost cell update routine for 2D mesh with array assignments

GhostExchange/GhostExchange_ArrayAssign/GhostExchange.cc

```
190    int icount;
191    if (nleft != MPI_PROC_NULL){
192        icount = 0;
193        for (int j = jlow; j < jhgh; j++){
194            for (int ll = 0; ll < nhalo; ll++){
195                xbuf_left_send[icount++] = x[j][ll];
196            }
197        }
198    }
199    if (nrght != MPI_PROC_NULL){
200        icount = 0;
201        for (int j = jlow; j < jhgh; j++){
202            for (int ll = 0; ll < nhalo; ll++){
```

> Fills the send buffers

```
203                      xbuf_rght_send[icount++] =
                             x[j][isize-nhalo+ll];
204              }
205          }
206      }
207
208      MPI_Irecv(&xbuf_rght_recv, bufcount,
                  MPI_DOUBLE, nrght, 1001,
209                  MPI_COMM_WORLD, &request[0]);
210      MPI_Isend(&xbuf_left_send, bufcount,
                  MPI_DOUBLE, nleft, 1001,
211                  MPI_COMM_WORLD, &request[1]);
212
213      MPI_Irecv(&xbuf_left_recv, bufcount,
                  MPI_DOUBLE, nleft, 1002,
214                  MPI_COMM_WORLD, &request[2]);
215      MPI_Isend(&xbuf_rght_send, bufcount,
                  MPI_DOUBLE, nrght, 1002,
216                  MPI_COMM_WORLD, &request[3]);
217      MPI_Waitall(4, request, status);
218
219      if (nrght != MPI_PROC_NULL){
220          icount = 0;
221          for (int j = jlow; j < jhgh; j++){
222              for (int ll = 0; ll < nhalo; ll++){
223                  x[j][isize+ll] =
                         xbuf_rght_recv[icount++];
224              }
225          }
226      }
227      if (nleft != MPI_PROC_NULL){
228          icount = 0;
229          for (int j = jlow; j < jhgh; j++){
230              for (int ll = 0; ll < nhalo; ll++){
231                  x[j][-nhalo+ll] =
                         xbuf_left_recv[icount++];
232              }
233          }
234      }
```

Fills the send buffers

Performs the communication between left and right neighbors

Copies the receive buffers into the ghost cells

The MPI_Irecv and MPI_Isend calls now use a count and the MPI_DOUBLE data type rather than the generic byte type of MPI_Pack. We also need to know the data type for copying data into and out of the communication buffer.

8.4.3 *Ghost cell exchanges in a three-dimensional (3D) stencil calculation*

You can also do a ghost cell exchange for a 3D stencil calculation. We'll do that in listing 8.22. The setup is a little more complicated, however. The process layout is first calculated as xcoord, ycoord, and zcoord values. Then the neighbors are determined, and the sizes of the data on each processor calculated.

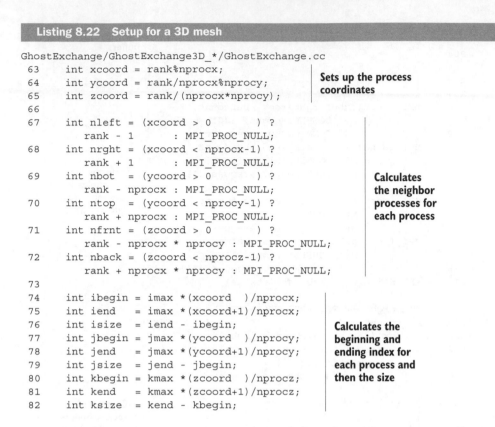

Listing 8.22   Setup for a 3D mesh

```
GhostExchange/GhostExchange3D_*/GhostExchange.cc
63    int xcoord = rank%nprocx;
64    int ycoord = rank/nprocx%nprocy;            Sets up the process
65    int zcoord = rank/(nprocx*nprocy);          coordinates
66
67    int nleft = (xcoord > 0       ) ?
         rank - 1       : MPI_PROC_NULL;
68    int nrght = (xcoord < nprocx-1) ?
         rank + 1       : MPI_PROC_NULL;
69    int nbot  = (ycoord > 0       ) ?           Calculates
         rank - nprocx : MPI_PROC_NULL;          the neighbor
70    int ntop  = (ycoord < nprocy-1) ?           processes for
         rank + nprocx : MPI_PROC_NULL;          each process
71    int nfrnt = (zcoord > 0       ) ?
         rank - nprocx * nprocy : MPI_PROC_NULL;
72    int nback = (zcoord < nprocz-1) ?
         rank + nprocx * nprocy : MPI_PROC_NULL;
73
74    int ibegin = imax *(xcoord  )/nprocx;
75    int iend   = imax *(xcoord+1)/nprocx;
76    int isize  = iend - ibegin;                 Calculates the
77    int jbegin = jmax *(ycoord  )/nprocy;       beginning and
78    int jend   = jmax *(ycoord+1)/nprocy;       ending index for
79    int jsize  = jend - jbegin;                 each process and
80    int kbegin = kmax *(zcoord  )/nprocz;       then the size
81    int kend   = kmax *(zcoord+1)/nprocz;
82    int ksize  = kend - kbegin;
```

The ghost cell update, including the array copies into buffers, communication, and copying out is a couple of hundred lines long and can't be shown here. Refer to the code examples (https://github.com/EssentialsofParallelComputing/Chapter8) that accompany the chapter for the detailed implementation. We'll show an MPI data type version of the ghost cell update in section 8.5.1.

8.5   *Advanced MPI functionality to simplify code and enable optimizations*

The excellent design of MPI becomes apparent as we see how basic MPI components can be combined into higher-level functionality. We got a taste of this in section 8.3.3, when we created a new double-double type and a new reduction operator. This extensibility gives MPI important capabilities. We'll look at a couple of these advanced functions that are useful in common data parallel applications. These include

- *MPI custom data types*—Builds new data types from the basic MPI type building blocks.
- *Topology support*—A basic Cartesian regular grid topology and a more general graph topology are both available. We'll just look at the simpler MPI Cartesian functions.

8.5.1   *Using custom MPI data types for performance and code simplification*

MPI has a rich set of functions to create new, custom MPI data types from the basic MPI types. This allows the encapsulation of complex data into a single custom data type that you can use in communication calls. As a result, a single communication call can send or receive many smaller pieces of data as a unit. Here is a list of some of the MPI data type creation functions:

- `MPI_Type_contiguous`—Makes a block of contiguous data into a type.
- `MPI_Type_vector`—Creates a type out of blocks of strided data.
- `MPI_Type_create_subarray`—Creates a rectangular subset of a larger array.
- `MPI_Type_indexed` or `MPI_Type_create_hindexed`—Creates an irregular set of indices described by a set of block lengths and displacements. The `hindexed` version expresses the displacements in bytes instead of a data type for more generality.
- `MPI_Type_create_struct`—Creates a data type encapsulating the data items in a structure in a portable way that accounts for padding by the compiler.

You'll find a visual illustration to be helpful in understanding some of these data types. Figure 8.6 shows some of the simpler and more commonly used functions including `MPI_Type_ contiguous`, `MPI_Type_vector`, and `MPI_Type_create_subarray`.

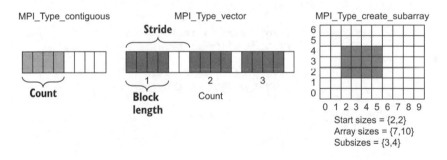

Figure 8.6   Three MPI custom data types with illustrations of the arguments used in their creation

Once a data type is described and made into a new data type, it must be initialized before it is used. For this purpose, there are a couple of additional routines to commit and free the types. A type must be committed before use and it must be freed to avoid a memory leak. The routines include

- `MPI_Type_Commit`—Initializes the new custom type with needed memory allocation or other setup
- `MPI_Type_Free`—Frees any memory or data structure entries from the creation of the data type

We can greatly simplify the ghost cell communication by defining a custom MPI data type as was shown in figure 8.6 to represent the column of data and to avoid the MPI_Pack calls. By defining an MPI data type, an extra data copy can be avoided. The data can be copied from its regular location straight into the MPI send buffers. Let's see how this is done in listing 8.23. Listing 8.24 shows the second part of the program.

We first set up the custom data types. We use the MPI_Type_vector call for sets of strided array accesses. For the contiguous data for the vertical type when we include corners, we use the MPI_Type_contiguous call, and in lines 139 and 140, we free the data type at the end before the MPI_Finalize.

Listing 8.23   Creating a 2D vector data type for the ghost cell update

```
GhostExchange/GhostExchange_VectorTypes/GhostExchange.cc
 56    int jlow=0, jhgh=jsize;
 57    if (corners) {
 58        if (nbot == MPI_PROC_NULL) jlow = -nhalo;
 59        if (ntop  == MPI_PROC_NULL) jhgh = jsize+nhalo;
 60    }
 61    int jnum = jhgh-jlow;
 62
 63    MPI_Datatype horiz_type;
 64    MPI_Type_vector(jnum, nhalo, isize+2*nhalo,
                       MPI_DOUBLE, &horiz_type);
 65    MPI_Type_commit(&horiz_type);
 66
 67    MPI_Datatype vert_type;
 68    if (! corners){
 69      MPI_Type_vector(nhalo, isize, isize+2*nhalo,
                       MPI_DOUBLE, &vert_type);
 70    } else {
 71      MPI_Type_contiguous(nhalo*(isize+2*nhalo),
                         MPI_DOUBLE, &vert_type);
 72    }
 73    MPI_Type_commit(&vert_type);
...
139    MPI_Type_free(&horiz_type);
140    MPI_Type_free(&vert_type);
```

You can then write the ghostcell_update more concisely and with better performance using the MPI data types as in the following listing. If we need to update corners, a synchronization is needed between the two communication passes.

Listing 8.24   2D ghost cell update routine using the vector data type

```
GhostExchange/GhostExchange_VectorTypes/GhostExchange.cc
197    int jlow=0, jhgh=jsize, ilow=0, waitcount=8, ib=4;
198    if (corners) {
199        if (nbot == MPI_PROC_NULL) jlow = -nhalo;
200        ilow = -nhalo;
201        waitcount = 4;
202        ib = 0;
```

```
203     }
204
205     MPI_Request request[waitcount];
206     MPI_Status status[waitcount];
207
208     MPI_Irecv(&x[jlow][isize], 1,
209         horiz_type, nrght, 1001,
            MPI_COMM_WORLD, &request[0]);
210     MPI_Isend(&x[jlow][0],      1,
211         horiz_type, nleft, 1001,
            MPI_COMM_WORLD, &request[1]);
212
213     MPI_Irecv(&x[jlow][-nhalo],      1,
214         horiz_type, nleft, 1002,
            MPI_COMM_WORLD, &request[2]);
215     MPI_Isend(&x[jlow][isize-nhalo], 1,
216         horiz_type, nrght, 1002,
            MPI_COMM_WORLD, &request[3]);
217
218     if (corners)
            MPI_Waitall(4, request, status);
219
220     MPI_Irecv(&x[jsize][ilow],    1,
221         vert_type, ntop, 1003,
            MPI_COMM_WORLD, &request[ib+0]);
222     MPI_Isend(&x[0     ][ilow],    1,
223         vert_type, nbot, 1003,
            MPI_COMM_WORLD, &request[ib+1]);
224
225     MPI_Irecv(&x[      -nhalo][ilow], 1,
226         vert_type, nbot, 1004,
            MPI_COMM_WORLD, &request[ib+2]);
227     MPI_Isend(&x[jsize-nhalo][ilow], 1,
228         vert_type, ntop, 1004,
            MPI_COMM_WORLD, &request[ib+3]);
229
230     MPI_Waitall(waitcount, request, status);
```

Send left and right using the custom horiz_type MPI data type

Synchronize if corners are sent.

Updates ghost cells on top and bottom

The reason for using MPI data types is usually given as better performance. It does allow MPI implementation to avoid an extra copy in some cases. But from our perspective, the biggest reason for MPI data types is the cleaner, simpler code and fewer opportunities for bugs.

The 3D version using MPI data types is a little more complicated. We use MPI_ Type_create_subarray in the following listing to create three custom MPI data types to be used in the communication.

Listing 8.25 Creating an MPI subarray data type for 3D ghost cells

```
GhostExchange/GhostExchange3D_VectorTypes/GhostExchange.cc
109     int array_sizes[] = {ksize+2*nhalo, jsize+2*nhalo, isize+2*nhalo};
110     if (corners) {
```

```
111        int subarray_starts[] = {0, 0, 0};
112        int hsubarray_sizes[] =
               {ksize+2*nhalo, jsize+2*nhalo,
                nhalo};
113        MPI_Type_create_subarray(3,
               array_sizes, hsubarray_sizes,
114            subarray_starts, MPI_ORDER_C,
               MPI_DOUBLE, &horiz_type);
115
116        int vsubarray_sizes[] =
               {ksize+2*nhalo, nhalo,
                isize+2*nhalo};
117        MPI_Type_create_subarray(3,
               array_sizes, vsubarray_sizes,
118            subarray_starts, MPI_ORDER_C,
               MPI_DOUBLE, &vert_type);
119
120        int dsubarray_sizes[] =
               {nhalo, jsize+2*nhalo,
                isize+2*nhalo};
121        MPI_Type_create_subarray(3,
               array_sizes, dsubarray_sizes,
122            subarray_starts, MPI_ORDER_C,
               MPI_DOUBLE, &depth_type);
123      } else {
124        int hsubarray_starts[] = {nhalo,nhalo,0};
125        int hsubarray_sizes[] = {ksize, jsize,
                                    nhalo};
126        MPI_Type_create_subarray(3,
               array_sizes, hsubarray_sizes,
127            hsubarray_starts, MPI_ORDER_C,
               MPI_DOUBLE, &horiz_type);
128
129        int vsubarray_starts[] = {nhalo, 0,
                                     nhalo};
130        int vsubarray_sizes[] = {ksize, nhalo,
                                    isize};
131        MPI_Type_create_subarray(3,
               array_sizes, vsubarray_sizes,
132            vsubarray_starts, MPI_ORDER_C,
               MPI_DOUBLE, &vert_type);
133
134        int dsubarray_starts[] = {0, nhalo,
                                     nhalo};
135        int dsubarray_sizes[] = {nhalo, ksize,
                                    isize};
136        MPI_Type_create_subarray(3,
               array_sizes, dsubarray_sizes,
137            dsubarray_starts, MPI_ORDER_C,
               MPI_DOUBLE, &depth_type);
138      }
139
140    MPI_Type_commit(&horiz_type);
141    MPI_Type_commit(&vert_type);
142    MPI_Type_commit(&depth_type);
```

Creates a horizontal data type using MPI_Type_create_subarray

Creates a depth data type using MPI_Type_create_subarray

Creates a vertical data type using MPI_Type_create_subarray

Creates a depth data type using MPI_Type_create_subarray

The following listing shows that the communication routine using these three MPI data types is pretty concise.

Listing 8.26 The 3D ghost cell update using MPI data types

GhostExchange/GhostExchange3D_VectorTypes/GhostExchange.cc

```
334    int waitcount = 12, ib1 = 4, ib2 = 8;
335    if (corners) {
336       waitcount=4;
337       ib1 = 0, ib2 = 0;
338    }
339
340    MPI_Request request[waitcount*nhalo];
341    MPI_Status status[waitcount*nhalo];
342
343    MPI_Irecv(&x[-nhalo][-nhalo][isize],    1,
344             horiz_type, nrght, 1001,
             MPI_COMM_WORLD, &request[0]);
345    MPI_Isend(&x[-nhalo][-nhalo][0],        1,
346             horiz_type, nleft, 1001,
             MPI_COMM_WORLD, &request[1]);
347
348    MPI_Irecv(&x[-nhalo][-nhalo][-nhalo],   1,
349             horiz_type, nleft, 1002,
             MPI_COMM_WORLD, &request[2]);
350    MPI_Isend(&x[-nhalo][-nhalo][isize-1], 1,
351             horiz_type, nrght, 1002,
             MPI_COMM_WORLD, &request[3]);
352    if (corners)
          MPI_Waitall(4, request, status);
353
354    MPI_Irecv(&x[-nhalo][jsize][-nhalo],    1,
355             vert_type, ntop, 1003,
             MPI_COMM_WORLD, &request[ib1+0]);
356    MPI_Isend(&x[-nhalo][0][-nhalo],        1,
357             vert_type, nbot, 1003,
             MPI_COMM_WORLD, &request[ib1+1]);
358
359    MPI_Irecv(&x[-nhalo][-nhalo][-nhalo],   1,
360             vert_type, nbot, 1004,
             MPI_COMM_WORLD, &request[ib1+2]);
361    MPI_Isend(&x[-nhalo][jsize-1][-nhalo], 1,
362             vert_type, ntop, 1004,
             MPI_COMM_WORLD, &request[ib1+3]);
363    if (corners)
          MPI_Waitall(4, request, status);
364
365    MPI_Irecv(&x[ksize][-nhalo][-nhalo],    1,
366             depth_type, nback, 1005,
             MPI_COMM_WORLD, &request[ib2+0]);
367    MPI_Isend(&x[0][-nhalo][-nhalo],        1,
368             depth_type, nfrnt, 1005,
             MPI_COMM_WORLD, &request[ib2+1]);
369
```

Ghost cell update for the horizontal direction.

Ghost cell update for the vertical direction.

Synchronize if corners are needed in the update.

Ghost cell update for the depth direction.

```
370    MPI_Irecv(&x[-nhalo][-nhalo][-nhalo],  1,
                 depth_type, nfrnt, 1006,
371              MPI_COMM_WORLD, &request[ib2+2]);
372    MPI_Isend(&x[ksize-1][-nhalo][-nhalo], 1,
                 depth_type, nback, 1006,
373              MPI_COMM_WORLD, &request[ib2+3]);
374    MPI_Waitall(waitcount, request, status);
```

Ghost cell update for the depth direction.

8.5.2   *Cartesian topology support in MPI*

In this section, we'll show you how the topology functions in MPI work. The operation is still the ghost exchange shown in figure 8.5, but we can simplify the coding by using Cartesian functions. Not covered are general graph functions for unstructured applications. We'll start with the setup routines before moving on to the communication routines.

The setup routines need to set the values for the process grid assignments and then to set the neighbors as was done in listings 8.18 and 8.22. As shown in listing 8.24 for 2D and listing 8.25 for 3D, the process sets the dims array to the number of processors to use in each dimension. If any of the values in the dims array are zero, the MPI_Dims_create function calculates some values that will work. Note that the number of processes in each direction does not take into account the mesh size and may not produce good values for long, narrow problems. Consider the case of a mesh that is 8x8x1000 and give it 8 processors; the process grid will be 2x2x2, resulting in a mesh domain of 4x4x500 on each process.

MPI_Cart_create takes the resulting dims array and an input array, periodic, that declares whether a boundary wraps to the opposite side and vice-versa. The last argument is the reorder argument that lets MPI reorder processes. It is zero (false) in this example. Now we have a new communicator that contains information about the topology.

Getting the process grid layout is just a call to MPI_Cart_coords. Getting neighbors is done with a call to MPI_Cart_shift with the second argument specifying the direction and the third argument the displacement or number of processes in that direction. The output is the ranks of the adjacent processors.

Listing 8.27   2D Cartesian topology support in MPI

```
GhostExchange/CartExchange_Neighbor/CartExchange.cc
43 int dims[2] = {nprocy, nprocx};
44 int periodic[2]={0,0};
45 int coords[2];
46 MPI_Dims_create(nprocs, 2, dims);
47 MPI_Comm cart_comm;
48 MPI_Cart_create(MPI_COMM_WORLD, 2, dims, periodic, 0, &cart_comm);
49 MPI_Cart_coords(cart_comm, rank, 2, coords);
50
51 int nleft, nrght, nbot, ntop;
52 MPI_Cart_shift(cart_comm, 1, 1, &nleft, &nrght);
53 MPI_Cart_shift(cart_comm, 0, 1, &nbot,  &ntop);
```

The 3D Cartesian topology setup is similar but with three dimensions as the following listing shows.

Listing 8.28 3D Cartesian topology support in MPI

```
GhostExchange/CartExchange3D_Neighbor/CartExchange.cc
65 int dims[3] = {nprocz, nprocy, nprocx};
66 int periods[3]={0,0,0};
67 int coords[3];
68 MPI_Dims_create(nprocs, 3, dims);
69 MPI_Comm cart_comm;
70 MPI_Cart_create(MPI_COMM_WORLD, 3, dims, periods, 0, &cart_comm);
71 MPI_Cart_coords(cart_comm, rank, 3, coords);
72 int xcoord = coords[2];
73 int ycoord = coords[1];
74 int zcoord = coords[0];
75
76 int nleft, nrght, nbot, ntop, nfrnt, nback;
77 MPI_Cart_shift(cart_comm, 2, 1, &nleft, &nrght);
78 MPI_Cart_shift(cart_comm, 1, 1, &nbot,  &ntop);
79 MPI_Cart_shift(cart_comm, 0, 1, &nfrnt, &nback);
```

If we compare this code to the versions in listing 8.19 and 8.23, we see that the topology functions do not save a lot of lines of code or greatly reduce the programming complexity in this relatively simple example for the setup. We can also leverage the Cartesian communicator created in line 70 of listing 8.28 to do the neighbor communication as well. That is where the greatest reduction of lines of code is seen. The MPI function has the following arguments:

```
int MPI_Neighbor_alltoallw(const void *sendbuf,
                           const int sendcounts[],
                           const MPI_Aint sdispls[],
                           const MPI_Datatype sendtypes[],
                           void *recvbuf,
                           const int recvcounts[],
                           const MPI_Aint rdispls[],
                           const MPI_Datatype recvtypes[],
                           MPI_Comm comm)
```

There are a lot of arguments in the neighbor call, but once we get these all set up, the communication is concise and done in a single statement. We'll go over all the arguments in detail because these can be difficult to get right.

The neighbor communication call can use either a filled buffer for the sends and receives or do the operation in place. We'll show the in-place method. The send and receive buffers are the 2D x array. We will use an MPI data type to describe the data block, so the counts will be an array with the value of one for all four Cartesian sides for 2D or six sides for 3D. The order of the communication for the sides is bottom, top, left, right for 2D and front, back, bottom, top, left, right for 3D, and is the same for both send and receive types.

The data block is different for each direction: horizontal, vertical, and depth. We use the convention of standard perspective drawings with x going to the right, y upwards, and z (the depth) going back into the page. But within each direction, the data block is the same but with different displacements to the start of the data block. The displacements are in bytes, which is why you will see the offsets multiplied by 8, the data type size of a double-precision value. Now let's look at how all this gets put into code for the setup of the communication for the 2D case in the following listing.

Listing 8.29   2D Cartesian neighbor communication setup

```
GhostExchange/CartExchange_Neighbor/CartExchange.c
55    int ibegin = imax *(coords[1]   )/dims[1];
56    int iend    = imax *(coords[1]+1)/dims[1];
57    int isize   = iend - ibegin;
58    int jbegin = jmax *(coords[0]   )/dims[0];
59    int jend    = jmax *(coords[0]+1)/dims[0];
60    int jsize   = jend - jbegin;
61
62    int jlow=nhalo, jhgh=jsize+nhalo,
          ilow=nhalo, inum = isize;
63    if (corners) {
64       int ilow = 0, inum = isize+2*nhalo;
65       if (nbot == MPI_PROC_NULL) jlow = 0;
66       if (ntop == MPI_PROC_NULL) jhgh = jsize+2*nhalo;
67    }
68    int jnum = jhgh-jlow;
69
70    int array_sizes[] = {jsize+2*nhalo, isize+2*nhalo};
71
72    int subarray_sizes_x[] = {jnum, nhalo};
73    int subarray_horiz_start[] = {jlow, 0};
74    MPI_Datatype horiz_type;
75    MPI_Type_create_subarray (2, array_sizes,
          subarray_sizes_x, subarray_horiz_start,
76       MPI_ORDER_C, MPI_DOUBLE, &horiz_type);
77    MPI_Type_commit(&horiz_type);
78
79    int subarray_sizes_y[] = {nhalo, inum};
80    int subarray_vert_start[] = {0, jlow};
81    MPI_Datatype vert_type;
82    MPI_Type_create_subarray (2, array_sizes,
          subarray_sizes_y, subarray_vert_start,
83       MPI_ORDER_C, MPI_DOUBLE, &vert_type);
84    MPI_Type_commit(&vert_type);
85
86    MPI_Aint sdispls[4] = {
          nhalo  *(isize+2*nhalo)*8,
87       jsize  *(isize+2*nhalo)*8,
88       nhalo  *8,
89       isize  *8};
90    MPI_Aint rdispls[4] = {
          0,
```

Calculates the global begin and end indices and the local array size

Includes the corner values if these are requested

Creates the data block to communicate in the horizontal direction using the subarray function

Creates the data block to communicate in the vertical direction using the subarray function

Bottom row is nhalo above start.

Top row is jsize above start.

Displacements are from bottom left corner of memory block in bytes.

Left column is nhalo right of start.

Right column is isize right of start.

Bottom ghost row is 0 above start.

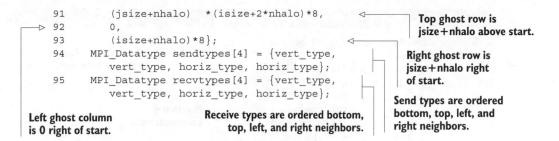

```
91          (jsize+nhalo)  *(isize+2*nhalo)*8,
92          0,
93          (isize+nhalo)*8};
94     MPI_Datatype sendtypes[4] = {vert_type,
            vert_type, horiz_type, horiz_type};
95     MPI_Datatype recvtypes[4] = {vert_type,
            vert_type, horiz_type, horiz_type};
```

Top ghost row is jsize+nhalo above start.

Right ghost row is jsize+nhalo right of start.

Send types are ordered bottom, top, left, and right neighbors.

Left ghost column is 0 right of start.

Receive types are ordered bottom, top, left, and right neighbors.

The setup for the 3D Cartesian neighbor communication uses the MPI data types from listing 8.25. The data types define the block of data to be moved, but we need to define the offset in bytes to the start location of the data block for the send and receive. We also need to define the arrays for the sendtypes and recvtypes in the proper order as in the next listing.

Listing 8.30 3D Cartesian neighbor communication setup

```
GhostExchange/CartExchange3D_Neighbor/CartExchange.c
154     int xyplane_mult = (jsize+2*nhalo)*(isize+2*nhalo)*8;
155     int xstride_mult = (isize+2*nhalo)*8;
156     MPI_Aint sdispls[6] = {
            nhalo  *xyplane_mult,
157         ksize  *xyplane_mult,
158         nhalo  *xstride_mult,
159         jsize  *xstride_mult,
160         nhalo  *8,
161         isize  *8};
162     MPI_Aint rdispls[6] = {
            0,
163         (ksize+nhalo)  *xyplane_mult,
164         0,
165         (jsize+nhalo)  *xstride_mult,
166         0,
167         (isize+nhalo)*8};
168     MPI_Datatype sendtypes[6] = {
            depth_type, depth_type,
            vert_type, vert_type,
            horiz_type, horiz_type};
169     MPI_Datatype recvtypes[6] = {
            depth_type, depth_type,
            vert_type, vert_type,
            horiz_type, horiz_type};
```

Front is nhalo behind front.

Back is ksize behind front.

Right column is isize.

Send and receive types are ordered front, back, bottom, top, left, and right.

Displacements are from bottom left corner of memory block in bytes.

Bottom row is nhalo above start.

Top row is jsize above start.

Left column is nhalo right of start.

Front ghost is 0 from front.

Back ghost is ksize+nhalo behind front.

Bottom ghost row is 0 above start.

Top ghost row is jsize+nhalo above start.

Left ghost column is 0 right of start.

Right ghost row is jsize+nhalo right of start.

The actual communication is done with a single call to the MPI_Neighbor_alltoallw as shown in listing 8.31. There is also a second block of code for the corner cases that requires a couple of calls with a synchronization in between to ensure the corners are properly filled. The first call does only the horizontal direction and then waits for completion before doing the vertical direction.

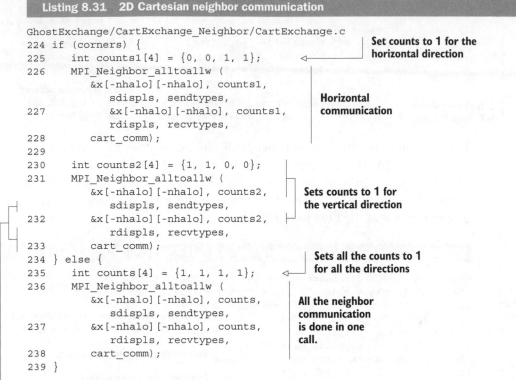

Listing 8.31   2D Cartesian neighbor communication

```
GhostExchange/CartExchange_Neighbor/CartExchange.c
224 if (corners) {
225     int counts1[4] = {0, 0, 1, 1};
226     MPI_Neighbor_alltoallw (
            &x[-nhalo][-nhalo], counts1,
            sdispls, sendtypes,
227         &x[-nhalo][-nhalo], counts1,
            rdispls, recvtypes,
228         cart_comm);
229
230     int counts2[4] = {1, 1, 0, 0};
231     MPI_Neighbor_alltoallw (
            &x[-nhalo][-nhalo], counts2,
            sdispls, sendtypes,
232         &x[-nhalo][-nhalo], counts2,
            rdispls, recvtypes,
233         cart_comm);
234 } else {
235     int counts[4] = {1, 1, 1, 1};
236     MPI_Neighbor_alltoallw (
            &x[-nhalo][-nhalo], counts,
            sdispls, sendtypes,
237         &x[-nhalo][-nhalo], counts,
            rdispls, recvtypes,
238         cart_comm);
239 }
```

Set counts to 1 for the horizontal direction

Horizontal communication

Sets counts to 1 for the vertical direction

Sets all the counts to 1 for all the directions

All the neighbor communication is done in one call.

Vertical communication

The 3D Cartesian neighbor communication is similar but with the addition of the z coordinate (depth). The depth comes first in the counts and types arrays. In the phased communication for corners, the depth comes after horizontal and vertical ghost cell exchanges as the next listing shows.

Listing 8.32   3D Cartesian neighbor communication

```
GhostExchange/CartExchange3D_Neighbor/CartExchange.c
346 if (corners) {
347     int counts1[6] = {0, 0, 0, 0, 1, 1};
348     MPI_Neighbor_alltoallw(
            &x[-nhalo][-nhalo][-nhalo], counts1,
            sdispls, sendtypes,
349         &x[-nhalo][-nhalo][-nhalo], counts1,
            rdispls, recvtypes,
350         cart_comm);
351
352     int counts2[6] = {0, 0, 1, 1, 0, 0};
353     MPI_Neighbor_alltoallw(
            &x[-nhalo][-nhalo][-nhalo], counts2,
            sdispls, sendtypes,
354         &x[-nhalo][-nhalo][-nhalo], counts2,
            rdispls, recvtypes,
355         cart_comm);
```

Horizontal ghost exchange

Vertical ghost exchange

```
356
357    int counts3[6] = {1, 1, 0, 0, 0, 0};
358    MPI_Neighbor_alltoallw(
           &x[-nhalo][-nhalo][-nhalo], counts3,
               sdispls, sendtypes,
359        &x[-nhalo][-nhalo][-nhalo], counts3,
               rdispls, recvtypes,
360        cart_comm);
361 } else {
362    int counts[6] = {1, 1, 1, 1, 1, 1};
363    MPI_Neighbor_alltoallw(
           &x[-nhalo][-nhalo][-nhalo], counts,
               sdispls, sendtypes,
364        &x[-nhalo][-nhalo][-nhalo], counts,
               rdispls, recvtypes,
365        cart_comm);
366 }
```

Depth ghost exchange (lines 357–360)

All neighbors at once (lines 362–365)

8.5.3 *Performance tests of ghost cell exchange variants*

Let's try out these ghost cell exchange variants on a test system. We'll use two Broadwell nodes (Intel® Xeon® CPU E5-2695 v4 at 2.10GHz) with 72 virtual cores each. We could run this on more compute nodes with different MPI library implementations, halo sizes, mesh sizes, and with higher performance communication interconnects for a more comprehensive view of how each ghost cell exchange variant performs. Here's the code:

```
mpirun -n 144 --bind-to hwthread ./GhostExchange -x 12 -y 12 -i 20000 \
       -j 20000 -h 2 -t -c
mpirun -n 144 --bind-to hwthread ./GhostExchange -x 6 -y 4 -z 6 -i 700 \
       -j 700 -k 700 -h 2 -t -c
```

The options to the GhostExchange program are

- -x (processes in the x-direction)
- -y (processes in the y-direction)
- -z (processes in the z-direction)
- -i (mesh size in the i- or x-direction)
- -j (mesh size in the j- or y-direction)
- -k (mesh size in the k- or z-direction)
- -h (width of halo cells, usually 1 or 2)
- -c (include the corner cells)

Exercise: Ghost cell tests

The accompanying source code is set up to run the whole set of ghost cell exchange variations. In the batch.sh file, you can change the halo size and whether you want corners. The file is set up to run all of the test cases 11 times on two Skylake Gold nodes with 144 total processes.

(continued)

```
cd GhostExchange
./build.sh
./batch.sh |& tee results.txt
./get_stats.sh > stats.out
```

You can then generate plots with the provided scripts. You need the matplotlib library for the Python plotting scripts. The results are for the median run time.

```
python plottimebytype.py
python plottimeby3Dtype.py
```

The following figure shows the plots for the small test cases. The MPI data type versions appear a little faster even at this small scale, indicating that perhaps a data copy is being avoided. The larger gain for the MPI Cartesian topology calls and MPI data types is that the ghost exchange code is greatly simplified. The use of these more advanced MPI calls does require more setup effort, but this is just done once at startup.

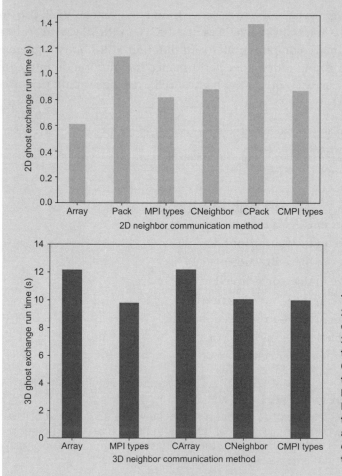

The relative performance of 2D and 3D ghost exchanges on two nodes with a total of 144 processes. The MPI data types in the MPI types and CNeighbor are a little faster than the buffer explicitly filled by loops of array assignments. In the 2D ghost exchanges, the pack routines are slower, although in this case, the explicitly filled buffer is faster than the MPI data types.

8.6 Hybrid MPI plus OpenMP for extreme scalability

The combination of two or more parallelization techniques is called a hybrid parallelization, in contrast to all MPI implementations that are also called pure MPI or MPI-everywhere. In this section, we'll look at Hybrid MPI plus OpenMP, where MPI and OpenMP are used together in an application. This usually amounts to replacing some MPI ranks with OpenMP threads. For larger parallel applications reaching into thousands of processes, replacing MPI ranks with OpenMP threads potentially reduces the total size of the MPI domain and the memory needed for extreme scale. However, the added performance of the thread-level parallelism layer might not always be worth the added complexity and development time. For this reason, hybrid MPI plus OpenMP implementations are normally the domain of extreme applications in both size and performance needs.

8.6.1 The benefits of hybrid MPI plus OpenMP

When performance becomes critical enough for the added complexity of hybrid parallelism, there can be several advantages of adding an OpenMP parallel layer to MPI-based code. For example, these advantages might be

- Fewer ghost cells to communicate between nodes
- Lower memory requirements for MPI buffers
- Reduced contention for the NIC
- Reduced size of tree-based communications
- Improved load balancing
- Accessing all hardware components

Spatially-decomposed parallel applications using subdomains with ghost (halo) cells will have fewer total ghost cells per node when you add thread-level parallelism. This leads to a reduction in both memory requirements and communication costs, especially on a many-core architecture like Intel's Knights Landing (KNL). Using shared-memory parallelism can also improve performance by reducing contention for the network interface card (NIC) by avoiding the unnecessary copying of data used by MPI for on-node messages. Additionally, many MPI algorithms are tree-based, scaling as $\log_2 n$. Reducing the run time by $2n$ threads decreases the depth of the tree and incrementally improves performance. While the remaining work still has to be done by threads, it impacts performance by allowing less synchronization and communication latency costs. Threads can also be used to improve load balance within a NUMA region or a compute node.

In some cases, a hybrid parallel approach is not only advantageous, but necessary to access the full hardware performance potential. For example, some hardware, and perhaps memory controller functionality, can only be accessed by threads and not processes (MPI ranks). The many-core architectures of Intel's Knights Corner and Knights Landing architectures have had these concerns. In *MPI + X + Y*, where *X* is threading and *Y* is a GPU language, we often match the ranks to the number of GPUs.

OpenMP allows the application to continue to access the other processors for on-CPU work. There are other solutions to this, such as MPI_COMM groups and MPI-shared memory functionality or simply driving the GPU from multiple MPI ranks.

In summary, while it can be attractive to run codes with MPI-everywhere on modern many-core systems, there are concerns about scalability as the number of cores grows. If you are looking for extreme scalability, you will want an efficient implementation of OpenMP in your application. We covered our design of high-level OpenMP that is much more efficient in the previous chapter in sections 7.2.2 and 7.6.

8.6.2 MPI plus OpenMP example

The first steps to a hybrid MPI plus OpenMP implementation is to let MPI know what you will be doing. This is done in the MPI_Init call right at the beginning of the program. You should replace the MPI_Init call with the MPI_Init_thread call like this:

```
MPI_Init_thread(&argc, &argv, int thread_model required,
                int *thread_model_provided);
```

The MPI standard defines four thread models. These models give different levels of thread safety with the MPI calls. In increasing order of thread safety:

- MPI_THREAD_SINGLE—Only one thread is executed (standard MPI)
- MPI_THREAD_FUNNELED—Multithreaded but only the main thread makes MPI calls
- MPI_THREAD_SERIALIZED—Multithreaded but only one thread at a time makes MPI calls
- MPI_THREAD_MULTIPLE—Multithreaded with multiple threads making MPI calls

Many applications perform communication at the main loop level, and OpenMP threads are applied to key computational loops. For this pattern, MPI_THREAD_FUNNELED works just fine.

> **NOTE** It's best to use the lowest level of thread safety that you need. Each higher level imposes a performance penalty because the MPI library has to place mutexes or critical blocks around send and receive queues and other basic parts of MPI.

Now let's see what changes are needed to our stencil example to add OpenMP threading. We chose the CartExchange_Neighbor example to modify for this exercise. The following listing shows that the first change is to modify the MPI initialization.

Listing 8.33 MPI initialization for OpenMP threading

```
HybridMPIPlusOpenMP/CartExchange.cc
26 int provided;
27 MPI_Init_thread(&argc, &argv,           MPI initialization for
      MPI_THREAD_FUNNELED, &provided);     OpenMP threading
28
```

```
29 int rank, nprocs;
30 MPI_Comm_rank(MPI_COMM_WORLD, &rank);
31 MPI_Comm_size(MPI_COMM_WORLD, &nprocs);
32 if (rank == 0) {
33    #pragma omp parallel
34    #pragma omp master
35       printf("requesting MPI_THREAD_FUNNELED"
                  " with %d threads\n",
36                omp_get_num_threads());
37    if (provided != MPI_THREAD_FUNNELED){
38       printf("Error: MPI_THREAD_FUNNELED"
                  " not available. Aborting ...\n");
39       MPI_Finalize();
40       exit(0);
41    }
42 }
```

Line 35–36 — **Prints number of threads to check if what we want**

Line 37 — **Checks if this MPI supports our requested thread safety level**

The mandatory change is using `MPI_Init_thread` instead of `MPI_Init` on line 27. The additional code checks that the requested thread safety level is available and exits if it is not. We also print the number of threads on the main thread of rank zero. Now onto the changes in the computational loop shown in the next listing.

Listing 8.34 Addition of OpenMP threading and vectorization to computational loops

```
HybridMPIPlusOpenMP/CartExchange.cc
157  #pragma omp parallel for
158  for (int j = 0; j < jsize; j++){
159     #pragma omp simd
160     for (int i = 0; i < isize; i++){
161        xnew[j][i] = ( x[j][i] + x[j][i-1] + x[j][i+1]
                            + x[j-1][i] + x[j+1][i] )/5.0;
162     }
163  }
```

Line 157 — **Adds OpenMP threading for outer loop**

Line 159 — **Adds SIMD vectorization for inner loop**

The changes required to add OpenMP threading are the addition of a single pragma at line 157. As a bonus, we show how to add vectorization for the inner loop with another pragma inserted at line 159.

You can now try running this hybrid MPI plus OpenMP+Vectorization example on your system. But to get good performance, you will need to control the placement of the MPI ranks and the OpenMP threads. This is done by setting affinity, a topic that we will cover in greater depth in chapter 14.

DEFINITION *Affinity* assigns a preference for the scheduliing of a process, rank, or thread to a particular hardware component. This is also called *pinning* or *binding*.

Setting the affinity for your ranks and threads becomes more important as the complexity of the node increases and with hybrid parallel applications. In earlier examples, we used `--bind-to core` and `--bind-to hwthread` to improve performance and reduce variability in run-time performance caused by ranks migrating from one core to another. In OpenMP, we used environment variables to set placement and affinities. An example is

```
export OMP_PLACES=cores
export OMP_CPU_BIND=true
```

For now, start with pinning the MPI ranks to sockets so that the threads can spread to other cores as we showed in our ghost cell test example for the Skylake Gold processor. Here's how:

```
export OMP_NUM_THREADS=22
mpirun -n 4 --bind-to socket ./CartExchange -x 2 -y 2 -i 20000 -j 20000 \
-h 2 -t -c
```

We run 4 MPI ranks that each spawn 22 threads as specified by the OMP_NUM_THREADS environment variable for a total of 88 processes. The --bind-to socket option to mpirun tells it to bind the processes to the socket where these are placed.

8.7   Further explorations

Although we have covered a lot of material in this chapter, there are still many more features that are worth exploring as you get more experience with MPI. Some of the most important are mentioned here and left for your own study.

- *Comm groups*—MPI has a rich set of functions that create, split, and otherwise manipulate the standard MPI COMM_WORLD communicator into new groupings for specialized operations like communication within a row or task-based subgroups. For some examples of the use of communicator groups, see listing 16.4 in section 16.3. We use communication groups to split the file output into multiple files and break the domain into row and column communicators.

- *Unstructured mesh boundary communications*—An unstructured mesh needs to exchange boundary data in a similar manner to that covered for a regular, Cartesian mesh. These operations are more complex and not covered here. There are many sparse, graph-based communication libraries that support unstructured mesh applications. One example of such a library is the L7 communication library developed by Richard Barrett now at Sandia National Laboratories. It is included with the CLAMR mini-app; see the l7 subdirectory at https://github.com/LANL/CLAMR.

- *Shared memory*—The original MPI implementations sent data over the network interface in nearly all cases. As the number of cores grew, MPI developers realized that they could do some of the communication in shared memory. This is done behind the scenes as a communication optimization. Additional shared memory functionality continues to be added with MPI shared memory "windows." This functionality had some problems at first, but it is becoming mature enough to use in applications.

- *One-sided communication*—Responding to other programming models, MPI added one-sided communication in the form of `MPI_Puts` and `MPI_Gets`. Contrary to the original MPI message-passing model, where both the sender and receiver have to be active participants, the one-sided model allows just one or the other to conduct the operation.

8.7.1 Additional reading

If you want more introductory material on MPI, the text by Peter Pacheco is a classic:

Peter Pacheco, *An introduction to parallel programming* (Elsevier, 2011).

You can find thorough coverage of MPI authored by members of the original MPI development team:

William Gropp, et al., "Using MPI: portable parallel programming with the message-passing interface," Vol. 1 (MIT Press, 1999).

For a presentation of MPI plus OpenMP, there is a good lecture from a course by Bill Gropp, one of the developers of the original MPI standard. Here's the link:

http://wgropp.cs.illinois.edu/courses/cs598-s16/lectures/lecture36.pdf

8.7.2 Exercises

1. Why can't we just block on receives as was done in the send/receive in the ghost exchange using the pack or array buffer methods in listings 8.20 and 8.21, respectively?
2. Is it safe to block on receives as shown in listing 8.8 in the vector type version of the ghost exchange? What are the advantages if we only block on receives?
3. Modify the ghost cell exchange vector type example in listing 8.21 to use blocking receives instead of a `waitall`. Is it faster? Does it always work?
4. Try replacing the explicit tags in one of the ghost exchange routines with `MPI_ANY_TAG`. Does it work? Is it any faster? What advantage do you see in using explicit tags?
5. Remove the barriers for the synchronized timers in one of the ghost exchange examples. Run the code with the original synchronized timers and the unsynchronized timers.
6. Add the timer statistics from listing 8.11 to the stream triad bandwidth measurement code in listing 8.17.
7. Apply the steps to convert high-level OpenMP to the hybrid MPI plus OpenMP example in the code that accompanies the chapter (HybridMPIPlusOpenMP directory). Experiment with the vectorization, number of threads, and MPI ranks on your platform.

Summary

- Use the proper send and receive point-to-point messages. This avoids hangs and gets good performance.
- Use collective communication for common operations. This makes for concise programming, avoids hangs, and improves performance.
- Use ghost exchanges to link together subdomains from various processors. The exchanges make the subdomains act as a single global computational mesh.
- Add more levels of parallelism through combining MPI with OpenMP threads and vectorization. The additional parallelism helps give better performance.

Part 3

GPUs: Built to accelerate

The following chapters on GPU computing discuss using GPUs for scientific computing. The topics include

- In chapter 9, you'll gain an understanding of the GPU architecture and its benefits for general-purpose computation.
- In chapter 10, you'll learn how to build a mental representation of the programming model for GPUs.
- In chapters 11 and 12, you'll explore the available GPU programming languages. In chapter 11, we present basic examples in OpenACC and OpenMP, and in chapter 12, we cover a broad range of GPU languages, from lower level native languages like CUDA, OpenCL, and HIP to higher level ones like SYCL, Kokkos, and Raja.
- In chapter 13, you'll learn about profiling tools and developing a work-flow model that enhances programmer productivity.

GPUs were built to accelerate computation. With a single-minded focus on improving the frame rate for computer animation, GPU hardware developers went to great lengths to increase numerical operation throughput. These devices are simply general-purpose extreme accelerators for any massively parallel operation. They are called graphics processing units because they were developed for that application.

Fast forward to today, and many software developers have realized that the acceleration provided by GPUs is just as applicable for a wide variety of application domains. While at the University of North Carolina in 2002, Mark Harris coined the term *general-purpose graphics processing units* (GPGPUs) to try and capture the idea that GPUs are suitable for more than graphics alone. Major markets for GPUs have sprung up for bitcoin mining, machine learning, and high-performance computing. Small modifications to the GPU hardware, such as double-precision floating-point units and tensor operations, have customized the basic GPU designs for each of these markets. No longer are GPUs just for graphics.

Each GPU model that is released targets a different market segment. With high-end GPU models commanding prices of up to $10,000, these are not the same hardware models that you will find in mass-market computers. Though GPUs are used in many more applications than they were originally intended for, it is still difficult to see them completely replacing the general-purpose functionality of a CPU within the near future, as a single operation is better suited for the CPU.

If we were to come up with a new name for GPUs, how would we capture their functionality in a broad sense? The commonality across all the use domains is that, in order for it to make sense to use GPUs, there must be a lot of work that can be done simultaneously. And by a lot, we mean thousands or tens of thousands of simultaneous parallel operations. GPUs are really *parallel accelerators*. Maybe we should call them Parallel Processing Units (PPUs) or Parallel Processing Accelerators (PPAs) to capture a better idea of their functionality. But, we'll stick with the term GPUs with the understanding that they are so much more. Seeing GPUs in this light, you can understand why they are of such importance for the parallel computing community.

GPUs are simpler devices to design and manufacture than CPUs, so the design cycle time is half that of the CPUs. The crossover point for many applications for GPU performance relative to CPUs was about 2012. Since then, GPU performance has been improving at about twice the rate of CPUs. In very rough numbers, GPUs today can provide a ten times speedup over CPUs. Of course, there is a lot of variability in this speedup by the type of application and the quality of code implementation. The trends are clear—GPUs will continue to show greater speedups for those applications that can fit its massively parallel architecture.

To help you understand these new hardware devices, we go over the essential parts of their hardware design in chapter 10. We then try to help you develop a mental model of how to approach them. It is important to gain this understanding before tackling a project for GPUs. We have seen numerous porting efforts fail because programmers thought they could just move the most expensive loop to the GPU and they would see fantastic speedups. Then when their application runs slower, they abandon the effort. Transferring data to the GPU is expensive; therefore, large parts of your application must be ported to the device to see any benefit. A simple performance model and analysis before the GPU implementation would have tempered programmers' initial expectations and cautioned them to plan for sufficient time and effort to achieve success.

Perhaps the biggest impediment to beginning a GPU implementation is the constantly shifting landscape of programming languages. It seems like a new language gets released every few months. Although these languages bring a high degree of innovation, this constant evolution makes it difficult for application developers. However, taking a closer look at the languages shows that there are more similarities than differences, often converging on a couple of common designs. While we expect a few more years of language thrashing, many of the language variations are akin to dialects rather than completely different languages. In chapter 11, we cover the pragma-based languages. In chapter 12, we survey native GPU languages and a new class of performance portability languages that heavily leverage C++ constructs. Though we present a variety of language implementations, we suggest you initially pick a couple of languages to get some hands-on experience with those. Much of your decision on which languages to experiment with will be dependent on the hardware that you have readily available.

You can check out the examples at https://github.com/EssentialsofParallelComputing for each of these chapters. (In fact, we highly encourage you to do so.) One of the barriers for GPU programming is access to hardware and getting it set up properly. The installation of system software to support the GPUs can sometimes be difficult. The examples have lists of the software packages for the GPUs from the vendors that can get you started. But you will want to install the software for the GPU in your system and, in the examples, comment out the rest. It will take some trial and error. In chapter 13, we discuss different workflows and alternatives such as setting up Docker containers and virtual machines (VMs). These options may provide a way to set up a development environment on your laptop or desktop, especially if you are using Windows or MacOS.

If you don't have local hardware available, you can try out a cloud service with GPUs. Some such as Google cloud ($200-300 credit) even have free trials. These services even have marketplace add-ons that let you set up an HPC cluster with GPUs. One example of an HPC cloud service with GPUs is the Fluid Numerics Google Cloud Platform. For testing out Intel GPUs, Intel has set up cloud services for trial services as well. For information, we recommend these sites:

- Fluid-Slurm Google Cloud Cluster at https://console.cloud.google.com/marketplace/details/fluid-cluster-ops/fluid-slurm-gcp
- Intel cloud version of oneAPI and DPCPP at https://software.intel.com/cn-us/oneapi (you must register to use).

GPU architectures and concepts

Why do we care about graphics processing units (GPUs) for high-performance computing? GPUs provide a massive source of parallel operations that can greatly exceed that which is available on the more conventional CPU architecture. To exploit their capabilities, it is essential that we understand GPU architectures. Though GPUs have often been used for graphical processing, GPUs are also used for general-purpose parallel computing. This chapter provides an overview of the hardware on a GPU-accelerated platform.

What systems today are GPU accelerated? Virtually every computing system provides the powerful graphics capabilities expected by today's users. These GPUs range from small components of the main CPU to large peripheral cards taking up a large part of space in a desktop case. HPC systems are increasingly coming equipped with multiple GPUs. On occasion, even personal computers used for simulation or gaming can sometimes connect two GPUs for higher graphics performance. In this chapter, we present a conceptual model that identifies key hardware components of a GPU accelerated system. Figure 9.1 shows these components.

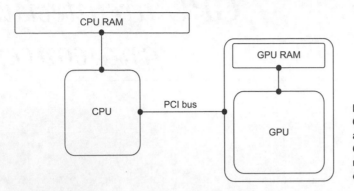

Figure 9.1   Block diagram of GPU-accelerated system using a dedicated GPU. The CPU and GPU each have their own memory. The CPU and GPU communicate over a PCI bus.

Due to inconsistent terminology in the community, there is added complexity in understanding GPUs. We will use the terminology established by the OpenCL standard because it was agreed to by multiple GPU vendors. We will also note alternate terminology that is in common use, such as that used by NVIDIA. Let's look at a few definitions before continuing our discussion:

- *CPU*—The main processor that is installed in the socket of the motherboard.
- *CPU RAM*—The "memory sticks" or dual in-line memory modules (DIMMs) containing Dynamic Random-Access Memory (DRAM) that are inserted into the memory slots in the motherboard.
- *GPU*—A large peripheral card installed in a Peripheral Component Interconnect Express (PCIe) slot on the motherboard.
- *GPU RAM*—Memory modules on the GPU peripheral card for exclusive use of the GPU.
- *PCI bus*—The wiring that connects the peripheral cards to the other components on the motherboard.

We'll introduce each component in a GPU-accelerated system and show how to calculate the theoretical performance for each. We'll then examine their actual performance with small micro-benchmark applications. This will help to establish how some hardware components can cause bottlenecks that prevent you from accelerating an application with GPUs. Armed with this information, we'll conclude the chapter with a discussion of the types of applications that benefit most from GPU acceleration and what your goals should be to see performance gains when porting an application to run on GPUs. For this chapter, you'll find the source code at https://github.com/EssentialsofParallelComputing/Chapter9.

9.1 The CPU-GPU system as an accelerated computational platform

GPUs are everywhere. They can be found in cell phones, tablets, personal computers, consumer-grade workstations, gaming consoles, high performance computing centers, and cloud computing platforms. GPUs provide additional compute power on most modern hardware and accelerate many operations you may not even be aware of. As the name suggests, GPUs were designed for graphics-related computations. Consequently, GPU design focuses on processing large blocks of data (triangles or polygons) in parallel, which is a requirement for graphics applications. Compared to CPUs that can handle tens of parallel threads or processes in a clock cycle, GPUs are capable of processing thousands of parallel threads simultaneously. Because of this design, GPUs offer a considerably higher theoretical peak performance that can potentially reduce the time to solution and the energy footprint of an application.

Computational scientists, always on the lookout for computational horsepower, were attracted to using GPUs to perform more general-purpose computing tasks. Because GPUs were designed for graphics, the languages originally developed to program them, like OpenGL, focused on graphics operations. To implement algorithms on GPUs, programmers had to reframe their algorithms in terms of these operations, which was time-consuming and error-prone. Extending the use of the graphics processor to non-graphics workloads became known as general-purpose graphics processing unit (GPGPU) computing.

The continued interest and success of GPGPU computing led to the introduction of a flurry of GPGPU languages. The first to gain wide adoption was the Compute Unified Device Architecture (CUDA) programming language for NVIDIA GPUs, which was first introduced in 2007. The dominant open standard GPGPU computing language is the Open Computing Language (OpenCL), developed by a group of vendors led by Apple and released in 2009. We'll cover both CUDA and OpenCL in chapter 12.

Despite the continual introduction of GPGPU languages, or maybe because of it, many computational scientists have found the original, native, GPGPU languages difficult to use. As a result, higher-level approaches using directive-based APIs gained a large following and spurred corresponding development efforts by vendors. We'll cover examples of directive-based languages like OpenACC and OpenMP (with the new target directive) in chapter 11. For now, we summarize the new directive-based GPGPU languages, OpenACC and OpenMP, as an unqualified success. These languages and APIs have allowed programmers to focus more on developing their applications, rather than expressing their algorithm in terms of graphics operations. The end result has often been tremendous speedups in scientific and data science applications.

GPUs are best described as accelerators, long used in the computing world. First let's define what we mean by an accelerator.

> **DEFINITION** An *accelerator* (hardware) is a special-purpose device that supplements the main general-purpose CPU in speeding up certain operations.

A classic example of an accelerator is the original PC that came with the 8088 CPU. It had the option and a socket for the 8087 coprocessor that would do floating-point operations in hardware rather than software. Today, the most common hardware accelerator is the graphics processor, which can be either a separate hardware component or integrated on the main processor. The distinction of being called an accelerator is that it is a special-purpose rather than a general-purpose device, but that difference is not always clear-cut. A GPU is an additional hardware component that can perform operations alongside a CPU. GPUs come in two flavors:

- *Integrated GPUs*—A graphics processor engine that is contained on the CPU
- *Dedicated GPUs*—A GPU contained on a separate peripheral card

Integrated GPUs are built directly into the CPU chip. Integrated GPUs share RAM resources with the CPU. Dedicated GPUs are attached to the motherboard via a Peripheral Component Interconnect (PCI) slot. The PCI slot is a physical component that allows data to be transmitted between the CPU and GPU. It is commonly referred to as the PCI bus.

9.1.1 Integrated GPUs: An underused option on commodity-based systems

Intel® has long included an integrated GPU with their CPUs for the budget market. They fully expected that users wanting real performance would buy a discrete GPU. The Intel integrated GPUs have historically been relatively weak in comparison to AMD's (Advanced Micro Devices, Inc.) integrated version. This has recently changed with Intel claiming that the integrated graphics on their Ice Lake processor are on a par with AMD integrated GPUs.

The AMD integrated GPUs are called Accelerated Processing Units (APUs). These are a tightly coupled combination of the CPU and a GPU. The source of the GPU design originally came from the AMD purchase of the ATI graphics card company in 2006. In the AMD APU, the CPU and GPU share the same processor memory. These GPUs are smaller than a discrete GPU, but still (proportionally) give GPU graphics (and compute) performance. The real target for AMD for APUs is to provide a more cost-effective, but performant system for the mass market. The shared memory is also attractive because it eliminates the data transfer over the PCI bus, which is often a serious performance bottleneck.

The ubiquitous nature of the integrated GPU is important. For us, it means that now many commodity desktops and laptops have the ability to accelerate computations. The goal on these systems is a relatively modest performance boost and, perhaps, to reduce the energy cost or to improve battery life. But for extreme performance, the discrete GPUs are still the undisputed performance champions.

9.1.2   *Dedicated GPUs: The workhorse option*

In this chapter, we will focus primarily on GPU accelerated platforms with dedicated GPUs, also called *discrete GPUs*. Dedicated GPUs generally offer more compute power than integrated GPUs. Additionally, these GPUs can be isolated to execute general-purpose computing tasks. Figure 9.1 conceptually illustrated a CPU-GPU system with a dedicated GPU. A CPU has access to its own memory space (CPU RAM) and is connected to a GPU via a PCI bus. It is able to send data and instructions over the PCI bus for the GPU to work with. The GPU has its own memory space, separate from the CPU memory space.

In order for work to be executed on the GPU, at some point, data must be transferred from the CPU to the GPU. When the work is complete, and the results are going to be written to file, the GPU must send data back to the CPU. The instructions the GPU must execute are also sent from CPU to GPU. Each one of these transactions is mediated by the PCI bus. Although we won't discuss *how* to make these actions happen in this chapter, we'll discuss the hardware performance limitations of the PCI bus. Due to these limitations, a poorly designed GPU application can potentially have worse performance than that with CPU-only code. We'll also discuss the internal architecture of the GPU and the performance of the GPU with regards to memory and floating-point operations.

9.2   *The GPU and the thread engine*

For those of us who have done thread programming over the years on a CPU, the graphics processor is like the ideal thread engine. The components of this thread engine are

- A seemingly infinite number of threads
- Zero time cost for switching or starting threads
- Latency hiding of memory accesses through automatic switching between work groups

Let's look at the hardware architecture of a GPU to get an idea of how it performs this magic. To show a conceptual model of a GPU, we abstract the common elements from different GPU vendors and even between design variations from the same vendor. We must remind you that there are hardware variations that are not captured by these abstract models. Adding to this plethora of terminology currently in use, it is not surprising that it is difficult for a newcomer to the field to understand GPU hardware and programming languages. Still, this terminology is relatively sane compared to the graphics world with vertex shaders, texture mapping units, and fragment generators. Table 9.1 summarizes the rough equivalence of terminology, but beware that because the hardware architectures are not exactly the same, the correspondence in terminology varies depending on the context and user.

Table 9.1   Hardware terminology: A rough translation

Host	OpenCL	AMD GPU	NVIDIA/CUDA	Intel Gen11
CPU	Compute device	GPU	GPU	GPU
Multiprocessor	Compute unit (CU)	Compute unit (CU)	Streaming multi-processor (SM)	Subslice
Processing core (Core for short)	Processing element (PE)	Processing element (PE)	Compute cores or CUDA cores	Execution units (EU)
Thread	Work Item	Work Item	Thread	
Vector or SIMD	Vector	Vector	Emulated with SIMT warp	SIMD

The last row in table 9.1 shows the hardware layer that implements a single instruction on multiple data, commonly referred to as SIMD. Strictly speaking, the NVIDIA hardware does not have vector hardware, or SIMD, but emulates this through a collection of threads in what it calls a warp in a single instruction, multi-thread (SIMT) model. You may want to refer back to our initial discussion of parallel categories in section 1.4 to refresh your memory on these different approaches. Other GPUs can also perform SIMT operations on what OpenCL and AMD call subgroups, which are equivalent to the NVIDIA warps. We'll discuss this more in chapter 10, which explicitly looks at GPU programming models. This chapter, however, will focus on the GPU hardware, its architecture, and concepts.

Often, GPUs also have hardware blocks of replication, some of which are listed in table 9.2, to simplify the scaling of their hardware designs to more units. These units of replication are a manufacturing convenience, but often show up in the specification lists and discussions.

Table 9.2   GPU hardware replication units by vendor

AMD	NVIDIA/CUDA	Intel Gen11
Shader Engine (SE)	Graphics processing cluster	Slice

Figure 9.2 depicts a simplified block diagram of a single node system with a single multiprocessor CPU and two GPUs. A single node can have a wide variety of configurations, composed of one or more multiprocessor CPUs with an integrated GPU, and from one to six discrete GPUs. In OpenCL nomenclature, each GPU is a compute device. But compute devices can also be CPUs in OpenCL.

> **DEFINITION**   A *compute device* in OpenCL is any computational hardware that can perform computation and supports OpenCL. This can include GPUs, CPUs, or even more exotic hardware such as embedded processors or field-programmable gate arrays (FPGAs).

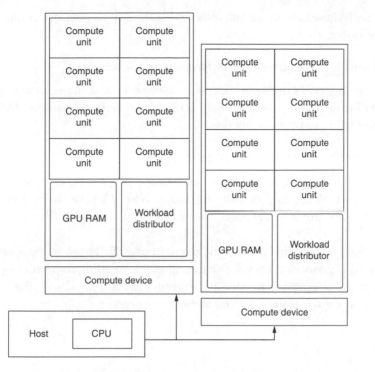

Figure 9.2 **A simplified block diagram of a GPU system showing two compute devices, each having separate GPU, GPU memory, and multiple compute units (CUs). The NVIDIA CUDA terminology refers to CUs as streaming multiprocessors (SMs).**

The simplified diagram in figure 9.2 is our model for describing the components of a GPU and is also useful when understanding how a GPU processes data. A GPU is composed of

- GPU RAM (also known as *global memory*)
- Workload distributor
- Compute units (CUs) (SMs in CUDA)

CUs have their own internal architecture, often referred to as the *microarchitecture*. Instructions and data received from the CPU are processed by the workload distributor. The distributor coordinates instruction execution and data movement onto and off of the CUs. The achievable performance of a GPU depends on

- Global memory bandwidth
- Compute unit bandwidth
- The number of CUs

In this section, we'll explore each of the components for our model of a GPU. With each component, we will also discuss models for theoretical peak bandwidth.

Additionally, we'll show how to use micro-benchmark tools to measure actual performance of components.

9.2.1 *The compute unit is the streaming multiprocessor (or subslice)*

A GPU compute device has multiple CUs. (CU, *compute unit*, is the term agreed to by the community for the OpenCL standard.) NVIDIA calls them *streaming multiprocessors* (SMs), and Intel refers to them as *subslices*.

9.2.2 *Processing elements are the individual processors*

Each CU contains multiple graphics processors called processing elements (PEs) in OpenCL, or CUDA cores (or Compute Cores) as NVIDIA calls them. Intel refers to them as execution units (EUs), and the graphics community calls them shader processors.

Figure 9.3 shows a simplified conceptual diagram of a PE. These processors are not equivalent to a CPU processor; they are simpler designs, needing to perform graphics operations. But the operations needed for graphics include nearly all the arithmetic operations that a programmer uses on a regular processor.

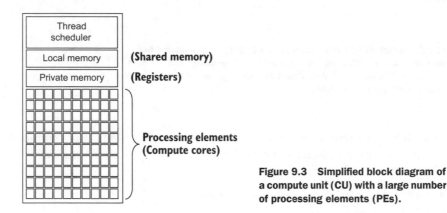

Figure 9.3   Simplified block diagram of a compute unit (CU) with a large number of processing elements (PEs).

9.2.3 *Multiple data operations by each processing element*

Within each PE, it might be possible to perform an operation on more than one data item. Depending on the details of the GPU microprocessor architecture and the GPU vendor, these are referred to as SIMT, SIMD, or vector operations. A similar type of functionality can be provided by ganging PEs together.

9.2.4 *Calculating the peak theoretical flops for some leading GPUs*

With an understanding of the GPU hardware, we can now calculate the peak theoretical flops for some recent GPUs. These include the NVIDIA V100, AMD Vega 20, AMD Arcturus, and the integrated Gen11 GPU on the Intel Ice Lake CPU. Table 9.3 lists the specifications for these GPUs. We'll use these specifications to calculate the theoretical performance of each device. Then, knowing the theoretical performance, you can make comparisons on how each performs. This can help you with purchasing decisions or with estimating how much faster or slower another GPU might be with your calculations. Hardware specifications for many GPU cards can be found at Tech-PowerUp: https://www.techpowerup.com/gpu-specs/.

For NVIDIA and AMD, the GPUs targeted to the HPC market have the hardware cores to perform one double-precision operation for every two single-precision operations. This relative flop capability can be expressed as a ratio of 1:2, where double precision is 1:2 of single precision on top-end GPUs. The importance of this ratio is that it tells you that you can roughly double your performance by reducing your precision requirements from double precision to single. For many GPUs, half precision has a ratio of 2:1 to single precision or double the flop capability. The Intel integrated GPU has 1:4 double precision relative to single precision, and some commodity GPUs have 1:8 ratios of double precision to single precision. GPUs with these lower ratios of double precision are targeted at the graphics market or for machine learning. To get these ratios, take the FP64 row and divide by the FP32 row.

Table 9.3 Specifications for recent discrete GPUs from NVIDIA, AMD, and an integrated Intel GPU

GPU	NVIDIA V100 (Volta)	NVIDIA A100 (Ampere)	AMD Vega 20 (MI50)	AMD Arcturus (MI100)	Intel Gen11 Integrated
Compute units (CUs)	80	108	60	120	8
FP32 cores/CU	64	64	64	64	64
FP64 cores/CU	32	32	32	32	
GPU clock nominal/boost	1290/1530 MHz	1410 MHz	1200/1746 MHz	1000/1502 MHz	400/1000 MHz
Subgroup or warp size	32	32	64	64	
Memory clock	876 MHz	1215 MHz	1000 MHz	1200 MHz	Shared memory
Memory type	HBM2 (32 GB)	HBM2(40 GB)	HBM2	HBM2 (32 GB)	LPDDR4X-3733
Memory data width	4096 bits	5120 bits	4096 bits	4096 bits	384 bits
Memory bus type	NVLink or PCIe 3.0x16	NVLink or PCIe Gen 4	Infinity Fabric or PCIe 4.0x16	Infinity Fabric or PCIe 4.0x16	Shared memory
Design Power	300 watts	400 watts	300 watts	300 watts	28 watts

The peak theoretical flops can be calculated by taking the clock rate times the number of processors times the number of floating-point operations per cycle. The flops per cycle accounts for the fused-multiply add (FMA), which does two operations in one cycle.

$$\text{Peak Theoretical Flops (GFlops/s)}$$
$$= \text{Clock rate MHZ} \times \text{Compute Units} \times \text{Processing units}$$
$$\times \text{Flops/cycle}$$

Example: Peak theoretical flop for some leading GPUs

Theoretical Peak Flops for NVIDIA V100:

- $2 \times 1530 \times 80 \times 64\ /10^6 = 15.6$ TFlops (single precision)
- $2 \times 1530 \times 80 \times 32\ /10^6 = 7.8$ TFlops (double precision)

Theoretical Peak Flops for NVIDIA Ampere:

- $2 \times 1410 \times 108 \times 64\ /10^6 = 19.5$ TFlops (single precision)
- $2 \times 1410 \times 108\ xx\ 32\ /10^6 = 9.7$ TFlops (double precision)

Theoretical Peak Flops for AMD Vega 20 (MI50):

- $2 \times 1746 \times 60 \times 64\ /10^6 = 13.4$ TFlops (single precision)
- $2 \times 1746 \times 60 \times 32\ /10^6 = 6.7$ TFlops (double precision)

Theoretical Peak Flops for AMD Arcturus (MI100):

- $2 \times 1502 \times 120 \times 64\ /10^6 = 23.1$ TFlops (single precision)
- $2 \times 1502 \times 120 \times 32\ /10^6 = 11.5$ TFlops (double precision)

Theoretical Peak Flops for Intel Integrated Gen 11 on Ice Lake:

- $2 \times 1000 \times 64 \times 8\ /10^6 = 1.0$ TFlops (single precision)

Both the NVIDIA V100 and the AMD Vega 20 give impressive floating-point peak performance. The Ampere shows some additional improvement in floating-point performance, but it is the memory performance that promises greater increases. The MI100 from AMD shows a bigger jump in floating-point performance. The Intel integrated GPU is also quite impressive given that it is limited by the available silicon space and lower nominal design power of a CPU. With Intel developing plans for discrete graphics cards for several market segments, expect to see even more GPU options in the future.

9.3   *Characteristics of GPU memory spaces*

A typical GPU has different types of memory. Using the right memory space can make a big impact on performance. Figure 9.4 shows these memories as a conceptual diagram. It helps to see the physical locations of each level of memory to understand how it should behave. Although a vendor can put the GPU memory wherever they want, it must behave as shown in this diagram.

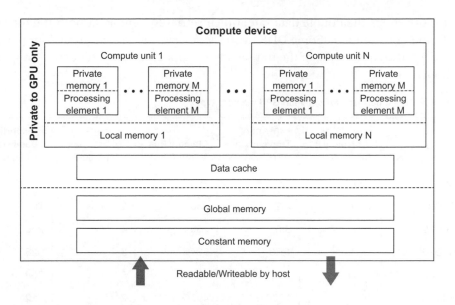

Figure 9.4 Rectangles show each component of the GPU and the memory that is at each hardware level. The host writes and reads the global and constant memory. Each of the CUs can read and write from the global memory and read from the constant memory.

The list of the GPU memory types and their properties are as follows.

- *Private memory (register memory)*—Immediately accessible by a single PE and only by that PE.
- *Local memory*—Accessible to a single CU and all of the PEs on that CU. Local memory can be split between a scratchpad that can be used as a programmable cache and, by some vendors, a traditional cache on GPUs. Local memory is around 64-96 KB in size.
- *Constant memory*—Read-only memory accessible and shared across all of the CUs.
- *Global memory*—Memory that's located on the GPU and accessible by all of the CUs.

One of the factors that makes GPUs fast is that they use specialized global memory (RAM), which provides higher bandwidth, whereas current CPUs use DDR4 memory and are just now moving to DDR5. GPUs use a special version called GDDR5 that gives higher performance. The latest GPUs are now moving to High-Bandwidth Memory (HBM2) that provides even higher bandwidth. Besides increasing bandwidth, HBM also reduces power consumption.

9.3.1 Calculating theoretical peak memory bandwidth

You can calculate the theoretical peak memory bandwidth for a GPU from the memory clock rate on the GPU and the width of the memory transactions in bits. Table 9.4 shows some of the higher values for each memory type. We also need to multiply by a factor of two for the double data rate, which retrieves memory at both the top of the cycle and at the bottom. Some DDR memory can even do more transactions per cycle. Table 9.4 also shows some of the transaction multipliers for different kinds of graphics memory.

Table 9.4   Specifications for common GPU memory types

Graphics Memory Type	Memory Clock (MHz)	Memory Transactions (GT/s)	Memory Bus Width (bits)	Transaction Multiplier	Theoretical Bandwidth (GB/s)
GDDR3	1000	2.0	256	2	64
GDDR4	1126	2.2	256	2	70
GDDR5	2000	8.0	256	4	256
GDDR5X	1375	11.0	384	8	528
GDDR6	2000	16.0	384	8	768
HBM1	500	1000.0	4096	2	512
HBM2	1000	2000.0	4096	2	1000

Calculating the theoretical memory bandwidth takes the memory clock rate times the number of transactions per cycle and then multiplies by the number of bits retrieved on each transaction:

$$\text{Theoretical Bandwidth} = \text{Memory Clock Rate (GHz)} \times \text{Memory bus (bits)} \times (1 \text{ byte}/8 \text{ bits}) \times \text{transaction multiplier}$$

Some specification sheets give the memory transaction rate in Gbps rather than the memory clock frequency. This rate is the transactions per cycle times the clock rate. Given this specification, the bandwidth equation becomes

$$\text{Theoretical Bandwidth} = \text{Memory Transaction Rate (Gbps)} \times \text{Memory bus (bits)} \times (1 \text{ byte}/8 \text{ bits})$$

Example: Theoretical bandwidth calculations
- For the NVIDIA V100 that operates at 876 MHz and uses HBM2 memory:

  Theoretical Bandwidth = 0.876 × 4096 × 1/8 × 2 = 897 GB/s

- For the AMD Radeon Vega20 (MI50) GPU that operates at 1000 MHz:

  Theoretical Bandwidth = 1.000 × 4096 × 1/8 × 2 = 1024 GB/s

9.3.2 *Measuring the GPU stream benchmark*

Because most of our applications scale with memory bandwidth, the STREAM Benchmark that measures memory bandwidth is one of the most important micro-benchmarks. We first used the STREAM Benchmark to measure the bandwidth on CPUs in section 3.2.4. The benchmark process is similar for the GPUs, but we need to rewrite the stream kernels in GPU languages. Fortunately, this has been done by Tom Deakin at the University of Bristol for a variety of GPU languages and hardware in his Babel STREAM code.

The Babel STREAM Benchmark code measures the bandwidth of a variety of hardware with different programming languages. We use it here to measure the bandwidth of an NVIDIA GPU using CUDA. Also available are versions in OpenCL, HIP, OpenACC, Kokkos, Raja, SYCL, and OpenMP with GPU targets. These are all different languages that can be used for GPU hardware like NVIDIA, AMD, and Intel GPUs.

Exercise: Measuring bandwidth using the Babel STREAM Benchmark

The steps to using the stream benchmark for CUDA on an NVIDIA GPU are

1 Clone the Babel STREAM Benchmark with

```
git clone git@github.com:UoB-HPC/BabelStream.git
```

2 Then type

```
make -f CUDA.make
./cuda-stream
```

The results for an NVIDIA V100 GPU are

Function	MBytes/sec	Min (sec)	Max	Average
Copy	800995.012	0.00067	0.00067	0.00067
Mul	796501.837	0.00067	0.00068	0.00068
Add	838993.641	0.00096	0.00097	0.00096
Triad	840731.427	0.00096	0.00097	0.00096
Dot	866071.690	0.00062	0.00063	0.00063

The process is similar for the AMD GPU:

1 Edit the OpenCL.make file and add the paths to your OpenCL header files and libraries.
2 Then type

```
make -f OpenCL.make
./ocl-stream
```

For the AMD Vega 20, the GPU bandwidth is slightly lower than the NVIDIA GPU.

```
Using OpenCL device gfx906+sram-ecc
```

Function	MBytes/sec	Min (sec)	Max	Average
Copy	764889.965	0.00070	0.00077	0.00072

(continued)

```
Mul         764182.281   0.00070      0.00076      0.00072
Add         764059.386   0.00105      0.00134      0.00109
Triad       763349.620   0.00105      0.00110      0.00108
Dot         670205.644   0.00080      0.00088      0.00083
```

9.3.3   *Roofline performance model for GPUs*

We introduced the roofline performance model for CPUs in section 3.2.4. This model accounts for both memory bandwidth and flop performance limits of the system. It is similarly useful for GPUs to understand their performance limits.

Exercise: Measuring bandwidth using the Empirical Roofline Toolkit

For this exercise, you will need access to an NVIDIA and/or an AMD GPU. A similar process can be used for other GPUs.

1   Get the roofline toolkit with

```
git clone https://bitbucket.org/berkeleylab/cs-roofline-toolkit.git
```

2   Then type

```
cd cs-roofline-toolkit/Empirical_Roofline_Tool-1.1.0
cp Config/config.voltar.uoregon.edu Config/config.V100_gpu
```

3   Edit these settings in Config/config.V100_gpu

```
ERT_RESULTS Results.V100_gpu
ERT_PRECISION FP64
ERT_NUM_EXPERIMENTS 5
```

4   Run

```
tests ./ert Config/config.V100_gpu
```

5   View the Results.config.V100_gpu/Run.001/roofline.ps file

```
cp Config/config.odinson-ocl-fp64.01 Config/config.Vega20_gpu
```

6   Edit these settings in Config/config.Vega20_gpu

```
ERT_RESULTS Results.Vega20_gpu
ERT_CFLAGS   -O3 -x c++ -std=c++11 -Wno-deprecated-declarations
             -I<path to OpenCL headers>
ERT_LDLIBS   -L<path to OpenCL libraries> -lOpenCL
```

7   Run

```
tests ./ert Config/config.Vega20_gpu
```

8   View the output in Results.config.Vega20_gpu/Run.001/roofline.ps

Figure 9.5 shows the results of the roofline benchmarks for both the NVIDIA V100 and the AMD Vega20 GPUs.

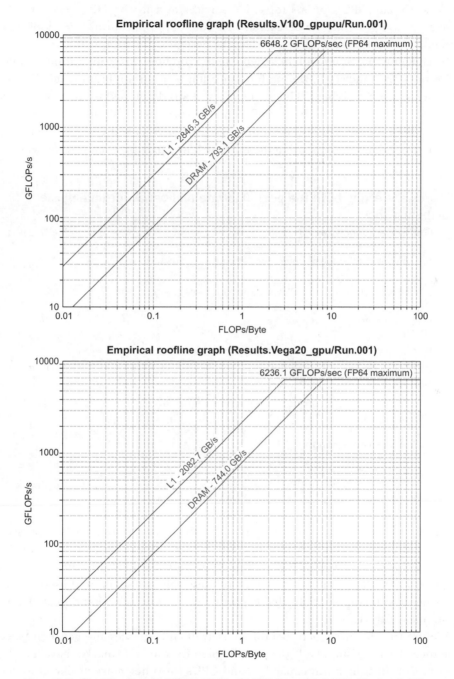

Figure 9.5   Roofline plots for NVIDIA V100 and AMD Vega 20 showing the bandwidth and flop limits for the two GPUs.

9.3.4 *Using the mixbench performance tool to choose the best GPU for a workload*

There are many GPU options for cloud services and in the HPC server market. Is there a way to figure out the best value GPU for your application? We'll look at a performance model that can help you select the best GPU for your workload.

By changing the independent variable in the roofline plot from arithmetic intensity to the memory bandwidth, the performance limits of an application relative to each GPU device are highlighted. The mixbench tool was developed to draw out the differences between the performance of different GPU devices. This information is really no different than that shown in the roofline model, but visually it has a different impact. Let's go through an exercise using the mixbench tool to show what you can learn.

Exercise: Getting both the peak flop rate and bandwidth using the mixbench tool

1 Get the mixbench code

```
git clone https://github.com/ekondis/mixbench.git
```

2 Check for CUDA or OpenCL and install if necessary.

```
cd mixbench; edit Makefile
```

3 Fix the path to the CUDA and/or OpenCL installations.
4 Set the executables to build. You can override the path to the CUDA installation with

```
make CUDA_INSTALL_PATH=<path>
```

5 Run either of the following:

```
./mixbench-cuda-ro
./mixbench-ocl-ro
```

The results of the benchmark are plotted as the compute rate in GFlops/sec with respect to the memory bandwidth in GB/sec (figure 9.6). Basically, the benchmark results in a horizontal line at the peak flop rate and a vertical dropoff at the memory bandwidth limit. The maximum of each of these values is taken and used to plot the single point at the upper right that captures both the peak flop and peak bandwidth capabilities of the GPU device.

We can run the mixbench tool for a variety of GPU devices and get their peak performance characteristics. GPU devices designed for the HPC market have a high double-precision floating-point capability, and GPUs for other markets like graphics and machine learning focus on single-precision hardware.

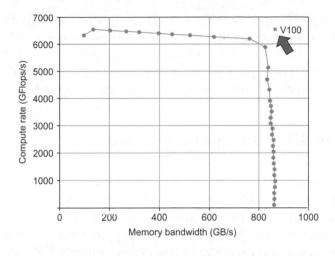
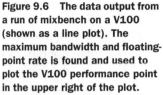

Figure 9.6 The data output from a run of mixbench on a V100 (shown as a line plot). The maximum bandwidth and floating-point rate is found and used to plot the V100 performance point in the upper right of the plot.

We can plot each GPU device in figure 9.7 along with a line representing the arithmetic or operational intensity of an application. Most typical applications are around a 1 flop/load intensity. At the other extreme, matrix multiplication has an arithmetic intensity of 65 flops/load. We show a sloped line for both of these types of applications in figure 9.7. If the GPU point is above the application line, we draw a vertical line down to the application line to find what the achievable application performance will be. For a device to the right and lower than the application line, we use a horizontal line to find the performance limit.

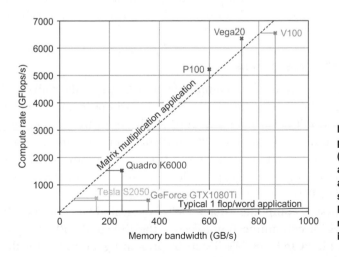
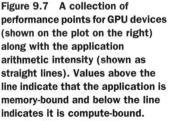

Figure 9.7 A collection of performance points for GPU devices (shown on the plot on the right) along with the application arithmetic intensity (shown as straight lines). Values above the line indicate that the application is memory-bound and below the line indicates it is compute-bound.

What the plot makes clear is the match in the GPU device characteristics relative to the application requirements. For the typical application that has a 1 flop/load arithmetic intensity, GPUs like the GeForce GTX 1080Ti, built for the graphics market, are a good match. The V100 GPU is more suited for the Linpack benchmark used for the TOP500 ranking of large computing systems because it's basically composed of matrix multiplications. GPUs like the V100 are specialized hardware specifically built for the HPC market and command a high price premium. For some applications with lower arithmetic intensity, the commodity GPUs designed for the graphics market can be a better value.

9.4   The PCI bus: CPU to GPU data transfer overhead

The PCI bus shown in figure 9.1 is needed to transfer data from the CPU to the GPU and back. The cost of the data transfer can be a significant limitation on the performance of operations moved to the GPU. It is often critical to limit the amount of data that gets transferred back and forth to get any speedup from the GPU.

The current version of the PCI bus is called PCI Express (PCIe). It has been revised several times in generations from 1.0 to 6.0 as of this writing. You should know which generation of the PCIe bus you have in your system to understand its performance limitation. In this section, we show two methods for estimating the bandwidth of a PCI bus:

- A back-of-the-envelope theoretical peak performance model
- A micro-benchmark application

The theoretical peak performance model is useful for quickly estimating what you might expect on a new system. The model has the benefit that you don't need to run any applications on the system. This is useful when you are just starting a project and would like to quickly estimate by hand the possible performance bottlenecks. In addition, the benchmark example shows that the peak bandwidth you can reach depends on how you make use of the hardware.

9.4.1   Theoretical bandwidth of the PCI bus

On dedicated GPU platforms, all data communication between the GPU and CPU occurs over the PCI bus. Because of this, it is a critical hardware component that can heavily influence the overall performance of your application. In this section, we go over the key features and descriptors of a PCI bus that you need to be aware of in order to calculate the theoretical PCI bus bandwidth. Knowing how to calculate this number on the fly is useful for estimating possible performance limitations when porting your application to GPUs.

The PCI bus is a physical component that attaches dedicated GPUs to the CPU and other devices. It allows for communication between the CPU and GPU. Communication occurs over multiple PCIe lanes. We'll start by presenting a formula for the theoretical bandwidth, and then explain each term.

$$\text{Theoretical Bandwidth (GB/s)} = \text{Lanes} \times \text{TransferRate (GT/s)} \times$$
$$\text{OverheadFactor(Gb/GT)} \times \text{byte/8 bits}$$

The theoretical bandwidth is measured in units of gigabytes per second (GB/s). It is calculated by multiplying the number of lanes and the maximum transfer rate for each lane and then converting from bits to bytes. The conversion is left in the formula because the transfer rates are usually reported in GigaTransfers per second (GT/s). The overhead factor is due to an encoding scheme used to ensure data integrity, reducing the effective transfer rate. For generation 1.0 devices, the encoding scheme had a cost of 20%, so the overhead factor would be 100%–20% or 80%. From generation 3.0 onward, the encoding scheme overhead drops to just 1.54%, so the achieved bandwidth becomes essentially the same as the transfer rate. Let's now dive into each of the terms in the bandwidth equation.

PCIe Lanes

The number of lanes of a PCI bus can be found by looking through manufacturer specifications, or you can use a number of tools available on Linux platforms. Keep in mind that some of these tools might require root privileges. If you do not have these privileges, it is best to consult your system administrator to find out this information. Nonetheless, we will present two options for determining the number of PCIe lanes.

A common utility available on Linux systems is lspci. This utility lists all the components attached to the motherboard. We can use the grep regular expression tool to filter out only the PCI bridge. The following command shows you the vendor information and the device name with the number of PCIe lanes. For this example, (x16) in the output indicates that there are 16 lanes.

```
$ lspci -vmm | grep "PCI bridge" -A2
Class:      PCI bridge
Vendor:     Intel Corporation
Device:     Sky Lake PCIe Controller (x16)
```

Alternatively, the dmidecode command provides similar information:

```
$ dmidecode | grep "PCI"
PCI is supported
Type: x16 PCI Express
```

Determining the maximum transfer rate

The maximum transfer rates for each lane in a PCIe bus can directly be determined by its design generation. Generation is a specification for the required performance of the hardware, much like 4G is an industry standard for cell-phones. The PCI Special Interest Group (PCI SIG) represents industry partners and establishes a PCIe specification that is commonly referred to as *generation* or *gen* for short. Table 9.5 shows the maximum transfer rate per PCI lanes and direction.

Table 9.5   PCI Express (PCIe) specifications by generation

PCIe Generation	Maximum Transfer Rate (bi-directional)	Encoding Overhead	Overhead factor (100%-encoding overhead)	Theoretical Bandwidth 16 lanes - GB/s
Gen1	2.5 GT/s	20%	80%	4
Gen2	5.0 GT/s	20%	80%	8
Gen3	8.0 GT/s	1.54%	98.46%	15.75
Gen4	16.0 GT/s	1.54%	98.46%	31.5
Gen5 (2019)	32.0 GT/s	1.54%	98.46%	63
Gen6 (2021)	64.0 GT/s	1.54%	98.46%	126

If you don't know the generation of your PCIe bus, you can use lspci to get this information. In all of the information output by lspci, we are looking for the link capacity for the PCI bus. In this output, link capacity is abbreviated LnkCap:

```
$ sudo lspci -vvv | grep -E 'PCI|LnkCap'
Output:

00:01.0 PCI bridge:
        Intel Corporation Sky Lake PCIe Controller (x16) (rev 07)
LnkCap: Port #2, Speed 8GT/s, Width x16, ASPM L0s L1, Exit Latency L0s
```

Now that we know the maximum transfer rate from this output, we can use this in the bandwidth formula. It's also helpful to know that this speed can also be aligned with the generation. In this case, the output indicates that we are working with a Gen3 PCIE system.

> **NOTE**   On some systems, the output from lspci and other system utilities may not give much information. The output is system specific and just reports the identification from each device. If you are unable to determine the characteristics from these utilities, your fallback might be to use the PCI benchmark code given in section 9.4.2 to determine the capabilities of your system.

OVERHEAD RATES

Transmitting data across the PCI bus requires additional overhead. Generation 1 and 2 standards stipulate that 10 bytes are transmitted for every 8 bytes of useful data. Starting with generation 3, the transfer transmits 130 bytes for every 128 bytes of data. The overhead factor is the ratio of the number of usable bytes over the total bytes transmitted (table 9.5).

REFERENCE DATA FOR PCIE THEORETICAL PEAK BANDWIDTH

Now that we have all of the necessary information, let's estimate the theoretical bandwidth through an example, using output shown in the previous sections.

> ## Example: Estimating the theoretical bandwidth
>
> We have identified that we have a Gen3 PCIe system with 16 lanes. Gen3 systems have a maximum transfer rate of 8.0 GT/s and an overhead factor of 0.985. With 16 lanes, the theoretical bandwidth is 15.75 GB/s as shown here.
>
> $$\text{Theoretical Bandwidth (GB/s)}$$
> $$= 16 \text{ lanes} \times 8.0 \text{ GT/s} \times 0.985 \text{ (Gb/GT)} \times \text{byte/8 bits}$$
> $$= 15.75 \text{ GB/s}$$

9.4.2 A benchmark application for PCI bandwidth

The equation for the theoretical PCI bandwidth gives the expected best peak bandwidth. In other words, this is the highest possible bandwidth that an application can achieve for a given platform. In practice, the achieved bandwidth can depend on a number of factors, including the OS, system drivers, other hardware components on the compute node, GPU programming API, and the size of the data block sent across the PCI bus. On most systems you have access to, it is likely that all but the last two choices are out of your control to modify. When developing your application, you are in control of the programming API and the size of the data blocks that are transmitted across the PCI bus.

With this in mind, we are left with the question how does the data block size influence the achieved bandwidth? This type of question is typically answered with a *micro-benchmark*. A micro-benchmark is a small program that is meant to exercise a single process or piece of hardware that a larger application will use. Micro-benchmarks help provide some indication of system performance.

In our situation, we want to devise a micro-benchmark that copies data from the CPU to the GPU and vice-versa. Because the data copy is expected to happen in microseconds to tens of microseconds, we will measure the time it takes to complete the data copy 1,000 times. This time will then be divided by 1,000 to obtain the average time to copy data between the CPU and GPU.

We will do a step-by-step walk through using a benchmark application to measure PCI bandwidth. Listing 9.1 shows the code that copies data from the host to the GPU. Writing in the CUDA GPU programming language will be covered in chapter 10, but the basic operation is clear from the function names. In listing 9.1, we take in the size of a flat 1-D array as input that we want to copy from CPU (host) to the GPU (device).

NOTE This code is available in the PCI_Bandwidth_Benchmark subdirectory at https://github.com/EssentialsofParallelComputing/Chapter9.

Listing 9.1   Copying data from CPU host to GPU device

```
PCI_Bandwidth_Benchmark.c
35 void Host_to_Device_Pinned( int N, double *copy_time )
36 {
37    float *x_host, *x_device;
38    struct timespec tstart;
39
40    cudaError_t status = cudaMallocHost((void**)&x_host, N*sizeof(float));
41    if (status != cudaSuccess)
42         printf("Error allocating pinned host memory\n");
43    cudaMalloc((void **)&x_device, N*sizeof(float));
44
45    cpu_timer_start(&tstart);
46    for(int i = 1; i <= 1000; i++ ){
47       cudaMemcpy(x_device, x_host, N*sizeof(float),
            cudaMemcpyHostToDevice);
48    }
49    cudaDeviceSynchronize();
50
51    *copy_time = cpu_timer_stop(tstart)/1000.0;
52
53    cudaFreeHost( x_host );
54    cudaFree( x_device );
55 }
```

Line 40 annotation: **Allocates pinned host memory for an array on the CPU**

Line 43 annotation: **Allocates memory for an array on the GPU**

Line 47 annotation: **Copies memory to the GPU**

Line 49 annotation: **Synchronizes the GPU so that the work completes**

Lines 53–54 annotation: **Frees the arrays**

In listing 9.1, the first step is to allocate memory for both the host and device copy. The routine on line 40 in this listing uses cudaMallocHost to allocate pinned memory on the host for faster data transfer. For the routine that uses regular pageable memory, the standard malloc and free calls are used. The cudaMemcpy routine transfers the data from the CPU host to the GPU. The cudaDeviceSynchronize call waits until the copy is complete. Before the loop, where we repeat the host to device copy, we capture the start time. We then execute the host-to-device copy 1,000 times and capture the current time again. The average time for copying from host to device is then calculated by dividing by 1,000. To keep things neat, we free the space held by the host and device arrays.

With the knowledge of the time it takes to transfer an array of size *N* from host to device, we can now call this routine multiple times, changing *N* each time. However, we're more interested in estimating the achieved bandwidth.

Recall that the bandwidth is the number of transmitted bytes per unit time. At the moment, we know the number of array elements and the time it takes to copy the array between the CPU and GPU. The number of bytes transmitted depends on the type of data stored in the array. For example, in an array of size *N* containing floats (4 bytes), the amount of data copied between CPU and GPU is 4*N*. If 4*N* bytes are transferred in time *T*, the achieved bandwidth is

$$B = 4N/T$$

This allows us to build a dataset showing the achieved bandwidth as a function of *N*. The subroutine in the following listing requires that the maximum array size is specified and then returns the bandwidth measured for each experiment.

> **Listing 9.2   Calling a CPU to GPU memory transfer for different array sizes**

```
PCI_Bandwidth_Benchmark.c
81 void H2D_Pinned_Experiments(double **bandwidth, int n_experiments,
          int max_array_size){
82    long long array_size;
83    double copy_time;
84
85    for(int j=0; j<n_experiments; j++){
86       array_size = 1;
87       for(int i=0; i<max_array_size; i++ ){
88
89          Host_to_Device_Pinned( array_size, &copy_time );
90
91          double byte_size=4.0*array_size;
92          bandwidth[j][i] = byte_size/(copy_time*1024.0*1024.0*1024.0);
93
94          array_size = array_size*2;
95       }
96    }
97 }
```

Repeats the experiments a few times — line 85

Calls CPU to GPU memory test and timing — line 89

Doubles the array size with each iteration — lines 87–94

Calculates bandwidth — lines 91–92

Here, we loop over array sizes, and for each array size, we obtain the average host-to-device copy time. The bandwidth is then calculated by the number of bytes copied divided by the time it takes to copy. The array contains floats, which have four bytes for each array element. Now, let's walk through an example that shows how you can use the micro-benchmark application to characterize the performance of your PCI Bus.

PERFORMANCE OF A GEN3 X16 ON A LAPTOP

We ran the PCI bandwidth benchmark application on a GPU accelerated laptop. On this system, the lspci command shows that it is equipped with a Gen3 x16 PCI bus:

```
$ sudo lspci -vvv | grep -E 'PCI|LnkCap'
00:01.0 PCI bridge: Intel Corporation Sky Lake PCIe Controller (x16)
                (rev 07)
           LnkCap: Port #2, Speed 8GT/s, Width x16, ASPM L0s L1,
                Exit Latency L0s
```

For this system, the theoretical peak bandwidth of the PCI Bus is 15.8 GB/s. Figure 9.8 shows a plot of the achieved bandwidth in our micro-benchmark application (curved lines) compared to the theoretical peak bandwidth (horizontal dashed lines). The shaded region around the achieved bandwidth indicates the +/− 1 standard deviation in bandwidth.

First, notice that when small chunks of data are sent across the PCI bus, the achieved bandwidth is low. Beyond array sizes of 10^7 bytes, the achieved bandwidth

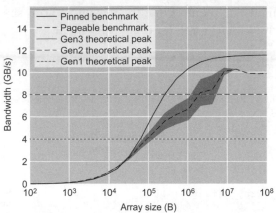

Figure 9.8   A theoretical peak bandwidth (horizontal lines) and an empirically measured bandwidth from the micro-benchmark application are shown for a Gen3 x16 PCIe system. The figure also shows results for both pinned and pageable memory.

approaches a maximum around 11.6 GB/s. Note also that the bandwidth with pinned memory is much higher than pageable memory, and pageable memory has a much wider variation of performance results for each memory size. It is helpful to know what pinned and pageable memory are to understand the reason for this difference.

- *Pinned memory*—Memory that cannot be paged from RAM and, thus, can be directly sent to the GPU without first making a copy
- *Pageable memory*—Standard memory allocations that can be paged out to disk

Allocating pinned memory reduces the memory available to other processes because the OS kernel can no longer make the memory page out to disk so other processes can use it. Pinned memory is allocated from the standard DRAM memory for the processor. The allocation process takes a little bit longer than a regular allocation. When using pageable memory, it must be copied into a pinned memory location before it can be sent. The pinned memory prevents it from being paged out to disk while the memory is being transferred. The example in this section shows that larger data transfers between the CPU and GPU can result in higher achieved bandwidth. Further, on this system, the maximum achieved bandwidth only reaches about 72% of the theoretical peak performance.

9.5   *Multi-GPU platforms and MPI*

Now that we've introduced the basic components of a GPU-accelerated platform, we'll discuss more exotic configurations that you might encounter. These exotic configurations come from the introduction of multiple GPUs. Some platforms offer multiple GPUs per node, connected to one or more CPUs. Others offer connections to multiple compute nodes over network hardware.

On the types of multi-GPU platforms (figure 9.9), it is usually necessary to use an MPI+GPU approach to parallelism. For data parallelism, each MPI rank is assigned to one of the GPUs. Let's look at a couple of possibilities:

- Single MPI rank drives each GPU
- Multiple MPI ranks multiplex their work on a GPU

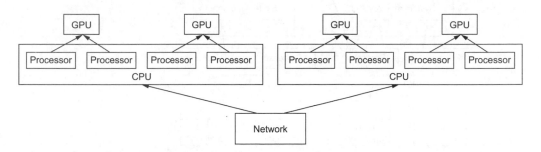

Figure 9.9 Here we illustrate a multi-GPU platform. A single compute node can have multiple GPUs and multiple processors. There can also be multiple nodes connected across a network.

Some of the early GPU software and hardware did not handle multiplexing efficiently, resulting in poor performance. With many of the performance problems fixed in the latest software, it is becoming increasingly attractive to multiplex MPI ranks onto the GPUs.

9.5.1   Optimizing the data movement between GPUs across the network

To use multiple GPUs, we have to send data from one GPU to another. Before we can discuss the optimization, we need to describe the standard data transfer process.

1 Copy the data from the GPU to the host processor
  a Move the data across the PCI bus to the processor
  b Store the data in CPU DRAM memory
2 Send the data in an MPI message to another processor
  a Stage the data from CPU memory to the processor
  b Move the data across the PCI bus to the network interface card (NIC)
  c Store the data from the processor to CPU memory
3 Copy the data from the second processor to the second GPU
  a Load the data from CPU memory to the processor
  b Send the data across the PCI bus to the GPU

As figure 9.10 shows, this is a lot of data movement and will be a major limitation to application performance.

In an NVIDIA GPUDirect®, CUDA adds the capability to send the data in a message. AMD has a similar capability called DirectGMA for GPU-to-GPU in OpenCL. The pointer to the data still has to be transferred, but the message itself gets sent over the PCI bus directly from one GPU to another GPU, thereby reducing the memory movement.

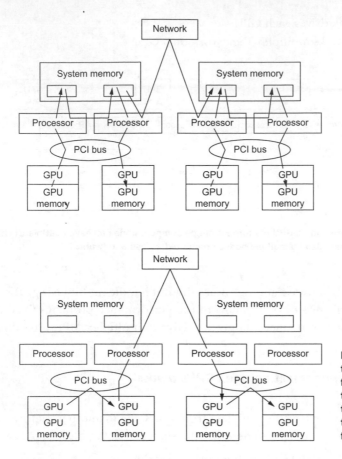

Figure 9.10   **On the top is the standard data movement for sending data from a GPU to other GPUs. On the bottom, the data movement bypasses the CPU when moving data from one GPU to another.**

9.5.2   *A higher performance alternative to the PCI bus*

There is little argument that the PCI bus is a major limitation for compute nodes with multi-GPUs. While this is mostly a concern for large applications, it also impacts heavy workloads such as in machine learning on smaller clusters. NVIDIA introduced NVLink® to replace GPU-to-GPU and GPU-to-CPU connections with their Volta line of P100 and V100 GPUs. With NVLink 2.0, the data transfer rates can reach 300 GB/sec. The new GPUs and CPUs from AMD incorporate Infinity Fabric to speed up data transfers. And Intel has been accelerating data transfers between CPUs and memory for some years.

9.6   *Potential benefits of GPU-accelerated platforms*

When is porting to GPUs worth it? At this point you've seen the theoretical peak performance for modern GPUs and how this compares to CPUs. Compare the roofline plot for the GPU in figure 9.5 to the CPU roofline plot in section 3.2.4 for both the floating-point calculation and the memory bandwidth limits. In practice, many applications do not reach these peak performance values. However, with the ceilings raised for GPUs, there is potential to outperform CPU architectures relative to a few metrics. These include the time to execute your application, energy consumption, cloud computing costs, and scalability.

9.6.1 *Reducing time-to-solution*

Suppose you have an existing code that runs on CPUs. You've spent a lot of time putting OpenMP or MPI into the code so that you can use all of the cores on the CPU. You feel like the code is well tuned, but a friend has told you that you might benefit more by porting your code to GPUs. You have more than 10,000 lines of code in your application, and you know that it will take considerable effort to get your code running on GPUs. At this point, you're interested in the prospect of running on GPUs because you like learning new things and you trust your friend's insights. Now, you have to make the case to your colleagues and your boss.

The important measure for your application is to reduce the time-to-solution for jobs that run days at a stretch. The best way to get across the impact of a reduction in time-to-solution is to look at an example. We'll use the Cloverleaf application as a proxy for this study.

Example: Considering an upgrade to your current workhorse system

Here are the steps to gather the performance of Cloverleaf on the base system. We use an Intel Ivybridge system (E5-2650 v2 @ 2.60GHz) with 16 physical cores. On average your application runs for about 500,000 cycles. You can get an estimate of the run time for a short sample run with these steps:

1 Clone Cloverleaf.git with

```
git clone --recursive git@github.com:UK-MAC/CloverLeaf.git CloverLeaf
```

2 Then enter these commands

```
cd CloverLeaf_MPI
make COMPILER=INTEL
sed -e '1,$s/end_step=2955/end_step=500/' InputDecks/clover_bm64.in\
        >clover.in
mpirun -n 16 --bind-to core ./clover_leaf
```

The run time for 500 cycles is 615.1 secs or 1.23 secs per cycle. This gives you a run time of 171 hours or 7 days and 3 hours.

Now let's get the run time for a couple of possible replacement platforms.

Example CPU replacement: Skylake Gold 6152 with 2.10GHz with 36 physical cores

The only difference for this run is that we increase the 16 processors to 36 for `mpirun` with this command:

```
mpirun -n 36 --bind-to core ./clover_leaf
```

The run time for the Skylake system is 273.3 secs or 0.55 secs per cycle. This would give a run time for the typical application problem of 76.4 hours or 3 days and 4 hours.

Not bad! Less than half the time as before. You are about ready to purchase this system but then think that maybe you should check out those GPUs that you have been hearing about.

Example GPU replacement: V100

CloverLeaf has a CUDA version that runs on the V100. You measure the performance with the following steps:

1   Clone Cloverleaf.git with

```
git clone --recursive git@github.com:UK-MAC/CloverLeaf.git CloverLeaf
```

2   Then type

```
cd CloverLeaf_CUDA
```

3   Add the CUDA architecture flags for Volta to the makefile to the current list of CODE_GEN architectures:

```
CODE_GEN_VOLTA=-arch=sm_70
```

4   Add the path to CUDA library CUDART, if necessary:

```
make COMPILER=GNU NV_ARCH=VOLTA
sed -e '1,$s/end_step=2955/end_step=500/' clover_bm64.in >clover.in
./clover_leaf
```

Whoa! The run is so fast you don't even have time to get a cup of coffee. But there it is: 59.3 secs! This is 0.12 secs per cycle or, for the full test problem size, a sweet 16.5 hours. Compared to the Skylake system, this is 4.6 times faster, and 10.4 times faster than the original Ivy Bridge system. Just imagine how much more work you could get done with an overnight turnaround instead of days!

Is this typical of the performance gains with GPUs? Performance gains for applications span a wide range, but these results are not unusual.

9.6.2 *Reducing energy use with GPUs*

Energy costs are becoming increasingly important for parallel applications. Where once the energy consumption of computers was not a concern, now the energy costs of running the computers, storage disks, and cooling system are fast approaching the same levels as the hardware purchase costs over the lifetime of the computing system.

In the race to Exascale computing, one of the biggest challenges is keeping the power requirements for the Exascale system to around 20 MW. For comparison, this is about enough power to supply 13,000 homes. There simply isn't enough installed power in data centers to go much beyond that. At the other end of the spectrum, smart phones, tablets, and laptops run on batteries with a limited amount of available energy (between charges). On these devices, it can be beneficial to focus on reducing energy costs for a computation to stretch out the battery life. Fortunately, aggressive efforts to reduce energy usage have kept the rate of an increase in power demands reasonable.

Accurately calculating the energy costs of an application is challenging without direct measurements of power usage. However, you can get a higher bound on the cost by multiplying the manufacturer's thermal design power (TDP) by the run time of the application and the number of processors used. TDP is the rate at which energy is expended under typical operational loads. The energy consumption for your application can be estimated using the formula

$$\text{Energy} = (N\,\text{Processors}) \times (R\,\text{Watts/Processor}) \times (T\,\text{hours})$$

where *Energy* is the energy consumption, *N* is the number of processors, *R* is the TDP, and *T* is the application's run time. Let's compare a GPU-based system to a roughly equivalent CPU system (table 9.6). We'll assume our application is memory bound, so we'll calculate the costs and energy consumption for a 10 TB/sec system.

Table 9.6 Designing a 10 TB/s bandwidth GPU and CPU system.

	NVIDIA V100	**Intel CPU Skylake Gold 6152**
Number	12 GPUs	45 processors (CPUs)
Bandwidth	12 × 850 GB/s = 10.2 TB/s	45 × 224 GB/s = 10.1 TB/s
Cost	12 × $11,000 = $132,000	45 × $3,800 = $171,000
Power	300 watt per GPU	140 watt per CPU
Energy for 1 day	86.4 kWhrs	151.2 kWhrs

To calculate the energy costs for one day, we take the specifications from table 9.6 and calculate the nominal energy costs.

Example: TDP for Intel's 22 core Xeon Gold 6152 Processor

Intel's 22 core Xeon Gold 6152 Processor has a TDP of 140 W. Suppose that your application uses 15 of these processors for 24 hours to run to completion. The estimated energy usage for your application is

Energy = (45 Processors) × (140 W/Processors) × (24 hrs) = 151.2 kWhrs

This is a significant amount of energy! Your energy consumption for this calculation is enough to power seven homes for the same 24 hours.

In general, GPUs have a higher TDP than CPUs (300 watts vs. 140 watts from table 9.6) so they consume energy at a higher rate. But GPUs can potentially reduce run time or require only a few to run your calculation. The same formula can be used as before, where N is now seen as the number of GPUs.

Example: TDP for a multi-GPU platform

Suppose that you've ported your application to a multi-GPU platform. You can now run your application on four NVIDIA Tesla V100 GPUs in 24 hrs. NVIDIA's Tesla V100 GPU has a maximum TDP of 300 W. The estimated energy usage for your application is

Energy = (12 GPUs) × (300 W/GPUs) × (24 hrs) = 86.4 kWhrs

In this example, the GPU accelerated application runs at a much lower energy cost compared to the CPU-only version. Note that in this case, even though the time to solution remains the same, the energy expense is cut by about 40%! We also see a 20% reduction in initial hardware costs, but we haven't accounted for the host CPU expense for the GPUs.

Now we can see there is great potential for a GPU system, but the nominal values that we used might be quite a ways from reality. We could further refine this estimate by getting measured performance and energy draws for our algorithm.

Achieving a reduction in energy cost through GPU accelerator devices requires that the application expose sufficient parallelism and that the device's resources are efficiently utilized. In the hypothetical example, we were able to reduce the energy usage in half when running on 12 GPUs for the same amount of time it takes to execute on 45 fully subscribed CPU processors. The formula for energy consumption also suggests other strategies for reducing energy costs. We'll discuss these strategies in a bit, but it's important to note that, in general, a GPU consumes more energy than a CPU per unit time. We'll start by examining the energy consumption between a single CPU processor and a single GPU.

Listing 9.3 shows how to plot the power and utilization for the V100 GPU.

Example: Monitoring GPU power consumption over application lifetime

Let's go back to the CloverLeaf problem that we ran earlier on the V100 GPU. We used the nvidia-smi (NVIDIA System Management Interface) tool to collect performance metrics for the run, including power and GPU utilization. To do this, we ran the following command before running our application:

```
nvidia-smi dmon -i 0 --select pumct -c 65 --options DT\
  --filename gpu_monitoring.log &
```

The following table shows the options for the nvidia-smi command.

dmon	Collects monitoring data.
-i 0	Queries GPU device 0.
--select pumct	Selects power [p], utilization [u], memory usage [m], clocks [c], PCI throughput [t]. You can also use -s as shorthand for --select.
-c 65	Collects 65 samples. Default time is 1 s.
-d <#>	Changes the sampling interval.
--options DT	Prepends monitoring data with date in YYYMMDD format and time in HH:MM::SS format, respectively.
--filename <name>	Writes output to the specified filename.
&	Puts the job in the background so you can run your application.

The shortened data output to the file looks like

```
Time       pwr gtemp mtemp   sm  mem enc dec     fb bar1 mclk pclk rxpci txpci
HH:MM:SS    W    C     C      %    %   %   %      MB   MB  MHz  MHz  MB/s  MB/s
21:36:47    64   43    41    24   28   0   0      0    0   877 1530    0     0
21:36:48   176   44    44    96  100   0   0  11181    0   877 1530    0     0
21:36:49   174   45    45   100  100   0   0  11181    0   877 1530    0     0
...
```

Listing 9.3   Plotting the power and utilization data from nvidia-smi

```
power_plot.py
 1 import matplotlib.pyplot as plt
 2 import numpy as np
 3 import re
 4 from scipy.integrate import simps
 5
 6 fig, ax1 = plt.subplots()
 7
```

```
 8 gpu_power = []
 9 gpu_time = []
10 sm_utilization = []
11
12 # Collect the data from the file, ignore empty lines
13 data = open('gpu_monitoring.log', 'r')
14
15 count = 0
16 energy = 0.0
17 nominal_energy = 0.0
18
19 for line in data:
20     if re.match('^ 2019',line):
21         line = line.rstrip("\n")
22         dummy, dummy, dummy, gpu_power_in, dummy, dummy,
    sm_utilization_in, dummy,
            dummy, dummy, dummy, dummy, dummy, dummy, dummy, dummy =
    line.split()
23         if (float(sm_utilization_in) > 80):
24             gpu_power.append(float(gpu_power_in))
25             sm_utilization.append(float(sm_utilization_in))
26             gpu_time.append(count)
27             count = count + 1
28             energy = energy + float(gpu_power_in)*1.0
29             nominal_energy = nominal_energy + float(300.0)*1.0
30
31 print(energy, "watts-secs", simps(gpu_power, gpu_time))
32 print(nominal_energy, "watts-secs", "  ratio
    ",energy/nominal_energy*100.0)
33
34 ax1.plot(gpu_time, gpu_power, "o", linestyle='-', color='red')
35 ax1.fill_between(gpu_time, gpu_power, color='orange')
36 ax1.set_xlabel('Time (secs)',fontsize=16)
37 ax1.set_ylabel('Power Consumption (watts)',fontsize=16, color='red')
38 #ax1.set_title('GPU Power Consumption from nvidia-smi')
39
40 ax2 = ax1.twinx()   # instantiate a second axes that shares the same x-axis
41
42 ax2.plot(gpu_time, sm_utilization, "o", linestyle='-', color='green')
43 ax2.set_ylabel('GPU Utilization (%)',fontsize=16, color='green')
44.
45 fig.tight_layout()
56 plt.savefig("power.pdf")
57 plt.savefig("power.svg")
58 plt.savefig("power.png", dpi=600)
59
60 plt.show()
```

Integrates power times time to get energy in watts/s

Gets the energy usage based on nominal power specification

Calculates the actual vs. nominal energy usage

Prints the calculated energy and uses the simps integration function from scipy

Figure 9.11 shows the resulting plot. At the same time, we integrate the area under the curve to get the energy usage. Note that even with the utilization at 100%, the power rate is only about 61% of the nominal GPU power specification. At idle, the GPU power consumption is around 20% of the nominal amount. This shows that the real power usage rate for GPUs is significantly lower than estimates based on nominal specifications. CPUs also are lower than the nominal amount, but probably not by as great a percentage of their nominal rate.

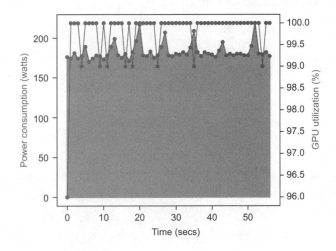

Figure 9.11 Power consumption for the CloverLeaf problem running on the V100. We integrate under the power curve to get 10.4 kJ for a run that lasted about 60 seconds. The rate of power consumption is about 61% of the nominal power specification for the V100 GPU.

WHEN WILL MULTI-GPU PLATFORMS SAVE YOU ENERGY?

In general, parallel efficiency drops off as you add more CPUs or GPUs (remember Amdahl's law from section 1.2?), and the cost for a computational job goes up. Sometimes, there are fixed costs (such as storage) associated with the overall run time of a job that are reduced if the job is finished sooner and the data can be transferred or deleted. The usual situation, however, is that you have a suite of jobs to run with a choice of how many processors for each job. The following example highlights the tradeoffs in this situation.

Example: Suite of parallel jobs to run

You have 100 jobs to run, roughly of the same type and length. You can run the jobs on either 20 processors or 40 processors. At 20 processors, the jobs take 10 hours each. The parallel efficiency in this processor range is about 80%. The cloud cluster you have access to has 200 processors. Let's look at two scenarios.

Case 1. Running 10 jobs at a time with 20 processors gives us this solution:

Total Suite Run Time = 10 hrs × 100/10 = 100 hrs

Case 2. Run 5 jobs at a time with 40 processors

Increasing the number of processors to 40 drops the run time to 5 hrs if parallel efficiency is perfect. But it is only 80% efficient, so the run time is 6.25 hrs. How did we

(continued)

get this number? Assume that 20 processors is the base case. For doubling the number of processors, the parallel efficiency formula is

$$P_{efficiency} = S/P_{mult} = 80\%$$

S is the speedup for the problem. The processor multiplier, P_{mult}, is a factor 2. Solving for the speedup, we get

$$S = 0.8 \times P_{mult} = 0.8 \times 2 = 1.6$$

Now we use the speedup equation to calculate the new time, *TN*:

$$S = T_{base}/T_{new}$$

We use T_{base} instead of T_{serial} for this form of the speedup equation. Parallel efficiency often decreases as we add processors, so we want the relationship at this point on the efficiency curve. Solving for T_{new}, we get

$$T_{new} = T_{base}/S = 10/1.6 = 6.25 \text{ hrs}$$

With this run time for 40 processors, we can now calculate the total suite run time:

$$\text{Total Suite Time} = 6.25 \text{ hrs} \times 100/5 = 125 \text{ hrs}$$

In summary, the scenario used in case 1 is much faster to accomplish the same amount of work.

This example shows that if we are optimizing the run time for a large suite of jobs, it is often better to use less parallelism. In contrast, if we are more concerned with the turnaround time for a single job, more processors will be better.

9.6.3 *Reduction in cloud computing costs with GPUs*

Cloud computing services from Google and Amazon let you match your workloads to a wide range of compute server types and demands.

- If your application is memory bound, you can use a GPU that has a lower flops-to-loads ratio at a lower cost.
- If you are more concerned with turnaround time, you can add more GPUs or CPUs.
- If your deadlines are less serious, you can use preemptible resources at a considerable reduction in cost.

As the cost of computing is more visible with cloud computing services, optimizing your application's performance becomes a higher priority. Cloud computing has the advantage of giving you access to a wider variety of hardware than you can have on-site and more options to match the hardware to the workload.

9.7   When to use GPUs

GPUs are not general-purpose processors. They are most appropriate when the computation workload is similar to a graphics workload—lots of operations that are identical. There are some areas where GPUs still do not perform well, although with each iteration of the GPU hardware and software, some of these are addressed.

- *Lack of parallelism*—To paraphrase Spiderman, "*With great power comes great need for parallelism.*" If you don't have the parallelism, GPUs can't do a lot for you. This is the first law of GPGPU programming.
- *Irregular memory access*—CPUs also struggle with this. The massive parallelism of GPUs brings no benefit to this situation. This is the second law of GPGPU programming.
- *Thread divergence*—Threads on GPUs all execute on each and every branch. This is a characteristic of SIMD and SIMT architectures (see section 1.4). Small amounts of short branching are fine, but wildly different branch paths do poorly.
- *Dynamic memory requirements*—Memory allocation is done on the CPU, which severely limits algorithms that require memory sizes determined on the fly.
- *Recursive algorithms*—GPUs have limited stack memory resources, and suppliers often state that recursion is not supported. However, a limited amount of recursion has been demonstrated to work in the mesh-to-mesh remapping algorithms in section 5.5.2.

9.8   Further explorations

GPU architectures continue to evolve with each iteration of hardware design. We suggest that you continue to track the latest developments and innovations. At the outset, GPU architectures were first and foremost for graphics performance. But the market has broadened into machine learning and computation as well.

9.8.1   Additional reading

For a much more detailed discussion of STREAM Benchmark performance and how it varies across parallel programming languages, we refer you to the following paper:

T. Deakin, J. Price, et al., "Benchmarking the achievable memory bandwidth of many-core processors across diverse parallel programming models," *GPU-STREAM*, v2.0 (2016). Paper presented at Performance Portable Programming models for Manycore or Accelerators (P^3MA) Workshop at ISC High Performance, Frankfurt, Germany.

A good resource on the roofline model for GPUs can be found at Lawrence Berkeley Lab. A good starting point is

Charlene Yang and Samuel Williams, "Performance Analysis of GPU-Accelerated Applications using the Roofline Model," GPU Technology Conference (2019) available at https://crd.lbl.gov/assets/Uploads/GTC19-Roofline.pdf.

In this chapter, we presented a simplified view of the mixbench performance model by assuming simple application performance requirements. The following paper presents a more thorough procedure to account for the complications of real applications:

> Elias Konstantinidis and Yiannis Cotronis, "A quantitative roofline model for GPU kernel performance estimation using micro-benchmarks and hardware metric profiling." *Journal of Parallel and Distributed Computing* 107 (2017): 37–56.

9.8.2   *Exercises*

1   Table 9.7 shows the achievable performance for a 1 flop/load application. Look up the current prices for the GPUs available on the market and fill in the last two columns to get the flop per dollar for each GPU. Which looks like the best value? If turnaround time for your application run time is the most important criterion, which GPU would be best to purchase?

Table 9.7   Achievable performance for a 1 flop/load application with various GPUs

GPU	Achievable Performance Gflops/sec	Price	Flops/$
V100	108.23		
Vega 20	91.38		
P100	74.69		
GeForce GTX1080Ti	44.58		
Quadro K6000	31.25		
Tesla S2050	18.50		

2   Measure the stream bandwidth of your GPU or another selected GPU. How does it compare to the ones presented in the chapter?

3   Use the likwid performance tool to get the CPU power requirements for the CloverLeaf application on a system where you have access to the power hardware counters.

Summary

- The CPU-GPU system can provide a powerful boost for many parallel applications. It should be considered for any application with a lot of parallel work.
- The GPU component of the system is in reality a general-purpose parallel accelerator. This means that it should be given the parallel part of the work.
- Data transfer over the PCI bus and memory bandwidth are the most common performance bottlenecks on CPU-GPU systems. Managing the data transfer and memory use is important for good performance.

- You'll find a wide range of GPUs available for different workloads. Selecting the most suitable model will give the best price to performance ratio.
- GPUs can reduce time-to-solution and energy costs. This can be a prime motivator in porting an application to GPUs.

GPU programming model

In this chapter, we will develop an abstract model of how work is performed on GPUs. This programming model fits a variety of GPU devices from different vendors and across the models from each vendor. It is also a simpler model than what occurs on the real hardware, capturing just the essential aspects required to develop an application. Fortunately, various GPUs have a lot of similarities in structure. This is a natural result of the demands of high-performance graphics applications.

The choice of data structures and algorithms has a long-range impact on the performance and ease of programming for the GPU. With a good mental model of the GPU, you can plan how data structures and algorithms map to the parallelism of the GPU. Especially for GPUs, our primary job as application developers is to expose as much parallelism as we can. With thousands of threads to harness, we need to fundamentally change the work so that there are a lot of small tasks to distribute across the threads. In a GPU language, as in any other parallel programming language, there are several components that must exist. These are a way to

- Express the computational loops in a parallel form for the GPU (see section 10.2)
- Move data between the host CPU and the GPU compute device (see section 10.2.4)
- Coordinate between threads that are needed for a reduction (see section 10.4)

Look for how these three components are accomplished in each GPU programming language. In some languages, you directly control some aspects, and in others, you rely on the compiler or template programming to implement the needed operations. While the operation of a GPU might seem mysterious, these operations are not all that different from what is necessary on a CPU for parallel code. We have to write loops that are safe for fine-grained parallelism, sometimes called do concurrent for Fortran or forall or foreach in C/C++. We have to think about data movement between nodes, processes, and the processor. We also have to have special mechanisms for reductions.

For native GPU computation languages like CUDA and OpenCL, the programming model is exposed as part of the language. These GPU languages are covered in chapter 12. In that chapter, you'll explicitly manage many aspects of parallelization for the GPU in your program. But with our programming model, you will be better prepared to make important programming decisions for better performance and scaling across a wide range of GPU hardware.

If you are using a higher-level programming language, such as the pragma-based GPU languages covered in chapter 11, do you really need to understand all the details of the GPU programming model? Even with pragmas, it is still helpful to understand how the work gets distributed. When you use a pragma, you are trying to steer the compiler and library to do the right thing. In some ways, this is harder than writing the program directly.

The goal of this chapter is to help you develop your application design for the GPU. This is mostly independent of the programming language for the GPU. There are questions you should answer up front. How will you organize your work and what kind of performance can be expected? Or the more basic question of whether your application should even be ported to the GPU or would it be better off staying with the CPU? GPUs, with their promise of an order-of-magnitude performance gains and lower energy use, are a compelling platform. But these are not a panacea for every application and use case. Let's dive into the details of the GPU's programming model and see what it can do for you.

NOTE We encourage you to follow along with the examples for this chapter at https://github.com/EssentialsofParallelComputing/Chapter10.

10.1   *GPU programming abstractions: A common framework*

The GPU programming abstractions are possible for a reason. The basic characteristics, which we explore in more detail in a bit, include the following. Then we'll take a quick look at some basic terminology for GPU parallelism.

- Graphics operations have massive parallelism
- Operations cannot be coordinated among tasks

10.1.1 *Massive parallelism*

Abstractions are based on what is necessary for high-performance graphics with GPUs. GPU workflows have some special characteristics that help to drive the commonality in the GPU-processing techniques. For a high frame rate and high-quality graphics, there are lots of pixels, triangles, and polygons to process and display.

Because of the large amounts of data, GPUs have massive parallelism. The operations on the data are generally identical, so GPUs use similar techniques to apply a single instruction to multiple data items to gain another level of efficiency. Figure 10.1 shows the common programming abstractions across various vendors and GPU models. These can be summarized as three or four basic techniques.

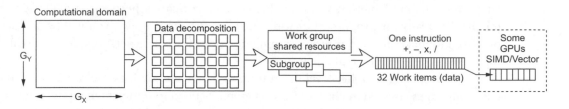

Figure 10.1   Our mental model for GPU parallelization contains the common programming abstractions across most GPU hardware.

We start with the computational domain and iteratively break up the work with the following components. We'll discuss each of these subdivisions of work in sections 10.1.4 through 10.1.8:

- Data decomposition
- Chunk-sized work for processing with some shared, local memory
- Operating on multiple data items with a single instruction
- Vectorization (on some GPUs)

One thing to note from these GPU parallel abstractions is that there are fundamentally three, or maybe four, different levels of parallelization that you can apply to a computational loop. In the original graphics use case, there is not much of a need to go beyond two or three dimensions and the corresponding number of parallelization levels. If your algorithm has more dimensions or levels, you must combine some computational loops to fully parallelize your problem.

10.1.2 Inability to coordinate among tasks

Graphics workloads do not require much coordination within the operations. But as we will see in later sections, there are algorithms such as reductions that require coordination. We will have to develop complicated schemes to handle these situations.

10.1.3 Terminology for GPU parallelism

The terminology for components of the GPU parallelism varies across vendors, adding a degree of confusion when reading programming documentation or articles. To help with cross-referencing the use of various terms, we summarize the official terms from each vendor in table 10.1.

Table 10.1 Programming abstractions and associated terminology for GPUs

OpenCL	CUDA	HIP	AMD GPU (HC compiler)	C++ AMP	CPU
NDRange (*N*-dimensional range)	grid	grid	extent	extent	Standard loop bounds or index sets with loop blocking
Work Group	block or thread block	block	tile	tile	loop block
Subgroup or Wavefront	warp	warp	wavefront	N/A	SIMD length
Work Item	thread	thread	thread	thread	thread

OpenCL is the open standard for GPU programming, so we use it as the base terminology. OpenCL runs on all of the GPU hardware and many other devices such as CPUs and even more exotic hardware such as field-programmable gate arrays (FPGAs) and other embedded devices. CUDA, the NVIDIA proprietary language for their GPUs, is the most widely used language for GPU computation and, thus, used in a great fraction of the documentation on programming GPUs. HIP (Heterogeneous-Computing Interface for Portability) is a portable derivative of CUDA developed by AMD for their GPUs. It uses similar terminology as CUDA. The native AMD Heterogeneous Compute (HC) Compiler and the C++ AMP language from Microsoft use a lot of the same terms. (C++ AMP is in maintenance mode and not under active development as of this writing.) When trying to get portable performance, it's also important to consider the corresponding features and terms for the CPU as shown in the last column in table 10.1.

10.1.4 Data decomposition into independent units of work: An NDRange or grid

The technique of data decomposition is at the heart of how GPUs obtain performance. GPUs break up the problem into many smaller blocks of data. Then they break it up again, and again.

GPUs must draw a lot of triangles and polygons to generate high frame rates. These operations are completely independent from each other. For this reason, the top-level data decomposition for computational work on a GPU also generates independent and asynchronous work.

With lots of work to do, GPUs hide latency (stalls for memory loads) by switching to another work group that is ready to compute. Figure 10.2 shows a case where only four subgroups (warps or wavefronts) can be scheduled due to resource limitations. When the subgroups hit a memory read and stall, execution switches to other subgroups. The execution switch, also called a context switch, is hiding latency with computation rather than with a deep cache hierarchy. *If you only have a single instruction stream on a single piece of data, a GPU will be slow because it has no way to hide the latency. But if you have lots of data to operate on, it's incredibly fast.*

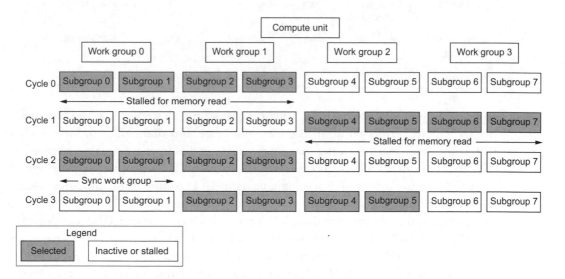

Figure 10.2 **The GPU subgroup (warp) scheduler switches to other subgroups to cover memory reads and instruction stalls. Multiple work groups allow work to be done even when a work group is being synchronized.**

Table 10.2 shows the device limitations for the current NVIDIA and AMD schedulers. For these devices, we want a high number of candidate work groups and subgroups to keep the processing elements busy.

Data movement and, in particular, moving data up and down the cache hierarchy, is a substantial part of the energy cost for a processor. Therefore, the reduction in the

Table 10.2 GPU subgroup (warp or wavefront) scheduler limitations

	NVIDIA Volta and Ampere	AMD MI50
Active number of subgroups per compute unit	64	40
Active number of work groups per compute unit	32	40
Selected subgroups for execution per compute unit	4	4
Subgroup (warp or wavefront) size	32	64

need for a deep cache hierarchy has some significant benefits. There is a large reduction in the energy usage. Also, a lot of precious silicon space is freed on the processor. This space can then be filled with more arithmetic logic units (ALUs).

We show the data decomposition operation in figure 10.3, where a 2D computational domain is split into smaller 2D blocks of data. In OpenCL, this is called an *NDRange*, short for *N*-dimensional range (the CUDA term, a *grid*, is a little more palatable). The NDRange in this case is a 3×3 set of tiles of size 8×8. The data decomposition process breaks up the global computational domain, G_y by G_x, into smaller blocks or tiles of size T_y by T_x.

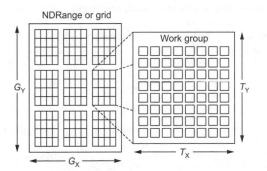

Figure 10.3 Breaking up the computational domain into small, independent work units

Let's work through an example to see what this step accomplishes.

Example: Data decomposition of a 1024×1024 2D computational domain

If we set a tile size of 16x8, the data decomposition will be as follows:

$NT_x = G_x/T_x = 1024/16 = 64$

$NT_y = G_y/T_y = 1024/8 = 128$

$NT = 64 \times 128 = 8{,}192$ tiles

This first level of the data decomposition begins to break up the dataset into a large number of smaller blocks or tiles. The GPUs make some assumptions of the

(continued)

characteristics of the work groups created by this data decomposition. These assumptions are that the work groups

- Are completely independent and asynchronous
- Have access to global and constant memory

Each work group that is created is an independent unit of work. This means that each of these work groups can be operated on in any order, providing a level of parallelism to spread out across the many compute units on a GPU. These are the same properties that we attributed to fine-grained parallelism in section 7.3.6. The same changes to loops for independent iterations for OpenMP and vectorization also enable GPU parallelism.

Table 10.3 shows examples of how this data decomposition might occur for 1D-, 2D-, and 3D-computational domains. The fastest changing tile dimension, T_x, should be a multiple of the cache line length, memory bus width, or subgroup (wavefront or warp) size for best performance. The number of tiles, NT, overall and in each dimension, results in a lot of work groups (tiles) to distribute across the GPU compute engines and processing elements.

Table 10.3   Data decomposition of the computational domain into tiles or blocks

	1D	Small 2D	Large 2D	3D
Global size	1,048,576	1024 × 1024	1024 × 1024	128 × 128 × 128
$T_z \times T_y \times T_x$	128	8 × 8	8 × 16	4 × 4 × 8
Tile size	128	64	128	128
$NT_z \times NT_y \times NT_x$	8,192	128 × 128	128 × 64	32 × 32 × 16
NT (number of work groups)	8,192	16,384	8,192	16,384

For algorithms that need neighbor information, the optimum tile size for memory accesses needs to be balanced against getting the minimum surface area for the tile (figure 10.4). Neighbor data must be loaded more than once for adjacent tiles, which makes this an important consideration.

Figure 10.4   Each work group needs to load neighbor data from the dashed rectangle, resulting in duplicate loads in the shaded regions where more duplicate loads will be needed for the case on the left. This must be balanced against optimum contiguous data loads in the x-direction.

10.1.5 Work groups provide a right-sized chunk of work

The work group spreads out the work across the threads on a compute unit. Each GPU model has a maximum size specified for the hardware. OpenCL reports this as `CL_DEVICE_MAX_WORK_GROUP_SIZE` in its device query. PGI reports it as `Maximum Threads per Block` in the output from its `pgaccelinfo` command (see figure 11.3). The maximum size for a work group is usually between 256 and 1,024. This is just the maximum. For computation, work group sizes are typically much smaller, so that there are more memory resources per work item or thread.

The work group is subdivided into subgroups or warps (figure 10.5). A subgroup is the set of threads that execute in lockstep. For NVIDIA, the warp size is 32 threads. For AMD it is called a wavefront, and the size is usually 64 work items. The work group size must be a multiple of the subgroup size.

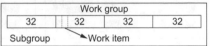

Figure 10.5   A multi-dimensional work group is linearized onto a 1D strip where it is broken up into subgroups of 32 or 64 work items. For performance reasons, work groups should be multiples of the subgroup size.

The typical characteristics of work groups on GPUs are that they

- Cycle through processing each subgroup
- Have local memory (shared memory) and other resources shared within the group
- Can synchronize within a work group or a subgroup

Local memory provides fast access and can be used as a sort of programmable cache or scratchpad memory. If the same data is needed by more than one thread in a work group, performance can generally be improved by loading it into the local memory at the start of the kernel.

10.1.6 Subgroups, warps, or wavefronts execute in lockstep

To further optimize the graphics operations, GPUs recognize that the same operations can be performed on many data elements. GPUs are therefore optimized by working on sets of data with a single instruction rather than with separate instructions for each. This reduces the number of instructions that need to be handled. This technique on the CPU is called *single instruction, multiple data* (SIMD). All GPUs emulate this with a group of threads where it is called *single instruction, multi-thread* (SIMT). See section 1.4 for the original discussion of SIMD and SIMT.

Because SIMT simulates SIMD operations, it is not necessarily constrained the same way as are SIMD operations by the underlying vector hardware. Current SIMT operations are executed in lockstep, with every thread in the subgroup executing all paths through branching if any one thread must go through a branch (figure 10.6). This is similar to how a SIMD operation is done with a mask. But because the SIMT operation is emulated, this could be relaxed with more flexibility in the instruction pipeline, where more than one instruction could be supported.

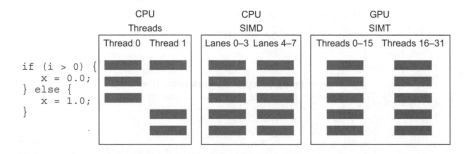

Figure 10.6   The shaded rectangles show the executed statements by threads and lanes. SIMD and SIMT operations execute all the statements in lockstep with masks for those that are false. Large blocks of conditionals can cause branch divergence problems for GPUs.

Small sections of conditionals for GPUs do not have a significant impact on overall performance. But if some threads take thousands of cycles longer than others, there's a serious issue. If threads are grouped such that all the long branches are in the same subgroup (wavefront), there will be little or no thread divergence.

10.1.7   *Work item: The basic unit of operation*

The basic unit of operation is called a work item in OpenCL. This work item can be mapped to a thread or to a processing core, depending on the hardware implementation. In CUDA, it is simply called a thread because that is how it is mapped in NVIDIA GPUs. Calling it a thread is mixing the programming model with how it is implemented in the hardware, but it is a little clearer to the programmer.

A work item can invoke another level of parallelism on GPUs with vector hardware units as figure 10.7 shows. This model of operation also maps to the CPU where a thread can execute a vector operation.

10.1.8   *SIMD or vector hardware*

Some GPUs also have vector hardware units and can do SIMD (vector) operations in addition to SIMT operations. In the graphics world, the vector units process spatial or color models. The use in scientific computation is more complicated and not

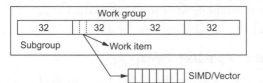

Figure 10.7 Each work item on an AMD or Intel GPU may be able to do a SIMD or Vector operation. This maps well over to the vector unit on a CPU as well.

necessarily portable between GPU hardware. The vector operation is done per work item, increasing the resource utilization for the kernel. But often there are additional vector registers to compensate for the additional work. Effective utilization of the vector units can provide a significant boost to performance when done well.

Vector operations are exposed in the OpenCL language and AMD languages. Because the CUDA hardware does not have vector units, the same level of support is not present in CUDA languages. Still, OpenCL code with vector operations will run on CUDA hardware, so it can be emulated in the CUDA hardware.

10.2 The code structure for the GPU programming model

Now we can begin to look at the code structure for the GPU that incorporates the programming model. For convenience and generality, we call the CPU the *host* and we use the term *device* to refer to the GPU.

The GPU programming model splits the loop body from the array range or index set that is applied to the function. The loop body creates the GPU kernel. The index set and arguments will be used on the host to make the kernel call. Figure 10.8 shows the transformation from a standard loop to the body of the GPU kernel. This example uses OpenCL syntax. But the CUDA kernel is similar, replacing the get_global_id call with

```
gid = blockIdx.x *blockDim.x + threadIdx.x
```

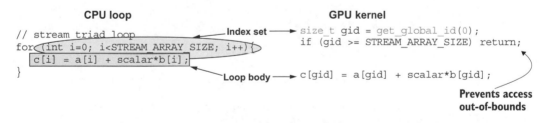

Figure 10.8 Correspondence between standard loop and the GPU kernel code structure

In the next four sections, we look separately at how the loop body becomes the parallel kernel and how to tie it back to the index set on the host. Let's break this down into four steps:

1 Extract the parallel kernel
2 Map from the local data tile to global data

3 Calculate data decomposition on the host into blocks of data

4 Allocate any required memory

10.2.1 *"Me" programming: The concept of a parallel kernel*

GPU programming is the perfect language for the "Me" generation. In the kernel, everything is relative to yourself. Take for example

```
c[i] = a[i] + scalar*b[i];
```

In this expression, there is no information about the extent of the loop. This could be a loop where i, the global i index, covers a range from 0 to 1,000 or just the single value 22. Each data item knows what needs to be done to itself and itself only. This is truly a "Me" programming model, where I care only about myself. What is so powerful about this is that the operations on each data element become completely independent. Let's look at the more complicated example of the stencil operator. Although we have two indices, both i and j, and some of the references are to adjacent data values, this line of code is still fully defined once we determine the values of i and j.

```
xnew[j][i] = (x[j][i] + x[j][i-1] + x[j][i+1] + x[j-1][i] + x[j+1][i])/5.0;
```

The separation of the loop body and the index set can be done in C++ with either functors or lambda expressions. In C++, lambda expressions have been around since the C++ 11 standard. Lambdas are used as a way for compilers to provide portability for single-source code to either CPUs or GPUs. Listing 10.1 shows the C++ lambda.

DEFINITION *Lambda expressions* are unnamed, local functions that can be assigned to a variable and used locally or passed to a routine.

Listing 10.1   C++ lambda for the stream triad

```
lambda.cc
 1 int main() {
 2     const int N = 100;
 3     double a[N], b[N], c[N];
 4     double scalar = 0.5;
 5
 6     // c, a, and b are all valid scope pointers on the device or host
 7
 8     // We assign the loop body to the example_lambda variable
 9     auto example_lambda = [&] (int i) {            ◁──── Lambda variable
10         c[i] = a[i] + scalar * b[i];               ◁──── Lambda body
11     };
12
13     for (int i = 0; i < N; i++)            ◁──── Arguments or index set for lambda
14     {
15         example_lambda(i);                 ◁──── Invokes lambda
16     }
17 }
```

The lambda expression is composed of four main components:

- *Lambda body*—The function to be executed by the call. In this case, the body is

  ```
  c[i] = a[i] + scalar * b[i];.
  ```

- *Arguments*—The argument (int i) used in the later call to the lambda expression.
- *Capture closure*—The list of variables in the function body that are defined externally and how these are passed to the routine, specified by [&] in listing 10.1. The & indicates that the variable is referred to by reference and an = sign says to copy it by value. A single & sets the default to variables by reference. We can more fully specify the variables with the capture specification of [&c, &a, &b, &scalar].
- *Invocation*—The for loop in lines 13 to 16 in listing 10.1 invokes the lambda over the specified array values.

Lambda expressions form the basis for more naturally generating code for GPUs in emerging C++ languages like SYCL, Kokkos, and Raja. We will briefly cover SYCL in chapter 12 as a higher-level C++ language (originally built on top of OpenCL). Kokkos from Sandia National Laboratories (SNL) and Raja, originating at Lawrence Livermore National Laboratory (LLNL), are two higher-level languages developed to simplify the writing of portable scientific applications for the broad array of today's computing hardware. We'll introduce Kokkos and Raja in chapter 12 as well.

10.2.2 Thread indices: Mapping the local tile to the global world

The key to how the kernel can compose its local operation is that, as a product of the data decomposition, we provide each work group with some information about where it is in the local and global domains. In OpenCL, you can get the following information:

- *Dimension*—Gets the number of dimensions, either 1D, 2D, or 3D, for this kernel from the kernel invocation
- *Global information*—Global index in each dimension, which corresponds to a local work unit, or the global size in each dimension, which is the size of the global computational domain in each dimension
- *Local (tile) information*—The local size in each dimension, which corresponds to the tile size in this dimension, or the local index in each dimension, which corresponds to the tile index in this dimension
- *Group information*—The number of groups in each dimension, which corresponds to the number of groups in this dimension, or the group index in each dimension, which corresponds to the group index in this dimension

Similar information is available in CUDA, but the global index must be calculated from the local thread index plus the block (tile) information:

```
gid = blockIdx.x *blockDim.x + threadIdx.x;
```

Figure 10.9 presents the indexing for the work group (block or tile) for OpenCL and CUDA. The function call for OpenCL is first, followed by the variable defined by

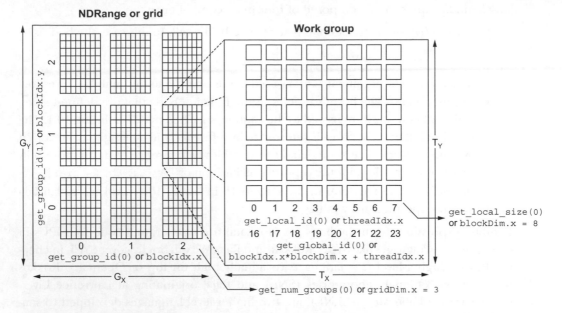

Figure 10.9   **Mapping of the index of individual work item to global index space. The OpenCL call is given first, followed by the variable defined in CUDA.**

CUDA. All of this indexing support is automatically done for you by the data decomposition for the GPU, greatly simplifying the handling of the mapping from the global space to the tile.

10.2.3 Index sets

The size of the indices for each work group should be identical. This is done by padding the global computational domain out to a multiple of the local work group size. We can do this with some integer arithmetic to get one extra work group and a padded global work size. The following example shows an approach using basic integer operations and then a second with the C $ceil$ intrinsic function.

$$global\_work\_size_x = ((global\_size_x + local\_work\_size_x - 1)/$$
$$local\_work\_size_x) * local\_work\_size_x$$

Example: Calculating work group sizes

This code uses the arguments for the kernel invocation to get uniform work group sizes.

```
int global_sizex = 1000;
int local_work_sizex = 128;
int global_work_sizex = ((global_sizex + local_work_sizex - 1)/
                         local_work_sizex) * local_work_sizex = 1024;
```

```
int number_work_groups_x = (global_size_x + local_work_size_x - 1)/
                            local_work_size_x = 8
// or, alternatively
int global_work_size_x = ceil(global_size_x/local_work_size_x) *
                         local_work_size_x = 1024;
int number_work_groups_x = ceil(global_size_x/local_work_size_x) = 8;
```

To avoid reading past the end of the array, we should test the global index in each kernel and skip the read if it is past the end of the array with something like

```
if (gid_x > global_size_x) return;
```

NOTE Avoiding out-of-bound reads and writes is important in GPU kernels because they lead to random kernel crashes with no error message or output.

10.2.4 How to address memory resources in your GPU programming model

Memory is still the most important concern impacting your application programming plan. Fortunately, there is a lot of memory on today's GPUs. Both the NVIDIA V100 and AMD Radeon Instinct MI50 GPUs support 32 GB of RAM. Compared to well-provisioned HPC CPU nodes with 128 GB of memory, a GPU compute node with 4–6 GPUs has the same memory. There is as much memory on GPU compute nodes as on CPUs. Therefore, we can use the same memory allocation strategy as we have for the CPU and not have to transfer data back and forth due to limited GPU memory.

Memory allocation for the GPU has to be done on the CPU. Often, memory is allocated for both the CPU and the GPU at the same time and then data is transferred between them. But if possible, you should allocate memory only for the GPU. This avoids expensive memory transfers back and forth from the CPU and frees up memory on the CPU. Algorithms that use a dynamic memory allocation present a problem for the GPU and need to be converted to a static memory algorithm, with the memory size known ahead of time. The latest GPUs do a good job of *coalescing* irregular or shuffled memory accesses into single, coherent cache-line loads when possible.

DEFINITION *Coalesced memory loads* are the combination of separate memory loads from groups of threads into a single cache-line load.

On the GPU, the memory coalescing is done at the hardware level in the memory controller. The performance gains from these coalesced loads are substantial. But also important is that a lot of the optimizations from earlier GPU programming guides are no longer necessary, significantly reducing the GPU programming effort.

You can get some additional speedup from using local (shared) memory for data that is used more than once. This optimization used to be important for performance, but the better cache on GPUs is making the speedup less significant. There are a couple of strategies on how to use the local memory, depending on whether you can predict the size of the local memory required. Figure 10.10 shows the regular grid approach on the left and the irregular grid for unstructured and adaptive mesh refinement on the right. The regular grid has four abutting tiles with overlapping halo regions. The adaptive mesh refinement shows only four cells; a typical GPU application would load 128 or 256 cells and then bring in the required neighbor cells around the periphery.

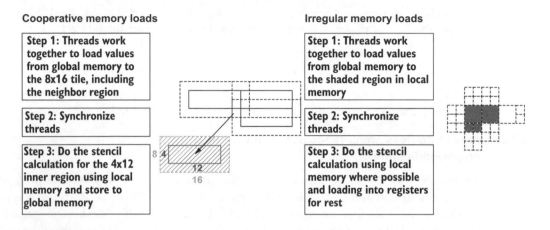

Cooperative memory loads

Step 1: Threads work together to load values from global memory to the 8x16 tile, including the neighbor region

Step 2: Synchronize threads

Step 3: Do the stencil calculation for the 4x12 inner region using local memory and store to global memory

Irregular memory loads

Step 1: Threads work together to load values from global memory to the shaded region in local memory

Step 2: Synchronize threads

Step 3: Do the stencil calculation using local memory where possible and loading into registers for rest

Figure 10.10   For stencils on regular grids, load all the data into local memory and then use local memory for the computation. The inner solid rectangle is the computational tile. The outer dashed rectangle encloses the neighboring data needed for the calculation. You can use cooperative loads to load the data in the outer rectangle into the local memory for each work group. Because irregular grids have an unpredictable size, load only the computed region into local memory and use registers for each thread for the rest.

The processes for the two cases are

- *Threads need the same memory loads as adjacent threads.* A good example of this is the stencil operation we use throughout the book. Thread i needs the i-1 and i+1 values, which means that multiple threads will need the same values. The best approach for this situation is to do cooperative memory loads. Copying the memory values from global memory to local (shared) memory results in a significant speedup.

- *An irregular mesh has an unpredictable number of neighbors, making it difficult to load into local memory.* One way to handle this is to copy the part of the mesh to be computed into local memory. Then load the neighbor data into registers for each thread.

These are not the only ways to utilize the memory resources on the GPU. It is important to think through the issues with regard to the limited resources and the potential performance benefits for your particular application.

10.3 Optimizing GPU resource usage

The key to good GPU programming is to manage the limited resources available for executing kernels. Let's look at a few of the more important resource limitations in table 10.4. Exceeding the available resources can lead to significant decreases in performance. The NVIDIA compute capability 7.0 is for the V100 chip. The newer Ampere A100 chip uses a compute capability of 8.0 with nearly identical resource limits.

Table 10.4   Some resource limitations on current GPUs

Resource limit	NVIDIA compute capability 7.0	AMD Vega 20 (MI50)
Maximum threads per work group	1024	256
Maximum threads per compute unit	2048	
Maximum work groups per compute unit	32	16
Local memory per compute unit	96 KB	64 KB
Register file size per compute unit	64K	256 KB vector
Maximum 32-bit registers per thread	255	

The most important control available to the GPU programmer is the work group size. At first, it would seem that using the maximum number of threads per work group would be desirable. But for computational kernels, the complexity of computational kernels in comparison to graphics kernels means that there are a lot of demands on compute resources. This is known colloquially as *memory pressure* or *register pressure*. Reducing the work group size gives each work group more resources to work with. It also gives more work groups for context switching, which we discussed in section 10.1.1. The key to getting good GPU performance is finding the right balance of work group size and resources.

> **DEFINITION**   *Memory pressure* is the effect of the computational kernel resource needs on the performance of GPU kernels. *Register pressure* is a similar term, referring to demands on registers in the kernel.

A full analysis of the resource requirements of a particular kernel and the resources available on the GPU requires an involved analysis. We'll give examples of a couple of these types of deep dives. In the next two sections, we look at

- How many registers a kernel uses
- How busy the multi-processors are kept, which is called occupancy

10.3.1 How many registers does my kernel use?

You can find out how many registers your code uses by adding the `-Xptxas="-v"` flag to the `nvcc` compile command. In OpenCL for NVIDIA GPUs, use the `-cl-nv-verbose` flag for the OpenCL compile line to get a similar output.

Example: Getting the register usage for your kernel on an NVIDIA GPU

First, we build BabelStream with the extra compiler flags:

```
git clone git@github.com:UoB-HPC/BabelStream.git
cd BabelStream
export EXTRA_FLAGS='-Xptxas="-v"'
make -f CUDA.make
```

The output from the NVIDIA compiler shows the register usage for the stream triad:

```
ptxas info    : Used 14 registers, 4096 bytes smem, 380 bytes cmem[0]
ptxas info    : Compiling entry function '_Z12triad_kernelIfEvPT_PKS0_S3_'
                for 'sm_70'
ptxas info    : Function properties for _Z12triad_kernelIfEvPT_PKS0_S3_
     0 bytes stack frame, 0 bytes spill stores, 0 bytes spill loads
```

In this simple kernel, we use 14 registers out of the 255 available on the NVIDIA GPU.

10.3.2 Occupancy: Making more work available for work group scheduling

We have discussed the importance of latency and context switching for good performance on the GPU. The benefit in "right-sized" work groups is that more work groups can be in flight at one time. For the GPU, this is important because when progress on a work group stalls due to memory latency, it needs to have other work groups that it can execute to hide the latency. To set the proper work group size, we need a measure of some sort. On GPUs, the measure used for analyzing work groups is called *occupancy*. Occupancy is a measure of how busy the compute units are during the calculation. The measure is complicated because it is dependent on a lot of factors, such as the memory required and the registers used. The precise definition is

$$\text{Occupancy} = \text{Number of Active Threads/Maximum Number of Threads Per Compute Unit}$$

Because the number of threads per subgroup is fixed, an equivalent definition is based on subgroups, also known as wavefronts or warps:

$$\text{Occupancy} = \text{Number of Active Subgroups/Maximum Number of Subgroups Per Compute Unit}$$

The number of active subgroups or threads is determined by the work group or thread resource that is exhausted first. Often this is the number of registers or local memory that is needed by a work group, preventing another work group from starting. We need a tool such as the CUDA Occupancy Calculator (presented in the following example) to do this well. NVIDIA programming guides focus a lot of attention on maximizing occupancy. While important, there just need to be enough work groups to switch between to hide latency and stalls.

Example: CUDA Occupancy Calculator

1 Download CUDA Occupancy Calculator spreadsheet from

https://docs.nvidia.com/cuda/cuda-occupancy-calculator/index.html

2 Enter the register count output from NVCC compiler (section 10.3.1) and work group size (1,024).

The following figure shows the results for the Occupancy Calculator. There are also plots on the spreadsheet for varying block size, register count, and local memory usage (not shown).

CUDA occupancy calculator

Just follow steps 1, 2, and 3 below! (or click here for help)

1.) Select compute capability (click):	7.0	(Help)
1.b) Select shared memory size config (bytes)	32768	

2.) Enter your resource usage:

Threads per block	1024	(Help)
Registers per thread	14	
Shared memory per block (bytes)	4096	

(Don't edit anything below this line)

3.) GPU occupancy data is displayed here and in the graphs:

Active threads per multiprocessor	2048	(Help)
Active warps per multiprocessor	64	
Active thread blocks per multiprocessor	2	
Occupancy of each multiprocessor	100%	

Physical limits for GPU compute capability: 7.0

Threads per warp	32
Max warps per multiprocessor	64
Max thread blocks per multiprocessor	32
Max threads per multiprocessor	2048
Maximum thread block size	1024
Registers per multiprocessor	65536
Max registers per thread block	65536
Max registers per thread	255
Shared memory per multiprocessor (bytes)	32768
Max shared memory per block	32768
Register allocation unit size	256
Register allocation granularity	warp
Shared memory allocation unit size	256
Warp allocation granularity	4

			= Allocatable
Allocated Resources	Per block	Limit per SM	Blocks per SM
Warps (Threads per block/Threads per warp)	32	64	2
Registers (Warp limit per SM due to per-warp reg count)	32	128	4
Shared memory (bytes)	4096	32768	8

Note: SM is an abbreviation for (streaming) multiprocessor

Maximum thread blocks per multiprocessor	Blocks/SM	* Warps/Block	= Warps/SM
Limited by max warps or max blocks per multiprocessor	2	32	64
Limited by registers per multiprocessor	4		
Limited by shared memory per multiprocessor	6		

Note: Occupancy limiter is shown in orange

Physical max warps/SM = 64
Occupancy = 64/64 = 100%

Output from CUDA Occupancy Calculator for the stream triad showing the resource usage for the kernel. The third block from the top shows the occupancy measures.

10.4 Reduction pattern requires synchronization across work groups

Up to now, the computational loops we have looked at over cells, particles, points, and other computational elements could be handled by the approach in figure 10.8, where the `for` loops are stripped from the computational body to create a GPU kernel. Making this transformation is quick and easy and can be applied to the vast majority of loops in a scientific application. But there are other situations where the code conversion to the GPU is exceedingly difficult. We'll look at algorithms that require a more sophisticated approach. Take for example, the single line of Fortran code using array syntax:

```
xmax = sum(x(:))
```

It looks so simple in Fortran, but it's far more complicated on the GPU. The source of the difficulty is that we cannot do cooperative work or comparisons across work groups. The only way to accomplish this is to exit the kernel. Figure 10.11 illustrates the general strategy that deals with this situation.

1. Calculate the sum for every work group and store into a scratch array (xblock) the size of global_size/work_group_size.

2a. Use a single work group and loop through array to find the sum per work item.

2b. Do a reduction within the work group to get the global sum.

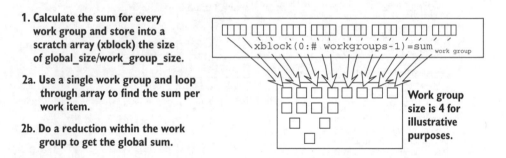

Figure 10.11 The reduction pattern on the GPU requires two kernels to synchronize multiple work groups. We exit the first kernel, represented by the rectangle, and then start another one the size of a single work group to allow thread cooperation for the final pass.

For ease of illustration, figure 10.11 shows an array 32 elements long. The typical array for this method would be hundreds of thousands or even millions of elements long so that it is much larger than the size of a work group. In the first step, we find the sum of each work group and store it in a scratch array the length of the number of work groups or blocks. The first pass reduces the size of the array by the size of our work group, which could be 512 or 1,024. At this point, we cannot communicate between work groups, so we exit the kernel and start a new kernel with just one work group. The remaining data might be greater than the work group size of 512 or 1,024, so we loop through the scratch array, summing up the values into each work item. We can communicate between the work items in the work group, so we can do a reduction to a single global value, summing along the way.

Complicated! The code to perform this operation on the GPU takes dozens of lines of code and two kernels to do the same operation that we can do in one line for the CPU. We'll see more of the actual code for a reduction in chapter 12 when we cover CUDA and OpenCL programming. The performance that is obtained on the GPU is faster than the CPU, but it takes a lot of programming work. And we'll start to see that one of the characteristics of GPUs is that synchronization and comparisons are hard to do.

10.5 Asynchronous computing through queues (streams)

We are going to see how we can more fully utilize a GPU by overlapping data transfer and computation. Two data transfers can occur at the same time as a computation on a GPU.

The basic nature of work on GPUs is asynchronous. Work is queued up on the GPU and, usually, only gets executed when a result or synchronization is requested. Figure 10.12 shows a typical set of commands sent to a GPU for a computation.

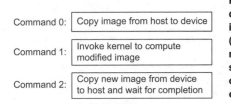

Figure 10.12 Work scheduled on a GPU in the default queue only gets completed when the wait for completion is requested. We scheduled the copy of a graphical image (a picture) to be copied to the GPU. Then we scheduled a mathematical operation on the data to modify it. We also scheduled a third operation to bring it back. None of these operations has to start until we demand the wait for completion.

We can also schedule work in multiple queues that are independent and asynchronous. The use of multiple queues as illustrated in figure 10.13 exposes the potential for overlapping data transfer and computation. Most of the GPU languages support some form of asynchronous work queues. In OpenCL the commands are queued, and in CUDA, the operations are placed in streams. While the potential for parallelism is created, whether it actually happens is dependent on the hardware capabilities and coding details.

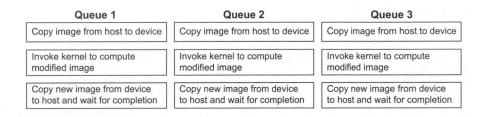

Figure 10.13 Staging work for three images in parallel queues

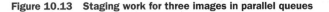

If we have a GPU capable of simultaneously performing these operations,

- Copying data from host to device
- Kernel computation(s)
- Copying data from device to host

then the work that is set up in three separate queues in figure 10.13 can overlap computation and communication as figure 10.14 shows.

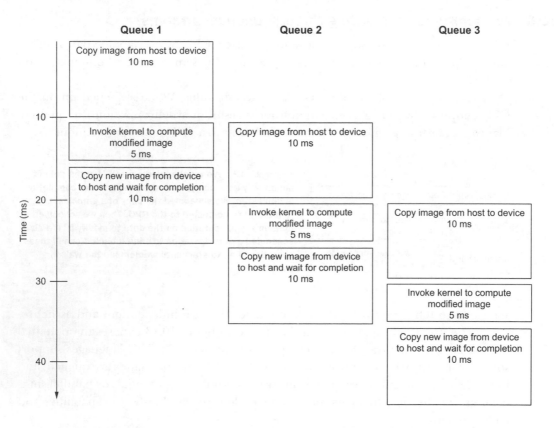

Figure 10.14   Overlapping computation and data transfers reduce the time for three images from 75 ms to 45 ms. This is possible because the GPU can do a computation, a data transfer from the host to the device, and another one from the device to the host simultaneously.

10.6   *Developing a plan to parallelize an application for GPUs*

Now we'll move on to using our understanding of the GPU programming model to develop a strategy for parallelization of our application. We'll use a couple of application examples to demonstrate the process.

10.6.1 Case 1: 3D atmospheric simulation

Your application is an atmospheric simulation ranging from 1024x1024x1024 to 8192x8192x8192 in size with x as the vertical dimension, y as the horizontal, and z as the depth. Let's look at the options you might consider:

- *Option 1: Distribute data in a 1D fashion across the z-dimension (depth).*

  For GPUs, we need tens of thousands of work groups for effective parallelism. From the GPU specification (table 9.3), we have 60–80 compute units of 32 double-precision arithmetic units for about 2,000 simultaneous arithmetic pathways. In addition, we need more work groups for latency hiding via context switching. Distributing data across the z-dimension gets us 1,024 to 8,192 work groups, which is low for a GPU parallelism.

  Let's look at the resources needed for each work group. The minimum dimensions would be a 1024x1024 plane, plus any required neighbor data in ghost cells. We'll assume one ghost cell in both directions. We would therefore need $1024 \times 1024 \times 3 \times 8$ bytes or 24 MiB of local data. Looking at table 10.4, GPUs have 64–96 KiB of local data, so we would not be able to preload data into local memory for faster processing.

- *Option 2: Distribute data in 2D vertical columns across y- and z-dimensions.*

  Distributing across two dimensions would give us over a million potential work groups, so we would have enough independent work groups for the GPU. For each work group, we would have 1,024 to 8,192 cells. We have our own cell plus 4 neighbors for $1024 \times 5 \times 8 = 40$ KiB minimum of required local memory. For larger problems and with more than one variable per cell, we would not have enough local memory.

- *Option 3: Distribute data in 3D cubes across x-, y-, and z-dimensions.*

  Using the template from table 10.3, for each work group, let's try using a 4x4x8 cell tile. With neighbors, this is $6 \times 6 \times 10 \times 8$ bytes for 2.8 KiB minimum of required local memory. We could have more variables per cell and can experiment with making the tile size a little larger.

  Total memory requirements for the 1024x1024x1024 cell tile $\times$ 8 bytes is 8 GiB. This is a large problem. GPUs have as much as 32 GiB of RAM, so the problem would possibly fit on one GPU. Larger size problems would require potentially up to 512 GPUs. So we should plan for distributed memory parallelism using MPI as well.

Let's compare this to the CPU where these design decisions would have different outcomes. We might have work to spread across 44 processes, each with fewer resource restrictions. While the 3D approach could work, the 1D and 2D will also be feasible. Now let's contrast that to an unstructured mesh where the data is all contained in 1D arrays.

10.6.2   *Case 2: Unstructured mesh application*

In this case, your application is a 3D unstructured mesh using tetrahedral or polygonal cells that range from 1 to 10 million cells. But the data is a 1D list of polygons with data such as x, y, and z that contains the spatial location. In this case, there's only one option: 1D data distribution.

Because the data is unstructured and contained in 1D arrays, the choices are simpler. We distribute the data in 1D with a tile size of 128. This gives us from 8,000 to 80,000 work groups, providing plenty of work for the GPU to switch between and hide latency. The memory requirements are 128×8 byte double-precision value = 1 KB, allowing space for multiple data values per cell.

We will also need space for some integer mapping and neighbor arrays to provide the connectivity between the cells. Neighbor data is loaded into registers for each thread so that we don't have to worry about the impact on local memory and possibly blowing past the memory limit. The largest size mesh at 10 million cells requires 80 MB, plus space for face, neighbor, and mapping arrays. These connectivity arrays can increase the memory usage significantly, but there should be plenty of memory on a single GPU to run computations on even the largest size meshes.

For best results, we will need to provide some locality for the unstructured data by using a data-partitioning library or by using a space-filling curve that keeps cells close to each other in the array that are close to each other spatially.

10.7   *Further explorations*

While the basic contours of the GPU programming model have stabilized, there are still a lot of changes occurring. In particular, the resources available for the kernels have slowly increased as the target uses broaden from 2D to 3D graphics and physics simulations for more realistic games. Markets such as scientific computing and machine learning are also becoming more important. For both these markets, custom GPU hardware has been developed: double precision for scientific computing and tensor cores for machine learning.

In our presentation, we've mostly discussed discrete GPUs. But there are also integrated GPUs as first discussed in section 9.1.1. The Accelerated Processing Unit (APU) is an AMD product offering. Both AMD's APU and Intel's integrated GPUs offer some advantages in reducing the memory transfer costs because these are no longer on the PCI bus. This is offset by the reduction in the silicon area for GPU transistors and a lower power envelope. Still, this capability has been underappreciated since it appeared. The primary development focus has been on the big discrete GPUs that are in the top-end HPC systems. But the same GPU programming languages and tools work equally as well with integrated GPUs. The critical limitation on developing new, accelerated applications is the widespread knowledge on how to program and exploit these devices.

Other mass-market devices such as Android tablets and cell phones have programmable GPUs with the OpenCL language. Some resources for these include

- Download OpenCL-Z and OpenCL-X benchmark applications from Google Play to see if your device supports OpenCL. Drivers may also be available from hardware vendors.
- Compubench (https://compubench.com) has performance results for some mobile devices that use OpenCL or CUDA.
- Intel has a nice site on programming with OpenCL for Android at https://software.intel.com/en-us/android/articles/opencl-basic-sample-for-android-os.

In recent years, GPU hardware and software have added support for other types of programming models, such as task-based approaches (see figure 1.25) and graph algorithms. These alternative programming models have long been an interest in parallel programming, but have struggled with efficiency and scale. There are critical applications, such as sparse matrix solvers, that cannot easily be implemented without further advances in these areas. But the fundamental question is whether enough parallelism can be exposed (revealed to the hardware) to utilize the massive parallel architecture of the GPUs. Only time will tell.

10.7.1 *Additional reading*

NVIDIA has long supported research into GPU programming. The CUDA C programming and best practices guides (available at https://docs.nvidia.com/cuda) are worth reading. Other resources include

- The GPU Gems series (https://developer.nvidia.com/gpugems) is an older set of papers that still contains a lot of relevant materials.
- AMD also has a lot of GPU programming materials at their GPUOpen site at

  https://gpuopen.com/compute-product/rocm/

  and at the ROCm site

  https://rocm.github.io/documentation.html

- AMD provides one of the better tables comparing terminology of different GPU programming languages available at https://rocm.github.io/languages.html.

Despite having about 65% of the GPU market (mostly integrated GPUs), Intel® is just beginning to be a serious player in GPU computation. They have announced a new discrete graphics board and will be the GPU vendor for the Aurora system at Argonne National Laboratory (to be delivered in 2022). The Aurora system is the first exascale system ever produced and has 6x the performance of the current top system in the world. The GPU is based on the Intel® Iris® X^e architecture, code named "Ponte Vecchio." With much fanfare, Intel has released its oneAPI programming initiative. The oneAPI toolkit comes with the Intel GPU driver, compilers, and tools. Go to https:// software.intel.com/oneapi for more information and downloads.

10.7.2 *Exercises*

1 You have an image classification application that will take 5 ms to transfer each file to the GPU, 5 ms to process, and 5 ms to bring back. On the CPU, the processing takes 100 ms per image. There are one million images to process. You have 16 processing cores on the CPU. Would a GPU system do the work faster?

2 The transfer time for the GPU in problem 1 is based on a third generation PCI bus. If you can get a Gen4 PCI bus, how does that change the design? A Gen5 PCI bus? For image classification, you shouldn't need to bring back a modified image. How does that change the calculation?

3 For your discrete GPU (or NVIDIA GeForce GTX 1060, if none), what size 3D application could you run? Assume 4 double-precision variables per cell and a usage limit of half the GPU memory so you have room for temporary arrays. How does this change if you use single precision?

Summary

- Parallelism on the GPU needs to be in the thousands of independent work items because there are thousands of independent arithmetic units. The CPU only needs parallelism in the tens of independent work items to distribute work across the processing cores. Thus, for the GPU, it is important to expose more parallelism in our applications to keep the processing units busy.

- Different GPU vendors have similar programming models driven by the needs of high-frame-rate graphics. Because of this, a general approach can be developed that is applicable across many different GPUs.

- The GPU programming model is particularly well suited for data parallelism with large sets of computational data but can be difficult for some tasks with a lot of coordination, such as reductions. The result is that many highly parallel loops port easily, but there are some that take a lot of effort.

- The separation of a computational loop into a loop body and the loop control, or index set, is a powerful concept for GPU programming. The loop body becomes the GPU kernel, and the CPU does the memory allocation, and invokes the kernel.

- Asynchronous work queues can overlap communication and computation. This can help to improve the utilization rate of the GPU.

Directive-based GPU programming

This chapter covers

- Selecting the best directive-based language for your GPU
- Using directives or pragmas to port your code to GPUs or other accelerator devices
- Optimizing the performance of your GPU application

There has been a scramble to establish standards for directive-based languages for programming for GPUs. The pre-eminent directive-based language, OpenMP, released in 1997, was the natural candidate to look to as an easier way to program GPUs. At that time, OpenMP was playing catchup and mainly focused on new CPU capabilities. To address GPU accessibility, in 2011, a small group of compiler vendors, (Cray, PGI and CAPS) along with NVIDIA as the GPU vendor, joined to release the OpenACC standard, providing a simpler pathway to GPU programming. Similar to what you saw in chapter 7 for OpenMP, OpenACC also uses pragmas. In this case, OpenACC pragmas direct the compiler to generate GPU code. A couple of years later, the OpenMP Architecture Review Board (ARB) added their own pragma support for GPUs to the OpenMP standard.

We'll work through some basic examples in OpenACC and OpenMP to give you an idea of how they work. We suggest that you try out the examples on your target system to see what compilers are available and their current status.

NOTE   As always, we encourage you to follow along with the examples for this chapter at https://github.com/EssentialsofParallelComputing/Chapter11.

Many programmers find themselves "on the fence" in regard to which directive-based language—OpenACC or OpenMP—they should use. Often, the choice is clear once you find out what is available on your system of choice. Keep in mind that the biggest hurdle to overcome is simply to start. If you later decide to switch GPU languages, the preliminary work will still prove valuable as the core concepts transcend the language. We hope that by seeing how little effort is required to generate GPU code using pragmas and directives, you will be encouraged to try it on some of your code. You may even experience a modest speedup with just a little effort.

The history of OpenMP and OpenACC

The development of OpenMP and OpenACC standards is mostly a friendly competition; some members of the OpenACC committee are also on the OpenMP committee. Implementations are still emerging, led by efforts at Lawrence Livermore National Laboratory, IBM, and GCC. Attempts have been made to merge the two approaches, but they continue to co-exist and will probably do so for the foreseeable future.

OpenMP is gaining steam and is believed to be the stronger long-term path, but for now, OpenACC has the more mature implementations and broader support by compilers. The following figure shows the full history of the standard's releases. Note that version 4.0 of the OpenMP standard is the first one to support GPU and accelerators.

OpenACC
- Version 1.0 Nov 2011
- Version 2.0 Jun 2013
- Version 2.5 Oct 2015
- Version 2.6 Nov 2017
- Version 2.7 Nov 2018

OpenMP with GPU support
- Version 4.0 July 2013
- Version 4.5 Nov 2015
- Version 5.0 Nov 2018
- Version 5.1 Nov 2020

Release dates of GPU pragma-based languages

11.1 Process to apply directives and pragmas for a GPU implementation

Directive or pragma-based annotations to C, C++, or Fortran applications provide one of the more attractive pathways to access the compute power of GPUs. Much like the OpenMP threading model covered in chapter 7, you can add just a few lines to your application and the compiler generates code that can run on the GPU or the CPU. As first covered in chapters 6 and 7, pragmas are preprocessor statements in C and C++ that give the compiler special instructions. These take the form

```
#pragma acc <directive> [clause]
#pragma omp <directive> [clause]
```

Directives in the form of special comments provide the corresponding capability for Fortran code. The directives start with the comment character, followed by either the acc or omp keyword to identify these as directives for OpenACC and OpenMP, respectively.

```
!$acc <directive> [clause]
!$omp <directive> [clause]
```

The same general steps are used for implementing OpenACC and OpenMP in applications. Figure 11.1 shows these steps and we'll detail them in the following sections.

Steps	CPU	GPU
Original	a[1000] for or do loop for or do loop free a	
1. Offload work to GPU	a[1000] #work pragma #work pragma free a	for or do loop (128 threads) for or do loop (128 threads)

2. Manage data movement to GPU	#data pragma{
	#work pragma
	#work pragma
	}
		a[1000]
		for or do loop (128 threads)
		for or do loop (128 threads)
		free a

3. Optimize GPU kernels	#data pragma{
	#work pragma
	#work pragma
	}
		a[1000]
		for or do loop (256 threads)
		for or do loop (64 threads)
		free a

Figure 11.1 Steps to implement a GPU port with the pragma-based languages. Offloading the work to a GPU causes data transfers that slow down the application until the data movement is reduced.

We summarize the three steps that we will use to convert a code to run on the GPU with either OpenACC or OpenMP as follows:

1 Move the computationally intensive work to the GPU. This forces data transfers between the CPU and GPU that will slow down the code, but the work has to be moved first.

2 Reduce the data movement between the CPU and GPU. Move allocations to the GPU if the data is only used there.

3 Tune the size of the workgroup, number of workgroups, and other kernel parameters to improve kernel performance.

At this point, you will have an application running much faster on the GPU. Further optimizations are possible to improve performance, although these tend to be more specific for each application.

11.2 OpenACC: The easiest way to run on your GPU

We'll start with getting a simple application running with OpenACC. We do this to show the basic details of getting things working. Then we'll work on how to optimize the application once it is running. As might be expected with a pragma-based approach, there is a large payoff for a small effort. But first, you have to work through the initial slowdown of the code. Don't despair! It is normal to encounter an initial slowdown on your journey to faster computations on a GPU.

Often the most difficult step is getting a working OpenACC compiler toolchain. Several solid OpenACC compilers are available. The most notable of the available compilers are listed as follows:[1]

- *PGI*—This is a commercial compiler, but note that PGI has a community edition for a free download.

- *GCC*—Versions 7 and 8 implement most of the OpenACC 2.0a specification. Version 9 implements most of the OpenACC 2.5 specification. The OpenACC development branch in GCC is working on OpenACC 2.6, featuring further improvements and optimizations.

- *Cray*—Another commercial compiler; it is only available on Cray systems. Cray has announced that they will no longer support OpenACC in their new LLVM-based C/C++ compiler as of version 9.0. A "classic" version of the compiler that supports OpenACC continues to be available.

For these examples, we'll use the PGI compiler (version 19.7) and CUDA (version 10.1). The PGI compiler is the most mature option among the more readily available compilers. The GCC compiler is another option but be sure to use the most recent version available. The Cray compiler is a great option if you have access to their system.

---

[1] One of the original OpenACC compilers, CAPS, went out of business in 2016 and is no longer available.

NOTE What if you don't have a suitable GPU? You can still try the examples by running the code on your CPU with the OpenACC generated kernels. Performance will be different, but the basic code should be the same.

With the PGI compiler, you can first get information on your system with the `pgaccelinfo` command. It also lets you know if your system and environment are in working order. After running the command, the output should look something like what is shown in figure 11.2.

```
CUDA Driver Version:          10010
NVRM version:                 NVIDIA UNIX x86_64 Kernel Module  418.87.00  Thu Aug  8 15:35:46 CDT 2019

Device Number:                0
Device Name:                  Tesla V100-SXM2-16GB
Device Revision Number:       7.0
Global Memory Size:           16914055168
Number of Multiprocessors:    80
Concurrent Copy and Execution: Yes
Total Constant Memory:        65536
Total Shared Memory per Block: 49152
Registers per Block:          65536
Warp Size:                    32
Maximum Threads per Block:    1024
Maximum Block Dimensions:     1024, 1024, 64
Maximum Grid Dimensions:      2147483647 x 65535 x 65535
Maximum Memory Pitch:         2147483647B
Texture Alignment:            512B
Clock Rate:                   1530 MHz
Execution Timeout:            No
Integrated Device:            No
Can Map Host Memory:          Yes
Compute Mode:                 default
Concurrent Kernels:           Yes
ECC Enabled:                  Yes
Memory Clock Rate:            877 MHz
Memory Bus Width:             4096 bits
L2 Cache Size:                6291456 bytes
Max Threads Per SMP:          2048
Async Engines:                2
Unified Addressing:           Yes
Managed Memory:               Yes
Concurrent Managed Memory:    Yes
Preemption Supported:         Yes
Cooperative Launch:           Yes
   Multi-Device:              Yes
PGI Default Target:           -ta=tesla:cc70
```

Figure 11.2 Output from the `pgaccelinfo` command shows the type of GPU and its characteristics.

11.2.1 Compiling OpenACC code

Listing 11.1 shows some excerpts from OpenACC makefiles. CMake provides the Find-OpenACC.cmake module called in line 18 in the listing. The full CMakeLists.txt file is included in the supplemental source code for the chapter in the OpenACC/StreamTriad directory at https://github.com/EssentialsofParallelComputing/Chapter11. We set some flags for compiler feedback and for the compiler to be less conservative about potential aliasing. Both a CMake file and a simple makefile are provided in the subdirectory.

Listing 11.1 Excerpts from OpenACC makefiles

```
OpenACC/StreamTriad/CMakeLists.txt
 8 if (NOT CMAKE_OPENACC_VERBOSE)
 9     set(CMAKE_OPENACC_VERBOSE true)
10 endif (NOT CMAKE_OPENACC_VERBOSE)
11
12 if (CMAKE_C_COMPILER_ID MATCHES "PGI")
13     set(CMAKE_C_FLAGS "${CMAKE_C_FLAGS} -alias=ansi")
14 elseif (CMAKE_C_COMPILER_ID MATCHES "GNU")
15     set(CMAKE_C_FLAGS "${CMAKE_C_FLAGS} -fstrict-aliasing")
16 endif (CMAKE_C_COMPILER_ID MATCHES "PGI")
17
18 find_package(OpenACC)          ◁─┤ CMake module sets compiler
19                                   │ flags for OpenACC
20 if (CMAKE_C_COMPILER_ID MATCHES "PGI")
21     set(OpenACC_C_VERBOSE "${OpenACC_C_VERBOSE} -Minfo=accel")
22 elseif (CMAKE_C_COMPILER_ID MATCHES "GNU")
23     set(OpenACC_C_VERBOSE
            "${OpenACC_C_VERBOSE} -fopt-info-optimized-omp")
24 endif (CMAKE_C_COMPILER_ID MATCHES "PGI")
25
26 if (CMAKE_OPENACC_VERBOSE)               ─┐ Adds compiler feedback
27   set(OpenACC_C_FLAGS                      │ for accelerator
        "${OpenACC_C_FLAGS} ${OpenACC_C_VERBOSE}")  │ directives
28 endif (CMAKE_OPENACC_VERBOSE)           ─┘
29
     < ... skipping first target ... >
33 # Adds build target of stream_triad with source code files
34 add_executable(StreamTriad_par1 StreamTriad_par1.c timer.c timer.h)
35 set_source_files_properties(StreamTriad_par1.c PROPERTIES COMPILE_FLAGS
─▷    "${OpenACC_C_FLAGS}")
36 set_target_properties(StreamTriad_par1 PROPERTIES LINK_FLAGS
─▷    "${OpenACC_C_FLAGS}")
```

Adds OpenACC flags to compile and link stream triad source

The simple makefiles can also be used for building the example codes by copying or linking these over to a Makefile by using either of these commands:

```
ln -s Makefile.simple.pgi Makefile
cp Makefile.simple.pgi Makefile
```

From the makefiles for the PGI and GCC compilers, we show the suggested flags for OpenACC:

```
Makefile.simple.pgi
 6 CFLAGS:= -g -O3 -c99 -alias=ansi -Mpreprocess -acc -Mcuda -Minfo=accel
 7
```

```
 8 %.o: %.c
 9    ${CC} ${CFLAGS} -c $^
10
11 StreamTriad: StreamTriad.o timer.o
12    ${CC} ${CFLAGS} $^ -o StreamTriad
```

```
Makefile.simple.gcc
 6 CFLAGS:= -g -O3 -std=gnu99 -fstrict-aliasing -fopenacc \
                             -fopt-info-optimized-omp
 7
 8 %.o: %.c
 9    ${CC} ${CFLAGS} -c $^
10
11 StreamTriad: StreamTriad.o timer.o
12    ${CC} ${CFLAGS} $^ -o StreamTriad
```

For PGI, the flags to enable OpenACC compilation for GCC are -acc -Mcuda. The Minfo=accel flag tells the compiler to provide feedback on accelerator directives. We also include the -alias=ansi flag to tell the compiler to be less concerned about pointer aliasing so that it can more freely generate parallel kernels. It is still a good idea to include the restrict attribute on arguments in your source code to tell the compiler that variables do not point to overlapping regions of memory. We also include a flag in both makefiles to set the C 1999 standard so that we can define loop index variables in a loop for clearer scoping. The -fopenacc flag turns on the parsing of the OpenACC directives for GCC. The -fopt-info-optimized-omp flag tells the compiler to provide feedback for code generation for the accelerator.

For the Cray compiler, OpenACC is on by default. You can use the compiler option -hnoacc if you need to turn it off. And the OpenACC compilers must define the _OPENACC macro. The macro is particularly important because OpenACC is still in the process of being implemented by many compilers. You can use it to tell what version of OpenACC your compiler supports and to implement conditional compilations for newer features by comparing against the compiler macro _OPENACC == yyyymm, where the version dates are

- Version 1.0: 201111
- Version 2.0: 201306
- Version 2.5: 201510
- Version 2.6: 201711
- Version 2.7: 201811
- Version 3.0: 201911

11.2.2 *Parallel compute regions in OpenACC for accelerating computations*

There are two different options for declaring an accelerated block of code for computations. The first is the kernels pragma that gives the compiler freedom to auto-parallelize the code block. This code block can include larger sections of code with several loops.

The second is the `parallel loop` pragma that tells the compiler to generate code for the GPU or other accelerator device. We'll go over examples of each approach.

USING THE KERNELS PRAGMA TO GET AUTO-PARALLELIZATION FROM THE COMPILER

The `kernels` pragma allows auto-parallelization of a code block by the compiler. It is often used first to get feedback from the compiler on a section of code. We'll cover the formal syntax for the `kernels` pragma, including its optional clauses. Then we'll look at the stream triad example we used in all of our programming chapters and apply the `kernels` pragma. First, we'll list the specification for the `kernels` pragma from the OpenACC 2.6 standard:

```
#pragma acc kernels [ data clause | kernel optimization | async clause |
                      conditional ]
```

where

```
data clauses - [ copy | copyin | copyout | create | no_create |
                 present | deviceptr | attach | default(none|present) ]
kernel optimization - [ num_gangs | num_workers | vector_length |
                        device_type | self ]
async clauses - [ async | wait ]
conditional - [ if ]
```

We'll discuss the data clauses in more detail in section 11.2.3, although you can also use the data clauses in the `kernel` pragma if these only apply to a single loop. We'll cover the kernel optimizations in section 11.2.4. And we'll briefly mention the async and conditional clauses in section 11.2.5.

We first start by specifying where we want the work to be parallelized by adding `#pragma acc kernels` around the targeted blocks of code. The `kernels` pragma applies to the code block following the directive or for the code in the next listing, the `for` loop.

> **Listing 11.2   Adding the `kernels` pragma**

```
OpenACC/StreamTriad/StreamTriad_kern1.c
 1 #include <stdio.h>
 2 #include <stdlib.h>
 3 #include "timer.h"
 4
 5 int main(int argc, char *argv[]){
 6
 7    int nsize = 20000000, ntimes=16;
 8    double* a = malloc(nsize * sizeof(double));
 9    double* b = malloc(nsize * sizeof(double));
10    double* c = malloc(nsize * sizeof(double));
11
12    struct timespec tstart;
13    // initializing data and arrays
14    double scalar = 3.0, time_sum = 0.0;          Inserts OpenACC
15 #pragma acc kernels                        ◁──┘  kernels pragma
```

```
16    for (int i=0; i<nsize; i++) {
17        a[i] = 1.0;
18        b[i] = 2.0;
19    }
20
21    for (int k=0; k<ntimes; k++){
22        cpu_timer_start(&tstart);
23        // stream triad loop
24 #pragma acc kernels
25        for (int i=0; i<nsize; i++){
26            c[i] = a[i] + scalar*b[i];
27        }
28        time_sum += cpu_timer_stop(tstart);
29    }
30
31    printf("Average runtime for stream triad loop is %lf msecs\n",
             time_sum/ntimes);
32
33    free(a);
34    free(b);
35    free(c);
36
37    return(0);
38 }
```

Inserts OpenACC kernels pragma → (points to line 24)

Code block for kernels pragma

The following output shows the feedback from the PGI compiler:

```
main:
    15, Generating implicit copyout(b[:20000000],a[:20000000])
        [if not already present]
    16, Loop is parallelizable
        Generating Tesla code
        16, #pragma acc loop gang, vector(128)
            /* blockIdx.x threadIdx.x */
    16, Complex loop carried dependence of a-> prevents parallelization
        Loop carried dependence of b-> prevents parallelization
    24, Generating implicit copyout(c[:20000000]) [if not already present]
        Generating implicit copyin(b[:20000000],a[:20000000])
        [if not already present]
    25, Complex loop carried dependence of a->,b-> prevents
        parallelization
        Loop carried dependence of c-> prevents parallelization
        Loop carried backward dependence of c-> prevents vectorization
        Accelerator serial kernel generated
        Generating Tesla code
        25, #pragma acc loop seq
    25, Complex loop carried dependence of b-> prevents parallelization
        Loop carried backward dependence of c-> prevents vectorization
```

What isn't clear in this listing is that OpenACC treats each for loop as if it has a #pragma acc loop auto in front of it. We have left the decision to the compiler to decide whether it could parallelize the loop. The output in bold indicates that the compiler doesn't think it can. The compiler is telling us it needs help. The simplest fix is to add a `restrict` attribute to lines 8-10 in listing 11.2.

```
 8    double* restrict a = malloc(nsize * sizeof(double));
 9    double* restrict b = malloc(nsize * sizeof(double));
10    double* restrict c = malloc(nsize * sizeof(double));
```

Our second choice for a fix to help the compiler is to change the directive to tell the compiler it is Ok to generate parallel GPU code. The problem is the default `loop` directive (`loop auto`), which we mentioned earlier. Here is the specification from the OpenACC 2.6 standard:

```
#pragma acc loop [ auto | independent | seq | collapse | gang | worker |
                   vector | tile | device_type | private | reduction ]
```

We cover many of these clauses in later sections. For now, we'll focus on the first three: auto, independent, and seq.

- auto lets the compiler do the analysis.
- seq, short for sequential, says to generate a sequential version.
- independent asserts that the loop can and should be parallelized.

Changing the clause from `auto` to `independent` tells the compiler to parallelize the loop:

```
15 #pragma acc kernels loop independent
   <Skipping unchanged code>
24 #pragma acc kernels loop independent
```

Note that we have combined the two constructs in these directives. You can combine valid individual clauses into a single directive, if you like. Now the output shows that the loop is parallelized:

```
main:
      15, Generating implicit copyout(a[:20000000],b[:20000000])
          [if not already present]
      16, Loop is parallelizable
          Generating Tesla code
          16, #pragma acc loop gang, vector(128)
             /* blockIdx.x threadIdx.x */
      24, Generating implicit copyout(c[:20000000]) [if not already present]
          Generating implicit copyin(b[:20000000],a[:20000000])
          [if not already present]
      25, Loop is parallelizable
          Generating Tesla code
          25, #pragma acc loop gang, vector(128)
             /* blockIdx.x threadIdx.x */
```

The important thing to note in this output is the feedback about data transfers (in bold). We'll discuss how to address this feedback in section 11.2.3.

TRY THE PARALLEL LOOP PRAGMA FOR MORE CONTROL OVER PARALLELIZATION

Next we'll cover how to use the parallel loop pragma. This is the technique we recommend that you use in your application. It is more consistent with the form used in other parallel languages such as OpenMP. It also generates more consistent and portable performance across compilers. Not all compilers can be counted on to perform an adequate job of analysis required by the kernels directive.

The parallel loop pragma is actually two separate directives. The first is the parallel directive that opens a parallel region. The second is the loop pragma that distributes the work across the parallel work elements. We'll look at the parallel pragma first. The parallel pragma takes the same clauses as the kernel directive. In the following example, we bolded the additional clauses for the kernel directive:

```
#pragma acc parallel [ clause ]
    data clauses - [ reduction | private | firstprivate | copy |
                    copyin | copyout | create | no_create | present |
                    deviceptr | attach | default(none|present) ]
    kernel optimization - [ num_gangs | num_workers |
                            vector_length | device_type | self ]
    async clauses - [ async | wait ]
    conditional - [ if ]
```

The clauses for the loop construct were mentioned earlier in the kernels section. The important thing to note is that the default for the loop construct in a parallel region is independent rather than auto. Again, as in the kernels directive, the combined parallel loop construct can take any clause that the individual directives can. With this explanation of the parallel loop construct, we move on to how it is added to the stream triad example as shown in the following listing.

Listing 11.3 Adding a parallel loop pragma

```
OpenACC/StreamTriad/StreamTriad_par1.c
12    struct timespec tstart;
13    // initializing data and arrays
14    double scalar = 3.0, time_sum = 0.0;
15 #pragma acc parallel loop
16    for (int i=0; i<nsize; i++) {
17        a[i] = 1.0;
18        b[i] = 2.0;             Inserts the
19    }                          parallel loop
20                               combined
21    for (int k=0; k<ntimes; k++){   construct
22        cpu_timer_start(&tstart);
23        // stream triad loop
24 #pragma acc parallel loop
25        for (int i=0; i<nsize; i++){
26            c[i] = a[i] + scalar*b[i];
27        }
28        time_sum += cpu_timer_stop(tstart);
29    }
```

The output from the PGI compiler is

```
main:
     15, Generating Tesla code
         16, #pragma acc loop gang, vector(128)
             /* blockIdx.x threadIdx.x */
     15, Generating implicit copyout(a[:20000000],b[:20000000])
         [if not already present]
     24, Generating Tesla code
         25, #pragma acc loop gang, vector(128)
             /* blockIdx.x threadIdx.x */
     24, Generating implicit copyout(c[:20000000]) [if not already present]
         Generating implicit copyin(b[:20000000],a[:20000000])
         [if not already present]
```

Even without the `restrict` attribute, the loop is parallelized because the default for the `loop` directive is the `independent` clause. This is different than the default for the `kernels` directive that we saw previously. Still, we recommend that you use the `restrict` attribute in your code to help the compiler generate the best code.

The output is similar to that from the previous `kernels` directive. At this point, the performance of the code will likely have slowed down due to the data movement we have shown in bold in this compiler output. Not to worry; we will speed it back up in the next step.

Before we move on to addressing the data movement, we'll take a quick look at reductions and the `serial` construct. Listing 11.4 shows the mass sum example first introduced in section 6.3.3. The mass sum is a simple reduction operation. Instead of the OpenMP SIMD vectorization pragma, we placed an OpenACC `parallel loop` pragma with the `reduction` clause before the loop. The syntax of the reduction is familiar because it is the same as was used by the threaded OpenMP standard.

Listing 11.4   Adding a `reduction` clause

```
OpenACC/mass_sum/mass_sum.c
 1 #include "mass_sum.h"
 2 #define REAL_CELL 1
 3
 4 double mass_sum(int ncells, int* restrict celltype,
 5                 double* restrict H, double* restrict dx,
                   double* restrict dy){
 6    double summer = 0.0;
 7 #pragma acc parallel loop reduction(+:summer)      ⟵——  Adds a reduction
 8    for (int ic=0; ic<ncells ; ic++) {                     clause to a parallel
 9        if (celltype[ic] == REAL_CELL) {                   loop construct
10            summer += H[ic]*dx[ic]*dy[ic];
11        }
12    }
13    return(summer);
14 }
```

There are other operators that you can use in a reduction clause. These include *, max, min, &, |, &&, and ||. For OpenACC versions up to 2.6, the variable or list of variables separated by commas are limited to scalars and not arrays. But OpenACC version 2.7 lets you use arrays and composite variables in the reduction clause.

The last construct we'll cover in this section is the one for serial work. Some loops cannot be done in parallel. Rather than exit the parallel region, we stay within it and tell the compiler to just do this one part in serial. This is done with the serial directive:

```
#pragma acc serial
```

Blocks of this code with the serial directive are executed by one gang of one worker with a vector length of one. Now, let's turn our attention to addressing the data movement feedback.

11.2.3 *Using directives to reduce data movement between the CPU and the GPU*

This section returns to a theme we have seen throughout this book. Data movement is more important than flops. Although we have sped up the computations by moving these to the GPU, the overall run time has slowed because of the cost of data movement. Addressing the excessive data movement will start yielding an overall speedup. To do this, we add the data construct to our code. In the OpenACC standard, v2.6, the specification for the data construct is as follows:

```
#pragma acc data [ copy | copyin | copyout | create | no_create | present |
                   deviceptr | attach | default(none|present) ]
```

You will also see references to clauses like present_or_copy or the shorthand pcopy that check for the presence of the data before making the copy. These are no longer necessary, though they are retained for backward compatibility. The standard clauses have incorporated this behavior beginning with version 2.5 of the OpenACC standard.

Many of the data clauses take an argument that lists the data to be copied or otherwise manipulated. The range specification for the array needs to be given to the compiler. An example of this is

```
#pragma acc data copy(x[0:nsize])
```

The range specification is subtly different for C/C++ and Fortran. In C/C++, the first argument in the specification is the start index, and the second is the length. In Fortran, the first argument is the start index, and the second argument is the end index.

There are two varieties of data regions. The first is the structured data region from the original OpenACC version 1.0 standard. The second, a dynamic data region, was introduced in version 2.0 of OpenACC. We'll look at the structured data region first.

STRUCTURED DATA REGION FOR SIMPLE BLOCKS OF CODE

The structured data region is delimited by a code block. This can be a natural code block formed by a loop or a region of code contained within a set of curly braces. In Fortran, the region is marked with a starting directive and ends with an ending directive. Listing 11.5 shows an example of a structured data region that starts with the directive on line 16 and is delimited by the opening brace on line 17 and the ending brace on line 37. We have included a comment on the ending brace in the code to help identify the block of code that the brace ends.

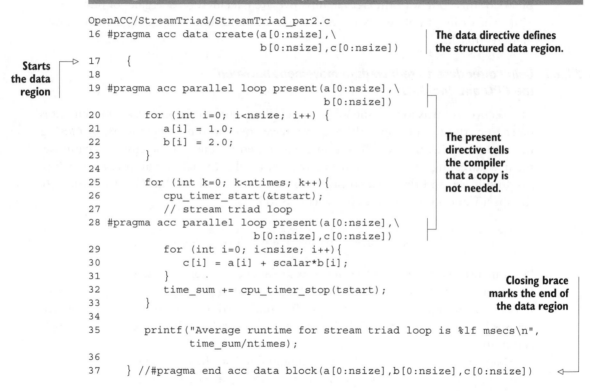

Listing 11.5   Structured data block pragma

```
OpenACC/StreamTriad/StreamTriad_par2.c
16 #pragma acc data create(a[0:nsize],\
                           b[0:nsize],c[0:nsize])
17    {
18
19 #pragma acc parallel loop present(a[0:nsize],\
                              b[0:nsize])
20       for (int i=0; i<nsize; i++) {
21          a[i] = 1.0;
22          b[i] = 2.0;
23       }
24
25       for (int k=0; k<ntimes; k++){
26          cpu_timer_start(&tstart);
27          // stream triad loop
28 #pragma acc parallel loop present(a[0:nsize],\
                              b[0:nsize],c[0:nsize])
29          for (int i=0; i<nsize; i++){
30             c[i] = a[i] + scalar*b[i];
31          }
32          time_sum += cpu_timer_stop(tstart);
33       }
34
35       printf("Average runtime for stream triad loop is %lf msecs\n",
                 time_sum/ntimes);
36
37    } //#pragma end acc data block(a[0:nsize],b[0:nsize],c[0:nsize])
```

Starts the data region

The data directive defines the structured data region.

The present directive tells the compiler that a copy is not needed.

Closing brace marks the end of the data region

The structured data region specifies that the three arrays are to be created at the start of the data region. These will be destroyed at the end of the data region. The two parallel loops use the `present` clause to avoid data copies for the compute regions.

DYNAMIC DATA REGION FOR A MORE FLEXIBLE DATA SCOPING

The structured data region, originally used by OpenACC, where memory is allocated and then there are some loops, does not work with more complicated programs. In particular, memory allocations in object-oriented code occur when an object is created. How do you put a data region around something with this kind of program structure?

To address this problem, OpenACC v2.0 added dynamic (also called unstructured) data regions. This dynamic data region construct was specifically created for more complex data management scenarios, such as constructors and destructors in C++. Rather than using scoping braces to define the data region, the pragma has an `enter` and an `exit` clause:

```
#pragma acc enter data
#pragma acc exit data
```

For the `exit data` directive, there is an additional `delete` clause that we can use. This use of the `enter/exit data` directive is best done where allocations and deallocations occur. The `enter data` directive should be placed just after an allocation, and the `exit data` directive should be inserted just before the deallocation. This more naturally follows the existing data scope of variables in an application. Once you want higher performance than what can be achieved from the loop-level strategy, these dynamic data regions become important. With the larger scope of the dynamic data regions, there is a need for an additional directive to update data:

```
#pragma acc update [self(x) | device(x)]
```

The `device` argument specifies that the data on the device is to be updated. The `self` argument says to update the local data, which is usually the host version of the data.

Let's look at an example using a dynamic data pragma in listing 11.6. The `enter data` directive is placed after the allocation at line 12. The `exit data` directive at line 35 is inserted before the deallocations. We suggest using dynamic data regions in preference to structured data regions in almost all but the simplest code.

Listing 11.6   Creating dynamic data regions

```
OpenACC/StreamTriad/StreamTriad_par3.c
8    double* restrict a = malloc(nsize * sizeof(double));
9    double* restrict b = malloc(nsize * sizeof(double));
10   double* restrict c = malloc(nsize * sizeof(double));
11
12 #pragma acc enter data create(a[0:nsize],\          Starts the dynamic data region
                    b[0:nsize],c[0:nsize])              after memory allocation
13
14   struct timespec tstart;
15   // initializing data and arrays
16   double scalar = 3.0, time_sum = 0.0;
17 #pragma acc parallel loop present(a[0:nsize],b[0:nsize])
18   for (int i=0; i<nsize; i++) {
19       a[i] = 1.0;
20       b[i] = 2.0;
21   }
22
23   for (int k=0; k<ntimes; k++){
24       cpu_timer_start(&tstart);
25       // stream triad loop
26 #pragma acc parallel loop present(a[0:nsize],b[0:nsize],c[0:nsize])
27       for (int i=0; i<nsize; i++){
28           c[i] = a[i] + scalar*b[i];
```

```
29        }
30        time_sum += cpu_timer_stop(tstart);
31     }
32
33     printf("Average runtime for stream triad loop is %lf msecs\n",
              time_sum/ntimes);
34
35 #pragma acc exit data delete(a[0:nsize],\.          Ends the dynamic data region
                     b[0:nsize],c[0:nsize])           before memory deallocation
36
37     free(a);
38     free(b);
39     free(c);
```

If you paid close attention to the previous listing, you will have noticed that the arrays a, b, and c are allocated on both the host and the device, but are only used on the device. In listing 11.7, we show one way to fix this by using the acc_malloc routine and then putting the deviceptr clause on the compute regions.

Listing 11.7   Allocating data only on the device

OpenACC/StreamTriad/StreamTriad_par4.c
```
 1 #include <stdio.h>
 2 #include <openacc.h>
 3 #include "timer.h"
 4
 5 int main(int argc, char *argv[]){
 6
 7     int nsize = 20000000, ntimes=16;
 8     double* restrict a_d =
          acc_malloc(nsize * sizeof(double));          Allocates memory
 9     double* restrict b_d =                           on the device. _d
          acc_malloc(nsize * sizeof(double));          indicates a device
10     double* restrict c_d =                           pointer.
          acc_malloc(nsize * sizeof(double));
11
12     struct timespec tstart;
13     // initializing data and arrays
14     const double scalar = 3.0;
15     double time_sum = 0.0;
16 #pragma acc parallel loop deviceptr(a_d, b_d)
17     for (int i=0; i<nsize; i++) {
18        a_d[i] = 1.0;                                  The deviceptr
19        b_d[i] = 2.0;                                  clause tells
20     }                                                 the compiler
21                                                       that memory
22     for (int k=0; k<ntimes; k++){                     is already on
23        cpu_timer_start(&tstart);                      the device.
24        // stream triad loop
25 #pragma acc parallel loop deviceptr(a_d, b_d,
                                       c_d)
26        for (int i=0; i<nsize; i++){
27           c_d[i] = a_d[i] + scalar*b_d[i];
28        }
```

```
29        time_sum += cpu_timer_stop(tstart);
30    }
31
32    printf("Average runtime for stream triad loop is %lf msecs\n",
             time_sum/ntimes);
33
34    acc_free(a_d);          Deallocates memory
35    acc_free(b_d);          on the device
36    acc_free(c_d);
37
38    return(0);
39 }
```

The output from the PGI compiler is now much shorter as shown here:

```
16 Generating Tesla code
17 #pragma acc loop gang, vector(128) /* blockIdx.x threadIdx.x */
25 Generating Tesla code
26 #pragma acc loop gang, vector(128) /* blockIdx.x threadIdx.x */
```

The data movement is eliminated and memory requirements on the host reduced. We still have some output giving feedback on the generated kernel that we will look at in section 11.2.4. This example (listing 11.7) works for 1D arrays. For 2D arrays, the deviceptr clause does not take a descriptor argument, so the kernel has to be changed to do its own 2D indexing in a 1D array.

When referencing data regions, you have available a rich set of data directives and data movement clauses that you can use to reduce unnecessary data movement. Still, there are more clauses and OpenACC functions that we have not covered that can be useful in specialized situations.

11.2.4 *Optimizing the GPU kernels*

Generally, you will have greater impact getting more kernels running on the GPU and reducing the data movement than optimizing the GPU kernels themselves. The OpenACC compiler does a good job at producing the kernels, and the potential gains from further optimizations will be small. Occasionally, you can help the compiler to improve the performance of key kernels enough for that to be worth some effort.

In this section, we'll go over the general strategies for these optimizations. First we'll go over the terminology used in the OpenACC standard. As figure 11.3 shows, OpenACC defines abstract levels of parallelism that apply over multiple hardware devices.

OpenACC defines these levels of parallelism:

- *Gang*—An independent work block that shares resources. A gang can also synchronize within the group but not across the groups. For GPUs, gangs can be mapped to CUDA thread blocks or OpenCL work groups.
- *Workers*—A warp in CUDA or work items within a work group in OpenCL.
- *Vector*—A SIMD vector on the CPU and a SIMT work group or warp on the GPU with contiguous memory references.

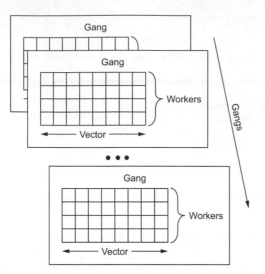
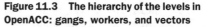

Figure 11.3   The hierarchy of the levels in OpenACC: gangs, workers, and vectors

Some examples of setting the level of a particular loop directive follow:

```
#pragma acc parallel loop vector
#pragma acc parallel loop gang
#pragma acc parallel loop gang vector
```

The outer loop must be a gang loop, and the inner loop should be a vector loop. A worker loop can appear in between. A sequential (seq) loop can appear at any level.

For most current GPUs, the vector length should be set to multiples of 32, so it is an integer multiple of the warp size. It should be no larger than the maximum threads per block, which is commonly around 1,024 on current GPUs (see the output from the pgaccelinfo command in figure 11.2). For the examples here, the PGI compiler sets the vector length to a reasonable value of 128. The value can be changed for a loop with the vector_length(x) directive.

In what scenario should you change the vector_length setting? If the inner loop of contiguous data is less than 128, part of the vector will go unused. In this case, reducing this value can be helpful. Another option would be to collapse a couple of the inner loops to get a longer vector as we will discuss shortly.

You can modify the worker setting with the num_workers clause. For the examples in this chapter, however, it is not used. Even so, it can be useful to increase it when shortening the vector length or for an additional level of parallelization. If your code needs to synchronize within the parallel work group, you should use the worker level, but OpenACC does not provide a user with a synchronization directive. The worker level also shares resources such as cache and local memory.

The rest of the parallelization is done with gangs, which are the asynchronous parallel level. Lots of gangs are important on GPUs to hide latency and for high occupancy. Generally, the compiler sets this to a large number, so there is no need for the user to override it. There is a num_gangs clause available in the remote chance you may need to do this.

Many of these settings will only be appropriate for a particular piece of hardware. The device_type(type) before a clause restricts it to the specified device type. The device type setting stays active until the next device type clause is encountered. For example

```
1 #pragma acc parallel loop gang \
2     device_type(acc_device_nvidia) vector_length(256) \
3     device_type(acc_device_radeon) vector_length(64)
4 for (int j=0; j<jmax; j++){
5         #pragma acc loop vector
6         for (int i=0; i<imax; i++){
7             <work>
8         }
9 }
```

For a list of valid device types, look at the openacc.h header file for PGI v19.7. Note that there is no acc_device_radeon in the lines from the openacc.h header file previously shown, so the PGI compiler does not support the AMD Radeon™ device. This means we need a C preprocessor ifdef around line 3 in the previous sample code to keep the PGI compiler from complaining.

```
Excerpt from openacc.h file for PGI
27 typedef enum{
28     acc_device_none          = 0,
29     acc_device_default       = 1,
30     acc_device_host          = 2,
31     acc_device_not_host      = 3,
32     acc_device_nvidia        = 4,
33     acc_device_pgi_opencl    = 7,
34     acc_device_nvidia_opencl = 8,
35     acc_device_opencl        = 9,
36     acc_device_current       = 10
37     } acc_device_t;
```

The syntax for the kernels directive is slightly different, with the parallel type applied to each loop directive individually and taking the int argument directly:

```
#pragma acc kernels loop gang
for (int j=0; j<jmax; j++){
        #pragma acc loop vector(64)
        for (int i=0; i<imax; i++){
            <work>
        }
}
```

Loops can be combined with the collapse(n) clause. This is especially useful if there are two small inner loops contiguously striding through data. Combining these allows you to use a longer vector length. The loops must be tightly nested.

DEFINITION   Two or more loops that have no extra statements between the for or do statements or between the end of the loops are *tightly-nested loops*.

An example of combining two loops in order to use a long vector is

```
#pragma acc parallel loop collapse(2) vector(32)
for (int j=0; j<8; j++){
      for (int i=0; i<4; i++){
         <work>
      }
}
```

OpenACC v2.0 added a tile clause that you can use for optimization. You can either specify the tile size or use asterisks to let the compiler choose:

```
#pragma acc parallel loop tile(*,*)
for (int j=0; j<jmax; j++){
      for (int i=0; i<imax; i++){
         <work>
      }
}
```

Now it is time to try out the various kernel optimizations. The stream triad example did not show any real benefits from our optimization attempts, so we will work with the stencil example used in many of the previous chapters.

The associated code for the stencil example for this chapter goes through the same first two steps of moving the computational loops to the GPU and then reducing the data movement. The stencil code also requires one additional change. On the CPU, we swap pointers at the end of the loop. On the GPU, in lines 45–50, we have to copy the new data back to the original array. The following listing takes up the stencil code example with these steps completed.

Listing 11.8   Stencil example with compute loops on the GPU and data motion optimized

```
OpenACC/Stencil/Stencil_par3.c
17 #pragma acc enter data create( \                    | Dynamic data
      x[0:jmax][0:imax], xnew[0:jmax][0:imax])         | region directives
18
19 #pragma acc parallel loop present( \
      x[0:jmax][0:imax], xnew[0:jmax][0:imax])
20    for (int j = 0; j < jmax; j++){
21       for (int i = 0; i < imax; i++){
22          xnew[j][i] = 0.0;                           Compute
23          x[j][i]    = 5.0;                            region
24       }                                               directives
25    }
26
27 #pragma acc parallel loop present( \
      x[0:jmax][0:imax], xnew[0:jmax][0:imax])
28    for (int j = jmax/2 - 5; j < jmax/2 + 5; j++){
29       for (int i = imax/2 - 5; i < imax/2 -1; i++){
```

```
30              x[j][i] = 400.0;
31          }
32      }
33
34      for (int iter = 0; iter < niter; iter+=nburst){
35
36          for (int ib = 0; ib < nburst; ib++){
37              cpu_timer_start(&tstart_cpu);
38 #pragma acc parallel loop present( \
            x[0:jmax][0:imax], xnew[0:jmax][0:imax])
39              for (int j = 1; j < jmax-1; j++){
40                  for (int i = 1; i < imax-1; i++){
41                      xnew[j][i]=(x[j][i]+x[j][i-1]+x[j][i+1]+
                                    x[j-1][i]+x[j+1][i])/5.0;
42                  }
43              }
44
45 #pragma acc parallel loop present( \
            x[0:jmax][0:imax], xnew[0:jmax][0:imax])
46              for (int j = 0; j < jmax; j++){
47                  for (int i = 0; i < imax; i++){
48                      x[j][i] = xnew[j][i];
49                  }
50              }
51              cpu_time += cpu_timer_stop(tstart_cpu);
52          }
53
54          printf("Iter %d\n",iter+nburst);
55      }
56
57 #pragma acc exit data delete( \
            x[0:jmax][0:imax], xnew[0:jmax][0:imax])
```

Compute region directives (annotation for lines 38–45)

Dynamic data region directives (annotation for line 57)

First, note that we are using the dynamic data region directives, so there are no braces wrapping the data region as we would see with the structured data region. The dynamic region begins the data region when it encounters the enter directive and ends when it reaches an exit directive, no matter what path occurs between the two directives. In this case, it is a straight line of execution from the enter to the exit directive. We'll add the collapse clause to the parallel loop to reduce the overhead for the two loops. The following listing shows this change.

Listing 11.9 Stencil example with a collapse clause

```
OpenACC/Stencil/Stencil_par4.c
36          for (int ib = 0; ib < nburst; ib++){
37              cpu_timer_start(&tstart_cpu);
38 #pragma acc parallel loop collapse(2)\
39          present(x[0:jmax][0:imax], xnew[0:jmax][0:imax])
40              for (int j = 1; j < jmax-1; j++){
41                  for (int i = 1; i < imax-1; i++){
42                      xnew[j][i]=(x[j][i]+x[j][i-1]+x[j][i+1]+
                                    x[j-1][i]+x[j+1][i])/5.0;
43                  }
```

Adds the collapse clause to the parallel loop directive (annotation for line 38)

```
44              }
45 #pragma acc parallel loop collapse(2)\
46      present(x[0:jmax][0:imax], xnew[0:jmax][0:imax])
47          for (int j = 0; j < jmax; j++){
48              for (int i = 0; i < imax; i++){
49                  x[j][i] = xnew[j][i];
50              }
51          }
52          cpu_time += cpu_timer_stop(tstart_cpu);
53
54      }
```

We can also try using the `tile` clause. We start out by letting the compiler determine the tile size as shown in lines 41 and 48 in the following listing.

Listing 11.10   Stencil example with a `tile` clause

```
OpenACC/Stencil/Stencil_par5.c
39          for (int ib = 0; ib < nburst; ib++){
40              cpu_timer_start(&tstart_cpu);
41 #pragma acc parallel loop tile(*,*) \        ◄─────   Adds the tile clause to the
42      present(x[0:jmax][0:imax], xnew[0:jmax][0:imax])        parallel loop directive
43          for (int j = 1; j < jmax-1; j++){
44              for (int i = 1; i < imax-1; i++){
45                  xnew[j][i]=(x[j][i]+x[j][i-1]+x[j][i+1]+
46                                      x[j-1][i]+x[j+1][i])/5.0;
46              }
47          }
48 #pragma acc parallel loop tile(*,*) \
49      present(x[0:jmax][0:imax], xnew[0:jmax][0:imax])
50          for (int j = 0; j < jmax; j++){
51              for (int i = 0; i < imax; i++){
52                  x[j][i] = xnew[j][i];
53              }
54          }
55          cpu_time += cpu_timer_stop(tstart_cpu);
56
57      }
```

The change in the run times from these optimizations is small relative to the improvement seen from the initial OpenACC implementation. Table 11.1 shows the results for the NVIDIA V100 GPU with the PGI compiler v19.7.

Table 11.1   Run times for the OpenACC stencil kernel optimizations

	OpenACC stencil kernel run time (secs)
Serial CPU code	5.237
Adding compute and data regions	0.818
Adding `collapse(2)` clause	0.802
Adding `tile(*,*)` clause	0.806

We tried changing the vector length to 64 or 256 and different tile sizes, but didn't see any improvement in the run times. More complex code can find more benefit from kernel optimizations, but note that any specialization of parameters such as vector length impacts portability by compilers for different architectures.

Another target for optimization is to implement a pointer swap at the end of the loop. The pointer swap is used in the original CPU code as a fast way to get data back to the original array. The copy of the data back to the original array doubles the run time on the GPU. The difficulty in pragma-based languages is that the pointer swap in a parallel region requires swapping both the host and the device pointers at the same time.

11.2.5 Summary of performance results for the stream triad

The run-time performance during the conversion to the GPU shows the typical pattern. Moving the computational kernels over to the GPU results in a slow down by about a factor of 3 as shown by the kernel 2 and parallel 1 implementations in table 11.2. In the kernel 1 case, the computational loop fails to parallelize. Running sequentially on the GPU, it was even slower. Once the data movement was reduced in kernel 3 and parallel 2–4, the run times showed a 67x speedup. The particular type of data region didn't matter so much for performance, but might be important to enable ports of additional loops in more complex codes.

Table 11.2 Run times from OpenACC stream triad kernel optimizations

	OpenACC stream triad kernel run time (ms)
Serial CPU code	39.6
Kernel 1. Fails to parallelize loop	1771
Kernel 2. Adds compute region	118.5
Kernel 3. Adds dynamic data region	0.590
Parallel 1. Adds compute region	118.8
Parallel 2. Adds structured data region	0.589
Parallel 3. Adds dynamic data region	0.590
Parallel 4. Allocates data only on device	0.586

11.2.6 Advanced OpenACC techniques

Many other features in OpenACC are available to handle more complex code. We'll cover these briefly so you know what capabilities are available.

HANDLING FUNCTIONS WITH THE OPENACC ROUTINE DIRECTIVE

OpenACC v1.0 required functions for use in kernels to be inlined. Version 2.0 added the `routine` directive with two different versions to make calling routines simpler. The two versions are

```
#pragma acc routine [gang | worker | vector | seq | bind | no_host |
                device_type]
#pragma acc routine(name)  [gang | worker | vector | seq | bind | no_host |
                device_type]
```

In C and C++, the `routine` directive should appear immediately before a function prototype or definition. The named version can appear anywhere before the function is defined or used. The Fortran version should include the `!#acc routine` directive within the function body itself or in the interface body.

AVOIDING RACE CONDITIONS WITH OPENACC ATOMICS

Many threaded routines have a shared variable that has to be updated by multiple threads. This programming construct is both a common performance bottleneck and a potential race condition. To handle this situation, OpenACC v2 provides atomics to allow only one thread to access a storage location at a time. The syntax and valid clauses for the atomic directive are

```
#pragma acc atomic [read | write | update | capture]
```

If you don't specify a clause, the default is an `update`. An example of the use of the atomic clause is

```
#pragma acc atomic
cnt++;
```

ASYNCHRONOUS OPERATIONS IN OPENACC

Overlapping OpenACC operations can help improve performance. The proper term for overlapping operations is *asynchronous*. OpenACC provides these asynchronous operations with the `async` and `wait` clauses and directives. The `async` clause is added to a work or data directive with an optional integer argument:

```
#pragma acc parallel loop async([<integer>])
```

The `wait` can be either a directive or a clause added to a work or data directive. The following pseudo-code in listing 11.11 shows how you can use this to launch the calculations on the x-faces and y-faces of a computational mesh and then wait for the results to update the cell values for the next iteration.

Listing 11.11 Async wait example in OpenACC

```
for (int n = 0; n < ntimes; ) {
   #pragma acc parallel loop async
     <x face pass>
```

```
#pragma acc parallel loop async
    <y face pass>
#pragma acc wait
#pragma acc parallel loop
    <Update cell values from face fluxes>
}
```

UNIFIED MEMORY TO AVOID MANAGING DATA MOVEMENT

Although unified memory is not currently part of the OpenACC standard, there are experimental developments with having the system manage memory movement. Such an experimental implementation of unified memory is available in CUDA and the PGI OpenACC compiler. Using the `-ta=tesla:managed` flag with the PGI compiler and recent NVIDIA GPUs, you can try out their unified memory implementation. While the coding is simplified, the performance impacts are still not known and will change as the compilers mature.

INTEROPERABILITY WITH CUDA LIBRARIES OR KERNELS

OpenACC provides several directives and functions to make it possible to interoperate with CUDA libraries. In calling libraries, it is necessary to tell the compiler to use the device pointers instead of host data. The `host_data` directive can be used for this purpose:

```
#pragma acc host_data use_device(x, y)
cublasDaxpy(n, 2.0, x, 1, y, 1);
```

We showed a similar example when we allocated memory using `acc_malloc` in listing 11.7. With `acc_malloc` or `cudaMalloc`, the pointer returned is already on the device. For this case, we used the `deviceptr` clause to pass the pointer to the data region.

One of the most common mistakes in programming GPUs in any language is confusing a device pointer and a host pointer. Try finding 86 Pike Place, San Francisco, when it is really 86 Pike Place, Seattle. The device pointer points to a different physical block of memory on the GPU hardware.

Figure 11.4 shows the three different operations we have covered to help you understand the differences. In the first case, the `malloc` routine returns a host pointer. The

Operation in host code	Host		Device	
malloc present(x_host)	x_host └─(dev *)x_host ──→ x_dev			x_dev
acc_malloc, cudaMalloc deviceptr(x_dev)	x_dev └─────────────→ x_dev			x_dev
host_data use_device(x_dev) dev_function(x_dev)	x_dev ◄───┐ x_dev └────────→ x_dev			x_dev
	host ptr	dev ptr	host ptr	dev ptr

Figure 11.4 Is it a device pointer or a host pointer? One points to the GPU memory and the other to the CPU memory, respectively. OpenACC keeps a map between arrays in the two address spaces and provides routines for retrieving each.

present clause converts this to a device pointer for the device kernel. In the second case, where we allocate memory on the device with `acc_malloc` or `cudaMalloc`, we are given a device pointer. We use the `deviceptr` clause to send it to the GPU without any changes. In the last case, we don't have a pointer on the host at all. We have to use the `host_data use_device(var)` directive to retrieve the device pointer to the host. This is done so that we have a pointer to send back to the device in the argument list for the device function.

It is good practice to append a `_h` or `_d` to pointers to clarify their valid context. In our examples, all pointers and arrays are assumed to be on the host except for those ending with `_d`, which is for any device pointer.

MANAGING MULTIPLE DEVICES IN OPENACC

Many current HPC systems already have multiple GPUs. We can also foresee that we will get nodes with different accelerators. The ability to manage which device we are using becomes more and more important. OpenACC gives us this capability through the following functions:

- `int acc_get_num_devices(acc_device_t)`
- `acc_set_device_type() / acc_get_device_type()`
- `acc_set_device_num() / acc_get_device_num()`

We have now covered as much of OpenACC as we can in a dozen pages. The skills we've shown you are enough to get you started on an implementation. There is a lot more functionality available in the OpenACC standard, but much of it is for more complex situations or low-level interfaces that are not necessary for entry-level applications.

11.3 OpenMP: The heavyweight champ enters the world of accelerators

The OpenMP accelerator capability is an exciting addition to the traditional threading model. In this section, we show you how to get started with these directives. We'll use the same examples as we did for the OpenACC section 11.2. By the end of this section, you should have some idea of how the two similar languages compare and which might be the better choice for your application.

Where do OpenMP's accelerator directives stand in comparison to OpenACC? The OpenMP implementations are notably less mature at this point, though rapidly improving. The currently available implementations for GPUs are as follows:

- Cray was first with an OpenMP implementation targeting NVIDIA GPUs in 2015. Cray now supports OpenMP v4.5.
- IBM fully supports OpenMP v4.5 on Power 9 processor and NVIDIA GPUs.
- Clang v7.0+ supports OpenMP v4.5 offloads to NVIDIA GPUs.
- GCC v6+ can offload to AMD GPUs; v7+ can offload to NVIDIA GPUs.

The two most mature implementations, Cray and IBM, are available only on their respective systems. Unfortunately, not everyone has access to systems from these vendors, but there are more widely available compilers. Two of these compilers, Clang and GCC, are in the throes of development with marginal versions available now. Look out for new developments with these compilers. The examples in this section use the IBM® XL 16 compiler and CUDA v10.

11.3.1 Compiling OpenMP code

We start with how to set up a build environment and compile an OpenMP code. CMake has an OpenMP module, but it does not have explicit support for the OpenMP accelerator directives. We include an OpenMPAccel module that calls the regular OpenMP module and adds the flags needed for the accelerator. It also checks the OpenMP version that is supported, and if it is not v4.0 or newer, it generates an error. This CMake module is included with the source code for the chapter.

Listing 11.12 shows excerpts from the main CMakeLists.txt file in this chapter. Feedback from most of the OpenMP compilers is weak right now, so setting the `-DCMAKE_OPENMPACCEL` flag for CMake will only have minimal benefit. We'll leverage other tools in these examples to fill in the gap.

Listing 11.12 Excerpts from an OpenMPaccel makefile

```
OpenMP/StreamTriad/CMakeLists.txt
10 if (NOT CMAKE_OPENMPACCEL_VERBOSE)
11     set(CMAKE_OPENMPACCEL_VERBOSE true)
12 endif (NOT CMAKE_OPENMPACCEL_VERBOSE)
13
14 if (CMAKE_C_COMPILER_ID MATCHES "GNU")
15     set(CMAKE_C_FLAGS "${CMAKE_C_FLAGS} -fstrict-aliasing")
16 elseif (CMAKE_C_COMPILER_ID MATCHES "Clang")
17     set(CMAKE_C_FLAGS "${CMAKE_C_FLAGS} -fstrict-aliasing")
18 elseif (CMAKE_C_COMPILER_ID MATCHES "XL")
19     set(CMAKE_C_FLAGS "${CMAKE_C_FLAGS} -qalias=ansi")
20 elseif (CMAKE_C_COMPILER_ID MATCHES "Cray")
21     set(CMAKE_C_FLAGS "${CMAKE_C_FLAGS} -h restrict=a")
22 endif (CMAKE_C_COMPILER_ID MATCHES "GNU")
23
24 find_package(OpenMPAccel)          ◁——  CMake module sets compiler flags
25                                           for OpenMP accelerator devices.
26 if (CMAKE_C_COMPILER_ID MATCHES "XL")
27     set(OpenMPAccel_C_FLAGS
         "${OpenMPAccel_C_FLAGS} -qreport")
28 elseif (CMAKE_C_COMPILER_ID MATCHES "GNU")      Adds compiler feedback
29     set(OpenMPAccel_C_FLAGS                      for accelerator
         "${OpenMPAccel_C_FLAGS} -fopt-info-omp")   directives
30 endif (CMAKE_C_COMPILER_ID MATCHES "XL")
31
32 if (CMAKE_OPENMPACCEL_VERBOSE)
33     set(OpenACC_C_FLAGS "${OpenACC_C_FLAGS} ${OpenACC_C_VERBOSE}")
34 endif (CMAKE_OPENMPACCEL_VERBOSE)
35
36 # Adds build target of stream_triad_par1 with source code files
37 add_executable(StreamTriad_par1 StreamTriad_par1.c timer.c timer.h)
```

```
38 set_target_properties(StreamTriad_par1 PROPERTIES
                         COMPILE_FLAGS ${OpenMPAccel_C_FLAGS})      ◁─┐
39 set_target_properties(StreamTriad_par1 PROPERTIES
                         LINK_FLAGS "${OpenMPAccel_C_FLAGS}")       ◁─┤
```

**Adds OpenMP accelerator flags for
compiling and linking of stream triad**

The simple makefile can also be used for building the example codes by copying or linking these over to Makefile with either of the following:

```
ln -s Makefile.simple.xl Makefile
cp Makefile.simple.xl Makefile
```

The following code snippet shows the suggested flags for the OpenMP accelerator directives in the simple makefiles for the IBM XL and GCC compilers:

```
Makefile.simple.xl
 6 CFLAGS:=-qthreaded -g -O3 -std=gnu99 -qalias=ansi -qhot -qsmp=omp \
         -qoffload -qreport
 7
 8 %.o: %.c
 9   ${CC} ${CFLAGS} -c $^
10
11 StreamTriad: StreamTriad.o timer.o
12   ${CC} ${CFLAGS} $^ -o StreamTriad

Makefile.simple.gcc
 6 CFLAGS:= -g -O3 -std=gnu99 -fstrict-aliasing \
 7           -fopenmp -foffload=nvptx-none -foffload=-lm -fopt-info-omp
 8
 9 %.o: %.c
10   ${CC} ${CFLAGS} -c $^
11
12 StreamTriad: StreamTriad.o timer.o
13   ${CC} ${CFLAGS} $^ -o StreamTriad
```

11.3.2 *Generating parallel work on the GPU with OpenMP*

Now we need to generate parallel work on the GPU. The OpenMP device parallel abstractions are more complicated than we saw with OpenACC. But this can also provide more flexibility in scheduling work in the future. For now, you should preface each loop with this directive:

```
#pragma omp target teams distribute parallel for simd
```

This is a long, confusing directive. Let's go over each of the parts as illustrated in figure 11.5. The first three clauses specify hardware resources:

- `target` gets onto the device
- `teams` creates a league of teams
- `distribute` spreads work out to teams

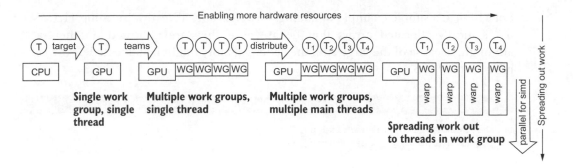

Figure 11.5 The `target`, `teams`, and `distribute` directives enable more hardware resources. The `parallel for simd` directive spreads out the work within each workgroup.

The remaining three are the parallel work clauses. All three clauses are necessary for portability. This is because the implementations by compilers spread out the work in different manners.

- `parallel` replicates work on each thread
- `for` spreads work out within each team
- `simd` spreads work out to threads (GCC)

For kernels with three nested loops, one way you can spread out the work is with the following:

```
k loop: #pragma omp target teams distribute
j loop: #pragma omp parallel for
i loop: #pragma omp simd
```

Each OpenMP compiler can spread out the work differently, thus requiring some variants of this scheme. The `simd` loop should be the inner loop across contiguous memory locations. Some simplification of this complexity is being introduced with the `loop` clause in OpenMP v5.0 as we will present in section 11.3.5. You can also add clauses to this directive:

```
private, firstprivate, lastprivate, shared, reduction, collapse,
        dist_schedule
```

Many of these clauses are familiar from OpenACC and behave the same way. One of the major differences from OpenACC is the default way that data is handled when entering a parallel work region. OpenACC compilers generally move all necessary arrays to the device. For OpenMP, there are two possibilities:

- Scalars and statically allocated arrays are moved onto the device by default before execution.
- Data allocated on the heap needs to be explicitly copied to and from the device.

Let's look at a simple example of adding a parallel work directive in listing 11.13. We use statically allocated arrays that behave as if they are allocated on the stack; although, because of the large size, the actual memory might be allocated by the compiler on the heap.

Listing 11.13   Adding OpenMP pragmas to parallelize work on the GPU

```
OpenMP/StreamTriad/StreamTriad_par1.c
 6 int main(int argc, char *argv[]){
 7
 8    int nsize = 20000000, ntimes=16;
 9    double a[nsize];                          Allocating
10    double b[nsize];                          static arrays
11    double c[nsize];                          on the host
12
13    struct timespec tstart;
14    // initializing data and arrays
15    double scalar = 3.0, time_sum = 0.0;
16 #pragma omp target teams distribute parallel for simd
17    for (int i=0; i<nsize; i++) {
18       a[i] = 1.0;
19       b[i] = 2.0;
20    }
21
22    for (int k=0; k<ntimes; k++){
23       cpu_timer_start(&tstart);
24       // stream triad loop
25 #pragma omp target teams distribute parallel for simd
26       for (int i=0; i<nsize; i++){
27          c[i] = a[i] + scalar*b[i];
28       }
29       time_sum += cpu_timer_stop(tstart);
30    }
31
32    printf("Average runtime for stream triad loop is %lf secs\n",
              time_sum/ntimes);
```

The feedback from the IBM XL compiler shows that the two kernels are offloaded to the GPU, but no other information is proffered. GCC gives no feedback at all. The IBM XL output is

```
"" 1586-672 (I) GPU OpenMP Runtime elided for offloaded kernel
              '__xl_main_l15_OL_1'
"" 1586-672 (I) GPU OpenMP Runtime elided for offloaded kernel
              '__xl_main_l23_OL_2'
```

To get some information on what the IBM XL compiler has done, we'll use the NVIDIA profiler:

```
nvprof ./StreamTriad_par1
```

The first part of the output is

```
==141409== Profiling application: ./StreamTriad_par1
==141409== Profiling result:
Time(%)  Time    Calls   Avg       Min       Max      Name
64.11% 554.30ms  7652   72.439us  1.2160us  79.039us  [CUDA memcpy DtoH]
34.79% 300.82ms  7650   39.323us  23.392us  48.767us  [CUDA memcpy HtoD]
 1.06% 9.1479ms    16  571.75us  571.39us  572.32us  __xl_main_123_OL_2
 0.04% 363.07us     1  363.07us  363.07us  363.07us  __xl_main_115_OL_1
```

From this output, we now know that there is a memory copy from the host to the device (`HtoD` in the output) and then back from the device to the host (`DtoH` in the output). The `nvprof` output from GCC is similar but without line numbers. More detail about the order in which the operations occur can be obtained with the following:

```
nvprof --print-gpu-trace ./StreamTriad_par1
```

Most programs are not written with statically allocated arrays. Let's take a look at a more commonly found case where the arrays are dynamically allocated as the following listing shows.

Listing 11.14 Parallel work directive with arrays dynamically allocated

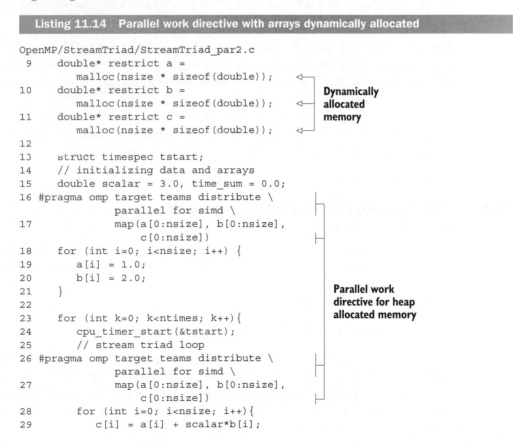

```
OpenMP/StreamTriad/StreamTriad_par2.c
 9    double* restrict a =
          malloc(nsize * sizeof(double));      ◁┐
10    double* restrict b =                       │  Dynamically
          malloc(nsize * sizeof(double));      ◁┤  allocated
11    double* restrict c =                       │  memory
          malloc(nsize * sizeof(double));      ◁┘
12
13    struct timespec tstart;
14    // initializing data and arrays
15    double scalar = 3.0, time_sum = 0.0;
16 #pragma omp target teams distribute \
              parallel for simd \
17            map(a[0:nsize], b[0:nsize],
                  c[0:nsize])
18    for (int i=0; i<nsize; i++) {
19      a[i] = 1.0;
20      b[i] = 2.0;
21    }
22
23    for (int k=0; k<ntimes; k++){
24      cpu_timer_start(&tstart);
25      // stream triad loop
26 #pragma omp target teams distribute \
              parallel for simd \
27            map(a[0:nsize], b[0:nsize],
                  c[0:nsize])
28      for (int i=0; i<nsize; i++){
29          c[i] = a[i] + scalar*b[i];
```

Parallel work directive for heap allocated memory

```
30        }
31        time_sum += cpu_timer_stop(tstart);
32     }
33
34     printf("Average runtime for stream triad loop is %lf secs\n",
                time_sum/ntimes);
35
36     free(a);
37     free(b);
38     free(c);
```

Note that lines 16 and 26 have added the map clause. If you try the directive without this clause, although it compiles fine with the IBM XLC compiler, at run time you'll get this message:

```
1587-164 Encountered a zero-length array section that points to memory
     starting at address 0x200020000010. Because this memory is not currently
     mapped on the target device 0, a NULL pointer will be passed to the
     device.
1587-175 The underlying GPU runtime reported the following error "an illegal
     memory access was encountered".
1587-163 Error encountered while attempting to execute on the target device
     0.  The program will stop.
```

The GCC compiler, however, both compiles and runs fine without the map directive. Thus, the GCC compiler moves heap allocated memory over to the device while IBM XLC does not. For portability, we should include the map clause in our application code.

OpenMP also has the reduction clause for the parallel work-region directives. The syntax is similar to that for the threaded OpenMP work directives and OpenACC. An example of the directive is as follows:

```
#pragma omp teams distribute parallel for simd reduction(+:sum)
```

11.3.3 *Creating data regions to control data movement to the GPU with OpenMP*

Now that we have the work moved over to the GPU, we can add data regions to manage the data movement to and from the GPU. The data movement directives in OpenMP are similar to those in OpenACC with both a structured and dynamic version. The form of the directive is

```
#pragma omp target data [ map() | use_device_ptr() ]
```

The work directives are wrapped in the structured data region as listing 11.15 shows. The data is copied over to the GPU, if not already there. The data is then maintained there until the end of the block (at line 35) and copied back. This greatly reduces the data transfers for every parallel work loop and should result in a net speedup in the overall application run time.

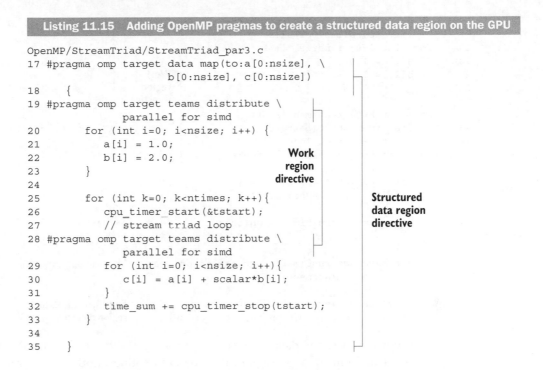

Listing 11.15   Adding OpenMP pragmas to create a structured data region on the GPU

```
OpenMP/StreamTriad/StreamTriad_par3.c
17 #pragma omp target data map(to:a[0:nsize], \
                   b[0:nsize], c[0:nsize])
18    {
19 #pragma omp target teams distribute \
            parallel for simd
20        for (int i=0; i<nsize; i++) {
21            a[i] = 1.0;
22            b[i] = 2.0;
23        }
24
25        for (int k=0; k<ntimes; k++){
26            cpu_timer_start(&tstart);
27            // stream triad loop
28 #pragma omp target teams distribute \
            parallel for simd
29            for (int i=0; i<nsize; i++){
30                c[i] = a[i] + scalar*b[i];
31            }
32            time_sum += cpu_timer_stop(tstart);
33        }
34
35    }
```

Work region directive

Structured data region directive

Structured data regions cannot handle more general-programming patterns. Both OpenACC and OpenMP (version 4.5) added dynamic data regions, often referred to as *unstructured* data regions. The form for the directive has enter and exit clauses with a map modifier to specify the data transfer operation (such as the defaults to and from):

```
#pragma omp target enter data map([alloc | to]:array[[start]:[length]])
#pragma omp target exit data map([from | release | delete]:
                              array[[start]:[length]])
```

In listing 11.16, we convert the omp target data directive to omp target enter data directive (line 13). The scope of the data on the GPU concludes when it encounters an omp target exit data directive (line 36). The effect of these directives is the same as the structured data region in listing 11.15. But the dynamic data region can be used in more complex data management scenarios like constructors and destructors in C++.

Listing 11.16   Using a dynamic OpenMP data region

```
OpenMP/StreamTriad/StreamTriad_par4.c
13 #pragma omp target enter data \
    map(to:a[0:nsize], b[0:nsize], c[0:nsize])
14
15    struct timespec tstart;
16    // initializing data and arrays
17    double scalar = 3.0, time_sum = 0.0;
```

Starts dynamic data region directive

```
18 #pragma omp target teams distribute \
              parallel for simd
19    for (int i=0; i<nsize; i++) {
20        a[i] = 1.0;
21        b[i] = 2.0;                           Work
22    }                                         region
23                                              directive
24    for (int k=0; k<ntimes; k++){
25        cpu_timer_start(&tstart);
26        // stream triad loop
27 #pragma omp target teams distribute \
              parallel for simd
28        for (int i=0; i<nsize; i++){
29            c[i] = a[i] + scalar*b[i];
30        }
31        time_sum += cpu_timer_stop(tstart);
32    }
33
34    printf("Average runtime for stream triad loop is %lf msecs\n",
              time_sum/ntimes);
35
36 #pragma omp target exit data \                Ends dynamic data
      map(from:a[0:nsize], b[0:nsize], c[0:nsize])   region directive
```

We can further optimize the data transfers by allocating on the device and deleting the arrays on exit from the data region, thereby eliminating another data transfer. When transfers are needed to move data back and forth from the CPU and the GPU, you can use the omp target update directive. The syntax for the directive is

```
#pragma omp target update [to | from] (array[start:length])
```

We should also recognize that in this example the CPU never uses the array memory. For memory that only exists on the GPU, we can allocate it there and then tell the parallel work regions that it is already there. There are a couple of ways we can do this. One is to use an OpenMP function call to allocate and free memory on the device. These calls look like the following and require the inclusion of the OpenMP header file:

```
#include <omp.h>
double *a = omp_target_alloc(nsize*sizeof(double), omp_get_default_device());
omp_target_free(a, omp_get_default_device());
```

We could also use the CUDA memory allocation routines. We need to include the CUDA run-time header file to use these routines:

```
#include <cuda_runtime.h>
cudaMalloc((void *)&a,nsize*sizeof(double));
cudaFree(a);
```

On the parallel work directives, we then need to add another clause to pass the device pointers to the kernels on the device:

```
#pragma omp target teams distribute parallel for is_device_ptr(a)
```

Putting this all together, we end up with the changes to the code shown in the following listing.

Listing 11.17   Creating arrays only on the GPU

```
OpenMP/StreamTriad/StreamTriad_par6.c
11    double *a = omp_target_alloc(nsize*sizeof(double),
                  omp_get_default_device());
12    double *b = omp_target_alloc(nsize*sizeof(double),
                  omp_get_default_device());
13    double *c = omp_target_alloc(nsize*sizeof(double),
                  omp_get_default_device());
14
15    struct timespec tstart;
16    // initializing data and arrays
17    double scalar = 3.0, time_sum = 0.0;
18 #pragma omp target teams distribute
              parallel for simd is_device_ptr(a, b, c)
19    for (int i=0; i<nsize; i++) {
20        a[i] = 1.0;
21        b[i] = 2.0;
22    }
23
24    for (int k=0; k<ntimes; k++){
25        cpu_timer_start(&tstart);
26        // stream triad loop
27 #pragma omp target teams distribute \
              parallel for simd is_device_ptr(a, b, c)
28        for (int i=0; i<nsize; i++){
29            c[i] = a[i] + scalar*b[i];
30        }
31        time_sum += cpu_timer_stop(tstart);
32    }
33
34    printf("Average runtime for stream triad loop is %lf msecs\n",
              time_sum/ntimes);
35
36    omp_target_free(a, omp_get_default_device());
37    omp_target_free(b, omp_get_default_device());
38    omp_target_free(c, omp_get_default_device());
```

OpenMP has another way to allocate data on the device. This method uses the `omp declare target` directive as shown in listing 11.18. We first declare the pointers to the array on lines 10-12 and then allocate these on the device with the following block of code (lines 14–19). A similar block is used on lines 42-47 for freeing the data on the device.

Listing 11.18   Using `omp declare` to create arrays only on the GPU

```
OpenMP/StreamTriad/StreamTriad_par8.c
10 #pragma omp declare target              Declares target
11    double *a, *b, *c;                    creates a pointer
12 #pragma omp end declare target          on the device
```

```
13
14 #pragma omp target
15    {
16        a = malloc(nsize* sizeof(double);      Allocates
17        b = malloc(nsize* sizeof(double);      data on the
18        c = malloc(nsize* sizeof(double);      device
19    }
   < unchanged code>
42 #pragma omp target
43    {
44        free(a);                  Frees
45        free(b);                  device
46        free(c);                  data
47    }
```

As we have seen, there are a lot of different options for data management for the GPU. We now have covered the most common data region directives and clauses in OpenMP. Recent additions to the OpenMP standard handle more complicated data structures and data transfers.

11.3.4 *Optimizing OpenMP for GPUs*

Let's switch to a stencil example for the kernel optimization like we did for OpenACC. There are a few things you can try for speeding up individual kernels, but for the most part, it is best to let the compiler do the optimization for portability reasons. The core part of the stencil kernel with the OpenMP data and work regions in the following listing is the starting point for the optimization work.

> **Listing 11.19   Initial OpenMP version of stencil**

```
OpenMP/Stencil/Stencil_par2.c
15    double** restrict x    = malloc2D(jmax, imax);
16    double** restrict xnew = malloc2D(jmax, imax);
17
18 #pragma omp target enter data \
      map(to:x[0:jmax][0:imax], \      OpenMP
          xnew[0:jmax][0:imax])        data region
19
20 #pragma omp target teams
21    {
22 #pragma omp distribute parallel for simd
23        for (int j = 0; j < jmax; j++){
24            for (int i = 0; i < imax; i++){
25                xnew[j][i] = 0.0;          Parallel
26                x[j][i]    = 5.0;          work
27            }                              directive
28        }
29
30 #pragma omp distribute parallel for simd
31        for (int j = jmax/2 - 5; j < jmax/2 + 5; j++){
32            for (int i = imax/2 - 5; i < imax/2 -1; i++){
33                x[j][i] = 400.0;
34            }
```

```
35          }
36      } // omp target teams
37
38      for (int iter = 0; iter < niter; iter+=nburst){
39
40          for (int ib = 0; ib < nburst; ib++){
41              cpu_timer_start(&tstart_cpu);
42 #pragma omp target teams distribute \
                    parallel for simd
43              for (int j = 1; j < jmax-1; j++){
44                  for (int i = 1; i < imax-1; i++){
45                      xnew[j][i]=(x[j][i]+
                            x[j][i-1]+x[j][i+1]+
                            x[j-1][i]+x[j+1][i])/5.0;
46                  }
47              }
48
49 #pragma omp target teams distribute \
                    parallel for simd
50              for (int j = 0; j < jmax; j++){
51                  for (int i = 0; i < imax; i++){
52                      x[j][i] = xnew[j][i];
53                  }
54              }
55              cpu_time += cpu_timer_stop(tstart_cpu);
56
57          }
58
59          printf("Iter %d\n",iter+nburst);
60      }
61
62 #pragma omp target exit data \
        map(from:x[0:jmax][0:imax], \
                xnew[0:jmax][0:imax])
63
64      free(x);
65      free(xnew);
```

Parallel work directive — lines 36–49 (bracket)

Stencil kernel — lines 43–47

Replaces swap with copy from new back to original — lines 50–54

OpenMP data region — line 62

Simply adding a single work directive for the 2D loop and the data construct is not enough to get the work efficiently generated for the GPU for version 16 of the IBM XL compiler. The run time is nearly twice as long as the serial version (see table 11.4 at the end of this section). You can use nvprof to find where the time is being spent. Here's the output:

```
==11376== Profiling application: ./Stencil_par2
==11376== Profiling result:
 Time(%)    Time  Calls    Avg       Min       Max     Name
 51.63%  9.73622s 1000  9.7362ms  9.6602ms  15.378ms  __xl_main_142_OL_3
 48.26%  9.10010s 1000  9.1001ms  9.0323ms  13.588ms  __xl_main_141_OL_2
  0.11%  20.439ms    1  20.439ms  20.439ms  20.439ms  __xl_main_118_OL_1
  0.00%  7.2960us    5  1.4590us  1.2160us  2.1440us  [CUDA memcpy DtoH]
  0.00%  5.3760us    2  2.6880us  2.5600us  2.8160us  [CUDA memcpy HtoD]

    < more output>
```

The first line shows that the third kernel is taking up more than 50% of the run time. The copy back to the original array is taking an additional 48% of the run time. It's the kernel code and not the data transfer that is causing the problem! To correct this, the first thing to try is to collapse the two nested loops into a single parallel construct. The changes for this include adding the collapse clause along with the number of loops to collapse on the work directives. This is shown on lines 22, 30, 42, and 49 in the next listing.

Listing 11.20   Using collapse for optimization

```
OpenMP/Stencil/Stencil_par3.c
20 #pragma omp target teams
21    {
22 #pragma omp distribute parallel \
              for simd collapse(2)
23       for (int j = 0; j < jmax; j++){
24          for (int i = 0; i < imax; i++){
25             xnew[j][i] = 0.0;
26             x[j][i]    = 5.0;
27          }
28       }
29
30 #pragma omp distribute parallel \
              for simd collapse(2)
31       for (int j = jmax/2 - 5; j < jmax/2 + 5; j++){
32          for (int i = imax/2 - 5; i < imax/2 -1; i++){
33             x[j][i] = 400.0;
34          }
35       }
36    }
37
38    for (int iter = 0; iter < niter; iter+=nburst){
39
40       for (int ib = 0; ib < nburst; ib++){
41          cpu_timer_start(&tstart_cpu);
42 #pragma omp target teams distribute \
              parallel for simd collapse(2)
43          for (int j = 1; j < jmax-1; j++){
44             for (int i = 1; i < imax-1; i++){
45                xnew[j][i]=(x[j][i]+x[j][i-1]+x[j][i+1]+
                                   x[j-1][i]+x[j+1][i])/5.0;
46             }
47          }
48
49 #pragma omp target teams distribute \
              parallel for simd collapse(2)
50          for (int j = 0; j < jmax; j++){
51             for (int i = 0; i < imax; i++){
52                x[j][i] = xnew[j][i];
53             }
54          }
55          cpu_time += cpu_timer_stop(tstart_cpu);
56
```

Adds collapse clause

```
57          }
58
59          printf("Iter %d\n",iter+nburst);
60      }
```

The run time is now faster than the CPU (see table 11.3), though not as fast as the version generated by the PGI OpenACC compiler (table 11.1). We expect that as the IBM XL compiler improves, this should get better. Let's try another approach of splitting the parallel work directives across the two loops as shown in the following listing.

Listing 11.21 Splitting work directives for optimization

```
OpenMP/Stencil/Stencil_par4.c
20 #pragma omp target teams
21    {
22 #pragma omp distribute
23       for (int j = 0; j < jmax; j++){
24 #pragma omp parallel for simd
25          for (int i = 0; i < imax; i++){
26             xnew[j][i] = 0.0;
27             x[j][i]    = 5.0;
28          }
29       }
30
31 #pragma omp distribute
32       for (int j = jmax/2 - 5; j < jmax/2 + 5; j++){
33 #pragma omp parallel for simd
34          for (int i = imax/2 - 5; i < imax/2 -1; i++){
35             x[j][i] = 400.0;
36          }
37       }
38    }
39
40    for (int iter = 0; iter < niter; iter+=nburst){
41
42       for (int ib = 0; ib < nburst; ib++){
43          cpu_timer_start(&tstart_cpu);
44 #pragma omp target teams distribute
45          for (int j = 1; j < jmax-1; j++){
46 #pragma omp parallel for simd
47             for (int i = 1; i < imax-1; i++){
48                xnew[j][i]=(x[j][i]+x[j][i-1]+x[j][i+1]+
49                           x[j-1][i]+x[j+1][i])/5.0;
50             }
51          }
52
53 #pragma omp target teams distribute
54          for (int j = 0; j < jmax; j++){
55 #pragma omp parallel for simd
56             for (int i = 0; i < imax; i++){
57                x[j][i] = xnew[j][i];
58             }
59          }
60          cpu_time += cpu_timer_stop(tstart_cpu);
```

Splits work over two loop levels

```
60
61        }
62
63        printf("Iter %d\n",iter+nburst);
64    }
```

The timing from the IBM XL compiler for the split parallel work directives is similar to the `collapse` clause. Table 11.3 shows the results of our experiments with kernel optimizations.

Table 11.3   Run times from OpenMP stencil kernel optimizations

	Open MP stencil kernel run time (secs)
Serial CPU code	5.497
Adding work directive	19.01
Adding compute and data regions	18.97
Adding `collapse(2)` clause	3.035
Splitting parallel directives	2.50

We also look at the run time results for the stream triad example from the IBM XL compiler v16 on a Power 9 processor with an NVIDIA V100 GPU in table 11.4. The performance on the CPU is different because, in one case, we used an Intel Skylake processor and, in this case, we are using a Power 9 processor. But it is encouraging to see that the performance of the stream kernel with OpenMP on the V100 GPU is essentially the same as that for the PGI OpenACC compiler in table 11.2.

Table 11.4   Run times from OpenMP stream triad kernel optimizations

	OpenMP stream triad kernel run time (ms)
Serial CPU code	15.9
Parallel 1. Compute region added	85.7
Parallel 3. Structured data region added	0.585
Parallel 4. Dynamic data region added	0.584
Parallel 8. Allocating data only on device	0.584

The performance of OpenMP with the IBM XL compiler is good on a simple 1D test problem but could be improved for the 2D stencil case. The focus thus far has been on correctly implementing the OpenMP standard for device offloading. We expect that performance will improve with each compiler release and with more compiler vendors offering OpenMP device offloading support.

11.3.5 *Advanced OpenMP for GPUs*

OpenMP has many additional advanced capabilities. OpenMP is also changing based on the experience with the early implementations on GPUs and as hardware continues to evolve. We'll cover just a few of the advanced directives and clauses that are important for

- Fine-tuning kernels
- Handling various important programming constructs (functions, scans, and shared access to variables)
- Asynchronous operations that overlap data movement and computation
- Controlling memory placement
- Handling complex data structures
- Simplifying work directives

CONTROLLING THE GPU KERNEL PARAMETERS IMPLEMENTED BY THE OPENMP COMPILER

We start by looking at clauses that can be used to fine-tune kernel performance. We can add these clauses to directives to modify the kernels that the compiler generates for the GPU:

- `num_teams` defines the number of teams generated by the `teams` directive.
- `thread_limit` adds the number of threads used by each team.
- `schedule` or `schedule(static,1)` specifies that the work items are distributed in a round-robin manner rather than in a block. This can help with memory load coalescing on the GPU.
- `simdlen` specifies the vector length or threads for the workgroup.

These clauses can be useful in special situations, but in general, it is better to leave the parameters for the compiler to optimize.

DECLARING AN OPENMP DEVICE FUNCTION

When we call a function within a parallel region on the device, we need a way to tell the compiler it should also be on the device. This is done by adding a `declare target` directive to the function. The syntax is similar to that for variable declarations. Here is an example:

```
#pragma omp declare target
int my_compute(<args>){
    <work>
}
```

NEW SCAN REDUCTION TYPE

We discussed the importance of the scan algorithm in section 5.6, where we also saw the complexity of implementing this algorithm on the GPU. This is a ubiquitous operation in parallel computing and complicated to write, so the addition of this type is helpful. The `scan` type will be available in version 5.0 of OpenMP.

```
int run_sum = 0;
#pragma omp parallel for simd reduction(inscan,+: run_sum)
for (int i = 0; i < n; ++i) {
   run_sum += ncells[i];
   #pragma omp scan exclusive(run_sum)
   cell_start[i] = run_sum;
   #pragma omp scan inclusive(run_sum)
   cell_end[i] = run_sum;
}
```

PREVENTING RACE CONDITIONS WITH OPENMP ATOMIC

It is normal in an algorithm that several threads access a common variable. It is often a bottleneck in the performance of routines. Atomics have provided this functionality in various compilers and thread implementations. OpenMP also provides an atomic directive. An example of the use of the directive is

```
#pragma omp atomic
   i++;
```

OPENMP'S VERSION OF ASYNCHRONOUS OPERATIONS

In section 10.5, we discussed the value of overlapping data transfer and computation through asynchronous operations. OpenMP also provides its version of these operations.

You create asynchronous device operations using the nowait clause on either a data or work directive. You can then use a depend clause to specify that a new operation cannot start until the previous operation is complete. These operations can be chained to form a sequence of operations. We can use a simple taskwait directive to wait for completion of all tasks:

```
#pragma omp taskwait
```

ACCESSING SPECIAL MEMORY SPACES

Memory bandwidth is often one of the most important performance limits. With pragma-based languages, it has not always been possible to control the placement of memory and the resulting memory bandwidth. The addition of features to give the programmer more control over this has been one of the more eagerly anticipated additions to OpenMP. With OpenMP 5.0, you will be able to target special memory spaces such as shared memory and high-bandwidth memory. The capability is through a new allocator clause modifier. The allocate clause takes an optional modifier as follows:

```
allocate([allocator:] list)
```

You can use the following pair of functions to directly allocate and free memory:

```
omp_alloc(size_t size, omp_allocator_t *allocator)
omp_free(void *ptr, const omp_allocator_t *allocator)
```

The OpenMP 5.0 standard specifies some predefined memory spaces for allocators as this table shows.

Memory space	Memory type description
`omp_default_mem_alloc/omp_default_mem_space`	Default system storage space
`omp_large_cap_mem_alloc/omp_large_cap_mem_space`	Large-capacity storage space
`omp_const_mem_alloc/omp_const_mem_space`	Storage for constant, unchanging data
`omp_high_bw_mem_alloc/omp_high_bw_mem_space`	High bandwidth memory
`omp_low_lat_mem_alloc/omp_low_lat_mem_space`	Storage with low latency

A set of functions is available to define new memory allocators. The two main routines are

```
omp_init_allocator
omp_destroy_allocator
```

These allocators take one of the predefined space arguments and allocator traits such as whether it should be pinned, aligned, private, nearby, or many others. Implementations of this capability are still under development. This functionality will be of increasing importance with new architectures, where there are special memory types with different latency and bandwidth performance characteristics.

DEEP COPY SUPPORT FOR TRANSFERRING COMPLEX DATA STRUCTURES

OpenMP 5.0 also adds a `declare mapper` construct that can do deep copies. *Deep copies* not only duplicate a data structure with pointers but also the data referred to by the pointers. Programs with complex data structures and classes have struggled with the difficulty of porting to GPUs. The ability to do deep copies greatly simplifies these implementations.

SIMPLIFYING WORK DISTRIBUTION WITH THE NEW LOOP DIRECTIVE

The OpenMP 5.0 standard introduces more flexible work directives. One of these is the `loop` directive that is simpler and closer to the functionality in OpenACC. The `loop` directive takes the place of `distribute parallel for simd`. With the `loop` directive, you are telling the compiler that the loop iterations can be executed concurrently, but you leave the actual implementation to the compiler. The following listing shows an example of using this directive in the stencil kernel.

Listing 11.22 Using the new `loop` directive in OpenMP 5.0

```
47 #pragma omp target teams          ◁──┐  Launches work on the
                                          GPU with multiple teams
48 #pragma omp loop                  ◁──┐
49          for (int j = 1; j < jmax-1; j++){   The loop parallelized
                                                as independent work
50 #pragma omp loop                  ◁──┘
```

```
51              for (int i = 1; i < imax-1; i++){
52                  xnew[j][i]=(x[j][i]+x[j][i-1]+x[j][i+1]+
                                x[j-1][i]+x[j+1][i])/5.0;
53              }
54          }
```

The `loop` clause is really a `loop independent` or `concurrent` clause that tells the compiler that iterations of the loop have no dependencies. The `loop` clause gives the compiler information or a descriptive clause rather than telling the compiler what to do, which is a prescriptive clause. Most compilers have not implemented this new feature, so we continue to work with the prescriptive clauses in the earlier examples in this chapter. If you're not familiar with these concepts, here's a definition of each:

- *Prescriptive directives and clauses*—Directives from the programmer that tell the compiler specifically what to do.
- *Descriptive directives and clauses*—Directives that give the compiler information about the following loop construct; also gives the compiler some freedom to generate the most efficient implementation.

OpenMP has traditionally used prescriptive clauses in its specifications. This reduces the variation between implementations and improves portability. But in the case of GPUs, it has led to the long, complex directives with subtle differentiation on whether synchronization is possible between threads and other hardware-specific features.

The descriptive approach is closer to the OpenACC philosophy and is not so burdened with the details of the hardware. This gives the compiler both the freedom and responsibility of how to properly and effectively generate code for the targeted hardware. Note that this is not only a significant shift for OpenMP, but an important one. If OpenMP continues to try and go down the path of prescriptive directives, as hardware complexity continues to grow, the OpenMP language will grow too complicated and the portability of codes will be reduced.

11.4 *Further explorations*

Both OpenACC and OpenMP are large languages with many directives, clauses, modifiers, and functions. Beyond the core functionality of these languages, there are few examples and sparse documentation. Indeed, many of the lesser used parts may not work in all compilers. You should test new functionality in a small example before adding it to a large application. To learn more about these languages, refer to the additional reading materials that follow. Also, be sure and get some hands-on experience with the exercises in section 11.4.2.

11.4.1 *Additional reading*

Because the OpenACC and OpenMP languages are still evolving, the best sources for additional materials are at the respective websites: https://openacc.org and https://openmp.org. Each site lists additional resources, including tutorials and presentations at leading HPC conferences.

OPENACC RESOURCES AND REFERENCES

OpenACC has been out a little longer than OpenMP and has more books and documentation. The starting place for the language is the OpenACC standard. At 150 pages, version 3.0 of the standard is very readable and relevant to the end user. It can be found on the openacc.org website. The following URL provides a link to *The OpenACC Application Programming Interface*, v3.0 (November, 2018):

> https://www.openacc.org/sites/default/files/inline-images/Specification/
> OpenACC.3.0.pdf.

The OpenACC site also has a document on programming and best practices. It is not linked to a particular version of the standard, but has not been updated since 2015. You'll find OpenACC-standard.org's *OpenACC Programming and Best Practices Guide* (June, 2015) here:

> https://www.openacc.org/sites/default/files/inline-files/OpenACC_Programming_
> Guide_0.pdf.

The leading book for OpenACC is

> Sunita Chandrasekaran and Guido Juckeland, *OpenACC for Programmers: Concepts and Strategies* (Addison-Wesley Professional, 2017).

OPENMP RESOURCES AND REFERENCES

Most of the books and guides to OpenMP predate device offloading capabilities, but the language specification thoroughly describes the OpenMP device offloading directives. At over 600 pages, it is more of a reference than a user's guide. Still, it is the go-to document for details on the features of the language.[2]

> OpenMP Architecture Review Board, *OpenMP Application Programming Interface*, Vol. 5.0 (November, 2018) at https://www.openmp.org/wp-content/uploads/Open MP-API-Specification-5.0.pdf.

A companion to the specification is the example guide. This guide gives short examples of how each feature should work, but not complete application-level cases:

> OpenMP Architecture Review Board, *OpenMP Application Programming Interface: Examples*, Vol. 5.0 (November, 2019) at https://www.openmp.org/wp-content/uploads/ openmp-examples-5.0.0.pdf.

With OpenMP still seeing significant changes and compilers still working on implementing v5.0 features, it is not surprising that there are few books that discuss the device offloading features. Ruud van der Pas and others recently completed a book that covers the new features of OpenMP up through v4.5.

---

[2] To get a relative comparison for the complexity of these pragma-based languages, the final draft of the C18 standard for the C language is just over 500 pages.

Ruud Van der Pas, Eric Stotzer, and Christian Terboven, *Using OpenMP—The Next Step: Affinity, Accelerators, Tasking, and SIMD* (MIT Press, 2017).

11.4.2 Exercises

1 Find what compilers are available for your local GPU system. Are both OpenACC and OpenMP compilers available? If not, do you have access to any systems that would allow you to try out these pragma-based languages?

2 Run the stream triad examples from the OpenACC/StreamTriad and/or the OpenMP/StreamTriad directories on your local GPU development system. You'll find these directories at https://github.com/EssentialsofParallelComputing/Chapter11.

3 Compare your results from exercise 2 to the BabelStream results at https://uob-hpc.github.io/BabelStream/results/. For the stream triad, the bytes moved are `3 * nsize * sizeof(datatype)`.

4 Modify the OpenMP data region mapping in listing 11.16 to reflect the actual use of the arrays in the kernels.

5 Implement the mass sum example from listing 11.4 in OpenMP.

6 For x and y arrays of size 20,000,000, find the maximum radius for the arrays using both OpenMP and OpenACC. Initialize the arrays with double-precision values that linearly increase from 1.0 to 2.0e7 for the x array and decrease from 2.0e7 to 1.0 for the y array.

Summary

- Pragma-based languages are the easiest way to port to the GPU. Using these gives you the quickest result with the least effort.

- The porting process is to move work to the GPU and then manage the data movement. This gets as much work as possible on the GPU while minimizing expensive data movement.

- The kernel optimization comes last and should mostly be left to the compiler. This produces the most portable and future-proof code.

- Track the latest developments of the pragma-based language and compilers. These compilers are still under rapid development and should continue improving.

GPU languages: Getting down to basics

This chapter covers

- Understanding the current landscape of native GPU languages
- Creating simple GPU programs in each language
- Tackling more complex multi-kernel operations
- Porting between various GPU languages

This chapter covers lower-level languages for GPUs. We call these native languages because they directly reflect features of the target GPU hardware. We cover two of these languages, CUDA and OpenCL, that are widely used. We also cover HIP, a new variant for AMD GPUs. In contrast to the pragma-based implementation, these GPU languages have a smaller reliance on the compiler. You should use these languages for more fine-tuned control of your program's performance. How are these languages different than those presented in chapter 11? Our distinction is that these languages have grown up from the characteristics of the GPU and CPU hardware, while the OpenACC and OpenMP languages started with high-level abstractions and rely on a compiler to map those to different hardware.

The set of native GPU languages, CUDA, OpenCL, and HIP, requires a separate source to be created for the GPU kernel. The separate source code is often similar to the CPU code. The challenges of having two different sources to maintain is a major difficulty. If the native GPU language only supports one type of hardware, then there can be even more source variants to maintain if you want to run on more than one vendor's GPU. Some applications have implemented their algorithms in multiple GPU languages and CPU languages. Thus, you can understand the critical need for more portable GPU programming languages.

Thankfully, portability is getting more attention with some of the newer GPU languages. OpenCL was the first open-standard language to run on a variety of GPU hardware and even CPUs. After an initial splash, OpenCL has not gotten as widespread an acceptance as originally hoped for. Another language, HIP, is designed by AMD as a more portable version of CUDA, which generates code for AMD's GPUs. As part of AMD's portability initiative, support for GPUs from other vendors is included.

The difference between these native languages and higher-level languages is blurring as new languages are introduced. The SYCL language, originally a C++ layer on top of OpenCL, is typical of these newer, more portable languages. Along with the Kokkos and RAJA languages, SYCL supports a single source for both CPU and GPU. We'll touch on these languages at the end of the chapter. Figure 12.1 shows the current picture of the interoperability for the GPU languages that we cover in this chapter.

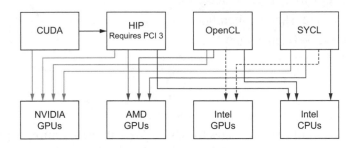

Figure 12.1   The interoperability map for the GPU languages shows an increasingly complex situation. Four GPU languages are shown at the top with the various hardware devices at the bottom. The arrows show the code generation pathways from the languages to the hardware. The dashed lines are for hardware that is still in development.

The focus on language interoperability is gaining traction as more diversity of GPUs appears in the largest HPC installations. The top Department of Energy HPC systems, Sierra and Summit, are provisioned with NVIDIA GPUs. In 2021, Argonne's Aurora system with Intel GPUs and Oak Ridge's Frontier system with AMD GPUs will be added to the list of Department of Energy HPC systems. With the introduction of the Aurora system, SYCL has emerged from near obscurity to become a major player with multiple implementations. SYCL was originally developed to provide a more natural C++ layer on top of OpenCL. The reason for the sudden emergence of SYCL was its adoption by Intel as part of the OneAPI programming model for Intel GPUs on the Aurora system. Because of SYCL's new-found importance, we cover SYCL in section 12.4. A similar growth in interest in other languages and libraries that provide portability across the GPU landscape is also prevalent.

We end the chapter with a brief look at a couple of these performance portability systems, Kokkos and RAJA, that were created to ease the difficulty of running on a wide range of hardware, from CPUs to GPUs. These work at a slightly higher level of abstraction, but promise a single source that will run everywhere. Their development has resulted from a major Department of Energy effort to support the porting of large scientific applications to newer hardware. The aim of RAJA and Kokkos is a one-time rewrite to create a single-source code base that is portable and maintainable through a time of great change in hardware design.

Last, we want to provide guidance on how to approach this chapter. We cover a lot of different languages in a short space. The proliferation of languages reflects the lack of cooperation among language developers at this point in time, as developers chase their immediate goals and hardware concerns. Rather than treat these languages as different languages, think of them as slightly different dialects of one or two languages. We recommend that you seek to learn a couple of these languages and appreciate the differences and similarities with the others. We will be comparing and contrasting the languages to help you see that they are not all that different once you get over the particular syntax of each and their quirks. We do expect that the languages will merge to a more common form because the current situation is not sustainable. We already see the beginnings of that with the push for more language portability driven by the needs of large applications.

12.1 *Features of a native GPU programming language*

A GPU programming language must have several basic features. It is helpful to understand what these features are so that you can recognize these in each GPU language. We summarize the necessary GPU language features here.

- *Detecting the accelerator device*—The language must provide a detection of the accelerator devices and a way to choose between those devices. Some languages give more control over the selection of devices than others. Even for a language such as CUDA, which just looks for an NVIDIA GPU, there must be a way to handle multiple GPUs on a node.
- *Support for writing device kernels*—The language must provide a way to generate the low-level instructions for GPUs or other accelerators. GPUs provide nearly identical basic operations as CPUs, so the kernel language should not be dramatically different. Rather than invent a new language, the most straightforward way is to leverage current programming languages and compilers to generate the new instruction set. GPU languages have done this by adopting a

particular version of the C or C++ language as a basis for their system. CUDA originally was based on the C programming language but now is based on C++ and has some support for the Standard Template Library (STL). OpenCL is based on the C99 standard and has released a new specification with C++ support.

The language design also needs to address whether to have the host and design source code in the same file or in different files. Either way, the compiler must distinguish between the host and design sources and must provide a way to generate the instruction set for the different hardware. The compiler must even decide *when* to generate the instruction set. For example, OpenCL waits for the device to be selected and then generates the instruction set with a just-in-time (JIT) compiler approach.

- *Mechanism to call device kernels from the host*—Ok, now we have the device code, but we also have to have a way of calling the code from the host. The syntax for performing this operation varies the most across the various languages. But the mechanism is only slightly more complicated than a standard subroutine call.
- *Memory handling*—The language must have support for memory allocations, deallocations, and moving data back and forth from the host to the device. The most straightforward way for this is to have a subroutine call for each of these operations. But another way is through the compiler detecting when to move the data and doing it for you behind the scenes. As this is such a major part of GPU programming, innovation continues to occur on the hardware and software side for this functionality.
- *Synchronization*—A mechanism must be provided to specify the synchronization requirements between the CPU and the GPU. Synchronization operations must also be provided within kernels.
- *Streams*—A complete GPU language allows the scheduling of asynchronous streams of operations along with the explicit dependencies between the kernels and the memory transfer operations.

This is not such a scary list. For the most part, native GPU languages do not look so different than current CPU code. Also recognizing these commonalities among native GPU language functionality helps you to become comfortable moving from one language to another.

12.2 CUDA and HIP GPU languages: The low-level performance option

We will begin with a look at two of the low level GPU languages, CUDA and HIP. These are two of the most common languages for programming GPUs.

Compute Unified Device Architecture (CUDA) is a proprietary language from NVIDIA that only runs on their GPUs. First released in 2008, it is currently the dominant native programming language for GPUs. With a decade of development, CUDA has a rich set of features and performance enhancements. The CUDA language closely reflects the architecture of the NVIDIA GPU. It does not purport to be a general accelerator language. Still, the concepts of most accelerators are similar enough for the CUDA language design to be applicable.

The AMD (formerly ATI) GPUs have had a series of short-lived programming languages. These have finally settled on a CUDA look-a-like that can be generated by "HIPifying" CUDA code with their HIP compiler. This is part of the ROCm suite of tools that provide extensive portability between GPU languages, including the OpenCL language for GPUs (and CPUs) discussed in section 12.3.

12.2.1 *Writing and building your first CUDA application*

We'll start with how to build and compile a simple CUDA application that runs on a GPU. We'll use the stream triad example we have used throughout the book that implements a loop for this calculation: C = A + scalar * B. The CUDA compiler splits the regular C++ code to pass to the underlying C++ compiler. It then compiles the remaining CUDA code. Code from these two paths is linked together into a single executable.

To follow along with this example, you might first need to install the CUDA software.[1] Each release of CUDA works with a limited range of compiler versions. As of CUDA v10.2, GCC compilers up through v8 are supported. If you are working with multiple parallel languages and packages, this constantly-battling-the-compiler-version issue is perhaps one of the most frustrating things about CUDA. But on a positive note, you can use much of your regular toolchain and build systems with just the version constraints and a few special additions.

We'll show three different approaches starting with a simple makefile and then a couple of different ways of using CMake. We encourage you to follow along with the examples for this chapter at https://github.com/EssentialsofParallelComputing/Chapter12.

You can select this simple makefile for CUDA by copying or linking it to Makefile, the default filename for make. The following listing shows the makefile itself.

1 To link to the file, type ln -s Makefile.simple Makefile
2 Build the application with make
3 Run the application with ./StreamTriad

Listing 12.1 A simple CUDA makefile

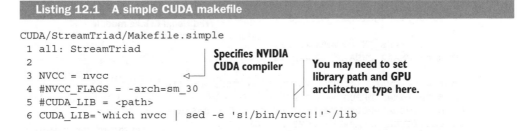

```
CUDA/StreamTriad/Makefile.simple
1 all: StreamTriad
2                                    Specifies NVIDIA
                                     CUDA compiler      You may need to set
3 NVCC = nvcc            ◄─┘                            library path and GPU
4 #NVCC_FLAGS = -arch=sm_30                             architecture type here.
5 #CUDA_LIB = <path>
6 CUDA_LIB=`which nvcc | sed -e 's!/bin/nvcc!!'`/lib
```

---

[1] See the CUDA installation guide for details (https://docs.nvidia.com/cuda/cuda-installation-guide-linux/).

```
 7 CUDA_LIB64=`which nvcc | sed -e 's!/bin/nvcc!!'`/lib64
 8
 9 %.o : %.cu                                          Implicit rule to compile
10   ${NVCC} ${NVCC_FLAGS} -c $< -o $@                 CUDA source files
11
12 StreamTriad: StreamTriad.o timer.o
13   ${CXX} -o $@ $^ -L${CUDA_LIB} -lcudart  ◄──┐ Link line
14                                               │ for CUDA
15 clean:                                        │ applications
16   rm -rf StreamTriad *.o
```

The key addition is a pattern rule on lines 9–10, which converts a file with a .cu suffix into an object file. We use the NVIDIA NVCC compiler for this operation. We then need to add the CUDA runtime library, CUDART, to the link line. You can use lines 4 and 5 to specify a particular NVIDIA GPU architecture and a special path to the CUDA libraries.

> **DEFINITION**   A *pattern rule* is a specification to the make utility that provides a general rule on how to convert any file with one suffix pattern to a file with another suffix pattern.

CUDA has extensive support in the CMake build system. Next, we cover both the old-style support and the new modern CMake approach that's recently emerged. We show the old-style method in listing 12.2. It has the advantage of more portability for systems with older CMake versions and the automatic detection of the NVIDIA GPU architecture. This latter feature of detecting the hardware device is such a convenience that the old-style CMake is the recommended approach at present. To use this build system, link the CMakeLists_old.txt to CMakeLists.txt:

```
ln -s CMakeLists_old.txt CMakeLists.txt
mkdir build && cd build
cmake ..
make
```

Listing 12.2   Old style CUDA CMake file

```
CUDA/StreamTriad/CMakeLists_old.txt
 1 cmake_minimum_required (VERSION 2.8)  ◄──┐ You need a minimum of
 2 project (StreamTriad)                     │ CMake v2.8 for CUDA support.
 3
 4 find_package(CUDA REQUIRED)   ◄──┐ Traditional CMake module
 5                                   │ sets compiler flags.
 6 set (CMAKE_CXX_STANDARD 11)
 7 set (CMAKE_CUDA_STANDARD 11)
 8
 9 # sets CMAKE_{C,CXX}_FLAGS from CUDA compile flags.
   # Includes DEBUG and RELEASE
10 set (CUDA_PROPAGATE_HOST_FLAGS ON) # default is on
11 set (CUDA_SEPARABLE_COMPILATION ON)  ◄──┐ Set to "on" for calling
12                                          │ functions in other compile
13 if (CMAKE_VERSION VERSION_GREATER "3.9.0")   │ units (default off)
```

```
14    cuda_select_nvcc_arch_flags(ARCH_FLAGS)          ◁    Detects and sets proper
15 endif()                                                  architecture flag for
16                                                          current NVIDIA GPU
17 set (CUDA_NVCC_FLAGS ${CUDA_NVCC_FLAGS}
         -O3 ${ARCH_FLAGS})                                 Sets the compiler flags for
18                                                          the NVIDIA compiler
19 # Adds build target of StreamTriad with source code files
20 cuda_add_executable(StreamTriad
       StreamTriad.cu timer.c timer.h)                      Sets the proper build
21                                                          and link flags for a
22 if (APPLE)                                               CUDA executable
23    set_property(TARGET StreamTriad PROPERTY BUILD_RPATH
          ${CMAKE_CUDA_IMPLICIT_LINK_DIRECTORIES})
24 endif (APPLE)
25
26 # Cleanup
27 add_custom_target(distclean COMMAND rm -rf CMakeCache.txt CMakeFiles
28                     Makefile cmake_install.cmake
                       StreamTriad.dSYM ipo_out.optrpt)
29
30 # Adds a make clean_cuda_depends target
   #    -- invoke with "make clean_cuda_depends"
31 CUDA_BUILD_CLEAN_TARGET()
```

Much of the CMake build system is standard. The separable compilation attribute on line 11 is suggested for a more robust build system for general development. You can then turn it off at a later stage to save a few registers in the CUDA kernels to get a small optimization in the generated code. The CUDA defaults are for performance, not for a more general, robust build. The automatic detection of the NVIDIA GPU architecture on line 14 is a significant convenience that keeps you from having to manually modify your makefile.

With version 3.0, CMake is undergoing a fairly major revision to its structure to what they call "modern" CMake. The key attributes of this style are a more integrated system and a per target application of attributes. Nowhere is it more apparent than in its support of CUDA. Let's take a look at the listing 12.3 to see how to use it. To use this build system for the modern, new style CMake support for CUDA, link the CMakeLists_new.txt to CMakeLists.txt:

```
ln -s CMakeLists_new.txt CMakeLists.txt
mkdir build && cd build
cmake ..
make
```

Listing 12.3   New style (modern) CUDA CMake file

```
CUDA/StreamTriad/CMakeLists_new.txt
 1 cmake_minimum_required (VERSION 3.8)    ◁    Requires
 2 project (StreamTriad)                        CMake v3.8
 3
 4 enable_language(CXX CUDA)    ◁    Enables CUDA as
 5                                   the language
```

```
 6 set (CMAKE_CXX_STANDARD 11)
 7 set (CMAKE_CUDA_STANDARD 11)           Manually sets the
 8                                        CUDA architecture
 9 #set (ARCH_FLAGS -arch=sm_30)   ◁
10 set (CMAKE_CUDA_FLAGS ${CMAKE_CUDA_FLAGS};    Sets the compile
       "-O3 ${ARCH_FLAGS}")                      flags for CUDA
11
12 # Adds build target of StreamTriad with source code files
13 add_executable(StreamTriad StreamTriad.cu timer.c timer.h)
14
15 set_target_properties(StreamTriad PROPERTIES    Sets the separable
      CUDA_SEPARABLE_COMPILATION ON)               compilation flag
16
17 if (APPLE)
18    set_property(TARGET StreamTriad PROPERTY BUILD_RPATH
         ${CMAKE_CUDA_IMPLICIT_LINK_DIRECTORIES})
19 endif(APPLE)
20
21 # Cleanup
22 add_custom_target(distclean COMMAND rm -rf CMakeCache.txt CMakeFiles
23                   Makefile cmake_install.cmake
                     StreamTriad.dSYM ipo_out.optrpt)
```

The first thing to note with this modern CMake approach is how much simpler it is than the old style. The key is the enabling of the CUDA as the language in line 4. From then on, little additional work needs to be done.

We can set the flags to compile for a specific GPU architecture as shown in lines 9–10. However, we don't have an automatic way to detect the architecture yet with the modern CMake style. Without an architecture flag, the compiler generates code and optimizes for the sm_30 GPU device. The sm_30 generated code runs on any device from Kepler K40 or newer, but it will not be optimized for the latest architectures. You can also specify multiple architectures in one compiler. Compiles will be slower, and the generated executable will be larger.

We can also set the separable compilation attribute for CUDA, but in a different syntax in which it applies to the specific target. The optimization flag on line 10, -O3, is only sent to the host compiler for the regular C++ code. The default optimization level for CUDA code is -O3 and seldom needs to be modified.

Overall, the process of building a CUDA program is easy and getting easier. Expect changes to the build to continue, however. Clang is adding native support for compiling CUDA code to give you another option besides the NVIDIA compiler. Now let's move on to the source code. We'll begin with the kernel for the GPU in the following listing.

Listing 12.4   CUDA version of stream triad: The kernel

```
CUDA/StreamTriad/StreamTriad.cu
 2 __global__ void StreamTriad(
 3                 const int n,
 4                 const double scalar,
```

```
 5                const double *a,
 6                const double *b,
 7                      double *c)
 8 {
 9     int i = blockIdx.x*blockDim.x+threadIdx.x;    ⟵——— Gets cell index
10
11     // Protect from going out-of-bounds     Protects from going
12     if (i >= n) return;                      ⟵  out-of-bounds
13
14     c[i] = a[i] + scalar*b[i];    ⟵——— stream triad body
15 }
```

As is typical with GPU kernels, we strip the `for` loop from the computational block. This leaves the loop body on line 14. We need to add the conditional at line 12 to prevent accessing out-of-bounds data. Without this protection, kernels can randomly crash without a message. And then, in line 9, we get the global index from the block and thread variables set by the CUDA run time. Adding the `__global__` attribute to the subroutine tells the compiler that this is a GPU kernel that will be called from the host. Meanwhile on the host side, we have to set up the memory and make the kernel call. The following listing shows this process.

Listing 12.5 CUDA version of stream triad: Set up and tear down

```
CUDA/StreamTriad/StreamTriad.cu
31     // allocate host memory and initialize
32     double *a = (double *)malloc(
                 stream_array_size*sizeof(double));
33     double *b = (double *)malloc(                   Allocates host
                 stream_array_size*sizeof(double));    memory
34     double *c = (double *)malloc(
                 stream_array_size*sizeof(double));
35
36     for (int i=0; i<stream_array_size; i++) {
37        a[i] = 1.0;                          Initializes arrays
38        b[i] = 2.0;
39     }
40
41     // allocate device memory. suffix of _d indicates a device pointer
42     double *a_d, *b_d, *c_d;
43     cudaMalloc(&a_d, stream_array_size*
                   sizeof(double));
44     cudaMalloc(&b_d, stream_array_size*     Allocates
                   sizeof(double));             device memory
45     cudaMalloc(&c_d, stream_array_size*
                   sizeof(double));
46
47     // setting block size and padding total grid size
       //    to get even block sizes
48     int blocksize = 512;                    Sets block size and
49     int gridsize =                          calculates number
          (stream_array_size + blocksize - 1)/ of blocks
          blocksize;
```

```
50
        < ... timing loop ... code shown below in listing 12.6 >

78      printf("Average runtime is %lf msecs data transfer is %lf msecs\n",
79             tkernel_sum/NTIMES, (ttotal_sum - tkernel_sum)/NTIMES);
80
81      cudaFree(a_d);
82      cudaFree(b_d);        Frees device
83      cudaFree(c_d);        memory
84
85      free(a);             Frees host
86      free(b);             memory
87      free(c);
88 }
```

First, we allocate memory on the host and initialize it on lines 31–39. We also need a corresponding memory space on the GPU to hold the arrays while the GPU is operating on those. For that, we use the cudaMalloc routine on lines 43–45. Now we come to some interesting lines (from 47–49) that are needed solely for the GPU. The block size is the size of the workgroup on the GPU. This is known by the tile size, block size, or workgroup size, depending on the GPU programming language being used (see table 10.1). The next line that calculates the grid size is characteristic of GPU code. We won't always have an array size that is an even integer multiple of the block size. So, we need to have an integer that is equal to or greater than the fractional number of blocks. Let's work through an example to understand what is being done.

Example: Calculating block size for the GPU

On line 3 in the following listing, we calculate the fractional number of blocks. For this example with an array size of 1,000, it is 1.95 blocks. Rather than truncate this to 1, which is what would happen with the default application of integer arithmetic, we need to round up to 2. If we just calculated array size divided by the block size, we would get integer truncation. So we have to cast each of these to a floating-point value to get floating-point division. We actually only need to cast one of the values, and the C/C++ standard requires the compiler to promote the other items. But in our programming conventions, a type conversion must be explicitly called for or it is a programming error. Compilers often don't flag these cases, but they can mask unintended situations.

The C ceil function used on lines 4 and 5 in the listing rounds up to the next integer value equal to or greater than the floating-point number. We can get the same result with integer arithmetic by adding one less than the block size and then performing integer division with truncation as is done on line 6. We choose to use this version because the integer form does not require any floating-point operations and should be faster.

```
1 int stream_array_size = 1000;
2 int blocksize = 512;
3 float frac_blocks = (float)stream_array_size/(float)blocksize;
```

```
>>>frac_blocks = 1.95
4 int nblocks = ceil(frac_blocks);
>>> nblocks = 2
```

or

```
5 int nblocks = ceil((float)stream_array_size/(float)blocksize);
```

or

```
6 int nblocks = (stream_array_size + blocksize - 1)/blocksize;
```

Now all the blocks but the last one have 512 values. The last block will be size 512, but will contain only 488 data items. The out-of-bounds check on line 12 of listing 12.4 keeps us from getting in trouble with this partially filled block. The last few lines in listing 12.5 free the device pointers and the host pointers. You must be careful to use cudaFree for the device pointers and the C library function, free, for host pointers.

All we have left is to copy memory to the GPU, call the GPU kernel, and copy the memory back. We do this in a timing loop (in listing 12.6) that can be executed multiple times to get a better measurement. Sometimes the first call to a GPU will be slower due to initialization costs. We can amortize it by running several iterations. If this is not sufficient, you can also throw away the timing from the first iteration.

> **Listing 12.6 CUDA version of stream triad: Kernel call and timing loop**

```
CUDA/StreamTriad/StreamTriad.cu
51 for (int k=0; k<NTIMES; k++){
52   cpu_timer_start(&ttotal);
53   cudaMemcpy(a_d, a, stream_array_size*              Copies array
        sizeof(double), cudaMemcpyHostToDevice);        data from host
54   cudaMemcpy(b_d, b, stream_array_size*              to device
        sizeof(double), cudaMemcpyHostToDevice);
55   // cuda memcopy to device returns after buffer available
56   cudaDeviceSynchronize();              <───         Synchronizes to get accurate
57                                                       timing for kernel only
58   cpu_timer_start(&tkernel);
59   StreamTriad<<<gridsize, blocksize>>>              Launches
        (stream_array_size, scalar, a_d, b_d, c_d);     StreamTriad kernel
60   cudaDeviceSynchronize();              <───
61   tkernel_sum += cpu_timer_stop(tkernel);            Forces completion
62                                                       to get timing
63   // cuda memcpy from device to host blocks for completion
     //   so no need for synchronize
64   cudaMemcpy(c, c_d, stream_array_size*              Copies array data back
        sizeof(double), cudaMemcpyDeviceToHost);        from device to host
65   ttotal_sum += cpu_timer_stop(ttotal);
66   // check results and print errors if found.
     //    limit to only 10 errors per iteration
67   for (int i=0, icount=0; i<stream_array_size && icount < 10; i++){
```

```
68        if (c[i] != 1.0 + 3.0*2.0) {
69            printf("Error with result c[%d]=%lf on iter %d\n",i,c[i],k);
70            icount++;
71        } // if not correct, print error
72    } // result checking loop
73 } // timing for loop
```

The pattern in the timing loop is composed of the following steps:

1 Copy data to the GPU (lines 53–54)
2 Call the GPU kernel to operate on the arrays (line 59)
3 Copy the data back (line 64)

We add some synchronization and timer calls to get an accurate measurement of the GPU kernel. At the end of the loop, we then put in a check for the correctness of the result. Once this goes into production, we can remove the timing, synchronization, and the error check. The call to the GPU kernel can easily be spotted by the triple chevrons, or angle brackets. If we ignore the chevrons and the variables contained within these, the line has a typical C subroutine call syntax:

```
StreamTriad(stream_array_size, scalar, a_d, b_d, c_d);
```

The values within the parentheses are the arguments to be passed to the GPU kernel. For example

```
<<<gridsize, blocksize>>>
```

So what are the arguments contained within the chevrons? These are the arguments to the CUDA compiler on how to break up the problem into blocks for the GPU. Earlier, on lines 48 to 49 of listing 12.2, we set the block size and calculated the number of blocks, or grid size, to contain all the data in the array. The arguments in this case are 1D. We can also have 2D or 3D arrays by declaring and setting these arguments as follows for an NxN matrix.

```
dim3 blocksize(16,16); dim3 blocksize(8,8,8);
dim3 gridsize( (N + blocksize.x - 1)/blocksize.x,
               (N + blocksize.y - 1)/blocksize.y );
```

We can speed up the memory transfers by eliminating a data copy. This is possible through a deeper understanding of how the operating system functions. Memory that is transferred over the network must be in a fixed location that cannot be moved during the operation. Normal memory allocations are placed into *pageable memory*, or memory that can be moved on demand. The memory transfer must first move the data into *pinned memory*, or memory that cannot be moved. We first saw the use of pinned memory in section 9.4.2 when benchmarking memory movement over the PCI bus. We can eliminate a memory copy by allocating our arrays in pinned memory rather than pageable memory. Figure 9.8 shows the difference in performance that we might obtain. Now, how do we make this happen?

CUDA gives us a function call, `cudaHostMalloc`, that does this for us. It is a straight-up replacement for the regular system `malloc` routines, with a slight change in arguments, where the pointer is returned as an argument as shown:

```
double *x_host = (double *)malloc(stream_array_size*sizeof(double));
cudaMallocHost((void**)&x_host, stream_array_size*sizeof(double));
```

Is there a downside to using pinned memory? Well, if you do use a lot of pinned memory, there is no place to swap in another application. Swapping out the memory for one application and bringing in another is a huge convenience for users. This process is called memory paging.

> **DEFINITION** *Memory paging* in multi-user, multi-application operating systems is the process of moving memory pages temporarily out to disk so that another process can take place.

Memory paging is an important advance in operating systems to make it seem like you have more memory than you really do. For example, it allows you to temporarily start up Excel while working on Word and not have to close down your original application. It does this by writing your data out to disk and then reading it back when you return to Word. But this operation is expensive, so in high performance computing, we avoid memory paging because of the severe performance penalty that it incurs. Some heterogeneous computing systems with both a CPU and a GPU are implementing unified memory.

> **DEFINITION** *Unified memory* is memory that has the appearance of being a single address space for both the CPU and the GPU.

By now, you have seen that the handling of separate memory spaces on the CPU and the GPU introduces much of the complexity of writing GPU code. With unified memory, the GPU runtime system handles this for you. There may still be two separate arrays, but the data is moved automatically. On integrated GPUs, there is the possibility that memory does not have to be moved at all. Still, it is advisable to write your programs with explicit memory copies so that your programs are portable to systems without unified memory. The memory copy is skipped if it is not needed on the architecture.

12.2.2 *A reduction kernel in CUDA: Life gets complicated*

When we need cooperation among GPU threads, things get complicated with lower-level, native GPU languages. We'll look at a simple summation example to see how we can deal with this. The example requires two separate CUDA kernels and is shown in listings 12.7–12.10. The following listing shows the first pass, where we sum up the values within a thread block and store the result back out to the reduction scratch array, `redscratch`.

Listing 12.7   First pass of a sum reduction operation

```
CUDA/SumReduction/SumReduction.cu (four parts)
23 __global__ void reduce_sum_stage1of2(
24                  const int     isize,        // 0  Total number of cells.
25                        double *array,        // 1
26                        double *blocksum,     // 2
27                        double *redscratch)   // 3     Scratchpad array in
28 {                                                     CUDA shared memory
29     extern __shared__ double spad[];           ←
30     const unsigned int giX  = blockIdx.x*blockDim.x+threadIdx.x;
31     const unsigned int tiX  = threadIdx.x;
32
33     const unsigned int group_id = blockIdx.x;
34
35     spad[tiX] = 0.0;
36     if (giX < isize) {                          Loads memory
37       spad[tiX] = array[giX];                   into scratchpad
38     }                                           array
39
40     __syncthreads();             ←—            Synchronizes threads before
41                                                using scratchpad data
42     reduction_sum_within_block(spad);     ←
43                                                Sets reduction
44     //  Write the local value back to an array  within thread block
45     //     the size of the number of groups
46     if (tiX == 0){                              One thread stores
47       redscratch[group_id] = spad[0];          result for block.
48       (*blocksum) = spad[0];
49     }
   }
```

We start out the first pass by having all of the threads store their data into a scratchpad array in CUDA shared memory (lines 35–38). All the threads in the block can access this shared memory. Shared memory can be accessed in one or two processor cycles instead of the hundreds required for main GPU memory. You can think of shared memory as a programmable cache or as scratchpad memory. To make sure all the threads have completed the store, we use a synchronization call on line 40.

Because the reduction sum within the block is going to be used in both reduction passes, we put the code in a device subroutine and call it on line 42. A *device subroutine* is a subroutine that is to be called from another device subroutine rather than from the host. After the subroutine, the resulting sum is stored back out into a smaller scratch array that we read in during the second phase. We also store the result on line 47 in case the second pass can be skipped. Because we cannot access the values in other thread blocks, we have to complete the operation in a second pass in another kernel. In this first pass, we have reduced the length of the data by our block size.

Let's move on to look at the common device code that we mentioned in the first pass. We will need a sum reduction for the CUDA thread block in both passes, so we write it as a general device routine. The code shown in the following listing can also be easily modified for other reduction operators and only needs small changes for HIP and OpenCL.

Listing 12.8   Common sum reduction device kernel

CUDA/SumReduction/SumReduction.cu (four parts)   **CUDA defines warpSize to be 32**

```
 1 #define MIN_REDUCE_SYNC_SIZE warpSize
 2
 3 __device__ void reduction_sum_within_block(double  *spad)
 4 {
 5    const unsigned int tiX  = threadIdx.x;
 6    const unsigned int ntX  = blockDim.x;
 7
 8    for (int offset = ntX >> 1; offset > MIN_REDUCE_SYNC_SIZE;
            offset >>= 1) {
 9       if (tiX < offset) {
10          spad[tiX] = spad[tiX] + spad[tiX+offset];
11       }
12       __syncthreads();
13    }
14    if (tiX < MIN_REDUCE_SYNC_SIZE) {
15       for (int offset = MIN_REDUCE_SYNC_SIZE; offset > 1; offset >>= 1) {
16          spad[tiX] = spad[tiX] + spad[tiX+offset];
17          __syncthreads();
18       }
19       spad[tiX] = spad[tiX] + spad[tiX+1];
20    }
21 }
```

Line 9 note: **Only use threads needed when greater than the warp size**

Synchronizes between every level of the pass

The common device routine that will be called from both passes is defined on line 3. It does a sum reduction within the thread block. The `__device__` attribute before the routine indicates that it will be called from a GPU kernel. The basic concept of the routine is a pair-wise reduction tree in $O(\log n)$ operations as figure 12.2 shows. The

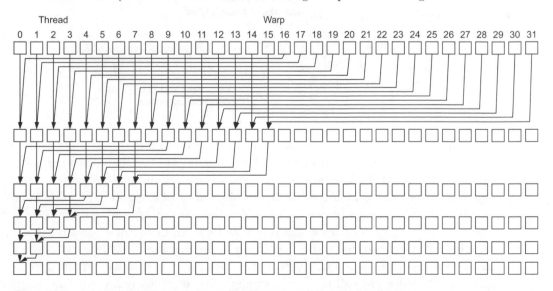

Figure 12.2   Pair-wise reduction tree for a warp that sums up values in log _n_ steps.

basic reduction tree from the figure is represented by the code on lines 15–18. We implement some minor modifications when the working set is larger than the warp size on lines 8–13 and for the final pass level on line 19 to avoid unnecessary synchronization.

The same pair-wise reduction concept is used for the full-thread block that can be up to 1,024 on most GPU devices, though 128 to 256 is more commonly used. But what do you do if your array size is greater than 1,024? We add a second pass that uses just a single thread block as the following listing shows.

Listing 12.9   Second pass for reduction operation

```
CUDA/SumReduction/SumReduction.cu (four parts)
51 __global__ void reduce_sum_stage2of2(
52                   const int    isize,
53                         double *total_sum,
54                         double *redscratch)
55 {
56    extern __shared__ double spad[];
57    const unsigned int tiX  = threadIdx.x;
58    const unsigned int ntX  = blockDim.x;
59
60    int giX = tiX;
61
62    spad[tiX] = 0.0;
63
64    // load the sum from reduction scratch, redscratch        Loads values into
65    if (tiX < isize) spad[tiX] = redscratch[giX];             scratchpad array
66
67    for (giX += ntX; giX < isize; giX += ntX) {       Loops by thread
68       spad[tiX] += redscratch[giX];                  block-size increments
69    }                                                  to get all the data
70                                Synchronizes when
71    __syncthreads();        ◄── scratchpad array is filled
72
73    reduction_sum_within_block(spad);    ◄──   Calls our common block
74                                               reduction routine
75    if (tiX == 0) {
76       (*total_sum) = spad[0];    ◄──   One thread sets the
77    }                                   total sum for return.
78 }
```

To avoid more than two kernels for larger arrays, we use one thread block and loop on lines 67–69 to read and sum any additional data into the shared scratchpad. We use a single thread block because we can synchronize within it, avoiding the need for another kernel call. If we are using thread block sizes of 128 and have a one million element array, the loop will sum in about 60 values into each location in shared memory ($1000000/128^2$). The array size is reduced by 128 in the first pass and then we sum into a scratchpad that is size 128, giving us the division by 128 squared. If we use larger block sizes, such as 1,024, we could reduce the loop from 60 iterations to a single read. Now we just call the same common thread block reduction that we used before. The result will be the first value in the scratchpad array. The last part of this is to set up and call these two kernels from the host. We'll see how this is done in the following listing.

Listing 12.10 Host code for CUDA reduction

CUDA/SumReduction/SumReduction.cu (four parts)

Calculates the block and grid sizes for the CUDA kernels

```
100 size_t blocksize = 128;
101 size_t blocksizebytes = blocksize*
                            sizeof(double);
102 size_t global_work_size = ((nsize + blocksize - 1) /blocksize) *
                            blocksize;
103 size_t gridsize = global_work_size/blocksize;
104
105 double *dev_x, *dev_total_sum, *dev_redscratch;
106 cudaMalloc(&dev_x, nsize*sizeof(double));
107 cudaMalloc(&dev_total_sum, 1*sizeof(double));
108 cudaMalloc(&dev_redscratch,
            gridsize*sizeof(double));
109
110 cudaMemcpy(dev_x, x, nsize*sizeof(double),
            cudaMemcpyHostToDevice);
111
112 reduce_sum_stage1of2
        <<<gridsize, blocksize, blocksizebytes>>>
        (nsize, dev_x, dev_total_sum,
         dev_redscratch);
113
114 if (gridsize > 1) {
115    reduce_sum_stage2of2
        <<<1, blocksize, blocksizebytes>>>
        (nsize, dev_total_sum, dev_redscratch);
116 }
117
118 double total_sum;
119 cudaMemcpy(&total_sum, dev_total_sum, 1*sizeof(double),
            cudaMemcpyDeviceToHost);
120 printf("Result -- total sum %lf \n",total_sum);
121
122 cudaFree(dev_redscratch);
123 cudaFree(dev_total_sum);
124 cudaFree(dev_x);
```

- **Allocates device memory for the kernel** (lines 106–108)
- **Copies the array to the GPU device** (line 110)
- **Calls the first pass of the reduction kernel** (line 112)
- **If needed, calls the second pass** (lines 114–115)

The host code first calculates the sizes for the kernel calls on lines 100–103. We then have to allocate the memory for the device arrays. For this operation, we need a scratch array where we can store the sums for each block from the first kernel. We allocate it on line 108 to be the grid size because that is the number of blocks that we have. We also need a shared memory scratchpad array that is the size of the block size. We calculate this size on line 101 and pass it into the kernel on lines 112 and 115 as the third parameter to the chevron operator. The third parameter is an optional parameter; this is the first time that we have seen it used. Take a look back at listing 12.9 (line 56) and listing 12.7 (line 29) to see where the corresponding code for the scratchpad is handled on the GPU device.

Trying to follow all the convoluted loops can be difficult. So we have created a version of the code that does the same loops on the CPU and prints its values as it goes along. It is in the CUDA/SumReductionRevealed directory at

https://github.com/EssentialsofParallelComputing/Chapter12

We don't have room to show all the code here, but you might find it useful to explore and print the values as it executes. We show an edited version of the output in the following example.

Example: CUDA/SumReductionRevealed

```
Calling first pass with gridsize 2 blocksize 128 blocksizebytes 1024

SYNCTHREADS after all values are in shared memory block
Data count is 200
 ====== ITREE_LEVEL 1 offset 64 ntX is 128 MIN_REDUCE_SYNC_SIZE 32 ====
Data count is reduced to 128
Sync threads when larger than warp
 ====== ITREE_LEVEL 2 offset 32 ntX is 128 MIN_REDUCE_SYNC_SIZE 32 ====
Sync threads when smaller than warp
Data count is reduced to 64
 ====== ITREE_LEVEL 3 offset 16 ntX is 128 MIN_REDUCE_SYNC_SIZE 32 ====
Sync threads when smaller than warp
Data count is reduced to 32
 ====== ITREE_LEVEL 4 offset 8 ntX is 128 MIN_REDUCE_SYNC_SIZE 32 ====
Sync threads when smaller than warp
Data count is reduced to 16
 ====== ITREE_LEVEL 5 offset 4 ntX is 128 MIN_REDUCE_SYNC_SIZE 32 ====
Sync threads when smaller than warp
Data count is reduced to 8
 ====== ITREE_LEVEL 6 offset 2 ntX is 128 MIN_REDUCE_SYNC_SIZE 32 ====
Sync threads when smaller than warp
Data count is reduced to 4
 ====== ITREE_LEVEL 7 offset 1 ntX is 128 MIN_REDUCE_SYNC_SIZE 32 ====
Data count is reduced to 2

Finished reduction sum within thread block

End of first pass

Synchronization in second pass after loading data
Data count is reduced to 2

 ====== ITREE_LEVEL 8 offset 1 ntX is 128 MIN_REDUCE_SYNC_SIZE 32 ====
Data count is reduced to 1

Finished reduction sum within thread block
```

```
Synchronization in second pass after reduction sum
Result -- total sum 19900
```

This example is for an array that is 200 integers long with each element initialized to its index value. We suggest that you follow along with the source code and figure 12.1 to understand what is happening. The start and end of the first pass and the second pass are printed. We can see the data count being reduced by a factor of two until there are only two left at the end of the first pass. The second pass quickly reduces this to a single value containing the summation.

We have shown this thread block reduction as a general introduction to kernels that require thread cooperation. You can see how complicated this is, especially compared to the single line needed for the intrinsic call in Fortran. In the process, we also gained a lot of speedup over the CPU and kept the data on the GPU for this operation. This algorithm can be further optimized, but you can also consider using some library services such as CUDA UnBound (CUB), Thrust, or other GPU libraries.

12.2.3 Hipifying the CUDA code

CUDA code only runs on NVIDIA GPUs. But AMD has implemented a similar GPU language and named it the Heterogeneous Interface for Portability (HIP). It is part of the Radeon Open Compute platform (ROCm) suite of tools from AMD. If you program in the HIP language, you can call the hipcc compiler that uses NVCC on NVIDIA platforms and HCC on AMD GPUs.

To try these examples, you may need to install the ROCm suite of software and tools. The install process frequently changes, so check for the latest instructions. There are some instructions that accompany the examples as well.

Example: Simple makefile for HIPifying a CUDA code

There are two versions of the makefile. One uses `hipify-perl` and the other uses `hipify-clang`. The `hipify-perl` is a simple Perl script. For more syntax-aware translation, you can try the `hipify-clang`. In either case, for more complex programs, you might need to manually complete the last modifications. We'll use the Perl version, so lets's start by linking Makefile.perl, shown in the following listing, to Makefile:

```
ln -s Makefile.perl Makefile
make
```

A simple makefile for HIP

```
HIP/StreamTriad/Makefile.perl
 1 all: StreamTriad
 2
 3 CXX = hipcc        ◁──┐  Sets the C++
                          compiler to hipcc
```

(continued)

```
 4
 5 %.cc : %.cu                      Converts the CUDA
 6   hipify-perl $^ > $@            code to HIP code
 7
 8 StreamTriad: StreamTriad.o timer.o
 9   ${CXX} -o $@ $^
10
11 clean:
12   rm -rf StreamTriad *.o StreamTriad.cc
```

The only real addition to the standard makefile is changing the compiler to hipcc and adding a pattern rule for converting the CUDA source code into HIP source code. We could just do the code conversion by manually invoking the hipify-perl script and then use the HIP version for both CUDA and AMD GPUs.

There is also good support for HIP in CMake, and HIP support has been available since version 2.8.3 of CMake. A typical CMakeLists file for HIP is shown in the following listing.

Listing 12.11   Building A HIP program with CMake

```
HIP/StreamTriad/CMakeLists.txt              Minimum version of
 1 cmake_minimum_required (VERSION 2.8.3)   CMake for HIP is 2.8.3
 2 project (StreamTriad)
 3                                          Sets a path to the
 6 if(NOT DEFINED HIP_PATH)                 HIP installation
 7    if(NOT DEFINED ENV{HIP_PATH})
 8        set(HIP_PATH "/opt/rocm/hip" CACHE PATH "Path to HIP install")
 9    else()
10        set(HIP_PATH $ENV{HIP_PATH} CACHE PATH "Path to HIP install")
11    endif()
12 endif()
13 set(CMAKE_MODULE_PATH "${HIP_PATH}/cmake" ${CMAKE_MODULE_PATH})
14
15 find_package(HIP REQUIRED)               Finds HIP using
16 if(HIP_FOUND)                            the path
17    message(STATUS "Found HIP: " ${HIP_VERSION})
20 endif()
21                                                      Sets the C++
22 set(CMAKE_CXX_COMPILER ${HIP_HIPCC_EXECUTABLE})      compiler to hipcc
23 set(MY_HIPCC_OPTIONS )
24 set(MY_HCC_OPTIONS )
25 set(MY_NVCC_OPTIONS )
26
27 # Adds build target of StreamTriad with source code files   Adds the executable,
28 HIP_ADD_EXECUTABLE(StreamTriad StreamTriad.cc               includes, and
                      timer.c timer.h)                         libraries
29 target_include_directories(StreamTriad PRIVATE ${HIP_PATH}/include)
30 target_link_directories(StreamTriad PRIVATE ${HIP_PATH}/lib)
31 target_link_libraries(StreamTriad hip_hcc)
```

```
32
33 # Cleanup
34 add_custom_target(distclean COMMAND rm -rf CMakeCache.txt CMakeFiles *.o
35     Makefile cmake_install.cmake StreamTriad.dSYM ipo_out.optrpt)
```

In the listing, we first try to set different path options for where the HIP install might be located and then call find_package for HIP on line 15. We then set the C++ compiler to hipcc on line 22. The HIP_ADD_EXECUTABLE command adds the build of our executable, and we round out the listing with settings for the HIP header files and libraries (lines 28–31). Now let's turn our attention to the HIP source in listing 12.12. We highlight the changes from the CUDA version of the source code given in listings 12.5–12.6.

> **Listing 12.12 The HIP differences for the stream triad**

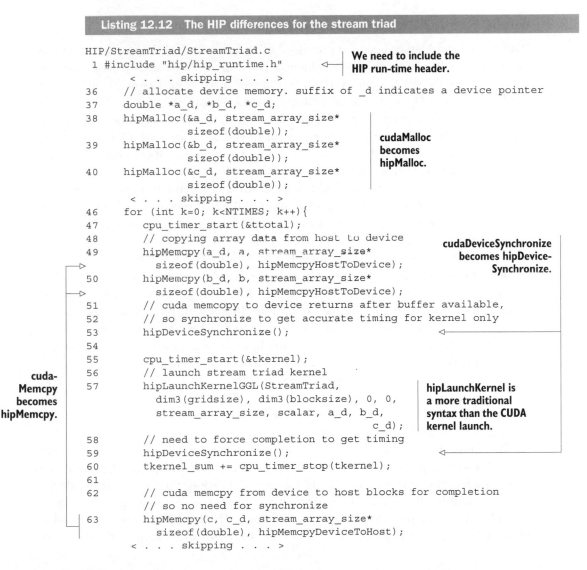

```
HIP/StreamTriad/StreamTriad.c
 1 #include "hip/hip_runtime.h"          ◁─┤  We need to include the
        < . . . skipping . . . >              HIP run-time header.
36     // allocate device memory. suffix of _d indicates a device pointer
37     double *a_d, *b_d, *c_d;
38     hipMalloc(&a_d, stream_array_size*
                sizeof(double));                   cudaMalloc
39     hipMalloc(&b_d, stream_array_size*          becomes
                sizeof(double));                   hipMalloc.
40     hipMalloc(&c_d, stream_array_size*
                sizeof(double));
        < . . . skipping . . . >
46     for (int k=0; k<NTIMES; k++){
47       cpu_timer_start(&ttotal);
48       // copying array data from host to device      cudaDeviceSynchronize
49       hipMemcpy(a_d, a, stream_array_size*           becomes hipDevice-
          sizeof(double), hipMemcpyHostToDevice);             Synchronize.
50       hipMemcpy(b_d, b, stream_array_size*
          sizeof(double), hipMemcpyHostToDevice);
51       // cuda memcopy to device returns after buffer available,
52       // so synchronize to get accurate timing for kernel only
53       hipDeviceSynchronize();                  ◁─────────────
54
55       cpu_timer_start(&tkernel);
56       // launch stream triad kernel
57       hipLaunchKernelGGL(StreamTriad,             hipLaunchKernel is
          dim3(gridsize), dim3(blocksize), 0, 0,     a more traditional
          stream_array_size, scalar, a_d, b_d,       syntax than the CUDA
                              c_d);                   kernel launch.
58       // need to force completion to get timing
59       hipDeviceSynchronize();                  ◁─────────────
60       tkernel_sum += cpu_timer_stop(tkernel);
61
62       // cuda memcpy from device to host blocks for completion
         // so no need for synchronize
63       hipMemcpy(c, c_d, stream_array_size*
          sizeof(double), hipMemcpyDeviceToHost);
        < . . . skipping . . . >
```

cuda-
Memcpy
becomes
hipMemcpy.

```
72      }
        < . . . skipping . . . >
75
76      hipFree(a_d);          hipFree replaces
77      hipFree(b_d);          cudaFree.
78      hipFree(c_d);
```

To convert from CUDA source to HIP source, we replace all occurrences of cuda in the source with hip. The only more significant change is to the kernel launch call, where HIP uses a more traditional syntax than the triple chevron used in CUDA. Oddly enough, the greatest changes are to use the correct terminology in the variable naming for the two languages.

12.3 *OpenCL for a portable open source GPU language*

With the overwhelming need for portable GPU code, a new GPU programming language, OpenCL, emerged in 2008. OpenCL is an open standard GPU language that can run on both NVIDIA and AMD/ATI graphic cards, as well as many other hardware devices. The OpenCL standard effort was led by Apple with many other organizations involved. One of the nice things about OpenCL is that you can use virtually any C or even C++ compiler for the host code. For the GPU device code, OpenCL initially was based on a subset of C99. Recently, the 2.1 and 2.2 versions of OpenCL added C++ 14 support, but implementations are still not available.

The OpenCL release took off with a lot of initial excitement. Finally, here was a way to write portable GPU code. For example, GIMP announced that it would support OpenCL as a way for GPU acceleration to be made available on many hardware platforms. The reality has been less compelling. Many feel that OpenCL is too low-level and verbose for widespread acceptance. It may even be that its eventual role is as the low-level portability layer for higher level languages. But its value as a portable language across a diverse set of hardware devices has been demonstrated by its acceptance within the embedded device community for field-programmable gate arrays (FPGAs). One of the reasons OpenCL is thought to be verbose is that the device selection is more complicated (and powerful). You have to detect and select the device you will run on. This can amount to a hundred lines of code just to get started.

Nearly everyone who uses OpenCL writes a library to handle the low-level concerns. We are no exception. Our library is called EZCL. Nearly every OpenCL call is wrapped with at least a light layer to handle the error conditions. Device detection, compiling code, and error handling consume a lot of lines of code.

We'll use an abbreviated version of our EZCL library, called EZCL_Lite, in our examples so that you can see the actual OpenCL calls. The EZCL_Lite routines are used to select the device and set it up for the application, then compile the device code and handle the errors. The code for these operations is too long to show here, so look at the examples in the OpenCL directory at https://github.com/Essentialsof ParallelComputing/Chapter12. The full EZCL library is also available in the directory.

The EZCL routines give detailed errors with calls and on which line in the source code that it occurs.

Before you start out trying the OpenCL code, check to see if you have the proper setup and devices. For this, you can use the `clinfo` command.

Example: Getting information about the OpenCL installation

Run the OpenCL info command:

```
clinfo
```

If you get the following output, OpenCL is not set up or you do not have an appropriate OpenCL device:

```
Number of platforms    0
```

If you don't have the `clinfo` command, try installing it with the appropriate command for your system. For Ubuntu, it is

```
sudo apt install clinfo
```

The examples that go along with the chapter include some brief hints for installation of OpenCL, but check for the latest information for your system. OpenCL has an extension that provides a detailed model for how each device should set up its driver in its Installable Client Driver (ICD) specification. This permits multiple OpenCL platforms and drivers to be available for an application.

12.3.1 Writing and building your first OpenCL application

The changes to a standard makefile to incorporate OpenCL are not too complicated. The typical changes are shown in listing 12.13. To use the simple makefile for OpenCL, type

```
ln -s Makefile.simple Makefile
```

Then build the application with `make` and run the application with ./StreamTriad.

Listing 12.13 OpenCL simple makefile

```
OpenCL/StreamTriad/Makefile.simple
 1 all: StreamTriad
 2
 3 #CFLAGS = -DDEVICE_DETECT_DEBUG=1      ◁─── Turns on device
 4 #OPENCL_LIB = -L<path>                      detection verbosity
 5
 6 %.inc : %.cl                           Pattern rule embeds
 7    ./embed_source.pl $^ > $@           the OpenCL source
 8
 9 StreamTriad.o: StreamTriad.c StreamTriad_kernel.inc
10
```

```
11 StreamTriad: StreamTriad.o timer.o ezclsmall.o
12   ${CC} -o $@ $^ ${OPENCL_LIB} -lOpenCL
13
14 clean:
15   rm -rf StreamTriad *.o StreamTriad_kernel.inc
```

The makefile includes a way to set the DEVICE_DETECT_DEBUG flag to print out detailed information on the GPU devices available. This flag turns on more verbosity in the ezcl_lite.c source code. It can be helpful for fixing problems with device detection or getting the wrong device. There is also the addition of a pattern rule on line 6 that embeds the OpenCL source into the program for use at run time. This Perl script converts the source into a comment and as a dependency on line 9. It will be included in the StreamTriad.c file with an include statement.

The embed_source.pl utility is one that we developed to link the OpenCL source directly into the executable. (See the chapter examples for the source to this utility.) The common way for OpenCL code to function is to have a separate source file that must be located at run time, which is then compiled once the device is known. Using a separate file creates problems with it not being able to be found or getting the wrong version of the file. We strongly recommend embedding the source into the executable to avoid these problems. We can also use CMake support for OpenCL in our build system as the following listing shows.

Listing 12.14   OpenCL CMake file

```
OpenCL/StreamTriad/CMakeLists.txt
 1 cmake_minimum_required (VERSION 3.1)
 2 project (StreamTriad)
 3
 4 if (DEVICE_DETECT_DEBUG)
 5    add_definitions(-DDEVICE_DETECT_DEBUG=1)
 6 endif (DEVICE_DETECT_DEBUG)
 7
 8 find_package(OpenCL REQUIRED)
 9 set(HAVE_CL_DOUBLE ON CACHE BOOL
        "Have OpenCL Double")
10 set(NO_CL_DOUBLE OFF)
11 include_directories(${OpenCL_INCLUDE_DIRS})
12
13 # Adds build target of StreamTriad with source code files
14 add_executable(StreamTriad StreamTriad.c ezclsmall.c ezclsmall.h
                   timer.c timer.h)
15 target_link_libraries(StreamTriad ${OpenCL_LIBRARIES})
16 add_dependencies(StreamTriad StreamTriad_kernel_source)
17
18 ########### embed source target ##############
19 add_custom_command(OUTPUT
 ${CMAKE_CURRENT_BINARY_DIR}/StreamTriad_kernel.inc
20    COMMAND ${CMAKE_SOURCE_DIR}/embed_source.pl
        ${CMAKE_SOURCE_DIR}/StreamTriad_kernel.cl
      > StreamTriad_kernel.inc
21        DEPENDS StreamTriad_kernel.cl ${CMAKE_SOURCE_DIR}/embed_source.pl)
```

CMake added OpenCL support with version 3.1.

Turns on device detection verbosity

Flags set CL_DOUBLE support

Custom command embeds OpenCL source into executable

```
22 add_custom_target(
           StreamTriad_kernel_source ALL DEPENDS        ◁————  Custom command
       ${CMAKE_CURRENT_BINARY_DIR}/                             embeds OpenCL source
           StreamTriad_kernel.inc)                       ◁————  into executable
23
24 # Cleanup
25 add_custom_target(distclean COMMAND rm -rf CMakeCache.txt CMakeFiles
26                   Makefile cmake_install.cmake StreamTriad.dSYM
                     ipo_out.optrpt)
27
28 SET_DIRECTORY_PROPERTIES(PROPERTIES ADDITIONAL_MAKE_CLEAN_FILES
                        "StreamTriad_kernel.inc")
```

OpenCL support in CMake was added at version 3.1. We added this version requirement at the top of the CMakelists.txt file on line 1. There are a few other special
things to note. For this example, we used the -DDEVICE_DETECT_DEBUG=1 option to the
CMake command to turn on the verbosity for the device detection. Also, we included
a way to turn on and off support for OpenCL double precision. We used this in the
EZCL_Lite code to set the just-in-time (JIT) compile flag for the OpenCL device code.
Last, we added a custom command in lines 19–22 for embedding the OpenCL device
source into the executable. The source code for the OpenCL kernel is in a separate
file called StreamTriad_kernel.cl as shown in the following listing.

Listing 12.15   OpenCL kernel

```
OpenCL/StreamTriad/StreamTriad_kernel.cl
 1 // OpenCL kernel version of stream triad
 2 __kernel void StreamTriad(                   ◁————  __kernel attribute
 3                const int n,                          indicates this is called
 4                const double scalar,                  from the host.
 5       __global const double *a,
 6       __global const double *b,
 7       __global       double *c)
 8 {                                            ┐  Gets the
 9    int i = get_global_id(0);        ◁────────┘  thread index
10
11    // Protect from going out-of-bounds
12    if (i >= n) return;
13
14    c[i] = a[i] + scalar*b[i];
15 }
```

Compare this kernel code to the kernel code for CUDA in listing 12.4. The OpenCL
code is nearly identical except that __kernel replaces __global__ on the subroutine
declaration, the __global attribute is added to the pointer arguments, and there's a
different way of getting the thread index. Also, the CUDA kernel code is in the same
.cu file as the source for the host, while the OpenCL code is in a separate .cl file. We
could have separated out the CUDA code into its own .cu file and put the host code in
a standard C++ source file. This would be similar to the structure we use for our
OpenCL application.

NOTE So many of the differences between the kernel codes for CUDA and OpenCL are superficial.

So how different is the OpenCL host-side code from the CUDA version? Let's take a look at the OpenCl version in listing 12.16 and compare it to the code in listing 12.5. There are two versions of the OpenCL stream triad: StreamTriad_simple.c without error checking and StreamTriad.c with error checking. The error checking adds a lot of lines of code that initially just get in the way of understanding what is going on.

Listing 12.16   OpenCL version of stream triad: Set up and tear down

```
OpenCL/StreamTriad/StreamTriad_simple.c
 5 #include "StreamTriad_kernel.inc"
 6 #ifdef __APPLE_CC__
 7 #include <OpenCL/OpenCL.h>              Apple has
 8 #else                                   to be
 9 #include <CL/cl.h>                       different.
10 #endif
11 #include "ezcl_lite.h"        ←         Our EZCL_Lite
   < . . . skipping code . . . >          support library
32    cl_command_queue command_queue;
33    cl_context context;
34    iret = ezcl_devtype_init(
             CL_DEVICE_TYPE_GPU, &command_queue,    Gets the GPU
             &context);                             device
35    const char *defines = NULL;
36    cl_program program =
         ezcl_create_program_wsource(context,       Creates the program
         defines, StreamTriad_kernel_source);       from the source
37    cl_kernel kernel_StreamTriad =                 Compiles the
         clCreateKernel(program, "StreamTriad",      StreamTriad kernel
         &iret);                                     in the source
38
39    // allocate device memory. suffix of _d indicates a device pointer
40    size_t nsize = stream_array_size*sizeof(double);
41    cl_mem a_d = clCreateBuffer(context,
         CL_MEM_READ_WRITE, nsize, NULL, &iret);
42    cl_mem b_d = clCreateBuffer(context,
         CL_MEM_READ_WRITE, nsize, NULL, &iret);
43    cl_mem c_d = clCreateBuffer(context,
         CL_MEM_READ_WRITE, nsize, NULL, &iret);
44
45    // setting work group size and padding
      //    to get even number of workgroups
46    size_t local_work_size = 512;
47    size_t global_work_size = ( (stream_array_size + local_work_size - 1)
         /local_work_size ) * local_work_size;
   < . . . skipping code . . . >
74    clReleaseMemObject(a_d);
75    clReleaseMemObject(b_d);
76    clReleaseMemObject(c_d);
77
```

Handles array memory (annotation for lines 41–76)

Work group size calculation is similar to CUDA. (annotation for lines 45–47)

```
78     clReleaseKernel(kernel_StreamTriad);
79     clReleaseCommandQueue(command_queue);
80     clReleaseContext(context);
81     clReleaseProgram(program);
```

Cleans up kernel and device-related objects

At the start of the program, we encounter some real differences at lines 34–37, where we have to find our GPU device and compile our device code. This is done for us behind the scenes in CUDA. Two of the lines of OpenCL code call our EZCL_Lite routines to detect the device and to create the program object. We made these calls because the amount of code required for these functions is too long to show here. The source for these routines is hundreds of lines long, though much of it is error checking.

> **NOTE** The source is available with the chapter examples in the OpenCL/ StreamTriad directory at https://github.com/EssentialsofParallelComputing/ Chapter12. Some of the error checking code has been left out of the short version, StreamTriad_simple.c, but it is in the long version of the code in the file StreamTriad.c.

The rest of the set up and tear down code follows the same pattern that we saw in the CUDA code, with a little more cleanup required, again related to the device and program source handling. Now, how does the section of code that calls the OpenCL kernel in the timing loop in listing 12.16 compare to the CUDA code from listing 12.6?

Listing 12.17 OpenCL version of stream triad: Kernel call and timing loop

```
OpenCL/StreamTriad/StreamTriad_simple.c
49     for (int k=0; k<NTIMES; k++){
50         cpu_timer_start(&ttotal);
51         // copying array data from host to device
52         iret=clEnqueueWriteBuffer(command_queue,
               a_d, CL_FALSE, 0, nsize, &a[0],
               0, NULL, NULL);
53         iret=clEnqueueWriteBuffer(command_queue,
               b_d, CL_TRUE, 0, nsize, &b[0],
               0, NULL, NULL);
54
55         cpu_timer_start(&tkernel);
56         // set stream triad kernel arguments
57         iret=clSetKernelArg(kernel_StreamTriad,
               0, sizeof(cl_int),
               (void *)&stream_array_size);
58         iret=clSetKernelArg(kernel_StreamTriad,
               1, sizeof(cl_double),
               (void *)&scalar);
59         iret=clSetKernelArg(kernel_StreamTriad,
               2, sizeof(cl_mem), (void *)&a_d);
60         iret=clSetKernelArg(kernel_StreamTriad,
               3, sizeof(cl_mem), (void *)&b_d);
61         iret=clSetKernelArg(kernel_StreamTriad,
               4, sizeof(cl_mem), (void *)&c_d);
```

Memory movement calls

Sets kernel arguments

```
62        // call stream triad kernel
63        clEnqueueNDRangeKernel(command_queue,
              kernel_StreamTriad, 1, NULL,          Calls the
              &global_work_size, &local_work_size,  kernel
              0, NULL, NULL);
64        // need to force completion to get timing
65        clEnqueueBarrier(command_queue);
66        tkernel_sum += cpu_timer_stop(tkernel);
67
68        iret=clEnqueueReadBuffer(command_queue,
              c_d, CL_TRUE, 0, nsize, c,           Synchronization
              0, NULL, NULL);                       barrier
69        ttotal_sum += cpu_timer_stop(ttotal);
70     }
```

What is happening on lines 57–61? OpenCL requires a separate call for every kernel argument. If we check the return code from each, it is even more lines. This is a lot more verbose than the single line 53 in listing 12.6 in the CUDA version. But there is a direct correspondence between the two versions. OpenCL is just more verbose in describing the operations to pass the arguments. Except for the device detection and program compilation, the programs are similar in their operations. The biggest difference is the syntax used in the two languages.

In listing 12.18, we show a rough call sequence for the device detection and the create program calls. What makes these routines long is the error checking and the handling required for special cases. For these two functions, it is important to have good error handling. We need the compiler report for an error in our source code or if it got the wrong GPU device.

Listing 12.18   OpenCL support library ezcl_lite

```
OpenCL/StreamTriad/ezcl_lite.c
/* init and finish routine */
cl_int ezcl_devtype_init(cl_device_type device_type,
   cl_command_queue *command_queue, cl_context *context);
clGetPlatformIDs -- first to get number of platforms and allocate
clGetPlatformIDs -- now get platforms
Loop on number of platforms and
   clGetDeviceIDs -- once to get number of devices and allocate
   clGetDeviceIDs -- get devices
   check for double precision support -- clGetDeviceInfo
End loop
clCreateContext
clCreateCommandQueue

/* kernel and program routines */
cl_program ezcl_create_program_wsource(cl_context context,
   const char *defines, const char *source);
     clCreateProgramWithSource
     set a compile string (hardware specific options)
     clBuildProgram
     Check for error, if found
```

```
        clGetProgramBuildInfo
        and printout compile report
    End error handling
```

We conclude this presentation on OpenCL with a nod to the many language interfaces that have been created for it. There are a C++, Python, Perl, and Java versions. In each of these languages, a higher-level interface has been created that hides some of the details in the C version of OpenCL. And, we highly recommend the use of our EZCL library or one of the many other middleware libraries for OpenCL.

There has been an unofficial C++ version available since OpenCL v1.2. The implementation is just a thin layer on top of the C version of OpenCL. Despite failure to get approval by the standards committee, it is completely usable by developers. It is available at https://github.com/KhronosGroup/OpenCL-CLHPP. The formal approval of C++ in OpenCL has only recently occurred, but we are still waiting on implementations.

12.3.2 Reductions in OpenCL

The sum reduction in OpenCL is similar to that in CUDA. Rather than step through the code, we'll just look at the differences in the kernel source. Shown first in figure 12.3 is the side-by-side difference of the sum_within_block, the common routine by both kernels.

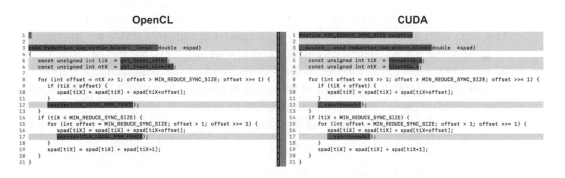

Figure 12.3   Comparison of OpenCL and CUDA reduction kernels: sum_within_block

The difference in this device kernel called by another kernel begins with the attributes on the declaration. CUDA requires a __device__ attribute on the declaration, while OpenCL does not. For the arguments, passing in the scratchpad array requires a __local attribute that CUDA does not need. The next difference is the syntax for getting the local thread index and block (tile) size (figure 12.3 on lines 5 and 6). The synchronization calls are also different. At the top of the routine, a warp size is defined by a macro to help with portability between NVIDIA and AMD GPUs. CUDA defines this as a warp-size variable. For OpenCL, it is passed in with a compiler define. We also change the terminology from block to tile in the actual code to stay consistent with each language's terminology.

The next routine is the first of two kernel passes, called stage1of2, in figure 12.4. This kernel is called from the host. The __global__ attribute for CUDA becomes __kernel for OpenCL. We also have to add the __global attribute to the pointer arguments for OpenCL.

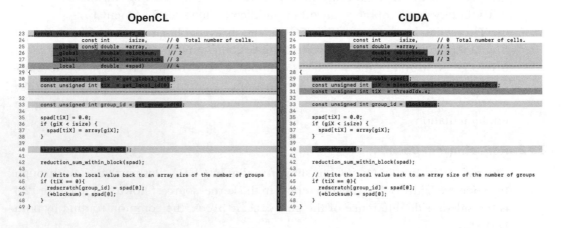

Figure 12.4   Comparison for the first of two kernel passes for the OpenCL and CUDA reduction kernels

The next difference is an important one to take note of. In CUDA, we declare the scratchpad in shared memory as an extern __shared__ variable in the body of the kernel. On the host side, the size of this shared memory space is given as a number of bytes in the optional third argument in the triple chevron brackets. OpenCL does this differently. It is passed as the last argument in the argument list with the __local attribute. On the host side, the memory is specified in the set argument call for the fourth kernel argument:

```
clSetKernelArg(reduce_sum_1of2, 4,
               local_work_size*sizeof(cl_double), NULL);
```

The size is the third argument in the call. The rest of the changes are in the syntax to set the thread parameters and the synchronization call. The last part of the comparison is the second pass of the sum reduction kernel in figure 12.5.

We've already seen all of the change patterns in the second kernel. We still have the differences in the declaration of the kernel and the arguments. The local scratch array also has the same differences as the kernel for the first pass. The thread parameters and the synchronization also have the same expected differences.

Looking back at the three comparisons in figures 12.3–5, it is what we didn't have to note that becomes apparent. The bodies of the kernels are essentially the same.

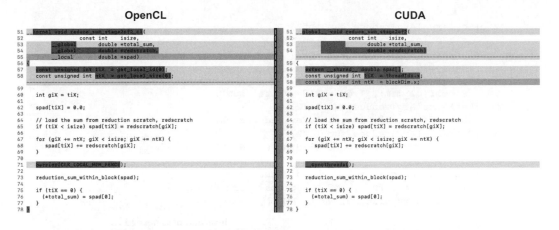

Figure 12.5 Comparison of the second pass for the reduction sum

The only difference is the syntax for the synchronization call. The host side code for the sum reduction in OpenCL is shown in the following listing.

Listing 12.19   Host code for the OpenCL sum reduction

```
OpenCL/SumReduction/SumReduction.c
20 cl_context context;
21 cl_command_queue command_queue;
22 ezcl_devtype_init(CL_DEVICE_TYPE_GPU, &command_queue, &context);
23
24 const char *defines = NULL;
25 cl_program program = ezcl_create_program_wsource(context, defines,
      SumReduction_kernel_source);
26 cl_kernel reduce_sum_1of2=clCreateKernel(
      program, "reduce_sum_stage1of2_cl", &iret);
27 cl_kernel reduce_sum_2of2=clCreateKernel(
      program, "reduce_sum_stage2of2_cl", &iret);
28
29 struct timespec tstart_cpu;
30 cpu_timer_start(&tstart_cpu);
31
32 size_t local_work_size = 128;
33 size_t global_work_size = ((nsize + local_work_size - 1)
      /local_work_size) * local_work_size;
34 size_t nblocks    = global_work_size/local_work_size;
35
36 cl_mem dev_x = clCreateBuffer(context, CL_MEM_READ_WRITE,
      nsize*sizeof(double), NULL, &iret);
37 cl_mem dev_total_sum = clCreateBuffer(context, CL_MEM_READ_WRITE,
      1*sizeof(double), NULL, &iret);
38 cl_mem dev_redscratch = clCreateBuffer(context, CL_MEM_READ_WRITE,
      nblocks*sizeof(double), NULL, &iret);
39
40 clEnqueueWriteBuffer(command_queue, dev_x, CL_TRUE, 0,
      nsize*sizeof(cl_double), &x[0], 0, NULL, NULL);
```

> **Two kernels to create from a single source**

```
41
42 clSetKernelArg(reduce_sum_1of2, 0,
       sizeof(cl_int), (void *)&nsize);
43 clSetKernelArg(reduce_sum_1of2, 1,
       sizeof(cl_mem), (void *)&dev_x);
44 clSetKernelArg(reduce_sum_1of2, 2,
       sizeof(cl_mem), (void *)&dev_total_sum);
45 clSetKernelArg(reduce_sum_1of2, 3,
       sizeof(cl_mem), (void *)&dev_redscratch);
46 clSetKernelArg(reduce_sum_1of2, 4,
       local_work_size*sizeof(cl_double), NULL);
47
48 clEnqueueNDRangeKernel(command_queue,
       reduce_sum_1of2, 1, NULL, &global_work_size,
       &local_work_size, 0, NULL, NULL);
49
50 if (nblocks > 1) {
51    clSetKernelArg(reduce_sum_2of2, 0,
          sizeof(cl_int), (void *)&nblocks);
52    clSetKernelArg(reduce_sum_2of2, 1,
          sizeof(cl_mem), (void *)&dev_total_sum);
53    clSetKernelArg(reduce_sum_2of2, 2,
          sizeof(cl_mem), (void *)&dev_redscratch);
54    clSetKernelArg(reduce_sum_2of2, 3,
          local_work_size*sizeof(cl_double), NULL);
55
56    clEnqueueNDRangeKernel(command_queue,
          reduce_sum_2of2, 1, NULL, &local_work_size,
          &local_work_size, 0, NULL, NULL);
57 }
58
59 double total_sum;
60
61 iret=clEnqueueReadBuffer(command_queue, dev_total_sum, CL_TRUE, 0,
       1*sizeof(cl_double), &total_sum, 0, NULL, NULL);
62
63 printf("Result -- total sum %lf \n",total_sum);
64
65 clReleaseMemObject(dev_x);
66 clReleaseMemObject(dev_redscratch);
67 clReleaseMemObject(dev_total_sum);
68
69 clReleaseKernel(reduce_sum_1of2);
70 clReleaseKernel(reduce_sum_2of2);
71 clReleaseCommandQueue(command_queue);
72 clReleaseContext(context);
73 clReleaseProgram(program);
```

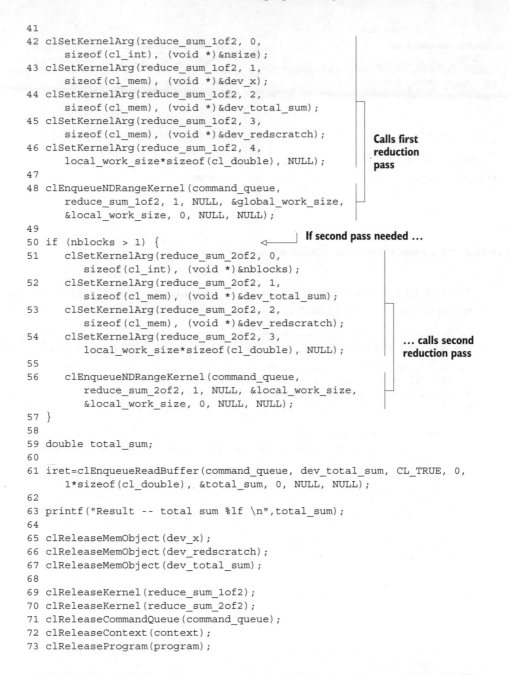

Calls first reduction pass

If second pass needed …

… calls second reduction pass

The call to the first kernel pass creates a local scratchpad array on line 46. The intermediate results are stored back into the redscratch array created on line 38. If there is more than one block, a second pass is needed. The redscratch array is passed back in to complete the reduction. Note that the kernel parameters in arguments 5 and 6 are set to `local_work_size` or a single work group. This is so a synchronization can be done across all the remaining data and another pass will not be needed.

12.4 *SYCL: An experimental C++ implementation goes mainstream*

SYCL started out in 2014 as an experimental C++ implementation on top of OpenCL. The goal of the developers creating SYCL is a more natural extension of the C++ language than the add-on feeling of OpenCL with the C language. It is being developed as a cross-platform abstraction layer that leverages the portability and efficiency of OpenCL. Its experimental language focus changed suddenly when Intel chose it as one of their major language pathways for the announced Department of Energy Aurora HPC system. The Aurora system will use the new Intel discrete GPUs that are under development. Intel has proposed some additions to the SYCL standard that they have prototyped in their Data Parallel C++ (DPCPP) compiler in their oneAPI open programming system.

You can get introduced to SYCL in several ways. Some of these even avoid having to install the software or having the right hardware. You might first try out the following cloud-based systems:

- Interactive SYCL provides a tutorial on the tech.io website at https://tech.io/playgrounds/48226/introduction-to-sycl/introduction-to-sycl-2.
- Intel provides a cloud version of oneAPI and DPCPP at https://software.intel.com/en-us/oneapi. You must register to use.

You can also download and install versions of SYCL from these sites:

- The ComputeCPP community edition at https://developer.codeplay.com/products/computecpp/ce/home/. You must register to download.
- The Intel DPCPP compiler at https://github.com/intel/llvm/blob/sycl/sycl/doc/GetStartedGuide.md
- Intel also provides Docker file setup instructions at https://github.com/intel/oneapi-containers/blob/master/images/docker/basekit-devel-ubuntu18.04/Dockerfile

We'll work with Intel's DPCPP version of SYCL. There are instructions to set up a VirtualBox installation of oneAPI with the examples that accompany this chapter in the README.virtualbox at https://github.com/EssentialsofParallelComputing/Chapter12. You should be able to run VirtualBox on nearly any operating system. Let's start off with a simple makefile for the DPCPP compiler as the following listing shows.

Listing 12.20 Simple makefile for DPCPP version of SYCL

```
DPCPP/StreamTriad/Makefile          ┐  Specifies dpcpp as
  1 CXX = dpcpp            ◄─────────┘  the C++ compiler
  2 CXXFLAGS = -std=c++17 -fsycl -O3  ◄──┐  Adds the SYCL option
  3                                      │  to the C++ flags
  4 all: StreamTriad
```

```
 5
 6 StreamTriad: StreamTriad.o timer.o
 7   $(CXX) $(CXXFLAGS) $^ -o $@
 8
 9 clean:
10   -rm -f StreamTriad.o StreamTriad
```

Setting the C++ compiler to the Intel dpcpp compiler takes care of the paths, libraries, and include files. The only other requirement is to set some flags for the C++ compiler. The following listing shows the SYCL source for our example.

Listing 12.21   Stream triad example for DPCPP version of SYCL

DPCPP/StreamTriad/StreamTriad.cc

```
 1 #include <chrono>                       ⎫ Includes the SYCL
 2 #include "CL/sycl.hpp"        ◄─────────┘ header file
 3
 4 namespace Sycl = cl::sycl;    ◄──┐ Uses the SYCL
 5 using namespace std;             └ namespace
 6
 7 int main(int argc, char * argv[])
 8 {
 9     chrono::high_resolution_clock::time_point t1, t2;
10
11     size_t nsize = 10000;
12     cout << "StreamTriad with " << nsize << " elements" << endl;
13
14     // host data
15     vector<double> a(nsize,1.0);        ⎫ Initializes the host
16     vector<double> b(nsize,2.0);        ⎬ side vectors to
17     vector<double> c(nsize,-1.0);       ⎭ constants
18
19     t1 = chrono::high_resolution_clock::now();
20                                              ⎫ Sets up the
21     Sycl::queue Queue(Sycl::cpu_selector{}); ◄─┘ device for CPU
22
23     const double scalar = 3.0;
24
25     Sycl::buffer<double,1> dev_a { a.data(),   ⎫ Allocates the
           Sycl::range<1>(a.size()) };           ⎬ device buffer
26     Sycl::buffer<double,1> dev_b { b.data(),   ⎬ and sets to the
           Sycl::range<1>(b.size()) };           ⎬ host buffer
27     Sycl::buffer<double,1> dev_c { c.data(),   ⎭
           Sycl::range<1>(c.size()) };
28
29     Queue.submit([&](Sycl::handler&   ⎫ Lambda for queue
           CommandGroup) {              └ submission
30
31         auto a = dev_a.get_access<Sycl::
               access::mode::read>(CommandGroup);   ⎫ Gets access
32         auto b = dev_b.get_access<Sycl::          ⎬ to device
               access::mode::read>(CommandGroup);   ⎬ arrays
33         auto c = dev_c.get_access<Sycl::          ⎭
               access::mode::write>(CommandGroup);
```

```
34
35          CommandGroup.parallel_for<class          Lambda for
                 StreamTriad>(Sycl::range<1>{nsize},   parallel for
                 [=] (Sycl::id<1> it){               kernel
36               c[it] = a[it] + scalar * b[it];
37          });
38      });                     Waits for
39      Queue.wait();       ←──┘  completion
40
41      t2 = chrono::high_resolution_clock::now();
42
        double time1 = chrono::duration_cast<
                    chrono::duration<double> >(t2 - t1).count();
43      cout << "Runtime is  " << time1*1000.0 << " msecs " << endl;
44 }
```

The first `Sycl` function selects a device and creates a queue to work on it. We ask for a CPU, though this code would also work for GPUs with unified memory.

```
Sycl::queue Queue(sycl::cpu_selector{});
```

We select a CPU for maximum portability so that the code runs on most systems. To make this code work on GPUs without unified memory, we would need to add explicit copies of data from one memory space to another. The default selector preferentially finds a GPU, but falls back to a CPU. If we want to only select a GPU or CPU, we could also specify other selectors such as

```
Sycl::queue Queue(sycl::default_selector{}); // uses the default device
Sycl::queue Queue(sycl::gpu_selector{});     // finds a GPU device
Sycl::queue Queue(sycl::cpu_selector{});     // finds a CPU device
Sycl::queue Queue(sycl::host_selector{});    // runs on the host (CPU)
```

The last option means that it will run on the host as if there were no SYCL or OpenCL code. The setup of the device and queue is far simpler than what we did in OpenCL. Now we need to set up device buffers with the SYCL buffer:

```
Sycl::buffer<double,1> dev_a { a.data(), Sycl::range<1>(a.size()) };
```

The first argument to the buffer is a data type, and the second is the dimensionality of the data. Then we give it the variable name, `dev_a`. The first argument to the variable is the host data array to use for initializing the device array, and the second is the index set to use. In this case, we specify a 1D range from 0 to the size of the a variable. On line 29, we encounter the first lambda to create a command group handler for the queue:

```
Queue.submit([&](Sycl::handler& CommandGroup)
```

We introduced lambdas in section 10.2.1. The lambda capture clause, `[&]`, specifies capturing outside variables used in the routine by reference. For this lambda, the capture gets `nsize`, `scalar`, `dev_a`, `dev_b`, and `dev_c` for use in the lambda. We could specify it with just the single capture setting of by reference, `[&]`, or with the following form, where we specify each variable that will be captured. Good programming practice would prefer the latter, but the lists can get long.

```
Queue.submit([&nsize, &scalar, &dev_a, &dev_b, &dev_c]
    (Sycl::handler& CommandGroup)
```

In the body of the lambda, we get access to the device arrays and rename them for use within the device routine. This is equivalent to a list of arguments for the command group handler. We then create the first task for the command group, a `parallel_for`. The `parallel_for` also is defined with a lambda.

```
CommandGroup.parallel_for<class StreamTriad>(Sycl::range<1>{nsize}, [=]
                                    (Sycl::id<1> it)
```

The name of the lambda is `StreamTriad`. We then tell it that we will operate over a 1D range that goes from 0 to *nsize*. The capture clause, `[=]`, captures the a, b, and c variables by value. Determining whether to capture by reference or value is tricky. But if the code gets pushed to the GPU, the original reference may be out of scope and no longer valid. We last create a 1D index variable, `it`, to iterate over the range.

12.5   *Higher-level languages for performance portability*

By now, you are seeing that the differences between CPU and GPU kernels are not all that big. So why not generate each of them using C++ polymorphism and templates? Well, that is exactly what a couple of libraries developed by Department of Energy research laboratories have done. These projects were started to tackle the porting of many of their codes to new hardware architectures. The Kokkos system was created by Sandia National Laboratories and has gained a wide following. Lawrence Livermore National Laboratory has a similar project by the name of RAJA. Both of these projects have already succeeded in their goal of a single-source, multi-platform capability.

These two languages have similarities in a lot of respects to the SYCL language that you saw in section 12.4. Indeed, they have borrowed concepts from each other as they strive for performance portability. Each of them provides libraries that are fairly light layers on top of lower-level parallel programming languages. We'll take a short look at each of them.

12.5.1   *Kokkos: A performance portability ecosystem*

Kokkos is a well-designed abstraction layer for languages such as OpenMP and CUDA. It has been in development since 2011. Kokkos has the following named execution spaces. These are enabled in the Kokkos build with the corresponding flag to CMake (or the option to build with Spack). Some of these are better developed than others.

Kokkos execution spaces	CMake/Spack-enabled flags
Kokkos::Serial	-DKokkos_ENABLE_SERIAL=On (default is on)
Kokkos::Threads	-DKokkos_ENABLE_PTHREAD=On
Kokkos::OpenMP	-DKokkos_ENABLE_OPENMP=On
Kokkos::Cuda	-DKokkos_ENABLE_CUDA=On
Kokkos::HPX	-DKokkos_ENABLE_HPX=On
Kokkos::ROCm	-DKokkos_ENABLE_ROCm=On

Exercise: Stream triad in Kokkos

For this exercise, we built Kokkos with the OpenMP backend and then built and ran the stream triad example. To start:

```
git clone https://github.com/kokkos/kokkos
mkdir build && cd build
cmake ../kokkos -DKokkos_ENABLE_OPENMP=On
```

Then go to the stream triad source directory for Kokkos and do an out-of-tree build with CMake:

```
mkdir build && cd build
export Kokkos_DIR=${HOME}/Kokkos/lib/cmake/Kokkos
cmake ..
make
export OMP_PROC_BIND-true
export OMP_PLACES=threads
```

The Kokkos build with CMake has been streamlined so that it is easy as the following listing. The `Kokkos_DIR` variable needs to be set to the location of the CMake configuration file for Kokkos.

Listing 12.22 Kokkos CMake file

```
Kokkos/StreamTriad/CMakeLists.txt
1 cmake_minimum_required (VERSION 3.10)
2 project (StreamTriad)
3
4 find_package(Kokkos REQUIRED)          ◁── Finds Kokkos and
5                                             sets the flags
6 add_executable(StreamTriad StreamTriad.cc)      Adds dependencies
7 target_link_libraries(StreamTriad Kokkos::kokkos)  ◁── and flags to build
```

Adding the CUDA option to the Kokkos build generates a version that runs on NVIDIA GPUs. There are many other platforms and languages that Kokkos can handle and more are being developed all the time.

The Kokkos stream triad example in listing 12.23 has some similarities to SYCL in that it uses C++ lambdas to encapsulate functions for either the CPU or GPU. Kokkos also supports functors for this mechanism, but lambdas are less verbose to use in practice.

Listing 12.23   Kokkos stream triad example

```
Kokkos/StreamTriad/StreamTriad.cc
 1 #include <Kokkos_Core.hpp>          <────  Includes the
 2                                             appropriate
 3 using namespace std;                        Kokkos header
 4
 5 int main (int argc, char *argv[])
 6 {
 7     Kokkos::initialize(argc, argv);{    <────  Initializes
 8                                                Kokkos
 9     Kokkos::Timer timer;
10     double time1;
11
12     double scalar = 3.0;
13     size_t nsize = 1000000;
14     Kokkos::View<double *> a( "a", nsize);
15     Kokkos::View<double *> b( "b", nsize);      Declares arrays
16     Kokkos::View<double *> c( "c", nsize);      with Kokkos::View
17
18     cout << "StreamTriad with " << nsize << " elements" << endl;
19
20     Kokkos::parallel_for(nsize,
            KOKKOS_LAMBDA (int i) {
21        a[i] = 1.0;
22     });
23     Kokkos::parallel_for(nsize,
            KOKKOS_LAMBDA (int i) {
24        b[i] = 2.0;
25     });                                      Kokkos
26                                              parallel_for
27     timer.reset();                           lambdas for
28                                              CPU or GPU
29     Kokkos::parallel_for(nsize,
            KOKKOS_LAMBDA (const int i) {
30        c[i] = a[i] + scalar * b[i];
31     });
32
33     time1 = timer.seconds();
34
35     icount = 0;
36     for (int i=0; i<nsize && icount < 10; i++){
37        if (c[i] != 1.0 + 3.0*2.0) {
38           cout << "Error with result c[" << i << "]=" << c[i] << endl;
39           icount++;
40        }
41     }
42
```

```
43        if (icount == 0)
              cout << "Program completed without error." << endl;
44        cout << "Runtime is  " << time1*1000.0 << " msecs " << endl;
45
46      }
47    Kokkos::finalize();        ◁──┐  Finalizes
48    return 0;                      │  Kokkos
49 }
```

The Kokkos program starts with Kokkos::initialize and Kokkos::finalize. These commands start up those things that are needed for the execution space, such as threads. Kokkos is unique in that it encapsulates flexible multi-dimensional array allocations as data views that can be switched depending on the target architecture. In other words, you can use a different data order for CPU versus GPU. We use Kokkos::View on lines 14–16, though this is only for 1D arrays. The real value comes with multidimensional arrays. The general syntax for Kokkos::View is

```
View < double *** , Layout , MemorySpace > name (...);
```

Memory spaces are an option for the template, but have a default appropriate for the execution space. Some memory spaces are

- HostSpace
- CudaSpace
- CudaUVMSpace

The layout can be specified, although it has a default appropriate for the memory space:

- For LayoutLeft, the leftmost index is stride 1 (default for CudaSpace)
- For LayoutRight, the rightmost index is stride 1 (default for HostSpace)

The kernels are specified using a lambda syntax on one of three data parallel patterns:

- parallel_for
- parallel_reduce
- parallel_scan

On lines 20, 23, and 29 in listing 12.23, we used the parallel_for pattern. The KOKKOS_LAMBDA macro replaces the [=] or [&] capture syntax. Kokkos takes care of specifying this for you and does it in a much more readable form.

12.5.2 *RAJA for a more adaptable performance portability layer*

The RAJA performance portability layer has the goal of achieving portability with a minimum of disruptions to existing Lawrence Livermore National Laboratory codes. In many ways, it is simpler and easier to adopt than other comparable systems. RAJA can be built with support for the following:

- -DENABLE_OPENMP=On (default on)
- -DENABLE_TARGET_OPENMP=On (default Off)

- -DENABLE_CUDA=On (default Off)
- -DENABLE_TBB=On (default Off)

RAJA also has good support for CMake as the following listing shows.

Listing 12.24   Raja CMake file

```
Raja/StreamTriad/CMakeLists.txt
 1 cmake_minimum_required (VERSION 3.0)
 2 project (StreamTriad)
 3
 4 find_package(Raja REQUIRED)
 5 find_package(OpenMP REQUIRED)
 6
 7 add_executable(StreamTriad StreamTriad.cc)
 8 target_link_libraries(StreamTriad PUBLIC RAJA)
 9 set_target_properties(StreamTriad PROPERTIES
                         COMPILE_FLAGS ${OpenMP_CXX_FLAGS})
10 set_target_properties(StreamTriad PROPERTIES
                         LINK_FLAGS "${OpenMP_CXX_FLAGS}")
```

The RAJA version of the stream triad takes only a few changes as the following listing shows. RAJA also heavily leverages lambdas to provide their portability to CPUs and GPUs.

Listing 12.25   Raja stream triad example

```
Raja/StreamTriad/StreamTriad.cc
 1 #include <chrono>
 2 #include "RAJA/RAJA.hpp"        ◁──  Includes Raja
 3                                      headers
 4 using namespace std;
 5
 6 int main(int RAJA_UNUSED_ARG(argc), char **RAJA_UNUSED_ARG(argv[]))
 7 {
 8    chrono::high_resolution_clock::time_point t1, t2;
 9    cout << "Running Raja Stream Triad\n";
10
11    const int nsize = 1000000;
12
13 // Allocate and initialize vector data.
14    double scalar = 3.0;
15    double* a = new double[nsize];
16    double* b = new double[nsize];
17    double* c = new double[nsize];
18
19    for (int i = 0; i < nsize; i++) {
20      a[i] = 1.0;
21      b[i] = 2.0;
22    }
23
24    t1 = chrono::high_resolution_clock::now();
25
```

```
26    RAJA::forall<RAJA::omp_parallel_for_exec>(
         RAJA::RangeSegment(0,nsize),[=](int i){
27      c[i] = a[i] + scalar * b[i];
28    });
29
30    t2 = chrono::high_resolution_clock::now();
31
   < ... error checking ... >
42    double time1 = chrono::duration_cast<
                       chrono::duration<double> >(t2 - t1).count();
43    cout << "Runtime is  " << time1*1000.0 << " msecs " << endl;
44 }
```

Raja forall using C++ lambda

The required changes for RAJA are to include the RAJA header file on line 2 and to change the computation loop to a `Raja::forall`. You can see that the RAJA developers provide a low-entry threshold to gaining performance portability. To run the RAJA test, we included a script that builds and installs RAJA as the following listing shows. The script then goes on to build the stream triad code with RAJA and runs it.

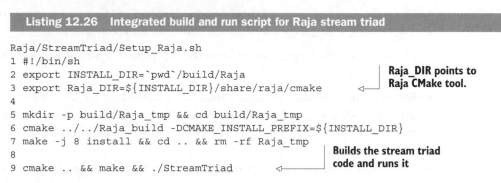

Listing 12.26 Integrated build and run script for Raja stream triad

```
Raja/StreamTriad/Setup_Raja.sh
1 #!/bin/sh
2 export INSTALL_DIR=`pwd`/build/Raja
3 export Raja_DIR=${INSTALL_DIR}/share/raja/cmake
4
5 mkdir -p build/Raja_tmp && cd build/Raja_tmp
6 cmake ../../Raja_build -DCMAKE_INSTALL_PREFIX=${INSTALL_DIR}
7 make -j 8 install && cd .. && rm -rf Raja_tmp
8
9 cmake .. && make && ./StreamTriad
```

Raja_DIR points to Raja CMake tool.

Builds the stream triad code and runs it

We covered a lot of different programming languages in this chapter. Think of these as dialects of a common language rather than completely different ones.

12.6 Further explorations

We have only begun to scratch the surface with all of these native GPU languages and performance portability systems. Even with the initial functionality shown, you can begin to implement some real application codes. If you're serious about using any of these in your applications, we strongly recommend availing yourself of the many additional resources for the language of your choice.

12.6.1 Additional reading

As the dominant GPU language for many years, there are many materials on CUDA programming. Perhaps the first place to go is the NVIDIA Developer's website at https://developer.nvidia.com/cuda-zone. There you'll find extensive guides on installing and using CUDA.

- The book by Kirk and Hwu has been one of the go-to references on NVIDIA GPU programming:

  David B. Kirk and W. Hwu Wen-Mei, *Programming massively parallel processors: a hands-on approach* (Morgan Kaufmann, 2016).

- AMD (https://rocm.github.io) has created a website that covers all aspects of their ROCm ecosystem.

- If you want to really learn more about OpenCL, we highly recommend the book by Matthew Scarpino:

  Matthew Scarpino, *OpenCL in action: how to accelerate graphics and computations* (Manning, 2011).

- A good source of additional information on OpenCL is https://www.iwocl.org, sponsored by the International Workshop on OpenCL (IWOCL). They also host an international conference annually. SYCLcon is also hosted through the same site.

- Khronos is the open standards body for OpenCL, SYCL, and related software. They host the language specifications, forums, and resource lists:

  Khronos Group, https://www.khronos.org/opencl/ and https://www.khronos.org/sycl/.

- For documentation and training materials on Kokkos, see their GitHub repository. Besides downloading the Kokkos software, you'll also find a companion repository (https://github.com/kokkos/kokkos-tutorials) for the tutorials they give around the country.

- The RAJA team (https://raja.readthedocs.io) has extensive documentation at their website.

12.6.2 *Exercises*

1 Change the host memory allocation in the CUDA stream triad example to use pinned memory (listings 12.1–12.6). Did you get a performance improvement?

2 For the sum reduction example, try an array size of 18,000 elements all initialized to their index value. Run the CUDA code and then the version in SumReductionRevealed. You may want to adjust the amount of information printed.

3 Convert the CUDA reduction example to HIP by hipifying it.

4 For the SYCL example in listing 12.20, initialize the a and b arrays on the GPU device.

5 Convert the two initialization loops in the RAJA example in listing 12.24 to the Raja:forall syntax. Try running the example with CUDA.

Summary

- Use straightforward modifications from the original CPU code for most kernels. This makes the writing of kernels simpler and easier to maintain.
- Careful design of cooperation and comparison in GPU kernels can yield good performance. The key to approaching these operations is breaking down the algorithm into steps and understanding the performance properties of the GPU.
- Think about portability from the start. You will avoid having to create more code versions every time you want to run your application on another hardware platform.
- Consider the single-source performance portability languages. If you need to run on a variety of hardware, these can be worth the initial difficulty in code development.

GPU profiling and tools

This chapter covers

- Available profiling tools for the GPU
- A sample workflow for these tools
- How to use the output from the GPU profiling tools

In this chapter, we will cover the tools and the different workflows that you can use to accelerate your application development. We'll show you how profiling tools for the GPU can be helpful. In addition, we'll discuss how to deal with the challenges of using profiling tools when working on a remote HPC cluster. Because the profiling tools continue to change and improve, we'll focus on the methodology rather than the details of any one tool. The main takeaway of this chapter will be understanding how to create a productive workflow when using the powerful GPU profiling tools.

13.1 An overview of profiling tools

Profiling tools allow for quicker optimization, improving hardware utilization, and a better understanding of the application performance and hotspots. We'll discuss how profiling tools expose bottlenecks and assist you in attaining better hardware usage. The following bulleted list highlights the commonly used tools in GPU profiling. We specifically show the NVIDIA tools for use with their GPUs because these tools have been around the longest. If you have a different vendor's GPU on your system, substitute their tools in the workflow. Don't forget about the standard Unix profiling tools such as gprof that we'll use later in section 13.4.2.

We encourage you to follow along with the examples for this chapter. The accompanying source code is at http://github.com/EssentialsOfParallelComputing/Chapter13, which shows examples of installing the software packages for tools from different hardware vendors. There are detailed lists of all the software that can be installed for each vendor. You will probably want to install the tools for the corresponding hardware.

> **NOTE** While a tool for another vendor might partially run on your system, its full functionality will be crippled.

- *NVIDIA nvidia-smi*—When trying to get a quick system profile from the command line, you can use nvidia-smi. As shown and explained in section 9.6.2, NVIDIA SMI (System Management Interface) allows for monitoring and collecting power and temperature during an application run. NVIDIA SMI gives you hardware information along with many other system metrics. The link to the SMI guide and options are in the "Further Explorations" section later in this chapter.
- *NVIDIA nvprof*—This NVIDIA Visual Profiler command-line tool collects and reports data on GPU performance. The data can also be imported into a visual profiling tool such as the NVIDIA Visual Profiler NVVP or other formats for application performance analysis. It shows performance metrics such as hardware-to-device copies, kernel usage, memory utilization, and many other metrics.
- *NVIDIA NVVP*—This NVIDIA Visual Profiler tool provides a visual representation of the application kernel performance. NVVP provides a GUI and guided analysis. It queries the same data the nvprof does, but represents the data to the user in a visual way, offering a quick timeline feature not as readily available on nvprof.
- *NVIDIA® Nsight™*—NSight is an updated version of NVVP that provides for a visual representation of CPU and GPU usage and application performance. Eventually, it may replace NVVP.
- *NVIDIA PGPROF*—The PGPROF utility originated with the Portland Group compiler. When the Portland Group was acquired by NVIDIA for their Fortran compiler, they merged Portland's profiler, PGPROF, with the NVIDIA tools.
- *CodeXL (originally AMD CodeXL)*—This GPUOpen profiler, debugger, and programming development workbench was originally developed by AMD. See the link to the CodeXL website in the "Additional Reading" section later in this chapter.

13.2   *How to select a good workflow*

Before beginning any complicated task, you must select the appropriate workflow. You might either be onsite with excellent connectivity, offsite with a slow home network, or somewhere in between. Each case requires a different workflow. In this section, we'll discuss four potential and efficient workflows for these different scenarios.

Figure 13.1 provides a visual representation of the four different workflows. Accessibility and connection speed are the determining factors in deciding which method you end up using. You can either run the tools with a graphics interface directly on the system, remotely with a client-server mode, or just avoid the problem by using command-line tools.

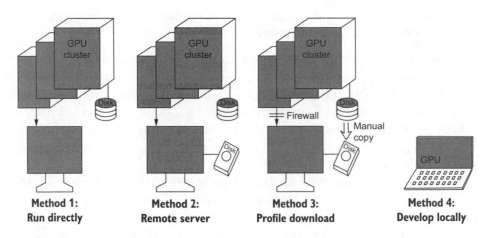

Figure 13.1   There are several different methods of using the profiling tools that give you alternatives for your application development situation.

When using profiling tools from a remote server, there is often a heavy delay in visualization and graphics interface response. Client-server mode separates the graphics interface so that it runs locally on your system. It then communicates with the server at the remote site to run the commands. This helps keep the interactive response of the graphical tool interface. For example, profiling tools such as NVVP can have a high latency when used on a remote server. Waiting minutes after every mouse click is not a very productive situation. Fortunately, the NVIDIA tools and many of the other tools give you several options to work around this problem. We go into greater detail on the different workflows in the following discussion.

- *Method 1: Run directly on the system*—When your network connection for your graphics application is fast, this is the preferred method because the storage requirements are pretty large. If you have a fast connection for graphics display, it is the most efficient way to work. But if your display network connection is slow, the response time for the graphics window is painful, and you will want to use one of the remote options. VNC, X2Go, and NoMachine can compress the graphics output and send it instead, sometimes making slower connections workable.

- *Method 2: Remote server*—This method runs the application with a command-line tool on the GPU system, then the files are transferred automatically to your local system. Firewalls, batch operations of the HPC system, and other network complications can make this method difficult or impossible to set up.
- *Method 3: Profile file download*—This method runs nvprof on an HPC site and downloads the files to your local computer. In this method, you manually transfer files to your local computer using secure copy (scp) or some other utility and then work on your local machine. When trying to profile multiple applications, it can be easier to take the raw data in a csv format and combine it into a single dataframe. Though this method may no longer be usable by the conventional profiling tools, you can do your own detailed analysis on the server or locally.
- *Method 4: Develop locally*—One of the great things about today's HPC hardware is that you often have similar hardware that you can use to develop an application locally. You might have a GPU from the same vendor but not as powerful as the GPU in the HPC system. You can optimize your application with the expectation that everything will be faster on the big system. You might also be able to develop your code on the CPU with some of the languages where debugging is easier.

The important thing to realize is that even if you are not on a fast connection to a computing site, you have some options when using development tools. Whichever method you use to do your porting and performance analysis, you should ensure that the versions of the software you use match. This is particularly important for CUDA and the NVIDIA nvprof and NVVP tools.

13.3 Example problem: Shallow water simulation

In this section, we'll work with a realistic example to show the code porting process and the use of some available tools. We'll use the problem from figure 1.9, where a volcanic eruption or earthquake might cause a tsunami to propagate outward. Tsunamis can travel thousands of miles across oceans with just a few feet of height, but when these reach the shore, they can be hundreds of meters high. These types of simulations are usually done after the event because of the time required to set up and run the problem. We'd prefer to simulate it in real time so that we can provide warnings to those who might be affected. Speeding up the simulation by running it on a GPU might provide this capability.

We'll first walk through the physics that occurs in this scenario then translate that into equations to numerically simulate the problem. The specific scenario we want to represent is the breaking off of a large mass of an island or other land mass, which falls into the ocean as figure 13.2 illustrates. This event actually happened with Anak Krakatau ("Child of Krakatau") in December, 2018.

Graphic courtesy of Cristian Gomez

Figure 13.2   The tsunami wave that occurred at Anak Krakatau on December 22, 2018, was caused by a sediment slide from the volcanic island.

For the December event, the landslide volume on the west flank of the Krakatau island was about 0.2 cubic km. This was smaller than earlier risk projections estimated. Additionally, wave heights were estimated to be over 100 meters. With the short distance from the source to the shore, there was little warning for those in the area, and with over 400 deaths, the event garnered world-wide news coverage.

Scientists performed many simulations prior to the event and even more afterward. You can view some of the visualizations and an analysis of the event at http://mng.bz/4Mqw. How were the simulations done? The basic physics required is only a small step in complexity from the stencil calculations that we have looked at throughout this book. A full-fledged simulation code might have a lot more sophisticated bells and whistles, but we can go a long way with simple physics. So let's take a look at the required physics behind the simulations.

The mathematical equations for the tsunami are relatively simple. These are conservation of mass and conservation of momentum. The latter is basically Newton's first law of motion: "An object at rest stays at rest and an object in motion stays in motion." The momentum equation uses the second law of motion, "Force is equal to the change in momentum." For the conservation of the mass equation, we basically have that the change in mass for a computational cell over a small increment in time is equal to the sum of the mass crossing the cell boundaries as shown here:

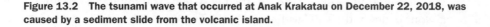

$$\frac{\partial M}{\partial t} + \frac{\partial(v_x M)}{\partial x} + \frac{\partial(v_y M)}{\partial y} = 0 \quad \text{(Conservation of mass)}$$

Where $\frac{\partial M}{\partial t}$ is the change in mass relative to time, and $\frac{v_x M}{\partial x}$ and $\frac{v_y M}{\partial x}$ are the mass fluxes (velocity * mass) across the x- and y-faces. Further, because water is incompressible, the density of water can be treated as constant. The mass of a cell is the volume * density. If we have cells that are all 1 meter × 1 meter, the volume is height × 1 meter × 1 meter. Putting this all together, everything is constant except for height, so we can replace mass with the height variable:

$$\text{Mass} = \text{Volume} \cdot \text{Density} = \text{Height} \cdot 1 \text{ Meter} \cdot 1 \text{ Meter} \cdot \text{Density} = \text{Constant} \cdot \text{Height}$$

Also using $u = v_x$ and $v = v_y$, we now get the standard form of the conservation law for the shallow water equations:

$$\frac{\partial h}{\partial t} + \frac{\partial(hu)}{\partial x} + \frac{\partial(hv)}{\partial y} = 0 \quad \text{(Conservation of mass)}$$

The conservation of momentum is similar but with momentum (*mom*) replacing the mass or height. We only show the *x* terms to fit the equation on the page like this:

$$\frac{\partial(mom_x)}{\partial t} + \frac{\partial}{\partial x}(v_x \cdot mom_x) + \frac{\partial}{\partial x}\left(\frac{1}{2}gh^2\right) = 0 \quad \text{(Conservation of x-momentum)}$$

The additional term of $1/2$ gh^2 is due to the work done on the system by gravity. According to Newton's second law, the external force creates additional momentum (F = ma). We'll look at how this term comes about with and without calculus. First, the acceleration in this case is gravity, and it causes a force acting on the column of water as figure 13.3 shows. Each additional meter of water height creates what is known as *hydrostatic pressure*, resulting in a higher pressure along the whole column of water. With calculus, we would integrate the pressure along the column to get the momentum created. This integration over the elevation (*z*) from 0 to the wave height (*h*) would be

$$p = \int_0^h gz\,dz = \frac{1}{2}gz^2\Big|_0^h = \frac{1}{2}gh^2 \qquad \text{(Integrate force over depth, z)}$$

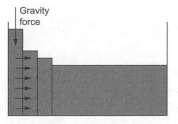

Gravity force

Figure 13.3   The force of gravity on the column of water creates flow and momentum.

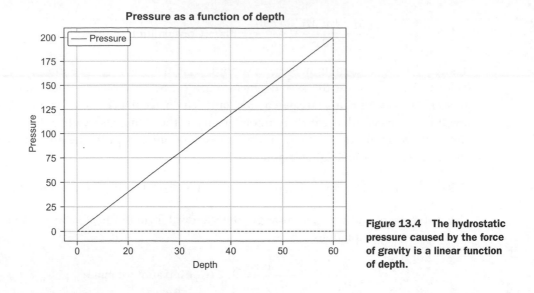

Figure 13.4   The hydrostatic pressure caused by the force of gravity is a linear function of depth.

There is also a much simpler derivation. In this case, the pressure is a linear function (figure 13.4). If we look at the height midpoint then apply the pressure difference at the height midpoint to the whole column, we can get the same solution. What we are doing is summing all of the pressure forces under the curve. The mathematical terminology for this is to integrate the function or perform a Riemann sum where you break the area under a curve into columns then add these. But this is all overkill. The area under the curve is a triangle, and we can use the area of a triangle or A = 1/2 bh.

$$p = mg \cdot h_{midpoint} = hg \cdot \frac{h}{2} = \frac{1}{2}gh^2 \quad \text{(Using hydrostatic pressure at height midpoint)}$$

Our resulting set of equations is

$$\frac{\partial h}{\partial t} + \frac{\partial(hu)}{\partial x} + \frac{\partial(hv)}{\partial y} = 0 \quad \text{(Conservation of mass)}$$

$$\frac{\partial(hu)}{\partial t} + \frac{\partial}{\partial x}\left(hu^2 + \frac{1}{2}gh^2\right) + \frac{\partial}{\partial y}(huv) = 0 \quad \text{(Conservation of x-momentum)}$$

$$\frac{\partial(hv)}{\partial t} + \frac{\partial}{\partial x}(hvu) + \frac{\partial}{\partial y}\left(hv^2 + \frac{1}{2}gh^2\right) = 0 \quad \text{(Conservation of y-momentum)}$$

If you are observant, you will notice cross-terms of the momentum fluxes for the y-momentum in the x-momentum equation and x-momentum in the y-momentum equation. In the conservation of x-momentum, the third term has x-momentum (hu)

moving across the *y*-face with the *y*-velocity (v). You can describe this as the advection, or flux, of the *x*-momentum with the velocity in the *y*-direction across the top and bottom faces of the computational cell. The flux of the *x*-momentum (hu) across the *x*-faces with the velocity *u* is in the second term as hu^2.

We also see that the newly created momentum is split across the two momentum equations with the new *x*-momentum in the *x*-momentum equation and the *y*-momentum in the *y*-momentum equation. These equations are then implemented as three stencil operations in our shallow water code, where for simplicity, we use $H = h$, $U = hu$, and $V = hv$. Now we have a simple scientific application that we can use for our demonstrations.

We have one more implementation detail. We use a numerical method that estimates the properties such as mass and momentum at the faces of each cell halfway through the timestep. We then use these estimates to calculate the amount of mass and momentum that moves into the cell during the timestep. This gives us a little more accuracy for the numerical solution.

Congratulations if you have worked your way through this discussion and gained some understanding. Now you have seen how we take the simple laws of physics and create a scientific application from those. You should always strive to understand the underlying physics and numerical method rather than treat the code as a set of loops.

13.4 A sample of a profiling workflow

Next, we reach the profiling step for the shallow water application. For this, we created a shallow water application based on the mathematical and physical equations presented in section 13.3. In many ways, the code is just three stencil calculations for the mass and two momentum equations. We have worked with a single, simple stencil equation since chapter 1, and the example code is included in https://github .com/EssentialsofParallelComputing/Chapter13.

13.4.1 Run the shallow water application

In this section, we show you how to run the shallow water code. We'll use the code to step through a sample workflow for porting your code to the GPU. First, some notes about the platforms:

- *macOS*—NVIDIA warns that CUDA 10.2 may be the last release to support macOS and only supports it up through macOS v10.13. As a result, NVVP is only supported through macOS v10.13. It sort of works with v10.14 but fails completely on v10.15 (Catalina). We suggest using VirtualBox https://www .virtualbox.org as a free virtual machine to try out the tools on Mac systems. We have also supplied a Docker container for macOS.
- *Windows*—NVIDIA still supports Microsoft Windows natively, but you can also use VirtualBox or Docker containers on Windows if you prefer.
- *Linux*—A direct installation on most Linux systems should work.

If you have a GPU on your local system, you can use the local workflow. If not, you will probably be running remotely on a compute cluster and transferring the files back for analysis.

If you want to use the graphics, you will need to install some additional packages. On an Ubuntu system, you can do this with the following commands. The first command is for installing OpenGL and freeglut for real-time graphics. The second is for installing ImageMagick® to handle the graphics file output that we can use for graphics stills. The graphics snapshots can also be converted into movies. The README .graphics file in the GitHub directory has more information on the graphics formats and the scripts in the examples that accompany this chapter.

```
sudo apt-get install libglu1-mesa-dev freeglut3-dev mesa-common-dev -y
sudo apt install cmake imagemagick libmagickwand-dev
```

We have found that real-time graphics can accelerate code development and debugging, so we included a sample of how to use them in the example code accompanying this chapter. For example, the real-time graphics output uses OpenGL to display the height of the water in the mesh, giving you immediate visual feedback. The real-time graphics code can also be easily extended to respond to keyboard and mouse interactions within the real-time graphics window.

This example is coded with OpenACC, so it is best to use the PGI compiler. A limited subset of the examples works with the GCC compiler due to its still-developing support of OpenACC. Compiling the example code is straightforward. We just use CMake and make.

1 To build the makefile, type

```
mkdir build && cd build
cmake ..
```

2 To turn on the graphics, type

```
cmake -DENABLE_GRAPHICS=1
```

3 Set the graphics file format with

```
export GRAPHICS_TYPE=JPEG
make
```

4 Then run the serial code with ./ShallowWater.

If you cannot get the graphics output to work, the program will run fine without it. But if you get it set up correctly, the real-time graphics output from the code displays a graphics window like that shown in figure 13.5. The graphics are updated every 100 iterations. The figure here shows a smaller mesh than the hard-coded size in the sample code. The lines represent the computational cells with the wave height higher on

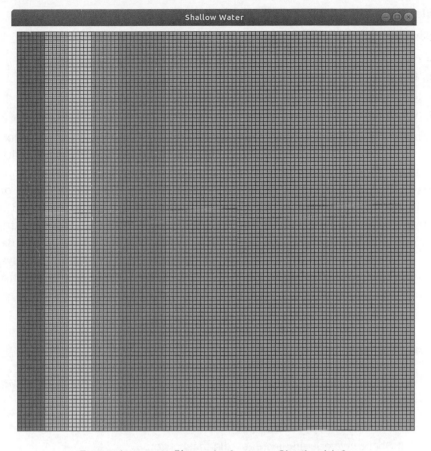

Figure 13.5 **Real-time graphics output from the shallow water application. The red stripes on the left indicate the beginning of the wave, where the landslide enters the water. The wave progresses to the right as it cross the ocean: orange, yellow, green, and blue. If you're reading this in black and white, the left shaded region corresponds to the red, and the far right shaded region corresponds to the blue. The lines are the outlines of the computational cells.**

the left. The wave travels to the right with the height, decreasing as it moves. The wave crosses the computational domain and reflects off the right face. Then it travels back and forth across the mesh. In a real calculation, there would be objects (such as shorelines) in the mesh.

If you have a system that can run OpenACC, the executables ShallowWater_par1 through ShallowWater_par4 will also be built. You can use these for the profiling exercises that follow.

13.4.2 *Profile the CPU code to develop a plan of action*

We described the parallel development cycle back in chapter 2 as

1 Profile
2 Plan
3 Implement
4 Commit

The first step is to profile our application. For most applications, we recommend using a high-level profiler such as the Cachegrind tool we introduced in section 3.3.1. Cachegrind shows the most time-consuming paths through the code and displays the results in an easy-to-interpret visual representation. However, for a simple program like the shallow water application, function-level profilers like Cachegrind are not effective. Cachegrind shows that 100% of the time is spent in the main function, which doesn't help us much. We need a line-by-line profiler for this particular situation. For this purpose, we draw upon the most well-known profiler on Unix systems—gprof. Later, when we have code that runs on the GPU, we will use the NVIDIA NVVP profiling tool to get the performance statistics. To get started, we just need a simple tool to profile an application running on the CPU.

Example: Profiling with gprof

1 Edit CMakeLists.txt by adding the -pg flag to the compiler flags (diff output shows the original line in the CMakeLists with a - symbol and the new line with a + symbol):

```
-set(CMAKE_C_FLAGS "${CMAKE_C_FLAGS} -g -O3")
+set(CMAKE_C_FLAGS "${CMAKE_C_FLAGS} -g -O3 -pg")
```

2 Edit ShallowWater.c and increase the mesh size:

```
-   int      nx = 500, ny = 200;
+   int      nx = 5000, ny = 2000;
```

3 Rebuild the ShallowWater executable by typing `make`.
4 Run the ShallowWater executable by typing `./ShallowWater`. You should get an output file called gmon.out.
5 Run the post-processing step by typing `gprof -l -pg ./ShallowWater`.

The output from gprof shows the loops that take the most time in the shallow water application (see the following figure).

Each sample counts as 0.01 seconds.

% time	cumulative seconds	self seconds	self calls	total Ts/call	Ts/call	name
42.95	140.38	140.38				main (ShallowWater.c:**207** @ 401885)
22.44	213.71	73.33				main (ShallowWater.c:**190** @ 401730)
22.34	286.74	73.03				main (ShallowWater.c:**172** @ 401500)
12.06	326.17	39.43				main (ShallowWater.c:**160** @ 401330)
< ... more output ...>						

The output from gprof. The loop at line 207 takes the most time and would make a good starting point for porting to the GPU.

We look up the loops for each of the line numbers in the profiling output in the figure and find that these correspond to the following operations:

- `ShallowWater.c:207` (second pass loop)
- `ShallowWater.c:190` (*y*-face pass)
- `ShallowWater.c:172` (*x*-face pass)
- `ShallowWater.c:160` (timestep calculation)

This tells us that we should concentrate our initial efforts on the computation of the second pass at the end of the main computation loop and work our way towards the top of the loop. There is a tendency to try and do everything all at once, but the safer approach is to work loop-by-loop and make sure the result is still correct. By focusing on the most expensive loops first, some performance improvement will be achieved earlier.

13.4.3 Add OpenACC compute directives to begin the implementation step

Now that we have profiled the application and developed a plan, the next step in the parallel development cycle is to begin the implementation of the plan. In this step, we begin the eagerly awaited modification of the code.

The implementation starts with porting the code to the GPU by moving the computation loop. We follow the same procedure used in section 11.2.2 to port the code to the GPU. The computations are moved by inserting the acc parallel loop pragma in front of every loop as shown on line 95 in the following listing.

Listing 13.1 Adding a loop directive

```
OpenACC/ShallowWater/ShallowWater_par1.c
 95 #pragma acc parallel loop
 96        for(int j=1;j<=ny;j++){
 97            H[j][0]=H[j][1];
 98            U[j][0]=-U[j][1];
 99            V[j][0]=V[j][1];
100            H[j][nx+1]=H[j][nx];
101            U[j][nx+1]=-U[j][nx];
102            V[j][nx+1]=V[j][nx];
103        }
```

We also need to replace the pointer swap on line 191 at the end of the loop with a data copy. This is not ideal because it introduces more data movement and is slower than a pointer swap. That being said, doing a pointer swap in OpenACC is tricky because the pointers on the host and device have to be switched simultaneously.

Listing 13.2 Replacing the pointer swap with a copy

```
OpenACC/ShallowWater/ShallowWater_par1.c
189        // Need to replace swap with copy
190 #pragma acc parallel loop
```

```
191        for(int j=1;j<=ny;j++){
192          for(int i=1;i<=nx;i++){
193              H[j][i] = Hnew[j][i];
194              U[j][i] = Unew[j][i];
195              V[j][i] = Vnew[j][i];
196          }
197        }
```

You will get better feedback of the performance of your application from a visual representation. At each step of the process, we run the NVVP profiling tool to get the graphical output of the performance trace.

Example: Getting a visual profile of your performance with the NVIDIA Visual Profiler (NVVP)

To acquire a visual performance timeline, we run the code with:

```
nvprof --export-profile ShallowWater_par1_timeline.prof
           ./ShallowWater_par1
```

Using the `nvprof` command saves a profiling timeline within the running directory:

```
nvvp ShallowWater_par1_timeline.prof
```

The `nvvp` command then imports the profile into the NVIDIA Visual Profiler suite with the graphical output shown in the following figure. You can copy the profile back to your local machine in between the two steps and view it locally if you like.

We'll first look at the visual profile to get a quick color-coded feel for the relative performance of our memory copies and computational kernels. This is the timeline shown at the top of the visual profiler window. At this point, pay particular attention to the lines MemCpy (HtoD) and MemCpy (DtoH), where the data transfer from the host to the device and the device to host are displayed. The guided analysis and OpenACC details panes that are at the bottom of this window are discussed in section 13.4.5.

The NVIDIA NVVP profiler output shows a timeline view of one computational cycle. You can see the device-to-hardware memory copies and vice versa. On the highlighted line, the output also shows compute regions.

If your network connection doesn't allow either using the graphical tool directly or transferring the profile data to your computer, you can always fall back to using nvprof in its text-based mode. You can get the same information from the text-based output, but there are always some insights that are clearer with the visual representation.

Figure 13.6 shows the ability to zoom into specific kernels to better identify performance metrics within certain compute cycles. Specifically, we zoomed into line 95 from listing 13.1 to show individual memory copies.

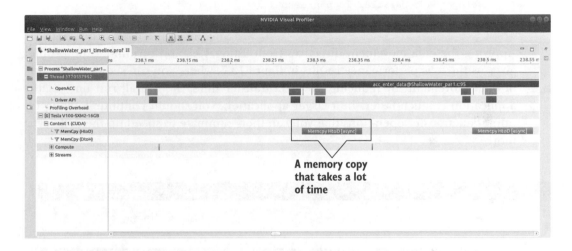

Figure 13.6 With NVIDIA's NVVP, you can zoom into specific copies in the timeline view. Here, you can see a zoomed in version of individual memory copies within each cycle. This allows you to see what lines these are on to help you easily refer back to the application.

13.4.4 Add data movement directives

The next step in porting the code to the GPU is the addition of data movement directives. This allows us to further improve the application performance by eliminating expensive memory copies. In this section, we will show you how it's done.

The Visual Profiler, NVVP, helps us to see where we need to focus our efforts. Start by looking for the large MemCpy time blocks and eliminating these one-by-one. As you remove the data transfer costs, your code will start to show speedups, recovering the performance lost during the application of compute directives in section 13.4.4.

In listing 13.3, we show an example of the data movement directives that we added. At the start of the data section, we use the `acc enter data create` directive to start a dynamic data region. The data will then exist on the device until we encounter an `acc exit data` directive. For each loop, we add the `present` clause to tell the compiler the data is already on the device. Refer to the example code for the chapter 13 in the file

OpenACC/ShallowWater/ShallowWater_par2.c for all the changes made to control the data movement.

Listing 13.3 Data movement directives

```
OpenACC/ShallowWater/ShallowWater_par2.c
51 #pragma acc enter data create( \
52         H[:ny+2][:nx+2],    U[:ny+2][:nx+2],    V[:ny+2][:nx+2], \
53         Hx[:ny][:nx+1],     Ux[:ny][:nx+1],     Vx[:ny][:nx+1], \
54         Hy[:ny+1][:nx],     Uy[:ny+1][:nx],     Vy[:ny+1][:nx], \
55         Hnew[:ny+2][:nx+2], Unew[:ny+2][:nx+2], Vnew[:ny+2][:nx+2])
   <...>
59   #pragma acc parallel loop present( \
60         H[:ny+2][:nx+2], U[:ny+2][:nx+2], V[:ny+2][:nx+2])
```

Applying the data movement directives from listing 13.3 and rerunning the profiler gives us the new performance results in figure 13.7, where you can see the reduction of data movement. By reducing the data transfer time, the overall run time of the application is much faster. In a larger application, you should continue looking for other data transfer operations that you can then eliminate to speed up the code even more.

Figure 13.7   This timeline from NVIDIA's Visual Profiler NVVP shows four iterations of the computation but now with data movement optimizations. What is interesting in this figure is not so much what you can see, but what is not there. The data movement that occurred in the previous figure is sharply reduced or no longer exists.

13.4.5 *Guided analysis can give you some suggested improvements*

For further insight, NVVP provides a guided analysis feature (figure 13.8). In this section, we'll discuss how to use this feature.

You must judge the suggestions from the guided analysis based on your knowledge of your application. In our example, we have few data transfers, so we will not be able to get memory copy and compute overlap mentioned in the top suggestion of Low Memcpy/Compute Overlap in figure 13.8. This is true of most of the other suggestions.

For example, for low kernel concurrency, we only have one kernel, so we can't have concurrency. Though our application is small and may not need these extra optimizations, these are good to note as they can be useful for larger applications.

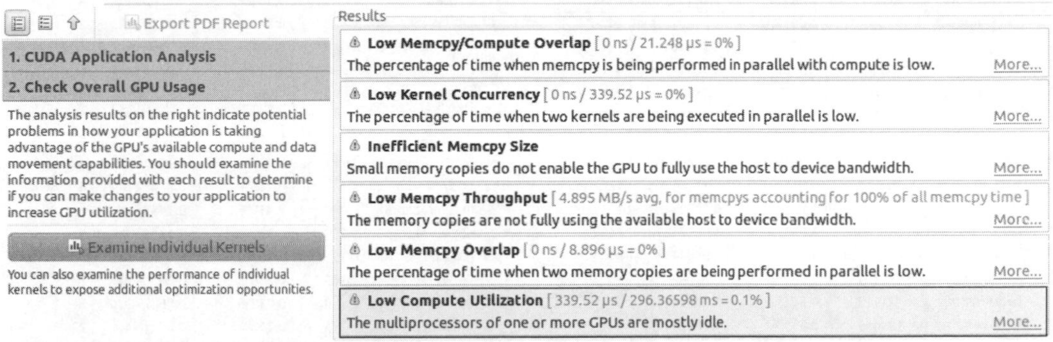

Figure 13.8 NVVP provides a guided analysis section as well. Here, the user can acquire insight for further optimizations. Note that the highlighted region shows low compute utilization.

Additionally, figure 13.8 shows low compute utilization for our application run. This is not unusual. This low GPU utilization is more indicative of the huge compute power available on the GPU and how much more it can do. To briefly go back to the performance measurements and analysis of our mixbench performance tool (section 9.3.4), we have a bandwidth-limited kernel so we will, at best, use 1–2% of the GPU's floating-point capability. In light of this, 0.1% compute utilization isn't so bad.

Another feature of the NVVP tool is an OpenACC Details window that gives the timings for each operation. One of the best ways to use this is by acquiring the before and after timings as figure 13.9 shows. The side-by-side comparisons give you a concrete measurement of improvement from the data movement directives.

With the OpenACC Details window opened, you'll note that the line numbers move within the profile. If we look at line 166 in the ShallowWater_par1 listing (on the left in figure 13.10), it takes 4.8% of the run time. The breakdown of the operations shows that a lot of that time is due to data transfer costs. The corresponding line of code in the ShallowWater_par2 listing is 181 (on the right in figure 13.10) and has the addition of the present data clause. We can see that the time for line 181 is only 0.81% and that this is largely due to the elimination of the data transfer costs. The compute construct takes about the same time in both cases at 0.16 ms as shown in the line labeled acc_compute_construct just below the highlighted line.

Analysis □ OpenACC Details ⊠			
Name	%	Time	Calls
ShallowWater_par1.c:190	10.53%	36.51828 ms	4816
▼ ShallowWater_par1.c:199	6.28%	21.77921 ms	2404
▶ acc_enqueue_download	5.125%	17.77496 ms	2400
▶ acc_wait	1.155%	4.00424 ms	4
▼ ShallowWater_par1.c:166	4.855%	16.83839 ms	2452
▶ acc_enqueue_upload	3.803%	13.19097 ms	2424
▶ acc_wait	0.972%	3.37148 ms	12
▶ acc_compute_construct	0.048%	0.16514 ms	4
▶ acc_enqueue_download	0.032%	0.1108 ms	12
▼ ShallowWater_par1.c:148	4.636%	16.07981 ms	2452
▶ acc_enqueue_upload	3.611%	12.52283 ms	2424
▶ acc_wait	0.963%	3.33845 ms	12
▶ acc_enqueue_download	0.033%	0.11467 ms	12
▶ acc_compute_construct	0.03%	0.10386 ms	4
▶ ShallowWater_par1.c:116	3.81%	13.21218 ms	2412
▶ ShallowWater_par1.c:75	0.85%	2.94674 ms	603
▶ ShallowWater_par1.c:104	0.645%	2.23644 ms	40
▶ ShallowWater_par1.c:115	0.541%	1.87769 ms	16
▶ ShallowWater_par1.c:65	0.515%	1.78728 ms	4
▶ ShallowWater_par1.c:53	0.347%	1.20382 ms	3
▶ ShallowWater_par1.c:66	0.323%	1.12113 ms	206
▶ ShallowWater_par1.c:202	0.306%	1.0627 ms	204

Analysis □ OpenACC Details ⊠			
Name	%	Time	Calls
ShallowWater_par2.c:51	3.208%	1.12397 ms	1
▶ acc_device_init	3.208%	1.12397 ms	1
▼ ShallowWater_par2.c:181	0.818%	0.28663 ms	8
▶ acc_compute_construct	0.457%	0.16025 ms	4
▶ acc_wait	0.361%	0.12638 ms	4
▼ ShallowWater_par2.c:126	0.776%	0.27193 ms	20
▶ acc_compute_construct	0.485%	0.1699 ms	4
▶ acc_enqueue_download	0.175%	0.06139 ms	4
▶ acc_enqueue_upload	0.063%	0.02196 ms	4
▶ acc_wait	0.053%	0.01869 ms	8
▼ ShallowWater_par2.c:161	0.471%	0.16494 ms	8
▶ acc_compute_construct	0.286%	0.10012 ms	4
▶ acc_wait	0.185%	0.06482 ms	4
▶ ShallowWater_par2.c:140	0.415%	0.14535 ms	8
▶ ShallowWater_par2.c:209	0.394%	0.13787 ms	8
▶ ShallowWater_par2.c:73	0.36%	0.12622 ms	5
▶ ShallowWater_par2.c:103	0.268%	0.09404 ms	8
▶ ShallowWater_par2.c:113	0.238%	0.08327 ms	8
▶ ShallowWater_par2.c:233	0.212%	0.07418 ms	2
▶ ShallowWater_par2.c:82	0.206%	0.07222 ms	5
▶ ShallowWater_par2.c:223	0.153%	0.05364 ms	4
▶ ShallowWater_par2.c:59	0.085%	0.02991 ms	2

Figure 13.9   NVVP's OpenACC Details window shows information on each OpenACC kernel and the cost of each operation. We can see the cost of the data transfer in the left window for version 1 of the code versus the time for the optimized data motion in version 2 on the right.

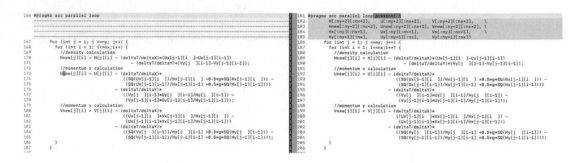

Figure 13.10   Side-by-side code comparison showing that line 166 in version 1 of the ShallowWater code is now line 181, which has the additional `present` clause.

13.4.6   *The NVIDIA Nsight suite of tools can be a powerful development aid*

NVIDIA is replacing their Visual Profiler tools (NVVP and nvprof) with the Nsight™ tool suite. The tool suite is anchored by two integrated development environments (IDEs):

1 Nsight Visual Studio Edition supports CUDA and OpenCL development in the Microsoft Visual Studio IDE.

2 Nsight Eclipse Edition adds the CUDA language to the popular open source Eclipse IDE.

Figure 13.11 shows our shallow water application in the Nsight Eclipse Edition development tool.

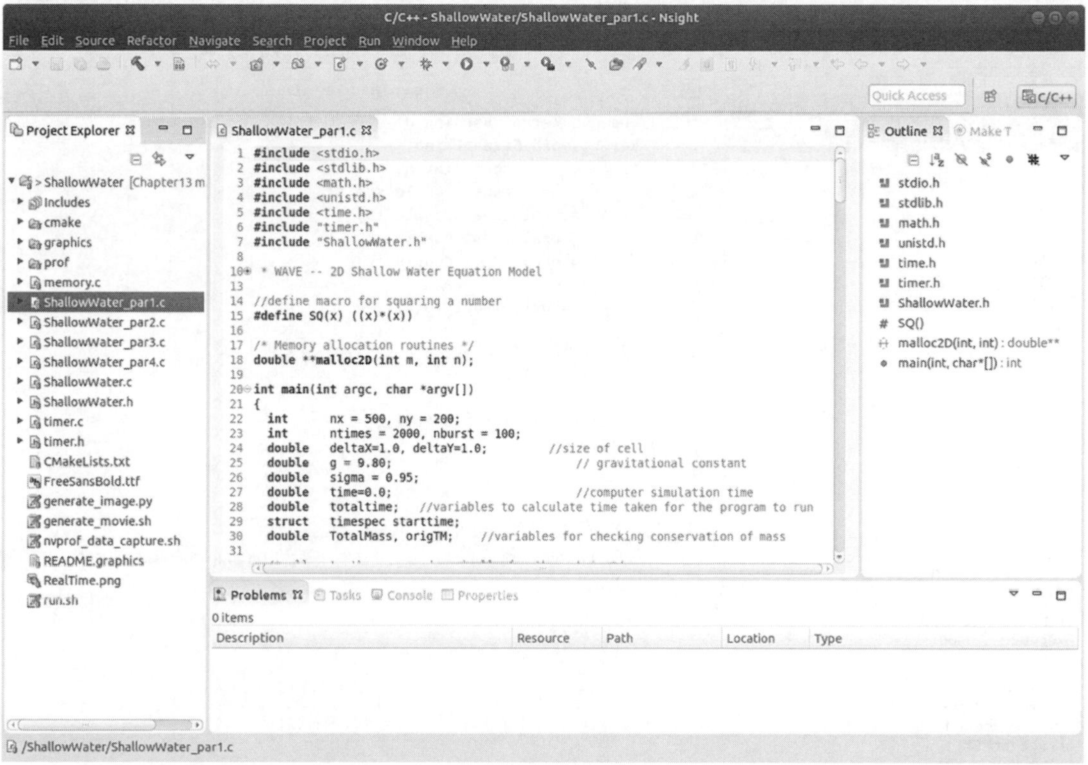

Figure 13.11 The NVIDIA Nsight Eclipse Edition application is a code development tool. This window in the tool shows the ShallowWater_par1 application.

The Nsight suite of tools also has single function components that can be downloaded by registered NVIDIA developers. These profilers incorporate the functionality from the NVIDIA Visual Profiler and add additional capabilities. The two components are

- Nsight Systems, a system-level performance tool, looks at overall data movement and computation.
- Nsight Compute, a performance tool, gives a detailed view of GPU kernel performance.

13.4.7 *CodeXL for the AMD GPU ecosystem*

AMD also has code development and performance analysis capabilities in their CodeXL suite of tools. As figure 13.12 shows, the application development tool is a full-featured code workbench. CodeXL also includes a profiling component (in the Profile menu) that helps with optimizing code for the AMD GPU.

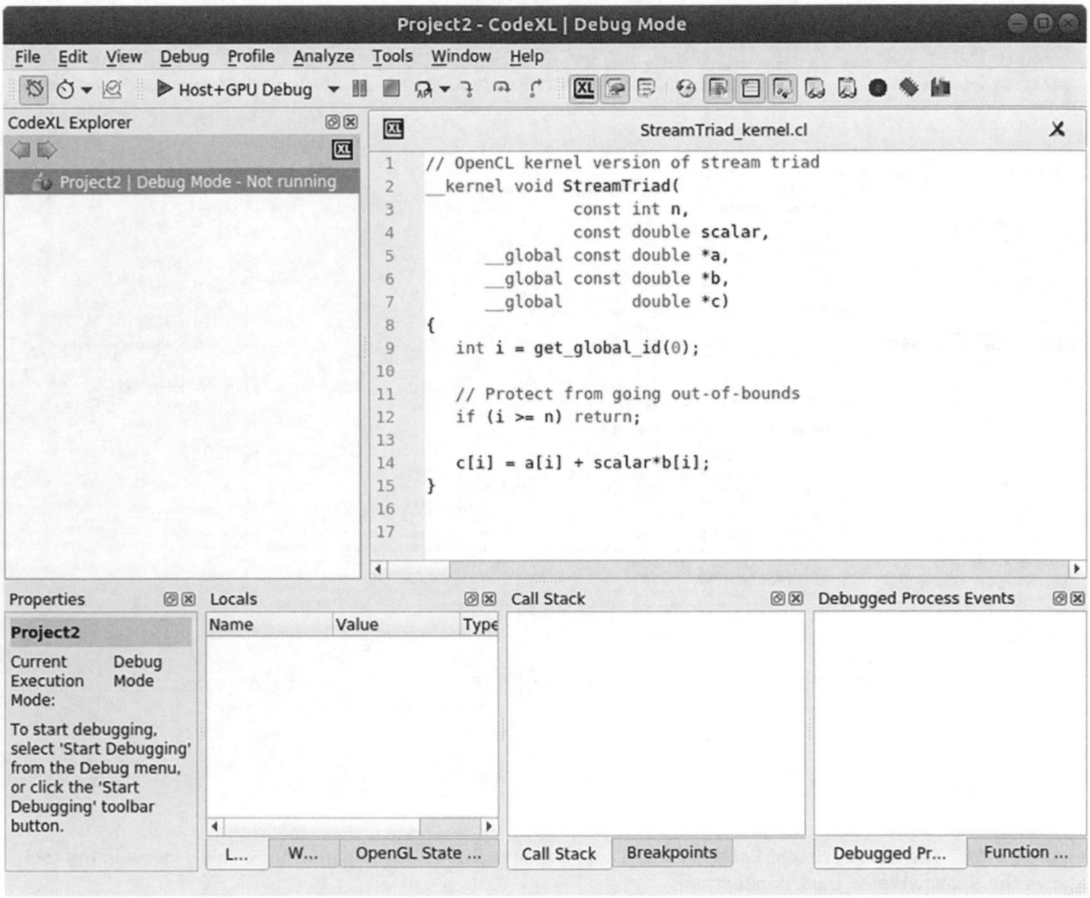

Figure 13.12   The CodeXL development tool supports compiling, running, debugging, and profiling.

These new tools from NVIDIA and AMD are still being rolled out. The availability of full-featured tools, including debuggers and profilers, will be a tremendous boost for GPU code development.

13.5 Don't get lost in the swamp: Focus on the important metrics

As with many profiling and performance measurement tools, the amount of information is initially overwhelming. You should focus on the most important metrics that you can gather from hardware counters and other measurement tools. In recent processors, the number of hardware counters has steadily grown, giving you insight into many aspects of processor performance that were previously hidden. We suggest the following three aspects as the most critical: occupancy, issue efficiency, and memory bandwidth.

13.5.1 Occupancy: Is there enough work?

The concept of occupancy is often mentioned as the top concern for GPUs. We first discussed this measure in section 10.3. For good GPU performance, we need enough work to keep compute units (CUs) busy. In addition, we need alternate work to cover stalls when workgroups hit memory-load waits (figure 13.13). As a reminder, CUs in OpenCL terminology are called streaming multiprocessors (SMs) in CUDA. The actual achieved occupancy is reported by the measurement counters. If you encounter low occupancy measures, you can modify the workgroup size and resource usage in the kernels to try and improve this factor. A higher occupancy is not always better. The occupancy just needs to be high enough so that there is alternate work for the CUs.

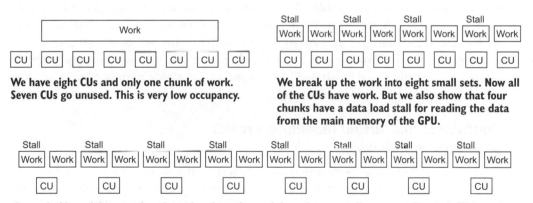

Figure 13.13 GPUs have a lot of compute units (CUs), also called streaming multiprocessors (SMs). We need to create a lot of work to keep the CUs busy, with enough extra work for handling stalls.

13.5.2 Issue efficiency: Are your warps on break too often?

Issue efficiency is the measurement of the instructions issued per cycle versus the maximum possible per cycle. To be able to issue an instruction, each CU scheduler must have an eligible wavefront, or warp, ready for execution. An *eligible wavefront* is an active wavefront that is not stalled. In some sense, it is an important result from having high enough occupancy so that there are lots of active wavefronts. The instructions can be floating point, integer or memory operations. Poorly written kernels with lots of stalls cause low-issue efficiency even if the occupancy is high. There are a variety of reasons for kernels to encounter stalls. There are also counters that can identify particular reasons for stalls. Some of the possibilities are

- *Memory dependency*—Waiting on a memory load or store
- *Execution dependency*—Waiting on a previous instruction to complete
- *Synchronization*—Blocked warp due to a synchronization call
- *Memory throttle*—Large number of outstanding memory operations
- *Constant miss*—Miss in the constants cache
- *Texture busy*—Fully utilized texture hardware
- *Pipeline busy*—Compute resources not available

13.5.3 Achieved bandwidth: It always comes down to bandwidth

Bandwidth is an important metric to understand because most applications are bandwidth limited. The best starting point is to look at the bandwidth measure. There are many memory counters available, allowing you to go as deep as you want. Comparing your achieved bandwidth measurements to the theoretical and measured bandwidth performance for your architecture from sections 9.3.1 through 9.3.3 can give you an estimate on how well your application is doing. You can use the memory measurements to determine whether it would be helpful to coalesce memory loads, to store values in the local memory (scratchpad), or to restructure code to reuse data values.

13.6 Containers and virtual machines provide alternate workflows

You are on a flight from somewhere to nowhere and just want to get some of your GPU code working. The latest software release doesn't work on your company-issued laptop. The workaround is to use a container or a virtual machine (VM) to run a different operating system or a different compiler version.

13.6.1 Docker containers as a workaround

Each of our chapters has an example Dockerfile and instructions for its use. The Dockerfile contains the commands to build a basic OS and then to install the necessary software that it needs.

Example: Building a Docker image with the supplied Dockerfile

The top-level directory for most chapters has a Dockerfile. In the directory for the chapter you are interested in, run the Docker `build` command and create a Docker container using the `-t` option to name it. In this example, we build the chapter 2 Docker container and name it `chapter2`:

```
docker build -t essentialsofparallelcomputing/chapter2 .
```

Now run the Docker container with the following command:

```
docker run -it --entrypoint /bin/bash
            essentialsofparallelcomputing/chapter2
```

Alternatively, use

```
./docker_run.sh
```

Some chapters have both a text-based and a graphics-based Dockerfile. To enable the text-based file, remove the Dockerfile and link in the text-based version with this command:

```
ln -s Dockerfile.Ubuntu20.04 Dockerfile
```

A Docker container is useful for dealing with software that does not work on your operating system. For example, for software that only runs on Linux, you can install a container on your Mac or Windows laptop that runs Ubuntu 20.0.4. Using a container works well for text-based, command-line software.

Containers also limit access to hardware devices such as GPUs. One option is to run the device kernels on the CPU for the GPU languages that have that capability. Doing this, we can at least test our software. If that is not enough for our needs, we can tackle some additional steps to try and get the graphics and GPU computation working. We'll start by looking at getting the graphics working. Running a graphical interface from a Docker build takes a little more effort.

Example: Running the Docker image with a GUI on macOS

Mac laptops do not have an X Window client built into their standard software. Therefore, you need to install an X Window client on your Mac if you have not done this already. The XQuartz package is an open source version of the original X Window that was included on older versions of macOS. You can install it with the brew package manager like this:

```
brew cask install xQuartz
```

(continued)

Now start XQuartz and look for the XQuartz menu bar at the top of the screen. If you don't see it, you might need to also start a sample X Window application such as xterm by using a right-click on the XQuartz icon. Then

1 Select the XQuartz menu bar and then the Preferences option
2 Go to the Security tab and select Allow Connections from Network Clients
3 Reboot your system to apply the settings.
4 Start XQuartz again

For chapters that require a GUI for tools or plots, the instructions are a little different. We use the Virtual Network Computing (VNC) software to enable the graphics capabilities through a web interface and VNC client viewers. You must use the docker_run.sh script to start the VNC server, then you need to start a VNC client on your local system. You can use one of a variety of VNC client packages, or you can open the graphics file through some browsers with the following in your browser toolbar site name:

```
http://localhost:6080/vnc.html?resize=downscale&autoconnect=1&password=
    <password>"
```

To test an application with a graphical interface such as NVVP, type nvvp. Or you might want to test the graphics with a simple X Window application such as xclock or xterm. We can also try to get access to the GPUs for computation. Access to the GPUs can be obtained by using the --gpus option or the older --device=/dev/<device name>. The option is a relatively new addition to Docker and, currently, is only implemented for NVIDIA GPUs.

Example: Accessing GPUs for computational work

To access a GPU for computation, add the --gpus option with an integer argument for the number of GPUs (gpus) to make available or all for all of the GPUs:

```
docker run -it --gpus all --entrypoint /bin/bash chapter13
```

For Intel GPUs, you can try

```
docker run -it --device=/dev/dri --entrypoint /bin/bash chapter13
```

Most of the chapters have prebuilt Docker containers. You can access the containers for each chapter at https://hub.docker.com/u/essentialsofparallelcomputing. You can retrieve the container for a chapter with the following command:

```
docker run -p 4000:80 -it --entrypoint /bin/bash
    essentialsofparallelcomputing/chapter2
```

There is also a prebuilt Docker container from NVIDIA that you can use as a starting point for your own Docker images. Visit the site at https://github.com/NVIDIA/nvidia-docker for up-to-date instructions. There is another site at NVIDIA with substantial container varieties at https://ngc.nvidia.com/catalog/containers. For ROCm, there are extensive instructions on Docker containers at https://github.com/RadeonOpenCompute/ROCm-docker. And Intel has a site for how to set up their oneAPI software in containers at https://github.com/intel/oneapi-containers. Some of their base containers are large and require a good internet connection.

The PGI compiler is important for OpenACC code development and some other GPU code development challenges as well. If you need the PGI compiler for your work, the container site for PGI compilers is at https://ngc.nvidia.com/catalog/containers/hpc:pgi-compilers. As you can see from the sites mentioned here, there are many resources for creating work environments with Docker containers. But this is also a rapidly evolving capability.

13.6.2 *Virtual machines using VirtualBox*

Using a virtual machine (VM) allows the user to create a guest OS within their own computer. The normal operating system is called a host, and the VM is called the guest. You can have more than one VM running as a guest. VMs use a more restrictive environment for the guest operating system than exists in the container implementations. Often, it is easier to set up GUIs in comparison to containers. Unfortunately, access to the GPU for computation is difficult or impossible. You might find VMs useful for GPU languages that have an option supporting computation on the host CPU processor.

Let's look at the process of setting up an Ubuntu guest operating system in VirtualBox. This example sets up the shallow water example running on the CPU with the PGI compiler in VirtualBox with graphics.

Example: Setting up an Ubuntu guest OS in VirtualBox

To set up your system for VirtualBox

1 Download VirtualBox for your system and install
2 Download the Ubuntu desktop and save it to your local disk

```
[ubuntu-20.04-desktop-amd64.iso]
```

3 Download the VBoxGuestAdditions.iso file, which may already be included in the VirtualBox download

Next, we set up the Ubuntu guest system. An automated script, autovirtualbox.sh, is included in the examples for this chapter to automate setting up the Ubuntu guest system in VirtualBox at https://github.com/EssentialsOfParallelComputing/Chapter13.git. Most of the other chapters have similar scripts. To set up the Ubuntu guest system, follow this process:

(continued)

1 Start VirtualBox and click New
2 Type in a name (chapter13, for example)
3 Select Linux and then Ubuntu 64-bit
4 Select the amount of memory (8192, for example)
5 Create a virtual hard disk
6 Select VDI VirtualBox Disk Image
7 Select Fixed Size Disk
8 Select 50 GB

Your new virtual machine should now be added to the list.

Now we are ready to install Ubuntu. The process is the same as setting up an Ubuntu system on your desktop.

Example: Installing Ubuntu
To install Ubuntu, follow these steps:

1 Start the Ubuntu VM by clicking the green start arrow
2 Select the iso file saved earlier by typing to ubuntu-20.04-desktop-amd64.iso from the options presented
3 Select Install Ubuntu
4 Select your keyboard and click Continue
5 Select Minimal Install, download updates, and install third-party software, then click Continue
6 Select Erase Disk and install Ubuntu and then click Install and select a time zone
7 Type the following into the text boxes: your name (chapter13, for example), your computer's name (chapter13-virtualbox), username (chapter13), and password (chapter13)
8 Select Require My Password to Log In and then select Continue

Time to get some coffee. When the installation is complete, restart your computer and follow these steps:

1 Sign back in
2 Click through What's New
3 Select the dots at bottom left and start a terminal
4 Edit Sudo Authorized Users configuration file with

```
sudo -i
visudo
```

and add the following in any blank line, `%vboxsf ALL=(ALL) ALL`, then exit

You may need to wait for updates or reboot and sign back in. Once logged back in install basic build tools with `sudo apt install build-essential dkms git -y`. Then

1 Make the VirtualBox window active and select the Devices pull-down menu from the window's menus at top of screen
2 Set the Shared Clipboard option to Bidirectional
3 Set the Drag and Drop option to Bidirectional
4 Install the guest additions by selecting the menu option virtualbox-guest-additions-iso
5 Remove the optical disk: from the desktop, right-click and eject the device or in the VirtualBox window, select Devices > Optical Disk and remove the disk from the virtual drive
6 Reboot and test by copying and pasting (copy on the Mac is Command-C and paste in Ubuntu is Shift-Ctrl-v)

Your Ubuntu guest system is now ready for downloading and installing software.

There are instructions for setting up virtual machines with the examples for each chapter. For this chapter, log back in and install the chapter examples:

```
git clone --recursive https://github.com/essentialsofparallelcomputing/
    Chapter13.git
cd Chapter13 && sh -v README.virtualbox
```

The commands in the README.virtualbox file install the software, and build and run the shallow water application. The real time graphics output should also work. You can also try the nvprof utility to profile the shallow water application as well.

13.7 *Cloud options: A flexible and portable capability*

When access to a specific GPU is limited (no supercomputer, laptop or desktop GPU, or remote server), you can make use of cloud computing.[1] Cloud computing refers to servers provided by large data centers. While most of these services are for more general users, some sites catering towards HPC-style services are beginning to appear. One of these sites is http://mng.bz/Q2YG. The Fluid Numerics Cloud cluster (fluid-slurm-gcp) setup on the Google Cloud Platform (GCP) has the Slurm batch scheduler and MPI. NVIDIA GPUs can be scheduled as well. Getting started can be a bit complicated. The Fluid Numerics site has some information to help with that process at http://mng.bz/XYwv.

The advantages of having hardware resources available on demand is often compelling. Google Cloud offers a $300 trial credit that should be more than sufficient for exploring the service. There are other cloud providers and add-on services that can provide exactly what you need, or you can customize the environment yourself. Intel

---

[1] See the README.cloud file in the examples for this chapter for the latest information on using the cloud.

has set up a cloud service for testing out Intel GPUs so that developers have access to both software and hardware for their oneAPI initiative and their DPCPP compiler that provides a SYCL implementation. You can try it out by going to https://software.intel .com/en-us/oneapi and registering to use it.

13.8   Further explorations

Incorporating a workflow and development environment is especially important for GPU code development. With the great variety of possible hardware configurations, the examples presented in this chapter will likely require some customization for your situation. Indeed, the configuration and setup of development systems is one of the challenges of GPU computing. You may even find that it is easier to use one of the pre-built Docker containers rather than figure out the process to configure and install software on your system.

We also suggest checking the most recent documentation relevant to your needs from the additional reading suggested in section 13.8.1. The tools and workflows are the fastest changing aspects of GPU programming. While the examples in this chapter will be generally relevant, the details are likely to change. Much of the software is so new that documentation on its use is still being developed.

13.8.1   Additional reading

The NVIDIA installation manual has some information on installing CUDA tools using a package manager at:

> https://docs.nvidia.com/cuda/cuda-installation-guide-linux/index.html#pack age-manager-installation

NVIDIA has a couple of resources on their profiling tools and the transition from NVVP to the Nsight tool suite at the following sites:

- NVIDIA NSight Guide at https://docs.nvidia.com/nsight-compute/Nsight Compute/index.html#nvvp-guide
- NVIDIA profiling tool comparison at https://devblogs.nvidia.com/migrat ing-nvidia-nsight-tools-nvvp-nvprof/

Other tools include the following:

- CodeXL has been released as open source under the GPUopen initiative. AMD has also removed its AMD brand from the tool to promote cross-platform development. For more information, see https://github.com/GPUOpen-Tools/ CodeXL.
- NVIDIA has a GPU Cloud with resources such as the PGI compilers in a container at https://ngc.nvidia.com/catalog/containers/hpc:pgi-compilers.
- AMD also has a webpage on setting up virtualization environments and containers. The virtualization instructions include a passthrough technique to get

access to the GPU for computation. You find this information at http://mng
.bz/MgWW

13.8.2 *Exercises*

1   Run nvprof on the stream triad example. You might try the CUDA version from
    chapter 12 or the OpenACC version from chapter 11. What workflow did you
    use for your hardware resources? If you don't have access to an NVIDIA GPU,
    can you use another profiling tool?

2   Generate a trace from nvprof and import it into NVVP. Where is the run time
    spent? What could you do to optimize it?

3   Download a prebuilt Docker container from the appropriate vendor for your sys-
    tem. Start up the container and run one of the examples from chapter 11 or 12.

Summary

- Improving performance is a high priority for scientific and big data applications. Performance tools can help you get the most out of your GPU hardware.
- There are many profiling tools available for GPU programming. You should try
  out the many new and emerging capabilities that are available.
- Workflows are essential for efficient GPU code development. Explore what
  works for you in your environment and the available GPU hardware.
- There are workarounds through the use of containers, virtual machines, and
  cloud computing to handle incompatibilities, computing needs, and access to
  GPU hardware. These workarounds give access to a large sampling of GPU vendor hardware that might not otherwise be available.

Part 4

High performance computing ecosystems

With today's high performance computing (HPC) systems, it is not enough for you to just learn parallel programming languages. You also need to understand many aspects of the ecosystem including the following:

- Placing and scheduling your processes for better performance
- Requesting and scheduling resources using an HPC batch system
- Writing and reading data in parallel on parallel file systems
- Making full use of the tools and resources to analyze performance and assist software development

These are just some of the important topics that surround the core parallel programming languages; forming a complementary set of capabilities we call the HPC ecosystem.

Our computing systems are exponentially growing in both complexity and the number of cores. Many of the considerations in HPC are also becoming important for high-end workstations. With so many processor cores, we need to control the placement and scheduling of processes within a node, a practice that is loosely called *process affinity* and done in conjunction with the OS kernel. As the number of cores on processors grows, the tools for controlling process affinity are quickly being developed to help with new concerns about process placement. We'll cover some of the techniques that are available for assigning process affinity in chapter 14.

Sophisticated resource management systems have become ubiquitous due to the growth in complexity of computing resources. These "batch systems" form a queue of requests for the resources and allocate these out, according to a priority system called a fair share algorithm. When you first get on an HPC system, the batch system can be confusing. Without knowing how to use a scheduler, you cannot deploy your applications on these large machines. This is why we think it's essential to go over the basics of using the most common batch systems in chapter 15.

We also don't just write out files the same way on HPC systems; we write these out in parallel to special filesystem hardware that can stripe the file writes across multiple disks simultaneously. For exploiting the power of these parallel filesystems, you need to learn about some of the software used for parallel file operations. In chapter 16, we show you how to use MPI-IO and HDF5, which are a couple of the more common parallel file software libraries. With data sets growing ever larger, the potential uses of parallel file software is expanding far outside the traditional HPC applications.

Chapter 17 covers a broad range of important tools and resources for the HPC application developer. You might find profilers of great value in helping your application performance. There is a wide range of profilers for different use cases and hardware such as GPUs. There are also tools that help with the software development process. These tools allow you to produce correct, robust applications. Additionally, many application developers can discover specialized approaches for their application from the wide variety of sample applications.

The capabilities of the HPC ecosystem are becoming more important as the complexity and scale of our computing platforms grow. The knowledge of how to use these capabilities has often been neglected. We hope that by covering these often overlooked aspects of high-performance computing in these four chapters, you will be able to get more productive use from your computing hardware.

Affinity:
Truce with the kernel

This chapter covers

- Why affinity is an important concern for modern CPUs
- Controlling affinity for your parallel applications
- Fine-tuning performance with process placement

We first encountered affinity in section 8.6.2 on the MPI (Message Passing Interface), where we defined it and briefly showed how to handle it. We repeat the definition here and also define process placement.

- *Affinity*—Assigns a preference for the scheduling of a process, rank or thread to a particular hardware component. This is also called *pinning* or *binding*.
- *Placement*—Assigns a process or thread to a hardware location.

We'll go into more depth about affinity, placement, and the order of threads or ranks in this chapter. Concerns about affinity are recent phenomena. In the past, with just a few processor cores per CPU, there wasn't that much to gain. As the number of processors grows and the architecture of a compute node gets more complicated, affinity has become more and more important. Still, the gains are relatively modest; perhaps the biggest benefit is in reducing the variation in performance from run to run and getting better on-node scaling. Occasionally, controlling affinity can avoid truly disastrous scheduling decisions by the kernel with respect to the characteristics of your application.

The decision of where to place a process or a thread is handled by the operating system kernel. Kernel scheduling has a rich history and is key to the development of multitasking, multi-user operating systems. It is due to these capabilities that you can fire up a spreadsheet, temporarily switch to a word processor, and then handle an important email. However, the scheduling algorithms developed for the general user are not always suitable for parallel computing. We can launch four processes for a four processor core system, but the operating system schedules those four processes any way it wants. It could place all four processes on the same processor, or it could spread them out across the four processors. Generally the kernel does something reasonable, but it can interrupt one of the parallel processes to perform a system function, causing all the other processes to idle and wait.

In chapter 1, figures 1.20 and 1.21, we showed question marks about where the processes get placed because we have no control over the placement of processors or threads on processors. At least until now. Recent releases of MPI, OpenMP, and batch schedulers have started to offer features to control placement and affinity. Although there is a lot of change in the options in some of the interfaces, things seem to be settling down with recent releases. However, you are advised to check the documentation for the releases that you use for any differences.

14.1   Why is affinity important?

Unlike most common desktop applications, parallel processes need to be scheduled together. This is referred to as gang scheduling.

> **DEFINITION**   *Gang scheduling* is a kernel scheduling algorithm that activates a group of processes at the same time.

Because parallel processes generally synchronize periodically during a run, scheduling a single thread that ends up waiting on another process that is not active has no benefit. The kernel scheduling algorithm has no information that a process is dependent on another's operation. This is true for MPI, OpenMP threads, and GPU kernels as well. The best approach for getting gang scheduling is to only allocate as many processes as there are processors and bind those processes to the processors. We cannot forget that the kernel and system processes need somewhere to run. Some advanced techniques reserve a processor just for system processes.

It is not enough to keep every parallel process active and scheduled. We also need to keep processes scheduled on the same Non-Uniform Memory Access (NUMA) domain to minimize memory access costs. With OpenMP, we typically go to a lot of trouble to "first touch" data arrays on the processor where the data is used (see section 7.1.1). If the kernel then moves your process to another NUMA domain, your efforts are all for naught. We saw in section 7.3.1 that the penalty for memory access in the wrong

NUMA domain can typically be a factor of two or more. It is a top priority for our processes to stay on the same memory domain.

Typically, a NUMA domain is aligned with the sockets on a node. If we can tell a process to schedule an affinity on the same socket, we'll always get the same, optimal memory access time for main memory. The need for NUMA region affinity, however, is dependent on your CPU architecture. Personal computing systems often have only one NUMA region, while large HPC systems often have far more processing cores per node with two CPU sockets and two or more NUMA regions.

While tying affinity to a NUMA domain optimizes our access time to main memory, we still can have less than optimal performance due to poor cache usage. A process fills the L1 and L2 cache with the memory that it needs. But then, if it gets swapped out to another processor on the same NUMA domain with a different L1 and L2 cache, cache performance suffers. The caches then need to be filled again. If you reuse data a lot, this causes a performance loss. For MPI, we want to lock processes or ranks to a processor. But with OpenMP, this causes all the threads to be launched on the same processor because the affinity is inherited by the spawned threads. With OpenMP, we want to have affinity for each thread to its processor.

Some processors also have a new feature called hyperthreads. Hyperthreads add another layer of complexity to the process placement considerations. First we need to define hyperthreading and what it is.

> **DEFINITION** *Hyperthreading*, an Intel technology, makes a single processor appear to be two virtual processors to the operating system through sharing of hardware resources between two threads.

Hyperthreads share a single physical core and its cache system. Because the cache is shared, there isn't as much penalty for movement between hyperthreads. But it also means that each virtual core has half the cache as a real physical core if the processes do not have any data in common. For our memory-bound applications, halving the cache can be a serious blow. Thus, the effectiveness of these virtual cores is mixed. Many HPC systems turn them off because some programs slow down with hyperthreads. Not all hyperthreads are equal either on the hardware or operating system level, so don't assume that if you didn't see a benefit on a previous implementation, you won't on your current system. If we use hyperthreads, we'll want the process placement to be close by so that the shared cache benefits both virtual processors.

14.2 *Discovering your architecture*

In order to leverage affinity for better performance, we need to know the details of our hardware architecture. The variety of hardware architectures makes this difficult; Intel alone has over a thousand CPU models. In this section, we introduce how to understand your architecture. This is a requirement before you can use affinity to exploit it.

You can get the best view of your architecture with the lstopo utility. We first saw lstopo in section 3.2.1 with the output for a Mac laptop in figure 3.2. The laptop is a simple architecture with four physical processing cores which, with hyperthreading enabled, appears as eight virtual cores to the operating systems. We can also see in figure 3.2 that the L1 and L2 caches are private to the physical core, and the L3 cache is shared across all of the processors. We also note that there is just one NUMA domain. Now let's take a look at a more complicated CPU. Figure 14.1 shows the architecture for an Intel Skylake Gold CPU.

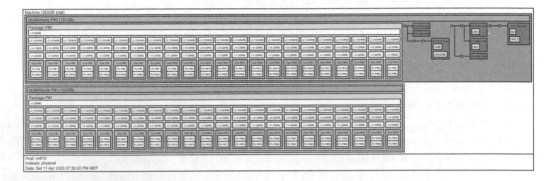

Figure 14.1   The Intel Skylake Gold architecture with two NUMA domains and 88 processing cores reveals the complexity of higher-end compute nodes.

The gray boxes in figure 14.1, each labeled core and containing two light rectangles labled PU for processing unit, are physical cores. Each of these gray boxes has two boxes inside that are the virtual processors created by hyperthreads. The L1 and L2 caches are private to each physical processor, while the L3 cache is shared across the NUMA domain. We also can see that the network and other peripherals at the right of the figure are closer to the first NUMA domain. We can get some information on most Linux or Unix systems with the lscpu command (figure 14.2).

The output from lscpu confirms that there are two threads per core and two NUMA domains. The processor numbering seems a little odd, but by having the first 22 processors on the first NUMA node and then skipping to include the next 22 processors on the second node, we leave the hyperthreads to be numbered last. Remember that the NUMA utilities definition of a node is different than our definition, where it is a separate, distributed memory system.

So what is the strategy for affinity and process placement for this architecture? Well, it depends on the application. Each application has different scaling and threading performance needs that must be considered. We will want to watch that we keep processes in their NUMA domains to get the optimal bandwidth to main memory.

```
Architecture:          x86_64
CPU op-mode(s):        32-bit, 64-bit
Byte Order:            Little Endian
CPU(s):                88
On-line CPU(s) list:   0-87
Thread(s) per core:    2
Core(s) per socket:    22
Socket(s):             2
NUMA node(s):          2
Vendor ID:             GenuineIntel
CPU family:            6
Model:                 85
Model name:            Intel(R) Xeon(R) Gold 6152 CPU @ 2.10GHz
Stepping:              4
CPU MHz:               1000.012
CPU max MHz:           3700.0000
CPU min MHz:           1000.0000
BogoMIPS:              4200.00
Virtualization:        VT-x
L1d cache:             32K
L1i cache:             32K
L2 cache:              1024K
L3 cache:              30976K
NUMA node0 CPU(s):     0-21,44-65
NUMA node1 CPU(s):     22-43,66-87
Flags:                 fpu vme de pse tsc msr pae mce cx8 apic sep mtrr pge mca cmov pat pse36 clflush dts acpi mmx
fxsr sse sse2 ss ht tm pbe syscall nx pdpe1gb rdtscp lm constant_tsc art arch_perfmon pebs bts rep_good nopl
xtopology nonstop_tsc aperfmperf eagerfpu pni pclmulqdq dtes64 monitor ds_cpl vmx smx est tm2 ssse3 sdbg fma cx16
xtpr pdcm pcid dca sse4_1 sse4_2 x2apic movbe popcnt tsc_deadline_timer aes xsave avx f16c rdrand lahf_lm abm
3dnowprefetch epb cat_l3 cdp_l3 invpcid_single intel_ppin intel_pt mba tpr_shadow vnmi flexpriority ept vpid fsgsbase
tsc_adjust bmi1 hle avx2 smep bmi2 erms invpcid rtm cqm mpx rdt_a avx512f avx512dq rdseed adx smap clflushopt clwb
avx512cd avx512bw avx512vl xsaveopt xsavec xgetbv1 cqm_llc cqm_occup_llc cqm_mbm_total cqm_mbm_local dtherm ida arat
pln pts pku ospke
```

Figure 14.2   Output from `lscpu` command for the Intel Skylake Gold processor.

14.3   *Thread affinity with OpenMP*

Thread affinity is vital when optimizing applications with OpenMP. Tying a thread to the location of the memory it uses is important to achieve good memory latency and bandwidth. We go to great effort to do *first touch* to get memory placed close to the thread as we discussed in section 7.1.1. If the threads are moving around to different processors, we lose all the benefits we should get from our extra effort.

With OpenMP v4.0, the affinity controls for OpenMP were expanded to include the `close`, `spread`, and `primary` keywords, in addition to the existing `true` or `false` options. Also added were three options for the OMP_PLACES environment variable, `sockets`, `cores`, and `threads`. In summary, we now have these affinity and placement controls:

- OMP_PLACES = [sockets|cores|threads] or an explicit list of places
- OMP_PROC_BIND = [close|spread|primary] or [true|false]

OMP_PLACES puts limits on where the threads can be scheduled. There is actually one option that is not listed: the `node`. It is the default and allows each thread to be scheduled anywhere in the "place." With more than one thread on the default place of the node, the possibility exists that the scheduler will move the threads or have collisions with two or more threads scheduled for one virtual processor. One sensible approach is not to have more threads than the quantity of the specified place. Perhaps the better rule is to specify a place that has a quantity greater than the desired number of threads. We'll show how that works in an example later in this section.

The OMP_PROC_BIND environment variable has five possible settings, but these have some overlap in meaning. The `close`, `spread`, and `primary` settings are specialized versions of `true`.

> **NOTE**   We also note that `primary` replaces the deprecated `master` keyword as of the OpenMP v5.1 standard. You may continue to encounter the old usage as compilers implement the new standard.

With the `false` setting, the kernel scheduler is free to move threads around. The `true` setting tells the kernel not to move the thread once it gets scheduled. But it can be scheduled anywhere within the place constraint and can vary from run to run. The `primary` setting is a special case that schedules threads on the main processor. The `close` setting schedules the threads close together and `spread` distributes the threads. The choice of which of these two settings to use has some subtle implications that you will see in the example for this section.

> **NOTE**   You can also set the placement with a detailed list. This is a more advanced use case that we won't go over here. The detailed list can give more fine-tuned control, but it is less portable to a different CPU type.

The OpenMP environment variables set the affinity and placement for the whole program. You can also set the affinity for individual loops through the addition of a clause on the `parallel` directive. The clause has this syntax:

```
proc_bind([primary|close|spread])
```

The following example shows these affinity controls in operation on our simple vector addition program from section 7.3.1. The affinity-reporting routines can also be added to your code to see the impact there.

> **Example: Vector addition with all possible settings of OMP_PLACES and OMP_PROC_BIND**
> For this example, we set every combination of OpenMP affinity and placement environment variables. We first modify the vector add from section 7.3.1 to call a routine that reports placement of threads shown in the following listing.

Modified vecadd_opt3.c for affinity study

```
OpenMP/vecadd_opt3.c
 1 #include <stdio.h>
 2 #include <time.h>
 3 #include "timer.h"
 4 #include "omp.h"
 5 #include "place_report_omp.h"
 6
 7 // large enough to force into main memory
 8 #define ARRAY_SIZE 80000000
 9 static double a[ARRAY_SIZE], b[ARRAY_SIZE], c[ARRAY_SIZE];
10
11 void vector_add(double *c, double *a, double *b, int n);
12
13 int main(int argc, char *argv[]){          Define to enable
14 #ifdef VERBOSE                              reporting
15    place_report_omp();         ◄           Call to placement
16 #endif                                     report
17    struct timespec tstart;
18    double time_sum = 0.0;
19 #pragma omp parallel
20    {
21 #pragma omp for
22       for (int i=0; i<ARRAY_SIZE; i++) {
23          a[i] = 1.0;
24          b[i] = 2.0;
25       }
26
27 #pragma omp masked
28       cpu_timer_start(&tstart);
29       vector_add(c, a, b, ARRAY_SIZE);
30 #pragma omp masked
31       time_sum += cpu_timer_stop(tstart);
32    } // end of omp parallel
33
34    printf("Runtime is %lf msecs\n", time_sum);
35 }
36
37 void vector_add(double *c, double *a, double *b, int n)
38 {
39 #pragma omp for
40    for (int i=0; i < n; i++){
41       c[i] = a[i] + b[i];
42    }
43 }
```

The main work is done in the place_report_omp subroutine. We use an ifdef around the call to easily turn the reporting on and off. So now let's take a look at the reporting routine in the next listing.

(continued)

Reporting place settings in OpenMP

```
OpenMP/place_report_omp.c
41 void place_report_omp(void)
42 {
43    #pragma omp parallel
44    {
45       if (omp_get_thread_num() == 0){
46          printf("Running with %d thread(s)\n",        ⟵ Reports number
                     omp_get_num_threads());                  of threads
47          int bind_policy = omp_get_proc_bind();       ⟵
48          switch (bind_policy)                             Queries
49          {                                                and reports
50             case omp_proc_bind_false:                     OMP_PROC_BIND
51                printf("  proc_bind is false\n");           setting
52                break;
53             case omp_proc_bind_true:
54                printf("  proc_bind is true\n");
55                break;
56             case omp_proc_bind_master:
57                printf("  proc_bind is master\n");
58                break;
59             case omp_proc_bind_close:
60                printf("  proc_bind is close\n");
61                break;
62             case omp_proc_bind_spread:
63                printf("  proc_bind is spread\n");
64          }
65          printf("  proc_num_places is %d\n",    Queries and reports overall
                     omp_get_num_places());          thread placement restrictions
66       }
67    }
68
69    int socket_global[144];
70    char clbuf_global[144][7 * CPU_SETSIZE];
71
72    #pragma omp parallel
73    {
74       int thread = omp_get_thread_num();
75       cpu_set_t coremask;
76       char clbuf[7 * CPU_SETSIZE];
77       memset(clbuf, 0, sizeof(clbuf));           Gets the affinity
78       sched_getaffinity(0, sizeof(coremask),     bit mask
                          &coremask);
                                                    Converts the bit mask to
79       cpuset_to_cstr(&coremask, clbuf);      ⟵  something we can print
80       strcpy(clbuf_global[thread],clbuf);
81       socket_global[omp_get_thread_num()] =      Gets the actual place
           omp_get_place_num();                     number to print
82       #pragma omp barrier
83       #pragma omp master
```

```
84          for (int i=0; i<omp_get_num_threads(); i++){
85            printf("Hello from thread %d: (core affinity = %s)"
                  " OpenMP socket is %d\n",
86                i, clbuf_global[i], socket_global[i]);
87          }
88      }
89  }
```

The CPU affinity bit mask needs to be converted to a more understandable format for printing out. The next listing shows that routine.

Routine to convert CPU bit mask to a C string

```
OpenMP/place_report_omp.c
12 static char *cpuset_to_cstr(cpu_set_t *mask, char *str)
13 {
14   char *ptr = str;
15   int i, j, entry_made = 0;
16   for (i = 0; i < CPU_SETSIZE; i++) {
17     if (CPU_ISSET(i, mask)) {
18       int run = 0;
19       entry_made = 1;
20       for (j = i + 1; j < CPU_SETSIZE; j++) {
21         if (CPU_ISSET(j, mask)) run++;
22         else break;
23       }
24       if (!run)
25         sprintf(ptr, "%d,", i);
26       else if (run == 1) {
27         sprintf(ptr, "%d,%d,", i, i + 1);
28         i++;
29       } else {
30         sprintf(ptr, "%d-%d,", i, i + run);
31         i += run;
32       }
33       while (*ptr != 0) ptr++;
34     }
35   }
36   ptr -= entry_made;
37   *ptr = 0;
38   return(str);
39 }
```

In the placement reporting routine, we query the OpenMP settings, report those, then show the placement and affinity for each thread. To try it out, compile the code with the verbose setting and run it with 44 threads or whatever number of threads makes sense on your system, and no special environment variable settings. The example code is at https://github.com/EssentialsofParallelComputing/Chapter14.git in the OpenMP subdirectory.

Example: Querying the OpenMP settings for the placement reporting routine

To query the OpenMP settings, report them, then show the placement and affinity for each thread, the steps are

```
mkdir build && cd build
cmake -DCMAKE_VERBOSE=on ..
make
export OMP_NUM_THREADS=44
./vecadd_opt3
```

Running this on the Intel Skylake-Gold with GCC 9.3 gives the following output.

```
Running with 44 thread(s)
  proc_bind is false                            Any processor
  proc_num_places is 0                          location
Hello from thread 0:  (core affinity = 0-87)  OpenMP socket is -1
Hello from thread 1:  (core affinity = 0-87)  OpenMP socket is -1
Hello from thread 2:  (core affinity = 0-87)  OpenMP socket is -1
Hello from thread 3:  (core affinity = 0-87)  OpenMP socket is -1
Hello from thread 4:  (core affinity = 0-87)  OpenMP socket is -1
   <... skipping output ...>
Hello from thread 42: (core affinity = 0-87)  OpenMP socket is -1
Hello from thread 43: (core affinity = 0-87)  OpenMP socket is -1
  0.022119
```

The output shows the affinity and placement report with no environment variables set. The threads are allowed to run on any processor from 0 to 87.

The core affinity allows the thread to run on any of the 88 virtual cores.

Let's see what happens when we place the threads on hardware cores and set the affinity binding to close.

```
export OMP_PLACES=cores
export OMP_PROC_BIND=close
./vecadd_opt3
```

The output with this affinity and placement settings is shown in Figure 14.3.

Wow! We can actually control the kernel! The threads are now pinned to the two virtual cores belonging to a single hardware core. The run time of 0.0166 ms is the last number in the output. This run time is a substantial improvement over the 0.0221 ms in the previous run for a 25% reduction in the computation time. You can experiment with various environment variable settings and see how the threads are placed on the node.

We are going to automate the exploration of all the settings and how they scale with different numbers of threads. We'll turn off the verbose option to reduce the

```
Running with 44 thread(s)
  proc_bind is close
  proc_num_places is 44                              Hardware core
Hello from thread 0:  (core affinity = 0,44)  OpenMP      socket is 0
Hello from thread 1:  (core affinity = 1,45)  OpenMP      socket is 1
Hello from thread 2:  (core affinity = 2,46)  OpenMP      socket is 2
Hello from thread 3:  (core affinity = 3,47)  OpenMP      socket is 3
Hello from thread 4:  (core affinity = 4,48)  OpenMP      socket is 4
    <... skipping output ...>
Hello from thread 42: (core affinity = 42,86) OpenM    P socket is 42
Hello from thread 43: (core affinity = 43,87) OpenM    P socket is 43
  0.016601
```

Figure 14.3 Affinity and placement report for `OMP_PLACES=cores` and `OMP_PROC_BIND=close`. Each thread can run on two possible virtual cores. These two processors belong to a single hardware core due to hyperthreading.

output that we have to deal with. Only the run time will print. Remove the previous build and rebuild the code as follows:

```
mkdir build && cd build
cmake ..
make
```

We then run the script in the following listing to get the performance for all cases.

Listing 14.1 Script to automate exploring all settings

```
OpenMP/run.sh
 1 #!/bin/sh
 2
 3 calc_avg_stddev()           ⟵┐ Calculates average and
 4 {                                standard deviation
 5    #echo "Runtime is $1"
 6    awk '{
 7      sum = 0.0; sum2 = 0.0        # Initialize to zero
 8      for (n=1; n <= NF; n++) {    # Process each value on the line
 9        sum += $n;                 # Running sum of values
10        sum2 += $n * $n            # Running sum of squares
11      }
12      print " Number of trials=" NF ",     avg=" sum/NF ", \
            std dev=" sqrt((sum2 - (sum*sum)/NF)/NF);
13      }' <<< $1
14 }
15
16 conduct_tests()       ⟵┘ Does the test
17 {
18    echo ""
19    echo -n `printenv |grep OMP_` ${exec_string}
20    foo=""
21    for index in {1..10}       ⟵┐ Repeats ten times
22    do                            to get statistics
23       time_result=`${exec_string}`
```

```
24          time_val[$index]=${time_result}
25          foo="$foo ${time_result}"
26      done
27      calc_avg_stddev "${foo}"
28  }
29
30  exec_string="./vecadd_opt3 "
31
32  conduct_tests
33
34  THREAD_COUNT="88 44 22 16 8 4 2 1"
35
36  for my_thread_count in ${THREAD_COUNT}        ◁──┐  Loops over number
37  do                                                │  of threads
38      unset OMP_PLACES
39      unset OMP_PROC_BIND
40      export OMP_NUM_THREADS=${my_thread_count}
41
42      conduct_tests
43
44      PLACES_LIST="threads cores sockets"
45      BIND_LIST="true false close spread primary"
46                                                       Loops over place
47      for my_place in ${PLACES_LIST}        ◁────────┘  settings
48      do
49          for my_bind in ${BIND_LIST}       ◁──┐  Loops over
50          do                                     │  affinity settings
51              export OMP_NUM_THREADS=${my_thread_count}
52              export OMP_PLACES=${my_place}
53              export OMP_PROC_BIND=${my_bind}
54
55              conduct_tests
56          done
57      done
58  done
```

Due to space, we show only a few of the results in figure 14.4. All of the values are the speedup from a single thread with no affinity or placement settings.

The first thing to note from figure 14.4 in our analysis is that the program is generally the fastest for all settings with only 44 threads. Overall, hyperthreading does not help. The exception is the close setting for threads because until we have more than 44 threads with this setting, there are no processes on the second socket. With threads only on the first socket, it limits the total memory bandwidth that can be obtained. At the full 88 threads, the close setting for threads gives the best performance, although by only a little bit. The close setting, in general, shows the same limited memory bandwidth effect due to only having threads on the first socket. You can also see that at larger process counts with process binding, the performance is higher than without process binding.

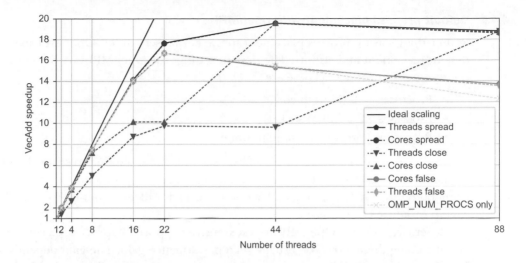

Figure 14.4 OpenMP affinity and placement settings of `OMP_PROC_BIND=spread` **boosts the parallel scaling by 50%. The lines are for various numbers of threads for a particular setting and are ordered roughly from high to low in the legend.**

Some key points to take away from this analysis

- Hyperthreading does not help with simple memory-bound kernels, but it also doesn't hurt.
- For memory-bandwidth-limited kernels on multiple sockets (NUMA domains), get both sockets busy.

We don't show the results for setting OMP_PROC_BIND to `primary` because it forces all the threads to be on the same processor and slows the program by as much as a factor of two. We also don't show setting OMP_PLACES to `sockets` because it has lower performance than those shown.

14.4 *Process affinity with MPI*

There are also benefits to applying affinity with MPI applications as discussed in section 14.2. It helps to get full memory bandwidth and cache performance by keeping the processes from being migrated to different processor cores by the operating system kernel. We will discuss affinity with OpenMPI because it has the most publicly available tools for affinity and process placement. Other MPI implementations like MPICH must be compiled with SLURM support enabled, which isn't as applicable to personal machines. We will discuss the command-line tools that can be used in more general situations in section 14.6. For now, let's move onward with our exploration of affinity in OpenMPI!

14.4.1 *Default process placement with OpenMPI*

Rather than leaving process placement to the kernel scheduler, OpenMPI specifies a default placement and affinity. The default settings for OpenMPI vary depending on the number of processes. These are

- Processes <= 2 (bind to core)
- Processes > 2 (bind to socket)
- Processes > processors (bind to none)

Some HPC centers might set other defaults such as always binding to cores. This binding policy may make sense for most MPI jobs but can cause problems with applications using both OpenMP threading and MPI. The threads will all be bound to a single processor, serializing the threads.

Recent versions of OpenMPI have extensive support for process placement and affinity. Using these tools, you usually get a performance gain. The gain depends upon how the process scheduler in the operating system is optimizing placement. Most schedulers are tuned for general computing, such as word processing and spreadsheets, but not parallel applications. Coaxing the scheduler to "do the right thing" potentially yields a benefit of 5–10%, but it can be a lot more.

14.4.2 *Taking control: Basic techniques for specifying process placement in OpenMPI*

For most use cases, it is sufficient to use simple controls to place processes and to bind these to hardware components. These controls are supplied to the `mpirun` command as options. Let's start with looking at distributing processes equally across a multi-node job. It is easiest to demonstrate this with an example.

Example: Distributing processes equally across multi-node jobs

We have an application that we want to run on 32 MPI ranks, but it is a memory-hungry application that needs half a terabyte of memory. A single node doesn't have enough memory, so how do we manage this?

If we look at the system details, each node has two sockets filled with Intel Broadwell (E52695) CPUs. Each CPU has 18 hardware cores that, with hyperthreading, gives us 36 virtual processors per socket. Each node has 128 GiB of memory.

- From the `lscpu` command

```
NUMA node0 CPU(s):     0-17,36-53
NUMA node1 CPU(s):     18-35,54-71
```

- From the /proc/meminfo file

```
MemTotal:        131728700 kB
```

For this example, we use our placement reporting tool for MPI applications. The two parts of the code are shown in the following listings.

Main MPI affinity code

```
MPI/MPIAffinity.c
 1 #include <mpi.h>
 2 #include <stdio.h>
 3 #include "place_report_mpi.h"
 4 int main(int argc, char **argv)
 5 {
 6    MPI_Init(&argc, &argv);
 7
 8    place_report_mpi();        ◄──┐  Inserts placement reporting
 9                                     call after MPI_Init
10    MPI_Finalize();
11    return 0;
12 }
```

We need to insert the call to our placement reporting subroutine after MPI is initialized. You can easily add this to your MPI application as well. Now let's look at the reporting subroutine in the next listing.

MPI placement reporting tool

```
MPI/place_report_mpi.c
40 void place_report_mpi(void)
41 {
42    int rank;
43    cpu_set_t coremask;
44    char clbuf[7 * CPU_SETSIZE], hnbuf[64];
45
46    memset(clbuf, 0, sizeof(clbuf));          Gets our
47    memset(hnbuf, 0, sizeof(hnbuf));          node name
48
49    MPI_Comm_rank(MPI_COMM_WORLD, &rank);     Gets the affinity
50                                              setting of our process
51    gethostname(hnbuf, sizeof(hnbuf));    ◄── Same cpuset_to_cstr routine
52    sched_getaffinity(0, sizeof(coremask),    from the vector addition
                      &coremask);               listing in section 14.3
53    cpuset_to_cstr(&coremask, clbuf);    ◄──
54    printf("Hello from rank %d, on %s. (core affinity = %s)\n",
55           rank, hnbuf, clbuf);
56 }
```

For our first run of our application, we simply ask mpirun to launch 32 processes:

```
mpirun -n 32 ./MPIAffinity | sort -n -k 4
```

We then have to sort the output by the data in the fourth column because the order of output by processes is random (done by the command sort -n -k 4). The output for this command with our placement report routine is shown in figure 14.5.

```
Hello from rank 0, on cn328. (core affinity = 0-17,36-53)
Hello from rank 1, on cn328. (core affinity = 18-35,54-71)
Hello from rank 2, on cn328. (core affinity = 0-17,36-53)
Hello from rank 3, on cn328. (core affinity = 18-35,54-71)
    <... skipping output ...>                            NUMA region
Hello from rank 28, on cn328. (core affinity = 0-17,36-53)
Hello from rank 29, on cn328. (core affinity = 18-35,54-71)
Hello from rank 30, on cn328. (core affinity = 0-17,36-53)
Hello from rank 31, on cn328. (core affinity = 18-35,54-71)
```

Figure 14.5   For mpirun -n 32**, all of our processes are on the cn328 node. The affinity is set to the NUMA region (socket).**

From the output in figure 14.5, we see that all the ranks were launched on node cn328. Referring to the default affinity settings for OpenMPI at the start of this section, for more than two ranks the affinity is set to bind to the socket. The output from the lscpu command shows our first NUMA region contains the virtual processing cores 0–17, 36–53. NUMA regions are usually aligned with each socket. In our output, we see that the core affinity equals 0–17, 36–53, confirming that the affinity was set to the socket.

Because our real application memory requirements are larger than the 128 GiB on the node, it fails when allocating memory. We thus need to find a way to spread out the processes. For this, we add another option, --npernode <#> or -N <#>, which tells MPI how many ranks to put on each node. We need to have four nodes to get enough memory for our problem, so we want eight processes per node.

```
mpirun -n 32 --npernode 8 ./MPIAffinity | sort -n -k 4
```

Figure 14.6 shows our placement report.

```
Hello from rank 0, on cn328. (core affinity = 0-17,36-53)
Hello from rank 1, on cn328. (core affinity = 18-35,54-71)
    < ... skipping output ... >
Hello from rank 8, on cn329. (core affinity = 0-17,36-53)
Hello from rank 9, on cn329. (core affinity = 18-35,54-71)    NUMA region
    < ... skipping output ... >
Hello from rank 16, on cn330. (core affinity = 0-17,36-53)
Hello from rank 17, on cn330. (core affinity = 18-35,54-71)
    < ... skipping output ... >
Hello from rank 24, on cn331. (core affinity = 0-17,36-53)
Hello from rank 25, on cn331. (core affinity = 18-35,54-71)
```

Figure 14.6   The MPI processes are spread out across the four nodes, cn328 through 331. The affinity is still tied to the NUMA region.

From the output in figure 14.6, we can see that we are running on four nodes. We should now have enough memory to run our application. Alternatively, we could specify how many ranks per socket with --npersocket. We have two sockets per node, so we want four ranks per socket, thus:

```
mpirun -n 32 --npersocket 4 ./MPIAffinity | sort -n -k 4
```

Figure 14.7 shows the output from the placement per socket.

```
Hello from rank 0, on cn328. (core affinity = 0-17,36-53)
Hello from rank 1, on cn328. (core affinity = 0-17,36-53)
Hello from rank 2, on cn328. (core affinity = 0-17,36-53)
Hello from rank 3, on cn328. (core affinity = 0-17,36-53)   NUMA region
Hello from rank 4, on cn328. (core affinity = 18-35,54-71)
Hello from rank 5, on cn328. (core affinity = 18-35,54-71)
Hello from rank 6, on cn328. (core affinity = 18-35,54-71)
Hello from rank 7, on cn328. (core affinity = 18-35,54-71)
Hello from rank 8, on cn329. (core affinity = 0-17,36-53)
Hello from rank 9, on cn329. (core affinity = 0-17,36-53)
   < ... skipping output ... >
```

Figure 14.7   With the placement set to four processes per socket, the order of the ranks changes. Now the four adjacent ranks are on the same NUMA region.

The placement report in figure 14.7 shows that the order of the ranks places adjacent ranks on the same NUMA domain instead of alternating the ranks between NUMA domains. That might be better if ranks are communicating with nearest neighbors.

So far, we have only worked on the placement of processes. Now let's try to see what we can do about the affinity and binding of the MPI processes. For this, we add the --bind-to [socket | numa | core | hwthread] option to mpirun:

```
mpirun -n 32 --npersocket 4 --bind-to core ./MPIAffinity | sort -n -k 4
```

We can see how this changes the affinity for the processes in the placement report in figure 14.8.

```
Hello from rank 0, on cn328. (core affinity = 0,36)
Hello from rank 1, on cn328. (core affinity = 1,37)
Hello from rank 2, on cn328. (core affinity = 2,38)
Hello from rank 3, on cn328. (core affinity = 3,39)   Hardware core
Hello from rank 4, on cn328. (core affinity = 18,54)
Hello from rank 5, on cn328. (core affinity = 19,55)
Hello from rank 6, on cn328. (core affinity = 20,56)
Hello from rank 7, on cn328. (core affinity = 21,57)
Hello from rank 8, on cn329. (core affinity = 0,36)
Hello from rank 9, on cn329. (core affinity = 1,37)
   < ... skipping output ... >
```

Figure 14.8   The affinity from binding to a core changes the affinity for the processes to a hardware core. Each hardware core represents two virtual cores because of hyperthreading. We get two locations for each process.

The placement results in figure 14.8 show that the process affinity is now restricted more than it was previously. There are two virtual cores that each process can schedule to run on. These two virtual cores belong to one hardware core, thus showing that the core binding option refers to a hardware core. Only four of the 18 processor cores on each socket are used. This is what we want so that there is more memory for each MPI rank. Let's try binding the process to the hyperthreads instead of to the core by using the `hwthread` option. This should force the scheduler to place processes on one, and only one, virtual core.

```
mpirun -n 32 --npersocket 4 --bind-to hwthread ./MPIAffinity | sort -n -k 4
```

Again, we use our placement report program to visualize the placement with the output shown in figure 14.9.

```
Hello from rank 0, on cn328. (core affinity = 0)
Hello from rank 1, on cn328. (core affinity = 36)
Hello from rank 2, on cn328. (core affinity = 1)
Hello from rank 3, on cn328. (core affinity = 37)    Processes
Hello from rank 4, on cn328. (core affinity = 18)    on a pair of
Hello from rank 5, on cn328. (core affinity = 54)    hyperthreads
Hello from rank 6, on cn328. (core affinity = 19)    on a single core
Hello from rank 7, on cn328. (core affinity = 55)
Hello from rank 8, on cn329. (core affinity = 0)
Hello from rank 9, on cn329. (core affinity = 36)
    < ... skipping output ... >
```

Figure 14.9   The process placement from the `hwthread` option limits where the processes can run to only one location.

Our last processor layout finally restricts where each process can run to a single location as shown in figure 14.9. That seems like a good result. But wait. Take a closer look. The first two ranks are placed on the pair of hyperthreads (0 and 36) of a single hardware core. This is not a good idea. That means the two ranks are sharing the cache and hardware components of that hardware core instead of having their own full complement of resources.

The `mpirun` command in OpenMPI also has a built-in option to report bindings. It is convenient for small problems, but the amount of output for nodes with a lot of processors and MPI ranks is hard to handle. Adding `--report-bindings` to the `mpirun` command used for figure 14.9 produces the output shown in figure 14.10.

The visual layout is a little easier to quickly understand, and there is a lot of information packed into the output. Each line indicates a rank in MPI_COMM_WORLD (MCW). The symbols between the forward slashes on the right side indicate the binding location for that process. The set of two dots between the forward slash symbols shows that there are two hyperthreads per core. The two sets of brackets delineate the two sockets on the node.

Binding location

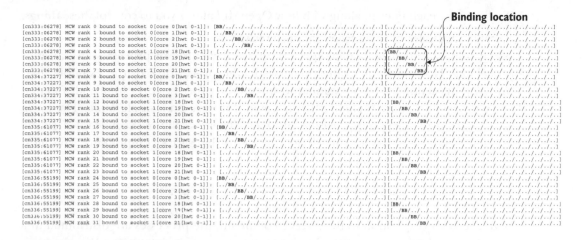

Figure 14.10   Placement report from the `--report-bindings` option to mpirun shows where ranks are bound with the letter *B*.

With the examples we explored in this section, you should be getting an idea of how to control placement and affinity. You should also have some tools to check that you are getting the placement and process bindings you expect.

14.4.3   Affinity is more than just process binding: The full picture

Now we will explore the full picture of affinity for parallel computing. We will use this as a way of introducing the advanced options offered in OpenMPI for even more control.

The concept of affinity is born out of how the operating system sees things. At the level of the operating system, you can set where each process is allowed to run. On Linux, this is done through either the `taskset` or the `numactl` commands. These commands, and similar utilities on other operating systems, emerged as the complexity of the CPU grew so that you could provide more information to the scheduler in the operating system. The directions might be taken as hints or requirements by the scheduler. Using these commands, you can pin a server process to a particular processor to be closer to a particular hardware component or to gain faster response. This focus on affinity alone is enough when dealing with a single process.

For parallel programming, there are additional considerations. We have a set of processes that we need to consider. Lets say we have 16 processors and we are running a four rank MPI job. Where do we put the ranks? Do we put these across the sockets, on all the sockets, pack them close together, or spread them out? Do we place certain ranks next to each other (ranks 1 and 2 together or ranks 1 and 4 together)? To be able to answer these questions, we need to address the following:

- Mapping (the placement of processes)
- Order of ranks (which ranks are close together)
- Binding (affinity or tying a process to a location or locations)

We'll go over each in turn, along with how OpenMPI allows you to control these things.

MAPPING PROCESSES TO PROCESSORS OR OTHER LOCATIONS

When thinking about a parallel application, we have a set of processes and a set of processors. How do we map the processes to the processors? In the example used throughout section 14.4.2, we wanted to spread the processes over four nodes so that every process has more memory than it would if it were on a single node. The more general form for mapping processes in OpenMPI is -mapby hwresource, where the argument hwresource is any of a large number of hardware components. The most common include the following:

```
--map-by [slot | hwthread | core | socket | numa | node]
```

With the --map-by option to the mpirun command, the processes are distributed in a round-robin fashion across this hardware resource. The default for the option is socket. Most of these hardware locations are self-explanatory except for slot. Slots are the list of possible locations for processes from the environment, the scheduler, or a host file. This form of the --map-by option is still limited in its meaning and, therefore, its effect.

A more general form uses an option called ppr or processes per resource, where n is the number of processes. Instead of a round-robin mapping by resource, you can specify a block of processes per hardware resource:

```
--map-by ppr:n:hwresource
```

Or, more explicitly

```
--map-by ppr:n:[slot | hwthread | core | socket | numa | node]
```

In our earlier examples, we used the simpler option of --npernode 8. In this more general form, it would be shorthand for

```
--map-by ppr:8:node
```

If the level of control from the previous options to mpirun is not sufficient, you can specify a list of processor numbers to map with the --cpu-list <logical processor numbers> option, where the processor numbers are a list that corresponds to the list from lstopo or lscpu. This option also binds the processes to the logical (virtual) processor at the same time.

ORDERING OF MPI RANKS

Another thing you might want to control is the ordering of your MPI ranks. You may want adjacent MPI ranks to be close to each other in physical processor space if they communicate a lot with each other. This reduces the cost of the communication between these ranks. Usually, it is sufficient to control this with the block size of the distribution during mapping, but you can get additional control with the `--rank-by` option:

```
--rank-by ppr:n:[slot | hwthread | core | socket | numa | node]
```

An even more general option is to use a rank file:

```
--rankfile <filename>
```

While you can fine-tune the placement of your MPI ranks with these commands and perhaps gain a couple of percent in performance, it is difficult to come up with the optimum formula.

BINDING PROCESSES TO HARDWARE COMPONENTS

The last piece to control is affinity itself. *Affinity* is the process of binding the process to the hardware resource. The option is similar to the previous ones:

```
--bind-to [slot | hwthread | core | socket | numa | node]
```

The default setting of `core` is sufficient for most MPI applications (without the `--bind-to` option the default is `socket` for greater than two processes as mentioned in section 14.4.1). But there are cases where that affinity setting causes problems.

As we saw in the example for figure 14.8, the affinity is set to the two hyperthreads on the hardware core. We might want to try `--map-to core --bind-to hwthread` to distribute the processes across the cores but bind each process more tightly to a single hyperthread. The performance difference from such fine-tuning is probably small. The greater problem comes when we try to implement a hybrid MPI and OpenMP application. It is important to realize that child processes inherit the affinity settings of their parent. If we use the options of `npersocket 4 --bind-to core` and then launch two threads, we have two locations for the threads to run (two hyperthreads per core), so we are Ok. If we launch four threads, these will share only two logical processor locations and performance will be limited.

We saw earlier in this section that there are a lot of options for controlling process, placement, and affinity. Indeed, there are too many combinations to even fully explore as we did in section 14.3 for OpenMP. In most cases, we should be satisfied with getting reasonable settings that reflect the needs of our applications.

14.5 Affinity for MPI plus OpenMP

Our goal in this section is to understand how to set affinity for hybrid MPI and OpenMP applications. Getting affinity right for these hybrid situations can be tricky. For this exploration, we've created a hybrid stream triad example with MPI and OpenMP. We have also modified the placement report used throughout this chapter to output information for hybrid MPI and OpenMP applications. The following listing shows the modified subroutine, `place_report_ mpi_omp.c`.

Listing 14.2   MPI and OpenMP placement reporting tool hybrid stream triad

```
StreamTriad/place_report_mpi_omp.c
41 void place_report_mpi_omp(void)
42 {
43    int rank;
44    MPI_Comm_rank(MPI_COMM_WORLD, &rank);
45
46    int socket_global[144];
47    char clbuf_global[144][7 * CPU_SETSIZE];
48
49    #pragma omp parallel
50    {
51       if (omp_get_thread_num() == 0 && rank == 0){
52          printf("Running with %d thread(s)\n",omp_get_num_threads());
53          int bind_policy = omp_get_proc_bind();
54          switch (bind_policy)
55          {
56             case omp_proc_bind_false:
57                printf("  proc_bind is false\n");
58                break;
59             case omp_proc_bind_true:
60                printf("  proc_bind is true\n");
61                break;
62             case omp_proc_bind_master:
63                printf("  proc_bind is master\n");
64                break;
65             case omp_proc_bind_close:
66                printf("  proc_bind is close\n");
67                break;
68             case omp_proc_bind_spread:
69                printf("  proc_bind is spread\n");
70          }
71          printf("  proc_num_places is %d\n",omp_get_num_places());
72       }
73
74       int thread = omp_get_thread_num();
75       cpu_set_t coremask;
76       char clbuf[7 * CPU_SETSIZE], hnbuf[64];
77       memset(clbuf, 0, sizeof(clbuf));
78       memset(hnbuf, 0, sizeof(hnbuf));
79       gethostname(hnbuf, sizeof(hnbuf));
80       sched_getaffinity(0, sizeof(coremask), &coremask);
81       cpuset_to_cstr(&coremask, clbuf);
82       strcpy(clbuf_global[thread],clbuf);
83       socket_global[omp_get_thread_num()] = omp_get_place_num();
84       #pragma omp barrier
85       #pragma omp master
86       for (int i=0; i<omp_get_num_threads(); i++){
87          printf("Hello from rank %02d,"
                    " thread %02d, on %s."
88                  " (core affinity = %2s)"                    Merges OpenMP
                    " OpenMP socket is %2d\n",                  and the MPI
89                  rank, i, hnbuf,                             affinity report
                    clbuf_global[i],
                    socket_global[i]);
```

```
90      }
91    }
92 }
```

We start this example by compiling the stream triad application. The stream triad code is at https://github.com/EssentialsofParallelComputing/Chapter14 in the Stream-Triad directory. Compile the code with

```
mkdir build && cd build
./cmake -DCMAKE_VERBOSE=1 ..
make
```

We ran this code on our Skylake Gold processor with 44 hardware processors and two hyperthreads each. We placed the two OpenMP threads on the hyperthreads and then an MPI rank on each hardware core. The following commands accomplish this layout:

```
export OMP_NUM_THREADS=2
mpirun -n 44 --map-by socket ./StreamTriad
```

The stream triad code has a call to our placement report from listing 14.2. Figure 14.11 shows the output.

NUMA domain

```
Hello from rank 00, thread 00, on cn618. (core affinity = 0-21,44-65) OpenMP socket is -1
Hello from rank 00, thread 01, on cn618. (core affinity = 0-21,44-65) OpenMP socket is -1
Hello from rank 01, thread 00, on cn618. (core affinity = 22-43,66-87) OpenMP socket is -1
Hello from rank 01, thread 01, on cn618. (core affinity = 22-43,66-87) OpenMP socket is -1
 < ... skipping output ... >
```

Figure 14.11   The MPI ranks are placed in a round-robin fashion across the sockets with two slots to accommodate the two OpenMP threads. The placement is restricted to a NUMA domain to keep memory close to the threads. The processes are not bound tightly to any particular virtual core, and the scheduler can move these around freely within the NUMA domain.

As the output in figure 14.11 shows, we succeeded in getting the ranks distributed across the NUMA domains in a round-robin manner, keeping the two threads together. This should give us good bandwidth from main memory. The affinity constraints are only sufficient to keep the processes within the NUMA domain and let the scheduler move the processes around as they wish. The scheduler can place thread 0 on any of 44 different virtual processors, including 0–21 or 44–65. The numbering can be confusing; 0 and 44 are two hyperthreads on the same physical core.

Now let's try to obtain more affinity constraints. For this, we need to use the form -mapby ppr:N:socket:PE=N. This command gives us the ability to spread out the processes with a specified spacing and specify how many MPI ranks to place on each socket. It is hard to unbundle the complexity of the option.

Let's start with the ppr:N:socket part. We want half of our MPI ranks on each socket. This should be 22 MPI ranks per socket or ppr:22:socket. The last part determines how many processors we want between the placement of processes. We want two threads for each MPI rank, so we want two virtual processors in each block. The specification is for hardware cores. It is important to know that each hardware core contains two virtual processors. Therefore, you only need one hardware core (PE=1). We then pin the threads to a hardware thread. For rank 0, we should get the first hardware core with the virtual processors 0 and 44. That gives us the following commands:

```
export OMP_NUM_THREADS=2
export OMP_PROC_BIND=true
mpirun -n 44 --map-by ppr:22:socket:PE=1 ./StreamTriad
```

Whew! That was complicated. Did we get it right? Well, let's check the output from the command as shown in figure 14.12.

Hyperthreads

```
Hello from rank 00, thread 00, on cn626. (core affinity = 0) OpenMP socket is 0
Hello from rank 00, thread 01, on cn626. (core affinity = 44) OpenMP socket is 1
Hello from rank 01, thread 00, on cn626. (core affinity = 1) OpenMP socket is 0
Hello from rank 01, thread 01, on cn626. (core affinity = 45) OpenMP socket is 1
 < ... skipping output ... >
```

Figure 14.12   The process and thread affinity are now constrained to a logical core, and the two OpenMP threads per rank are located on the hyperthread pairs (0 and 44 in the figure). The ranks are packed close in order to reduce communication costs for more complicated programs. The MPI ranks are pinned to hardware cores and the thread affinity is to the hyperthread.

From the output in figure 14.12, we have the threads locked down where we want them. We also have the MPI rank pinned to the hardware core. You can verify this by unsetting the OMP_PROC_BIND environment variable (unset OMP_PROC_BIND) and the output (figure 14.13) confirms that the rank is bound to two logical processors, composing a single hardware core.

Hardware core

```
Hello from rank 00, thread 00, on cn610. (core affinity = 0,44) OpenMP socket is -1
Hello from rank 00, thread 01, on cn610. (core affinity = 0,44) OpenMP socket is -1
Hello from rank 01, thread 00, on cn610. (core affinity = 1,45) OpenMP socket is -1
Hello from rank 01, thread 01, on cn610. (core affinity = 1,45) OpenMP socket is -1
< ... skipping output ... >
```

Figure 14.13   Output without OMP_PROC_BIND=true shows that the MPI ranks are pinned to hardware cores.

We've worked through one case and were able to get the affinity settings the way we wanted. But now you want to know if we can run more than two OpenMP threads and how the program performs. Let's take a look at a set of commands that test any number of threads that divides into the number of processors evenly. The following listing shows the key scripting commands.

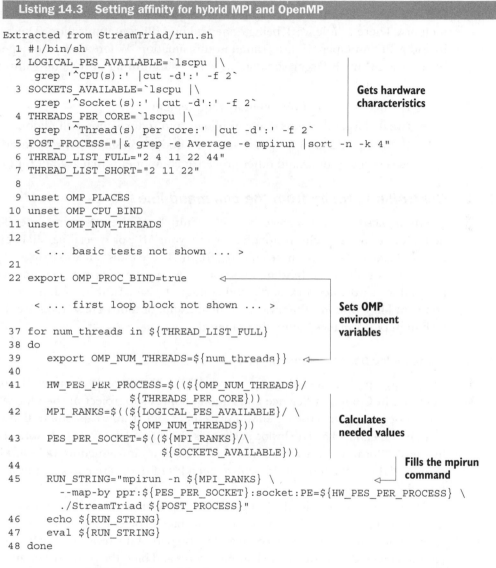

Listing 14.3 Setting affinity for hybrid MPI and OpenMP

```
Extracted from StreamTriad/run.sh
 1 #!/bin/sh
 2 LOGICAL_PES_AVAILABLE=`lscpu |\
   grep '^CPU(s):' |cut -d':' -f 2`
 3 SOCKETS_AVAILABLE=`lscpu |\
   grep '^Socket(s):' |cut -d':' -f 2`
 4 THREADS_PER_CORE=`lscpu |\
   grep '^Thread(s) per core:' |cut -d':' -f 2`
 5 POST_PROCESS="|& grep -e Average -e mpirun |sort -n -k 4"
 6 THREAD_LIST_FULL="2 4 11 22 44"
 7 THREAD_LIST_SHORT="2 11 22"
 8
 9 unset OMP_PLACES
10 unset OMP_CPU_BIND
11 unset OMP_NUM_THREADS
12
   < ... basic tests not shown ... >
21
22 export OMP_PROC_BIND=true

   < ... first loop block not shown ... >

37 for num_threads in ${THREAD_LIST_FULL}
38 do
39    export OMP_NUM_THREADS=${num_threads}}
40
41    HW_PES_PER_PROCESS=$((${OMP_NUM_THREADS}/
                ${THREADS_PER_CORE}))
42    MPI_RANKS=$((${LOGICAL_PES_AVAILABLE}/ \
                ${OMP_NUM_THREADS}))
43    PES_PER_SOCKET=$((${MPI_RANKS}/\
                ${SOCKETS_AVAILABLE}))
44
45    RUN_STRING="mpirun -n ${MPI_RANKS} \
        --map-by ppr:${PES_PER_SOCKET}:socket:PE=${HW_PES_PER_PROCESS} \
        ./StreamTriad ${POST_PROCESS}"
46    echo ${RUN_STRING}
47    eval ${RUN_STRING}
48 done

   < ... additional loop blocks ... >
```

Gets hardware characteristics

Sets OMP environment variables

Calculates needed values

Fills the mpirun command

To make the script portable, we grab the hardware characteristics using the `lscpu` command. We then set the desired OpenMP environment parameters. We could set OMP_PROC_BIND to `true`, `close`, or `spread` with the same result for this case, where all the slots are filled. Then we calculate the variables needed for the `mpirun` command and launch the job.

In the full stream triad example in listing 14.2, we tested a combination of thread sizes and MPI ranks that divide evenly into 88 processes. We followed that with 44 total processes where we skip the hyperthreads because we didn't really get any better performance with them (section 14.3). The performance results are pretty constant over the set of tests. That is because all that is being measured is the bandwidth from main memory. There is little work being done and no MPI communication. The benefits of hybrid MPI and OpenMP are limited in this situation. Where we would expect to see benefits is in much larger simulations where substituting an OpenMP thread for a MPI rank would

- Reduce the MPI buffer memory requirements
- Create larger domains that consolidate and reduce ghost cell regions
- Reduce contention for processors on a node for a single network interface
- Access vector units and other processor components that are not fully utilized

14.6   *Controlling affinity from the command line*

There are also general ways to control affinity from the command line. The command-line tools can help in situations where your MPI or special parallel application doesn't have built-in options to control affinity. These tools can also help with general-purpose applications by binding these close to important hardware components such as graphics cards, network ports, and storage devices. In this section, we cover two command-line options: the hwloc and likwid suite of tools. These tools are developed with high-performance computing in mind.

14.6.1   *Using hwloc-bind to assign affinity*

The hwloc project was developed by INRIA, the French National Institute for Research in Computer Science and Automation. A subproject of the OpenMPI project, hwloc implements the OpenMPI placement and affinity capabilities that we saw in sections 14.4 and 14.5. The hwloc package is also a standalone package with command-line tools. Because there are many hwloc tools, as an introduction, we'll just look at a couple of these. We'll use hwloc-calc to get a list of hardware cores and hwloc-bind to bind these.

Using hwloc-bind is simple. Just prefix the application with `hwloc-bind` and then add the hardware location where you want it to bind. For our application, we'll use the `lstopo` command. The `lstopo` command is also part of the hwloc tools. Here is our one-liner to launch the job on all the hardware cores and bind the processes to the cores:

```
for core in `hwloc-calc --intersect core --sep " " all`; do hwloc-bind \
    core:${core} lstopo --no-io --pid 0 & done
```

The `--intersect core` option only uses hardware cores. The `--sep " "` says to separate the numbers in the output with spaces instead of commas. The result of this command on our usual Skylake Gold processor launches 44 lstopo graphic windows, each looking similar to that in figure 14.14. Each window has the bound locations high-lighted in green.

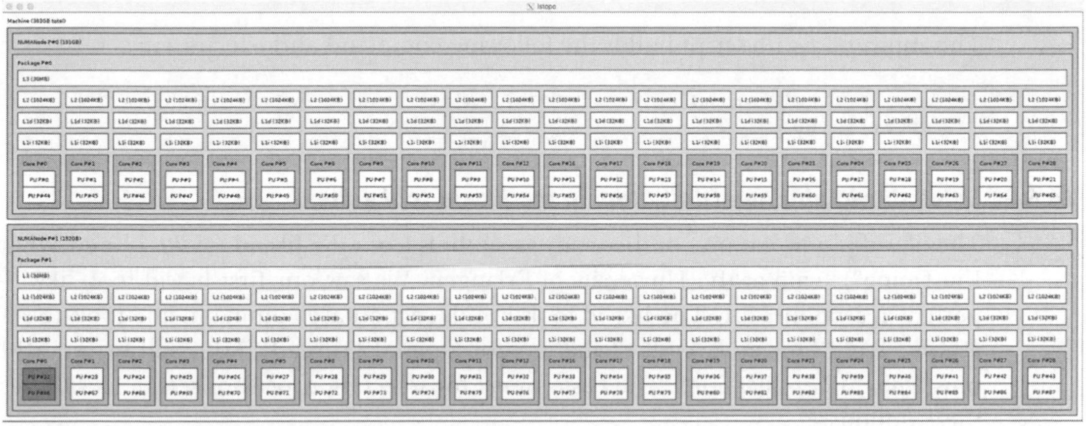

Figure 14.14 The lstopo image shows the bound location in green (shaded core) at the lower left. This shows that process 22 is bound to the 22nd and 66th virtual cores, which are hyperthreads for a single physical core.

We could use a similar command to launch two processes on the first core of each socket. For example

```
for socket in `hwloc-calc --intersect socket \
    --sep " " all`; do hwloc-bind \
    socket:${socket}.core:0 lstopo --no-io --pid 0 & done
```

The following listing shows how we can build a general-purpose `mpirun` command with binding.

Listing 14.4   Using hwloc-bind to bind processes

```
MPI/mpirun_distrib.sh
 1 #!/bin/sh
 2 PROC_LIST=$1
 3 EXEC_NAME=$2
 4 OUTPUT="mpirun "          ←┐ Initializes this
 5 for core in ${PROC_LIST}     string with mpirun
 6 do
 7     OUTPUT="$OUTPUT -np 1"\        Appends another
            " hwloc-bind core:${core}"\   MPI rank launch
            " ${EXEC_NAME} :"             with binding
 8 done
 9 OUTPUT=`echo ${OUTPUT} | sed -e 's/:$/\n/'`   ←┐ Strips last colon
10 eval ${OUTPUT}                                   and substitutes a
                                                    new line
```

Now we can launch our MPI affinity application from section 14.4 on the first core of each socket with this command:

```
./mpirun_distrib.sh "1 22" ./MPIAffinity
```

This mpirun_distrib script builds the following command and executes it:

```
mpirun -np 1 hwloc-bind core:1 ./MPIAffinity : -np 1 hwloc-bind core:22
  ./MPIAffinity
```

14.6.2   *Using likwid-pin: An affinity tool in the likwid tool suite*

The likwid-pin tool is one of the many great tools from the likwid ("Like I Knew What I'm Doing") team at the University of Erlangen. We saw our first likwid tool, likwid-perfctr in section 3.3.1. The likwid tools in this section are command-line tools to set affinity. We'll look at variants of the tool for OpenMP threads, MPI, and hybrid MPI plus OpenMP applications. The basic syntax for selecting processor sets in likwid uses these options:

- Default (physical numbering)
- N (node-level numbering)
- S (socket-level numbering)
- C (last level cache numbering)
- M (NUMA memory domain numbering)

To set the affinity, use this syntax: -c <N,S,C,M>:[n1,n2,n3-n4]. To get a list of the numbering schemes, use the command likwid-pin -p. Understanding how likwid-pin works is best gained from examples and experimentation.

PINNING OPENMP THREADS WITH LIKWID-PIN

This example shows how to use likwid-pin with OpenMP applications:

```
export OMP_NUM_THREADS=44
export OMP_PROC_BIND=spread
export OMP_PLACES=threads
./vecadd_opt3
```

To get this same pinning result with likwid-pin for OpenMP applications, we use the socket (S) option. In the following, we distribute 22 threads on each socket, where the two pin sets are separated and concatenated with the @ symbol:

```
likwid-pin -c S0:0-21@S1:0-21 ./vecadd_opt3
```

The OMP environment variables are not necessary when using likwid-pin and are mostly ignored. The number of threads is determined from the pin set lists. For this command, it is 44. We ran the vecadd example from section 14.3, configured with the -DCMAKE_VERBOSE option to get our placement report as figure 14.15 shows.

```
[pthread wrapper]
[pthread wrapper] MAIN -> 0
[pthread wrapper]  PIN MASK: 0->1 1->2 2->3 3->4 4->5 5->6 6->7 7->8 8->9 9->10
10->11 11->12 12->13 13->14 14->15 15->16 16->17 17->18 18->19 19->20 20->21
21->22 22->23 23->24 24->25 25->26 26->27 27->28 28->29 29->30 30->31 31->32
32->33 33->34 34->35 35->36 36->37 37->38 38->39 39->40 40->41 41->42 42->43
[pthread wrapper] SKIP MASK: 0x0
      threadid 47149577160576 -> core 1 - OK
      threadid 47149581363200 -> core 2 - OK
          < ... skipped output ... >
      threadid 47152378182656 -> core 42 - OK
      threadid 47152382389376 -> core 43 - OK
Running with 44 thread(s)
  proc_bind is false
  proc_num_places is 0                          Physical core
Hello from thread 0: (core affinity = 0) OpenMP socket is -1
Hello from thread 1: (core affinity = 1) OpenMP socket is -1
   < ... skipped output ... >
Hello from thread 42: (core affinity = 42) OpenMP socket is -1
Hello from thread 43: (core affinity = 43) OpenMP socket is -1
 0.016692
```

Figure 14.15 The likwid-pin output is at the top of the screen, followed by our placement report output. The output shows that the threads are pinned to the 44 physical cores.

Our placement report shows that the OMP environment variables are not set and that OpenMP has not placed and pinned the threads in the OpenMP sockets. And yet, we get the same placement and pinning from the likwid-pin tool with the same performance results. *We have just confirmed that the OMP environment variables are not necessary with likwid-pin as we claimed in the previous paragraph.* One thing to note is that if you set the OMP_NUM_THREADS environment variable to something other than the number of threads in the pin sets, the likwid tool distributes the threads from the OMP_NUM_THREADS variable across the processors specified in the pin sets. When there are more threads than processors, the tool wraps the thread placement around on the available processors.

PINNING MPI RANKS WITH LIKWID-MPIRUN

The likwid pinning functionality for MPI applications is included in the likwid-mpirun tool. You can use this tool as a substitute for mpirun in most MPI implementations. Let's look at the MPIAffinity example from section 14.4.

Example: Pinning MPI ranks with likwid-mpirun

Run the MPIAffinity example on 44 ranks and use the likwid-mpirun command to pin the ranks to the hardware cores. By default, likwid-mpirun pins the ranks to the cores, so we need to use the likwid-mpirun command to get what we usually want without any additional options:

```
likwid-mpirun -n 44 ./MPIAffinity |sort -n -k 4
```

Figure 14.16 shows the output from our placement report for this example.

```
WARN: Cannot extract OpenMP vendor from executable or commandline, assuming no OpenMP
Hello from rank 0, on cn630. (core affinity = 0)
Hello from rank 1, on cn630. (core affinity = 1)
 < ... skipping output ... .
Hello from rank 42, on cn630. (core affinity = 42)
Hello from rank 43, on cn630. (core affinity = 43)
```

Processor core

Figure 14.16   The placement report for likwid-mpirun shows that each rank is pinned to cores in numeric order.

That was easy! As figure 14.16 shows, likwid-mpirun pins the ranks to the hardware cores. Let's move on to an example where we have to provide some options to the command.

> **Example: Options for pinning MPI ranks with likwid-mpirun**
> We start with the basic command:
>
> ```
> likwid-mpirun -n 22  ./MPIAffinity |sort -n -k 4
> ```
>
> The ranks are distributed across the first 22 hardware cores on socket 0 and none on socket 1. We showed earlier that you need to distribute the processes across both sockets to get the full bandwidth from main memory. Adding the -nperdomain option lets us specify how many sockets per NUMA domain and the S:11 pin set gets the right numbers for 11 ranks on the socket. The command now looks like
>
> ```
> likwid-mpirun -n 22 -nperdomain S:11  ./MPIAffinity |sort -n -k 4
> ```

14.7   *The future: Setting and changing affinity at run time*

What if the user didn't need to worry about affinity? It is challenging to get users to use the complicated invocations to properly place and pin processes. It might make more sense in many cases to embed the pinning logic into the executable. One way to do this would be to query information about the hardware and set the affinity appropriately. Few applications have yet undertaken this approach, but we expect to see more that do in the future.

Some applications not only set their affinity at run time but also modify the affinity to adapt to changing characteristics during run time! This innovative technique was developed by Sam Gutiérrez of Los Alamos National Laboratory in his QUO library. Perhaps you have an application that uses all MPI ranks on a node, but it calls a library that uses a combination of MPI ranks and OpenMP threads. The QUO library provides a simple interface built on top of hwloc to set proper affinities. It can then push the settings onto a stack, quiesce the processors, and set a new binding policy. We'll look at examples of initiating process binding within your application and changing it during run time in the following sections.

14.7.1 Setting affinities in your executable

Setting your process placement and affinities in your application means that you no longer have to deal with complicated mpirun commands or portability between MPI implementations. Here we use the QUO library to implement this binding to all the cores on a Skylake Gold processor. The open source QUO library is available at https://github.com/LANL/libquo.git. First, we build the executable in the Quo directory and run the application with the number of hardware cores on your system:

```
make autobind
mpirun -n 44 ./autobind
```

The source code for autobind is shown in listing 14.5. The program has the following steps. Our placement reporting routine is called before and afterward to show the process bindings.

1 Initialize QUO
2 Set affinities to the hardware cores
3 Distribute the processes and bind these to the cores
4 Return to the initial affinities

Listing 14.5 Using QUO to bind processes from your executable

```
Quo/autobind.c
31 int main(int argc, char **argv)
32 {
33     int ncores, nnoderanks, noderank, rank, nranks;
34     int work_member = 0, max_members_per_res = 2, nres = 0;
35     QUO_context qcontext;
36
37     MPI_Init(&argc, &argv);                            Initializes QUO
38     QUO_create(&qcontext, MPI_COMM_WORLD);    ◁        context
39     MPI_Comm_size(MPI_COMM_WORLD, &nranks);
40     MPI_Comm_rank(MPI_COMM_WORLD, &rank);
41     QUO_id(qcontext, &noderank);
42     QUO_nqids(qcontext, &nnoderanks);
43     QUO_ncores(qcontext, &ncores);
44                                                        Gets system
45     QUO_obj_type_t tres = QUO_OBJ_NUMANODE;           information
46     QUO_nnumanodes(qcontext, &nres);
47     if (nres == 0) {
48         QUO_nsockets(qcontext, &nres);
49         tres = QUO_OBJ_SOCKET;
50     }
51
52     if ( check_errors(ncores, nnoderanks, noderank, nranks, nres) )
53         return(-1);
54
55     if (rank == 0)
56         printf("\nDefault binding for MPI processes\n\n");
57     place_report_mpi();          ◁——  Reports default bindings
58
```

```
59      SyncIt();
60      QUO_bind_push(qcontext,
                      QUO_BIND_PUSH_PROVIDED,          Sets new bindings
61                    QUO_OBJ_CORE, noderank);         to core
62      SyncIt();
63
64      QUO_auto_distrib(qcontext, tres,
                         max_members_per_res,          Distributes and
65                       &work_member);                binds MPI ranks
66      if (rank == 0)
67          printf("\nProcesses should be pinned to the hw cores\n\n");
68      place_report_mpi();        ⟵⎯  Reports new bindings
69
70      SyncIt();
71      QUO_bind_pop(qcontext);    ⟵⎯  Pops off the bindings
72      SyncIt();                        and returns to initial
73                                       settings
74      QUO_free(qcontext);
75      MPI_Finalize();
76      return(0);
77 }
```

We need to be careful to synchronize processes as we change the bindings. To ensure that, in the following listing, we use an MPI barrier and a micro sleep call in the `SyncIt` routine.

Listing 14.6   `SyncIt` subroutine

```
Quo/autobind.c
23 void SyncIt(void)
24 {
25     int rank;
26     MPI_Comm_rank(MPI_COMM_WORLD, &rank);   Standard MPI
27     MPI_Barrier(MPI_COMM_WORLD);    ⟵⎯      barrier
28     usleep(rank * 1000);    ⟵⎯  Additional micro sleep
29 }
```

The output from the autobind application (figure 14.17) clearly shows the bindings changed from sockets to the hardware cores.

14.7.2 *Changing your process affinities during run time*

Suppose we have an application with one part that wants to use all MPI ranks and another part that works best with OpenMP threads. To handle this, we need to switch the affinities during run time. This is the scenario that QUO is designed for! The steps for this include

1 Initialize QUO
2 Set the process bindings to cores for MPI region
3 Expand the bindings to the whole node for the OpenMP region
4 Return to the settings for MPI

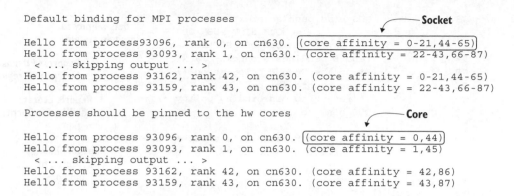

```
Default binding for MPI processes                          ┌── Socket
                                                           ↓
Hello from process93096, rank 0, on cn630.  (core affinity = 0-21,44-65)
Hello from process 93093, rank 1, on cn630.  (core affinity = 22-43,66-87)
 < ... skipping output ... >
Hello from process 93162, rank 42, on cn630. (core affinity = 0-21,44-65)
Hello from process 93159, rank 43, on cn630. (core affinity = 22-43,66-87)

Processes should be pinned to the hw cores                 ┌── Core
                                                           ↓
Hello from process 93096, rank 0, on cn630.  (core affinity = 0,44)
Hello from process 93093, rank 1, on cn630.  (core affinity = 1,45)
 < ... skipping output ... >
Hello from process 93162, rank 42, on cn630. (core affinity = 42,86)
Hello from process 93159, rank 43, on cn630. (core affinity = 43,87)
```

Figure 14.17　The output from the autobind demo shows cores initially bound to sockets, but afterwards, these are bound to hardware cores.

Let's see how this is done with Quo in the following listing.

Listing 14.7　Dynamic affinity demo switching from MPI to OpenMP

```
Quo/dynaffinity.c
45 int main(int argc, char **argv)
46 {
47     int rank, noderank, nnoderanks;
48     int work_member = 0, max_members_per_res = 44;
49     QUO_context qcontext;
50
51     MPI_Init(&argc, &argv);
52     MPI_Comm_rank(MPI_COMM_WORLD, &rank);        ┐ Initializes
53     QUO_create(&qcontext, MPI_COMM_WORLD);    ◄──┘ QUO context
54
55     node_info_report(qcontext, &noderank, &nnoderanks);
56
57     SyncIt();
58     QUO_bind_push(qcontext,
                     QUO_BIND_PUSH_PROVIDED,      ┐ Sets affinities to
59                   QUO_OBJ_CORE, noderank);      ┘ hardware cores
60     SyncIt();
61
62     QUO_auto_distrib(qcontext, QUO_OBJ_SOCKET,
                     max_members_per_res,          ┐ Distributes and
63                   &work_member);                ┘ binds MPI ranks
64
65     place_report_mpi_quo(qcontext);       ◄──   ┐ Reports process affinities
66                                                 ┘ for all MPI regions
67     /* change binding policies to accommodate OMP threads on node 0 */
68     bool on_rank_0s_node = rank < nnoderanks;
69     if (on_rank_0s_node) {
70         if (rank == 0) {
71             printf("\nEntering OMP region...\n\n");
72             // expands the caller's cpuset
               //    to all available resources on the node.
```

```
73              QUO_bind_push(qcontext,
                         QUO_BIND_PUSH_OBJ,
                         QUO_OBJ_SOCKET, -1);
74              report_bindings(qcontext, rank);
75              /* do the OpenMP calculation */
76              place_report_mpi_omp();
77              /* revert to old binding policy */
78              QUO_bind_pop(qcontext);
79          }
80          /* QUO_barrier because it's cheaper than
               MPI_Barrier on a node. */
81          QUO_barrier(qcontext);
82      }
83      SyncIt();
84
85      // Wrap-up
86      QUO_free(qcontext);
87      MPI_Finalize();
88      return(0);
89 }
```

Line 73 annotation: **Sets affinity to whole system**

Line 74 annotation: **Reports CPU masks for OpenMP region**

Line 78 annotation: **Reports process affinities for OpenMP region**

Line 81 annotation: **Pops off bindings and returns to MPI bindings**

We can run the dynaffinity application with the number of hardware cores on our system with

```
make dynaffinity
mpirun -n 44 ./dynaffinity
```

We again use our reporting routines to check the process bindings for the MPI region and for OpenMP. Figure 14.18 displays the output.

The output in figure 14.18 shows that the process bindings changed between the MPI and the OpenMP regions, accomplishing a dynamic modification of the affinities during run time.

```
Nodeinfo: nnodes 1 nnoderanks 44 nsockets 2 ncores 44 nhwthreads 88  ── Hardware core

Hello from process 96779, rank 0, on cn630. (core affinity = 0,44) cbind [0x00001000,0x00000001]
Hello from process 96781, rank 1, on cn630. (core affinity = 1,45) cbind [0x00002000,0x00000002]
  <... skipping output ...>
Hello from process 96851, rank 42, on cn630. (core affinity = 42,86) cbind [0x00400000,0x00000400,0x0]
Hello from process 96849, rank 43, on cn630. (core affinity = 43,87) cbind [0x00800000,0x00000800,0x0]

Entering OMP region...

rank 0's cpuset: 0x00ffffff,0xffffffff,0xffffffff
Running with 44 thread(s)
proc_bind is false
proc_num_places is 0                              ── Any processor core
Hello from rank 00, thread 00, on cn625. (core affinity = 0-87) OpenMP socket is -1
Hello from rank 00, thread 01, on cn625. (core affinity = 0-87) OpenMP socket is -1
  <... skipping output ...>
Hello from rank 00, thread 42, on cn625. (core affinity = 0-87) OpenMP socket is -1
Hello from rank 00, thread 43, on cn625. (core affinity = 0-87) OpenMP socket is -1
```

Figure 14.18 For the MPI region, the processes are bound to the hardware cores. When we enter the OpenMP region, the affinities are expanded to the whole node.

14.8   Further explorations

The handling of process placement and bindings is relatively new. Watch for presentations in the MPI and OpenMP communities for additional developments in this area. In the next section, we list some of the most current materials on affinity that we recommend for additional reading. We'll follow the additional reading with some exercises to explore the topic further.

14.8.1   Additional reading

The process placement reporting programs used in this chapter for OpenMP, MPI, and MPI plus OpenMP are modified from the xthi.c program used in training for several HPC sites. Here are references to papers and presentations that use it to explore affinities:

- Y. He, B. Cook, et al., "Preparing NERSC users for Cori, a Cray XC40 system with Intel many integrated cores" In *Concurrency Computat: Pract Exper.*, 2018; 30:e4291 (https://doi.org/10.1002/cpe.4291).
- Argonne National Laboratory, "Affinity on Theta," at https://www.alcf.anl.gov/support-center/theta/affinity-theta.
- National Energy Research Scientific Computing Center (NERSC), "Process and Thread Affinity," at https://docs.nersc.gov/jobs/affinity/.

Here's a good presentation on OpenMP that includes a discussion on affinity and how to handle it:

T. Mattson and H. He, "OpenMP: Beyond the common core," at http://mng.bz/aK47.

We only covered part of the options for the mpirun command in OpenMPI. For exploring more capabilities, see the man page for OpenMPI:

https://www.open-mpi.org/doc/v4.0/man1/mpirun.1.php.

Portable Hardware Locality (hwloc) is a subproject of The Open MPI Project. It is a standalone package that works equally well with either OpenMPI or MPICH and has become the universal hardware interface for most MPI implementations and many other parallel programming software applications. For further information, see the following references:

- The hwloc project main page https://www.open-mpi.org/projects/hwloc/, where you'll also find some key presentations.
- B. Goglin, "Understanding and managing hardware affinities with Hardware Locality (hwloc)," *High Performance and Embedded Architecture and Compilation* (HiPEAC, 2013), http://mng.bz/gxYV.

The "Like I Knew What I'm Doing" (likwid) suite of tools is well regarded for its simplicity, usability, and good documentation. Here is a good starting point to investigate these tools further:

> University of Erlangen-Nuremberg's performance monitoring and benchmarking suite, https://github.com/RRZE-HPC/likwid/wiki.

This conference presentation about the QUO library gives a more complete overview and the philosophy behind it:

> S. Gutiérrez et al., "Accommodating Thread-Level Heterogeneity in Coupled Parallel Applications," https://github.com/lanl/libquo/blob/master/docs/slides/gutierrez-ipdps17.pdf, 2017 International Parallel and Distributed Processing Symposium (IPDPS17).

14.8.2 Exercises

1   Generate a visual image of a couple of different hardware architectures. Discover the hardware characteristics for these devices.

2   For your hardware, run the test suite using the script in listing 14.1. What did you discover about how to best use your system?

3   Change the program used in the vector addition (vecadd_opt3.c) example in section 14.3 to include more floating-point operations. Take the kernel and change the operations in the loop to the Pythagorean formula:

```
c[i] = sqrt(a[i]*a[i] + b[i]*b[i]);
```

How do your results and conclusions about the best placement and bindings change? Do you see any benefit from hyperthreads now (if you have those)?

4   For the MPI example in section 14.4, include the vector add kernel and generate a scaling graph for the kernel. Then replace the kernel with the Pythagorean formula used in exercise 3.

5   Combine the vector add and Pythagorean formula in the following routine (either in a single loop or two separate loops) to get more data reuse:

```
c[i] = a[i] + b[i];
d[i] = sqrt(a[i]*a[i] + b[i]*b[i]);
```

How does this change the results of the placement and binding study?

6   Add code to set the placement and affinity within an application from one of the previous exercises.

Summary

- There are tools that show your process placement. These tools can also show you the affinity for your processes.
- Use process placement for your parallel applications. This gives you full main memory bandwidth for your application.
- Select a good process ordering for your OpenMP threads or MPI ranks. A good ordering reduces communication costs between processes.
- Use a binding policy for your parallel processes. Binding each process keeps the kernel from moving your process and losing the data it has loaded into cache.
- It is possible to change affinity within your application. This can accommodate code sections that would do better with different process affinities.

Batch schedulers: Bringing order to chaos

15

This chapter covers

- The role of batch schedulers in high performance computing
- Submitting a job to a batch scheduler
- Linking job submissions for long runs or more complex workflows

Most high performance computing systems use batch schedulers to schedule the running of applications. We'll give you a brief idea why in the first section of this chapter. Because schedulers are ubiquitous on high-end systems, you should have at least a basic understanding of them to be able to run jobs at high-performance computing centers and even smaller clusters. We'll cover the purpose and usage of the batch schedulers. We won't go into how to set up and manage them (that's a whole other beast). Set up and management is a topic for system administrators and we are just lowly system users.

What if you don't have access to a system with a batch scheduler? We don't recommend installing a batch scheduler just to try out these examples. Rather, count your blessings and keep the information in this chapter handy for when the need arises. If your demand for computational resources grows and you begin using a larger multi-user cluster, you can come back to this chapter.

There are many different batch schedulers, and each installation has its own unique customizations. We'll discuss two batch schedulers that are freely available: the Portable Batch System (PBS) and the Simple Linux Utility for Resource Management (Slurm). There are variants of each of these, including commercially supported versions.

The PBS scheduler originated at NASA in 1991 and was released as open source under the name OpenPBS in 1998. Subsequently, commercial versions, PBS Professional by Altair and PBS/TORQUE by Adaptive Computing Enterprises, were forked off as separate versions. Freely available versions are still available and in common use on smaller clusters. Larger high performance computing sites tend to have similar versions but with a support contract.

The Slurm scheduler originated at Lawrence Livermore National Laboratory in 2002 as a simple resource manager for Linux clusters. It later was spun off into various derivative versions such as the SchedMD version.

Schedulers can also be customized with plugins or add-ins that provide additional functionality, support for special workloads, and improved scheduling algorithms. You'll also find a number of strictly commercial batch schedulers, but their functionality is similar to those presented here. The basic concepts of each scheduler implementation are much the same, and often, many details vary from site to site. Portability of batch scripts can still be a bit of a challenge and require some customization for each system.

15.1 The chaos of an unmanaged system

You just got your latest cluster up for your group and the software is running. Soon, you'll have a dozen of your colleagues logging in and launching jobs. Ka-Boom—you have multiple parallel jobs on compute nodes colliding with each other, slowing these down, and sometimes, causing some jobs to crash. Palpable tension is in the air and tempers are short.

As high performance computing systems grow in size and number of users, it becomes necessary to add some management to the system to bring order to chaos and get the most performance from the hardware. Installation of a batch scheduler can save the day (figure 15.1). User jobs can be run, and the exclusive use of the hardware as a resource becomes a reality. However, the use of a batch system is not a panacea. While this type of software offers much to the users of the cluster or high performance computing system, batch schedulers require significant system administration time and the establishment of different queues and policies. With good policies, you can obtain privately allocated compute nodes for your exclusive use for a fixed block of time.

The order provided by the system management software is absolutely essential for achieving performance on your parallel applications. The historical work on batch schedulers in Beowulf clusters (mentioned in section 15.6.1) gives a good perspective on the importance of schedulers. In the late 1990s, Beowulf clusters emerged as a widespread movement to build computing clusters out of commodity computers. The Beowulf community soon realized that it was not enough to have a collection of computing hardware; it was necessary to have some software control and management to make it a productive resource.

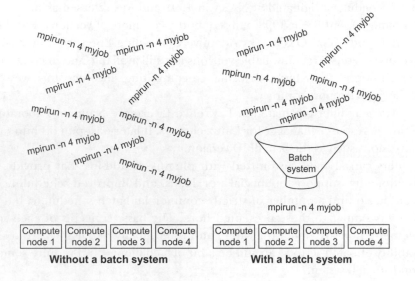

Figure 15.1   Batch systems are like the supermarket checkout queueing system for a computer cluster. These help to make better use of the resources and bring more efficiency to your jobs.

15.2 *How not to be a nuisance when working on a busy cluster*

Busy clusters have lots of users and lots of work. A batch system is often implemented to manage the workload and get the most out of the system. These clusters are a different environment than a standalone, single-user workstation. When working on these busy clusters, it is essential to know how to effectively use the system while being considerate of other users. We'll give you some of the stated and unstated social rules so as to not become a pariah on the busy cluster. But first, let's consider how these typical systems are set up.

15.2.1 *Layout of a batch system for busy clusters*

Most clusters have some nodes set aside to be front ends. These front-end nodes are also called *login nodes* because that is where you will be when you log in to the system. The rest of the system is then set up as back-end nodes that are controlled and allocated by the batch system. These back-end nodes are organized into one or more queues. Each queue has a set of policies for things like the size of jobs (such as the number of processors or memory) and how long these jobs can run.

15.2.2 How to be courteous on busy clusters and HPC sites: Common HPC pet peeves

For interactive work

- Check the load on your front end with the top command and move to a lightly loaded front-end node. There is usually more than one front-end node with numbers such as fe01, fe02, and fe03.
- Watch for heavy file-transfer jobs on the front end. Some sites have special queues for these types of jobs. If you get a node that has heavy file usage, you may find that your compiles or other jobs might take much longer than usual even if the load does not appear to be high.
- Some sites want you to compile on the back end and others on the front end. Check the policies on your cluster.
- Don't tie up nodes with batch interactive sessions and then go off to attend a meeting for several hours.
- Rather than get a second batch interactive session, export an X terminal or shell from your first session.
- For light work, look for queues for shared usage that allow over-subscription.
- Many sites have special queues for debugging. Use these when you need to debug, but don't abuse these debug queues.

For big jobs

- Big parallel jobs should be run on the back-end nodes through the batch system queues.
- Keep the number of jobs in the queue small: don't monopolize the queues.
- Try to run your big jobs during non-work hours so other users can get interactive nodes for their work.

For storage

- Store large files in the appropriate place. Most sites have large parallel file systems, scratch, project, or work directories for output from calculations.
- Move files to long-term storage for your site.
- Know the purging policies for file storage. Large sites will purge files in some of the scratch directories on a periodic basis.
- Clean up your files regularly and keep file systems below 90% full. File system performance drops off as file systems become full.

NOTE Don't be afraid to send private messages to users who are causing problems, but be courteous. They may not realize that their work is bringing many workflows to a standstill.

Further cluster wisdom includes the following:

- Heavy usage of the front-end nodes can cause instabilities and crashes. These instabilities affect the whole system as jobs can no longer be scheduled for the back-end nodes.
- Often projects get resource allocations that are used for prioritizing jobs using a "fair-share" scheduling algorithm. In these cases, you may need to submit an application for the resources that you need for your project.
- Each site can set policies that implement rules, but these cannot cover every situation. You should follow the spirit of the rules as well as the actual implementation. In other words, don't game the system. It is not an inanimate object but rather your fellow users. They are also trying to get work done.
- Rather than gaming the system, you should optimize your code and your file storage. The savings will allow you to get more work done and will let others get their work done on the cluster as well.
- Submitting several hundred jobs into a queue when only a few can run at a time is inconsiderate. We generally submit a maximum of ten or so at a time and then submit additional jobs when each of those completes. There are many ways of doing this through shell scripts or even the batch dependency techniques (discussed later in this chapter).
- For jobs that require run times much longer than the maximum batch time allowed, you should implement checkpointing (section 15.4). *Checkpointing* catches batch termination signals or uses wall clock timings to get the most effective use of the whole batch time. A subsequent job then starts where the last one stopped.

15.3 *Submitting your first batch script*

In this section, we'll go through the process of submitting your first batch script. Batch systems require a different way of thinking. Instead of just launching a job whenever you want, you have to think about organizing your work. Planning results in better use of resources even before your jobs get submitted. How do you use these batch systems? As figure 15.2 shows, there are two basic system modes.

Most of the commands used in one mode can also be used in the other. Let's work through a couple of examples to see how these modes function. We'll work with the Slurm batch scheduler in this first set of examples. We'll start with an interactive example and modify the example into a batch file form.

The interactive command-line mode is generally used for program development, testing, or short jobs. For submitting longer production jobs, it is more common to use a batch file to submit a batch job. The batch file allows the user to run applications overnight or unattended. Batch scripts can even be written to automatically restart jobs if there is some catastrophic system event. We'll show the translation in syntax from the command-line option to a batch script. But first we need to go over the basic structure of a batch script.

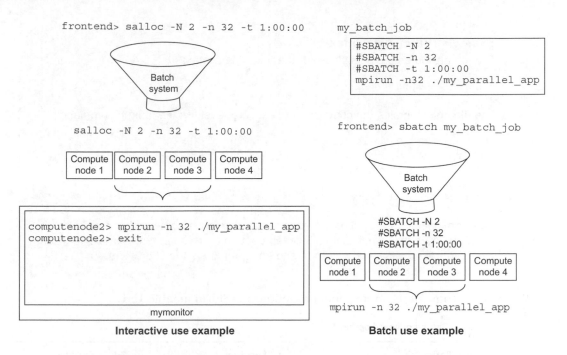

Figure 15.2 Batch systems are typically used in either an interactive mode or a batch usage model.

Example: Interactive command line

Let's start on the front end of the cluster, where everybody logs in. Now we want two compute nodes (-N 2) with a total of 32 processors (-n 32) for an hour (-t 1:00:00). Notice the difference in capitalization for number of nodes (*N*) and number of processors (*n*). Also, you can limit your run to specified minutes, although many systems have a minimum and maximum run-time policy. Some systems even have minimums and maximums for the number of compute nodes you use. The `salloc` command for this specific request would be

```
frontend> salloc -N 2 -n 32 -t 1:00:00
```

The `salloc` command allocates and logs into two compute nodes. Note that the following command prompt changes to indicate that we are a on different system. The specific prompt is highly dependent on your system and environment settings. Once we have two nodes, we can launch our parallel application with:

```
computenode22> mpirun -n 32 ./my_parallel_app
```

This example shows starting up a parallel job with mpirun. As mentioned in section 8.1.3, the command to start a parallel job might be different on your system. When we are done, we just exit:

```
computenode22> exit
```

Example: Batch file syntax

The job attributes are specified with the following syntax:

```
#SBATCH <option>
```

The file also contains the commands to execute, such as the mpirun command:

```
mpirun -n 32 ./my_parallel_app
```

The batch file is then submitted with the `sbatch` command:

```
sbatch < my_batch_job or sbatch my_batch_job
```

You can specify the options either on the interactive command line or with the SBATCH keyword. There is both a long-form option and a short-form syntax. For example, `time=1:00:00` is the long form and `-t=1:00:00` is the short form.

We show some of the more common options for Slurm in table 15.1.

Table 15.1   Slurm command options

Option	Function	Example
`[--time|-t]=hr:min:sec`	Requests a maximum run time	`-t=8:00:00`
`[--nodes|-N]=#`	Requests a number of nodes	`--nodes=2`
`[--ntasks|-n]=nprocs`	Requests a number of processors	`-n=8`
`[--job-name|-J]=name`	Names your job	`-J=job22`
`[--output|-o]=filename`	Writes standard output to the specified filename	`-o=run.out`
`[--error|-e]=filename`	Writes error output to the specified filename	`-e=run.err`
`[--exclusive]`	Specifies the exclusive use of nodes	`--exclusive`
`[--oversubscribe|-s]`	Indicates the oversubscribe resources	`--oversubscribe`

Let's go ahead and put this all together into our first full Slurm batch script as the following listing shows. This example is included with the associated code for the book at https://github.com/EssentialsofParallelComputing/Chapter15. As always, we encourage you to follow along with the examples for this chapter.

Listing 15.1   Slurm batch script for a parallel job

```
1 #!/bin/sh
2 #SBATCH -N 1        ←──┐  Specifies one compute node
3 #SBATCH -n 4        ←──┘  Indicates four processors
5 #SBATCH -t 01:00:00 ←───── Runs job one hour
6
7 # Do not place bash commands before the last SBATCH directive
```

```
 8 # Behavior can be unreliable
 9
10 mpirun -n 4 ./testapp &> run.out
```

The -N on line 2 can alternatively be specified with --nodes. The -N has a different meaning in other batch schedulers and MPI implementations, leading to incorrect values and errors. You should be on the lookout for inconsistencies in syntax for the set of batch systems and MPIs that you use. We then submit this job with sbatch < first_slurm_batch_job. We'll get the equivalent of the batch job in an interactive job with

```
frontend> salloc -N 1 -n 4 -t 01:00:00
computenode22> mpirun -n 4 ./testapp
computenode22> exit
```

NOTE The options are the same in both the batch file and on the command line.

We need to make a special mention of the exclusive and oversubscribe options. One of the major reasons for using a batch system is to get exclusive use of the resource for more efficient application performance. Nearly every major computing center sets the default behavior to exclusive use of the resource. But the configuration may set one partition to be shared for particular use cases. You can use these command options, exclusive and oversubscribe, for the sbatch and srun commands to request a different behavior than the system configuration. However, you cannot override the shared configuration setting for a partition.

Most large computing systems are composed of many nodes with identical characteristics. It is, however, increasingly common to have systems with a variety of node types. Slurm provides commands that can request nodes with special characteristics. For example, you can use --mem=<#> to get large memory nodes with the requested size in MB. There are many other special requests that can be made through the batch system. A batch script for the PBS batch scheduler is similar, but with a different syntax. Some of the most common PBS options are shown in table 15.2.

Table 15.2 PBS command options

Option	Function	Example
-l [nodes|walltime|cput|mem |ncpus|ppn|procs]	Catch-all for parallel requirements	-l nodes=2,procs=4
-N <name>	Names the job	-N job22
-o <filename>	Writes standard output to the specified filename	-o run.out
-e <filename>	Writes error output to the specified filename	-e run.err

Table 15.2   PBS command options *(continued)*

Option	Function	Example
-q <queue>	Queues for job submission (queue names are site specific)	-q standard
-j	Joins standard and error output	-j -o run.out

The -l option is a catch-all that is used for a variety of options. Let's put together the equivalent PBS batch script for the same job as in listing 15.1. The following listing shows the PBS script.

Listing 15.2   PBS batch script for a parallel job

```
1 #!/bin/sh
2 #PBS -l nodes=1                    PBS keywords
3 #PBS -l procs=4                    and syntax
5 #PBS -l walltime=01:00:00
6
7 # Do not place bash commands before the last PBS directive
8 # Behavior can be unreliable
9
10 mpirun -n 4 ./testapp &> run.out
```

For PBS, we submit the job with qsub < first_pbs_batch_job. To get an interactive allocation in PBS, we use the -I option to qsub:

```
frontend> qsub -I -l nodes=1,procs=4,walltime=01:00:00
computenode22> mpirun -n 4 ./testapp &> run.out
computenode22> exit
```

You may need to specify a queue or other site-specific information for these examples. Many sites have different queues for long, short, large, and other specialized situations. Consult the local site documentation for these important details.

We've seen a couple of batch scheduler commands in the previous discussion. To effectively use the system, you will need more commands, found below. These batch scheduler commands check on the status of your job, get information on the system resources, and cancel jobs. We summarize the most common commands for both the Slurm and PBS schedulers next.

Slurm reference guide

- salloc [--nodes|-N]=N [-ntasks|-n]=N allocates nodes for a batch job:

  ```
  frontend> salloc -N 1 -n 32
  ```

- sbatch submits a batch job to the batch scheduler (see examples earlier in this section).

- `scancel` cancels a job either running or waiting in queue:

```
frontend> scancel <SLURM_JOB_ID>
```

- `sinfo` provides information on the status of the system controlled by the batch scheduler:

```
frontend> sinfo
PARTITION AVAIL   TIMELIMIT   NODES   STATE NODELIST
standard*   up     4:00:00       1   drain n02
standard*   up     4:00:00       5    resv n[03-07]
standard*   up     4:00:00       2   alloc n[08-09]
standard*   up     4:00:00       1    idle n01
debug       up     1:00:00       1    idle n10
```

- `squeue` shows the jobs in the queue and their status (such as running or waiting to run). Most common usage is `squeue -u <username>` for just your own user jobs or `squeue` for all jobs.

```
frontend> squeue
JOBID PARTITION    NAME    USER ST     TIME  NODES NODELIST(REASON)
35456   standard   sim_2    jrr PD     0:00      1 (Resources)
35455   standard   sim_1    jrr  R  2:26:54      1 n08
```

- `srun [--nodes|-N]=N [--ntasks|-n]=N <exec>`, a replacement for mpirun, contains additional capabilities for placement and binding. If the affinity plugin is enabled, these additional options are available:

```
--sockets-per-node=S
--cores-per-socket=C
--threads-per-core=T
--ntasks-per-core=n
--ntasks-per-socket=n
--cpu-bind=[threads|cores|sockets]
--exclusive
--share
```
For example

```
frontend> srun -N 1 -n 16 --cpu-bind=cores my_exec
```

- `scontrol` views or modifies Slurm components:

```
frontend> scontrol show job <SLURM_JOB_ID>
JobID=35456 JobName=sim2
  UserID=jrr <...and much more...>
```

The following table lists some environment variables in Slurm that can be useful in your batch scripts.

(continued)

Slurm environment variable	Function
SLURM_NTASKS	Formerly SLURM_NPROCS, the total number of processors requested
SLURM_CPUS_ON_NODE	CPUs on node
SLURM_JOB_CPUS_PER_NODE	CPUS requested for each node
SLURM_JOB_ID	Job ID
SLURM_JOB_NODELIST	List of nodes allocated for job
SLURM_JOB_NUM_NODES	Number of nodes for job
SLURM_SUBMIT_DIR	Directory from which job was submitted
SLURM_TASKS_PER_NODE	Number of tasks to be started on each node

PBS reference guide

- qsub submits a batch job, where
  - -I is an interactive job
  - The batch equivalent for this command is #PBS interactive=true.
  - -W block=true waits until job completion
  - The batch equivalent is #PBS block=true.
  - qdel deletes a batch job: frontend> qdel <job ID>
  - qsig sends a signal to the batch job: frontend> qsig 23 56
  - qstat shows the status of batch jobs

    ```
    frontend> qstat or qstat -u jrr

                                              Req'd Elap
    JobID    User   Queue Jobname Sess NDS  TSK Mem Time S Time
    -------- ------ ----- ------- ---- ---- --- --- ---- - ----
    56.base  jrr    standard sim2 --   --    1  -- 0:30 R 0:02
    ```

- qmsg sends a message to a batch job:

    ```
    frontend> qmsg "message to standard error" 56
    ```

The following table lists some environment variables in PBS that can be useful in your batch scripts.

PBS environment variable	Function
PBS_JOBDIR	Job execution directory
PBS_TMPDIR	Temporary directory or scratch space
PBS_O_WORKDIR	Current working directory where qsub command was executed
PBS_JOBID	Job ID

15.4 Automatic restarts for long-running jobs

Most high-performance computing sites limit the maximum time that a job can run. So how do you run longer jobs? The typical approach is for applications to periodically write out their state into files and then a follow-on job is submitted that reads the file and starts at that point in the run. This process, as illustrated in figure 15.3, is referred to as *checkpointing* and *restarting*.

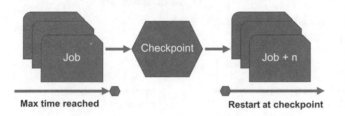

Max time reached   Restart at checkpoint

Figure 15.3 A checkpoint file that saves the state of the calculation is written out to disk at the conclusion of a batch job and then the next batch job reads the file and restarts the calculation where the previous job left off.

The checkpointing process is useful for dealing with a limited time for a batch job and for handling system crashes or other job interruptions. You might restart your jobs manually for a small number of cases, but as the number of restarts gets larger, it becomes a real burden. If this is the case, you should add the capability to automate the process. It takes a fair amount of effort to do this and requires changes to your application and more sophisticated batch scripts. We show a skeleton application where we have done this.

First, the batch script needs to signal your application that it is reaching the end of its allocated time. Then the script needs to resubmit itself recursively until your job reaches completion. The following listing shows such a script for Slurm.

Listing 15.3 Batch script to automatically restart

```
AutomaticRestarts/batch_restart.sh
 1 #!/bin/sh
    < ... usage notes ... >
13 #SBATCH -N 1
14 #SBATCH -n 4
15 #SBATCH --signal=23@160
```

Sends application a signal 23 (SIGURG) 160 s before termination

```
16 #SBATCH -t 00:08:00
17
18 # Do not place bash commands before the last SBATCH directive
19 # Behavior can be unreliable
20
21 NUM_CPUS=${SLURM_NTASKS}
22 OUTPUT_FILE=run.out
23 EXEC_NAME=./testapp                    Maximum number of
24 MAX_RESTARTS=4                         script submissions
25
26 if [ -z ${COUNT} ]; then
27    export COUNT=0                          Counts the
28 fi                                         number of
29                                            submissions
30 ((COUNT++))
31 echo "Restart COUNT is ${COUNT}"
32
33 if [ ! -e DONE ]; then                 Checks for DONE file
34    if [ -e RESTART ]; then             Checks for
35       echo "=== Restarting ${EXEC_NAME} ===" \    RESTART file
                >> ${OUTPUT_FILE}
36       cycle=`cat RESTART`              Gets the iteration number
37       rm -f RESTART                    for the command line
38    else
39       echo "=== Starting problem ===" \
                >> ${OUTPUT_FILE}
40       cycle=""
41    fi
42
43    mpirun -n ${NUM_CPUS} ${EXEC_NAME} \    Invokes MPI job with
                ${cycle} &>> ${OUTPUT_FILE}    command-line arguments
44    STATUS=$?
45    echo "Finished mpirun" \
                >> ${OUTPUT_FILE}
46                                           Exits if reached
47    if [ ${COUNT} -ge ${MAX_RESTARTS} ]; then    maximum restarts
48       echo "=== Reached maximum number of restarts ===" \
                >> ${OUTPUT_FILE}
49       date > DONE
50    fi
51
52    if [ ${STATUS} = "0" -a ! -e DONE ]; then
53       echo "=== Submitting restart script ===" \
                >> ${OUTPUT_FILE}
54       sbatch <batch_restart.sh      Submits next
55    fi                               batch job
56 fi
```

This script has a lot of moving parts. Much of this is to avoid a runaway situation where more batch jobs are submitted than needed. The script also requires cooperation with the application. This cooperation includes these tasks:

- The batch system sends a signal and the application catches it.
- The application writes out to a file named DONE when complete.

- The application writes out the iteration number to a file named RESTART.
- The application writes out a checkpoint file and reads it on restart.

The signal number might need to vary depending on what the batch system and MPI already use. We also caution you not to put shell commands before any of the Slurm commands. While the script might seem to work, we found that the signals did not function properly; therefore, order does matter and you won't always get an obvious failure. Listing 15.4 shows a skeleton of an application code in C to demonstrate the automatic restart functionality.

NOTE   The example codes at https://github.com/EssentialsofParallelComputing/Chapter15 also contain a Fortran example of an automatic restart.

Listing 15.4   Sample application for testing

```
AutomaticRestarts/testapp.c
 1 #include <unistd.h>
 2 #include <time.h>
 3 #include <stdio.h>
 4 #include <stdlib.h>
 5 #include <signal.h>
 6 #include <mpi.h>
 7
 8 static int batch_terminate_signal = 0;          ◁──── Global variable for batch signal
 9 void batch_timeout(int signum){                 ◁────┐
10     printf("Batch Timeout : %d\n",signum);           │ Callback function sets the global variable
11     batch_terminate_signal = 1;                 ◁────┘
12     return;
13 }
14
15 int main(int argc, char *argv[])
16 {
17     MPI_Init(&argc, &argv);
18     char checkpoint_name[50];
19     int mype, itstart = 1;
20     MPI_Comm_rank(MPI_COMM_WORLD, &mype);
21
22     if (argc >=2) itstart = atoi(argv[1]);      ◁──── If a restart, reads the checkpoint file
           // < ... read restart file ... >
24
25     if (mype ==0) signal(23, batch_timeout);    ◁──── Sets the callback function for signal 23
26
27     for (int it=itstart; it < 10000; it++){
28         sleep(1);                               ◁──── Stands in for computational work
29
30         if ( it%60 == 0 ) {                     ◁──── Writes out checkpoint every 60 iterations
               // < ... write out checkpoint file ... >
40         }
41         int terminate_sig = batch_terminate_signal;
42         MPI_Bcast(&terminate_sig, 1, MPI_INT, 0, MPI_COMM_WORLD);
43         if ( terminate_sig ) {
               // < ... write out RESTART and              Writes out special checkpoint
               //     special checkpoint file ... >        file and a file named RESTART
```

```
54         MPI_Finalize();
55         exit(0);
56      }
57
58   }
59
           // < ... write out DONE file ... >    <──┐
67   MPI_Finalize();
68   return(0);
69 }
```

Writes out DONE file when application meets completion criteria

This may appear to be a short and simple code, but there is a lot packed into these lines. A real application would need hundreds of lines to fully implement checkpointing and restart, completion criteria, and input handling. We also caution that developers need to carefully check their code to prevent runaway conditions. The signal timing also needs to be tuned for how long it takes to catch the signal, complete the iterations, and write out the restart file. For our little skeleton for an automatic restart application, we start the submission with

```
sbatch < batch_restart.sh
```

and get the following output:

```
=== Starting problem ===
App launch reported: 2 (out of 2) daemons - 0 (out of 4) procs
 60 Checkpoint: Mon May 11 20:06:08 2020
120 Checkpoint: Mon May 11 20:07:08 2020
180 Checkpoint: Mon May 11 20:08:08 2020
240 Checkpoint: Mon May 11 20:09:08 2020
Batch Timeout : 23
297 RESTART: Mon May 11 20:10:05 2020
Finished mpirun
=== Submitting restart script ===
=== Restarting ./testapp ===
App launch reported: 2 (out of 2) daemons - 0 (out of 4) procs
300 Checkpoint: Mon May 11 20:10:11 2020
 < ... skipping output ... >
1186 RESTART: Mon May 11 20:25:05 2020
Finished mpirun
=== Reached maximum number of restarts ===
```

From the output, we see that the application writes out periodic checkpoint files every 60 iterations. Because the stand-in for computation work is actually a `sleep` command of 1 s, the checkpoints are 1 min apart. After approximately 300 s, the batch system sends the signal and the test application reports that it was caught. At that point, the script writes out a file named RESTART that contains the iteration number. The script then writes out a message that the restart script was resubmitted. The output also shows the application starting back up. In the output, we skipped showing the additional restarts and just showed the message that the maximum number of restarts has been reached.

15.5 Specifying dependencies in batch scripts

Do batch systems have built-in support for sequences of batch jobs? Most have a dependency feature that allows you to specify how one job depends on another. Using this dependency capability, we can get our subsequent jobs submitted earlier in the queue by submitting the next batch job *prior* to running our application. As figure 15.4 shows, this may give us higher priority for starting up the next batch job, depending on the policies of the site. Regardless, your jobs will be in the queue, and you don't have to worry about whether the next job will be submitted.

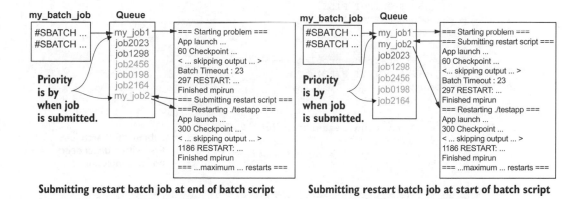

Figure 15.4 Automatic restart submitted at start of batch job will have more time in queue, which can give your restart job higher priority than one submitted at end of batch job (dependent on local scheduling policies).

We can make this change to the batch script by adding the dependency clause (on line 33 in the following listing). This batch script is submitted first, before we begin our work, but with a dependency on the completion of this current batch job.

> **Listing 15.5 Batch script to submit first to restart script**

```
Prestart/batch_restart.sh
 1 #!/bin/sh
    < ... usage notes ... >
13 #SBATCH -N 1
14 #SBATCH -n 4
15 #SBATCH --signal=23@160
16 #SBATCH -t 00:08:00
17
18 # Do not place bash commands before the last SBATCH directive
19 # Behavior can be unreliable
20
21 NUM_CPUS=4
22 OUTPUT_FILE=run.out
```

```
23 EXEC_NAME=./testapp
24 MAX_RESTARTS=4
25
26 if [ -z ${COUNT} ]; then
27    export COUNT=0
28 fi
29
30 ((COUNT++))
31 echo "Restart COUNT is ${COUNT}"
32
33 if [ ! -e DONE ]; then
34    if [ -e RESTART ]; then
35       echo "=== Restarting ${EXEC_NAME} ===" \
               >> ${OUTPUT_FILE}
36       cycle=`cat RESTART`
37       rm -f RESTART
38    else
39       echo "=== Starting problem ===" \
               >> ${OUTPUT_FILE}
40       cycle=""
41    fi
42
43    echo "=== Submitting restart script ===" \
             >> ${OUTPUT_FILE}
44    sbatch --dependency=afterok:${SLURM_JOB_ID} \
             <batch_restart.sh
45
46    mpirun -n ${NUM_CPUS} ${EXEC_NAME} ${cycle} \
            &>> ${OUTPUT_FILE}
47    echo "Finished mpirun" \
             >> ${OUTPUT_FILE}
48
49    if [ ${COUNT} -ge ${MAX_RESTARTS} ]; then
50       echo "=== Reached maximum number of restarts ===" \
             >> ${OUTPUT_FILE}
51       date > DONE
52    fi
53 fi
```

Submit this batch job first with a dependency on its completion ← *(pointing to line 44)*

This listing showed how to use dependencies in your batch scripts for the simple case of a checkpoint/restart, but dependencies are useful for many other situations. More complicated workflows might have pre-processing steps that need to complete before the main work and then a post-processing step afterward. Some more complex workflows need more than a dependency on whether the previous job completed. Fortunately, batch systems provide other types of dependencies between jobs. Table 15.3 shows the various possible options. PBS has similar dependencies for batch jobs that can be specified with -W depend=<type:job id>.

Table 15.3 Dependency options for batch jobs

Dependency option	Function
after	Job can begin after specified job(s) have started.
afterany	Job can begin after specified job(s) have terminated with any status.
afternotok	Job can begin after specified job(s) have failed.
afterok	Job can begin after specified job(s) have successfully completed.
singleton	Job can begin after all jobs with same name and user have completed.

15.6 *Further explorations*

There are general reference materials for the Slurm and PBS schedulers, but you should also look at the documentation for your site. Many sites have customized set-ups and added commands and features for their specific needs. If you think you might want to set up a computing cluster with a batch system, you may want to research new initiatives such as OpenHPC and the Rocks Cluster distributions that have recently been released for different HPC computing niches.

15.6.1 *Additional reading*

Both freely available and commercially supported versions of Slurm are available from SchedMD. Not surprisingly, the SchedMD site has a lot of documentation on Slurm. Another good reference site is Lawrence Livermore National Laboratory where Slurm was originally developed.

- SchedMD and Slurm documentation at https://slurm.schedmd.com.
- Blaise Barney, "Slurm and Moab," Lawrence Livermore National Laboratory, https://computing.llnl.gov/tutorials/moab/.

The best information on PBS is the PBS User Guide:

Altair Engineering, PBS User Guide, https://www.altair.com/pdfs/pbsworks/PBS UserGuide2021.1.pdf.

Though somewhat dated, the following online reference to setting up a Beowulf cluster is a good historical perspective on the emergence of cluster computing and how to set up cluster management, including the PBS batch scheduler:

Edited by William Gropp, Ewing Lusk, Thomas String, *Beowulf Cluster Computing with Linux*, 2nd ed. (Massachusetts Institute of Technology, 2002, 2003), http://etutorials.org/Linux+systems/cluster+computing+with+linux/.

Here are some sites with information on current HPC software management systems:

- OpenHPC, http://www.openhpc.community.
- Rocks Cluster, http://www.rocksclusters.org.

15.6.2 Exercises

1 Try submitting a couple of jobs, one with 32 processors and one with 16 processors. Check to see that these are submitted and whether they are running. Delete the 32 processor job. Check to see that it got deleted.

2 Modify the automatic restart script so that the first job is a preprocessing step to set up for the computation before the restarts run the simulation.

3 Modify the simple batch script in listing 15.1 for Slurm and 15.2 for PBS to clean up on failure by removing a file called simulation_database.

Summary

- Batch schedulers allocate resources so that you can use a parallel cluster efficiently. It is important to learn how to use these to run on larger, high-performance computing systems.

- There are many commands to query your job and its status. Knowing these commands allows you to better utilize the system.

- You can use automatic restarts and chaining of jobs to run larger simulations and workflows. Adding this capability to your application makes it possible to scale to problems that you would not otherwise be able to do.

- Batch job dependencies give the capability of controlling complex workflows. By using dependencies between multiple jobs, you can stage data, preprocess it for a calculation, or launch a post-processing job.

16

File operations
for a parallel world

This chapter covers

- Modifying a parallel application for standard file operations
- Writing out data using parallel file operations with MPI-IO and HDF5
- Tuning parallel file operations for different parallel filesystems

Filesystems create a streamlined workflow of retrieving, storing, and updating data. For any computing work, the product is the output, whether it be data, graphics, or statistics. This includes final results but also intermediate output for graphics, checkpointing, and analysis. Checkpointing is a special need on large HPC systems with long-running calculations that might span days, weeks, or months.

DEFINITION *Checkpointing* is the practice of periodically storing the state of a calculation to disk so that the calculation can be restarted in the event of system failures or because of finite length run times in a batch system

When processing data for highly parallel applications, there needs to be a safe and performant way of reading and storing data at run time. Therein lies the need to understand file operations in a parallel world. Some of the concerns you should keep in mind are correctness, reducing duplicate output, and performance.

It is important to be aware that the scaling of the performance of filesystems has not kept up with the rest of the computing hardware. We are scaling calculations up to billions of cells or particles, which is putting severe demands on the filesystems. With the advent of machine learning and data science, many more applications need big data that requires large files sets and complex workflows with intermediate file storage.

Adding an understanding of file operations to your HPC toolset is becoming more and more important. In this chapter, we introduce how to modify file operations for a parallel application so that you are writing out data efficiently and making the best use of the available hardware. Though this topic may not be heavily covered in many parallel tutorials, we think it's a baseline essential for today's parallel applications. You will learn how to speed up the file-writing operation by orders of magnitude while maintaining correctness. We will also look at the different software and hardware that are typically used for large HPC systems. We will use the example of writing out the data from the domain decomposition of a regular grid with halo cells using different parallel file software. We encourage you to follow along with the examples for this chapter at https://github.com/EssentialsOfParallelComputing/Chapter16.git.

16.1 The components of a high-performance filesystem

We first review what hardware comprises a high-performance filesystem. Traditionally, file operations store data to a hard disk with a mechanical mechanism that writes a series of bits to a magnetic substrate. Like many other parts of HPC systems, the storage hardware has become more complex with deeper hierarchies of hardware and different performance characteristics. This evolution of storage hardware is similar to the deepening of the cache hierarchy for processors as these increased in performance. The storage hierarchy also helps to cover the large disparity in bandwidth at the processor level, compared to mechanical disk storage. This is because it is much harder to reduce the size of mechanical components than electrical circuits. The introduction of solid-state drives (SSDs) and other solid-state devices has helped to provide a way around the scaling of physical spinning disks.

Let's first specify what might comprise an HPC storage system as illustrated in figure 16.1. Typical storage hardware components include the following:

- *Spinning disk*—Electro-mechanical device where data is stored in an electro-magnetic layer through the movement of a mechanical recording head.
- *SSD*—A solid-state drive (SSD) is a solid-state memory device that can replace a mechanical disk.
- *Burst buffer*—Intermediate storage hardware layer composed of NVRAM and SSD components. It is positioned between the compute hardware and the main disk storage resources.
- *Tape*—A magnetic tape with auto-loading cartridges.

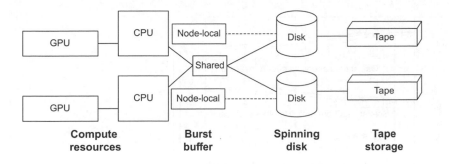

Figure 16.1 **Schematic showing positioning of burst buffer hardware in between the compute resources and disk storage. Burst buffers can either be node-local or shared among nodes via a network.**

The storage schematic in figure 16.1 illustrates the storage hierarchy between the compute system and the storage system. Burst buffers are inserted in between the compute hardware and the main disk storage to cover the increasing gap in performance. Burst buffers can either be placed on each node or on the IO nodes and shared via a network with the other compute nodes.

With the rapid development of solid-state storage technology, the burst buffer designs will continue to evolve in the near future. Besides helping with the gap in latency and bandwidth performance, new storage designs are increasingly driven by the need to reduce power requirements as systems grow in size. A magnetic tape has traditionally been used for long-term storage, but some designs have even looked at a "dark disk," where spinning disks are used but turned off when not needed.

16.2 Standard file operations: A parallel-to-serial interface

Let's first take a look at standard file operations. For our parallel applications, the conventional file-handling interface is still a serial operation. It is not practical to have a hard disk for every processor. Even a file per process is only viable in limited situations and at small scale. The result is that for every file operation, we go from parallel to serial. A file operation needs to be treated as a reduction (or expansion for reads) in the number of processes, requiring special handling for parallel applications. You can handle this parallelism with some simple modifications to standard file input and output (IO).

A large portion of the modifications for parallel applications is at the file-operation interface. We should first review our prior examples that involved file operations. For an example of file input, section 8.3.2 shows how to read in data on one process and then broadcast it to other processes. In section 8.3.4, we used an MPI gather operation so that output from processes is written out in a deterministic order.

(Pro tip) To avoid later complications, the first step you should take in parallelizing an application is to go through the code and insert an if (rank == 0) in front of

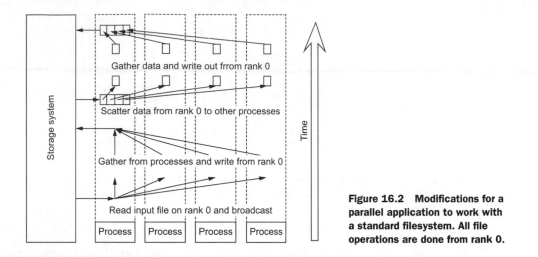

Figure 16.2   Modifications for a parallel application to work with a standard filesystem. All file operations are done from rank 0.

every input and output statement. While going through the code, you should identify which file operations need additional treatment. These operations include the following (illustrated in figure 16.2).

- Opening files on only one process and then broadcasting the data to other processes
- Distributing data that needs to be partitioned across processes with a scatter operation
- Ensuring that output should come from only one process
- Collecting the distributed data with a gather operation before it is output

A common inefficiency is to open a file on every process; you can imagine it being equivalent to a dozen people trying to open a door at the same time. While your program might not crash, it causes problems at scale (imagine 1,000 people opening that same door). There's a lot of contention for the file metadata and the lock for correctness that it causes, which can take minutes at larger process counts. We can avoid this contention by opening the file on just one process. By adding parallel communication calls at each of the transition points from serial to parallel and parallel to serial, we can make modest parallel applications work using standard files. This is sufficient for the vast majority of parallel applications.

As our applications grow in size, we can no longer easily gather or scatter the data to a single process. Our biggest limitation is memory; we don't have enough memory resources on a single process to bring the data from thousands of other processes down to just one. Thus, we have to have a different, more scalable approach to file operations. That is the subject of the next two sections on MPI file operations, called MPI-IO, and Hierarchical Data Format v5 (HDF5). In these sections, we show how these two libraries permit a parallel application to treat file operations in a parallel manner. There are other parallel file libraries that we will mention in section 16.5.

16.3 MPI file operations (MPI-IO) for a more parallel world

The best way to learn MPI-IO is to see how it is used in a realistic scenario. We'll take a look at the example of writing out a regular mesh that has been distributed across processors with halo cells using MPI-IO. Through this example, you will become familiar with the basic structure that occurs with MPI-IO and some of its more common function calls.

The first parallel file operations were added to MPI in the MPI-2 standard in the late 1990s. The first widely available implementation of the MPI file operations, ROMIO, was led by Rajeev Thakur at Argonne National Laboratory (ANL). ROMIO can be used with any MPI implementation. Most MPI distributions include ROMIO as a standard part of their software release. MPI-IO has a lot of functions, all beginning with the prefix `MPI_File`. In this section, we will cover just a subset of the most commonly used operations (see table 16.1).

There are different ways to use MPI-IO. We are interested in the highly parallel version, the collective form that has the processes work together to write to their section of the file. In order to do this, we'll utilize the ability to create a new MPI data type that was first introduced in section 8.5.1.

The MPI-IO library has both a shared file pointer across all processes and independent file pointers for each process. Using the shared pointer causes a lock to be applied for each process and serializes the file operations. To avoid the locks, we use the independent file pointers for better performance.

File operations are broken down into collective and non-collective operations. Collective operations use the MPI collective communication calls, and all members of the communicator must make the call or it will hang. *Non-collective calls* are serial operations that are invoked separately for every process. Table 16.1 shows some general purpose operations and the respective commands for each.

Table 16.1 MPI general file routines

Command	Description
`MPI_File_open`	Collective file open
`MPI_File_seek`	Moves individual file pointers to this location in file
`MPI_File_set_size`	Allocates the file space specified
`MPI_File_close`	Collective file close
`MPI_File_set_info`	Communicates hints to the MPI-IO library for more optimized MPI operations

The file open and close operations are self-explanatory. The seek operation moves the individual file pointer to the specified location for each process. You can use `MPI_File_set_info` to communicate both general- and vendor-specific hints. There is also an `MPI_File_delete`, but it is a non-collective call. In this case, we mean a non-collective call to be a serial call: every process deletes the file. For C and C++ programs, the remove function works just as well. Calling `MPI_File_set_size` with the expected size of your file can be more efficient than the file being incrementally increased in size with each write.

We'll start by looking at the independent file operations for the read and write operations. When each process operates on its independent file pointer, it's known as an *independent file operation*. Independent file operations are useful for writing out replicated data across processes. For this common data, you can write it out from a single rank with the routines in table 16.2.

Table 16.2   MPI independent file routines

Command	Description
`MPI_File_read`	Each process reads from its current file pointer position.
`MPI_File_write`	Each process writes to its current file pointer position.
`MPI_File_read_at`	Moves the file pointer to the specified location and reads the data
`MPI_File_write_at`	Moves the file pointer to the specified location and writes the data

You should write out distributed data with collective operations (table 16.3). When processes operate collectively on the file, it's known as a *collective file operation*. The write and read functions are similar to the independent file operations but with an `_all` appended to the function name. To make the best use of the collective operations, we need to create complex MPI data types. The `MPI_File_set_view` function is used to set the data layout in the file.

Table 16.3   MPI collective file routines

Command	Description
`MPI_File_set_view`	View of file visible to each process. Sets file pointers to zero.
`MPI_File_read_all`	All processes collectively read from their current, independent file pointer.
`MPI_File_write_all`	All processes collectively write from their current, independent file pointer.
`MPI_File_read_at_all`	All processes move to specified file location and read the data.
`MPI_File_write_at_all`	All processes move to specified file location and write the data.

For this example, we'll break up the code into four blocks. (The full code for this example is included with the code for the chapter.) To begin, we must start with the creation of an MPI data type for the memory layout of the data and another for the file layout; these are referred to as memspace and filespace, respectively. Figure 16.3 shows these data types for a smaller 4×4 version of our example. For simplicity, we only show four processes, each with a 4×4 grid surrounded by a one cell halo. The halo depth size in the figure is ng, short for number of ghost cells.

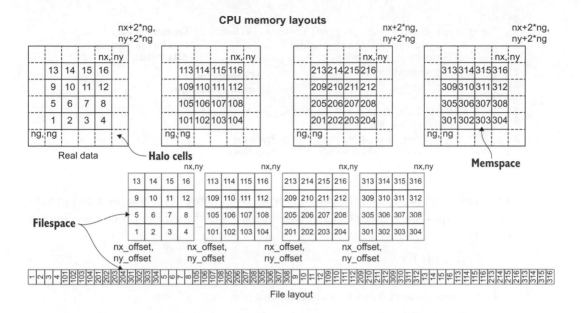

Figure 16.3 The 4x4 blocks of data from each process written without the halo cells to contiguous sections of the output file. The top row is the memory layout on the process, referred to as the *memspace*. The middle row is the memory in the file with the halo cells stripped off, referred to as the *filespace*. The memory in the file is actually linear, so it takes the form in the last row.

The first block of code in listing 16.1 shows the creation of these two data types. This only needs to be done once at the start of the program. The data types should then be freed at the end of the program in the finalize routine.

Listing 16.1 Setting up MPI-IO dataspace types

```
MPI_IO_Examples/mpi_io_block2d/mpi_io_file_ops.c
10 void mpi_io_file_init(int ng, int ndims, int *global_sizes,
11     int *global_subsizes, int *global_starts, MPI_Datatype *memspace,
       MPI_Datatype *filespace){
12   // create data descriptors on disk and in memory
13
14   // Global view of entire 2D domain -- collates decomposed subarrays
15   MPI_Type_create_subarray(ndims,
        global_sizes, global_subsizes,
16      global_starts, MPI_ORDER_C, MPI_DOUBLE,
        filespace);
17   MPI_Type_commit(filespace);
18
19   // Local 2D subarray structure -- strips ghost cells on node
20   int ny = global_subsizes[0], nx = global_subsizes[1];
21   int local_sizes[]    = {ny+2*ng,   nx+2*ng};
22   int local_subsizes[] = {ny,        nx};
23   int local_starts[]   = {ng,        ng};
```

Creates the data type for the file data layout

Commits the file data type

```
24
25   MPI_Type_create_subarray(ndim, local_sizes,        │ Creates the data
         local_subsizes, local_starts,                  │ type for the memory
26       MPI_ORDER_C, MPI_DOUBLE, memspace);            │ data layout
27   MPI_Type_commit(memspace);          ◄───   Commits the
28 }                                            memory data type
29
30 void mpi_io_file_finalize(MPI_Datatype *memspace,
         MPI_Datatype *filespace){
31   MPI_Type_free(memspace);       │ Frees the
32   MPI_Type_free(filespace);      │ data types
33 }
```

In this first step, we created the two data types from figure 16.1. Now we need to write these data types out to the file. There are four steps to the writing process as shown in listing 16.2:

1 Create the file
2 Set the file view
3 Write out each array with collective call
4 Close the file

Listing 16.2   Writing an MPI-IO file

```
MPI_IO_Examples/mpi_io_block2d/mpi_io_file_ops.c
35 void write_mpi_io_file(const char *filename, double **data,
36     int data_size, MPI_Datatype memspace, MPI_Datatype filespace,
       MPI_Comm mpi_io_comm){
37   MPI_File file_handle = create_mpi_io_file(            │ Creates
38     filename, mpi_io_comm, (long long)data_size);       │ the file
39
40   MPI_File_set_view(file_handle, file_offset,
41     MPI_DOUBLE, filespace, "native",                    │ Sets file view
         MPI_INFO_NULL);
42   MPI_File_write_all(file_handle,          │ Writes out
       &(data[0][0]), 1, memspace,           │ arrays
       MPI_STATUS_IGNORE);
43   file_offset += data_size;
44
45   MPI_File_close(&file_handle);      ◄───   Closes the file
46   file_offset = 0;
47 }
48
49 MPI_File create_mpi_io_file(const char *filename, MPI_Comm mpi_io_comm,
50         long long file_size){
51   int file_mode = MPI_MODE_WRONLY | MPI_MODE_CREATE |
                     MPI_MODE_UNIQUE_OPEN;
52
53   MPI_Info mpi_info = MPI_INFO_NULL;   // For MPI IO hints
54   MPI_Info_create(&mpi_info);
55   MPI_Info_set(mpi_info,              │ Communicates hints
       "collective_buffering", "1");    │ for collective operation
```

```
56    MPI_Info_set(mpi_info,
          "striping_factor", "8");              Communicates
57    MPI_Info_set(mpi_info,                     hints for striping on
          "striping_unit", "4194304");          Lustre filesystem
58
59    MPI_File file_handle = NULL;
60    MPI_File_open(mpi_io_comm, filename, file_mode, mpi_info,
                    &file_handle);
61    if (file_size > 0)                          Preallocates file space
        MPI_File_set_size(file_handle, file_size);   for better performance
62    file_offset = 0;
63    return file_handle;
64  }
```

There are a few optimizations that can be provided during the open with hints in an
`MPI_Info` object (line 53). A hint could be that the file operations should be done
using collective operations, `collective_buffering`, as on line 55. Or a hint can be
one that's filesystem specific to stripe across eight hard disks, `striping_factor = 8`, as
on line 56. We will discuss hints more in section 16.6.1.

We can also preallocate the file space, as shown on line 61, so that it doesn't have
to be increased during the writes. Reading the file has the same four steps as the writing process listed previously and is shown in the following listing.

Listing 16.3   Reading an MPI-IO file

```
MPI_IO_Examples/mpi_io_block2d/mpi_io_file_ops.c
66 void read_mpi_io_file(const char *filename, double **data, int data_size,
67     MPI_Datatype memspace, MPI_Datatype filespace, MPI_Comm mpi_io_comm){
68   MPI_File file_handle = open_mpi_io_file(        Opens the file
         filename, mpi_io_comm);
69
70   MPI_File_set_view(file_handle, file_offset,
71       MPI_DOUBLE, filespace, "native",           Sets file view
         MPI_INFO_NULL);
72   MPI_File_read_all(file_handle,
         &(data[0][0]), 1, memspace,                Collective read
         MPI_STATUS_IGNORE);                        of arrays
73   file_offset += data_size;
74
75   MPI_File_close(&file_handle);        ◁──┐ Closes the file
76   file_offset = 0;
77 }
78
79 MPI_File open_mpi_io_file(const char *filename, MPI_Comm mpi_io_comm){
80   int file_mode = MPI_MODE_RDONLY | MPI_MODE_UNIQUE_OPEN;
81
82   MPI_Info mpi_info = MPI_INFO_NULL; // For MPI IO hints
83   MPI_Info_create(&mpi_info);
84   MPI_Info_set(mpi_info, "collective_buffering", "1");
85
86   MPI_File file_handle = NULL;
87   MPI_File_open(mpi_io_comm, filename, file_mode, mpi_info,
                   &file_handle);
```

```
88    return file_handle;
89 }
```

The read operation requires fewer hints and settings than the write operation. This is because some of the settings for a read are determined from the file. So far, these MPI-IO file operations have been written in a general form that can be called for any problem. Now let's take a look at the main application code in the following listing that sets up the calls.

Listing 16.4   Main application code

MPI_IO_Examples/mpi_io_block2d/mpi_io_block2d.c

```
 9 int main(int argc, char *argv[])
10 {
11   MPI_Init(&argc, &argv);
12
13   int rank, nprocs;
14   MPI_Comm_rank(MPI_COMM_WORLD, &rank);
15   MPI_Comm_size(MPI_COMM_WORLD, &nprocs);
16
17   // for multiple files, subdivide communicator and
18   //    set colors for each set
18   MPI_Comm mpi_io_comm = MPI_COMM_NULL;
19   int nfiles = 1;
20   float ranks_per_file = (float)nprocs/(float)nfiles;
21   int color = (int)((float)rank/ranks_per_file);
22   MPI_Comm_split(MPI_COMM_WORLD, color, rank, &mpi_io_comm);
23   int nprocs_color, rank_color;
24   MPI_Comm_size(mpi_io_comm, &nprocs_color);
25   MPI_Comm_rank(mpi_io_comm, &rank_color);
26   int row_color = 1, col_color = rank_color;
27   MPI_Comm mpi_row_comm, mpi_col_comm;
28   MPI_Comm_split(mpi_io_comm, row_color, rank_color, &mpi_row_comm);
29   MPI_Comm_split(mpi_io_comm, col_color, rank_color, &mpi_col_comm);
30
31   // set the dimensions of our data array and the number of ghost cells
32   int ndim = 2, ng = 2, ny = 10, nx = 10;
33   int global_subsizes[] = {ny, nx};
34
35   int ny_offset = 0, nx_offset = 0;
36   MPI_Exscan(&nx, &nx_offset, 1, MPI_INT, MPI_SUM, mpi_row_comm);
37   MPI_Exscan(&ny, &ny_offset, 1, MPI_INT, MPI_SUM, mpi_col_comm);
38   int global_offsets[] = {ny_offset, nx_offset};
39
40   int ny_global, nx_global;
41   MPI_Allreduce(&nx, &nx_global, 1, MPI_INT, MPI_SUM, mpi_row_comm);
42   MPI_Allreduce(&ny, &ny_global, 1, MPI_INT, MPI_SUM, mpi_col_comm);
43   int global_sizes[] = {ny_global, nx_global};
44   int data_size = ny_global*nx_global;
45
46   double **data = (double **)malloc2D(ny+2*ng, nx+2*ng);
47   double **data_restore = (double **)malloc2D(ny+2*ng, nx+2*ng);
   < ... skipping data initialization ... >
54
```

```
55    MPI_Datatype memspace = MPI_DATATYPE_NULL,
                     filespace = MPI_DATATYPE_NULL;
56    mpi_io_file_init(ng, global_sizes,                  Initializes and sets
         global_subsizes, global_offsets,                up the data types
57       &memspace, &filespace);
58
59    char filename[30];
60    if (ncolors > 1) {
61      sprintf(filename,"example_%02d.data",color);
62    } else {
63      sprintf(filename,"example.data");
64    }
65
66    // Do the computation and write out a sequence of files
67    write_mpi_io_file(filename, data,
         data_size, memspace, filespace,                  Writes out
         mpi_io_comm);                                     the data
68    // Read back the data for verifying the file operations
69    read_mpi_io_file(filename, data_restore,
70       data_size, memspace, filespace,                  Reads
         mpi_io_comm);                                     the data
71
72    mpi_io_file_finalize(&memspace, &filespace);       Closes the file and
73                                                         frees the data types
  < ... skipping verification code ... >
105
106   free(data);
107   free(data_restore);
108
109   MPI_Comm_free(&mpi_io_comm);
110   MPI_Comm_free(&mpi_row_comm);
111   MPI_Comm_free(&mpi_col_comm);
112   MPI_Finalize();
113   return 0;
114 }
```

This setup takes a little explanation. This code supports the ability to write out more than one MPI data file. This is commonly called NxM file writes where N processes write out M files and where M is greater than one but much smaller than the number of processes (figure 16.4). The reason for this technique is that at larger problem sizes, writing to a single file does not always scale well.

We can break up the processes into groups by colors as shown in figure 16.4. In lines 17–22 in listing 16.4, we set up a new communicator based on M colors, where M is the number of files. The number of files is set on line 19 and our color is computed on lines 20 and 21. We use a floating-point type for ranks_per_file to handle an uneven division of the ranks. We then get our new rank within our color. Each communication group on the right side of figure 16.4 has 4,096 processes or ranks. The order of the ranks is the same as in the global communication group. If there is more than one file, the filenames include a color number on lines 59–64. This code currently only sets one color and only writes one file as shown on the left side of figure 16.4, but it is written to support more files.

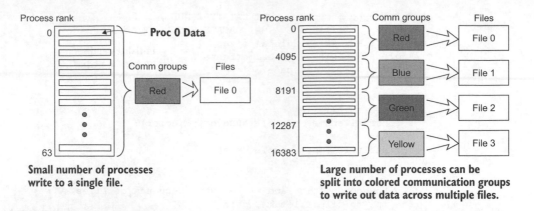

Figure 16.4 **At large sizes, the processes can be broken up into communication groups by colors so they write out to separate files. The ranks of the subgroups are in the same order as the ranks in the original communicator.**

We also need to know where the starting *x* and *y* values are for each process. For data decompositions that have the same number of rows and columns for each process, the calculation only needs to know the location of the process in the global set. But when the number of rows and columns varies across processes, we need to sum all the sizes below our position. As we have previously discussed in section 5.6, this operation is a common parallel pattern called a *scan*. To do this calculation, in lines 22–34 we create communicators for each row and column. These perform an exclusive scan operation to get the starting location of *x* and *y* for each process. In this code, we only partition the data in the x-coordinate direction to keep it a little simpler. The global and process sizes in the array `subsizes` are set in lines 27–44. This includes the data offsets calculated using the exclusive scans.

Now that we have all the necessary information about the data decomposition, we can call our `mpi_io_file_init` subroutine on line 52 to set up the MPI data types for the memory and filesystem layout. This only has to be done once, at startup. We are then free to call our subroutines for writes, `write_mpi_io_file`, and reads, `read_mpi_io_file`, on lines 63 and 65. We can call these as many times as needed during the run. In our example code, we then verify the data read in, compare it to the original data, and print an error if it occurs. Finally, we open the file on a single process and use a standard C binary read to show how the data is laid out in the file. This is done by reading each value from the file in sequential order and printing it out.

Now to compile and run the example. The build is a standard CMake build, and we'll run it on four processors.

```
mkdir build && cd build
cmake ..
make
mpirun -n 4 ./mpi_io_block2d
```

Figure 16.5 shows the output from a standard C binary read for the 10×10 grid on each processor.

```
x[0][ ]   1   2   3   4   5   6   7   8   9  10 101 102 103 104 105 106 107 108 109 110
        201 202 203 204 205 206 207 208 209 210 301 302 303 304 305 306 307 308 309 310
x[1][ ]  11  12  13  14  15  16  17  18  19  20 111 112 113 114 115 116 117 118 119 120
        211 212 213 214 215 216 217 218 219 220 311 312 313 314 315 316 317 318 319 320
x[2][ ]  21  22  23  24  25  26  27  28  29  30 121 122 123 124 125 126 127 128 129 130
        221 222 223 224 225 226 227 228 229 230 321 322 323 324 325 326 327 328 329 330
x[3][ ]  31  32  33  34  35  36  37  38  39  40 131 132 133 134 135 136 137 138 139 140
        231 232 233 234 235 236 237 238 239 240 331 332 333 334 335 336 337 338 339 340
x[4][ ]  41  42  43  44  45  46  47  48  49  50 141 142 143 144 145 146 147 148 149 150
        241 242 243 244 245 246 247 248 249 250 341 342 343 344 345 346 347 348 349 350
x[5][ ]  51  52  53  54  55  56  57  58  59  60 151 152 153 154 155 156 157 158 159 160
        251 252 253 254 255 256 257 258 259 260 351 352 353 354 355 356 357 358 359 360
x[6][ ]  61  62  63  64  65  66  67  68  69  70 161 162 163 164 165 166 167 168 169 170
        261 262 263 264 265 266 267 268 269 270 361 362 363 364 365 366 367 368 369 370
x[7][ ]  71  72  73  74  75  76  77  78  79  80 171 172 173 174 175 176 177 178 179 180
        271 272 273 274 275 276 277 278 279 280 371 372 373 374 375 376 377 378 379 380
x[8][ ]  81  82  83  84  85  86  87  88  89  90 181 182 183 184 185 186 187 188 189 190
        281 282 283 284 285 286 287 288 289 290 381 382 383 384 385 386 387 388 389 390
x[9][ ]  91  92  93  94  95  96  97  98  99 100 191 192 193 194 195 196 197 198 199 200
        291 292 293 294 295 296 297 298 299 300 391 392 393 394 395 396 397 398 399 400
```

Figure 16.5 Output from a small binary read code for the MPI-IO shows what the file contains. With MPI-IO, we had to write a small utility to check the file contents.

16.4 *HDF5 is self-describing for better data management*

With traditional data file formats, the data is meaningless without the code that is used to write and read the file. The Hierarchical Data Format (HDF), version 5, takes a different approach. HDF5 provides a self-describing parallel data format. HDF5 is called self-describing because the name and characteristics are stored in the file with the data. In HDF5, with the description of the data contained in the file, you no longer need the source code and can read the data by just querying the file. HDF5 also has a rich set of command-line utilities (such as h5ls and h5dump) that you can use to query the contents of a file. You will find that the utilities are useful when checking that your files are properly written.

We want to write data in binary format because of speed and precision. But because it is in binary format, it is difficult to check if the data is correctly written. If we read the data back in, the problem could be in the reading process as well. A utility that can query the file provides a way to check the write operation separately from the read. In figure 16.4 in the previous section on MPI-IO, we needed a small program to read the contents of the file. For HDF5, it is unnecessary because the utility is already provided. In figure 16.6 (shown later in this section), we used the h5dump command-line utility to look at the contents. You can avoid the need to write code for many common operations by using the already existing HDF5 utilities.

The parallel HDF5 code is implemented by using MPI-IO. Because it is built on MPI-IO, the structure of HDF5 is similar. Although similar, the terminology and individual function calls are different enough to cause some difficulty. We'll cover the functions that are needed to write a similar parallel file-handling routine as we did for MPI-IO. The HDF5 library is divided into lower-level functionality groupings. These functional groups are conveniently distinguished by prefixes for all of the calls in the group. The first group is the obligatory file handling operations (table 16.4) that collectively handle file open and close operations.

Table 16.4 HDF5 collective file routines

Command	Description
H5Fcreate	Collective file open that will create the file if it doesn't exist
H5Fopen	Collective file open of a file that already exists
H5Fclose	Collective file close

Next, we need to define new memory types. These are used to specify the portions of data to write and their layout. In HDF5, these memory types are called dataspaces. The dataspace operations in table 16.5 include ways to extract patterns from a multidimensional array. You can find information on the many additional routines in the further reading section at the end of the chapter (16.7.1).

Table 16.5 HDF5 dataspace routines

Command	Description
H5Screate_simple	Creates a multidimensional array type
H5Sselect_hyperslab	Creates a hyperslab region type of parts of a multidimensional array
H5Sclose	Releases a dataspace

There are other dataspace operations, including point-based operations, that we haven't covered here. Now we need to apply these dataspaces to a set of multidimensional arrays (table 16.6). In HDF5, a multidimensional array is called a *dataset,* which is generally a multidimensional array or some other form of data within the application.

Table 16.6 HDF5 dataset routines

Command	Description
H5Dcreate2	Creates the space for a dataset in the file
H5Dopen2	Opens an existing dataset as described within the file
H5Dclose	Closes the dataset within the file

Table 16.6 HDF5 dataset routines *(continued)*

Command	Description
H5Dwrite	Writes a dataset to the file using `filespace` and `memspace`
H5Dread	Reads a dataset from the file using `filespace` and `memspace`

There is only one operation group left that we need. This group, called *property lists*, gives you a way to modify or supply hints to operations as table 16.7 shows. We can use property lists for setting attributes to use collective operations with reads or writes. Property lists can also be used to pass hints to the underlying MPI-IO library.

Table 16.7 HDF5 property list routines

Command	Description
H5Pcreate	Creates a property list
H5Pclose	Frees a property list
H5Pset_dxpl_mpio	Sets the data transfer property list
H5Pset_coll_metadata_write	Sets the collective metadata writes for all processes in a group
H5Pset_fapl_mpio	Stores the MPI-IO properties to the file-access property list
H5Pset_all_coll_metadata_ops	Sets the parallel metadata read operations in the file access property list

Let's move on to an example. We start this HDF5 example with the code to create the file and the memory dataspaces. The following listing shows this process. All the arguments to HDF5 are bolded in the listing.

Listing 16.5 Setting up HDF5 dataspace types

```
HDF5Examples/hdf5block2d/hdf5_file_ops.c
11 void hdf5_file_init(int ng, int ndims, int ny_global, int nx_global,
12    int ny, int nx, int ny_offset, int nx_offset, MPI_Comm mpi_hdf5_comm,
13    hid_t *memspace, hid_t *filespace){
14   // create data descriptors on disk and in memory
15   *filespace = create_hdf5_filespace(ndims,
         ny_global, nx_global, ny, nx,                    Creates the file
16       ny_offset, nx_offset, mpi_hdf5_comm);            dataspace
17   *memspace =
           create_hdf5_memspace(ndims ny, nx, ng);     ←──┐ Creates the memory
18 }                                                       │ dataspace
19
20 hid_t create_hdf5_filespace(int ndims, int ny_global, int nx_global,
21    int ny, int nx, int ny_offset, int nx_offset,
         MPI_Comm mpi_hdf5_comm){
22   // create the dataspace for data stored on disk
     //    using the hyperslab call
```

```
23    hsize_t dims[] = {ny_global, nx_global};
24
25    hid_t filespace = H5Screate_simple(ndims,          Creates the
                            dims, NULL);                 filespace object
26
27    // determine the offset into the filespace for the current process
28    hsize_t  start[] = {ny_offset, nx_offset};
29    hsize_t stride[] = {1,          1};
30    hsize_t  count[] = {ny,         nx};
31
32    H5Sselect_hyperslab(filespace, H5S_SELECT_SET,     Selects the filespace
33                 start, stride, count, NULL);          hyperslab
34    return filespace;
35  }
36
37  hid_t create_hdf5_memspace(int ndims, int ny, int nx, int ng) {
38    // create a memory space in memory using the hyperslab call
39    hsize_t dims[] = {ny+2*ng, nx+2*ng};
40
41    hid_t memspace = H5Screate_simple(ndims, dims, NULL);   ◁──┐  Creates the
42                                                                 memspace
43    // select the real data out of the array                     object
44    hsize_t  start[] = {ng,   ng};
45    hsize_t stride[] = {1,    1};
46    hsize_t  count[] = {ny,   nx};
47
48    H5Sselect_hyperslab(memspace, H5S_SELECT_SET,      Creates the
49                 start, stride, count, NULL);          memspace hyperslab
50    return memspace;
51  }
52
53  void hdf5_file_finalize(hid_t *memspace, hid_t *filespace){
54    H5Sclose(*memspace);
55    *memspace = H5S_NULL;
56    H5Sclose(*filespace);
57    *filespace = H5S_NULL;
58  }
```

In listing 16.5, we used the same pattern when creating the two dataspaces: create the data object, set the data size arguments, and then select a rectangular region of the array. First, we created the global array space with the H5Screate_simple call. For the file dataspace, we set the dimensions to the global array size of nx_global and ny_global on line 23 and then used those sizes on line 25 to create the dataspace. We then selected a region of the file dataspace for each processor with the H5Sselect_hyperslab calls on lines 32 and 48. A similar process is then done for the memory dataspace.

Now that we have the dataspaces, the process of writing out the data into the file is straightforward. We open the file, create the dataset, and write it. If there are more datasets, we continue to write these out, and when finished, we close the file. The following listing shows how this is done.

Listing 16.6   Writing to an HDF5 file

```
HDF5Examples/hdf5block2d/hdf5_file_ops.c
60 void write_hdf5_file(const char *filename, double **data1,
61     hid_t memspace, hid_t filespace, MPI_Comm mpi_hdf5_comm) {
62   hid_t file_identifier = create_hdf5_file(
       filename, mpi_hdf5_comm);                         Calls the subroutine
63                                                         to create the file
64   // Create property list for collective dataset write.
65   hid_t xfer_plist = H5Pcreate(H5P_DATASET_XFER);
66   H5Pset_dxpl_mpio(xfer_plist, H5FD_MPIO_COLLECTIVE);
67                                                         Calls the subroutine
68   hid_t dataset1 = create_hdf5_dataset(                to create the dataset
       file_identifier, filespace);
69   //hid_t dataset2 = create_hdf5_dataset(file_identifier, filespace);
70
71   // write the data to disk using both the memory space
     //   and the data space.
72   H5Dwrite(dataset1, H5T_IEEE_F64LE,                   Writes the
       memspace, filespace, xfer_plist,                  dataset
73       &(data1[0][0]));
74   //H5Dwrite(dataset2, H5T_IEEE_F64LE,
     //       memspace, filespace, xfer_plist,
75   //       &(data2[0][0]));
76
77   H5Dclose(dataset1);
78   //H5Dclose(dataset2);
79
80   H5Pclose(xfer_plist);
81                                                        Closes the objects
82   H5Fclose(file_identifier);          <————            and the data file
83 }
84
85 hid_t create_hdf5_file(const char *filename, MPI_Comm mpi_hdf5_comm){
86   hid_t file_creation_plist = H5P_DEFAULT;
87   // set the file access template for parallel IO access
88   hid_t file_access_plist   = H5P_DEFAULT;             <——
89   file_access_plist = H5Pcreate(H5P_FILE_ACCESS);          Creates file
90                                                            access property
91   // set collective mode for metadata writes
92   H5Pset_coll_metadata_write(file_access_plist, true);
93                                                        Creates MPI
94   MPI_Info mpi_info = MPI_INFO_NULL;     <————         IO hints
95   MPI_Info_create(&mpi_info);
96   MPI_Info_set(mpi_info, "striping_factor", "8");
97   MPI_Info_set(mpi_info, "striping_unit", "4194304");
98
99   // tell the HDF5 library that we want to use MPI-IO to do the writing
100  H5Pset_fapl_mpio(file_access_plist, mpi_hdf5_comm, mpi_info);
101
102  // Open the file collectively
103  // H5F_ACC_TRUNC - overwrite existing file.
     //    H5F_ACC_EXCL - no overwrite
104  // 3rd argument is file creation property list. Using default here
105  // 4th argument is the file access property list identifier
```

Creates file creation property list

```
106    hid_t file_identifier = H5Fcreate(filename,
107       H5F_ACC_TRUNC, file_creation_plist,
          file_access_plist);
108
109    // release the file access template
110    H5Pclose(file_access_plist);
111    MPI_Info_free(&mpi_info);
112
113    return file_identifier;
114 }
115
116 hid_t create_hdf5_dataset(hid_t file_identifier, hid_t filespace){
117    // create the dataset
118    hid_t link_creation_plist    = H5P_DEFAULT;
119    hid_t dataset_creation_plist = H5P_DEFAULT;
120    hid_t dataset_access_plist   = H5P_DEFAULT;
121    hid_t dataset = H5Dcreate2(
122       file_identifier,           // Arg 1: file identifier
123       "data array",              // Arg 2: dataset name
124       H5T_IEEE_F64LE,            // Arg 3: datatype identifier
125       filespace,                 // Arg 4: filespace identifier
126       link_creation_plist,       // Arg 5: link creation property list
127       dataset_creation_plist,    // Arg 6: dataset creation property list
128       dataset_access_plist);     // Arg 7: dataset access property list
129
130    return dataset;
131 }
```

HDF5 routine creates the file. (lines 106–107)

Creates the link creation property list (line 118)

Creates the dataset creation property list (line 118)

Creates the dataset access property list (line 120)

HDF5 routine creates the dataset. (line 121)

In listing 16.6, the main write_hdf5_file routine uses the filespace dataspace that we created in listing 16.5. We then wrote out the dataset with the H5Dwrite routine on line 72, using both the memspace and filespace dataspaces. We also created and passed in a property list to tell HDF5 to use collective MPI-IO routines. Finally, on line 82, we closed the file. We also closed the property list and dataset on previous lines to avoid memory leaks. For the routine to create the file, we finally call H5Fcreate on line 106, but we need several lines to set up the hints. We wrapped the property list setup for the collective write and the MPI-IO hints along with the call and put these into a separate routine. We also took the same approach with the HDF5 call on line 121 for creating the dataset so we could detail the different property lists that you can use.

The routine to read the HDF5 data file, shown in the following listing, has the same basic pattern as the earlier write operation. The biggest difference between this listing and listing 16.6 is that there are fewer hints and attributes needed.

Listing 16.7   Reading an HDF5 file

```
HDF5Examples/hdf5block2d/hdf5_file_ops.c
135 void read_hdf5_file(const char *filename, double **data1,
136    hid_t memspace, hid_t filespace, MPI_Comm mpi_hdf5_comm) {
137    hid_t file_identifier =
          open_hdf5_file(filename, mpi_hdf5_comm);
138
139    // Create property list for collective dataset write.
```

Calls the subroutine to open the file (lines 137)

```
140    hid_t xfer_plist = H5Pcreate(H5P_DATASET_XFER);
141    H5Pset_dxpl_mpio(xfer_plist, H5FD_MPIO_COLLECTIVE);
142
143    hid_t dataset1 =
           open_hdf5_dataset(file_identifier);
144    // read the data from disk using both the memory space
       //    and the data space.
145    H5Dread(dataset1, H5T_IEEE_F64LE, memspace,
146      filespace, H5P_DEFAULT, &(data1[0][0]));
147    H5Dclose(dataset1);
148
149    H5Pclose(xfer_plist);
150
151    H5Fclose(file_identifier);
152 }
153
154 hid_t open_hdf5_file(const char *filename, MPI_Comm mpi_hdf5_comm){
155   // set the file access template for parallel IO access
156   hid_t file_access_plist = H5P_DEFAULT;   // File access property list
157   file_access_plist = H5Pcreate(H5P_FILE_ACCESS);
158
159   // set collective mode for metadata reads (ops)
160   H5Pset_all_coll_metadata_ops(file_access_plist, true);
161
162   // tell the HDF5 library that we want to use MPI-IO to do the reading
163   H5Pset_fapl_mpio(file_access_plist, mpi_hdf5_comm, MPI_INFO_NULL);
164
165   // Open the file collectively
166   // H5F_ACC_RDONLY - sets access to read or write
       //    on open of an existing file.
167   // 3rd argument is the file access property list identifier
168   hid_t file_identifier = H5Fopen(filename,
         H5F_ACC_RDONLY, file_access_plist);
169
170   // release the file access template
171   H5Pclose(file_access_plist);
172
173   return file_identifier;
174 }
175
176 hid_t open_hdf5_dataset(hid_t file_identifier){
177   // open the dataset
178   hid_t dataset_access_plist = H5P_DEFAULT;
179   hid_t dataset = H5Dopen2(
180     file_identifier,           // Arg 1: file identifier
181     "data array",              // Arg 2: dataset name to match for read
182     dataset_access_plist);     // Arg 3: dataset access property list
183
184   return dataset;
185 }
```

Callout annotations:
- **Calls the subroutine to create the dataset** (line 143)
- **Reads the dataset** (lines 145–146)
- **Closes the objects and the data file** (lines 149–151)
- **HDF5 routine opens the file.** (line 168)
- **Creates dataset access property list** (line 178)
- **HDF5 routine creates the dataset.** (line 179)

Because the file already exists, we use an open call on line 168 in listing 16.7 to specify read-only mode. (Using read-only mode allows additional optimizations.) The accessed file already has some attributes that were specified during the write. Some of these attributes do not need to be specified in the read. The HDF5 listings so far might comprise a general-purpose library within an application. The next listing shows the calls that would be placed at different points in the main application.

> **Listing 16.8   Main application file**

```
HDF5Examples/hdf5block2d/hdf5block2d.c
52    hid_t memspace = H5S_NULL, filespace = H5S_NULL;
53    hdf5_file_init(ng, ndims, ny_global,           Sets up the memory
          nx_global, ny, nx, ny_offset, nx_offset,   and file dataspaces
54        mpi_hdf5_comm, &memspace, &filespace);
55
56    char filename[30];
57    if (ncolors > 1) {
58      sprintf(filename,"example_%02d.hdf5",color);
59    } else {
60      sprintf(filename,"example.hdf5");
61    }
62
63    // Do the computation and write out a sequence of files
64    write_hdf5_file(filename, data, memspace,        Writes the
                      filespace, mpi_hdf5_comm);       HDF5 data file
65    // Read back the data for verifying the file operations
66    read_hdf5_file(filename, data_restore,           Reads in the data from
          memspace, filespace, mpi_hdf5_comm);         the HDF5 data file
67
68    hdf5_file_finalize(&memspace, &filespace);   ◄——  Frees the dataspace
                                                        objects
```

In listing 16.8, the initialization operation to set up the dataspaces on line 53 can be done once, at the start of your program. Then you might write out the data in your program at periodic intervals for graphics and checkpointing. The read would then typically be done when restarting from a checkpoint at the start of a run. Lastly, the finalize call should be done at the end of the program before terminating the calculation. Now to compile and run the example. The build is a standard CMake build. We'll run it on four processors:

```
mkdir build && cd build
cmake ..
make
mpirun -n 4 ./hdf5block2d
```

In a single install, the HDF5 package can be either installed as a parallel or as a serial version but not both. A common problem is to link the wrong version into your application. We added some special code to the CMake build system to preferentially select a parallel version as the next listing shows. The program then fails if the HDF5 version is not parallel so that we don't get an error during the build.

Listing 16.9   Checking for a parallel HDF5 package

```
HDF5Examples/hdf5block2d/CMakeLists.txt
14 set(HDF5_PREFER_PARALLEL true)
15 find_package(HDF5 1.10.1 REQUIRED)
16 if (NOT HDF5_IS_PARALLEL)
17     message(FATAL_ERROR " -- HDF5 version is not parallel.")
18 endif (NOT HDF5_IS_PARALLEL)
```

The example code does a verification test to check that the data read back from the file is the same as the data that we started with. We can also use the h5dump utility to print the data in the file. You can use the following command to look at your data file. Figure 16.6 shows the output from the command.

```
h5dump -y example.hdf5
```

```
HDF5 "example.hdf5" {
GROUP "/" {
   DATASET "data array" {
      DATATYPE  H5T_IEEE_F64LE
      DATASPACE  SIMPLE { ( 10, 40 ) / ( 10, 40 ) }
      DATA {
         1, 2, 3, 4, 5, 6, 7, 8, 9, 10, 101, 102, 103, 104, 105, 106, 107, 108,
         109, 110, 201, 202, 203, 204, 205, 206, 207, 208, 209, 210, 301, 302,
         303, 304, 305, 306, 307, 308, 309, 310,
         11, 12, 13, 14, 15, 16, 17, 18, 19, 20, 111, 112, 113, 114, 115, 116,
         117, 118, 119, 120, 211, 212, 213, 214, 215, 216, 217, 218, 219, 220,
         311, 312, 313, 314, 315, 316, 317, 318, 319, 320,
         21, 22, 23, 24, 25, 26, 27, 28, 29, 30, 121, 122, 123, 124, 125, 126,
         127, 128, 129, 130, 221, 222, 223, 224, 225, 226, 227, 228, 229, 230,
         321, 322, 323, 324, 325, 326, 327, 328, 329, 330,
         31, 32, 33, 34, 35, 36, 37, 38, 39, 40, 131, 132, 133, 134, 135, 136,
         137, 138, 139, 140, 231, 232, 233, 234, 235, 236, 237, 238, 239, 240,
         331, 332, 333, 334, 335, 336, 337, 338, 339, 340,
         41, 42, 43, 44, 45, 46, 47, 48, 49, 50, 141, 142, 143, 144, 145, 146,
         147, 148, 149, 150, 241, 242, 243, 244, 245, 246, 247, 248, 249, 250,
         341, 342, 343, 344, 345, 346, 347, 348, 349, 350,
         51, 52, 53, 54, 55, 56, 57, 58, 59, 60, 151, 152, 153, 154, 155, 156,
         157, 158, 159, 160, 251, 252, 253, 254, 255, 256, 257, 258, 259, 260,
         351, 352, 353, 354, 355, 356, 357, 358, 359, 360,
         61, 62, 63, 64, 65, 66, 67, 68, 69, 70, 161, 162, 163, 164, 165, 166,
         167, 168, 169, 170, 261, 262, 263, 264, 265, 266, 267, 268, 269, 270,
         361, 362, 363, 364, 365, 366, 367, 368, 369, 370,
         71, 72, 73, 74, 75, 76, 77, 78, 79, 80, 171, 172, 173, 174, 175, 176,
         177, 178, 179, 180, 271, 272, 273, 274, 275, 276, 277, 278, 279, 280,
         371, 372, 373, 374, 375, 376, 377, 378, 379, 380,
         81, 82, 83, 84, 85, 86, 87, 88, 89, 90, 181, 182, 183, 184, 185, 186,
         187, 188, 189, 190, 281, 282, 283, 284, 285, 286, 287, 288, 289, 290,
         381, 382, 383, 384, 385, 386, 387, 388, 389, 390,
         91, 92, 93, 94, 95, 96, 97, 98, 99, 100, 191, 192, 193, 194, 195, 196,
         197, 198, 199, 200, 291, 292, 293, 294, 295, 296, 297, 298, 299, 300,
         391, 392, 393, 394, 395, 396, 397, 398, 399, 400
      }
   }
}
}
```

Figure 16.6   Using the h5dump command-line utility shows what is contained in the HDF5 file without having to write any code.

16.5 *Other parallel file software packages*

In this section, we briefly cover a couple of the more common parallel file software packages: PnetCDF and Adios. PnetCDF, short for Parallel Network Common Data Form, is another self-describing data format that is popular in the Earth Systems community and among organizations funded by the National Science Foundation (NSF). While originally a completely separate software source, the parallel version is built on top of HDF5 and MPI-IO. The decision of whether to use PnetCDF or HDF5 is strongly influenced by your community. Because the files generated by your application are often used by others, using the same data standard is important.

ADIOS, or the Adaptable Input/Output System, is also a self-describing data format from Oak Ridge National Laboratory (ORNL). ADIOS has its own native binary format, but it can also use HDF5, MPI-IO, and other file-storage software.

16.6 *Parallel filesystem: The hardware interface*

With increasing data demands, more complex filesystems become necessary. In this section, we will introduce these parallel filesystems. A parallel filesystem can greatly speed up file writes and reads by spreading out the operations across several hard disks with multiple file writers or readers. While we now have some parallelism at the filesystem, it is not a simple situation. There is still a mismatch between the application parallelism and the parallelism provided by the filesystem. Because of this, the management of the parallel operations is complex and highly dependent on the hardware configurations and application demands. To deal with the complexity, many of the parallel filesystems use an object-based file structure. Object-based filesystems are a natural fit for these challenges. But the performance and robustness of the parallel filesystem is often limited by the metadata describing the locations of the file data.

> **DEFINITION**   *Object-based filesystem* is a system that's organized based on objects rather than on files in a folder. An object-based filesystem requires a database or metadata to store all the information describing the object.

The writing of parallel file operations is highly intertwined with the parallel filesystem software. This requires the knowledge of which parallel filesystem is being used and the settings available for that installation and filesystem. Tuning your parallel file software can sometimes yield significant performance gains.

16.6.1 *Everything you wanted to know about your parallel file setup but didn't know how to ask*

As you get into the interaction of the parallel file operations with the filesystem, it is helpful to see more information about the parallel library settings. The settings can be set differently for each installation. You can also get some high-level statistics that can help with debugging performance issues.

Most MPI-IO libraries are one of two implementations, either ROMIO, which is distributed with MPICH and many system vendor implementations, or OMPIO, which is the default on newer versions of OpenMPI. Let's first go over how to get information from OpenMPI's OMPIO plugin or how to switch back to using ROMIO. To extract information on OpenMPI's OMPIO settings, use the following commands:

- `--mca io [ompio|romio]`
  Specifies the IO plugin, either OMPIO or ROMIO. Older releases use ROMIO as the default plugin, while OMPIO is the default on newer releases.
- `ompi_info --param <component> <plugin> --level <int>`
  Displays information on the local OpenMPI configuration for that plugin.
- `--mca io_ompio_verbose_info_parsing 1`
  Shows the hints parsed from a program's `MPI_Info_set` calls.

First, you can get the names of the IO plugins with the `ompi_info` command. We just want the IO component plugins, so we filter the output for these:

```
ompi_info |grep "MCA io:"
MCA io: romio321 (MCA v2.1.0, API v2.0.0, Component v4.0.3)
MCA io: ompio (MCA v2.1.0, API v2.0.0, Component v4.0.3)
```

Then you can get the individual settings available for each plugin. Using the `ompi_info` command, we get the following abbreviated output:

```
ompi_info --param io ompio --level 9 | grep ": parameter"

MCA io ompio: parameter "io_ompio_priority" (current value: "30" …
MCA io ompio: parameter "io_ompio_delete_priority" (current value: "30" …
MCA io ompio: parameter "io_ompio_record_file_offset_info" (current value: "0" …
MCA io ompio: parameter "io_ompio_coll_timing_info" (current value: "1" …
MCA io ompio: parameter "io_ompio_cycle_buffer_size" (current value: "536870912" …
MCA io ompio: parameter "io_ompio_bytes_per_agg" (current value: "33554432" …
MCA io ompio: parameter "io_ompio_num_aggregators" (current value: "-1" …
MCA io ompio: parameter "io_ompio_grouping_option" (current value: "5" …
MCA io ompio: parameter "io_ompio_max_aggregators_ratio" (current value: "8" …
MCA io ompio: parameter "io_ompio_aggregators_cutoff_threshold" (current value: "3"
    …
MCA io ompio: parameter "io_ompio_overwrite_amode" (current value: "1" …
MCA io ompio: parameter "io_ompio_verbose_info_parsing" (current value: "0"
...
```

You can also verify how the `MPI_Info_set` calls are interpreted by the MPI-IO library with the following run-time option. This can be a good way to check that your code is correctly written for your filesystem and parallel file operation libraries.

```
mpirun --mca io_ompio_verbose_info_parsing 1 -n 4 ./mpi_io_block2d
File: example.data info: collective_buffering value true enforcing using
    individual fcoll component
< ... repeated three more times ... >
```

For the ROMIO parallel file software included with MPICH, we have different mechanisms to query the software installation. Cray adds some additional environment variables for their implementations of ROMIO. We'll list some of these and then see examples that use these.

- ROMIO recognizes the following hint:
  - ROMIO_PRINT_HINTS=1
- Cray provides these additional environment variables:
  - MPICH_MPIIO_HINTS_DISPLAY=1
  - MPICH_MPIIO_STATS=1
  - MPICH_MPIIO_TIMERS=1

The following shows the output when using ROMIO_PRINT_HINTS:

```
export ROMIO_PRINT_HINTS=1; mpirun -n 4 ./mpi_io_block2d
key = cb_buffer_size            value = 16777216
key = romio_cb_read             value = automatic
key = romio_cb_write            value = automatic
key = cb_nodes                  value = 1
key = romio_no_indep_rw         value = false
key = romio_cb_pfr             value = disable
key = romio_cb_fr_types        value = aar
key = romio_cb_fr_alignment    value = 1
key = romio_cb_ds_threshold    value = 0
key = romio_cb_alltoall        value = automatic
key = ind_rd_buffer_size        value = 4194304
key = ind_wr_buffer_size        value = 524288
key = romio_ds_read             value = automatic
key = romio_ds_write            value = automatic
key = striping_unit             value = 4194304
key = cb_config_list            value = *:1
key = romio_filesystem_type     value = NFS:
key = romio_aggregator_list     value = 0
key = cb_buffer_size            value = 16777216
key = romio_cb_read             value = automatic
key = romio_cb_write            value = automatic
key = cb_nodes                  value = 1
key = romio_no_indep_rw         value = false
key = romio_cb_pfr             value = disable
key = romio_cb_fr_types        value = aar
key = romio_cb_fr_alignment    value = 1
key = romio_cb_ds_threshold    value = 0
key = romio_cb_alltoall        value = automatic
key = ind_rd_buffer_size        value = 4194304
key = ind_wr_buffer_size        value = 524288
key = romio_ds_read             value = automatic
key = romio_ds_write            value = automatic
key = cb_config_list            value = *:1
key = romio_filesystem_type     value = NFS:
key = romio_aggregator_list     value = 0

export MPICH_MPIIO_HINTS_DISPLAY=1; srun -n 4 ./mpi_io_block2d
PE 0: MPICH MPIIO environment settings:
PE 0:    MPICH_MPIIO_HINTS_DISPLAY                 = 1
PE 0:    MPICH_MPIIO_HINTS                         = NULL
```

```
PE 0:    MPICH_MPIIO_ABORT_ON_RW_ERROR          = disable
PE 0:    MPICH_MPIIO_CB_ALIGN                   = 2
PE 0:    MPICH_MPIIO_DVS_MAXNODES               = -1
PE 0:    MPICH_MPIIO_AGGREGATOR_PLACEMENT_DISPLAY  = 0
PE 0:    MPICH_MPIIO_AGGREGATOR_PLACEMENT_STRIDE   = -1
PE 0:    MPICH_MPIIO_MAX_NUM_IRECV              = 50
PE 0:    MPICH_MPIIO_MAX_NUM_ISEND              = 50
PE 0:    MPICH_MPIIO_MAX_SIZE_ISEND             = 10485760
PE 0: MPICH MPIIO statistics environment settings:
PE 0:    MPICH_MPIIO_STATS                      = 0
PE 0:    MPICH_MPIIO_TIMERS                     = 0
PE 0:    MPICH_MPIIO_WRITE_EXIT_BARRIER         = 1
MPIIO WARNING: DVS stripe width of 8 was requested but DVS set it to 1
See MPICH_MPIIO_DVS_MAXNODES in the intro_mpi man page.
PE 0: MPIIO hints for example.data:
         cb_buffer_size             = 16777216
         romio_cb_read              = automatic
         romio_cb_write             = automatic
         cb_nodes                   = 1
         cb_align                   = 2
         romio_no_indep_rw          = false
         romio_cb_pfr               = disable
         romio_cb_fr_types          = aar
         romio_cb_fr_alignment      = 1
         romio_cb_ds_threshold      = 0
         romio_cb_alltoall          = automatic
         ind_rd_buffer_size         = 4194304
         ind_wr_buffer_size         = 524288
         romio_ds_read              = disable
         romio_ds_write             = automatic
         striping_factor            = 1
         striping_unit              = 4194304
         direct_io                  = false
         aggregator_placement_stride = -1
         abort_on_rw_error          = disable
         cb_config_list             = *:*
         romio_filesystem_type      = CRAY ADIO:

export MPICH_MPIIO_STATS=1; srun -n 4 ./mpi_io_block2d
+----------------------------------------------------------+
| MPIIO write access patterns for example.data
|    independent writes      = 0
|    collective writes       = 4
|    independent writers      = 0
|    aggregators             = 1
|    stripe count            = 1
|    stripe size             = 4194304
|    system writes           = 2
|    stripe sized writes      = 0
|    aggregators active       = 4,0,0,0 (1, <= 1, > 1, 1)
|    total bytes for writes   = 3600
|    ave system write size    = 1800
|    read-modify-write count  = 0
|    read-modify-write bytes  = 0
|    number of write gaps     = 0
```

```
|   ave write gap size      = NA
| See "Optimizing MPI I/O on Cray XE Systems" S-0013-20 for explanations.
+--------------------------------------------------------+
+--------------------------------------------------------+
| MPIIO read access patterns for example.data
|   independent reads       = 0
|   collective reads        = 4
|   independent readers     = 0
|   aggregators             = 1
|   stripe count            = 1
|   stripe size             = 524288
|   system reads            = 1
|   stripe sized reads      = 0
|   total bytes for reads   = 3200
|   ave system read size    = 3200
|   number of read gaps      = 0
|   ave read gap size       = NA
| See "Optimizing MPI I/O on Cray XE Systems" S-0013-20 for explanations.
+--------------------------------------------------------+
```

16.6.2   *General hints that apply to all filesystems*

It is sometimes useful to give some hints about the type of file operations you will use in your application. You can modify the parallel file settings with environment variables, a hints file, or at run time with `MPI_Info_set`. This provides the appropriate method for handling different scenarios if you don't have access to the program source to add the `MPI_Info_set` command. To set parallel file options in this case, use the following commands:

- Cray MPICH

  ```
  MPICH_MPIIO_HINTS="*:<key>=<value>:<key>=<value>
  ```

  For example

  ```
  export MPICH_MPIIO_HINTS=\
     "*:striping_factor=8:striping_unit=4194304"
  ```

- ROMIO

  ```
  ROMIO_HINTS=<filename>
  ```

  For example: `ROMIO_HINTS=romio-hints`

  where the romio-hints file includes

  ```
  striping_factor 8       // file is broken into 8 parts and
                          // is written in parallel to 8 disks
  striping_unit 4194304   // the size in bytes of each
                          // block to be written
  ```

- OpenMPI OMPI

  ```
  OMPI_MCA_<param_name> <value>
  ```

  For example: export `OMPI_MCA_io_ompio_verbose_info_parsing=1`

The OpenMPI mca run-time option as an argument to the mpirun command is

```
mpirun --mca io_ompio_verbose_info_parsing 1 -n 4 <exec>
```

The default location of the OpenMPI file is in $HOME/.openmpi/mca-params.conf or it can be set with the following:

```
--tune <filename>
mpirun --tune mca-params.conf -n 2 <exec>
```

The most important hint that you can set is whether to use collective operations or data sieving. We'll first look at the collective operations and then the data sieving operations.

Collective operations harness MPI collective communication calls and use a two-phase I/O approach that collects the data for aggregators that then write or read from your file. Use the following commands for collective I/O:

- ROMIO and OMPIO
  - cb_buffer_size=integer specifies the buffer size in bytes for a two-phase collective I/O. It should be a multiple of the page size.
  - cb_nodes=integer sets the maximum number of aggregators.
- ROMIO only
  - romio_cb_read=[enable|automatic|disable] specifies when to use collective buffering for reads.
  - romio_cb_write=[enable|automatic|disable] specifies when to use collective buffering for writes.
  - cb_config_list=*:<integer> sets the number of aggregators per node.
  - romio_no_indep_rw=[true|false] specifies whether to use any independent I/O. If none are allowed, no file operations (including file open) will be done on non-aggregator nodes.
- OMPIO only
  - collective_buffering=[true|false] uses collective operations when writing from a parallel job to the filesystem.

Data sieving does a single read (or write), spanning a file block and then parcels out the data to the individual process reads. This avoids a lot of smaller reads and the contention between file readers that might occur. Use the following commands for data sieving with ROMIO:

- romio_ds_read=[enable|automatic|disable]
- romio_ds_write=[enable|automatic|disable]
- ind_rd_buffer_size=integer (bytes for read buffer)
- ind_wr_buffer_size=integer (bytes for write buffer)

16.6.3 *Hints specific to particular filesystems*

Some hints only apply to a particular filesystem, such as Lustre or GPFS. We can detect the filesystem type from within our program and set the appropriate hints for the filesystem. The fs_detect.c program in the examples does this. This program uses the `statfs` command as the next listing shows and you can find it in the examples directory for this chapter.

Listing 16.10   Filesystem detection program

```
MPI_IO_Examples/mpi_io_block2d/fs_detect.c
 1 #include <stdio.h>
 2 #ifdef __APPLE_CC__
 3 #include <sys/mount.h>
 4 #else
 5 #include <sys/statfs.h>
 6 #endif
 7 // Filesystem types are listed in the system
   //    include directory in linux/magic.h
 8 // You will need to add any additional
   //    parallel filesystem magic codes
 9 #define LUSTRE_MAGIC1        0x858458f6
10 #define LUSTRE_MAGIC2        0xbd00bd0
11 #define GPFS_SUPER_MAGIC     0x47504653
12 #define PVFS2_SUPER_MAGIC    0x20030528
13 #define PAN_KERNEL_FS_CLIENT_SUPER_MAGIC   \
                          0xAAD7AAEA
14
15 int main(int argc, char *argv[])
16 {
17   struct statfs buf;
18   statfs("./fs_detect", &buf);
19   printf("File system type is %lx\n",buf.f_type);
20 }
```

> **Magic numbers for parallel filesystem type** (lines 9–13)

> **Gets filesystem type** (line 18)

We included the magic number for some of the parallel filesystems in this listing. When using this for other applications, replace the filename on line 18 with an appropriate filename for the directory where your files are written. Build the fs_detect program and then run the following command to get the filesystem type:

```
mkdir build && cd build
cmake ..
make
grep `./fs_detect | cut -f 4 -d' '` /usr/include/linux/magic.h ../fs_detect.c
```

Now we are ready for the filesystem-specific hints. We don't list all the possible hints. You can get the current list by using the commands previously shown.

LUSTRE FILESYSTEM: THE MOST COMMON FILESYSTEM IN HIGH PERFORMANCE COMPUTING CENTERS
Lustre is the dominant filesystem on the largest high performance computing systems. Originating at Carnegie Mellon University, its primary development and ownership has been passed through Intel, HP, Sun, Oracle, Intel, Whamcloud, and others.

In this process, it has passed from commercial to open source and back. Currently it is under the Open Scalable File Systems (OpenSFS) and European Open File Systems (EOFS) banners.

Lustre is built on the concept of object storage with Object Storage Servers (OSSs) and Object Storage Targets (OSTs). When we specify a `striping_factor` of 8 on line 56 of listing 16.2 and line 96 of listing 16.6, we are telling the ROMIO library to use Lustre to break up the writes (and reads) into eight pieces and send them to eight OSTs, effectively writing out the data in eight-way parallelism. The `striping_unit` hint tells ROMIO and Lustre to use 4 MiB stripe sizes. Lustre also has Metadata Servers (MDS) and Metadata Targets (MDT) to store the critical descriptions of where each part of the file is stored. For striping operations, use the following:

- MPICH (ROMIO)
  - `striping_unit=<integer>` sets the stripe size in bytes.
  - `striping_factor=<integer>` sets the number of stripes, where `-1` is automatic.
- OpenMPI (OMPIO)
  - `fs_lustre_stripe_size=<integer>` sets the stripe size in bytes.
  - `fs_lustre_stripe_width=<integer>` sets the number of stripes, where `-1` is automatic.

We can confirm the Lustre parameters for OpenMPI with a command-line query:

```
ompi_info --param fs lustre --level 9
MCA fs lustre: parameter "fs_lustre_priority" (current value: "20" …
MCA fs lustre: parameter "fs_lustre_stripe_size" (current value: "0" …
MCA fs lustre: parameter "fs_lustre_stripe_width" (current value: "0" …
```

GPFS: A FILESYSTEM FROM IBM

IBM systems have the General Parallel File System (GPFS), also part of their Spectrum Scale product, that offers striping and parallel file operations on their systems. GPFS is an enterprise storage product with the corresponding support infrastructure and services. GPFS stripes across all available devices by default. The MPI hints may not have as much effect on this filesystem, however. For MPICH (ROMIO), use this command to help with large memory writes/reads:

```
IBM_largeblock_io=true
```

DATAWARP: A FILESYSTEM FROM CRAY

Cray's DataWarp integrates burst buffer hardware on top of another parallel filesystem, such as their version of Lustre. Taking advantage of burst buffers is still in its infancy, though, but Cray has been a leader in this effort.

PANASAS® : A COMMERCIAL FILESYSTEM REQUIRING FEWER HINTS FROM USERS

Panasas® is a commercial parallel filesystem that is composed of object storage and metadata servers. Panasas has also contributed to the extension to the Network File System

(NFS) to support parallel operations. Panasas was used in some of the top-ten computing systems at LANL, although it is not so prevalent there today. For MPICH (ROMIO), use these commands to set the strip size and the number of stripes, respectively:

- `panfs_layout_stripe_unit=<integer>`
- `panfs_layout_total_num_comps=<integer>`

ORANGEFS (PVFS): THE MOST POPULAR OPEN-SOURCE FILESYSTEM

OrangeFS, previously known as the Parallel Virtual File System (PVFS), is an open source parallel filesystem from Clemson University and Argonne National Laboratory. It is popular on Beowulf clusters. Besides being a scalable parallel filesystem, OrangeFS has been integrated into the Linux kernel. You can use the following commands for MPICH (ROMIO) to set the stripe size (in bytes) and to number the stripes (with –1 being automatic), respectively:

- `striping_unit=<integer>`
- `striping_factor=<integer>`

BEEGFS: A NEW OPEN SOURCE FILESYSTEM THAT IS GAINING IN POPULARITY

BeeGFS, formerly FhGFS, was developed at the Fraunhofer Center for High Performance Computing and is freely available. It is popular because of its open source characteristics.

DISTRIBUTED APPLICATION OBJECT STORAGE (DAOS): SETTING NEW BENCHMARKS FOR PERFORMANCE

Intel is developing their new, open source DAOS object-storage technology under the Department of Energy (DOE) FastForward program. DAOS ranks first in the 2020 ISC IO500 supercomputing file-speed list (https://www.vi4io.org). It's scheduled to be deployed on the Aurora supercomputer, Argonne National Laboratory's first exascale computing system, in 2021. DAOS is supported in the ROMIO MPI-IO library, available with MPICH, and is portable to other MPI libraries.

WEKAIO: A NEWCOMER FROM THE BIG DATA COMMUNITY

WekaIO is a fully POSIX-compliant filesystem that provides a large shared namespace with highly optimized performance, low latency, and high bandwidth, and uses the latest solid-state hardware components. WekaIO is an attractive filesystem for applications that require large amounts of high-performing data file manipulation and is popular in the big data community. WekaIO took top honors in the 2019 SC IO500 supercomputing file speed list.

CEPH FILESYSTEM: AN OPEN SOURCE DISTRIBUTED STORAGE SYSTEM

Ceph originated at Lawrence Livermore National Laboratory. The development is now led by RedHat for a consortium of industrial partners and has been integrated into the Linux kernel.

NETWORK FILESYSTEM (NFS): THE MOST COMMON NETWORK FILESYSTEM

NFS is the dominant cluster filesystem for the networks in local organizations. It is not a recommended system for highly parallel file operations, although with the proper settings, it functions correctly.

16.7 Further explorations

Much of the current documentation on parallel file operations is in presentations and academic conferences. One of the best conferences is the Parallel Data Systems Workshop (PDSW), held in conjunction with The International Conference for High Performance Computing, Networking, Storage, and Analysis (otherwise known as the yearly Supercomputing Conference).

You can use the micro benchmarks, IOR and mdtest, to check the best performance of a filesystem. The software is documented at https://ior.readthedocs.io/en/latest/ and hosted by LLNL at https://github.com/hpc/ior.

16.7.1 Additional reading

The addition of the MPI-IO functions to MPI is described in the following text. It remains one of the best descriptions of MPI-IO.

William Gropp, Rajeev Thakur, and Ewing Lusk. *Using MPI-2: Advanced Features of the Message Passing Interface* (MIT Press, 1999).

There are a couple of good books on writing high performance parallel file operations. We recommend the following:

- Prabhat and Quincey Koziol, editors, *High Performance Parallel I/O* (Chapman and Hall/CRC, 2014).
- John M. May, *Parallel I/O for High Performance Computing* (Morgan Kaufmann, 2001).

The HDF Group maintains the authoritative website on HDF5. You can get more information at

The HDF Group, https://portal.hdfgroup.org/display/HDF5/HDF5.

NetCDF remains popular within certain HPC application segments. You can get more information on this format at the NetCDF site hosted by Unidata. Unidata is one of the University Corporation for Atmospheric Research (UCAR)'s Community Programs (UCP).

Unidata, https://www.unidata.ucar.edu/software/netcdf/.

A parallel version of NetCDF, PnetCDF, was developed by Northwestern University and Argonne National Laboratory independently from Unidata. More information on PnetCDF is at their GitHub documentation site:

Northwestern University and Argonne National Laboratory, https://parallel-netcdf.github.io.

ADIOS is one of the leading parallel file operations libraries maintained by a team led by Oak Ridge National Laboratory (ORNL). To learn more, see their documentation at the following website:

Oak Ridge National Laboratory, https://adios2.readthedocs.io/en/latest/index.html.

Some good presentations on tuning performance for filesystems include

- Philippe Wautelet, "Best practices for parallel IO and MPI-IO hints" (CRNS/ IDRIS, 2015), http://www.idris.fr/media/docs/docu/idris/idris_patc_hints_ proj.pdf.
- George Markomanolis, ORNL Spectrum Scale (GPFS) https://www.olcf.ornl .gov/wp-content/uploads/2018/12/spectrum_scale_summit_workshop.pdf.

16.7.2 Exercises

1 Check for the hints available on your system using the techniques described in section 16.6.1.
2 Try the MPI–IO and HDF5 examples on your system with much larger datasets to see what performance you can achieve. Compare that to the IOR micro benchmark for extra credit.
3 Use the h5ls and h5dump utilities to explore the HDF5 data file created by the HDF5 example.

Summary

- There is a proper way to handle standard file operations for parallel applications. The simple techniques introduced in this chapter, where all IO is performed from the first processor, are sufficient for modest parallel applications.
- The use of MPI-IO is an important building block for parallel file operations. MPI-IO can dramatically speed up the writing and reading of files.
- There are advantages of using the self-describing parallel HDF5 software. The HDF5 format can improve how your application manages data while also getting fast file operations.
- There are ways to query and set the hints for the parallel file software and filesystem. This can improve your file writing and reading performance on particular systems.

Tools and resources
for better code

This chapter covers
- Potential tools for your development toolbelt
- Various resources to guide your application development
- Common tools to work on large computing sites

Why a whole chapter on tools and resources? Though we've mentioned tools and resources in previous chapters, this chapter further discusses the wide variety and alternatives available to high-performance computing programmers. From version control systems to debugging, the available capabilities, whether commercial or open source, are essential to enable the rapid iterations of parallel application development. Nonetheless, these tools are not mandatory. Having an understanding of and embedding these into your workflow often yields tremendous benefits, far outweighing the time spent learning how to use them.

Tools are an important piece of the high-performance computing development process. Not every tool works on every system; therefore, availability of alternatives is important. In the previous chapters, we wanted to focus on the process and not get bogged down in the details of how to use every possible tool. We chose to present the simplest, most available tool for each need. We also preferred the command-line and text-based tools over the fancy graphical interface tools because using graphics interfaces over slow networks can be difficult or even impossible. Graphical tools also tend to be more vendor- or system-centric and often change. Despite these drawbacks, we include many of these vendor tools in this chapter because they can greatly improve your code development for high-performance computing applications.

Resources such as a wide variety of benchmark applications, are valuable because applications don't come in just one flavor. For these specialized application domains, we need more appropriate benchmarks and mini-apps that explore the best approach for algorithm development and the right programming pattern for each architecture. We strongly recommend that you learn from these resources rather than reinventing the techniques from scratch. For most of the tools, we give brief instructions on installation and where to find some documentation. We also provide more detail in the companion code for this chapter at https://github.com/EssentialsofParallelComputing/Chapter17.

We are strongly vendor-agnostic and stress portability as well. Although we cover a lot of tools, it just isn't possible to go into detail on all of them. In addition, the rate of change for these tools exceeds that of the rest of the high-performance computing ecosystem. History has shown that the support for good tool development is fickle. Thus, the tools come and go and change ownership more quickly than documentation can be updated.

For a quick reference, table 17.1 provides a summary of the tools we cover in this chapter. These are shown in their corresponding categories to help you find the best tools for your needs. We included a wide variety of tools because there may be only one that works on a particular hardware or operating system or may have specialized capabilities. We have chosen to give more details on some of the simpler, more useful and commonly used tools in the following sections of this chapter as indicated in the table.

Table 17.1   Summary of tools covered in this chapter

17.1 Version control systems	17.1.1 Centralized version control	Subversion CVS
	17.1.2 Distributed version control	Git Mercurial
17.2 Timer routines	`clock_gettime` (with a `CLOCK_MONOTONIC` type) `clock_gettime` (with a `CLOCK_REALTIME` type) `gettimeofday` `getrusage` `host_get_clock_service` (for MacOS C++ high resolution clock)	
17.3 Profilers	17.3.1 Simple text-based profilers	Likwid gprof gperftools timemory Open|SpeedShop

Table 17.1 Summary of tools covered in this chapter

	17.3.2 High-level profilers	Kcachegrind Arm MAP
	17.3.3 Medium-level profilers	Intel® Advisor Intel® Vtune CrayPat AMD µProf NVIDIA Visual Profiler CodeXL
	17.3.4 Detailed profilers	HPCToolkit Open|SpeedShop TAU
17.5 Memory error tools	Free software	17.5.1 Valgrind 17.5.2 Dr. Memory
	17.5.3 Commercial software	Purify Insure++ Intel® Inspector TotalView memory checker
	17.5.4 Compiler-based	MemorySanitizer (LLVM) AddressSanitizer (LLVM) ThreadSanitizer (LLVM) mtrace (GCC)
	17.5.5 Out-of-bounds checkers	Dmalloc Electric Fence Memwatch
	17.5.6 GPU memory tools	CUDA-MEMCHECK
17.6 Thread checkers	17.6.1 Intel® Inspector 17.6.2 Archer	
17.7 Debuggers	Commercial	17.7.1 TotalView 17.7.2 ARM DDT
	17.7.3 Linux debuggers	GDB cgdb DDD
	17.7.4 GPU debuggers	CUDA-GDB ROCgdb
17.8 File operation profiler	Darshan	
17.9 Package managers	17.9.1 MacOS	Homebrew MacPorts
	17.9.2 HPC	Spack
17.10 Modules	17.10.1 Modules 17.10.2 Lmod	

17.1   *Version control systems: It all begins here*

Version control for software is one of the most basic of software engineering practices and critically important when developing parallel applications. We covered the role of version control in parallel application development in section 2.1.1. Here, we go into more detail on the various version control systems and their characteristics. Version control systems can be broken down into two major categories, distributed and centralized, as figure 17.1 shows.

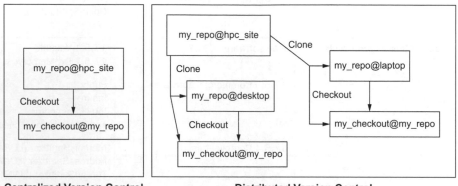

Centralized Version Control   Distributed Version Control

Figure 17.1   Selecting a type of version control is dependent on your work pattern. Centralized version control is for when everyone is at a location with access to a single server. Distributed version control gives you a full copy of your repository on your laptop and desktop and allows you to go worldwide and mobile.

In a centralized version control system there is just one central repository. This requires a connection to the repository site to do any operations on the repository. In a distributed version control system, various commands, such as `clone`, create a duplicate (remote) version of the repository and a checkout of the source. You can commit your changes to your local version of the repository while traveling, then push or merge the changes into the main repository at a later time. No wonder distributed version control systems have gained popularity in recent years. That said, these also come with another layer of complexity.

17.1.1   *Distributed version control fits the more mobile world*

Many code teams are scattered across the globe or on the move all the time. For them, a distributed version control system makes the most sense. The two most common freely-available distributed version control systems are Git and Mercurial. There are several other smaller distributed version control systems as well. All of these implementations support a variety of developer workflows.

Despite claims to be easy to learn, these are complex tools to fully understand and use properly. It would take a full book to cover each of these. Fortunately, there are many web tutorials and books that cover their use. A good starting point for Git resources is the Git SCM site: https://git-scm.com.

Mercurial is a bit simpler and has a cleaner design than Git. Additionally, the Mercurial website has a lot of tutorials to get you started.

- Mercurial at https://www.mercurial-scm.org/wiki/Mercurial
- Bryan O'Sullivan, *Mercurial: The Definitive Guide* (O'Reilly Media, 2009), http://hgbook.red-bean.com

There are also some commercially distributed version control systems. Perforce and ClearCase are the best known. With these products, you can get more support, which might be important for your organization.

17.1.2 *Centralized version control for simplicity and code security*

While there are many centralized version control systems that have been developed over a long history of software configuration management, the two most commonly used today are Concurrent Versions System (CVS) and Subversion (SVN). Both are a bit dated these days as interest has shifted towards distributed version control. If used in the proper way for a centralized repository, however, these are both effective and much simpler to use.

Centralized version control also provides better security for proprietary codes by having only one place where the repository needs to be protected. For this reason, centralized version control is still popular in the corporate environment, where limiting access to the source code history is of paramount importance. CVS has a simple branching operation that works well. There is documentation at the CVS website and a widely available book:

- CVS (Free Software Foundation, Inc., 1998) at https://www.nongnu.org/cvs/
- Per Cederqvist, *Version Management with CVS* (Network Theory Ltd, December, 2002), available at various sites online and in print

Subversion was developed as a replacement for CVS. Although in many respects, it is an improvement over CVS, the branching function is a bit weaker than that in CVS. There is a good book on Subversion and development is ongoing:

Ben Collins-Sussman, Brian W. Fitzpatrick, and C. Michael Pilato, *Version Control with Subversion* (Apache Software Foundation, 2002), http://svnbook.red-bean.com

17.2 *Timer routines for tracking code performance*

It is helpful to put internal timers into your application to track performance as you work on it. We show a representative timing routine in listings 17.1 and 17.2 that you can use in C, C++, and Fortran with a Fortran wrapper routine. This routine uses the `clock_gettime` routine with a `CLOCK_MONOTONIC` type to avoid problems with clock time adjustments.

Listing 17.1   Timer header file

```
timer.h
1 #ifndef TIMER_H
2 #define TIMER_H
3 #include <time.h>
4
5 void cpu_timer_start1(struct timespec *tstart_cpu);
6 double cpu_timer_stop1(struct timespec tstart_cpu);
7 #endif
```

Listing 17.2   Timer source file

```
timer.c
 1 #include <time.h>
 2 #include "timer.h"
 3
 4 void cpu_timer_start1(struct timespec *tstart_cpu)
 5 {
 6     clock_gettime(CLOCK_MONOTONIC, tstart_cpu);        ◁
 7 }
 8 double cpu_timer_stop1(struct timespec tstart_cpu)
 9 {
10     struct timespec tstop_cpu, tresult;
11     clock_gettime(CLOCK_MONOTONIC, &tstop_cpu);        ◁
12     tresult.tv_sec = tstop_cpu.tv_sec - tstart_cpu.tv_sec;
13     tresult.tv_nsec = tstop_cpu.tv_nsec - tstart_cpu.tv_nsec;
14     double result = (double)tresult.tv_sec +
                        (double)tresult.tv_nsec*1.0e-9;
15
16     return(result);
17 }
```

Calls clock_gettime requesting a monotonic clock

There are other timer implementations that you can use if you need an alternative routine. Portability is one reason you may want another implementation. The clock _gettime routine has been supported on the macOS since Sierra 10.12, which has helped with some of the portability issues.

ALTERNATIVE TIMER IMPLEMENTATIONS

If you are using C++ with 2011 standards, you can use the high resolution clock, std::chrono::high_resolution_clock. Here we show a list of alternative timers you can use with portability across C, C++, and Fortran.

- clock_gettime with the CLOCK_MONOTONIC type
- clock_gettime with the CLOCK_REALTIME type
- gettimeofday
- getrusage
- host_get_clock_service for MacOS
- clock std:chrono_high_resolution_clock (C++ high resolution, C++ 2011 standard)

> **Example: Experiment with timers**
>
> Use the code at https://github.com/EssentialsofParallelComputing/Chapter17 in the timers directory. In that directory, run the following commands:
>
> ```
> mkdir build && cd build
> cmake ..
> make
> ./runit.sh
> ```
>
> This example builds the various timer implementations and runs them. This example gives you some ideas for alternate options if the default version does not work or doesn't behave well on your system.

The `clock_gettime` function has two versions. Although the `CLOCK_MONOTONIC` is preferred, it's not a required type for Portable Operating System Interface (POSIX), the standard for portability across operating systems. In the timers directory of the examples that accompany this chapter, we include a version with the `CLOCK_REALTIME` timer type. The `gettimeofday` and `getrusage` functions are widely portable and might work on systems where `clock_gettime` does not.

17.3 *Profilers: You can't improve what you don't measure*

A profiler is a programmer tool that measures some aspect of the performance of an application. We covered profiling earlier in sections 2.2 and 3.3 as a key part of the application development process and introduced a couple of the simpler profiling tools. In this section, we'll cover some of the alternative profiling tools that you might consider for your application development and introduce you to how to use some more of the simpler profilers. Profilers are important tools in developing parallel applications when:

- You want to work on a section of code that has the most impact in improving the performance of your application. This section of code is often referred to as the *bottleneck.*
- You want to measure your performance improvement on various architectures. After all, we are all about performance in high performance computing applications.

Profilers come in a variety of shapes and sizes. We'll break down our discussion into categories that reflect their broad characteristics. It is important to use a tool from the appropriate category. It is not advisable to use a heavy-weight profiling tool when all you want is to find the biggest bottleneck. The wrong tool will bury you in an avalanche of information that will leave you digging yourself out for hours or days. Save the heavy-weight tools when you really need to dive down into the low-level details of your application. We suggest starting with simple profilers and working up to the detailed profilers when needed. Our categories of profilers follow this simple-to-complex hierarchy with some subjective judgment where each profiling tool falls in the list.

Table 17.2   Categories of profiling tools (simple to complex)

Simple text-based profilers	Returns a short text-based summary of performance
High-level profilers	A top-down profiler that highlights the routines needing improvement, often in a graphical user interface
Medium-level profilers	Profilers that give a manageable amount of performance data
Detailed profilers	Bury me with data, please

High-level is not indicative of high-detail; these tools give the 25,000 ft picture of an application's performance. We find ourselves returning to the simpler profiling tools, such as the simple text-based and high-level profilers because these are quick to use and don't take up most of the day.

17.3.1 *Simple text-based profilers for everyday use*

Simple text-based profilers like LIKWID, gprof, gperftools, timemory, and Open|Speed-Shop are easy to incorporate into your daily application development workflow. These provide a quick insight on performance.

The likwid (Like I Knew What I'm Doing) suite of tools was first introduced in section 3.3.1 and also used in chapters 4, 6, and 9. We used it extensively because of its simplicity. There is ample documentation at the likwid website:

likwid performance tools at https://hpc.fau.de/research/tools/likwid/

The venerable gprof tool has been a mainstay for profiling applications on Linux for many years. We used it in section 13.4.2 for a quick profile of our application. Gprof uses a sampling approach to measure where the application is spending its time. It is a command-line tool that is enabled by adding -pg when compiling and linking your application. Then, when your application runs, it produces a file called gmon.out at completion. The command-line gprof utility then displays the performance data as text output. Gprof comes with most Linux systems and is part of the GCC and Clang/LLVM compilers. Gprof is relatively dated, but is readily available and simple to use. The gprof documentation is fairly simple and is widely available at the following site:

GNU Binutils documentation from The Free Software Foundation at https://sourceware.org/binutils/docs/gprof/index.html

The gperftools suite (originally Google Performance Tools) is a newer profiling tool similar in functionality to gprof. The suite of tools also comes with TCMalloc, a fast malloc for applications that use threads. It also throws in a memory leak detector and a heap profiler. The gperftools CPU profiler has a website that has a short introduction to the tool:

> Gperftools (Google) at https://gperftools.github.io/gperftools/cpuprofile.html

The timemory tool from the National Energy Research Scientific Computing Center (NERSC) is a simple tool built on top of many other performance measurement interfaces. The simplest tool in this suite, timem, is a replacement for the Linux `time` command, which can also output additional information such as the memory used and the number of bytes read and written. Notably, it has an option to automatically generate a roofline plot. The tool has extensive use information at its documentation website:

> timemory documentation at https://timemory.readthedocs.io

Open|SpeedShop has a command-line option and Python interface that might make it a possible substitute for these simple tools. It is a more powerful tool, which we'll discuss in section 17.3.4.

17.3.2 *High-level profilers for quickly identifying bottlenecks*

High-level tools are the best choice for a quick overview of the performance of your application. These tools distinguish themselves by focusing on identifying the high-cost parts of your code and giving a robust graphics-based overview of application performance. Unlike the simple profilers, you must often step out of your workflow and start a graphics application in order to use these high-level profilers.

We first talked about Cachegrind in section 3.3.1. Cachegrind specializes in showing you the high-cost paths through your code, enabling you to focus on the performance critical parts. It has a simple graphical user interface that is easy to understand.

> Cachegrind, a cache and branch-prediction profiler (Valgrind™ Developers) at https://valgrind.org/docs/manual/cg-manual.html

Another good high-level profiler is the Arm MAP profiler, previously named Allinia Map or Forge Map. MAP is a commercial tool and its parent firm has changed a few times. It utilizes a graphic user interface that gives more detail than KCachegrind, but still focuses on the most salient details. The MAP tool has a companion tool, the DDT debugger, that comes in the Arm Forge suite of high-performance computing tools. We'll discuss the DDT debugger later in the chapter in section 17.7.2. There is extensive documentation, tutorials, webinars, and a user guide at the ARM website:

> Arm MAP (Arm Forge) at http://mng.bz/n2x2

17.3.3   *Medium-level profilers to guide your application development*

Medium-level profilers are often used when trying to fine-tune optimizations. Many of the graphical user interface tools designed to guide your application development fall into this category. These include Intel® Advisor, VTune, CrayPat, AMD μProf, NVIDIA Visual Profiler, and CodeXL (formerly a Radeon tool and now part of the GPUOpen initiative). We start with the more general and popular tools for CPUs and then work into the specialized tools for GPUs.

Intel® Advisor is targeted at guiding the use of vectorization with Intel compilers. It shows which loops are vectorized and suggests changes to vectorize others. While it is especially useful for vectorizing code, it is also good for general profiling. Advisor is a proprietary tool, but recently has been made freely available for many users. You can install Intel Advisor using the Ubuntu package manager. You need to add the Intel package and then use apt-get to install the version with OneAPI.

```
wget -q https://apt.repos.intel.com/intel-gpg-keys/GPG-PUB-KEY-INTEL-SW-
    PRODUCTS-2023.PUB
apt-key add GPG-PUB-KEY-INTEL-SW-PRODUCTS-2023.PUB
rm -f GPG-PUB-KEY-INTEL-SW-PRODUCTS-2023.PUB
echo "deb https://apt.repos.intel.com/oneapi all main" >>
    /etc/apt/sources.list.d/oneAPI.list
echo "deb [trusted=yes arch=amd64]
     https://repositories.intel.com/graphics/ubuntu bionic
    main" >> /etc/apt/sources.list.d/intel-graphics.list
apt-get update
apt-get install intel-oneapi-advisor
```

Complete instructions on installing the Intel OneAPI software from its package repository can be found at http://mng.bz/veO4.

Intel® VTune is a general-purpose optimization tool that helps to identify bottlenecks and potential improvements. It is also another proprietary tool that's freely available. VTune can be installed with apt-get from the OneAPI suite.

```
wget -q https://apt.repos.intel.com/intel-gpg-keys/GPG-PUB-KEY-INTEL-SW-
    PRODUCTS-2023.PUB
apt-key add GPG-PUB-KEY-INTEL-SW-PRODUCTS-2023.PUB
rm -f GPG-PUB-KEY-INTEL-SW-PRODUCTS-2023.PUB
echo "deb https://apt.repos.intel.com/oneapi all main" >>
    /etc/apt/sources.list.d/oneAPI.list
echo "deb [trusted=yes arch=amd64]
     https://repositories.intel.com/graphics/ubuntu bionic
    main" >> /etc/apt/sources.list.d/intel-graphics.list
apt-get update
apt-get install intel-oneapi-vtune
```

The CrayPat tool is a proprietary tool that is only available on Cray Operating Systems. It is an excellent command-line tool that gives simple feedback on optimization of loops and threading. If you are working on one of the many high-performance computing sites that use the Cray Operating System, this tool may be worth investigating. Unfortunately, it is not available elsewhere.

AMD µProf is the profiling tool from AMD for their CPUs and APUs. Accelerated Processing Unit (APU) is the AMD term for a CPU with an integrated GPU that was first introduced when AMD bought out ATI, manufacturer of the Radeon GPU. The integrated unit is more tightly coupled than a typical integrated GPU and is part of the Heterogeneous System Architecture concept from AMD. You can install the AMD µProf tool with package installers on Ubuntu or Red Hat Enterprise Linux. The download requires a manual acceptance of the EULA. To install AMD µProf, follow these steps:

1 Go to https://developer.amd.com/amd-uprof/
2 Scroll down to the bottom of the page and select the appropriate file
3 Accept the EULA to start the download with the package manager

```
Ubuntu: dpkg --install amduprof_x.y-z_amd64.deb
RHEL: yum install amduprof-x.y-z.x86_64.rpm
```

More details on installation are given in the user guide, which is available at the AMD developer website: https://developer.amd.com/wordpress/media/2013/12/User_Guide.pdf.

NVIDIA Visual Profiler is part of the CUDA software suite. It is being incorporated into the NVIDIA® Nsight suite of tools. We covered this tool in section 13.4.3. The NVIDIA tools can be installed on the Ubuntu Linux distribution with the following commands:

```
wget -q https://developer.download.nvidia.com/
    compute/cuda/repos/ubuntu1804/x86_64/cuda-repo-ubuntu1804_10.2.89-
    1_amd64.deb
dpkg -i cuda-repo-ubuntu1804_10.2.89-1_amd64.deb
apt-key adv --fetch-keys https://developer.download.nvidia.com/
    compute/cuda/repos/ubuntu1804/x86_64/7fa2af80.pub
apt-get update
apt-get install cuda-nvprof-10-2 cuda-nsight-systems-10-2 cuda-nsight-
    compute-10-2
```

CodeXL is the GPUOpen code development workbench with profiling support for Radeon GPUs. It is part of the GPUOpen open source initiative begun by AMD. The CodeXL tool combines both debugger and profiler functionality. The CPU profiling has been moved to the AMD µProf tool so that the CodeXL tool could be moved to an open source status. Follow the instructions to install CodeXL on Ubuntu or RedHat Linux distributions.

```
wget https://github.com/GPUOpen-Archive/
         CodeXL/releases/download/v2.6/codexl-2.6-302.x86_64.rpm
RHEL or CentOS: rpm -Uvh --nodeps codexl-2.6-302.x86-64.rpm
Ubuntu: apt-get install rpm
        rpm -Uvh --nodeps codexl-2.6-302.x86-64.rpm
```

17.3.4 *Detailed profilers give the gory details of hardware performance*

There are several tools that produce detailed application profiling. If you need to extract every bit of performance from your application, you should learn to use at least one of these tools. The challenge with these tools is that they produce so much information, it can be time-consuming to understand and use the results. You will also need to have some hardware architecture expertise to really make sense of the profiling data. The tools from this category should be used after you have gotten what you can out of the simpler profiling tools. The detailed profilers that we cover in this section are HPCToolkit, Open|SpeedShop, and TAU.

HPCToolkit is a powerful, detailed profiler developed as an open source project by Rice University. HPCToolkit uses hardware performance counters to measure performance and presents the data using graphical user interfaces. The development for extreme scale on the latest high-performance computing systems is sponsored by the Department of Energy (DOE) Exascale Computing Project. Its hpcviewer GUI shows performance data from a code perspective while the hpctraceviewer presents a time trace of the code execution. More information and detailed user guides are available at the HPCToolkit website. HPCToolkit can be installed with the Spack package manager with `spack install hpctoolkit`.

HPCToolkit at http://hpctoolkit.org

Open|SpeedShop is another profiler that can produce detailed program profiles. It has both a graphical user interface and a command-line interface. The Open|SpeedShop tool runs on all the latest high-performance computing systems as a result of DOE funding. It has support for MPI, OpenMP, and CUDA. Open|Speedshop is open source and can be freely downloaded. Their website has detailed user guides and tutorials. Open|Speedshop can be installed with the Spack package manager with `spack install openspeedshop`.

Open|Speedshop at https://openspeedshop.org

TAU is a profiling tool developed primarily at the University of Oregon. This freely available tool has a graphical user interface that is easy to use. TAU is used on many of the largest high-performance computing applications and systems. There is extensive documentation on using TAU at the tool's website. TAU can be installed with the Spack package manager with `spack install tau`.

Performance Research Lab (University of Oregon) at http://www.cs.uoregon.edu/research/tau/home.php

17.4 Benchmarks and mini-apps: A window into system performance

We noted the value of benchmarks and mini-apps for assessing the performance of your applications in chapter 3. Benchmarks are more appropriate for measuring the performance of a system. Mini-apps are more focused on application areas and how best to implement the algorithms for various architectures, but the difference between these can be blurred at times.

17.4.1 Benchmarks measure system performance characteristics

The following is a list of benchmarks that can be useful measures for your potential system performance. We have extensively used the STREAM Benchmark in our performance studies, but there may be more appropriate benchmarks for your application. For example, if your application loads a single data value from scattered memory locations, the Random benchmark would be the most appropriate.

- Linpack at http://www.netlib.org/benchmark/hpl/—Used for the Top 500 High Performance Computers list.
- STREAM at https://www.cs.virginia.edu/stream/ref.html—A benchmark for memory bandwidth. You can find a version in the Git repository at https://github.com/jeffhammond/STREAM.git.
- Random at http://icl.cs.utk.edu/projectsfiles/hpcc/RandomAccess/—A benchmark for random memory access performance.
- NAS Parallel Benchmarks at http://www.nas.nasa.gov/publications/npb.html—NASA benchmarks, first released in 1991, include some of the most heavily used benchmarks for research.
- HPCG at http://www.hpcg-benchmark.org/software/—New conjugate gradient benchmark developed as an alternative to Linpack. HPCG gives a more realistic performance benchmark for current algorithms and computers.
- HPC Challenge Benchmark at http://icl.cs.utk.edu/hpcc/—A composite benchmark.
- Parallel Research Kernels at https://github.com/ParRes/Kernels—Various small kernels from typical scientific simulation codes and in several parallel implementations.

17.4.2 Mini-apps give the application perspective

Applications have had to make many adaptations for new architectures. With the use of mini-apps, you can highlight the performance of a simple application type on a target system. This section presents a list of mini-apps developed by the Department of Energy (DOE) laboratories, which might be a valuable reference implementation for your application.

The DOE laboratories have been tasked with the development of exascale computers, which provide the leading edge of high-performance computing. These laboratories have created mini-apps and proxy applications for hardware designers and application developers to experiment with how to get the most out of these exascale systems. Each of these mini-apps has a different purpose. Some reflect the performance of a large application, while others are meant for algorithmic exploration. To begin, let's define a couple of terms to help us categorize the mini-apps.

- *Proxy mini-app*—An extract or smaller form of a larger application that captures its performance characteristics. Proxies are useful to hardware vendors in a co-design process as a smaller application that they can use in the hardware design process.
- *Research mini-app*—A simpler form of a computational approach that is useful for researchers to explore alternative algorithms and methods for improved performance and new architectures.

The categorization of mini-apps is not perfect. Each author of a mini-app has their own reason for their creation, which often doesn't fit into neat categories.

EXASCALE PROJECT PROXY APPS: A CROSS-SECTION OF SAMPLE APPLICATIONS

The DOE has developed some sample applications for use in benchmarking systems, performance experiments, and algorithm development. Many of these have been organized by the DOE Exascale Computing Project at https://proxyapps.exascaleproject.org/.

- *AMG*—Algebraic multi-grid example
- *ExaMiniMD*—Proxy application for particle and molecular dynamics codes
- *Laghos*—Unstructured, compressible shock hydrodynamics
- *MACSio*—Scalable I/O tests
- *miniAMR*—Block-based adaptive mesh refinement mini-app
- *miniQMC*—Quantum Monte Carlo mini-app
- *NEKbone*—Incompressible Navier-Stokes solver using spectral elements
- *PICSARlite*—Electromagnetic particle-in-cell
- *SW4lite*—3D seismic modeling kernels
- *SWFFT*—Fast Fourier transform
- *Thornado-mini*—Finite element, moment-based radiation transport
- *XSBench*—Kernel from a Monte Carlo neutronics app

The Exascale Project proxy applications are selected from the many proxy applications developed by national laboratories. In the following sections, we list other proxy and mini-applications developed by various national laboratories for scientific applications that are important to the mission for their research laboratory. These applications are made available to the public and hardware developers as part of the national codesign strategy. The *codesign process* is where hardware developers and application developers work closely together in a feedback loop that iterates the features of these exascale systems.

Often, the applications that these mini-apps mirror tend to be proprietary and, therefore, cannot be shared outside the corresponding laboratory. With the release of some of these mini-apps, we recognize that current applications are more complex and stress the hardware in different ways than the simple kernels previously available.

LAWRENCE LIVERMORE NATIONAL LABORATORY PROXIES

Lawrence Livermore National Laboratory has been one of the leading proponents of proxy development. Their LULESH proxy is one of the most heavily studied by vendors and academic researchers. Some of the Lawrence Livermore National Laboratory proxies include

- LULESH—Explicit Lagrangian shock hydrodynamics on an unstructured mesh representation
- Kripke—Sweep-based deterministic transport
- Quicksilver—Monte Carlo particle transport

For more detail on the Lawrence Livermore National Laboratory proxies, see their website at https://computing.llnl.gov/projects/co-design/proxy-apps.

LOS ALAMOS NATIONAL LABORATORY PROXY APPLICATIONS

Los Alamos National Laboratory also has many interesting proxy applications. Some of the more popular are listed here.

- *CLAMR*—Cell-based adaptive mesh refinement mini-app
- *NuT*—Monte Carlo proxy for neutrino transport
- *Pennant*—Unstructured mesh hydrodynamics mini-app
- *SNAP*—SN (Discrete Ordinates) application proxy

For more detail on the Los Alamos National Laboratory proxies, see their website at https://www.lanl.gov/projects/codesign/proxy-apps/lanl/index.php.

SANDIA NATIONAL LABORATORIES MANTEVO SUITE OF MINI-APPS

Sandia National Laboratories has put together a branded mini-app suite called Mantevo, which includes their mini-apps and a few from other organizations such as the United Kingdom's Atomic Weapons Establishment (AWE). Here is list of their mini-apps:

- *CloverLeaf*—Cartesian grid compressible fluids hydrocode mini-app
- *CoMD*—Molecular dynamics mini-app
- *EpetraBenchmarkTest*—Dense math-solver kernels
- *MiniAero*—Unstructured compressible Navier-Stokes
- *miniFE*—Proxy application for unstructured implicit finite element codes
- *miniGhost*—Proxy application for ghost cell updates
- *miniSMAC2D*—Body-fitted incompressible Navier-Stokes solver
- *miniXyce*—Circuit simulation mini-app
- *TeaLeaf*—Proxy application for unstructured implicit finite element codes

More information on the Mantevo min-app suite is available at https://mantevo .github.io.

17.5 Detecting (and fixing) memory errors for a robust application

For robust applications, you need a tool to detect and report memory errors. In this section, we discuss the capabilities and the pros and cons of a number of tools that detect and report memory errors. The memory errors that occur in applications can be broken down into these categories:

- *Out-of-bound errors*—Attempting to access memory beyond the array bounds. Fence-post checkers and some compilers can catch these errors.
- *Memory leaks*—Allocating memory and never freeing it. Malloc replacement tools are good at catching and reporting memory leaks.
- *Uninitialized memory*—Memory that is used before it is set. Because memory is not set before its use, it has whatever value is in memory from previous use. The result is that the behavior of the application can vary from run to run. This type of error is difficult to find, and tools specifically designed to catch these are essential.

Only a few tools handle all of these categories of memory errors. Most of the tools handle the first two categories to some degree. Uninitialized memory checks are an important check and supported by just a few tools. We'll cover those tools first.

17.5.1 Valgrind Memcheck: The open source standby

Valgrind checks uninitialized memory with its default Memcheck tool. We first presented Valgrind for this purpose in section 2.1.3. Valgrind is a good choice both because it is open source and freely available and because it is one of the best tools at detecting memory errors in all three categories.

It's best to use Valgrind with the GCC compiler. The GCC team uses it for their development, and as a result cleaned up their generated code so that a suppression file for false positives is not needed for their serial applications. For parallel applications, you can also suppress the false positives detected by Valgrind with OpenMPI by using a suppression file provided by the OpenMPI package. For example

```
mpirun -n 4 valgrind \
    --suppressions=$MPI_DIR/share/openmpi/openmpi-valgrind.supp <my_app>
```

There are only a few command-line options, and the Valgrind tool often suggests which options to use in its report. For more information on the usage, see the Valgrind website (https://valgrind.org).

17.5.2 *Dr. Memory for your memory ailments*

Yes, really, that's its name. Dr. Memory is a similar tool to Valgrind but newer and faster. Like Valgrind, Dr. Memory detects memory errors and problems within your program. It is an open source project, freely available across a variety of chip architectures and operating systems.

There are many other tools besides Dr. Memory in this suite of run-time tools. Because Dr. Memory is a relatively simple tool, we'll present a quick example of how to use it. Let's first set up Dr. Memory for use.

Example: Using Dr. Memory to detect memory errors

Go to https://github.com/DynamoRIO/drmemory/wiki/Downloads and download the latest version for Linux:

```
tar -xzvf DrMemory-Linux-2.3.0-1.tar.gz
```

Then add it to your path with

```
export PATH=${HOME}/DrMemory-Linux-2.3.0-1/bin64:$PATH
```

We'll try out Dr. Memory on the example in the repository at https://github.com/EssentialsofParallelComputing/Chapter17. The following listing is a copy of the code from listing 4.1 of chapter 4. The code is just a fragment to check that the syntax correctly compiles.

Listing 17.3   DrMemory test example

```
DrMemory/memoryexample.c
 1 #include <stdlib.h>
 2
 3 int main(int argc, char *argv[])
 4 {
 5   int j, imax, jmax;
 6
 7   // first allocate a column of pointers of type pointer to double
 8   double **x = (double **)
        malloc(jmax * sizeof(double *));          Uninitialized memory
 9                                                 read of variable jmax
10   // now allocate each row of data              Memory leak for variable x
11   for (j=0; j<jmax; j++){
12       x[j] = (double *)malloc(imax * sizeof(double));
13   }
14 }
```

Running this example takes just a few commands. Retrieve the code from the supplemental examples for the chapter and build it:

```
git clone --recursive \
    https://github.com/EssentialsofParallelComputing/Chapter17
cd DrMemory
make
```

Now run the example by executing `drmemory`, followed by two dashes and then the name of the executable: `drmemory -- memoryexample`. Figure 17.2 shows the report that Dr. Memory produces.

```
                                               Uninitialized memory report
~~Dr.M~~ Dr. Memory version 2.3.0
~~Dr.M~~
~~Dr.M~~ Error #1: UNINITIALIZED READ: reading register edx
~~Dr.M~~ # 0 main              [Chapter17/DrMemory/memoryexample.c:11]
~~Dr.M~~ Note: @0:00:00.401 in thread 146899
~~Dr.M~~ Note: instruction: cmp  %eax %edx
~~Dr.M~~                              Memory leak report
~~Dr.M~~ Error #2: LEAK 8 direct bytes 0x0000000000607710-0x0000000000607718 + 33567080 indirect bytes
~~Dr.M~~ # 0 replace_malloc   [/drmemory_package/common/alloc_replace.c:2577]
~~Dr.M~~ # 1 main             [Chapter17/DrMemory/memoryexample.c:8]
~~Dr.M~~
~~Dr.M~~ ERRORS FOUND:
~~Dr.M~~       0 unique,      0 total unaddressable access(es)
~~Dr.M~~       1 unique,      2 total uninitialized access(es)
~~Dr.M~~       0 unique,      0 total invalid heap argument(s)
~~Dr.M~~       0 unique,      0 total warning(s)
~~Dr.M~~       1 unique,      1 total, 33567088 byte(s) of leak(s)
~~Dr.M~~       0 unique,      0 total,      0 byte(s) of possible leak(s)
~~Dr.M~~ ERRORS IGNORED:
~~Dr.M~~      24 unique,     46 total,  14053 byte(s) of still-reachable allocation(s)
~~Dr.M~~           (re-run with "-show_reachable" for details)
~~Dr.M~~ Details:
Chapter17/DrMemory/DrMemory-Linux-2.3.0-1/drmemory/logs/DrMemory-memoryexample.146899.000/results.txt
```

Figure 17.2   Report from Dr. Memory shows that an uninitialized read at line 11 and a memory leak for memory allocated at line 8.

Dr. Memory correctly flags that `jmax` was not initialized when used on line 11. It also shows a leak on line 12. To fix these, we initialize `jmax` and then free each `x[j]` pointer and the `x` array, then try again with `drmemory -- memoryexample`. Figure 17.3 shows the report.

```
~~Dr.M~~ Dr. Memory version 2.3.0
~~Dr.M~~
~~Dr.M~~ NO ERRORS FOUND:       No errors reported!
~~Dr.M~~       0 unique,      0 total unaddressable access(es)
~~Dr.M~~       0 unique,      0 total uninitialized access(es)
~~Dr.M~~       0 unique,      0 total invalid heap argument(s)
~~Dr.M~~       0 unique,      0 total warning(s)
~~Dr.M~~       0 unique,      0 total,      0 byte(s) of leak(s)
~~Dr.M~~       0 unique,      0 total,      0 byte(s) of possible leak(s)
~~Dr.M~~ ERRORS IGNORED:
~~Dr.M~~      24 unique,     46 total,  14053 byte(s) of still-reachable allocation(s)
~~Dr.M~~           (re-run with "-show_reachable" for details)
~~Dr.M~~ Details:
Chapter17/DrMemory/DrMemory-Linux-2.3.0-1/drmemory/logs/DrMemory-memoryexample.147746.000/results.txt
```

Figure 17.3   This Dr. Memory report shows that the uninitialized memory error and the leak are fixed.

The report from Dr. Memory in figure 17.3 shows no errors after our fix. Note that Dr. Memory does not flag that `imax` is uninitialized. For more information on Dr. Memory for Windows, Linux, and Mac, see https://drmemory.org.

17.5.3 *Commercial memory tools for demanding applications*

Purify and Insure++ are commercial tools that detect memory errors, including some form of uninitialized memory check. TotalView includes a memory checker in its most recent versions. If you have a demanding application that requires extreme quality code, and you are looking for vendor support for your memory checking tool, one of these commercial tools may be a good choice.

17.5.4 *Compiler-based memory tools for convenience*

Many compilers are incorporating memory tools into their products. The LLVM compiler has a set of tools that includes memory checker functionality. This includes MemorySanitizer, AddressSanitizer, and ThreadSanitizer. GCC includes the mtrace component which detects memory leaks.

17.5.5 *Fence-post checkers detect out-of-bounds memory accesses*

Several tools place blocks of memory before and after memory allocations to detect out-of-bounds memory accesses and to also track memory leaks. These types of memory checkers are referred to as fence-post memory checkers. These are fairly simple tools to implement and are usually provided as a library. Additionally, these tools are portable and easy to add to a regular regression testing system.

Here we discuss dmalloc in detail and how to use a fence-post memory checker. Electric Fence and Memwatch are two other packages that provide fence-post memory checks and have an analogous use model, but dmalloc is the best known fence-post memory checker. It replaces the malloc library with a version that provides memory checking.

Example: Setting up dmalloc

To download and install dmalloc, run the following code:

```
wget https://dmalloc.com/releases/dmalloc-5.5.2.tgz
tar -xzvf dmalloc-5.5.2.tgz
cd dmalloc-5.5.2/
./configure --prefix=${HOME}/dmalloc
make
make install
```

To add dmalloc to your executable path, on the command line or in your environment setup file, set your PATH variable:

```
export PATH=${PATH}:${HOME}/dmalloc/bin
```

(continued)

Set the DMALLOC_OPTIONS variable. The backticks execute the command and set the variable.

```
export `dmalloc -l logfile -i 100 low`
```

The DMALLOC_OPTIONS variable should now be set in your environment. It may look something like this:

```
DMALLOC_OPTIONS=debug=0x4e48503,inter=100,log=logfile
```

We need to add these changes to the makefile to link in the dmalloc library and include the header file:

```
CFLAGS = -g -std=c99 -I${HOME}/dmalloc/include -DDMALLOC \
        -DDMALLOC_FUNC_CHECK
LDLIBS=-L${HOME}/dmalloc/lib -ldmalloc
```

For our source code in the following listing, we added the dmalloc header file with an `include` directive on line 3 so that we get line numbers in our report.

Listing 17.4   Dmalloc example code

```
Dmalloc/mallocexample.c
 1 #include <stdlib.h>
 2 #ifdef DMALLOC
 3 #include "dmalloc.h"        ←  Includes the
 4 #endif                         dmalloc header file
 5
 6 int main(int argc, char *argv[])
 7 {
 8    int imax=10, jmax=12;
 9
10    // first allocate a block of memory for the row pointers
11    double *x = (double *)malloc(imax*sizeof(double *));
12
13    // now initialize the x array to zero
14    for (int i = 0; i < jmax; i++) {      Writes past the
15       x[i] = 0.0;                        end of the x array
16    }
17    free(x);
18    return(0);
19 }
```

We've included an out-of-bounds access on the x array on lines 14 and 15. Now we can build our executable and run it:

```
make
./mallocexample
```

But the output to the terminal reports a failure:

```
debug-malloc library: dumping program, fatal error
   Error: failed OVER picket-fence magic-number check (err 27)
Abort trap: 6
```

Let's get more information about the problem from the log file shown in figure 17.4.

```
1595103932: 1: Dmalloc version '5.5.2' from 'http://dmalloc.com/'
1595103932: 1: flags = 0x4e48503, logfile 'logfile'
1595103932: 1: interval = 100, addr = 0, seen # = 0, limit = 0
1595103932: 1: starting time = 1595103932
1595103932: 1: process pid = 22944
1595103932: 1:   error details: checking user pointer
1595103932: 1: pointer '0x10a4eaf88' from 'unknown' prev access 'mallocexample.c:11'
1595103932: 1:   dump of proper fence-top bytes: 'i\336\312\372'
1595103932: 1:   dump of '0x10a4eaf88'+64:
'\000\000\000\000\000\000\000\000\000\000\000\000\000\000\000\000\000\000\000\000'
1595103932: 1: next pointer '0x10a4eb000' (size 0) may have run under from 'unknown'
1595103932: 1: ERROR: _dmalloc_chunk_heap_check: failed OVER picket-fence magic-number check (err
27)
```

Out-of-bounds memory report

Figure 17.4 The dmalloc log file shows an out-of-bounds memory access at line 11.

Dmalloc has detected the out-of-bounds access. Great! You can find more information on dmalloc at its website (https://dmalloc.com).

17.5.6 *GPU memory tools for robust GPU applications*

GPU vendors are developing memory tools for detecting memory errors for applications running on their hardware. NVIDIA has released a corresponding tool, and other GPU vendors are sure to follow. The NVIDIA CUDA-MEMCHECK tool checks for out-of-bounds memory references, data race detections, synchronization usage errors, and uninitialized memory. The tool can be run as a standalone command:

```
cuda-memcheck [--tool memcheck|racecheck|initcheck|synccheck] <app_name>
```

Documentation on the tool usage is available on the NVIDIA website:

> CUDA-MEMCHECK, CUDA Toolkit Documentation at https://docs.nvidia.com/cuda/cuda-memcheck/index.html

17.6 *Thread checkers for detecting race conditions*

Tools to detect thread race conditions (also called *data hazards*) are critical in developing OpenMP applications. It is impossible to develop robust OpenMP applications without a race detection tool. Yet, there are few tools that can detect race conditions. Two tools that are effective are Intel Inspector and Archer, which we discuss next.

17.6.1 *Intel® Inspector: A race condition detection tool with a GUI*

Intel® Inspector is a tool with a graphical user interface that is effective at detecting race conditions in OpenMP code. We discussed Intel Inspector earlier in section 7.9. Though Inspector is an Intel proprietary tool, it is now freely available. On Ubuntu, it can be installed from the OneAPI suite from Intel:

```
wget -q https://apt.repos.intel.com/intel-gpg-keys/GPG-PUB-KEY-INTEL-SW-
    PRODUCTS-2023.PUB
apt-key add GPG-PUB-KEY-INTEL-SW-PRODUCTS-2023.PUB
rm -f GPG-PUB-KEY-INTEL-SW-PRODUCTS-2023.PUB
echo "deb https://apt.repos.intel.com/oneapi all main" >>
    /etc/apt/sources.list.d/oneAPI.list
echo "deb [trusted=yes arch=amd64]
    https://repositories.intel.com/graphics/ubuntu bionic
    main" >> /etc/apt/sources.list.d/intel-graphics.list
apt-get install intel-oneapi-inspector
```

17.6.2 *Archer: A text-based tool for detecting race conditions*

Archer is an open source tool built on LLVM's ThreadSanitizer (TSan) and adapted for detecting thread race conditions in OpenMP. Using the Archer tool is basically just replacing the compiler command with `clang-archer` and linking in the Archer library with `-larcher`. Archer outputs its report as text.

You can manually install Archer with the LLVM compiler, or install with the Spack package manager using `spack install archer`. We have included some build scripts with the accompanying examples at https://github.com/EssentialsofParallelComputing/Chapter17 for installation. Once the Archer tool is installed, you can build our example in the Archer subdirectory of the examples. In the example, we use one of the stencil codes from section 7.3.3. We then modify the CMake build system by changing the compiler command to `clang-archer` and by adding the Archer libraries to the link command as the following listing shows.

> **Listing 17.5   Archer example code**

```
Archer/CMakeLists.txt
 1 cmake_minimum_required (VERSION 3.0)
 2 project (stencil)
 3
 4 set (CC clang-archer)          ◁── Sets the compiler
 5                                     command to clang-archer
 6 set (CMAKE_C_STANDARD 99)
 7
 8 set(CMAKE_C_FLAGS "${CMAKE_C_FLAGS} -g -O3")
 9
10 find_package(OpenMP)
11
12 # Adds build target of stencil with source code files
13 add_executable(stencil stencil.c timer.c timer.h malloc2D.c malloc2D.h)
14 set_target_properties(stencil PROPERTIES
      COMPILE_FLAGS ${OpenMP_C_FLAGS})
```

```
15 set_target_properties(stencil PROPERTIES LINK_FLAGS "${OpenMP_C_FLAGS}
        -L${HOME}/archer/lib -larcher")
```
⟵ **Adds the archer libraries to LINK_FLAGS**

Compile the code and run it is as before:

```
mkdir build && cd build
cmake ..
make
./stencil
```

We get the Archer tool output mixed in with the normal output as figure 17.5 shows.

```
==================
WARNING: ThreadSanitizer: data race (pid=59460)
  Atomic read of size 1 at 0x7b6800031140 by main thread:
    #0 pthread_mutex_lock
/projects/kitsune/packages/llvm-7.0.0-full-package/projects/compiler-rt/lib/tsan/../sanitizer_common/sanitizer_common_i
nterceptors.inc:4071 (stencil+0x440237)
    #1 __kmp_resume_64 <null> (libomp.so+0x7d4e4)
    #2 __libc_start_main <null> (libc.so.6+0x22554)
  Previous write of size 1 at 0x7b6800031140 by thread T64:
    #0 pthread_mutex_init
/projects/kitsune/packages/llvm-7.0.0-full-package/projects/compiler-rt/lib/tsan/rtl/tsan_interceptors.cc:1184
(stencil+0x42924a)
    #1 __kmp_suspend_initialize_thread(kmp_info*) <null> (libomp.so+0x7e9e3)
  Location is heap block of size 1504 at 0x7b6800030c00 allocated by main thread:
    #0 malloc
/projects/kitsune/packages/llvm-7.0.0-full-package/projects/compiler-rt/lib/tsan/rtl/tsan_interceptors.cc:664
(stencil+0x4533bc)
    #1 ___kmp_allocate <null> (libomp.so+0x1c127)
    #2 __libc_start_main <null> (libc.so.6+0x22554)
  Thread T64 (tid=59525, running) created by main thread at:
    #0 pthread_create
/projects/kitsune/packages/llvm-7.0.0-full-package/projects/compiler-rt/lib/tsan/rtl/tsan_interceptors.cc:965
(stencil+0x428e5b)
    #1 __kmp_create_worker <null> (libomp.so+0x7b358)
    #2 __libc_start_main <null> (libc.so.6+0x22554)
< ... skipping output ... >

Iter 7000
Iter 8000
Iter 9000
Timing is init nan flush 61.890046 stencil 60.155356 total nan
ThreadSanitizer: reported 8 warnings
```

Figure 17.5   Output from the Archer data race detection tool

There are some reports of race conditions reported at startup that appear to be false positives, but no additional messages during the run. For more information, check out the following documentation:

- "Archer PRUNERS: Providing Reproducibility for Uncovering Non-deterministic Errors in Runs on Supercomputers" (2017), https://pruners.github.io/archer/
- Archer repository at https://github.com/PRUNERS/archer

17.7   Bug-busters: Debuggers to exterminate those bugs

You spend much of your application development time fixing bugs. This is especially true in parallel application development. Any tool that helps with this process is vitally important. Parallel programmers also need additional capabilities targeted at dealing with multiple processes and threads.

The debuggers used for large parallel applications at high performance computing sites generally include a couple of commercial offerings. This includes the powerful and easy-to-use TotalView and Arm DDT debuggers. But most code development is initially done on laptops, desktops, and local clusters outside of large centers, so you may not have access to a commercial debugger on these smaller systems. The non-commercial debuggers available for smaller clusters, desktops, and laptops are more limited in parallel programming features and harder to use. In this section, we begin with a discussion of the commercial debuggers.

17.7.1   TotalView debugger is widely available at HPC sites

TotalView has extensive support for leading high performance computing systems, including MPI and OpenMP threading. TotalView has some support for debugging NVIDIA GPUs using CUDA. It uses a graphical user interface and is easy to navigate; it also has a great depth of features that take some exploration. TotalView is generally invoked by prefixing the command line with `totalview`. The `-a` flag indicates that the rest of the arguments are to be passed to the application:

```
totalview mpirun -a -n 4 <my_application>
```

Lawrence Livermore National Laboratory has a good tutorial on Totalview. Detailed information is available at the TotalView websites:

- TotalView (Lawrence Livermore National Laboratory) at https://computing .llnl.gov/tutorials/totalview/
- TotalView (Perforce) at https://totalview.io

17.7.2   DDT is another debugger widely available at HPC sites

The ARM DDT debugger is another popular commercial debugger used at high performance computing sites. It has extensive support for MPI and OpenMP. It also has some support for debugging CUDA code. The DDT debugger uses a graphical user interface that is very intuitive. In addition, DDT has support for remote debugging. In this case, the graphical client interface is run on your local system, and the application that is being debugged is remotely launched on the high performance computing system. To start a debug session with DDT, just prepend `ddt` to your command line:

```
ddt <my_application>
```

The Texas Advanced Computing Center has a good introduction to DDT. There is also more information at the DDT websites:

- ARM DDT Debugger tutorials (TACC, Texas Advanced Computing Center) at https://portal.tacc.utexas.edu/tutorials/ddt
- ARM DDT (ARM Forge) at https://www.arm.com/products/development-tools/server-and-hpc/forge/ddt

17.7.3 *Linux debuggers: Free alternatives for your local development needs*

The standard Linux debugger, GDB, is ubiquitous on Linux platforms. Its command-line interface requires some work to learn. For a serial executable, GDB runs with the command

```
gdb <my_application>
```

GDB does not have built-in parallel MPI support. You may be able to debug parallel jobs by launching multiple GDB sessions with the `mpirun` command. The xterms cannot be launched in all environments, so this is not a fool-proof technique.

```
mpirun -np 4 xterm -e gdb ./<my_application>
```

Many higher-level user interfaces are built on top of GDB. The simplest of these is cgdb, which is a curses-based interface that has a strong similarity to the vi editor. The curses interface is a character-based windows system. It has the advantage of better network performance characteristics than a full-fledged, bit-mapped graphical user interface. cgdb is widely available along with its documentation here:

cgdb, the curses debugger, at https://cgdb.github.io

A full graphical user interface to GDB is available in the DataDisplayDebugger, known as DDD. The DDD debugger website gives more information on DDD and other similar debuggers:

DDD, the DataDisplayDebugger, at https://www.gnu.org/software/ddd/

Neither cgdb nor DDD includes explicit parallel support. Other higher-level user interfaces such as the Eclipse IDE provide a parallel debugger interface on top of the GDB debugger. The Eclipse IDE is available for a wide range of languages and provides the foundation for programming tools for CPUs and GPUs.

Desktop IDEs (Eclipse Foundation) at https://www.eclipse.org/ide/

17.7.4 *GPU debuggers can help crush those GPU bugs*

The availability of debuggers for the development of GPU code is a critical game changer. The development of GPU code has been seriously hampered by the difficulty of debugging on GPUs. The GPU debugging tools discussed in this section are still immature, but any capability is sorely needed. These GPU debuggers heavily leverage the open source tools such as GDB and DDD introduced in the previous section.

CUDA-GDB: A DEBUGGER FOR THE NVIDIA GPUs

CUDA has a command-line debugger based on GDB called CUDA-GDB. There is also a version of CUDA-GDB with a graphical user interface in NVIDIA's Nsight™ Eclipse tool as part of their CUDA toolkit. CUDA-GDB has also been integrated into DDD and Emacs. To use CUDA-GDB with DDD, launch DDD using ddd --debugger cuda-gdb. You'll find the CUDA-GDB documentation at https://docs.nvidia.com/cuda/cuda-gdb/.

ROCGDB: A DEBUGGER FOR THE RADEON GPUs

The AMD ROCm debugger, part of the Radeon Open Compute initiative, is based on the GDB debugger but with initial support for the AMD GPUs. The ROCm website has documentation on ROCgdb, but it is largely the same as the GDB debugger.

- The site for the AMD ROCm debugger is at https://rocmdocs.amd.com/en/latest/ROCm_Tools/ROCgdb.html.
- The ROCm website is https://rocmdocs.amd.com.
- Check for updates for the ROCm debugger in the ROCgdb User Guide at https://github.com/RadeonOpenCompute/ROCm/blob/master/Debugging%20with%20ROCGDB%20User%20Guide%20v4.1.pdf.

17.8 *Profiling those file operations*

Filesystem performance is often an afterthought with high performance computing application development. In today's world of big data, and with filesystem performance lagging other parts of the computing system, filesystem performance is a growing issue. The necessary tools for measuring filesystem performance are scarce. The Darshan tool was developed to fill this gap. Darshan, an HPC I/O characterization tool, specializes at profiling an application's use of the filesystem. Since its release, Darshan has achieved widespread use at high performance computing centers.

Example: Installing the Darshan tool

In this example, you install the Darshan tool into your home directory. You may want to build the run-time tools on your compute cluster and the analysis tools on another system such as your laptop. The analysis tools require portions of a LaTex distribution and some simple graphics utilities that might not be on the computer cluster. If you run into problems with missing utilities, the DockerFile with accompanying examples at https://github.com/EssentialsofParallelComputing/Chapter17.git lists all the packages necessary for running the analysis tools. To begin, download and unpack the Darshan distribution:

```
wget ftp://ftp.mcs.anl.gov/pub/darshan/releases/darshan-3.2.1.tar.gz
tar -xvf darshan-3.2.1.tar.gz
```

Load or install your MPI package. If it is not installed in the standard location, set the paths with the following export commands:

```
export CFLAGS=-I<MPI_INCLUDE_PATH>
export LDFLAGS=-L<MPI_LIB_PATH>
```

Build the Darshan run-time tools:

```
cd darshan-3.2.1/darshan-runtime
./configure --prefix=${HOME}/darshan --with-log-path=${HOME}/darshan-logs
        --with-jobid-env=SLURM_JOB_ID --enable-mpiio-mod
make
make install
```

Now build the Darshan analysis tools:

```
cd ../darshan-util
./configure --prefix=${HOME}/darshan
make
make install
```

Then set the path to the Darshan executables:

```
export PATH=${PATH}:${HOME}/darshan/bin
```

Run the Darshan script to set up the date directories in the Darshan log directory:

```
darshan-mk-log-dirs.pl
```

Add the Darshan libraries to your build using your LINK_FLAGS. You can get the proper flags by executing the darshan-config utility with the --dyn-ld-flags option:

```
darshan-config --dyn-ld-flags
```

In the CMake build system, we can capture the output from the command and use it to set our DARSHAN_LINK_FLAGS variable:

```
execute_process(COMMAND darshan-config --dyn-ld-flags
        OUTPUT_STRIP_TRAILING_WHITESPACE
        OUTPUT_VARIABLE DARSHAN_LINK_FLAGS)
```

Then we add the DARSHAN_LINK_FLAGS to the LINK_FLAGS variable:

```
set_target_properties(mpi_io_block2d PROPERTIES LINK_FLAGS
        "${MPI_C_LINK_FLAGS} ${DARSHAN_LINK_FLAGS}")
```

We made these changes to the CMakeLists.txt file in the MPI_IO_Examples/mpi_io_block2d directory at https://github.com/EssentialsofParallelComputing/Chapter17.git. This is the same MPI-IO example we presented in section 16.3 but with a larger 1000x1000 mesh and with the verification code commented out. Now you can build and run the executable as before:

```
mkdir build && cd build
cmake ..
make
mpirun -n 4 mpi_io_block2d
```

You should find the Darshan logs organized by date in your ~/darshan-logs subdirectories.

Example: Using the Darshan analysis tool

You can run the Darshan analysis tool on the generated Darshan log file:

```
darshan-job-summary.pl <darshan log file>
```

You'll find the output will have the same file name as the log file, but with a .pdf extension added. You can look at the output with your favorite PDF viewer.

The Darshan analysis tool outputs a few pages of text and graphics information on the file operations in your application in portable document format (PDF). We show a part of the output in figure 17.6.

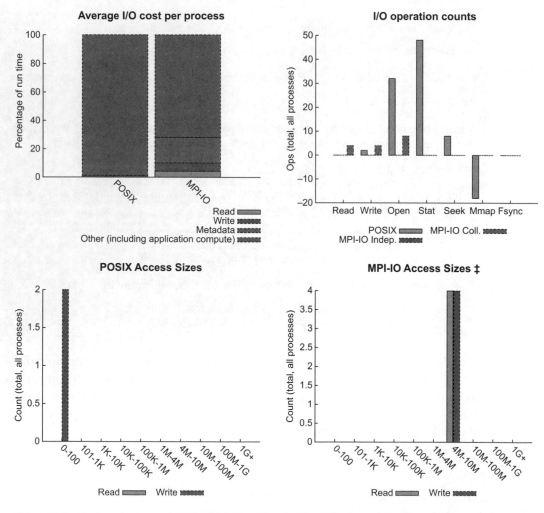

Figure 17.6   The graphs are part of the output from the Darshan I/O characterization tool. Both the standard iO (POSIX) and MPI-IO are shown. From the graph on the upper right, we can confirm that MPI-IO used collective rather than independent operations.

We built the run-time tool with support for both POSIX and MPI-IO profiling. POSIX, an acronym for Portable Operating System Interface, is the standard for portability for a wide range of system-level functions such as regular filesystem operations. For our modified test, we turned off all of the verification and other standard IO operations so that we can focus on the MPI-IO parts of the code. We also made the arrays larger. This test was done on the NFS filesystem that is used for our home directory. In the figure, we can see that we did both an MPI-IO write and read and that the write is slightly slower than the read. We can also see that the cost of the MPI metadata operations is much higher. The writing of file metadata records information about where the file is located, its permissions, and its access times. By its nature, writing metadata is a serial operation.

Darshan also has some support for profiling HDF5 file operations. You can get more information on the Darshan HPC I/O characterization tool at the project website:

> https://www.mcs.anl.gov/research/projects/darshan/

17.9 Package managers: Your personal system administrator

Package managers have become critical tools for simplifying software package installation on a variety of systems. These tools first appeared on Linux systems with the Red Hat package manager to manage software installation, but these have since become widespread in many operating systems. Using package managers to install tools and device drivers can greatly simplify the installation process and keep your system more stable and up-to-date.

Linux operating systems heavily rely on the use of package management. You should use your Linux package system to install software whenever possible. Unfortunately, not all software packages, and particularly vendor device drivers, are set up for installing with package managers. Without the use of a package manager, software installation is more difficult and error-prone. Most high performance computing software packages for Linux are distributed as Debian (.deb) or as Red Hat Package Manager (.rpm) package formats. These package formats can be installed on most Linux distributions.

17.9.1 Package managers for macOS

For the Mac operating system (macOS), the two major package managers are Homebrew and MacPorts. In general, both are good choices for installing software packages. Because macOS is a derivative of the Berkeley Software Distribution (BSD) Unix, many open source tools are available. But with recent changes to macOS to improve security, some tools have dropped support for the latest releases for the platform. And with recent changes to the Mac hardware, there may be significant changes to package management. More information on Homebrew and MacPorts is available at their respective websites:

- Homebrew at https://brew.sh
- MacPorts at https://www.macports.org

17.9.2   *Package managers for Windows*

The heavily proprietary Windows operating system has long been a mixed bag for software installation and support. Some software has been well supported and other software not at all. Things are changing at Microsoft as it embraces the open source movement. Windows is just now coming to the party with its new Windows Subsytem Linux (WSL). WSL sets up a Linux environment within a shell and should permit most Linux software to work without changes. A recent announcement that WSL would support transparent access to the GPU has generated excitement in the high performance community. Of course, the main targets are gaming and other mass-market applications, but we'll be happy to ride the coattails if possible.

17.9.3   *The Spack package manager: A package manager for high performance computing*

So far, we have discussed package managers focused around specific computing platforms. The challenges of a tool for high performance computing are much greater than those for traditional package managers because of the larger number of operating systems, hardware, and compilers that need to be simultaneously supported. It took until 2013, when Todd Gamblin at Lawrence Livermore National Laboratory released the Spack package manager, to address these issues. One of this book's authors contributed a couple of packages to the Spack list when there were fewer than a dozen packages in the whole system. Now there are over 4,000 supported packages and many of these are unique to the high performance computing community.

Example: Quick-start guide to Spack

To install Spack, type

```
git clone https://github.com/spack/spack.git
```

Then add to your environment the path and setup script. You can add these to your ./bash_profile or ./bashrc file so that you will have Spack ready to go at anytime.

```
export SPACK_ROOT=/path/to/spack
source $SPACK_ROOT/share/spack/setup-env.sh
```

To configure Spack, first set up Spack for your compilers:

```
spack compiler find
```

If the compiler is loaded from a module, add the load to the Spack compiler configuration

```
spack config edit compilers
```

or edit

```
~/.spack/linux/compiler.yaml
```

> You may want to add some of the system packages that already exist to the default configuration so these don't get built. To do this, use your favorite editor and edit
>
> ```
> ~/.spack/linux/packages.yaml
> ```

You'll find many Spack commands. Table 17.3 provides a few to get you started.

Table 17.3 Using Spack

Command	Description
`spack list`	Lists available packages
`spack install <package_name>`	Installs the requested package
`spack find`	Lists the packages that have already been built
`spack load <package_name>`	Loads the package into your environment

Spack has extensive documentation and an active development community. Check their site for up-to-date information: https://spack.readthedocs.io.

17.10 *Modules: Loading specialized toolchains*

The realities of software development on large computing sites are that these sites have to simultaneously support multiple environments. Because of this, you can load different versions of the GCC and MPI for testing. You might be able to load these different development toolchains, but the software modules do *not* come with the extensive testing that is done with most vendor distributions.

> **WARNING** Errors with toolchain software installed from the Modules package can occur. The advantages for high performance applications, however, are largely worth the potential difficulties.

Now let's look at the typical commands you might use with a toolchain system installed with the Modules package as table 17.4 shows.

Table 17.4 Toolchain module commands: Quick start

Command	Description
`module avail`	Lists modules available on the system
`module list`	Lists modules that are loaded into your current environment
`module purge`	Unloads all modules and restores the environment to before modules loaded
`module show <module_name>`	Shows what changes will be done to your environment

Table 17.4   Toolchain module commands: Quick start *(continued)*

Command	Description
`module unload <module_name>`	Unloads the module and removes changes to the environment
`module swap <module_name> <module_name>`	Replaces one module package with another

Because the `module show` command displays the actions executed by the module, let's look at a couple of examples for the GCC compiler suite and for CUDA.

Example: module show gcc/9.3.0

```
/opt/modulefiles/centos7/gcc/9.3.0:
module-whatis      This loads the GCC 9.3.0 environment.
prepend-path PATH /projects/opt/x86_64/gcc/9.3.0/bin
prepend-path LD_LIBRARY_PATH
    /opt/x86_64/gcc/9.3.0/lib64:/opt/x86_64/gcc/9.3.0/lib
prepend-path MANPATH /opt/x86_64/gcc/9.3.0/share/man
setenv      CC gcc
setenv      CXX g++
setenv      CPP cpp
setenv      FC gfortran
setenv      F77 gfortran
setenv      F90 gfortran
conflict    gcc
```

In this example, the GCC v9.3.0 module adds the GCC 9.3.0 directory to the path with `prepend-path` and to the environment with the LD_LIBRARY_PATH setting. It also sets some environment variables with `setenv` to direct which compiler to use.

Example: module show cuda/10.2

```
/opt/modulefiles/centos7/cuda/10.2:
conflict    cuda
module-whatis      load NVIDIA CUDA 10.2 environment
module-whatis      Modifies: PATH, LD_LIBRARY_PATH
module-whatis      IMPORTANT: the OpenCL libraries are
    installed by the NVIDIA driver, not this module
setenv      CUDA_PATH /opt/centos7/cuda/10.2
setenv      CUDADIR /opt/centos7/cuda/10.2
setenv      CUDA_INSTALL_PATH /opt/centos7/cuda/10.2
setenv      CUDA_LIB /opt/centos7/cuda/10.2/lib64
setenv      CUDA_INCLUDE /opt/centos7/cuda/10.2/include
setenv      CUDA_BIN /opt/centos7/cuda/10.2/bin
prepend-path PATH /opt/centos7/cuda/10.2/bin
prepend-path LD_LIBRARY_PATH /opt/centos7/cuda/10.2/lib64
setenv      OPENCL_LIBS /opt/centos7/cuda/10.2/lib64
```

```
setenv      OPENCL_INCLUDE /opt/centos7/cuda/10.2/include
setenv      CUDA_SDK /opt/centos7/cuda/10.2/samples
```

This CUDA module example sets paths, include directories, and library locations. It also sets the paths for the NVIDIA OpenCL implementation.

As you can see from the examples of these Modules commands, the modules are simply setting some environment variables. This is why Modules is not foolproof. Here are some important hints for using Modules that we learned the hard way. We begin with the following:

- *Consistency is important.* Set the same modules for compiling and running your code. If the path to the library changes, your code may crash or give you the wrong results.
- *Automate as much as possible.* If you neglect to do so, your first build (or run) will fail before you realize you forgot to load your modules.

Also, there are different approaches to loading module files. Each is filled with advantages and disadvantages. These approaches are

- Shell startup scripts
- Interactive at command line
- Batch submission scripts

Use interactive shell startup scripts, not batch startup scripts (e.g., load Modules in a .login file instead of a .cshrc). Parallel jobs propagate their environment to remote nodes. If you load Modules in the wrong shell startup script, your remote nodes can have different modules than your head node. This could have unexpected consequences.

Use `module purge` in batch scripts before loading Modules. If you have Modules loaded, the module load can fail because of a conflict, potentially causing your program to fail. (Note that it is unreliable to use `module purge` on Cray systems.)

Set run paths in program builds. Embedding run paths in your executable through the `rpaths` link option or other build mechanisms, helps to make your application less sensitive to changing Modules environments and paths. The disadvantage is that your application may not run on another system if the compilers are not in the same location. Note that this technique does not help with getting the wrong version of a program such as mpirun from your PATH variable.

Load specific versions of compilers (e.g., GCC v9.3.0 rather than just GCC). Often a particular compiler version is set as default, but this will change at some point, breaking your application or build. Also, defaults are not going to be the same on all systems.

There are two major software packages that implement basic Modules commands. The first is called module, often called TCL modules, and the second is Lmod. We discuss these in the following sections.

17.10.1 TCL modules: The original modules system for loading software toolchains

Yeah, this is confusing. The Modules package created the category that now more or less uses the same name—module. In 1991, John Furlani at Sun Microsystems created module and then released it as open source software. The module tool is written in the Tool Command Language, better known as TCL. It has proven to be an essential component at major computing centers. The module document is at https://modules .readthedocs.io/en/stable/module.html.

17.10.2 Lmod: A Lua-based alternative Modules implementation

Lmod is a Lua-based Modules system that dynamically sets up a user's environment. It is a newer implementation of the environment modules concept. The lmod documentation is at https://lmod.readthedocs.io/en/latest.

17.11 Reflections and exercises

We wish we had the time and space to go through in better detail how to use each of these tools. Unfortunately, it would take another book (even several books) to explore the world of tools for high performance computing.

We have gone through some of the simpler tools, presenting both their power and usefulness. Just like you shouldn't judge a book by its cover, don't judge a tool by the fancy interface. Instead, you should look at what the tool does and how easy it is to use. Our experience has been that fancy user interfaces, instead of functionality, often become the goal. In addition, tools should be simple. We have grown weary of facing another 600-page quick start guide to just learn the next tool. Yes, the tool might be great and do wondrous things, but an application developer has a lot of other things to master as well. The best tools can be picked up and made useful in a couple of hours.

Now we turn some of the effort over to you to try these tools, and hopefully, you will find some that will expand your developer's toolset. The addition of just a couple of tools makes you a better and more effective programmer. Here are a few exercises to get you started.

1   Run the Dr. Memory tool on one of your small codes or one of the codes from the exercises in this book.
2   Compile one of your codes with the dmalloc library. Run your code and view the results.
3   Try inserting a thread race condition into the example code in section 17.6.2 and see how Archer reports the problem.
4   Try the profiling exercise in section 17.8 on your filesystem. If you have more than one filesystem, try it on each. Then change the size of the array in the example to 2000x2000. How does it change the filesystem performance results?
5   Install one of the tools using the Spack package manager.

Summary

- Better software development practices start with version control. Creating a solid software development environment results in faster and better code development.
- Use timers and profilers to measure the performance of your applications. Measuring performance is the first step towards improving application performance.
- Explore the various mini-apps to see programming examples relevant to your application area. Learning from these examples will help you avoid reinventing the methods and improve your application.
- Use tools that help with detecting problems in your application. This improves your program quality and robustness.

appendix A
References

We have already provided a list of additional resources at the end of each chapter that we suggest for learning more about topics covered in the chapter. In each chapter, we placed the materials that we think would be most valuable to most readers. The references in this appendix are for those interested in the source materials that were used in developing the book. The citations are partially to give credit to the original authors of research and technical reports. These are also important for those conducting more in-depth research on a particular topic.

A.1   Chapter 1: Why parallel computing?

- Amdahl, Gene M. "Validity of the single processor approach to achieving large scale computing capabilities." Proceedings of the April 18–20, 1967, Spring Joint Computer Conference. (1967):483–48. https://doi.org/10.1145/1465482.1465560.
- Flynn, Michael J. "Some Computer Organizations and Their Effectiveness." In *IEEE Transactions on Computers*, Vol. C-21, no. 9 (September, 1972): 948–960.
- Gustafson, John L. "Reevaluating Amdahl's Law." In *Communications of the ACM*, Vol. 31, no. 5 (May, 1988):532–533. http://doi.acm.org/10.1145/42411.42415.
- Horowitz, M., Labonte, F., and Rupp, K., et al. "Microprocessor Trend Data." Accessed February 20, 2021. https://github.com/karlrupp/microprocessor-trend-data.

A.2   Chapter 2: Planning for parallelism

- CMake. https://cmake.org/.

A.3   Chapter 3: Performance limits and profiling

Tools

- Empirical Roofline Toolkit (ERT). https://bitbucket.org/berkeleylab/cs-roofline-toolkit.
- 4Intel® Advisor. https://software.intel.com/en-us/advisor.
- likwid. https://github.com/RRZE-HPC/likwid.
- STREAM download. https://github.com/jeffhammond/Stream.git.
- Valgrind. http://valgrind.org/.

Articles

- McCalpin, J. D. "STREAM: Sustainable Memory Bandwidth in High Performance Computers." Accessed February 20, 2021. https://www.cs.virginia.edu/stream/.
- Peise, Elmar. "Performance Modeling and Prediction for Dense Linear Algebra." arXiv:1706.01341 (June, 2017). Preprint: https://arxiv.org/abs/1706.01341.
- Williams, S. W., D. Patterson, et. al. "The Roofline Model: A pedagogical tool for auto-tuning kernels on multicore architectures." In *Hot Chips, A Symposium on High Performance Chips*, Vol. HC20 (August 10, 2008).

A.4   Chapter 4: Data design and performance models

Resources

- Data-oriented design. https://github.com/dbartolini/data-oriented-design.

Articles and books

- Bird, R. "Performance Study of Array of Structs of Arrays." Los Alamos National Lab (LANL). Paper in preparation.
- Garimella, Rao, and Robert W. Robey. "A Comparative Study of Multi-material Data Structures for Computational Physics Applications," no. LA-UR-16-23889. Los Alamos National Lab (LANL) (January, 2017).
- Hennessy, John L., and David A. Patterson. *Computer architecture: A Quantitative Approach.* 5th ed. San Francisco, CA, USA: Morgan Kaufmann, 2011.
- Hofmann, Johannes, Jan Eitzinger, and Dietmar Fey. "Execution-Cache-Memory Performance Model: Introduction and Validation." arXiv:1509.03118 (March, 2017). Preprint: https://arxiv.org/abs/1509.03118.
- Hollman, David, Bryce Lelbach, H. Carter Edwards, et al. "mdspan in C++: A Case Study in the Integration of Performance Portable Features into International Language Standards." IEEE/ACM International Workshop on Performance, Portability and Productivity in HPC (P3HPC) (November, 2019):60–70.
- Treibig, Jan, and Georg Hager. "Introducing a performance model for bandwidth-limited loop kernels." International Conference on Parallel Processing and Applied Mathematics (May, 2009):615–624.

A.5   *Chapter 5: Parallel algorithms and patterns*

- Ahrens, Peter, Hong Diep Nguyen, and James Demmel. "Efficient Reproducible Floating Point Summation and BLAS." In *EECS Department, University of California, Berkeley, Techical Report*, No. UCB/EECS-2015-229 (December, 2015).

- Alcantara, Dan A., Andrei Sharf, Fatemeh Abbasinejad, et al. "Real-time parallel hashing on the GPU." In *ACM Transactions on Graphics (TOG)*, Vol. 28, no. 5 (December, 2009):154.

- Anderson, Alyssa. "Achieving Numerical Reproducibility in the Parallelized Floating Point Dot Product." (April, 2014). https://digitalcommons.csbsju.edu/honors_theses/30/.

- Blelloch, Guy E. "Scans as primitive parallel operations." In *IEEE Transactions on computers*, Vol. 38, no. 11 (November, 1989):1526–1538.

- Blelloch, Guy E. *Vector models for data-parallel computing.* Cambridge, MA, USA: The MIT Press, 1990.

- Chapp, Dylan, Travis Johnston, and Michela Taufer. "On the Need for Reproducible Numerical Accuracy through Intelligent Runtime Selection of Reduction Algorithms at the Extreme Scale." 2015 IEEE International Conference on Cluster Computing (October, 2015):166–175.

- Cleveland, Mathew A., Thomas A. Brunner, et al. "Obtaining identical results with double precision global accuracy on different numbers of processors in parallel particle Monte Carlo simulations." In *Journal of Computational Physics*, Vol. 251 (October, 2013):223–236.

- Harris, Mark, Shubhabrata Sengupta, and John D. Owens. "Parallel Prefix Sum (Scan) with CUDA." In *GPU Gems 3*, no. 39 (April, 2007):851-876.

- Lessley, Brenton. "Data-Parallel Hashing Techniques for GPU Architectures." In *Eurographics Conference on Visualization* (EuroVis), Vol. 37, no. 3 (July, 2018).

A.6   *Chapter 8: MPI: The parallel backbone*

- Hoefler, Torsten, and Jesper Larsson Traff. "Sparse collective operations for MPI." 2009 IEEE International Symposium on Parallel & Distributed Processing (July, 2009):18.

- Thakur, Rajeev, and William Gropp. "Test suite for evaluating performance of multithreaded MPI communication." In *Parallel Computing*, Vol. 35, no. 12 (December, 2009):608–617.

A.7   *Chapter 9: GPU architectures and concepts*

- Yang, Charlene, Thorsten Kurth, and Samuel Williams. "Hierarchical Roofline analysis for GPUs: Accelerating performance optimization for the NERSC-9 Perlmutter system." In *Concurrency and Computation: Practice and Experience* (November, 2019). https://doi.org/10.1002/cpe.5547.

A.8   Chapter 10: GPU programming model

- CUDA Toolkit Documentation. "Compute Capabilities." CUDA C++ Programming Guide, v11.2.1 (NVIDIA Corporation, 2021). https://docs.nvidia.com/cuda/cuda-c-programming-guide/index.html#compute-capabilities.

A.9   Chapter 12: GPU languages: Getting down to basics

- Harris, Mark. "Optimizing Parallel Reduction in CUDA." (NVIDIA Corporation). https://developer.download.nvidia.com/assets/cuda/files/reduction.pdf.

A.10   Chapter 13: GPU profiling and tools

- BBC News. "Indonesia tsunami: How a volcano can be the trigger." BBC Global News Ltd (December, 2018). http://mng.bz/y92d.

A.11   Chapter 14: Affinity: Truce with the kernel

- Broquedis, François, Jérôme Clet-Ortega, et al. "hwloc: A Generic Framework for Managing Hardware Affinities in HPC Applications." Proceedings of the 18th Euromicro International Conference on Parallel, Distributed and Network-based Processing (PDP2010). IEEE Computer Society Press (February, 2010):180–186. https://ieeexplore.ieee.org/document/5452445.
- Hewlett Packard Enterprise, Original process placement program, xthi.c. CLE User Application Placement Guide (CLE 5.2.UP04) S-2496, pg 87. http://mng.bz/MgWB.
- "OpenMP Application Programming Interface," v5.0. OpenMP Architecture Review Board (November, 2018). https://www.opcnmp.org/wp-content/uploads/OpenMP-API-Spccification-5.0.pdf.
- Samuel K. Gutiérrez, "Adaptive Parallelism for Coupled, Multithreaded Message-Passing Programs." (December, 2018). https://www.cs.unm.edu/~samuel/publications/2018/skgutierrez-dissertation.pdf.
- Samuel K. Gutiérrez, Davis, Kei, et al. "Accommodating Thread-Level Heterogeneity in Coupled Parallel Applications." Proceedings of the IEEE International Parallel and Distributed Processing Symposium (May, 2017). https://github.com/lanl/libquo/blob/master/docs/publications/quo-ipdps17.pdf.
- Squyres, Jeff. "Process Placement." (September, 2014). Accessed February 20, 2021. https://github.com/open-mpi/ompi/wiki/ProcessPlacement.
- Treibig, J., G. Hager and G. Wellein. "LIKWID: A lightweight performance-oriented tool suite for x86 multicore environments." arXiv:1004.4431 (June, 2010). Preprint: http://arxiv.org/abs/1004.4431.

A.12   *Chapter 16: File operations for a parallel world*

Tools

- BeeGFS (The leading parallel file system). https://www.beegfs.io/c/.
- Lustre®. OpenSFS and EOFS. http://lustre.org.
- The OrangeFS Project. http://www.orangefs.org.
- Panasas PanFS Parallel File System. https://www.panasas.com/panfs-architecture/panfs/.

Articles and books

- Gropp, William. "Lecture 33: More on MPI I/O Best practices for parallel IO and MPI-IO hints." Accessed February 20, 2021. http://wgropp.cs.illinois.edu/courses/cs598-s15/lectures/lecture33.pdf.
- Mendez, Sandra, Sebastian Lührs, et al. "Best Practice Guide—Parallel I/O." Accessed February 20, 2021. https://prace-ri.eu/wp-content/uploads/Best-Practice-Guide_Parallel-IO.pdf.
- Thakur, Rajeev, Ewing Lusk, and William Gropp. *Users guide for ROMIO: A high-performance, portable MPI-IO implementation.* ANL/MCS-TM-234. Artonne, IL, USA: Argonne National Laboratory (October, 1997).
- Thakur, Rajeev, William Gropp, and Ewing Lusk. "Data sieving and collective I/O in ROMIO." Proceedings. Frontiers' 99. Seventh Symposium on the Frontiers of Massively Parallel Computation (February, 1999):182–189.

A.13   *Chapter 17: Tools and resources for better code*

- Stepanov, Evgeniy, and Konstantin Serebryany. "MemorySanitizer: fast detector of uninitialized memory use in C++." 2015 IEEE/ACM International Symposium on Code Generation and Optimization (CGO) (February, 2015):46–55.

appendix B
Solutions to exercises

B.1 Chapter 1: Why parallel computing?

1 What are some other examples of parallel operations in your daily life? How would you classify your example? What does the parallel design appear to optimize for? Can you compute a parallel speedup for this example?

Answer: Examples of parallel operations in daily life include multi-lane highways, class registration queues, and mail delivery. There are many others.

2 For your desktop, laptop, or cellphone, what is the theoretical parallel processing power of your system in comparison to its serial processing power? What kinds of parallel hardware are present in it?

Answer: It can be hard to penetrate the marketing and hype and find the real specifications. Most devices, including handheld, have multi-core processors and at least an integrated graphics processor. Desktops and laptops have some vector capabilities except for very old hardware.

3 Which parallel strategies do you see in the store checkout example in figure 1.1? Are there some present parallel strategies that are not shown? How about in your examples from exercise 1?

Answer: Multiple instruction, multiple data (MIMD), distributed data, pipeline parallelism, and out-of-order execution with specialized queues.

4 You have an image-processing application that needs to process 1,000 images daily, which are 4 mebibytes (MiB, 2^{20} or 1,048,576 bytes) each in size. It takes 10 min in serial to process each image. Your cluster is composed of multi-core nodes with 16 cores and a total of 16 gibibytes (GiB, 2^{30} bytes, or 1024 mebibytes) of main memory storage per node. (Note that we use the

619

proper binary terms, MiB and GiB, rather than MB and GB, which are the metric terms for 10^6 and 10^9 bytes, respectively.)

a What parallel processing design best handles this workload?

b Now customer demand increases by 10x. Does your design handle this? What changes would you have to make?

Answer: Threading on a single compute node along with vectorization. 4MiB × 1000 = 4 Gb. But to process 16 images at a time, only 64 MiB is needed, well under 1 GiB on each node (workstation) of the cluster. The time would be 10 min × 1000 or 167 min in serial and 10.4 min on 16 cores in parallel. Vectorization could reduce this to under 5 min. A demand increase of 10x would make this 100 min. This may be Ok, but it might also be time to think about message passing or distributed computing.

5 An Intel Xeon E5-4660 processor has a thermal design power of 130 W; this is the average power consumption rate when all 16 cores are used. Nvidia's Tesla V100 GPU and AMD's MI25 Radeon GPU have a thermal design power of 300 W. Suppose you port your software to use one of these GPUs. How much faster should your application run on the GPU to be considered more energy efficient than your 16-core CPU application?

Answer: 300 W / 130 W. It needs to have a 2.3x speedup to be more energy efficient.

B.2   Chapter 2: Planning for parallelism

1 You have a wave height simulation application that you developed during graduate school. It is a serial application and because it was only planned to be the basis for your dissertation, you didn't incorporate any software engineering techniques. Now you plan to use it as the starting point for an available tool that many researchers can use. You have three other developers on your team. What would you include in your project plan for this?

Answer: The preparation steps would include

– Establishing a version control system with Git
– Creating a set of tests with known results
– Running memory correctness tools on the tests in the test suite
– Profiling the hardware and your application
– Creating a plan for the next step in your agile management strategy

2 Create a test using CTest

Answer: To create a test using CTest, because CTest detects any error status from a command, a test can be made from a build instruction. Sometimes installing the CTest files will strip the executable bit from the permissions and cause the test to fail with no clear error message. To avoid this, we can add a test to detect if the CTest script is executable. In the following code, the $0 is the CTest script with the full path so that it works for out-of-tree builds.

– In CMakeLists.txt, add

```
enable_testing()

add_test(NAME make WORKING_DIRECTORY ${CMAKE_BINARY_DIRECTORY}
         COMMAND ${CMAKE_CURRENT_SOURCE_DIR}/build.ctest)
```

– Add the build.ctest file with

```
#!/bin/sh
if [ -x $0 ]
then
    echo "PASSED - is executable"
else
    echo "Failed - ctest script is not executable"
    exit -1
fi
```

3 Fix the memory errors in listing 2.2

Answer: You can fix the memory errors in listing 2.2 by changing or adding the following lines:

```
4     int ipos=0, ival;
7     for (int i = 0; i<10; i++){ iarray[i] = ipos; }
8     for (int i = 0; i<10; i++){
11    free(iarray);
```

4 Run valgrind on a small application of your choice

Answer: On your own

B.3   Chapter 3: Performance limits and profiling

1 Calculate the theoretical performance of a system of your choice. Include the peak flops, memory bandwidth, and machine balance in your calculation.

Answer: On your own

2 Download the Roofline Toolkit from https://bitbucket.org/berkeleylab/cs-roofline-toolkit.git and measure the actual performance of your selected system.

Answer: On your own

3 With the Roofline Toolkit, start with one processor and incrementally add optimization and parallelization, recording how much improvement you get at each step.

Answer: On your own

4 Download the STREAM benchmark from https://www.cs.virginia.edu/stream/ and measure the memory bandwidth of your selected system.

Answer: On your own

5 Pick one of the publicly available benchmarks or mini-apps listed in section 17.4 and generate a call graph using KCachegrind.

Answer: On your own

6 Pick one of the publicly available benchmarks or mini-apps listed in section 17.4 and measure its arithmetic intensity with either Intel Advisor or the likwid tools.

Answer: On your own

7 Using the performance tools presented in this chapter, determine the average processor frequency and energy consumption for a small application.

Answer: On your own

8 Using some of the tools from section 2.3.3, determine how much memory an application uses.

Answer: On your own

B.4   Chapter 4: Data design and performance models

1 Write a 2D contiguous memory allocator for a lower-left triangular matrix.

Answer: Listing B.4.1 shows the code to allocate a lower-left triangular array. Assume array indexing is C, with the lower left element at [0][0]. Also, the matrix must be a square matrix. We use the same code as in listing 4.3 but with the length of imax reduced by 1 for each row. Note that the number of elements in the triangular array can be calculated by jmax*(imax+1)/2.

Listing B.4.1   Triangular matrix allocation

ExerciseB.4.1/malloc2Dtri.c

```
 1 #include <stdlib.h>
 2 #include "malloc2Dtri.h"
 3
 4 double **malloc2Dtri(int jmax, int imax)
 5 {
 6    double **x =
         (double **)malloc(jmax*sizeof(double *) +      First allocate a block of
                                                         memory for the row
 7         jmax*(imax+1)/2*sizeof(double));              pointers and the 2D array
 8
 9    x[0] = (double *)(x + jmax);        ◄──    Now assign the start of the block of memory
                                                 for the 2D array after the row pointers
10
11    for (int j = 1; j < jmax; j++, imax--) {    ◄──        Reduce imax by 1
12       x[j] = x[j-1] + imax;    ◄──   Last, assign the memory    each iteration
13    }                                 location to point to for
14                                      each row pointer
```

```
15    return(x);
16 }
```

2 Write a 2D allocator for C that lays out the memory the same way as Fortran.

Answer: Let's assume that we want to address the array as x(j,i) in Fortran. The array will be addressed as x[i][j] in C. If we create a macro #define x(j,i) x[i-1][j-1], then the code could use the Fortran array notation. The 2D memory allocator from listing 4.3 can be used by interchanging i and j and imax and jmax. The following listing shows the resulting code.

Listing B.4.2 Triangular matrix allocation

Exercise4.2/malloc2Dfort.c
```
 1 #include <stdlib.h>
 2 #include "malloc2Dfort.h"
 3
 4 double **malloc2Dfort(int jmax, int imax)
 5 {
 6    double **x =                                    First allocate a block of
          (double **)malloc(imax*sizeof(double *) +   memory for the column
 7        imax*jmax*sizeof(double));                   pointers and the 2D array
 8
 9    x[0] = (double *)(x + imax);    ◄───  Now assign the start of the block of memory
10                                          for the 2D array after the column pointers
11    for (int i = 1; i < imax; i++) {
12        x[i] = x[i-1] + jmax;    ◄──  Last, assign the memory
13    }                                  location to point to for
14                                       each column pointer
15    return(x);
16 }
```

3 Design a macro for an Array of Structure of Arrays (AoSoA) for the RGB color model in section 4.1.

Answer: We want to retrieve the data with the normal array index and color name:

```
#define VV = 4
#define color(i,C) AOSOA[(i)/VV].C[(i)%4-1]
color(50,B)
```

4 Modify the code for the cell-centric full matrix data structure to *not* use a conditional and estimate its performance.

Answer: The following figure shows the code with the if statement removed. From this modified code, the performance model counts look like the following:

$$\text{Memops} = 2 * N_c N_m + 2 * N_c = 102 \, M \, \text{Memops}$$

```
1: for all cells, C, up to N_c do
2:     ave ← 0.0
3:     for all material IDs, m, up to N_m do
4:         ave ← ave + ρ[C][m] * f[C][m]        # 2N_c N_m loads (ρ, f)
                                                  # 2N_c N_m flops (+, *)
5:     end for
6:     ρ_ave[C] ← ave/V[C]                       # N_c stores (ρ_ave), N_c loads (V)
                                                  # N_c flops (/)
7: end for
```

Performance Model = 61.0 ms. This performance estimate is slightly faster than the version with the `if` statement.

5 How would an AVX-512 vector unit change the ECM model for the stream triad?

Answer: The performance analysis with the ECM model in section 4.4 uses an AVX-256 vector unit that could process all the needed floating-point operations in 1 cycle. The AVX-512 would still need 1 cycle but would only have half of its vector units busy and could do twice the work if it were present. Because the compute operation time, T_{OL}, remains at 1 cycle, the performance would not change at all.

B.5   *Chapter 5: Parallel algorithms and patterns*

1 A cloud collision model in an ash plume is invoked for particles within a 1 mm distance. Write pseudocode for a spatial hash implementation. What complexity order is this operation?

Answer: The pseudocode for the collision operation is as follows:

```
1. Bin particles into 1 mm spatial bins
2. For each bin
3.     For each particle, i, in the bin
4.         For all other particles, j, in this bin or adjacent bins
5.             if  |P_i - P_j| < 1 mm
6.                 compute collision
```

The operation is $O(N^2)$ in the local region, but as the mesh grows larger, the distance between the particles does not have to be computed for larger regions, thus, the operation approaches $O(N)$.

2 How are spatial hashes used by the postal service?

Answer: Zip codes. The hashing function encodes the state and region in the first three digits with the remaining two encoding first the large towns and then alphabetical order for the rest.

3 Big data uses a map-reduce algorithm for efficient processing of large data sets. How is it different than the hashing concepts presented here?

Answer: Although developed for different problem domains and scales, the map operation in the map-reduce algorithm is a hash. So these both do a hashing step followed by a second local operation. The spatial hash has a concept of a distance relationship between bins, whereas the map-reduce intrinsically does not.

4 A wave simulation code uses an AMR mesh to better refine the shoreline. The simulation requirements are to record the wave heights versus time for specified locations where buoys and shore facilities are located. Because the cells are constantly being refined, how could you implement this?

Answer: Create a perfect spatial hash with the bin size the same as the smallest cell and store the cell index in the bins underlying the cell. Calculate the bin for each station and get the cell index from the bin.

B.6   Chapter 6: Vectorization: FLOPs for free

1 Experiment with auto-vectorizing loops from the multimaterial code in section 4.3 (https://github.com/LANL/MultiMatTest.git). Add the vectorization and loop report flags and see what your compiler tells you.

Answer: On your own

2 Add OpenMP SIMD pragmas to help the compiler vectorize loops to the loop you selected in the first exercise.

Answer: On your own

3 For one of the vector intrinsic examples, change the vector length from four double precision values to an eight-wide vector width. Check the source code for this chapter for examples of working code for eight-wide implementations.

Answer: In kahan_fog_vector.cpp, change 4s to 8s and change Vec4d to Vec8d. Add `mprefer-vector-width=512 -DMAX_VECTOR_SIZE=512` to CXXFLAGS. The changed code and Makefile are included in the source code for this chapter.

4 If you are on an older CPU, does your program from exercise 3 successfully run? What is the performance impact?

Answer: For Intel 256-bit vector units, the Intel intrinsics do not work and must be commented out. The GCC and Fog versions still work, however. The timing results from a 2017 Mac laptop show the superiority of Agner Fog's vector class library with the eight-wide vectors producing better results than the four-wide. In contrast, the GCC implementation for the eight-wide vector is slower than the four-wide version. Here's the output:

```
SETTINGS INFO -- ncells 1073741824 log 30
Initializing mesh with Leblanc problem, high values first
  relative diff  runtime   Description
    8.423e-09    1.461642  Serial sum
            0    3.283697  Kahan sum with double double accumulator
```

```
                    4 wide vectors serial sum
                        -3.356e-09    0.408654    Serial sum (OpenMP SIMD pragma)
                        -3.356e-09    0.407457    Intel vector intrinsics Serial sum
                        -3.356e-09    0.402928    GCC vector intrinsics Serial sum
                        -3.356e-09    0.406626    Fog C++ vector class Serial sum
                    4 wide vectors Kahan sum
                                 0    0.872013    Intel Vector intrinsics Kahan sum
                                 0    0.873640    GCC vector extensions Kahan sum
                                 0    0.872774    Fog C++ vector class Kahan sum
                  8 wide vector serial sum
                        -1.986e-09    1.467707    8 wide GCC vector intrinsic Serial sum
                        -1.986e-09    0.586075    8 wide Fog C++ vector class Serial sum
                  8 wide vector Kahan sum
                        -1.388e-16    1.914804    8 wide GCC vector extensions Kahan sum
                        -1.388e-16    0.545128    8 wide Fog C++ vector class Kahan sum
                        -1.388e-16    0.687497    Agner C++ vector class Kahan sum
```

B.7   Chapter 7: OpenMP that performs

1 Convert the vector add example in listing 7.8 into a high-level OpenMP following the steps in section 7.2.2.

Answer: Converting to high-level OpenMP, we end up with the code shown in the following listing with just a single pragma to open the parallel region.

Listing B.7.1   High-level OpenMP

```
ExerciseB.7.1/vecadd.c
11 int main(int argc, char *argv[]){
12    #pragma omp parallel
13    {
14       double time_sum;
15       struct timespec tstart;
16       int thread_id = omp_get_thread_num();
17       int nthreads  = omp_get_num_threads();
18       if (thread_id == 0){
19          printf("Running with %d thread(s)\n",nthreads);
20       }
21       int tbegin = ARRAY_SIZE * ( thread_id     ) / nthreads;
22       int tend   = ARRAY_SIZE * ( thread_id + 1 ) / nthreads;
23
24       for (int i=tbegin; i<tend; i++) {
25          a[i] = 1.0;
26          b[i] = 2.0;
27       }
28
29       if (thread_id == 0) cpu_timer_start(&tstart);
30       vector_add(c, a, b, ARRAY_SIZE);
31       if (thread_id == 0) {
32          time_sum += cpu_timer_stop(tstart);
33          printf("Runtime is %lf msecs\n", time_sum);
34       }
35    }
36 }
```

```
37
38 void vector_add(double *c, double *a, double *b, int n)
39 {
40    int thread_id = omp_get_thread_num();
41    int nthreads = omp_get_num_threads();
42    int tbegin = n * ( thread_id     ) / nthreads;
43    int tend   = n * ( thread_id + 1 ) / nthreads;
44    for (int i=tbegin; i < tend; i++){
45       c[i] = a[i] + b[i];
46    }
47 }
```

2 Write a routine to get the maximum value in an array. Add an OpenMP pragma to add thread parallelism to the routine.

Answer: The reduction routine uses the `reduction(max:xmax)` clause as the following listing shows.

Listing B.7.2 OpenMP max reduction

ExerciseB.7.2/max_reduction.c
```
1 #include <float.h>
2 double array_max(double* restrict var, int ncells)
3 {
4    double xmax = DBL_MIN;
5    #pragma omp parallel for reduction(max:xmax)
6    for (int i = 0; i < ncells; i++){
7       if (var[i] > xmax) xmax = var[i];
8    }
9 }
```

3 Write a high-level OpenMP version of the reduction in the previous exercise.

Answer: In high-level OpenMP, we manually divide up the data. The data decomposition is done in lines 6-9 in listing B.7.3. Thread 0 allocates the xmax-_thread shared data array on line 13. Lines 18–22 find the maximum value for each thread and store the result in the xmax_thread array. Then, on lines 26–30, one thread finds the maximum across all the threads.

Listing B.7.3 High-level OpenMP

ExerciseB.7.3/max_reduction.c
```
 1 #include <stdlib.h>
 2 #include <float.h>
 3 #include <omp.h>
 4 double array_max(double* restrict var, int ncells)
 5 {
 6    int nthreads = omp_get_num_threads();
 7    int thread_id = omp_get_thread_num();
 8    int tbegin = ncells * ( thread_id     ) / nthreads;
 9    int tend   = ncells * ( thread_id + 1 ) / nthreads;
10    static double xmax;
```

```
11      static double *xmax_thread;
12      if (thread_id == 0){
13         xmax_thread = malloc(nthreads*sizeof(double));
14         xmax = DBL_MIN;
15      }
16  #pragma omp barrier
17
18      double xmax_thread_private = DBL_MIN;
19      for (int i = tbegin; i < tend; i++){
20         if (var[i] > xmax_thread_private) xmax_thread_private = var[i];
21      }
22      xmax_thread[thread_id] = xmax_thread_private;
23
24  #pragma omp barrier
25
26      if (thread_id == 0){
27         for (int tid=0; tid < nthreads; tid++){
28            if (xmax_thread[tid] > xmax) xmax = xmax_thread[tid];
29         }
30      }
31
32  #pragma omp barrier
33
34      if (thread_id == 0){
35         free(xmax_thread);
36      }
37      return(xmax);
38  }
```

B.8 *Chapter 8: MPI: The parallel backbone*

1   Why can't we just block on receives as was done in the send/receive in the ghost exchange using the pack or array buffer methods in listings 8.20 and 8.21, respectively?

Answer: The version using the pack or array buffers schedules the send, but returns before the data is copied or sent. The standard for the MPI_Isend says, "*The sender should not modify any part of the send buffer after a nonblocking send operation is called, until the send completes.*" The pack and array versions deallocate the buffers after the communication. So these versions might delete the buffers before these are copied, causing the program to crash. To be safe, the status of the send must be checked before the buffer is deleted.

2   Is it safe to block on receives as shown in listing 8.8 in the vector type version of the ghost exchange? What are the advantages if we only block on receives?

Answer: The vector version sends the data from the original arrays instead of making a copy. This is safer than the versions that allocate a buffer, which will be deallocated. If we only block on receives, the communication can be faster.

3   Modify the ghost cell exchange vector type example in listing 8.21 to use blocking receives instead of a waitall. Is it faster? Does it always work?

Answer: Even with the vector version of the ghost cell exchange, we have to be careful that we do not modify the buffers that are still in the process of being sent. The odds of this happening can be small when we are not sending corners. But it still can occur. To be absolutely safe, we need to check for completion of the sends before changing the arrays.

4 Try replacing the explicit tags in one of the ghost exchange routines with `MPI_ANY_TAG`. Does it work? Is it any faster? What advantage do you see in using explicit tags?

Answer: Using `MPI_ANY_TAG` for the tag argument works fine. It can be slightly faster though it is unlikely that it will be significant enough to be measurable. Using explicit tags adds another check that the right message is being received.

5 Remove the barriers in the synchronized timers in one of the ghost exchange examples. Run the code with the original synchronized timers and the unsynchronized timers.

Answer: Removing the barriers in the timers should give better performance and allow the processes to operate more independently (asynchronous). It can be more difficult to understand the timing measurements though.

6 Add the timer statistics from listing 8.11 to the stream triad bandwidth measurement code in listing 8.17.

Answer: On your own

7 Apply the steps to convert high-level OpenMP to the hybrid MPI plus OpenMP example in the code that accompanies the chapter (HybridMPIPlusOpenMP directory). Experiment with the vectorization, number of threads, and MPI ranks on your platform.

Answer: On your own

B.9 Chapter 9: GPU architectures and concepts

1 Table 9.7 shows the achievable performance for a 1 flop/load application. Look up the current prices for the GPUs available on the market and fill in the last two columns to get the flop per dollar for each GPU. Which looks like the best value? If turnaround time for your application runtime is the most important criteria, which GPU would be best to purchase?

Table 9.7 Achievable performance for a 1 flop/load application with various GPUs

GPU	Achievable Performance Gflops/sec	Price	Flops/$
V100	108.23		
Vega 20	91.38		

Table 9.7   Achievable performance for a 1 flop/load application with various GPUs (continued)

GPU	Achievable Performance Gflops/sec	Price	Flops/$
P100	74.69		
GeForce GTX1080Ti	44.58		
Quadro K6000	31.25		
Tesla S2050	18.50		

Answer: On your own

2 Measure the stream bandwidth of your GPU or another selected GPU. How does it compare to the ones presented in the chapter?

Answer: On your own

3 Use the likwid performance tool to get the CPU power requirements for the CloverLeaf application on a system where you have access to the power hardware counters.

Answer: On your own

B.10   *Chapter 10: GPU programming model*

1 You have an image classification application that will take 5 ms to transfer each file to the GPU, 5 ms to process and 5 ms to bring back. On the CPU, the processing takes 100 ms per image. There are one million images to process. You have 16 processing cores on the CPU. Would a GPU system do the work faster?

Answer:

Time on a CPU—100 ms × 1,000,000/16 /1,000 = 6,250 s
Time on a GPU—(5 ms + 5 ms + 5 ms) × 1,000,000/1,000 = 15,000 s
The GPU system would not be faster. It would take about 2.5 times as long.

2 The transfer time for the GPU in problem 1 is based on a third generation PCI bus. If you can get a Gen4 PCI bus, how does that change the design? A Gen 5 PCI bus? For image classification, you shouldn't need to bring back a modified image. How does that change the calculation?

Answer: A fourth-generation PCI bus is twice as fast as a third-generation PCI bus.

(2.5 ms + 5 ms + 2.5 ms) × 1,000,000/1,000 = 10,000 s

A fifth-generation PCI bus would be four times as fast as the original third-generation PCI bus.

(1.25 ms + 5 ms + 1.25 ms) × 1,000,000/1,000 = 7,500 s

If we don't have to transfer the results back, we are now just as fast on the GPU as on the CPU.

(1.25 ms + 5 ms) × 1,000,000/1,000 = 6,250 s

3 For your discrete GPU (or NVIDIA GeForce GTX 1060, if none), what size 3D application could you run? Assume 4 double-precision variables per cell and a usage limit of half the GPU memory so you have room for temporary arrays. How does this change if you use single precision?

Answer: An NVIDIA GeForce GTX 1060 has a memory size of 6 GiB. It has GDDR5 with a 192-bit wide bus and 8GHz memory clock.

(6 GiB/2/4 doubles/8bytes × $1024^3)^{1/3}$ = 465 × 465 × 465 3D mesh

For single precision

(6 GiB/2/4floats/4bytes × $1024^3)^{1/3}$ = 586 × 586 × 586 3D mesh

If we are dividing up our computational domain into this 3D mesh, this is a 25% improvement in resolution.

B.11 Chapter 11: Directive-based GPU programming

1 Find what compilers are available for your local GPU system. Are both Open-ACC and OpenMP compilers available? If not, do you have access to any systems that would allow you to try out these pragma-based languages?

Answer: On your own

2 Run the stream triad examples from the OpenACC/StreamTriad and/or the OpenMP/StreamTriad directories on your local GPU development system. You'll find these directories at https://github.com/EssentialsofParallelComputing/Chapter11.

Answer: On your own

3 Compare your results from exercise 2 to BabelStream results at https://uob-hpc.github.io/BabelStream/results/. For the stream triad, the bytes moved are `3 * nsize * sizeof(datatype)`.

Answer: From the performance results in the chapter for the NVIDIA V100 GPU

3 × 20,000,000 × 8 bytes/.586 ms) × (1000 ms/s) / (1,000,000,000 bytes/GB) = 819 GB/s

This is about 50% greater than the peak shown for the BabelStream benchmark for the NVIDIA P100 GPU.

4 Modify the OpenMP data region mapping in listing 11.16 to reflect the actual use of the arrays in the kernels.

Answer: The arrays are only used on the GPU, so these can be allocated there and deleted at the end. Therefore, the changes are

```
13 #pragma omp target enter data map(alloc:a[0:nsize], b[0:nsize],
                                          c[0:nsize])
36 #pragma omp target exit data map(delete:a[0:nsize], b[0:nsize],
                                          c[0:nsize])
```

The full listing of this change is in Stream_par7.c in the examples for the chapter.

5 Implement the mass sum example from listing 11.4 in OpenMP.

Answer: We just need to change the one pragma as the following listing shows.

Listing B.11.5 GPU version of OpenMP

ExerciseB.11.5/mass_sum.c
```
 1 #include "mass_sum.h"
 2 #define REAL_CELL 1
 3
 4 double mass_sum(int ncells, int* restrict celltype,
 5        double* restrict H, double* restrict dx, double* restrict dy){
 6    double summer = 0.0;
 7 #pragma omp target teams distribute \
               parallel for simd reduction(+:summer)
 8    for (int ic=0; ic<ncells ; ic++) {
 9       if (celltype[ic] == REAL_CELL) {
10          summer += H[ic]*dx[ic]*dy[ic];
11       }
12    }
13    return(summer);
14 }
```

6 For x and y arrays of size 20,000,000, find the maximum radius for the arrays using both OpenMP and OpenACC. Initialize the arrays with double-precision values that linearly increase from 1.0 to 2.0e7 for the x array and decrease from 2.0e7 to 1.0 for the y array.

Answer: The following listing shows a possible implementation of finding the maximum radius using OpenACC.

Listing B.11.6 OpenACC version of Max Radius

ExerciseB.11.6/MaxRadius.c or Chapter11/OpenACC/MaxRadius/MaxRadius.c
```
 1 #include <stdio.h>
 2 #include <math.h>
 3 #include <openacc.h>
 4
 5 int main(int argc, char *argv[]){
 6    int ncells = 20000000;
 7    double* restrict x = acc_malloc(ncells * sizeof(double));
 8    double* restrict y = acc_malloc(ncells * sizeof(double));
```

```
 9
10    double MaxRadius = -1.0e30;
11 #pragma acc parallel deviceptr(x, y)
12    {
13 #pragma acc loop
14        for (int ic=0; ic<ncells; ic++) {
15            x[ic] = (double)(ic+1);
16            y[ic] = (double)(ncells-ic);
17        }
18
19 #pragma acc loop reduction(max:MaxRadius)
20        for (int ic=0; ic<ncells ; ic++) {
21            double radius = sqrt(x[ic]*x[ic] + y[ic]*y[ic]);
22            if (radius > MaxRadius) MaxRadius = radius;
23        }
24    }
25    printf("Maximum Radius is %lf\n",MaxRadius);
26
27    acc_free(x);
28    acc_free(y);
29 }
```

B.12 *Chapter 12: GPU languages: Getting down to basics*

1 Change the host memory allocation in the CUDA stream triad example to use pinned memory (listings 12.1–12.6). Did you get a performance improvement?

Answer: To get pinned memory, replace `malloc` in the host-side memory allocation with `cudaHostMalloc` and the free memory with `cudaFreeHost` as listing B.12.1 shows. In the listing, we only display the lines that need to be changed. Compare the performance to the code from chapter12 in CUDA/StreamTriad directory. The data transfer time should be at least a factor of two times faster with pinned memory.

> **Listing B.12.1   Pinned memory version of stream triad**

```
ExerciseB.12.1/StreamTriad.cu
31    // allocate host memory and initialize
32    double *a, *b, *c;
33    cudaMallocHost(&a,stream_array_size*sizeof(double));
34    cudaMallocHost(&b,stream_array_size*sizeof(double));
35    cudaMallocHost(&c,stream_array_size*sizeof(double));
       < ... steam triad code ... >
86    cudaFreeHost(a);
87    cudaFreeHost(b);
88    cudaFreeHost(c);
```

2 For the sum reduction example, try an array size of 18,000 elements all initialized to their index value. Run the CUDA code and then the version in SumReductionRevealed. You may want to adjust the amount of information printed.

Answer: On your own

3 Convert the CUDA reduction example to HIP by hipifying it.

Answer: On your own

4 For the SYCL example in listing 12.20, initialize the a and b arrays on the GPU device.

Answer: The following listing shows a version with the a and b arrays initialized on the GPU.

Listing B.12.4   Initializing arrays a and b in SYCL

```
14   // host data
15   vector<double> a(nsize);
16   vector<double> b(nsize);
17   vector<double> c(nsize);
18
19   t1 = chrono::high_resolution_clock::now();
20
21   Sycl::queue Queue(sycl::cpu_selector{});
22
23   const double scalar = 3.0;
24
25   Sycl::buffer<double,1> dev_a { a.data(), Sycl::range<1>(a.size()) };
26   Sycl::buffer<double,1> dev_b { b.data(), Sycl::range<1>(b.size()) };
27   Sycl::buffer<double,1> dev_c { c.data(), Sycl::range<1>(c.size()) };
28
29   Queue.submit([&](sycl::handler& CommandGroup) {
30
31       auto a =
            dev_a.get_access<Sycl::access::mode::write>(CommandGroup);
32       auto b =
            dev_b.get_access<Sycl::access::mode::write>(CommandGroup);
33       auto c =
            dev_c.get_access<Sycl::access::mode::write>(CommandGroup);
34
35       CommandGroup.parallel_for<class StreamTriad>(
            Sycl::range<1>{nsize}, [=] (Sycl::id<1> it) {
36           a[it] =  1.0;
37           b[it] =  2.0;
38           c[it] = -1.0;
39       });
40   });
41   Queue.wait();
42
43   Queue.submit([&](sycl::handler& CommandGroup) {
44
45       auto a = dev_a.get_access<Sycl::access::mode::read>(CommandGroup);
46       auto b = dev_b.get_access<Sycl::access::mode::read>(CommandGroup);
47       auto c =
            dev_c.get_access<Sycl::access::mode::write>(CommandGroup);
48
49       CommandGroup.parallel_for<class StreamTriad>(
            Sycl::range<1>{nsize}, [=] (Sycl::id<1> it) {
```

```
50              c[it] = a[it] + scalar * b[it];
51         });
52    });
53    Queue.wait();
54
55    t2 = chrono::high_resolution_clock::now();
```

5 Convert the two initialization loops in the Raja example in listing 12.24 to the Raja:forall syntax. Try running the example with CUDA.

Answer: The initialization loop needs the changes shown in the following listing. Then the stream triad code is built and run the same way as in section 12.5.2.

> **Listing B.12.5   Adding Raja to the initialization loop of stream triad**

```
ExerciseB.12.5/StreamTriad.cc
19 RAJA::forall<RAJA::omp_parallel_for_exec>(RAJA::RangeSegment(0,
      nsize), [=] (int i) {
20   a[i] = 1.0;
21   b[i] = 2.0;
22 });
```

With these changes, the run time compared to the original version in section 12.5.2 drops from around 6.59 ms to 1.67 ms.

B.13   Chapter 13: GPU profiling and tools

1 Run nvprof on the STREAM Triad example. You might try the CUDA version from chapter 12 or the OpenACC version from chapter 11. What workflow did you use for your hardware resources? If you don't have access to an NVIDIA GPU, can you use another profiling tool?

Answer: On your own

2 Generate a trace from nvprof and import it into NVVP. Where is the run time spent? What could you do to optimize it?

Answer: On your own

3 Download a prebuilt Docker container from the appropriate vendor for your system. Start up the container and run one of the examples from chapter 11 or 12.

Answer: On your own

B.14   Chapter 14: Affinity: Truce with the kernel

1 Generate a visual image of a couple of different hardware architectures. Discover the hardware characteristics for these devices.

Answer: Use the lstopo tool to generate an image of your architecture.

2 For your hardware, run the test suite using the script in listing 14.4. What do you discover about how to best use your system?

Answer: On your own

3 Change the program used in the vector addition (vecadd_opt3.c) example in section 14.3 to include more floating-point operations. Take the kernel and change the operations in the loop to the Pythagorean formula:

```
c[i] = sqrt(a[i] * a[i] + b[i] * b[i]);
```

How do your results and conclusions about the best placement and bindings change? Do you see benefit from hyperthreads now (if you have those)?

Answer: On your own

4 For the MPI example in section 14.4, include the vector add kernel and generate a scaling graph for the kernel. Then replace the kernel with the Pythagorean formula used in exercise 3.

Answer: On your own

5 Replace the kernel with the Pythagorean formula used in exercise 3.

Answer: On your own

6 Combine the vector add and Pythagorean formula in the following routine (either in a single loop or two separate loops) to get more data reuse:

```
c[i] = a[i] + b[i];
d[i] = sqrt(a[i]*a[i] + b[i]*b[i]);
```

How does this change the results of the placement and binding study?

Answer: On your own

7 Add code to set the placement and affinity within the application from one of the previous exercises.

Answer: On your own

B.15   *Chapter 15: Batch schedulers: Bringing order to chaos*

1 Try submitting a couple of jobs, one with 32 processors and one with 16 processors. Check to see that these are submitted and whether they are running. Delete the 32 processor job. Check to see that it got deleted.

Answer: On your own

2 Modify the automatic restart script so that the first job is a preprocessing step to set up for the computation and the restarts are for running the simulation.

Answer: To insert a preprocessing step, we need to insert another conditional case as the following listing shows on lines 31–36 and then use the PREPRO-CESS_DONE file to indicate that the preprocessing has been done.

Listing B.15.2a Inserting preprocessing step and then automatically restarting

```
ExerciseB.15.2/Preprocess_then_restart.sh
 1 #!/bin/sh
 2 #SBATCH -N 1
 3 #SBATCH -n 4
 4 #SBATCH --signal=23@160
 5 #SBATCH -t 00:08:00
 6
 7 # Do not place bash commands before the last SBATCH directive
 8 # Behavior can be unreliable
 9
10 NUM_CPUS=4
11 OUTPUT_FILE=run.out
12 EXEC_NAME=./testapp
13 MAX_RESTARTS=4
14
15 if [ -z ${COUNT} ]; then
16     export COUNT=0
17 fi
18
19 ((COUNT++))
20 echo "Restart COUNT is ${COUNT}"
21
22 if [ ! -e DONE ]; then
23     if [ -e RESTART ]; then
24         echo "=== Restarting ${EXEC_NAME} ==="            >> ${OUTPUT_FILE}
25         cycle=`cat RESTART`
26         rm -f RESTART
27     elif [ -e PREPROCESS_DONE ]; then
28         echo "=== Starting problem ==="                   >> ${OUTPUT_FILE}
29         cycle=""
30     else
31         echo "=== Preprocessing data for problem ==="     >> ${OUTPUT_FILE}
32         mpirun -n ${NUM_CPUS} ./preprocess_data          &>> ${OUTPUT_FILE}
33         date > PREPROCESS_DONE
34         sbatch \                                          ┤ Submits first
              --dependency=afterok:${SLURM_JOB_ID} \          calculation job
              <preprocess_then_restart.sh                     after preprocess
35         exit
36     fi
37
38     echo "=== Submitting restart script ==="             >> ${OUTPUT_FILE}
39     sbatch \                                              ┤ Submits
           --dependency=afterok:${SLURM_JOB_ID} \             restart job
           <preprocess_then_restart.sh
40
41     mpirun -n ${NUM_CPUS} ${EXEC_NAME} ${cycle}          &>> ${OUTPUT_FILE}
42     echo "Finished mpirun"                               >> ${OUTPUT_FILE}
43
```

```
44   if [ ${COUNT} -ge ${MAX_RESTARTS} ]; then
45       echo "=== Reached maximum number of restarts ===" >> ${OUTPUT_FILE}
46       date > DONE
47   fi
48 fi
```

Often the preprocessing step needs a different number of processors. In this case, we can use a separate batch script for the preprocessing, shown in the following listing.

Listing B.15.2b   Smaller preprocessing step and then automatic restart

```
ExerciseB.15.2/Preprocess_batch.sh
 1 #!/bin/sh
 2 #SBATCH -N 1
 3 #SBATCH -n 1
 5 #SBATCH -t 01:00:00
 6
 7 sbatch --dependency=afterok:${SLURM_JOB_ID} <batch_restart.sh
 9
10 mpirun -n 4 ./preprocess &> preprocess.out
```

3   Modify the simple batch script in listing 15.1 for Slurm and 15.2 for PBS to clean up on failure by removing a file called simulation_database.

Answer: Change the Slurm batch script to check the status of the command and remove the simulation database. There are several different ways to do the cleanup. Here are three. The first two in listings B.15.3a and b use the exit code from the mpirun command.

Listing B.15.3a   OpenACC version of Max Radius

```
ExerciseB.15.3/batch_simple_error.sh
 1 #!/bin/sh
 2 #SBATCH -N 1
 3 #SBATCH -n 4
 5 #SBATCH -t 01:00:00
 6
 7 mpirun -n 4 ./testapp &> run.out || \
     rm -f simulation_database
```

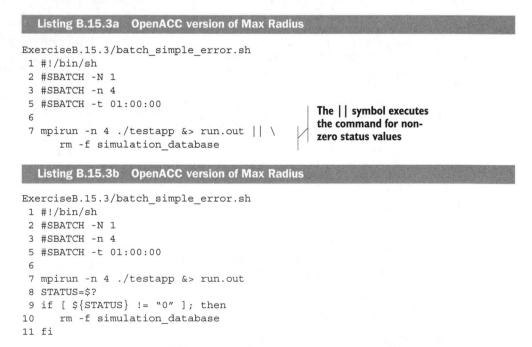

The || symbol executes the command for non-zero status values

Listing B.15.3b   OpenACC version of Max Radius

```
ExerciseB.15.3/batch_simple_error.sh
 1 #!/bin/sh
 2 #SBATCH -N 1
 3 #SBATCH -n 4
 5 #SBATCH -t 01:00:00
 6
 7 mpirun -n 4 ./testapp &> run.out
 8 STATUS=$?
 9 if [ ${STATUS} != "0" ]; then
10    rm -f simulation_database
11 fi
```

The third version in listing B.15.3.b uses the status condition of the batch job through a dependency flag to invoke a cleanup job. The types of errors that are handled are different than the first two methods.

Listing B.15.3b   OpenACC version of Max Radius

```
ExerciseB.15.3/batch.sh
 1 #!/bin/sh
 2 #SBATCH -N 1
 3 #SBATCH -n 4
 5 #SBATCH -t 01:00:00
 6
 7 sbatch --dependency=afternotok:${SLURM_JOB_ID} <batch_cleanup.sh
 9
10 mpirun -n 4 ./testapp &> run.out

ExerciseB.15.3/batch_cleanup.sh
 1 #!/bin/sh
 2 #SBATCH -N 1
 3 #SBATCH -n 1
 5 #SBATCH -t 00:10:00
 6 rm -f simulation_database
```

B.16   *Chapter 16: File operations for a parallel world*

1   Check for the hints available on your system using the techniques described in section 16.6.1.

Answer: On your own

2   Try the MPI–IO and HDF5 examples on your system with much larger datasets to see what performance you can achieve. Compare that to the IOR micro benchmark for extra credit.

Answer: On your own

3   Use the h5ls and h5dump utilities to explore the HDF5 data file created by the example.

Answer: On your own

B.17   *Chapter 17: Tools and resources for better code*

1   Run the Dr. Memory tool on one of your small codes or one of the codes from the exercises in this book.

Answer: On your own

2   Compile one of your codes with the dmalloc library. Run your code and view the results.

Answer: On your own

3   Try inserting a thread race condition into the example code in section 17.6.2
    and see how Archer reports the problem.

Answer: On your own

4   Try the profiling exercise in section 17.8 on your filesystem. If you have more
    than one filesystem, try it on each one. Then change the size of the array in the
    example to 2000x2000. How does it change the filesystem performance results?

Answer: On your own

5   Install one of the tools using the Spack package manager.

Answer: On your own

appendix C
Glossary

3DNow! An AMD vector instruction set that first supported single-precision operations.

Affinity. Assigning a preference for the placement of a process, rank, or thread to a particular hardware component. This is also called pinning or binding.

Algorithmic complexity. A measure of the number of operations that it would take to complete an algorithm. Algorithmic complexity is a property of the algorithm and is a measure of the amount of work or operations in a procedure.

Aliasing. Where pointers point to overlapping regions of memory. In this situation, the compiler cannot tell if it is the same memory, and in these instances, it would be unsafe to generate vectorized code or other optimizations.

Anti-flow dependency. A variable within the loop is written after being read, known as a write-after-read (WAR).

Arithmetic intensity. The number of floating-point operations (flops) relative to the memory loads (data) that your application or kernel (loop) performs. The arithmetic intensity is an important measure to understand the limiting characteristics of an application.

Asymptotic notation. An expression that specifies the limiting bound on performance. Basically, does the run time grow linearly or worse with the size of a problem? The notation uses various forms of O, such as $O(n)$, $O(n \log_2 n)$ or $O(n^2)$. The O can be thought of as "order" as in "scales on an order of."

Asynchronous. This call is non-blocking and only initiates an operation.

Auto-vectorization. The vectorization of the source code by the compiler for standard C, C++, or Fortran language source code.

AVX. Advanced Vector Extensions (AVX) is a 256-bit vector hardware unit and instruction set.

AVX2. An improvement to AVX hardware to support fused multiply adds (FMA).

AVX512. Extends the AVX hardware to 512-bit vector widths.

Bandwidth. The best rate at which data can be moved through a given path in the system. This can refer to memory, disk, or network throughput.

Binary data format. The machine representation of the data that is used by the processor and stored in main memory. Usually this term refers to the data format staying in binary form when it is written out to the hard disk.

Blocking. An operation that does not complete until a specific condition is fulfilled.

Branch miss. The cost encountered when the predicted branch in an if statement is incorrect.

Bucket. A storage location holding a collection of values. Hashing techniques are used to store the values for keys in a bucket because there might be multiple values for that location.

Cache. A faster block of memory that is used to reduce the cost of accessing the slower main memory by storing blocks of data or instructions that might be needed.

Cache eviction. The removal of blocks of data, called cache lines, from one of the various levels of the cache hierarchy.

Cache line. The block of data loaded into cache when memory is accessed.

Cache misses. Occur when the processor tries to access a memory address and it is not in the cache. The system then has to retrieve the data from main memory at a cost of 100s of cycles of time.

Cache thrashing. A condition where one memory load evicts another and then the original data is needed again, causing loading, eviction, and reloading of data.

Cache update storms. On a multiprocessor system, when one processor modifies data that is in another processor's cache, the data has to be reloaded on those other processors.

Call stack. The list of called subroutines that has to be unwound by a return at the end of the subroutine where it jumps back to the previous calling routine.

Capacity misses. The misses that are caused by the limited size of the cache.

Catastrophic cancellation. The subtraction of two almost equal numbers, causing the result to have only a few significant digits.

Centralized version control system. A version control system implemented as a single centralized system.

Checkpoint/Restart. The periodic writing out of the state of an application followed by the starting up of the application in a later job.

Checkpointing. The practice of periodically storing the state of a calculation to disk so that the calculation can be restarted due to system failures or finite length run times in a batch system. See checkpoint/restart.

Clock cycle. The small intervals of time between operations in the computer based on the clock frequency of the system.

Cluster. A small group of distributed memory nodes connected by a commodity network.

Coalesced memory loads. The combination of separate memory loads from groups of threads into a single cache-line load.

Coarse-grained parallelism. A type of parallelism where the processor operates on large blocks of code with infrequent synchronization.

Code coverage. A metric of how many lines of the source code are executed and, therefore, "covered" by running a test suite. It is usually expressed as a percentage of the source lines of code.

Coherency misses. Cache updates needed to synchronize the caches between multiprocessors when data is written to one processor's cache that is also held in another processor's cache.

Cold cache. A cache that does not have any of the data to be operated on in cache from a previous operation when the current operation begins.

Collisions (hash). When more than one key wants to store its value in the same bucket.

Commit tests. A test suite that is run prior to committing any code to the repository.

Compact hash. A hash that is compressed into a smaller memory size. A compact hash must have a way to handle collisions.

Comparative speedups. Short for *comparative performance speedups between architectures.* This is the relative performance between two hardware architectures, often based on a single node or a fixed power envelope.

Compressed sparse data structures. A space-efficient way to represent a data space that is sparse. The most notable example is the Compressed Sparse Row (CSR) format used for sparse matrices.

Compulsory misses. Cache misses are those that are necessary to bring in the data when it is first encountered.

Computational complexity. The number of steps needed to complete an algorithm. This complexity measure is an attribute of the implementation and the type of hardware that is being used for the calculation.

Computational kernel. A section of the application that is both computationally intensive and conceptually self-contained.

Computational mesh. A collection of cells or elements that covers the simulation region.

Compute device (OpenCL). Any computational hardware that can perform computation and supports OpenCL is a compute device. This can include GPUs, CPUs, or even more exotic hardware such as embedded processors or FPGAs.

Concurrency. The operation of parts of a program in any order with the same result. Concurrency was originally developed to support concurrent computing or timesharing by interleaving computing on a limited set of resources.

Conflict misses (cache). Misses caused by the loading of another block of memory into a cache line that is still needed by the CPU.

Contiguous memory. Memory that is composed of an uninterrupted sequence of bytes.

Continuous integration. An automatic testing process that is invoked with every commit to the repository.

Core. Core or computational core is the basic element of the system that does the mathematical and logical operations.

CPU. The discrete processing device (the central processing unit) composed of one or more computational cores that is placed on the socket of a circuit board to provide the main computational operations.

Data parallel. A type of parallelism where the data is partitioned among the processors or threads and operated on in parallel.

Dedicated GPU. A GPU on a separate peripheral card. Also known as a discrete GPU.

Dereferencing. An operation where the memory address is obtained from the pointer reference so that the cache line is for the memory data instead of for the pointer.

Descriptive directives and clauses. These directives give the compiler information about the following loop construct and give the compiler some freedom to generate the most efficient implementation.

Direct-mapped cache. A cache for which a memory address has only one location in the cache where it can be loaded. This can lead to conflicts and evictions if another block of memory also maps to this location. See N-way set associative cache for a type of cache that avoids this problem.

Directive. An instruction to a Fortran compiler to help it interpret the source code. The form of the instruction is a comment line starting with !$.

Discretization. The process of breaking up a computational domain into smaller cells or elements, forming a computational mesh. Calculations are then performed on each cell or element.

Distributed array. An array that is partitioned and split across the processors. For example, an array containing 100 values might be divided up across four processors with 25 values on each processor.

Distributed computing. Applications and loosely coupled workflows that span multiple computers and use communication across the network to coordinate the work. Examples of distributed computing applications include searches via browsers on the internet and multiple clients interacting with a database on a server.

Distributed memory. More than one block of memory, each existing in its own address space and control.

Distributed version control system. A version control system that allows multiple repository databases rather than a single centralized system.

Domain-boundary halos. Halo cells used for imposing a specific set of boundary conditions

Dope vector. The metadata for an array in Fortran composed of the start, stride, and length for each dimension. The meaning is from the slang "give me the dope on" or information on someone or something.

DRAM. Dynamic Random Access Memory. This memory needs to have its state refreshed frequently and the data it stores is lost when the power is turned off.

Dynamic range. The range of the working set of real numbers in a problem.

Eviction. See cache eviction.

Fine-grained parallelism. A type of parallelism where computational loops or other small blocks of code are operated on by multiple processors or threads and may need frequent synchronization.

First touch. The first touch of an array causes the memory to be allocated. It is allocated near to the thread location where the touch occurs. Prior to the first touch, the memory only exists as an entry in virtual memory. The physical memory that corresponds to the virtual memory is created when it is first accessed.

Flow dependency. A variable within the loop is read after being written, known as a read-after-write (RAW).

FLOPs. Floating-point operations such as addition, subtraction, and multiplication on single- or double-precision data types.

Flynn's Taxonomy. A categorization of computer architectures based on whether the data and instructions are either single or multiple.

Gather memory operation. Memory loaded into a cache line or vector unit from noncontiguous memory locations.

Generation (PCIe). The PCI Special Interest Group (PCI SIG) is a group representing industry partners that establishes a PCI Express Specification, commonly referred to as *generation* or *gen* for short.

Ghost cells. A set of cells that contain adjacent processor(s) data for use on the local processor so that the processor can operate in large blocks without issuing communication calls.

Global sum issue. The difference in a global sum in a parallel calculation compared to a serial or run on a different number of processors.

GNU Compiler Collection (GCC). An open-source, publically available compiler suite, including C, C++, Fortran, and many other languages.

GNU's Not Unix (GNU). A free, Unix-like operating system.

Graphical user interface (GUI). An interface composed of visual elements and interactive components that can be manipulated with a mouse or other advanced input devices.

Graphics processing unit (GPU) or general-purpose graphics processing unit (GPGPU), integrated or discrete (external). A device whose primary purpose is drawing graphics to the computer monitor. It is composed of many streaming multiprocessors and its own RAM memory, capable of executing tens of thousands of threads in one clock cycle.

HAL. A small rogue computer that precedes IBM in lexicographic order. HAL is a fictional computer in Arthur C. Clarke's *2001: A Space Odyssey*. HAL goes rogue because it interprets its instructions differently than intended, with deadly consequences. HAL is just one letter off from IBM. HAL's lesson is to be careful with your programming; you never know what the results might be.

Halo cells. Any set of cells surrounding a computational mesh domain.

Hang. When one or more processors is waiting on an event that can never occur.

Hash or hashing. A computer data structure that maps a key to a value.

Hash load factor. The number of filled buckets divided by the total number of buckets in the hash.

Hash sparsity. The amount of empty space in a hash.

Heap. A region of memory for the program that is used to provide dynamic memory for the program. The `malloc` routines and the `new` operator get memory from this region. The second region of memory is stack memory.

High Performance Computing (HPC). Computing that focuses on extreme performance. The computing hardware is generally more tightly coupled. The term High Performance Computing has mostly replaced the older nomenclature of supercomputing.

Hyperthreading. An Intel technology that makes a single processor appear to be two virtual processors to the operating system through sharing of hardware resources between two threads.

Inline (routines). Rather than make a function call, compilers insert the code at the call point to avoid call overhead. This only works for smaller routines and for simpler code.

Interconnects. The connections between compute nodes, also called a *network*. Generally the term refers to higher performance networks that tightly couple the operations on a parallel computing system. Many of these interconnects are vendor proprietary and include specialized topologies such as fat-tree, switches, torus, and dragonfly designs.

Inter-process communication (IPC). Communication between processes on a computer node. The various techniques to communicate between processes form the backbone of client/server mechanisms in distributed computing.

Instruction cache. The storage of instructions in fast memory close to the processor. Instructions can be for memory movement, or integer or floating-point operations. The data that is operated on has its own separate data cache.

Integrated GPU. A graphics processor engine that is contained on the CPU.

Lambda expressions. An unnamed, local function that can be assigned to a variable and used locally or passed to a routine.

Lanes (vector lanes). Pathways for data in a vector operation. For a 256-bit vector unit operating on double-precision values, there are four lanes allowing four simultaneous operations with one instruction in one clock cycle.

Latency. The time required for the first byte or word of data to be transferred (see also memory latency).

Load factor (hash). The fraction of a hash that is filled with entries.

Machine balance. The ratio of flops to memory loads that a computer system can perform.

Main memory. Also called DRAM or RAM, it is the large block of memory for the compute node.

Memory latency. The time it takes to retrieve the first byte of memory from a level of the memory hierarchy.

Memory leaks. Allocating memory and never freeing it. Malloc replacement tools are good at catching and reporting memory leaks.

Memory overwrites. Writing to memory that is not owned by a variable in the program.

Memory paging. In multi-user, multi-application operating systems, the process of moving memory pages temporarily out to disk so that another process can take place.

Memory pressure. The effect of the computational kernel resource needs on performance of GPU kernels. Register pressure is a similar term, referring to demands on registers in the kernel.

Method invocation. In object-oriented programming, the call to a piece of code within the object that operates on data in the object. These small pieces of code are called methods and the call to these is termed an invocation.

MIMD. Multiple instruction, multiple data is a component of Flynn's Taxonomy represented by a multi-core system.

Minimal perfect hash. A hash with one and only one entry in each bucket.

MISD. Multiple instruction, single data is a component of Flynn's Taxonomy describing a redundant computer for high reliability or a parallel pipeline parallelism.

MMX. Earliest x86 vector instruction set released by Intel.

Motherboard. The main system board of a computer.

Multi-core. A CPU that contains more than one computational core.

Network. The connections between compute nodes over which data flows.

Node. A basic building block of a compute cluster with its own memory and a network to communicate with other compute nodes and to run a single image of an operating system.

Non-Uniform Memory Access (NUMA). On some computing nodes, blocks of memory are closer to some processors than others. This situation is called Non-Uniform Memory Access (NUMA). Often this is the case when a node has two CPU sockets with each socket having its own memory. The access to the other block of memory typically takes twice the time as its own memory.

N-way set associative cache. A cache that allows N locations for a memory address to be mapped into the cache. This reduces the conflicts and evictions associated with direct-mapped cache.

Object-based filesystem. A system that is organized based on objects rather than based on files in a folder. An object-based filesystem requires a database or metadata to store all the information describing the object.

Operations (OPs). Operations can be integer, floating-point, or logic.

Out-of-bounds (memory access). Attempting to access memory beyond the array bounds. Fence-post checkers and some compilers can catch these errors.

Output dependency. A variable is written to more than once in the loop.

Pageable memory. Standard memory allocations that can be paged out to disk. See pinned memory for an alternative type that cannot be paged out.

Parallel algorithm. A well-defined, step-by-step computational procedure that emphasizes concurrency to solve a problem.

Parallel computing. Computing that operates on more than one thing at a time.

Parallel pattern. A common, independent, concurrent component of code that occurs in diverse scenarios with some frequency. By themselves, these components generally do not solve complete problems of interest.

Parallel speedup. Performance of a parallel implementation relative to a baseline serial run.

Parallelism. The operation of parts of a program across a set of resources at the same time.

Pattern rule. A specification to the make utility that gives a general rule on how to convert any file with one suffix pattern to a file with another suffix pattern.

PCI bus. Peripheral Component Interconnect bus is the main data pathway between components on the system board, including the CPU, main memory, and the communication network.

Peel loop. A loop to execute for misaligned data so that the main loop would then have aligned data. Often the peel loop is conditionally executed at run time if the data is discovered to be misaligned.

Perfect hash. A hash where there are no collisions; there is at most one entry in each bucket.

Perfectly nested loops. Loops that only have statements in the innermost loop. That means that there are no extraneous statements before or after each loop block.

Performance model. A simplified representation of how the operations in a program can be converted into an estimate of the code's run time.

Pinned memory. Memory that cannot be paged out from RAM. It is especially useful for memory transfers because it can be directly sent without making a copy.

POSIX standard. The Portable Operating System Interface (POSIX) standard is an IEEE standard for Unix and Unix-like operating systems to facilitate portability. The standard specifies the basic operations that should be provided by the OS.

Pragma. An instruction to a C or C++ compiler to help it interpret the source code. The form of the instruction is a preprocessor statement starting with #pragma.

Prescriptive directives and clauses. These are directives from the programmer that tell the compiler specifically what to do.

Private variable (OpenMP). In the context of OpenMP, a private variable is local and only visible to its thread.

Process. An independent unit of computation that has ownership of a portion of memory and control over resources in user space.

Processing core or (simply) core. The most basic unit capable of performing arithmetic and logical operations.

Profilers. A programming tool that measures the performance of an application.

Profiling. The run-time measurement of some aspects of application performance; most commonly, the time it takes to execute parts of a program.

Race conditions. A situation where multiple outcomes are possible and the result is dependent on the timing of the contributors.

Random access memory (RAM). Main system memory where any needed data can be retrieved without having to read sequentially through the data.

Reduction operation. Any operation where a multidimensional array from 1 to N dimensions is reduced to a least one dimension smaller and often to a scalar value.

Register pressure. Register pressure refers to the effect of register needs on the performance of GPU kernels.

Regression tests. Test suites that are run at periodic intervals such as nightly or weekly.

Relaxed memory model. The value of the variables in main memory or caches of all the processors are not updated immediately.

Remainder loop. A loop that executes after the main loop to handle a partial set of data that is too small for a full vector length.

Remote procedure call (RPC). A call to the system to execute another command.

Replicated array. A dataset that is duplicated across all the processors.

Scalar operation. An operation on a single value or one element of an array.

Scatter memory operation. Store from a cache line or vector unit to non-contiguous memory locations.

Shared memory. A block of memory that is accessible and modifiable by multiple processes or threads of execution. The block of memory is from the programmer's perspective.

Shared variable (OpenMP). In the context of OpenMP, a shared variable is visible and modifiable by any thread.

SIMD. Single instruction, multiple data is a component of Flynn's Taxonomy describing a parallelism such as that found in vectorization, where a single instruction is applied across multiple data items.

SIMT. Single instruction, multiple thread is a variant of SIMD, where multiple threads operate concurrently on multiple data.

SISD. Single instruction, single data is a component of Flynn's Taxonomy that describes a traditional serial architecture.

Socket. The location where a processor is inserted on a motherboard. Motherboards normally are either single or dual socket, allowing one or two processors to be installed, respectively.

Source code repository. Storage for source code that tracks changes and can be shared between a project's code developers.

Spatial locality. Data with nearby locations in memory that are often referenced close together.

SSE. Streaming SIMD Extensions, a vector hardware and instruction set released by Intel that first supported floating-point operations.

SSE2. An improved SSE instruction set that supports double-precision operations.

Stack memory. Memory within a subroutine is often created by pushing the objects onto the stack after the stack pointer. These are usually small memory objects that exist for only the duration of the routine and disappear at the end of the routine when the instruction pointer jumps back to the previous location.

Streaming kernels. Blocks of computational code that load data in a nearly optimal way to effectively use the cache hierarchy.

Streaming multiprocessor (SM). Usually used to describe the multiprocessors of a GPU that are designed for streaming operations. These are tightly-coupled, symmetric processors (SMP) that have a single instruction stream operating on multiple threads.

Streaming store. A store of a value directly to main memory, bypassing the cache hierarchy.

Stride (arrays). Distance between indexed elements in an array. In C, in the x dimension, the data is contiguous or a stride of 1. In the y dimension, the data has a stride of the length of the row.

Super-linear speedup. Performance that is better than the ideal strong scaling curve. This can happen because the smaller array sizes fit into a higher level of cache, resulting in better cache performance.

Symmetric processors (SMP). All cores of the multicore processor operate in unison in a single-instruction, multiple-thread (SIMT) fashion.

Task. Work that is divided into separate pieces and parceled out to individual processes or threads.

Task parallel. A form of parallelism where processors or threads work on separate tasks.

Temporal locality. Recently referenced data that is likely to be referenced in the near future.

Test-driven development (TDD). A process of code development where the tests are created first.

Test suite. A set of problems that exercise parts of an application to guarantee that parts of the code are still working.

Thread. A separate instruction pathway through a process created by having more than one instruction pointer.

Tightly-nested loops. Two or more loops that have no extra statements between the for or do statements or the end of the loops.

Time complexity. Time complexity takes into account the actual cost of an operation on a typical modern computing system. The largest adjustment for time is to consider the cost of memory loads and caching of data.

Translation lookaside buffer (TLB). The table of entries to translate virtual memory addresses to physical memory. The limited size of the table means that only recently used page locations are held in memory, and a TLB miss occurs if it is not present, incurring a significant performance hit.

Unified memory. Memory that has the appearance of being a single address space for both the CPU and the GPU.

Unit testing. Testing of each individual component of a program.

Uninitialized memory. Memory that is used before its values are set.

User space. The scope of control of operations for a program such that it is isolated from the purview of the operating system.

Validated results. Results of a calculation that are compared favorably to experimental or real-world data.

Vector (SIMD) instruction set. The set of instructions that extend the regular scalar processor instructions to utilize the vector processor.

Vector lane. A pathway through a vector operation on vector registers for a single data element much like a lane on a multi-lane freeway.

Vector length. The number of operations done in a single cycle by a vector unit.

Vector operation. An operation on two or more elements of an array with a single operation or instruction being supplied to the processor.

Vector width. The width of the vector unit, usually expressed in bits.

Vectorization. The process of grouping operations together so more than one can be done at a time.

Version Control System. A database that tracks the changes to your source code, simplifies the merging of multiple developers, and provides a way to roll back changes.

Warm cache. When a cache has data to be operated on in the cache from a previous operation as the current operation begins.

Warp. An alternate term for a thread workgroup.

Word (size). The size of the basic type being used. For single precision, this is four bytes and for double, it is eight bytes.

Workgroup. A group of threads operating together with a single instruction queue.

Figure C.1   Desktop motherboard with Intel CPU and discrete NVIDIA GPU

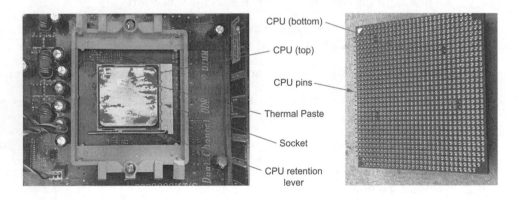

Figure C.2   Intel CPU installed in socket and underside with CPU data pins. The data transfer to the CPU is limited by the number of pins that can be physically fit onto the surface of the CPU.

index

RELATED MANNING TITLES

Modern Fortran
by Milan Curcic
Foreword by Damian Rouson

ISBN 9781617295287
416 pages, $59.99
October 2020

Concurrency in .NET
by Riccardo Terrell

ISBN 9781617292996
568 pages, $59.99
June 2018

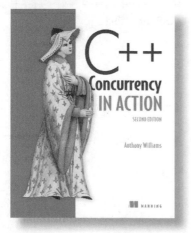

C++ Concurrency in Action, Second Edition
by Anthony Williams

ISBN 9781617294693
592 pages, $69.99
February 2019

For ordering information go to www.manning.com